START-UP AT THE NEW MET

Leontyne Price as Cleopatra in *Antony and Cleopatra*. Photography by Louis Mélançon. Courtesy Metropolitan Opera Archives.

START-UP AT THE NEW MET

The Metropolitan
Opera Broadcasts
1966–1976

by

Paul Jackson

Author of

Saturday Afternoons at the Old Met:
The Metropolitan Opera Broadcasts, 1931–1950

Sign-off for the Old Met:
The Metropolitan Opera Broadcasts, 1950–1966

aɸ

AMADEUS
PRESS

Published in 2006 by Amadeus Press
512 Newark Pompton Turnpike
Pompton Plains, New Jersey 07444

Printed in the United States of America

Library of Congress Cataloging-in-Publication Data is available upon request.

ISBN 1-57467-147-2

www.amadeuspress.com

For Lee, my wife

Contents

Illustrations

The Metropolitan Opera at Lincoln Center. Photography by Louis Mélançon. Courtesy Metropolitan Opera Archives.

Preface

How perverse of me to have left Mr. Bing dangling between the old Met and the new Met. We last saw him on the final day of the 1965–66 season, with his company gathered around him, celebrating the glorious history of the old house. His thoughts undoubtedly were on the seasons to come at Lincoln Center. The first six of them would be under his continuing stewardship. It will be well to bind up the Bing regime and, in this, my last go at the broadcasts, round out the decade of performances by adding another four seasons (1972–76). Those four seasons are years of turmoil for the company. They hold Schuyler Chapin's troubled three years at the helm until in the fourth season Anthony Bliss grabs hold of the administrative rudder and steadies the Metropolitan barque. And during the final half of our chronicle decade, yet another force enters upon the Metropolitan scene. His first steps are modest, but he moves ever with purposeful intent. James Levine begins to make his presence felt in the last year of Mr. Bing's tenure. Thereafter his influence increases with each year, until, beginning with the 1976–77 season, the artistic well-being of the Metropolitan is placed in his hands and he is named music director of the company. A new Metropolitan era is thereby legitimized, for the Levine reign will endure into the twenty-first century. Thus, the decade under consideration makes a tidy period in which to consider the musical accomplishments of the company as apparent in the broadcast seasons. To leave the chronology at the point when Levine officially takes hold seems to me an appropriate place to end my accounts of the broadcasts.

Though I do not repeat here the acknowledgments noted in the previous two volumes, I wish to reaffirm my gratitude to all persons and institutions I have previously cited. I cannot forgo, however, citing with special affection two institutions, namely, Drake University (whose grant several decades ago fostered this project) and the Immortal Performances Recorded Music Society. In addition, I wish to thank those companies and foundations, both large and small, and especially the multitude of individual listeners who have been so generous in supporting the Metropolitan Opera radio broadcasts throughout these years. To Ellen Godfrey, radio network producer for the Metropolitan Opera, I express my gratitude for gaining permission to quote from the colorful and informative intermissions of the broadcasts. My thanks also to F. Paul Driscoll, editor in chief of *Opera News*, who kindly granted permission to use a number of quotations from that magazine. A special word of gratitude must be given to the Metropolitan Opera Archives (Robert Tuggle, archivist) and specifically to John Pennino, assistant archivist, who facilitated the selection of the sixty-nine photographs supplied by the Archives. All other photographs and memorabilia are from the author's collection. Richard Caniell, Madeleine McCarthy, and Roger Gross are a few of the many individuals who rendered specific services. To John Cerullo, publisher, and the staff of Amadeus Press (designer Clare Cerullo and proofreader Gail Siragusa must be cited by name), I extend regards and appreciation for their efforts on my behalf. Carol Flannery, editorial director, deserves all thanks for her knowing professional supervision of the production process. And a special expression of gratitude is reserved for Rosalie Wieder, my expert copyeditor and most enjoyable production cohort. In addition, many readers have written me about the *Old Met* books, often relating in detail their fond memories of those earlier years. I thank them for their responses and their joyful recountings.

Once again, I cannot close without expressing my abiding love and deep gratitude to my wife for her constant support in these endeavors.

Randolph Center, Vermont

METROPOLITAN OPERA

OPENING NIGHT   LINCOLN CENTER PLAZA

Friday Evening, September 16, 1966, at 8:00

THE NATIONAL ANTHEM

OPENING REMARKS

> JOHN D. ROCKEFELLER 3RD, CHAIRMAN OF THE BOARD,
> LINCOLN CENTER FOR THE PERFORMING ARTS
> ANTHONY A. BLISS, PRESIDENT, METROPOLITAN OPERA ASSOCIATION

WORLD PREMIERE

SAMUEL BARBER

Antony and Cleopatra

Opera in three acts
The text of William Shakespeare adapted by Franco Zeffirelli
Conductor: Thomas Schippers
Designed and directed by Franco Zeffirelli

Cleopatra	Leontyne Price
Antony	Justino Díaz
Charmian	Rosalind Elias
Iras	Belén Amparán
Caesar	Jess Thomas
Octavia	Mary Ellen Pracht
Enobarbus	Ezio Flagello
Agrippa	John Macurdy
Mardian	Andrea Velis
Clown	Clifford Harvuot
Messenger	Paul Franke
Soothsayer	Lorenzo Alvary
Lepidus	Robert Nagy
Maecenas	Russell Christopher
Dolabella	Gene Boucher
Thidias	Robert Goodloe
Decretas	Louis Sgarro
Alexas	Raymond Michalski
Scarus	Ron Bottcher (debut)
A Captain	Dan Marek
A Soldier of Caesar	Gabor Carelli
1st Guard	Robert Schmorr
2nd Guard	Edward Ghazal
3rd Guard	Norman Scott
Demetrius	Norman Giffin
Canidius	Lloyd Strang
A Soldier of Antony	John Trehy
1st Watchman	Paul De Paola
2nd Watchman	Luis Forero
A Sentinel	Peter Sliker
Eros	Bruce Scott (debut)

Choreography by Alvin Ailey (debut)
Sally Brayley, Nira Paaz, Rhodie Jorgenson, Hope Clarke (debut),
Jan Mickens, Lance Westergard and Corps de Ballet
Chorus Master: Kurt Adler
Musical Preparation: Ignace Strasfogel *and* Lawrence Smith

This production of ANTONY AND CLEOPATRA *was made possible by a generous
and deeply appreciated gift from The Francis Goelet Foundation*

KNABE PIANO USED EXCLUSIVELY

*The audience is respectfully, but urgently, requested
not to interrupt the music with applause*

Program for the premiere of *Antony and Cleopatra* on opening night of the Metropolitan Opera at
Lincoln Center.

CHAPTER ONE

At Long Last, a New Home

Opening nights have their own peculiar mystique. Add to the mix the world premiere of an American opera and more than the usual suspense accrues to the evening. When combined with the initial viewing and sounding of a new opera house, the occasion positively moves beyond the trying into the realm of the apprehensive, prompting in management and opera-lovers equal parts hope and terror. Even so, on 16 September 1966 the Metropolitan Opera felt reasonably ready to show off its new Lincoln Center home to the opening night audience that filled the enormous space of the house. Fortunately for the record, millions of radio listeners were eager participants as well.

The journey from Broadway and Thirty-ninth Street, cradle of the old Met and its home since the company's birth in 1883, to upper Manhattan had been fraught with problems that daunted even Rudolf Bing. After sixteen years at the helm of one of the world's leading opera companies, the general manager was an old hand at handling and untangling crises large and small. But this time he was playing for bigger stakes. Problems with the intricate machinery of the house complicated, even momentarily threatened, the strenuous cycle of nine new productions that the usually cautious impresario had projected. In addition to the opening night premiere of Samuel Barber's *Antony and Cleopatra*, three more were scheduled for the first week. He says he "overplanned the season," not having realized that production designers, fascinated by their new toy, would be seduced into excessive exploitation of the stage's seemingly boundless resources.[1] "And then the machinery didn't work," Bing—with his characteristic honesty—lamented. To lessen the congestion, the house premiere of *Die Frau ohne Schatten,* a monster offering, was moved to a later date. But the malaise ran deep. While some problems submitted to ingenious solutions, others, most particularly relations between management and labor unions, would remain stubbornly obdurate for years. Foremost in the minds of all on this evening of celebration was the threat of the musicians union to strike the day after the opening night unless management met its demands. Their members had played for two years without a contract.

As the festivities began troubles were, at least momentarily, set aside. We can enter into the spirit of the occasion. Milton Cross, perhaps feeling a mite unsettled in his new broadcast booth, welcomes us to "the most eagerly awaited musical event of our time." The veteran announcer was never afraid to show his colors—he loved the Met. He invites us to tour the house with assistant manager Herman Krawitz as our guide. Since 1962 Krawitz had overseen construction ("from top to bottom") of the new home. In *Opera News* he had suggested that readers might best understand the makeup of the new house if they would conjure up "a forty-four-story office building and lay it on its side."[2] A hint of it dimensions, usage, and practicality may be gleaned from the fact that fifteen fully assembled operas could be ready to move from the basement space onto an elevator and up to the stage without delay. With a stage area six times as large as that of the old Met, the audience would see stage pictures three times as large. The backstage area held a plethora of rehearsal spaces, and the miracles of modern technology that clothe and feed the greedy main stage needed only a set designer's imagination to call them forth.

As luck would have it, the best-laid plans not only went astray, they all but wandered off the planet. Human frailty, rather than a technological misfire, caused one of the highly touted miracles to remain earthbound. When the turntable that propelled the revolving stage was loaded with the chorus and sets for the Sphinx scene of *Antony and Cleopatra*, it broke down. Its use was suspended for the first season; sets had to be rebuilt and new staging improvised for several of the new productions. Those expedients alone would be enough to take the starch out of any manager's optimism. Despite the backstage turmoil, permanent improvements were obvious to the eager audience members. Sightlines were excellent for all 3,788 seats. Mr. Bing had insisted that every patron, even those in the Family Circle, must be able to see the conductor's head. Cross tells us that standee positions are to be reserved, a new feature calculated to warm the aging hearts of those (like me) who once raced upstairs to the Family Circle or pushed on to other areas, eagerly seeking to claim a favorite viewing spot.

Now Mr. Bing takes over the radio microphone, introducing the leading artists of the performance (and gently chiding prima donna Leontyne Price about the expensive costumes for her Cleopatra). Good humor is the watchword of the evening. During the lengthy first intermission, Edward Downes, perennial quizmaster of the opera broadcasts, interviews a few of the numerous distinguished guests. Mrs. Lyndon B. Johnson, wife of the president, cites "the feeling of electricity in the air," but not before Downes has given pride of place to Mrs. August Belmont, onetime savior of the company and, at age eighty-eight, the grand old dame of the Metropolitan Opera Guild. Speaking by phone from Northeast Harbor, Maine, she lauds the "dedication and courage and hard work" that have brought this great fulfillment. More important than accolades is the imprimatur of Wallace K. Harrison, the architect of the new theater, who, when asked about the acoustics, ventures a quiet "I think it works . . . we are all very happy." He feels it was "just luck" that, despite its magnitude, the house seems intimate. Representatives of the Juilliard School and the Texaco Company (the oil giant and sponsor of the opening night broadcast as well as twenty-seven consecutive seasons of the Saturday afternoon broadcasts) step up to the mike to offer congratulations. One or two artists from the Met's glorious past are called upon: Lotte Lehmann thinks "the singers sing with great ease" from the new stage.

To promote its array of new productions, the company trots out an impressive group of designers, including Sir Cecil Beaton (for *La Traviata*), Beni Montresor (*La Gioconda*), and Robert O'Hearn (*Die Frau ohne Schatten*). The latter's partner, stage director Nathaniel Merrill, spills the beans about the broken turntable ("a slightly sore subject"). With a smile in his voice—and a bit hard-heartedly—he notes that the breakdown won't affect their production. Rather than the turntable, *Die Frau* will utilize a different technology, i.e., the ascent and descent capabilities of the machinery, when moving between the two worlds of Strauss' epic opera. Proudly tooting his own horn, he claims that he and O'Hearn are "the only ones who are using the stage as a dramatic impetus, not merely to move large quantities of scenery from one place to another." Most honored of the designers is Marc Chagall, whose vibrant lobby murals will give joy to opera lovers even longer than his colorful settings for *Die Zauberflöte*. In French, he tells Downes that his affection for the American people motivated his conception and execution of the murals.

But now to the heart of the evening: Barber's *Antony and Cleopatra*. The program not ungenerously credits the text to William Shakespeare, as adapted by Franco Zeffirelli. The troubling facts about the premiere have become part of operatic lore. Like Bing in his retirement recollections, contemporaneous reports deemed the opera, in its stage incarnation, to have been too grandly conceived and executed. The expanse of the new stage (particularly its cavernous depth) and its extensive machinery were as tempting to designers as Circe's magic cup was to unwitting tasters. Fortunately for our famous designer/director's long and successful career, succumbing led not to swinehood but merely a singed reputation. Certainly, the complex stage machinery would have been envied by even a seventeenth-century *deus*, whether in or out of his machine. His godly intervention would have been welcome on an evening when miraculous solutions were sorely needed.

Zeffirelli generally was regarded as the villain of the occasion. He had devised a dramaturgy that, throughout the opera's sixteen-plus scenes, would allow him to display not only the prodigious resources of the new Met but his equally prodigious virtuosity. As librettist, he had played a dominant role in determining the form of the opera and, creature of the theater that he was (and is), he could not but relish the scenic and action possibilities of his playbook. Of course, display is bound to be a prime component of any new work that inaugurates an opera house. Its wares are meant to be set forth with flair. Yet another opera with an Egyptian locale and spectacular production demands was intended to serve a similar function, the inauguration of the khedive's Cairo Opera House in 1869. War may have delayed the premiere of *Aida* until 1871 (the Cairo house opened with *Rigoletto*), but even Zeffirelli, seized as he was by an attack of elephantiasis—the condition would become chronic—and apparently guilty of rehearsal ineptitude, could not keep *Antony* off the opening-night boards.

It well may be that Barber's work, at least in its original state, would not have enjoyed greater success in a less overblown production. Improved regard for the opera's musical setting has come about only after major revisions of libretto and music (with the astute Gian Carlo Menotti, as theater-wise as Zeffirelli, playing Svengali). The modifications diminished the ceremonial portions and focused upon the personal relationship of the lovers. (Productions of the new version occurred at the Juilliard School in 1975, at Menotti's Spoleto Festival in Charleston, South Carolina, in 1983, and at the Chicago Lyric Opera in 1991.) Thus, quite apart from Zeffirelli's zealous tyranny, the tepid initial reception of the opera

Antony and Cleopatra
17 September 1966

Cleopatra
Leontyne Price
Charmian
Rosalind Elias
Iras
Belén Amparán
Caesar
Jess Thomas
Antony
Justino Díaz
Enobarbus
Ezio Flagello
Conductor
Thomas Schippers

may be attributed to Barber, who was simply the wrong man for the job. That is, if the job was to deliver a pièce d'occasion wherein the ceremonial was highlighted at the expense of the personal. Even without reference to his instrumental works, it was apparent that intimate, lyrical expression was his métier. *Vanessa*, premiered by the Met in 1958, had confirmed that predilection. Then, too, unlike that of many of his contemporaries, Barber's musical imagination had been most convincingly stimulated by the set musical forms that had served composers, instrumental and operatic, long and well. For maximum eloquence, those forms need a certain time span to accumulate nuances and deepen expression. And there Barber was done in. Rather than the admittedly problematic scenic investiture, it is the rapid changes of scene, wherein each episode is of short duration, that are the major culprits. Moreover, within the brief formats fashioned by Zeffirelli, the need for narrative exposition takes precedence over amplification of affect; such a dramaturgical procedure is bound to diminish opera's prime appeal, namely, the expansive expression of passions. Even without the distraction of Zeffirelli's stage pictures in the initial acts of the opera, the musical setting (though never less than skillful and sometimes more than that) too often seems inconsequential or merely a conventional response to familiar stage moods. Should battle music be required, Barber can serve it up in exciting and time-honored fashion; to support an exotic or seductive mood, he knows he should plug the winds into serpentine mode; if Antony (played by the young Puerto Rican bass-baritone Justino Díaz) must leap on a table and sing a drinking song, the composer can supply a craggy syllabic piece with male chorus background. A lot of this seems music off the rack.

In no way do I mean to minimize the composer's skills or ignore his precious gifts. At any given moment, the orchestration in itself can be wonderfully colored and evocative. And, even in the initial acts, a few moments radiate the full flavor of his lyrical talent. Cleopatra's 'Give me some music,' the opera's first extended piece, makes its effect, though its musical profile is somewhat indistinct. The episode that mirrors the vision of Cleopatra's barge is wonderfully replete, Barber's music as laden with sensuous sounds as the beauteous queen lying in her gliding pavilion is perfumed by the bard's scented purple sails. Give Barber a topic that sets his imagination aflame and he burns hot. Zeffirelli, too, wove his dramaturgical wand to fine effect when he caused the barge vision to migrate from Shakespeare's original placement to the opera's first-act curtain. (Cross tells us that the barge is seen "slowly coming toward the audience"—a stage effect made possible by the 120-foot-deep stage. The sets and costumes, he assures us "are just out of this world . . . so beautiful and colorful.") Antony's companion, Enobarbus, who, after deserting his friend, dies of a broken heart, is provided near the end of act two with a quasi-lyrical set piece that resonates, especially as it comes from the resonant throat of Ezio Flagello. And Antony is finally given his due in the touching episode wherein he learns of Cleopatra's purported death. Accompanied by steady drum beats with occasional plaintive flute solos, his long scene (a mix of arioso and recitativo accompagnato) by its simplicity touches the heart and provides a moving conclusion to the act.

Of course, the third act is the prima donna's province—and as Cleopatra, Leontyne Price is entirely worthy of that abused title. There Barber gives us something to remember. Now the expressive power of opera is released, its potent incense penetrates the airwaves, envelopes us in its spell as Barber makes believers of us all. Time is now on his side and the several set pieces of the act rouse him to vivid expression. The lovely trio ('My Lord, noblest of men') for Cleopatra, Charmian (Rosalind Elias), and Iras (Belén Amparan) prepares us for the queen's grand lament ('Give me my robe. . . . I have immortal longings'), a dirge wherewith the composer serves not only his own best gifts but Price's generous allotment as well. Her broadly declaimed phrases and stunning high notes mate well with the expansive melodic orchestral lines. When, after the asp has done its work, Elias takes up the lament, she astonishes with the grandeur and beauty of her singing as Charmian follows her mistress in death. (Perhaps Barber rewarded the mezzo-soprano with this vibrant moment as a token of gratitude for her memorable portrayal of Erika in his *Vanessa*.) The lengthy choral peroration that follows provides a lofty close to an opera, flawed in its earliest stages, but worthy of respect by evening's end.

Thomas Schipper's control of the score is absolute. His reading is rhythmically trenchant in the livelier episodes and yet sensitive to the beauties of Barber's scoring in the more reflective moments. Barring the seemingly obligatory brass blurp or two, the orchestra is in superior form. A large and well-qualified cast peoples the new stage. Of the many cameo portraits, a few standouts should be mentioned: John Macurdy, who arranges Antony's ill-fated marriage to Octavia (Mary Ellen Pracht, singing with resplendent tone and unexpected assurance); Paul Franke, ever the assertive messenger; Robert Goodloe, his clear-toned baritone making plausible Antony's jealousy; and Clifford Harvuot, the rustic who brings Cleopatra figs and snake and thus genially abets the denouement. The occasional comic scenes do not come off. There Elias' chest voice and comedic manner are annoying and Alvary's slurred diction makes the Soothsayer unintelligible. In general, the intelligibility quotient is markedly low for most players; yet Elias, Harvuot, Raymond Michalski, Andrea Velis, Gene Boucher, Flagello, and (at least with some frequency) Díaz all shine in text clarity. In assigning the lover function to a bass, the composer shortchanged his leading tenor. Jess Thomas, as Caesar, not only doesn't get the girl but has little to do, and most of that boring. His strong, marbled tenor, while decidedly corporeal, does lend vitality to Caesar's praise for the dead Antony.

The opulence of Díaz's bass-baritone is quite remarkable. His tone is vibrant and securely focused, quite unlike the airless sonority associated with the later stages of his long career. Virility of manner and timbre make him a believable general and wooer, though in love's "soft hours" greater variety of nuance and dynamics would have made his Antony a more interesting fellow. Happily, Shakespeare supplied the Roman with enough of a profile to remedy the deficiency that Barber evidently was unwilling or unable to supply on his own. Though Antony has several extended monologues that well exploit Díaz's firm voice (I especially like his affecting soliloquy on the battlefield after Cleopatra deserts and takes her fleet back to Egypt), the singer is denied an expansive, song-filled air.

Barber, as we have seen, takes far better care of his Cleopatra and both queen and Price are the beneficiaries. From the lift of the curtain, Price is in marvelous vocal form and entirely committed to the evening's work. Occasionally, her diction seems rather off center (her "a" vowels are decidedly trying), and when the composer wants a bit of quick rhythmic play she responds with chesty, nasal strokes that don't mate well with the remainder of her luscious instrument. Nevertheless, at this relatively early point in her career, the voice generally retains uniformity of timbre, richly somber and smoldering on the staff until it soars effortlessly to a silvery top. As expected, her high notes are glorious. Barber supplies her with a cornucopia's overflow of them and we can be grateful for every one, especially in those moments when musical interest lies fallow. Cleopatra's set pieces (later arranged for concert performance by the composer) will serve Price well in future orchestral appearances. Subsidiary benefits must be counted on the plus side when evaluating the opera's worth.

Bing, undeterred by mishaps and setbacks, resolutely had led the company to its new home. He deserves the last word. In his memoirs, the manager admits that Zeffirelli was "somewhat doubtful" about the music that Barber had provided. "We all were," he confessed.[3] But the manager was a ready man with a gambler's throw. Sixteen years earlier, on his first Met opening night, he had risked his American career on the unlikely choice of Verdi's long-neglected *Don Carlo* and won big. At the new Met, his initial winnings for the opening night venture were slight, but in later years critical response to the revised *Antony and Cleopatra* began to run in his favor. Time's croupier may yet grant him greater reward.

Bing survived the tribulations of the move to Lincoln Center with his customary resilience. In fact, the season ahead held a series of artistic triumphs that would have gratified the heart and satisfied the ego of the most curmudgeonly impresario. And even on that freighted opening night, there was good news. The general manager earned the evening's heartiest applause when he appeared onstage after the second act to spread the word: an agreement had been reached with the musicians' union and the strike was over. The season would go on.

Leonie Rysanek as the Empress in *Die Frau ohne Schatten*. Photography by Louis Mélançon. Courtesy Metropolitan Opera Archives.

CHAPTER TWO

Baptism by Fire:
The Inaugural Season

Antony and Cleopatra had proved to be rather more than the new Met could handle and somewhat less than critics and opera lovers had hoped for, but the Metropolitan premiere of *Die Frau ohne Schatten* elicited paeans of praise from the press and general rejoicing from the public. Before the broadcast of 17 December 1966 rolled around, the editor of *Opera News* could claim that every performance was sold out.[1] Even the house organ was mystified by the unanimity of response for, though diehard Straussians revered *Die Frau*, they were outnumbered by a larger body of informed opinion makers who considered the opera to be oversized and undernourished. Hence the forty-seven-year lapse between the Vienna and Metropolitan premieres. With characteristic chutzpah, the San Francisco Opera had lessened the gap by introducing American audiences to the work in 1959. Mr. Bing may have been brave—and we know he was willing to wager—but he was no crusader.

As the broadcast performance makes clear, the attractions of the work are many. Most appetizing are the feast of orchestral sonorities, both ear-splitting and heartrendingly simple, and vocalism often flamboyant, occasionally touching. When, at the final curtain, Cross, in a masterpiece of understatement, admits to the radio audience that the opera's plot is "a rather complicated story," he feels compelled to add (perhaps too optimistically) "but I think you understand it now." The burden that the opera bears is twofold, both components rooted in Hofmannsthal's philosophic and mythic ramblings. These verbal perambulations can defy (or at least inhibit) comprehension; of even greater moment, they failed to inspire the composer at critical moments of the opera, most notably in portions of the last act. While deeming the work "full of picturesque and poetical happy thoughts," Romain Rolland, a Strauss confidant in the early years and sometime partisan, regretted its reliance upon the "German disease of musical development, of repetition"—a not unexpected judgment from the French perspective.[2] Erich Leinsdorf was more to the point, calling Strauss the champion purveyor of operatic "stuffing."[3] As for Hofmannsthal, Rolland dismissed him as theatrically incompetent: "his obscure thought trails an icy shadow." A few years after the premiere,

Die Frau ohne Schatten
17 December 1966

Empress
Leonie Rysanek
Dyer's Wife
Christa Ludwig
Nurse
Irene Dalis
Emperor
James King
Barak
Walter Berry
Messenger
William Dooley
Conductor
Karl Böhm

Hofmannsthal himself was willing to admit that the second act was "wearying and oppressive."[4] Most recent critics have found that, taken pound for pound, the opera's musical substance far outweighs any lumps of stuffing.

A singular achievement of librettist and composer is their creation of five genuinely memorable operatic roles—twentieth-century opera holds few enough of them. The 1919 Vienna premiere cast featured Maria Jeritza and Lotte Lehmann (Empress and Dyer's Wife) with Lucie Weidt (Nurse), Karl Aagard-Oestwig (Emperor), and the Strauss/Hofmannsthal pair's unsurpassed Ochs, Richard Mayr (Barak). The Metropolitan assembled a comparable quintet of singers eminently equipped to meet the challenges posed by the unabashedly grandiloquent creators. Management surrounded them with a corps of their best supporting players. Standouts are Paul Franke, Clifford Harvuot, and Lorenzo Alvary as characterful brothers to the put-upon Barak, Robert Nagy, a stout-voiced tenor tempter, and Mary Ellen Pracht as a secure-voiced Guardian. Only Belén Amparan muffs her critical, if miniscule, assignment; her pronouncements of forgiveness are too casual to carry conviction. As guide for the admirable crew onstage the Met had to hand the period's prime Straussian, Karl Böhm. An intimate of the aged composer and fervent proponent of his late works, Böhm brings not only authority and command to his task but a seeming belief in the master's witchery. Probably it is that element of faith which enables him to ride over the opera's languors ("Bavarian phlegm," according to Rolland) and then, reaching the haven of inspired creativity, propel the symphonic interludes to breathtaking effect.[5] Better yet, he allows the welcome chamber music intimacies of the score ample expressive space. The gap between these polarities may occasionally widen so as to test the opera's tensile strength (in particular, the tumultuous episodes can seem overly thrusting), but the individual profiles of flamboyance and intimacy are convincingly conveyed.

With a sure hand at the helm, the artists onstage deliver with comparable assurance. We may even expand the quintet of principals by one since the Bote is sung by William Dooley. What a beautiful baritone he owns! To cast a company Onegin, Mandryka, and Jokanaan as the messenger is further evidence of management's strong commitment to the production. The male contingent is doubly enhanced by two newcomers to our airwaves. Tenor James King, Kansas-born and a latecomer to—but longtime survivor in—opera, makes a capital first impression as the Emperor. He had come to the company in January 1966 as Florestan, having appeared in Berlin, Salzburg, Vienna, and Bayreuth during the short five-year duration of his career. Stern-voiced, as befits a mortal who turns to stone, his singing is refreshingly clean in sound and line, thus delivering us from the wheezes and sneezes that too many Teutonic specialists have, of necessity, favored. The Emperor prefers hunting to loving, and this tenor, responding in kind, appropriately supplies song strongly voiced and unclouded by nuance. King as Kaiser deserves that upgrading since his outpouring of firm tone and clear diction in the second-act solo scene is enhanced by yet another rarity in contemporary heroic tenors, a confident top voice. That Strauss converts to fustian Bacchus mode in the final scene is no fault of King's. He complies admirably.

Our other newcomer, Walter Berry, plays in quite another fashion and one rather more inviting. His instrument and manner bring into relief a certain lack of graciousness in the tenor's music making. The Met program designates the Austrian as baritone, while *Grove* insists on the bass-baritone category. Since 1950 a regular member of the Vienna Staatsoper and much-prized guest at German and American houses, Berry had made his Met debut in the current production at the October premiere. During a Met career of moderate duration he would sing Barak an amazing twenty-nine times, a total that confirms his primacy in the role. His portrayal is in all respects quite wonderful. The voice is more than handsome, entirely dependable both high and low, and capable of notable warmth, the latter an all-important asset in rendering Barak's imperturbable benevolence. The musical niceties of the role are impeccably handled. In particular, the singer's overall subtle expansion of line effectively contrasts with his rhythmic vitality in the dyer's plebeian ditty. Barak is the heart of the opera and Berry's seasoned artistry and sympathetic portrayal pulsate with charity.

If I characterize Irene Dalis' portrait of the Nurse as heartless, I mean it as high praise for her mesmerizing and virtuoso reading of this pivotal role. Evil is the Amme's sphere, her hatred of mankind its motivating force. Dalis sees her as "an instrument of Fate" and capable of a variety of interpretations—but evil is always the constant.[6] The mezzo-soprano was a veteran of two earlier productions (San Francisco and Hamburg), and her authority, vocal control throughout the music's extensive range, and clear diction lend unfailing dramatic focus to every scene in which she appears. Two enhancing qualities in particular should be cited. Unlike some interpreters of the role whose soprano-like timbre negates the Nurse's vileness, Dalis' instrument maintains a bronze tincture throughout its entire compass; from the moment of her initial appearance the dark timbre inherently reinforces the Amme's malevolence. (But how craftily instrument and manner are recast in beauty's image when the Nurse tempts the Dyer's Wife.) At the opposite pole, Dalis flies over the skittering vocal line that Strauss fashioned for the Nurse with utmost security—at one point several brief melismas are deftly executed. With this remarkable portrayal the mezzo-soprano's status is appreciably elevated.

Leonie Rysanek's stature in the role of Empress needs no enhancement. To this day her portrait of the tormented Kaiserin, the role Hofmannsthal regarded as the "most important" in the opera, is remembered as a supreme operatic achievement.[7] Strauss granted the shadowless spirit flights of tone and fierce pronouncements that can only be fully realized by a singer who plays with bold impetuosity and is unfettered by fear when invading the upper range. There you have Rysanek in all her glory. Above all, incandescence is the quality that distinguishes her portrayal. As she enters, her instrument exudes an ethereal shimmer. She appears to have gained firmer control over the lower voice and, notwithstanding a few glancing pitches and an occasional scoop to a top note, is in excellent vocal form. Even when the middle or low voice fails to sound with immediacy and security, its suggestive weirdness seems to complement the opera's aura of fantasy. Of course, there are a pair of her notorious screams (Strauss himself wanted the effect), even a Grand Guignol gasp, and she is prodigal with her searing top tones. Dramatically, the portrayal is fully developed. I found her despair after dreaming of her husband's petrification particularly moving. Indeed, throughout the second act the successive stages of the Empress' human progress (each one, according to Hofmannsthal, a "flaming beacon") are fully illumed.[8] Her third-act vocalism is less consistent. Some wayward sounds obtrude, the voice does not seem well-tuned—a "beacon" or two wears a shade. But the reverent tenor of her quiet address to her father is effective. She regains her form in the finale—those top tones can always

James King as the Emperor, Leonie Rysanek as the Empress, Walter Berry as Barak, and Christa Ludwig as the Dyer's Wife in *Die Frau ohne Schatten*. Photography by Louis Mélançon. Courtesy Metropolitan Opera Archives.

enchain us. A favorite since her 1959 debut, Rysanek deserves the unqualified embrace she receives from the audience at the curtain's fall.

The mounting of *Die Frau ohne Schatten* provided the opportunity for the estimable artist Christa Ludwig to return to the house. She had been absent for five seasons. In an earlier two-season foray with the company, the Berlin-born singer had first appeared as Cherubino, but Octavian, Amneris, and Brangäne were other Met roles more representative of her future career path. This time she appears in soprano guise (though still listed in the program as mezzo-soprano). Her initial Met seasons, while well received, had brought her no particular American acclaim, but by the time of her return Ludwig's warm-toned, firmly centered instrument and sterling musicianship guaranteed her a prominent position on the roster. In the role of the Dyer's Wife, her eloquent song and adept characterization (whether as disgruntled spouse or wandering penitent) amply confirm her right to membership in the star-filled Met company. Unlike Rysanek, Ludwig owns a voice secure throughout its entire range (how odd that in her memoirs, she avers that her vocal cords were "always peevish").[9] Moreover, it is remarkably all-of-a-piece in its tonal coloration. The latter attribute can court boredom over the long term, especially if the personality is short on volatility. But Miss Ludwig's personal warmth, her obvious Gemütlichkeit, are too welcoming to permit inattention on our part. Her way of playing is quite different from that of Rysanek. Ludwig is always dramatically alert to the disagreeable nature of her role, but her tonal homogeneity makes the virago's shrewishness comparatively palatable over a long afternoon. The manner is shrewish, not the voice. And she is undaunted by the elevated tessitura; only an occasional slight hardening of timbre (and the timbre is so agreeable) on a very top tone suggests that she will not long continue her flirtation with the soprano *Fach*. Writing of her performances as the Dyer's Wife, she does in fact gratefully acknowledge that the experienced Böhm "helped her" over the climaxes.[10] She is at her best in the opening scene of the third act where, as the voices of unborn children haunt the wife and the loss of Barak is driven home, mental anguish consumes her. At last, the humanity that is Ludwig's innate gift is allowed to surface.

At the end of the second act, Mr. Cross confesses that the scenes are "really beyond my description," so "spectacularly beautiful" are they. Of course, in assessing the afternoon's performance, I of necessity have left the stage picture out of the equation. And the opportunity to exploit the enormous scenic resources of the new house, to savor its technological miracles, was foremost in the decision to mount the forbidding *Die Frau*. In meeting those indulgent goals, designer Robert O'Hearn and his director partner Nathaniel Merrill achieved what the *Times'* critic called a "convincing union between literalism and modernism."[11] *Antony and Cleopatra* suffered from overproduction, but *Die Frau* demanded grand scenic gestures. Strauss himself would probably have relished the Met's gargantuan display. Believing that the celebrated designer Alfred Roller had let him down in the Viennese production, the composer informed Hofmannsthal before the Berlin premiere that he wanted the "magic tricks" to be spectacular. "The music alone can't do everything," he conceded.[12] His collaborator agreed that Roller had "no sense of the fantastic."[13] The Met team was not lacking in that department and audiences reveled in the luxuriousness of the decor. The elaborate production would return in the 1968–69 and 1970–71 seasons (to the airwaves as well) with the principal artists repeating their triumphs of the premiere season.

Elektra
10 December 1966

Elektra
Birgit Nilsson
Chrysothemis
Leonie Rysanek
Klytämnestra
Regina Resnik
Aegisth
James King
Orest
William Dooley
Conductor
Thomas Schippers

Strauss, though regarded by the musical elite as the lesser of the recognized pair of German operatic masters, was favored with a second grand spread. Wagnerites had to be content with a new production of *Lohengrin*, while the palates of Strauss devotees, salivating over the unfamiliar *Frau*, were further stimulated by a new production of *Elektra*. Considering its subject matter, the opera can hardly be called friendly, but in 1952 its febrile witchery had enthralled radio audiences when the formidable Astrid Varnay made revenge, if not attractive, remarkably welcome in its inevitability. Inge Borkh, in 1961, clothed dementia in fashionable eroticism, but her effort was hampered by conductor Joseph Rosenstock, whose pedestrian podium manner was far removed from the acute guidance of Fritz Reiner in the earlier revival. The new production (grandly decadent in Rudolf Heinrich's sets) was entrusted to Thomas Schippers, whose leadership, sound enough, settles somewhere between the extremes of mediocrity and genius proffered by his two predecessors. Indeed, on the broadcast of 10 December 1966 sound seems his ultimate goal, for he charges headlong through the more blatant passages of the decibel-packed score in heavy boots. Inevitably, the inhabitants of ancient Mycenae feel their blunt imprint.

Fortunately, his charges are a trio of sopranos whose natural vocal endowment makes them virtually impervious to orchestral sabotage. William Dooley, his Orest, is less bountifully equipped and could therefore have been more carefully tended. Nevertheless, the baritone's sympathetic timbre and musico-dramatic sensitivity supply the balm that the prodigal brother must radiate when, in the final moments of the opera, he enters the soprano-charged ether. The manly tenor of James King (his casting an instance of managerial largesse) proves uncommonly attractive as the petulant Aegisth. Not so the weak-toned Guardian of Gerhard Pechner; even the reliable Charles Anthony sounds hard-pressed as the Young Servant. The quintet of maids (well stocked with ghastly glottals) augments the pervasive *Schrecklichkeit*.

Of the principals, Rysanek's Chrysothemis is the only holdover from the 1961 airing. Hers is a justly celebrated portrayal and once again it registers high on the thrill meter. Only in the central portion of her first solo do we briefly suffer the blight that here continues to afflict her lower voice. Her fiercely energetic manner and outsized vocalism, glorious in themselves, are so potent as to occasionally threaten to steal some of the thunder that rightly belongs to her much-abused sister. But, of course, Birgit Nilsson can more than hold her own in the thunder department. When the two sopranos celebrate their brother's triumphant matricide, the airwaves bristle with ravishing tone (Rysanek's province) and thrusting sonance (Nilsson's bounteous store). Resnik experiences a bit of tremulousness at her entrance—interchange between registers is the cause. Beyond that momentary caution, her Klytämnestra is a magnificent creation. In an interview in the broadcast issue of *Opera News*, the mezzo-soprano reminds us that the tormented mother is a "tragic figure," not merely a "physical wreck. . . . After all, she is a queen."[14] The dignity of Resnik's stage impersonation resonates in her commanding voice. Its size and luxuriant coloration quickly become fully responsive to the artist's imaginative demands. We are spared the more familiar vocal caricature, replete with vocal tricks. In the mesmerizing episode where the mother slips into nostalgia and Elektra craftily draws her further into remembrance of earlier familial times, Resnik endows the scene with multiple, subtle layers of characterization.

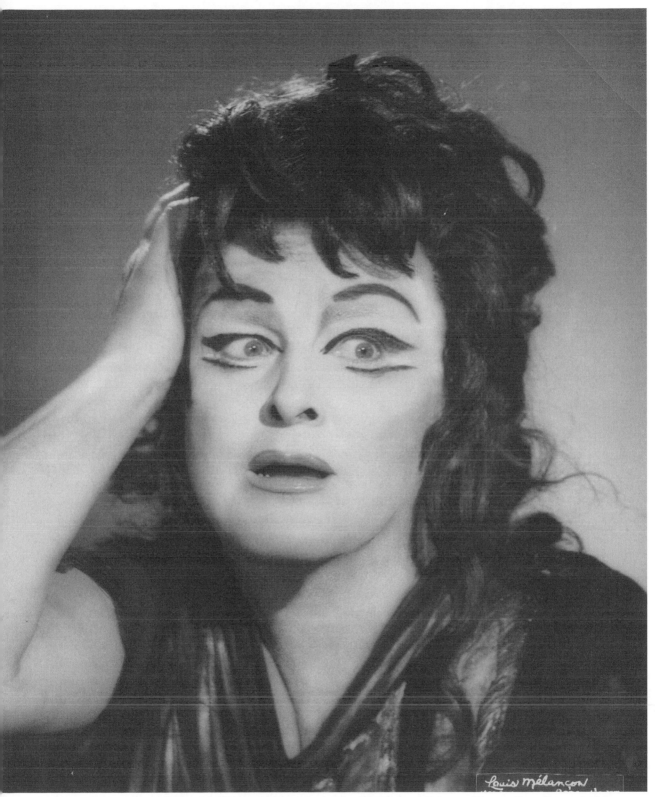

Birgit Nilsson as Elektra. Photography by Louis Mélançon. Courtesy Metropolitan Opera Archives.

The number of Wagner operas in the Met's yearly repertory continued to be limited by the drought of superior male Wagnerians. Of Nilsson's heroines, only Isolde figured in the current list, and since her elevated rank in the hierarchy of divas demanded a new production, Elektra seemed an inevitable choice for the soprano's prodigious gifts. She had first undertaken the role the previous year in Stockholm and thereafter repeated it in Wieland Wagner's Vienna mounting. Her success as Salome at the Met in the previous two seasons was further certification of her Straussian credentials. And, as heard on the broadcast, her craggy Elektra is certainly a success. For most of the opera (all but the recognition scene) the heroine operates at full throttle and no Met soprano ever had less fear of stripping her vocal gears than our Swedish paragon. Splendid moments abound. Not only is her ever-resilient upper voice radiantly deployed, but the mid and lower voice has a welcome burnishment; its often opulent color and constant solidity are effective aids in negotiating the many patches of low tessitura that are especially prominent in the opening monologue. She has studied hard to suggest the netherworld of Elektra's hatred (a domain obviously quite foreign to her optimistic temperament). To that end, she introduces a number of telling dramatic touches such as striking gutteral laughs and a sneering, cynical taunting of Aegisth. Yet, in the long run, some of her effects are oddly annoying, in part because her timbre—and perhaps her creative genes—do not allow much variation of her brilliant Nordic tone. But her thrilling, forthright vocalism in the duet with her newly discovered brother is immensely satisfying. Disappointment does finally surface when she cannot summon the requisite lyricism, the all-enveloping tenderness for the cathartic episode of the opera, namely, Elektra's aria after she recognizes Orest. Here a number of quiet, sympathetic, incredibly lovely, silvery top tones do much to create the requisite mood. If sweetness does not live in the tone, affection certainly motivates the intent and governs the manner. Still, the overall shape of the phrases is insufficiently pliant, the tone a mite too self-contained to redeem this heroine quite as fully as Strauss intended. That reservation acknowledged, it is tremendously reassuring to know from the moment of the curtain's rise that we are in safe hands with Nilsson. This soprano meets the formidable challenges of this fearsome role head-on and conquers them.

Fortune smiled on opera lovers (and Strauss) when she allowed the convergence of three such potent artists as Nilsson, Rysanek, and Resnik on this broadcast afternoon—a serendipitous time frame, indeed. Next up in the line of new productions was *Lohengrin* (8 December premiere) and there, too, artists of merit were nigh. In the broadcast schedule, the Wagner operas were clustered together, with *Die Meistersinger von Nürnberg* (14 January) played a week before *Lohengrin*. *Tristan*, the only other offering in the repertory, was not broadcast. The previously cited heroic tenor drought in the Teutonic area evidently caused management to shy away from certain documentation and the millions of listeners that the broadcast would have guaranteed. And rightly so: in nine scheduled house performances Ticho Parly, Pekka Nuotio, and Karl Liebl were valiant, but vanquished. Regrettably, Nilsson's Isolde would be absent from the airwaves from February 1963 to December 1971.

Nor is the *Meistersinger* broadcast quite the treat the Met had served up in earlier years. Joseph Rosenstock is at the helm, as he had been in 1963. He tramps through the miraculous aural landscape with his destination clearly in mind and

Die Meistersinger
14 January 1967

Eva
Jean Fenn
Magdalene
Mildred Miller
Walther
Sándor Kónya
David
Murray Dickie
Hans Sachs
Giorgio Tozzi
Kothner
William Walker
Beckmesser
Karl Dönch
Pogner
Ezio Flagello
Conductor
Joseph Rosenstock

delivers his charges safely there, but he neglects to savor the view en route. Wagner's expressive ideas need more breathing space. The multiple and varied felicities of remembered airings with Fritz Reiner, Rudolf Kempe, and Karl Böhm do linger in the ear. Of the principal singers, only Kónya, Karl Dönch, and Ezio Flagello were 1963 participants, but even they are new to this chronicle in these roles. A healthy American contingent fills the ranks. In addition to Flagello's Pogner, Jean Fenn (Eva), Mildred Miller (Magdalena), William Walker (Kothner), Clifford Harvuot (Nightwatchman), and all the second-rank mastersingers (including Andrea Velis, Gabor Carelli, Robert Nagy, Louis Sgarro, and Norman Scott) look for guidance to the newly minted Sachs of Giorgio Tozzi. A novel cosmopolitan touch is added by the broadcast debut of a Scot, tenor Murray Dickie, as David.

Sachs' put-upon apprentice can be a trial not only to his master but to the audience as well. A character part of some length, the role of David requires considerable tenorial skill in addition to the expected sprightly demeanor and knowing manner. More than most broadcast Davids, Dickie has that elusive combination, although an occasional bray of top tone causes aural discomfort. But his long experience in the role (including performances under Sir Thomas Beecham) and idiomatic delivery (perfected at the Vienna Staatsoper and Salzburg) are fully apparent, especially in the final act. In yet another role of the character *Fach*, Karl Dönch offers a virtuoso turn as Beckmesser. If (as opposed to the more congenial interpretation currently in favor), you prefer the traditional portrayal of the town clerk-critic (staccato tones, spitted consonants, a mean-spirited nasality when at his nastiest), he is your man. As the aspirant to Eva's hand assures Sachs, "Beckmesser; keiner besser!" but neither the cobbler nor we can swallow that bit of self-promotion. Still, Dönch has a decent baritone and employs it rather frequently—especially as he begins his contest song—so that the conception is well balanced and ultimately successful. Harvuot fulfills Wagner's intent when he utters the Watchman's second warning in "a weak, quavering voice," and Walker is an efficient Kothner, singing rather than barking the role. As father Pogner, Flagello may not be a song contestant, but he would surely win if he were. Vocally he is always on the winning team. Is there a more beautiful bass voice to be heard on the mid-sixties' broadcasts? His Italianate tones and warm manner may create a double image for his character (how could this father have offered his daughter a choice between celibacy and an arranged marriage?), but they are tremendously reassuring to us and undoubtedly cosseted his willful daughter.

The quintet of amorists (count as number five the tempted Sachs) are a respectable group, but several are not entirely comfortable in this mating game. Dickie knows the rules. So does Miller, ever the dependable musician and wise in the ways of the stage. And her tutelage early in her career in the German houses allows her Magdalena to make her points effectively. But her attractive timbre flirts with the soprano mode. The coloration has the virtue of making Magdalena seem more marriageable than many aging, dowdy-voiced mezzos have suggested, but the voice proves a little light for the ensemble assignments. Miss Fenn's Eva suffers from the same decibel lack. The soprano must have made a lovely stage picture. She, too, knows what is expected of her and moves through the role with assurance. Wagner posed a problem for all players of his adorable heroine: he alloted her limited time in the spotlight. But an Eva, in the few, but rapturous, moments that are hers, must project a star quality if the drama is to enrapture us in turn and its musical counterpart to flower fully. Fenn fails in this key requisite. She owns a fine lyric instrument, its attractive timbre not inapt for an idiomatic Eva (though it lacks the shimmer of light-voiced portrayers like Seefried and the puissance of a Della Casa or De los Angeles). The voice is well trained, firmly focused, and without wobble—those are attributes that warrant gratitude. But her firmly delivered act-two outburst in Sachs' studio doesn't startle, doesn't cause the spine to tingle. (Recall Rethberg's thrilling sounding of this episode.) Fenn might have been expected to launch the quintet lovingly, but there her rather ordinary manner (the sixteenth notes remain mere conduits to the next tone in her phraseology) cannot capture nor, indeed, amplify the serenity of the blessed dawn image. Nor has Tozzi well prepared the magical moment, for he employs full voice at 'Die selige "Morgentraum."' Wagner marked it *piano*. Fortunately, on this afternoon, our noble knight is worthy of his station. If Gigli had undertaken Stolzing he may have sounded and played the role rather as Kónya does. The latter's succulent tenor is doubly welcome for returning what too often has been a trial for the audience to the stage contest where it belongs. Oh, he can be excessively casual with rhythms here and there, unexpectedly introduce an Italianate sob, drop a few words, chew on his German vowels until they turn Hungarian, and treat the repetitive circular phrases in the practice lieds as though pitch doesn't matter (it's only a rehearsal, isn't it?). But when it comes to the real thing, he delivers. There Kónya's high As crown his efforts and assure him the prize. Beautiful tone, heft in the big moments, consummate aplomb, even an appropriate character touch now and then, make him a Stolzing worthy of any Eva, let alone this one.

Kónya is one with his role. The same cannot be said of Tozzi. It is perhaps too much to expect that he should be at ease in this lengthy, complex assignment when he has only added it to his repertory this season. Moreover, he has been asked to sing his first Metropolitan Sachs on the Saturday afternoon broadcast, a testing beyond the norm for the most searching, experienced artist. And he is a bass singing what is at best a bass-baritone role, and one frequently sung by baritones. (The broadcast history thus far has included Friedrich Schorr, Paul Schöffler, and Otto Edelmann, all normally classified as bass-baritones, and Herbert Janssen, a lyric baritone.) Though Sachs is all too human (I call it his most attractive quality), he possesses godlike attributes. So must the singing actor who portrays him. Stamina beyond the ordinary, a timbre that encompasses both sturdiness and warmth, and powers of imagination, both musical and dramatic, are needed if success is to be gained.

Now in the middle of his forties and of his two-decades-plus Met career, Tozzi possesses several, but unfortunately not all, of those attributes. Stamina is his to a remarkable degree, for he has as much voice at the end of the afternoon as at the opening (only a single top tone betrays a hint of strain in the final peroration). And he has the range for the role, the top notes firmly sung and of excellent quality. Though he is a bass, his tone is warm, not stern, and owns a certain airiness as though the timbre is penetrated by light; this is a welcome asset for any Sachs, baritone or bass or in between, and it allows Tozzi to project the good humor, the well-being of the hero cobbler with unaffected ease. When heartiness is called for, Tozzi supplies it in abundance—his 'Tralalei's ring out wonderfully. When it comes to imaginative powers, we enter uncertain territory. It may be the newness of the assignment that accounts for deficiency there. The core of Sachs is revealed in the monologues of the second and third acts. Tozzi has not yet fully digested them. He manages the agitated section of the 'Wahn' monologue in acceptable fashion, but the introspective moments there and in the 'Flieder' monologue (and they are the heart of these set pieces) are unconvincing to a marked degree, lacking in legato and variety of expression. He is unable to command a mezza voce—when singing softly, in fact, he seems and sounds ill at ease; perhaps his support is not adequate to sustain the tone. That may also be the cause of the discrepancies in pitch which surface both in minor and critical moments—unfortunately, it affects the opening and close of the 'Flieder' monologue. Tozzi probably turned gratefully to solving Walther's problems for there he is a secure and ingratiating teacher of the miscreant lover. Let us hope that in the remaining ten performances of Sachs which the Met allotted him that the bass was able to bring the introspective episodes to a par with his captivating merry moods. The voice is a fine one for the role, and we desperately need a grand Sachs.

Orchestra and chorus are in good form, but it must be said that, in spite of their efforts, the festive spirit is not well sustained throughout the long afternoon. Senseless cuts of a page here or two pages there do not help. Above all, *Meistersinger* must be cast from strength and cannot be treated as a repertory piece.

On paper, the broadcast of *Lohengrin* on 21 January 1967 holds a brighter prospect. There Ingrid Bjoner, Ludwig, Kónya, Berry, Sherrill Milnes, and John Macurdy respond to Böhm's leadership as the maestro conducts his first Met series of the romantic favorite.

Wieland Wagner was the progenitor of the new mounting. *Opera News* appropriately coined a birthing term ("conceived by") in assigning to him the production credit. But the midwife was Wieland's Bayreuth assistant, Peter Lehmann. The grandson of the composer and originator of the new Bayreuth production style had died several weeks before the Met *Lohengrin* was unveiled on 8 December. His reshaping of nineteenth-century Wagner production values had been applauded in Europe for a decade and a half, but, even with some of the more startling symbolist effects diluted for the New York public, their modest abstraction evidently proved unsettling to the Met public. (Even in more recent times, that conservative body retains a fondness for the trappings of nineteenth-century realistic settings: Robert Wilson's evocative, but bare-bones production of *Lohengrin* in 1998 became a cause célèbre when the normally civil Met patrons booed at the premiere.) *Opera News* confidently proclaimed "on December 8, the new Bayreuth came to America," but it enjoyed only immigrant status.[15] After only two seasons, its green card expired and the production was retired.

Aural gratification, however, is the privilege of the broadcast audience. For them, the only acknowledgement of the visual concept is what may be the sound of a chorister keeling over in the second act—chorus members were ringed on circular tiers and stood immobile throughout the opera. A salutary side effect of that oratorio-like setting is the exemplary choral work throughout the afternoon. Under Böhm's leadership, chorus and orchestra are again in capital form. The conductor never allows Romantic sentimentality to inhibit the dynamism of his conception. The extensive ensemble scenes, in particular, feel the charge. (He goes so far as to propel the conclusion of the first-act finale with a startling accelerando—shades of the fondly remembered Bodanzky routs of the thirties!) The maestro keeps his soloists on the run as well, but they are well equipped for the course.

Lohengrin
21 January 1967

Elsa
Ingrid Bjoner
Ortrud
Christa Ludwig
Lohengrin
Sándor Kónya
Telramund
Walter Berry
Herald
Sherrill Milnes
King Henry
John Macurdy
Conductor
Karl Böhm

Kónya evidently was out of sorts at the premiere, but this broadcast portrayal holds many of the virtues of his 1964 airing. Buttery tone may turn his legato into a taffy-pull—the German consonants indolently loll when they ought to crisp the line—but that oddly appealing trait will be considered no demerit by Wagnerites who have suffered reams of tonal bleakness from tenors of more idiomatic diction. The Hungarian tenor ably supplies the contrasting requisites of the role. That is, he has the heft for the thrusting phrases that dot the score when Lohengrin assumes a commanding stance, but his gentle, honeyed tone in itself conjures the innate purity of a knight of the Grail. When the two modes come together, as in his noble, but contained, act-two voicing of 'Komm, lass in Freude dort diese thränen fliessen!,' Kónya is the very aural picture of a gracious hero. He is a touch casual interpretively now and then. A salutary effect of his nonchalance is the intimacy that permeates the bridal chamber duet. I sense that he is pacing himself carefully through the rigorous demands of the final act. His lyrical reading of 'In fernem Land' conjures an aptly ethereal aura in this evocation of remote Montsalvat while his easy manner preserves its narrative character. In the 1880s, Hugo Wolf, the composer of impeccable songs, demeaned himself—people do—by criticizing the creative work of others in the *Wiener Salonblatt*; when he heard the elusive knight of the estimable Heinrich Vogl (Wagner's first Loge and Siegmund), he found him "too much the mortal."[16] Kónya escapes that trap—so much so that more declamatory thrust for Lohengrin's final revelation of his origin and name would add a fillip to a finely conceived and, in large part, still well-executed portrayal.

Elsa served for Norwegian soprano Ingrid Bjoner's debut role at the Met in 1961. In successive seasons she had appeared as Eva, Donna Anna, Ariadne, the Countess, and the Empress in *Frau*; Fidelio and Turandot were in her Met future, as were Brünnhilde and Elektra in other venues. From that lineup one might deem her an asset in the grand ensembles (she proves to be), but question management's judgment in casting her as the demure Elsa in so prominent a new production. Portrayers of the Brabantine ought to be either radiant of manner (Lehmann-esque, at best) or tonally gleaming (à la Lemnitz), and preferably both, as was Steber in her palmy days. Without one or the other of these attributes, Elsa is a hard heroine to like, let alone love. Miss Bjoner cannot register in either category. She has a healthy voice, but it is more an all-purpose soprano, rather dowdy of tone in the lower octave, yet bright and more attractive in the upper regions (and secure there). Her manner is that of a self-sufficient Hausfrau. Interpretively, she seems quite matter-of-fact until assertiveness causes her sound to turn shrewish. From her rendering of the dream aria one might think Elsa merely had a restless sleep, so lacking in wondrous remembrance is her conception. Her second-act encounter with Ortrud is an improvement, especially after she descends from the tower to comfort the unhappy wife. But she remains the weak link in a cast of superior quality.

The remaining male members of the group are select. House bass John Macurdy's burgeoning Met career notches a step higher with his sympathetic portrayal of King Henry. More than many a bass in the Teutonic repertory he modifies dynamics and tonal color in response to textual cues, and thus his monarch is not only benevolent, but more interesting. Early on, one or two top tones get away from him, but elsewhere his voice is firm and resonant. The Herald has served as a youthful vehicle for many a promising baritone but few were destined to figure so

prominently in multiple Metropolitan ventures as Sherrill Milnes. He is no shooting star destined for a brief orbit, however blazing his beginnings (and plagued
his end). Consider that, between his December 1965 debut as Valentin in the old
house and his broadcast Herald he has been a Met Yeletsky, Fernando, Amonasro,
Jack Rance, Gérard, Renato, Ashton, *Samson* High Priest, and Escamillo, with
Germont and a pivotal role in the upcoming premiere of *Mourning Becomes Electra*
on the docket before the current season ends. Barnaba and Don Carlo would be
added in the fall of 1967. Some of this largesse had come about in the course of
serving as a replacement for another baritone, but his ability to accommodate so
varied a repertory with assurance and quality was testimony to his native intelligence and musical training. And years on the Boris Goldovsky touring circuit had
broadened his repertory and solidified his stage know-how. "Those years taught
me to take the pace and pressure of the profession," he confidently opined in a
prebroadcast interview.[17] He was right: his Herald fairly reeks of self-assurance.
Wagner offers him little opportunity for characterization—a herald's job is to
declaim and Milnes does it splendidly. His longtime admirers may be surprised at
the bright cast of the voice, its narrower-bore focus an attractive alternative to the
burred timbre of his maturity. He even manages to discover a few opportunities
for vocal expression and offer an occasional phrase caress.

Of late, we are not used to hearing prime baritones as the now belligerent,
now groveling Telramund. Usurpers are merely expected to implement their villainy with brutish tone. In bygone days, Friedrich Schorr and Herbert Janssen did
not conform to that prescription and, happily, Walter Berry is in their line. We
know his virtues from his remarkably sympathetic Barak. His Count of Brabant is
strong of voice and intense in manner, but no conventional malefactor. Through
richness of tone and musical integrity this baritone evokes a modicum of sympathy for a husband in thrall to a 'fürchterliches Weib.' By their imaginative play
and superb vocalism, Berry and Christa Ludwig (in life his real wife and certainly
no "frightful" spouse), make their scene outside the palace gates the high point of
the afternoon. The mezzo-soprano follows her triumph as the Dyer's Wife with
another superb portrayal. The voice is so round, so firmly anchored, so consistent
in timbre and size throughout its entire compass that one can only marvel at its
uniform excellence. She easily navigates the tessitura of the part (the role is often
taken by dramatic sopranos) and is fearless in her conquest of its widely ranging
phrases, as fresh-voiced in her final assault after Lohengrin reveals his name as in
her opening gambits. Nor is she afraid to employ a broad portamento to assist
her efforts; in the more exuberant or trying phrases she occasionally swathes its
curves or angles with a broad brush of sound, preferring to preserve tonal continuity rather than articulate notes or text with absolute precision. The process aids
projection and does preserve dramatic intensity during critical moments. But she
is no mere unloader of tone, however resounding. More than many an Ortrud, she
introduces varieties of dynamics and subtleties of timbre to bring her husband to
heel: she either converts him to her evil pursuits with secretive, wheedling whispers or taunts him with scornful bursts of plangent tone. Elsa, too, falls under her
spell as Ludwig cajoles her with utterance pathetic, yet demanding. In her memoirs, she confides that singing Ortrud "beautifully" allows the audience to experience a more sympathetic response to the sorceress.[18] She achieves that goal. Of
course, her fearless 'Entweihte Götter!' reaps applause—her tone seems to spring

from the roots of her being. Amazingly, she maintained that she "never found the role difficult," and her performance gives credence to the claim.[19] A ragged attack or two mars 'Der Rache Werk' as the stage spouses implore the gods to aid them in their vengeance. Surely their faulty unison is not an unconscious harbinger of the divorce that lies in their future.

Die Zauberflöte
4 March 1967

Pamina
Judith Raskin
Queen
Roberta Peters
First Lady
Mary Ellen Pracht
Tamino
George Shirley
Papageno
Theodor Uppman
Speaker
Walter Cassel
Sarastro
John Macurdy
Conductor
Josef Krips

After naming the premiere of *Die Frau ohne Schatten* the acknowledged triumph of the opening season, I must acknowledge that the new production of *Die Zauberflöte* is a strong competitor for that honor. Kolodin, writing in the *Saturday Review*, went so far as to name it Mr. Bing's "most sophisticated venture" with the company.[20] Tipping the scales in favor of that judgment was the remarkable production of Marc Chagall, an investiture (complemented by Günther Rennert's staging) that filled cynical critics with wonder and would continue to dazzle audiences for many seasons. The radio audience could only imagine the colorful components of Chagall's production—though assuredly many could fill the void by drawing upon their acquaintance with his widely disseminated graphic art—and therefore it seems appropriate to adhere to my earlier judgment in awarding the palm to the Strauss premiere. The introduction of a work new to the house tips the scales in its favor.

The specific musical character of the 19 February 1967 *Zauberflöte* premiere cannot be judged, though the presence of such experienced Mozarteans as Pilar Lorengar, Lucia Popp, Nicolai Gedda, and Hermann Prey guaranteed a high measure of authentic style and lovely vocalism. By intent, management excused the European principals and subsidiary Americans and introduced an all-American cast for the third performance and the broadcast on 4 March. Double casts were necessary since, in addition to many performances by both contingents in the regular series, a number of student performances were also scheduled. The Chagall sets assuredly were prime movers in that regard. Josef Krips led both the premiere and broadcast. The widely respected conductor, heard in his debut appearances at the Met, brought with him elements of the Viennese Mozart style that he himself had helped to shape in his long association with the Staatsoper and other houses in the city of his birth. I remember him well. In the mid-fifties, from my perch in the Musikverein's Orgelgalerie, I had looked long and appreciatively into his benevolent, rather cherubic, face as he conducted the complete Beethoven symphonies and subsidiary works (including Nilsson's commanding traversal of 'Ah! perfido'). That benevolence, auditory rather than visual this time, governs his idiomatic broadcast reading of the many-sided marvel that Mozart fashioned out of Schikaneder's hodgepodge script. An occasional imprecision—a nonsynchronized tympanum upbeat, a faulty wind attack on an opening chord, even a fleeting divergence between pit and stage (Kolodin thought the lack of coordination shocking at the premiere)—does not diminish the warmth and authority of his interpretation. He lovingly shapes the specific topics of Mozart's varied text, sometimes so carefully that the gear shifts show, but by the second act complete fluidity obtains. He returned the following season to conduct the first two performances of the opera but thereafter the work fell to Rosenstock. Regrettably, Krips' Met career was limited to four seasons, his only charges three Mozart operas. But his *Figaro* and *Giovanni* also would make it to the airwaves.

Until the Chagall production, the opera had always been broadcast in English and Americans had figured prominently in the cast lists. Uppman and Peters are the longtime survivors of those *Magic Flute* airings and their portrayals once again prove their worth. The California baritone is heard here in his fifth consecutive broadcast as Papageno and he would rack up another pair before his career ends. The broadcast tally and Metropolitan record (60 performances) confirm the hold he had on the role from the fifties through the seventies. (Prey, John Reardon, and Donald Gramm would garner single broadcast outings before Uppman's finale in 1977.) His portrayal is as fresh as ever, lively in dialogue, endearing in song, with his pliant head voice augmenting delight and expert German diction lending new colors to his birdcatcher's finely gauged whimsy. Peters, too, knows every inch of the Queen's rocky terrain. She negotiates the coloratura hurdles of her arias without a trace of fear at their difficulties. Her technique is as impregnable as Asteria's chastity, though a few squeaks above high C blight her on-the-mark staccatos. Krips adopts a slower tempo for 'Der Hölle Rache' than she evidently prefers, even slowing down for the treacherous moments; he thus hampers the soprano, one of the few who can knock out the filigree effortlessly in tempo. She gamely tries to project evil intent (as much as her vocal size will allow), but naturally she is more successful in 'O zitt're nicht,' where the mother's goodness is still plausible. New to the broadcasts in their assignments are Nedda Casei (Third Lady), Loretta Di Franco (a piquant Papagena), Armored Men Michalski and Franke (demoted from Monostatos and showing the reason why), and, in that role, Andrea Velis, a capital, vocally nasty Moor. Three well-tutored boys replace the Met's customary women as genii. Heard in the 1964 broadcast, but new to my chronicles, are Shirley Love (Second Lady), Mary Ellen Pracht (a First Lady of sweet tone, but rather small-voiced for a role that once called for a Steber or Amara), Walter Cassel, and George Shirley. The role of the Sprecher allows Cassel, largely a veteran of major character parts, to discard his burly manner for once; he delivers a surprisingly cultivated performance, both in tone and manner.

Macurdy and Judith Raskin are heard in new broadcast assignments as Sarastro and Pamina. We have come to expect from the wise priest a flood of rolling black tones that descend into a vocal abyss with nary a care and rock-solid authority. Nothing else apparently will do for these hymnal arias. The character of the Detroit bass' instrument, however, conjures a decidedly youthful sorcerer. The voice is neither black nor assertive in its lowest range and thus his efforts in those godlike moments do not meet expectations. But elsewhere (and even in the higher regions of the hymns), his tone is sympathetic. Dare we hope that it may have been more reassuring to the beleaguered Pamina than the impressive grandeur of a Gottlob Frick? Raskin is a charming Pamina, her sweet, girlish tone a delight, its purity suggesting the heroine's helpless plight and in itself evoking pathos. But she is a determined heroine as well, straightforward in her desires, by true intervallic leaps and pointed tones adding spine to the role. The girl was, after all, her mother's daughter. She doesn't coddle 'Ach, ich fühls,' but bravely traverses its meandering paths; eschewing sentiment, she chooses rather to register bewildered innocence. The voice is a mite light, perhaps even white, for the Pamina of one's dreams, but she satisfies day-world needs.

I have saved for last the serendipitous best—that is, the performance that gives complete satisfaction not only for its quality but for its novelty. On the broadcasts, tenor George Shirley has appeared as Ferrando (1962) and Tamino (1964), but thus far we have met him only in lesser roles (Isolde's taunting Steers-

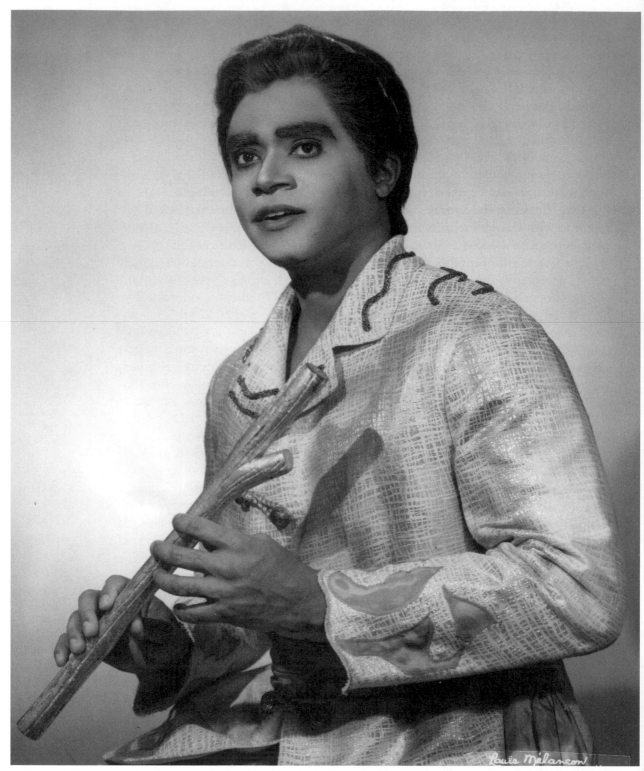

George Shirley as Tamino in *Die Zauberflöte*. Photography by Louis Mélançon. Courtesy Metropolitan Opera Archives.

man, Beppe, and Narraboth), all appealingly done. In fact, by the 1967 *Zau berflöte*, Shirley had undertaken at the Met roles as diverse as Almaviva, Elvino, Rodolfo, the French Des Grieux, and Gabriele. Obviously, his is a worthy talent. The voice has an appealing timbre, manly yet touched with light, and a curious kind of sweetness. It ascends into the higher range without perceptible strain or timbral break and operates with ease in that region. He is an impeccable musician, adept at fast passagework, alive to textual dictates and mood changes and able to suggest them by vocal means. The 'Bildnis' aria is delivered with complete aplomb (and appropriate interpretive gestures in response to the text), yet elsewhere he summons uncommon passion for a prince who is afraid of a snake. How commanding in recitative is his Tamino when he approaches the temple doors! In the two critical episodes where Mozart employs his innovative Germanic idiom (the first with Cassel, the second in the trio with Raskin and Macurdy), Shirley is deeply committed and quite moving; there he is abetted by Krips, who is particularly convincing in these elevated moments of the score. At the other end of the spectrum, Shirley sings the flute melody with artless grace as the animals cavort. Is it overreaching to suggest that he might be a Rosvaenge in the making? Would that the Met had been his home for longer than his allotted twelve consecutive seasons so that we could know the answer.

The broadcast may not have had quite the glamor of the premiere but the American contingent under Krips' hand delivered a performance of substantial quality. Cross is right to hail the final chorus of rejoicing over "the triumph of courage, virtue, beauty, and wisdom." The tormented amorists of the composer's *Don Giovanni* honor those high-minded qualities rather less than the denizens of Sarastro's domain. The gratification of their desires, though more easily attainable, proves more elusive. Still, in this opera, it is the chase that matters, as the broadcast songsters of 28 January 1967 demonstrate once again. Even among the inaugural season's spate of new productions, the company's 1957 mounting remains one of Bing's prime achievements and the current musical rendering retains the high standard of the decade-old premiere.

Böhm's duties this season are many, as we have seen. Hearing his spacious yet dramatic traversal of *Don Giovanni* provides a familiar pleasure. The overture is commandingly done, the interpretation even a bit imperious at times. Otherwise, his tempos tend toward the leisurely, the singers readily accommodated (Siepi occasionally presses a bit, but not unduly) and theatrical impact agreeably wedded with classical restraint. The Italian bass and Uppman are Böhm's only remaining cohorts from the 1957 premiere and both deliver characteristic performances. Amidst the rumble of three sonorous basses—baritone Giovannis are no longer impresarios' preferred seducers—Uppman's heady baritone lends needed timbral contrast and, of greater importance, his comic stance is dramatically inviting. An expressive touch here and there adds interest to the rather limited musical means that Mozart settled on his peasant bridegroom. The composer better served the bride, but Laurel Hurley fails to make the most of his largesse. Her 'Batti, batti, o bel Masetto' is unattractive in timbre (sadly, her once-vibrant tone sounds scratchy and lacking in resonance on sustained notes) and awkward at times, while the frequently sounded F at the top of the staff repeatedly veers under pitch. She fares much better with 'Vedrai, carino.' There her tone regains some of its wonted luster.

Don Giovanni
28 January 1967

Donna Anna
Joan Sutherland
Donna Elvira
Pilar Lorengar
Zerlina
Laurel Hurley
Don Ottavio
Nicolai Gedda
Don Giovanni
Cesare Siepi
Leporello
Fernando Corena
Masetto
Theodor Uppman
Commandant
Bonaldo Giaiotti
Conductor
Karl Böhm

Siepi, of course, has the lion's share of the afternoon's work and he shoulders it with remarkable good humor. His manner is all affability. This rake converts corruption of damsels into a gentlemanly occupation. The ins and outs of the role are intimately known to him and he makes no false moves (unless you count those that Da Ponte intentionally fixed on Giovanni). Vocally, he is in superb form, his instrument well channeled, its plummy resonance almost never overburdening the classical poise of Mozart's phrases. The opening of 'Là ci darem' is seduction personified. One might hope for an airier tone (mezza voce would be welcome) in the Serenade, but Siepi's legato and timbral control are plausible alternatives. Böhm's staid tempo in the champagne tribute is rather inhibiting so the basso is denied his familiar virtuoso turn, but the little aria remains an expertly declaimed lark. Ezio Flagello plays his much-put-upon servant without recourse to buffo tricks. The portrait may lose a touch of fetching comedy and volubility, but the gain in musicality and dramatic impact is worth it. His imposing voice more readily encompasses the broader phrases of 'Madamina!' than most buffo specialists; oddly, he substitutes the text of the reprise for the opening of the andante con moto section. Flagello loves to sing and, in effect, he leaves the characterization to Böhm, whose orchestra makes the most of Mozart's sardonic instrumental commentary. Of course, Flagello has fun mimicking Siepi's refulgent sonority as he dons Giovanni's cloak—and so do we, especially when he adroitly inserts his own timbre in a brief aside.

Glancing at his repertory, one might think that Gedda is the house's tenor-of-all-work. He is much more than a reliable using-horse in Bing's well-run stable. Adaptability, while a virtue much prized by management, is hardly the value of values. Gedda's artistry, however, rises as high as his repertory is wide. His versatility is quite amazing. In his first decade with the company, Gedda's list had included roles as diverse as Adméte, Hoffmann, Pelléas, Des Grieux, Roméo, Dimitri, Lensky, Tamino, Barinkay, Nemorino, Elvino, Edgardo, the Duke of Mantua, Pinkerton, and Kodanda in Menotti's *The Last Savage*. Amid all that diversity he had his specialties. One thinks of him most fondly as the tenor who invariably rewards Francophiles, while the mordant fall of Lensky's phrases lingers longest in the ear. And on recordings, he is the unique purveyor of Viennese operetta Schwung. Don Ottavio had been an early assignment. He appeared in Berman's new production only ten days after his 1957 debut as Faust. The 1961 broadcast fell to him, but veteran Jan Peerce had a lock on the role for the next three airings. Gedda plays Ottavio with magnificent assurance, as though a lover's reward were a foregone conclusion. As if to leave no doubt of consummation, he forswears the customary mooning stance and attacks 'Dalla sua pace' with firm tone and *forte* dynamic, reserving his *piano* for the reprise. However eager I am to sanctify this most intelligent of artists, I confess that occasionally I am put off by the hint of the bumptious in Gedda's conception of line: some will prefer to describe the demerit as vigor or avoidance of preciosity. If that posture costs him (and, more importantly, us) some of the expected Mozartean suavity of tone and line, he offers compensations. 'Il mio tesoro' is tossed off with an impressive combination of ease and brio; even at Böhm's unhurried pace, every note of the trying fioritura is firmly in place. In the concluding vaudeville, he matches Sutherland note for note in their conjoint sixteenths. Unfortunately, for the time being, that musical union will be Ottavio's only reward. Undoubtedly, the tenor took the news of Anna's reticence with composure. Giaiotti's Commandant (heard in the 1963 broadcast) is newly reported here. Few stone guests have mirrored their concrete state as convincingly as does the Italian with his firm, sepulchral utterance. Böhm's rock-steady rhythmic progress abets the lava-like flow of the two basses' tone as repentance and pride face off.

Pilar Lorengar will enjoy a Metropolitan career of respectable duration. Following appearances in Milan, Buenos Aires, Tokyo, and San Francisco and lengthier residencies at Glyndebourne and the Deutsche Oper in West Berlin (where Carl Ebert was her mentor), the Spanish soprano had come to New York as Donna Elvira in 1960. Previous to her broadcast debut in this performance, she had added only Alice Ford, but Pamina, the Countess, Violetta, Butterfly, and Marguerite would soon give the Met public a fuller measure of her abilities. As heard on this January afternoon, her song may be an acquired taste. Elvira has a shrewish makeup and some have chosen to play her that way, but I doubt that Miss Lorengar consciously cultivates that pose. Yet, at her entry the pointed tone is rather grievously aggravated by a rapid, very pronounced vibrato. Like a wine poured before it enjoys breathing time but whose initial sharpness lessens as the minutes pass, Lorengar's voice loses its excessive pungency, the vibrato eventually comes under control, and one falls under the spell of its crystalline ring. (In some ways she calls to mind Steber's timbre and manner, though agitation never afflicted the American soprano's performances to this degree.) She is a musicianly singer as well, and dramatically vivid—the agitated manner befits Elvira's emotional state. All fioritura passages are readily accommodated. In fact, the extensive, intricate passagework of 'Mi tradì' is so easily negotiated that her reading (notwithstanding some welcome variety in intermediate passages) is a bit placid. On the other hand, in Lorengar's throat, the aria seems a more natural utterance than we have heard from most sopranos. One can't help but eagerly look forward to future appearances by this appealing artist.

The jewel of the performance is Sutherland's singing of Donna Anna's arias. Since her triumphant 1961 debut as Lucia the diva's Met appearances had been limited to repetitions of that role, plus Amina and Violetta. All three portrayals were broadcast. Her assumption of Anna presents the reigning coloratura soprano in territory almost a half-century removed from the bel canto milieu that has been her natural habitat. She has the principal attributes for the role: a voice of size that can amplify the grand emotions of an *opera seria* heroine and agility to negotiate the fioritura minefield of 'Non mi dir.' It must be admitted that her proverbial mushy diction is uncommonly prominent at some moments. How she opens the closed vowels, and dodges words like 'mio' and even consonants that might trouble the flow of tone! But the distinction of her singing in the accompanied recitatives and arias is so rare that praise must be her full portion.

Where most sopranos simulate vengeance in 'Or sai chi l'onore' by hurling their voices onto the uppermost notes of the aria and emphasizing its bracing rhythms, Sutherland laces the phrases with appoggiaturas and sustains the mood of a troubled daughter more than that of an avenging force. In a few brief passages, she introduces a lovely, unexpected effect with a quiet remembrance of the murdered father. She has no need to assault the repeated As that crown many phrases they are hers to command, firmly and fully and with radiant tone. To hear all the little subsidiary runs so clearly articulated is a bonus. Her way with the piece is original and highly effective. Like other astute artists (with an assist, no doubt, from husband Bonynge) she has devised an interpretation that suits her means. On this afternoon, the mask trio is an unadulterated treat by all participants. Lorengar is particularly fine here, her tone lovely, settled, and on the mark, while Sutherland's negotiation of the ascending and descending runs is a marvel of ease and beauty. To go further, her 'Non mi dir' is a revelation. Yes, she takes forever in the preceding accompanied recitative and the lack of crisp diction is again annoying. (I take solace in recalling that Hugo Wolf—I have him on my mind—decried the purportedly unimpeachable Lilli Lehmann's indistinct diction as "unbearable" when he heard her Anna and Norma. "Baby-talk" was his derisive term for it. [21]) As if offered in retribution, Sutherland's vault to 'Abbastanza' is powerful and bracing. Oddly she detaches the initial 'Non' from 'mi dir,' violating the full phrase length, but thereafter all is glory. The embellishments of the larghetto are effortlessly and beautifully integrated into Mozart's long-limbed phrases and the tessitura is accommodated with splendid tone. Never on the broadcasts has the allegretto moderato been so handily negotiated, with no tempo hesitations required to aid the singer. Her articulation of the many two-note slurs (not a common feature of most interpretations) graces many a phrase. The staccatos are in tempo (for once they don't sound silly) while the concluding phrase is broadly declaimed in triumph rather than in the more familiar gasp of relief at reaching the trial's end. A concluding low trill puts the cap on a portrayal of marked individuality and distinction.

Stepping back a century in time but holding within the Spanish frame, we travel from the environs of Da Ponte's Seville north to the more violent landscape of Biscay and Aragon. There the passions are equally rampant and as rudimentary, but they blaze rather more flamboyantly. Verdi unflaggingly fanned their flames in *Il Trovatore*, but Francesco Molinari-Pradelli evidently can't stand the heat. Under his stodgy leadership, the 18 February 1967 performance moves at a sluggish pace. The churning energy that is the hallmark of the opera is consistently reined in, the fires damped down. Give the maestro, now in his second Met season, credit for a unified conception; his modest tempos are applied in just proportions throughout the entire opera. Thus the composer's scrupulously formal construct is acknowledged and (perhaps unduly) respected.

For a good deal of the afternoon the singers seem to be merely going through their paces, as though the conductor's restraint has sucked their vitality or diminished their commitment. For they are an able group: Arroyo, Cvejic, Tucker, Merrill. The lead-off man, Raymond Michalski, is a musicianly Ferrando. That attribute may not be the perfect complement for the burly soldier's grisly narrative, but the young bass' perfectly placed voice, deft articulation of Verdi's repetitive rhythmic patterns, and sensitivity to textual content give life to what is too often merely a dull curtain-raiser. Even when that condition obtains, the optimistic opera buff looks for redress from Azucena. A barn-burner turn may or may not have been Verdi's intent—for him, the old gypsy is the heart and soul of the opera—but the opportunities for aggrandizement are there for mezzos with the goods and the will to display them. Biserka Cvejic is not of their ilk, in either regard. Her goods are limited and she does not counterfeit them in an attempt to appease the gallery. She is a respectable provincial Azucena, her tone a bit haggard as she begins, and no more successful than most mezzos within the confined compass of 'Stride la vampa!'. She avoids chest tone (hers is merely functional). Soon

Il Trovatore
18 February 1967

Leonora
Martina Arroyo
Azucena
Biserka Cvejic
Manrico
Richard Tucker
Di Luna
Robert Merrill
Ferrando
Raymond Michalski
Conductor
Francesco Molinari-Pradelli

the voice settles and her gentle tones, while occasionally breathy, are pleasant to the ear. The fourth-act scene with her "son" is nicely done. Throughout the afternoon it is the caring mother rather than the vengeful fanatic who holds the stage. Half an Azucena shortchanges the aficionados but she gets a decent hand at her solo bow at the opera's end (a brave high note as she turns the tables on Di Luna helps). A few performances at the beginning of the next season will terminate the Yugoslav's Met career.

Miss Arroyo is quite another story. Now in her third season as a Met principal, she is in excellent voice from start to finish, the top octave ever free and opulent, indeed quite glorious. And she has managed to lend body to the middle and lower voice, mustering nasal resonance to mask the infantile tone that previously limited projection in that area. The new manner somewhat inhibits interpretive freedom and textual clarity but it proves to be a serviceable response to need. A rather neutral reading of 'Tacea la notte placida' holds some beautiful arched phrases and leads to a modest, yet fluent cabaletta (with a notably even ascending and descending scale and a utilitarian concluding trill). She caps the ensuing trio with an on-the-button high D-flat. The little arioso at the cloister is equally lovely in tone but not phased for maximum effect. That arioso and the fourth-act aria betray one aspect of Arroyo's stylistic deficiencies. Sopranos who wish to make the Verdi terrain their private property ideally should possess in their interpretive arsenal equal parts lineal plasticity and dramatic thrust. At least one or the other is a must. The poised suspension of movement, momentary yet seemingly everlasting, so often gives the Verdi line its unique expressivity. Arroyo has not yet acquired this mesmerizing skill. Perhaps she will eventually discover its power. That she is unresponsive to text and dramatic situation also becomes clear in her unimaginative treatment of the repetitive, mounting three-note phrases suggestive of Leonora's exhilaration as Manrico arrives to save her from the Count ('E deggio e posso crederlo?'). Arroyo could be counting embroidery stitches. Of course, Molinari-Pradelli's plodding tempo would make it almost impossible for any soprano to achieve the proper effect there and in the *concertato* that follows. (In a betrayal of the score, Tucker, like most tenors, joins Arroyo in the magnificent vaulting phrase that ends the act.)

Despite these cavils, Miss Arroyo's pristine vocalism is the main treat of the afternoon. 'D'amor sull'ali rosee' holds no technical terrors for her: the little trills are sound, the top C is effortless (legitimate opulence replaces the remembered Milanov *pianissimo* at the phrase apex), the cadenza is fluent and more complete than most. Her failure in the preceding accompanied recitative to distinguish between Leonora's dismissal of Ruiz, her fear of the night's threatening dark, and the sighing breezes that are to carry her love to the imprisoned Manrico is lamentable, but the soprano's vocal aplomb in the aria must be cherished. Neither soprano nor tenor generates much excitement in a prosaic Miserere. There, Verdi's menacing death chords atrophy under Molinari-Pradelli's baton.

In contrast to the little-known Cvejic and newcomer Arroyo, a pair of old pros tackle the male roles. Tucker and Merrill, often heard in recital together in the late stages of their careers, are respectively enjoying their twenty-third and twenty-second Met seasons. And well seasoned they are in more ways than one. Their professional know-how and solid vocal techniques are blemished by occasional touches of hamming (the tenor's blight) and ham-handedness (a baritone curse on which Merrill has no monopoly). The accusation is not meant to denigrate their immense natural gifts nor their stageworthy qualities but merely to recognize an essential (to them) part of their performance style. They love to please the crowd. Some will value them the more for their heartiness. On this afternoon, even that quality is not enough to prevent some heavy vocal lifting in the early acts until their much-used instruments are massaged into shape. (In his opening gambit, Tucker does manage the tricky offstage serenade better than most.) How our tenor loves to shudder out the numerous exclamations ('Orrore!' is a favored one) that pepper the text! How he spits his way through the recitatives! He comes into his own when Verdi provides lyrical bounty, for he knows how to conduct a line in masterly fashion. Alas! even there the desire to do so is not always upon him. After a fine start (including a splendid extended phrase in the lead-in), he turns the lyrical effusion of 'Ah si, ben mio' into a dramatic, teary turn. Who can gainsay the star tenor from making the most of his moment in the spotlight? Undeniably, something grand (and vocally sound) has transpired. He has pleased his crowd. 'Di quella pira' (taken down a half-step) is not really his meat. He probably knew it, for he did not undertake Manrico at the Met until his twentieth season; eventually his list would include a not inconsiderable twenty-six troubadours. However game his heart and fiery, even pugnacious, his manner (and he brings a welcome spirit to this too pedestrian afternoon), he has neither the heft nor the metal for the call to battle. The initial high B is decidedly hollow but he manages a stout closing shot. He is in his best vocal form by the time he must comfort the imprisoned Azucena. And when Leonora promises him his freedom he lofts a splendid denunciation at her supposed perfidy. Above all, he never forgets what is expected of a tenor.

The final act does in fact contain some lovely work from all participants. Earlier on, Merrill's familiar Di Luna sounds more like the villainous Barnaba than a lovesick aristocrat. In many ways this opera is a throwback to the bel canto era, but Merrill's vocalism on this afternoon is far from that ideal. His voice is rather thick and unwieldy in the early acts, and whenever menace is apposite he relies on a newly developed snarl to deploy tone, a manner quite removed from the mellow richness we have come to expect from him. In his big aria, he, too, prefers a half-step downward transposition (the aging singer's proverbial—and often well-earned—safety-net). Now the voice begins to limber up and, though the ease of his top tones is departing with the years, he provides a big-time moment. And *his* crowd loves it. He really does not need to overblow his tone, willy-nilly employ raised pitch accents, or aimlessly huff away. His still-splendid instrument can speak for itself.

One accepts on faith that early listeners found *Trovatore* excessively gloomy. Verdi's response that "in life isn't everything death?" would seem to confirm that view.[22] It hardly finds an echo in the broadcast's rather superficial traipse through the score. Or is the fault in us? Have we become too jaded from overexposure to the jaunty anvil's clang, the tenor's heady call to arms, the theatrically effective Miserere, the humble 'Home to Our Mountains' (that favorite transcription for beginning piano students), and the stagey trappings of a vengeance-driven gypsy to believe, as undoubtedly the composer did and wanted us to? (Other than death, he wrote, "What else exists?") I want to believe again. Down the line surely we will find a more informing reading of the score. In the meantime, on to *Rigoletto*, a work that continues to inspire belief even in our time. In the father–daughter relationship Verdi did find something more than death to celebrate.

Roberta Peters.

Rigoletto
8 April 1967
Gilda
Roberta Peters
Maddalena
Belén Amparán
Duke
Nicolai Gedda
Rigoletto
Cornell MacNeil
Sparafucile
Bonaldo Giaiotti
Conductor
Lamberto Gardelli

An earlier (8 April 1967) broadcast of *Rigoletto* provides the opportunity, thus far neglected in my chronicle, to appraise one of the most familiar characterizations of the Bing era. The frequency of Roberta Peters' appearances as Gilda before the footlights and over the airwaves alone ensures remembrance in Metropolitan history. What prompted this currency? Fortunately, in this broadcast we hear her in her prime, at a time when artistic maturity and vocal certitude are joined in a gratifying equilibrium, the hoped-for upward path of the former and the normally inevitable downward curve of the latter poised in happy neutrality. Her colleagues include MacNeil (previously heard as the jester in 1960 and 1964 broadcasts), Giaiotti (also a veteran), and, in new radio portrayals, Amparan (Maddalena), Michalski (Monterone), Goodloe (Marullo), and, most notably, Gedda as the Duke of Mantua.

New on the podium is Lamberto Gardelli, currently at the Met for a three-season span. The maestro, Swedish born but with obvious roots in Italy and now in his early fifties, has a wealth of experience to sustain him. Apprenticeship with the revered Tullio Serafin certified his credentials, while lengthy tenures with the Swedish Royal Opera and the Budapest Opera, plus appearances at the Berlin Staatsoper and Glyndebourne, ensured repertory expertise. A composer of operas as well as a podium fixture, Gardelli is more concerned with overall structure than momentary excitement. His tempos are just and his baton reliably articulates traditional musical postures, including orchestral accelerandos and occasional hesitancies that allow the singers to spin tone. (The traditional Met cuts regrettably are in place as well.) Even so, accompaniment figures sometimes lack buoyancy—Gedda, for instance, several times signals that a snappier pace would be more to his liking. But the newcomer's command of all his forces is entirely assured; the agreement between stage and pit is remarkably precise. The 'Zitti' chorus, which can run off the rails, is deftly executed—in general, the men sing well throughout the afternoon. Toscanini tensility may be in short supply in the earlier acts, but Gardelli's storm music is atmospherically potent and cumulative energy in the final act allows the opera to progress to a satisfactory close.

Giaiotti's villain and Michalski's victim are dependably sturdy participants, the former's coal-black instrument sufficiently menacing in itself. The languorous line of the cello solo that underpins Sparafucile's murder proposition is staidly drawn—a touch of insouciance in its line would augment the black humor of the scene. Michalski's attractive instrument easily negotiates Monterone's high tessitura. Amparan's tones are alternatively suggestive, as any reputable Maddalena's ought to be, or blowzy-veiled, as too many voices in the part have been. Goodloe's well-focused delivery of Marullo's lines and vocal character mark him as in the Cehanovsky line of supporting player.

Except for a touch of raw tone in the 'Ah! veglia, o donna' duet and a decidedly disturbing patch of off-pitch (sharp) singing in the 'Piangi!' duet (both with Gilda), MacNeil is in fine fettle, both vocally and interpretively. Of course, those are notable exceptions, since the father–daughter relationship is at the heart of the opera. Nevertheless, the baritone's portrayal is grandly conceived (even threatening in its power at climactic moments), musically sensitive (indeed, he is more faithful to Verdi's markings than most interpreters), and quite affecting when the father's fears and grief surface. A Rigoletto who not only observes but executes with ease the composer's crescendo and diminuendo on the repeated notes of 'quel vecchio maledivami!' must be applauded. And he knowingly underplays certain emotional scenes, as when initially he quietly pleads with the courtiers to leave him with his distraught daughter. At a few critical episodes the American's caressing mezza voce is an effective expressive tool, one not available to many of his colleagues. Basically, his is a broad-shouldered voice. Top tones are thrust forth with surety and splendid density (no slow beat, either); a few stunning high A-flats must have satisfied the hunger of those fans who demand a goodly portion of red meat from a Verdi baritone. Predictably, his rousing delivery of 'Cortigiani, vil razza dannata' is the high point of his portrayal. The rough edges of his vocalism may be exposed here and there, but on this afternoon MacNeil is an all-purpose baritone.

The Duke of Mantua is yet another new Metropolitan assumption for Gedda. He would sing it only a few times during his lengthy career with the company. Understandably, management believed his unique gifts were best employed in rarer venues. His portrayal is remarkably assured, the rakish character of the libertine almost brazenly set forth. Not many Dukes have conveyed with comparable potency so strong a belief in the nobleman's rights, such an inherent disdain for the sensibilities of others. Of course, that means the charm that other celebrated interpreters have purveyed, an appeal that legitimizes the ruler's case of conquest and Gilda's love for him, is minimized. Still, the Swedish tenor, brilliant technician and superb musician that he is, offers some delicious nuances (diminuendos abound) and deft vocal feats (the ornaments are tidily etched). Most remarkable is his sounding of the final cadential tones (marked *dolcissimo*) of 'Parmi veder le lagrime' in a caressing *voix mixte*. The maneuver is seldom attempted, not only due to its difficulty but because the quiet close is certain to dilute applause for lack of a big finish. (Unfortunately, the cabaletta, where Gedda, unlike many tenors, would be expected to shine, is deleted.) The aria's introductory dramatic recitative is delivered with conviction and the challenges of the aria itself, in particular its taxing tessitura, are surmounted with notable vocal splendor and legato phrasing. Though he has forfeited the big finish of 'Parmi veder,' our tenor takes care of any grandstand deficiency with a sprinkling elsewhere of brilliant top tones that are as securely placed and emphatically thrust forth as a fencer's coup de grâce. The crowning feat is a dead center high D-flat at the conclusion of 'Addio, speranza ed anima'; the preceding cantabile is well sung, though hardly bewitching, while the cabaletta is tailor-made for Gedda's talents. Oddly, 'La donna è mobile' would appear not to be to his taste. Perhaps its simple structure, its melodic and philosophic nonchalance, are foreign to his particular intelligence. Gedda's delivery of the piece seems excessively callow, though the trumpeted top note at its close and fleet, well-articulated cadenza command positive response—which the audience readily supplies. In contrast, the reprise, lightly delivered as the rake drops into sleep, is delightful. The quartet belongs to the tenor and here the Duke's charm might be expected to dominate. Braggadocio, however, is Gedda's wooing weapon. Crude desire, obviously the rake's motivation, is more overtly stressed than most tenors prefer to betray in this cherished musico-dramatic ensemble. A notable example of Gedda's scrupulous regard for the composer's directives (in this case, 'palpitar' is marked *stentando*—laboring—with strong accents placed over each note) occurs when he, aided by aspirates, emphatically presses the stepwise ascending notes. Gedda's execution sounds unattractive, though it is accurate and honorable in the intent. As with other roles of this repertory, I do find that the tenor's Italian style is rather strenuous—text can be overaccented and suavity of phrase diluted by rhythmic assertiveness. Some will also find the glare of his timbre wearing in the aggregate. But for bravado and technical finish, the Swedish tenor is in a league of his own.

Peters' secure traversal of her role is a foregone conclusion, but not for that is it any less to be honored. I have not always found the diva's voice and art entirely beguiling, but on this occasion there is much to admire. The still-young soprano (at this time a few weeks short of her thirty-sixth birthday but already enjoying her seventeenth Met season) has always been remarkable for the technical assurance and consistency of her portrayals. She has analyzed the inherent character of her instrument with a thoroughness that commands respect; her control of register adjustment, mixing of chest and head voice, application of nasal resonance where necessary to stabilize or project tone, and numerous other facets of tone management are absolute. The result is both satisfying for its secure vocalism and a bit off-putting in its calculation. For a few, the voice, and its usage, can suggest a masterly fabrication. But her years at the Met have neither wearied tone nor decreased range, though the upper voice can narrow excessively and occasionally even acquire a slight whine. Overall, on this afternoon the voice (except for a tinny, pinched E in alt) is basically attractive, its canny mix of registers in midvoice lending warmth in that area; her tone, however, lacks spin, a vivifying tonal float, so that Gilda's girlish charm and filial piety are shortchanged. If her tone lacks buoyancy, still, often enough it casts an aura all its own. The effect may be compared to the tonal glow, the gratifying hue, of Ingres' remarkable pencil drawings. There, though color is lacking, the sheen of glistening graphite (especially in combination with the artist's fluidity of line) is satisfying in itself. In similar fashion, Miss Peters' instrument has its own satisfactions.

All the notes are in place on this afternoon, remarkably so in her exact delivery of the intricacies of 'Caro nome.' The performance's grandest ovation is her reward. (Unfortunately, in the aria's pendant, rather than drawing a quiet trill in midvoice as Verdi directed—an enchanting effect when properly executed—she, like a few other sopranos, adopts an arpeggiated, trilled ascent to the aforementioned high E.) Her staccatos are always on the mark, and in moments of agitation her rhythmic sense is bracingly accurate. To her credit, on this afternoon, the soprano often acts with the voice, that is, she applies realistic touches to notes and phrases, intending thereby (and, for the most part, succeeding) to make audible ecstasy, anguish, remorse, and other emotions. 'Tutte le feste,' in which Gilda confesses her shame to her father, reveals her theatrical skill; the soprano knows how to plot a scene and score points effectively. 'Lassù in cielo' lacks the ultimate celestial glow, both in tone and arched line, but it is affectingly traced and touching in its way. In a gratifying coincidence, I have to hand the *Times*' account of the diva's 17 November 2000 recital (at Alice Tully Hall) in celebration of the fiftieth anniversary of her Met debut. The event was partially marred by the soprano having contracted a cold, but such longevity confirms the thoroughness of her tutelage and her astute management of an important career.

With the conductor exhibiting a preference for orderly progress, the soprano and tenor shining first and foremost as technicians, and Italianate timbral warmth in short supply, the *Rigoletto* performance is a bit hard-edged to my mind. But the

Tito Gobbi as Iago in *Otello*. Photography by Louis Mélançon. Courtesy Metropolitan Opera Archives.

professional know-how and interpretive aplomb exhibited by all parties (including baritone MacNeil) are qualities any house worldwide would prize.

There are baritones who are all voice and some who are all style and a few who offer a magical union of these prime ingredients. When sonic sublimity, however, is not quite your portion, but the vocal material is distinctive and sufficient to your means and your means are infinitely varied and imaginative, then you are a rare operatic creature. And your name is Tito Gobbi. Though the Italian baritone had first appeared on the Met stage more than a decade earlier (debut as Scarpia in January 1956), he is met for the first time on the broadcasts in *Otello* on 11 March 1967. Such managerial parsimony toward the radio audience might cause the gorge to rise. In fact, Gobbi never had a full-fledged Metropolitan career; in New York he sang only thirty-three performances (twelve more on tour) of four roles over a disjunct two-decade period. Recall that as early as 1951 Bing declined to hire him, citing to his amanuensis and confidant, Max Rudolf, the artist's purported failure in appearances with the San Francisco Opera in the late forties.[23] Two appearances would be his paltry broadcast allotment.

After extolling Gobbi so handsomely and regretting his absence from the airwaves, I am forced to backtrack a bit. Reputation, regrettably, is rather too often confounded by actuality, especially when artists enter their mid-fifties. Long and successful careers take their toll on most instruments. That may be the case with Gobbi on this afternoon. Not that he doesn't have plenty of voice for Iago and dispense it with generosity. And, above all, he knows how to deliver a performance. But if one follows the score (a pursuit that, while increasing knowledge, frequently can diminish enjoyment—and understanding— if one becomes lost in minutiae), one discovers that he is more Boito's servant than Verdi's. In the drinking song, he cannot articulate cleanly the downward scales on 'beva,' and he aspirates the concluding notes—a small point in the face of his command of rhythm and complete immersion in the scene. He tosses off the increasingly complex verses with as much panache as he undoubtedly downed the beaker of wine. From the first, he is all villain—perhaps vocal necessity now requires the single focus. Still, he delivers a brand of malevolence that would intimidate the devil himself. Diction rather than legato is his primary tool. The *piano* dynamic and mezza voce seem almost beyond his resources at this point in his career and those assets are vital to Iago's musical (hence dramatic) character. In 'Era la notte' he employs mezza voce only in the first phrase and, unfortunately, Tibbett's magical voicing of this entire passage remains in the ear. Gobbi's fine soft high E on 'sogno' is doubly welcome—it is not only skillfully negotiated but marvelously suggestive of Cassio's furtive dream. But our baritone blatantly ignores even Verdi's notorious seven-*piano* marking at 'Seguia più vago l'incubo blando' (and we know this supremely intelligent artist had it at his command a half dozen years earlier in the Serafin recording). We are a world away from the scrupulous observance of dynamics and the songlike phraseology of Warren, the favored broadcast Iago of the fifties.

At the other extreme, in the monumental second-act duet Gobbi must counterfeit size with blatantly open tone, even as he has overblown his instrument (to the point of sharping at the end of the opening phrase) as he enunciates his Credo. But what a grand, heaven-defying statement it is! And he offers a bit of contrast as he subtly colors the concluding 'E poi' pair—has anyone ever drawn us so completely into the macabre center of Iago's soul? The 'gelosia' episode is delivered at

Otello
11 March 1967

Desdemona
Montserrat Caballé
Emilia
Shirley Love
Otello
James McCracken
Iago
Tito Gobbi
Lodovico
Raymond Michalski
Conductor
Zubin Mehta

full voice and in so grisly a fashion as to be almost comic. Is it effective?—indeed it is. But Iago's triumphant 'Ecco il Leone!' seems almost nondescript when we have had little but malignity for two hours. Still, the baritone shows off his virtuosity as he conjures the spider web of 'Questa è una ragna' (though conductor Mehta's articulation of this scherzo-like piece is hobbled by insufficient sparkle). And Gobbi's dramatic skill is mesmeric as Iago begins the entrapment of Otello. Here is an artist at work.

In spite of musical inaccuracies and vocal inadequacies, Boito's (to a lesser extent, Shakespeare's) villain is vividly set before us. The complete assurance of Gobbi's conception and portrayal, its sheer brio and flaunted stagecraft (unseen, but vividly conveyed by the vocal manner), provide an exhilarating, treasurable experience. He offers an individual countenance, the latter preferred by a favorite author (Elizabeth Bowen) to a mere face as "something not to pattern, a free surface for pleasure."[24] What would Verdi have thought of the Gobbi imprint? We know that he traveled to Paris to certify Victor Maurel's vocal condition before agreeing to his creation of Iago at the premiere.[25] The baritone had been a frequent participant in the composer's earlier premieres in several cities, but even long acquaintance and loyalty were not enough to gain Verdi's approval without a hearing. Evidently enough vocal quality remained (the baritone was only thirty-seven) to sustain Maurel's potent character-creating abilities. Would not the same apply to Gobbi? Still, the composer had his own ideas about his Shakespearean villain. He wanted him to be "absent-minded, *nonchalant*, indifferent about everything."[26] Gobbi certainly could play him that way—but not on this afternoon. We shall have the pleasure of hearing him in another Maurel creation, *Falstaff*, in the 1972 broadcast of Verdi's opera.

Earlier in the broadcast season, Zubin Mehta had taken charge of the spectacular Met *Turandot*. Happily, the grandiosity of that offering has not rubbed off on his *Otello*. Indeed, the conductor's penchant for extremes is apparent only in a few appropriate moments of orchestral bombast (though his tempo for Otello's farewell to glory is oddly a dozen points faster than the score's metronome mark). One hopes the wretched cut in the third-act *concertato* (28 pages of the vocal score) was not Mehta's idea. The conductor was new to the opera. Vickers, who assumed the role a few weeks after this broadcast, purportedly accused him of not having "studied" the score, in effect, of sight-reading at an early rehearsal.[27] His is, in fact, a rather neutral reading of this brimming score. But then, ensemble cohesion (notwithstanding a bit of looseness in the second-act choral ensemble) and a gracious acknowledgment of traditional interpretative gambits are usually more welcome than flashy idiosyncratic moves. He has worthy collaborators, even in the shorter roles. Michalski's Venetian ambassador wears a heavier vocal tunic than his agile Ferrando: here his voice takes on an unexpectedly somber cast. Shirley Love is able to project Emilia's last-act hysterics without sounding the shrew. And James McCracken and Montserrat Caballé prove their mettle in the leading roles.

I do not recall hearing McCracken in better vocal form. Banished are the tonal shudder (it sometimes suggested strangulation) that occasionally has blighted his portrayals. The timbre is free and vibrant in the upper octave, rich and somber in the baritonal range (the latter a welcome asset for any Otello). The several high Bs and single C that discomfort most tenors capable of meeting the heavy demands of the role are readily, even nonchalantly, sounded. And his is a near-ideal

Otello voice in its weight, assertiveness, range, and emotional content. Perhaps reflective of his unencumbered vocal estate, the decks have been cleared of most of the excesses apparent in his 1963 broadcast portrayal. He no longer is content merely to haphazardly spend his vocal wealth as generously as a drunken sailor in port scatters his hard-earned wages.

The terrifying entrance passage is fearlessly delivered with nary a bit of strain. He tries for a prescribed *piano* as he voices Otello's 'estasi' in the love duet and achieves a clean, resplendent 'Venere splende' at its close. A potent legato is his and he applies it generously throughout the afternoon; even the stentorian 'Sì, pel ciel' is grandly sung rather than grunted (and the preceding phrases are sonorously trumpeted). This time he begins the third-act 'Dio! mi potevi scagliar' quietly, maintaining its reflective quality for a goodly portion of the monologue (though the raised pitches and random *parlando,* which are foreign to Verdi's intent, are not entirely forsworn). A few intrusive breaths (before 'del ciel' and 'quel raggio') mar several heartrending phrases of the monologue, but in compensation he offers a genuine head tone at 'acqueto' in response to Verdi's *dolcissimo* notation. The crazed outbursts before the court and in the death scene are realistically delivered. If 'Niun mi tema' is not quite the wrenching catharsis a few others have achieved in this sublime moment, it is effective. In the five seasons since his return from Europe as a bona fide heroic tenor, McCracken had already taken on Canio, Manrico, Samson, Don José, Gherman, and Radamès, with Calàf and Don Alvaro in his near future. With Vickers and Corelli contending for most of these parts as well, the Met management undoubtedly relished a rare sense of security in the dramatic tenor department.

Of course, the soprano roster was even more providentially stocked. On hand were Tebaldi, Rysanek, Nilsson, Price, Arroyo, and Crespin. Enter the incandescent Montserrat Caballé. A single performance in the old house had sufficed for a debut (as Marguerite on 22 December 1965; she also appeared at the final gala). Now in her first full season (full is rather a misnomer since her Met appearances were never overlong, though double those of Gobbi), she offers Desdemona for her broadcast debut. The soprano had appeared precipitously on the New York scene in a concert version of *Lucrezia Borgia* at Carnegie Hall in 1965. The beauty and fluency of her singing created a sensation. In reality, she had been part of the European scene for a decade, singing a wide range of roles but seldom at first-rank houses. Her Desdemona is a markedly satisfying portrayal, one worthy of comparison with the several grand interpretations of the part over the previous three broadcast decades.

Right off she deploys her trademark *pianissimo* on the 'Amen risponda' in the love duet. She matches it with another effluxion on the 'Amen' at the end of the fourth-act prayer, holding it six beats beyond its prescribed length, one of the few signs of her wonted musical willfulness to surface on this afternoon. That quality would become more troubling as the years passed, but on this afternoon Miss Caballé is the complete artist. Her Desdemona seems the epitome of the feminine for her tones are ever lambent, her phrasing is exquisitely fashioned, and her manner appropriately suppliant. Her *forte* singing may be just a touch erratic early on, but by the time she reaches the quartet the line is secure and her tone full and vibrant. In contrast to some late career offerings, no harshness in the upper range disturbs the poise of the opera's grander phrases. Many moments confirm her dutiful mu-

Geraldine Farrar as Juliette in *Roméo et Juliette*.

sicianship; the trying descent from the top note in 'Vien ch'io t'allieti il core,' for instance, is delicately taken and moves in perfect union with the orchestral chords. Again, unlike later years where she was apt to abandon the text if articulation might cause even modest vocal discomfiture, she sounds the opening syllable of 'lagrime' at the crown of the crucial phrase of the third-act conflict. The opening section of the episode ('Esterrefatta fisso') could be more intense—the situation is replete with despair—but she comes into her own in the lyrical phrases that follow. And she commands the grand style as well—hear her bold descent from the high B-flat (the note commandingly taken) when Desdemona protests her innocence after Otello calls her a vile courtesan. One hoped for a more dramatic and fuller-voiced treatment of Desdemona's plight than Caballé offers in the opening measures of the grand *concertato*; but even there her ravishing tone in the upper octave makes up for deficiency in declamation. Of course, the Willow Song and Ave Maria are most affecting, the voice limpid, its seemingly boundless deliquescence exquisitely controlled. Notable are her mixing of the registers in the intoned phrases that open the prayer and her handling of the simple (and for that reason often trying) phrases in mid-voice; in contrast to many fine sopranos, her pitch is accurate. Unlike Gobbi, Caballé will be heard in a number of broadcast roles.

Sopranos are very much in the picture on this afternoon. On his "Biographies in Song" series, Francis Robinson repeats his 1961 tribute to Rosa Ponselle. This time she is to be honored on her seventieth birthday with a grand celebration in her hometown of Baltimore. In the absence (not the later permanent vice-presidential withdrawal) of the governor, Mrs. Spiro Agnew is to present an award to this "true goddess in the annals of song," to quote assistant manager Robinson. He reminds us of Geraldine Farrar's response to Lotte Lehmann's query as to how one gets a voice like Ponselle's: "Only by special arrangement with God." At the opera's close, Milton Cross provides a sad postscript when he reports that Farrar, "one of our beloved American sopranos," has died on this very day. She was eighty-five years old and had lived in her Connecticut home for many decades after her 1922 Metropolitan retirement. Reminding us that he shared the broadcast booth with her in the mid-1930s when she briefly returned to the house to serve as commentator, he mourns the passing of "a great lady and a great artist." In announcing the next broadcast, the normally unflappable Cross names Renata Scotti as Butterfly, perhaps an unconscious acknowledgment of the close association on and off stage of Farrar and golden age baritone Antonio Scotti in the early decades of the century. Even opera lovers without Cross' longtime associations will remember the *Otello* broadcast as one of the better Saturday afternoons at the opera in many a year.

The *Bohème* broadcast of 4 February holds promise as well with a solid group of male Bohemians (Sereni, Harvuot, Tozzi), Teresa Stratas' first broadcast Mimì, and an Italian tenor new to the airwaves. The promise is only partly honored. Initially (for much of the first act) we share the optimism that sustains the penniless crew in the garret but before long maestro Cleva's charges, choral and solo, turn wayward under his permissive hand. A certain looseness of ensemble (on occasion approaching sloppiness) infects the later stages of the opera.

But individual portraits have merit. Beverly Bower, the first Fanciulla in the new house at the tryout student performance in April, fails to reach the high Bs in the waltz song, but her healthy instrument provides a welcome change from slighter-voiced, more shrewish Musettas. Her lovely middle voice enhances the fourth-act prayer. Old hand Alvary (very Mittel-European in contrast to the heartier Italian buffo tradition) conjures an unusually miserly landlord, his nasal twang ('magra, magra') vividly mirroring Benoit's disaffection with 'lean' women. The lower-voiced Bohemians are a brawny group, hale of voice, hearty in manner, and ever adept at serving Momus, the god of banter. Harvuot effectively liquidates the parrot and is stalwart in ensemble thereafter. Tozzi is always a genial artist and thus his philosopher is more companionable than most philosophers I have known. The coat donation may be magnanimous on Colline's part, but the shabbiness of the garment is reflected in Tozzi's singing of the miniature aria; the shine is off both coat and song (excessive wear on the former and suspect pitch in the latter). Sereni is the star of this group. He is musicianly, disciplined, ever in character, and an uncommonly attractive lover and friend, in short, a standout in the long line of Metropolitan Marcellos. The manly burr of his voice, with its robust and, on this afternoon, burnished timbre, is his greatest asset. He sings the opening strains of the waltz song with a marvelously expansive swagger and, despite Raimondi's race-horse habits, maintains the mood of their pensive duet.

La Bohème
4 February 1967
Mimì
Teresa Stratas
Musetta
Beverly Bower
Rodolfo
Gianni Raimondi
Marcello
Mario Sereni
Colline
Giorgio Tozzi
Conductor
Fausto Cleva

Gianni Raimondi's broadcast debut was greatly anticipated since his appearance in the Zeffirelli-Karajan film had given a certain réclame to his Rodolfo. The tenor was no stranger to America—he had appeared with the San Francisco company as far back as 1957. La Scala and other Italian theaters were his home ground, but Vienna, Munich, Berlin, Dallas, and Buenos Aires knew him as well. Buttressed by almost two decades of a far-ranging professional career, Raimondi had entered the Met (Rodolfo) in 1965. On this afternoon, his reputed ease in the higher terrain was certified by a ringing high C in the aria and free emission thereafter whenever ranging above the staff. The suntanned timbre has appeal but for a good portion of the opera his tones have a curiously stopped quality. In particular, the several notes of the *passagio* (and even near neighbors) frequently skirt the lower side of the pitch, occasionally for entire phrases. One wonders if the voice is simply not in prime working order this afternoon. Indeed, as the opera progresses, the tenor seems disaffected, for he is careless about rhythm, hurries Cleva here and there, fails to nurture the Puccini grand line, and applies a conversational spurt in certain phrases where we are accustomed to hear a tenor display his honeyed wares. (Oddly, he alters the alignment of text and notes in the final phrase—'Vi piaccia dir!'— of the aria.) He has his moments, especially when the voice opens up and the timbre takes on a ring in the later scenes. The opening of the duet with Marcello is charming: he cossets Mimì affectingly, and his angry outbursts as he suspects that she has died are novel and effective. All in all, a curious performance. Looking back on her long career, Lucine Amara, who had partnered his Rodolfo and whose opinions of singers were always forthright, named him the "most memorable" Rodolfo of her many Bohemian lovers.[28] Cavaradossi in 1968 brought Raimondi's radio tally to two. During his four Met seasons he appeared also as the Duke, Pinkerton, Faust, and Edgardo before departing in 1969.

Befuddled but still optimistic, I turn to Mimì. This time no disappointment awaits. From the moment when Stratas enters the garret on to Mimì's death in its frigid ambience, she is in remarkably fine voice. Only a slight and occasional shallowness (hardly worthy of notice) in the very lowest notes betrays any insecurity. Her tone is refulgent on up through the topmost notes; indeed, it is almost voluptuous, a quality enhanced by a lubricious legato. Hence, her Mimì is not quite the reticent seamstress commonly met. This midinette is eager to take whatever life offers; since her song and manner are enchanting, she is certain to be offered plenty. And Raimondi seemingly recognizes a welcoming avidity in her portrayal. Not for him a dreamy, wonder-filled 'Che bella bambina!'—he is a rake on the scent, his utterance reeking of intent. Stratas' narrative is filled with lovely portamentos, a rather Muzio-like spin of tone, a neat enunciation of the high tone of 'primavere' (though she eschews the opening consonant of 'bacio'), and appropriate mood changes, including a deftly "talked" midsection to set up her paean to the sun. She has a tendency to overly open her vowels ('Germoglia') or to insert pseudo-vowels, as in the broad portamento on 'faccio' (it becomes 'fa-ahooh-ccio'). The tollgate encounter with Marcello, an episode that can prove strenuous for lyric sopranos, is met head-on and conquered with lush tone and a canny mix of passion and pathos—and she doesn't rant. All the climaxes are easily surmounted. Though Stratas is slight of person, aurally this Mimì is no fragile waif. But the soprano's soft luminosity of timbre ensures that her heroine remains endearing. Cleva moves the farewell along at a good clip. I don't find Stratas' reading of the aria as exquisite as I had expected. It is not quite the gem of the opera that a number of sopranos have made it—the mood is less pervasive, certain phrases are more talked than sung (with whispered 'Addio's). Nevertheless, her naturalistic interpretation is very fine in its own way. In the last act, she maintains the individualistic quality of her portrayal, deigning to suggest the frail, spent person only when recalling Rodolfo's 'Che gelida manina.' She employs chest voice at 'grande come il mare,' erupts in a burst of happiness upon receiving her little 'cuffietta,' and later when caressing the muff limns 'Oh come è bello e morbido' with limpid skill. 'Sto bene . . . Pianger così perchè' is bravely uttered before Mimì slips into the final slumber. Thus, the somewhat slipshod performance of the opera gains respect for Sereni's staunch Marcello and a Mimì worthy of the ages.

Broadcasts of *Trovatore*, *Rigoletto*, and *Bohème* indicate that business as usual governs the more familiar offerings. That is their common fate in a repertory house. Happily, *Meistersinger*, *Giovanni*, and *Otello* (all splendidly mounted productions from the earlier domain) confirm management's careful tending of some of its older assets. But, inevitably, the new Met shone best when exploiting the extravagant resources of the new house in productions where the aural and visual met on equal terms. The ordeal of the opening season is not quite over. Two mid-twentieth-century works, one a world premiere, offer further challenges to Bing and company.

Jon Vickers as Peter Grimes. Photography by Louis Mélançon. Courtesy Metropolitan Opera Archives.

CHAPTER THREE

The Met Goes Modern

New homes foster new habits. Or so they should. Having largely ignored contemporary opera for decades, in its opening Lincoln Center season the Metropolitan executed an astonishing about-face. Three of its nine new productions were mid-twentieth-century works, and two of the three were world premieres.

Peter Grimes had not been heard at the Met since 1949. Britten's first full-fledged opera had come to the Met in the final years of the Johnson regime. Its success was modest, but sufficient to allow repeat performances in a second season and two broadcasts. Americans Frederick Jagel (then at the end of an honorable Met career) and Regina Resnik (in her soprano guise) and Australian John Brownlee were the 1948 premiere principals, but Polyna Stoska took over as Ellen in both broadcasts, with young Brian Sullivan the second radio Grimes; Mack Harrell and aging idol Lawrence Tibbett divided Balstrode's chores. In all these performances the work was packed with effective portrayals with the notable exception (and it was a killing one) of a commanding portrait of the troubled fisherman himself. At that time, some regarded *Grimes* as merely "Britten's youthful attempt to write a repertory opera," a work of insufficient power and interest.[1] Before the curtain went up for the broadcast of 11 February 1967, however, Mr. Cross was able to inform the radio audience that "the New York critics were unanimous in their praise" of the revival. In a procedure quite out of the ordinary on the opera broadcasts, he offered proof of their regard by quoting the *Daily News'* Douglas Watt ("a thundering success") and, from the *World Journal Tribune*, Miles Kastendieck ("an absorbing experience . . . the season is the richer for its revival"). Cross' obvious delight in the triumph prepares us for the treat in store.

Bing had entrusted the production to a first-class team. Tyrone Guthrie, who had imaginatively staged one of the manager's early successes, *Carmen* in 1952, returned to perform the same service for *Grimes*. (His intermediate *Traviata* for Tebaldi was less auspicious.) New in the pit was the relatively young Colin Davis, destined to become one of the world's most distinguished maestros and already displaying a sure hand and a compelling vision, both essential for Britten's febrile child. The composer's sonic imagination evokes a correspondingly vivid response from Davis. Under the British conductor's illuminative care, the several interludes, now almost overly familiar to us from numerous symphonic readings, are more meaningful as heard within the context of the drama. Davis' pacing and

Peter Grimes
11 February 1967

Ellen Orford
Lucine Amara
Mrs. Sedley
Jean Madeira
Auntie
Lili Chookasian
Peter Grimes
Jon Vickers
Balstrode
Geraint Evans
Boles
Paul Franke
Swallow
Raymond Michalski
Conductor
Colin Davis

45

control of the opera are superb, and never more apparent than in the transitions between the widely disparate moods that the composer's astute theatrical pulse dictates. In tandem with Vickers' interpretive stance, Davis' reading intentionally brings the violence of the work (rather than what he called its "cloying sweetness") to the fore.[2] One of that incomparable old-fashioned breed who is at home in both the symphonic and opera spheres (a half-decade tenure as director of the Sadler's Wells company will soon be coupled with his stint as principal conductor of the BBC Symphony), Davis would seem to be just the tonic Bing's conducting staff needs. Unfortunately, his Met outings would be severely limited over the next two decades. The Met orchestra plays splendidly on this afternoon, but the chorus could profit from greater precision and resonance—the all-important climaxes do not carry the same theatrical wallop that other forces have engendered.

Though the opera lives or dies on the portrayal of its protagonist, the work demands numerous cameos that must be both individually graphic and yet readily integrated into an organic ensemble. The Met's character artists are up to the task. Notable portraits of the inhabitants of the Borough are contributed by Norman Scott (Hobson), Paul Franke (some strain apparent in the initial scenes, but thereafter a strong presence), tenor Robert Schmorr as an accommodating preacher, and Lili Chookasian (her Auntie takes for gospel that 'a joke's a joke and fun is fun'). Ray Michalski's beautiful voice again pleases, and his easy way with text and phrase as lawyer Swallow questions Grimes about the death of his apprentice removes some of the stodginess that infects the prologue. Jean Madeira's contralto is solid and slightly grotesque in Mrs. Sedley's emphatic denunciation of Grimes—one can believe her mean-spirited attack would drive the populace to violence. Balstrode may be considered a leading role and with Geraint Evans to portray him, he is indubitably that. But Britten has given him little opportunity to display his singing actor skills. The Welsh baritone makes the most of his few moments, however, invigorating the scene with his pungent diction and burly tone. If some of his village comrades seem a bit well-behaved, even overly civilized, for their occupations, Evans' rugged manner has the smell of the sea on it. In the captain's lengthy dialogue with Grimes his speech and tone convey the essence of a rough, upright life.

Lucine Amara (Ellen Orford) was said not to be well at the 20 January premiere and it may be that she has not regained her full resources at the broadcast three weeks later. At the outset, it must be noted that she is unsuited to the task that has been assigned her. One can be grateful for her beautiful vocalizing of the difficult embroidery aria in that she shows her marvelous vocal control and intelligent manipulation of her instrument. In fact, in the repeatedly descending phrases where tonal consistency is of utmost importance, one hears her formulate a quite unusual (for her) opulent color in the low voice. The climax is well managed as well, with a stunning crescendo at its apex. Perhaps because of stage placement, the soprano's voice is oddly remote and quite ineffectual in the sunny scene that opens the second act. Clarity of text is a problem for her at many moments in the opera—of course, that is a chronic soprano disease. Yet, it is apparent in this English-language opera that Amara's vocal method is not built upon the word. Her forte is a silken legato of tone, lovely in quality, and seamlessly conducted. That attribute does not mate well with the down-to-earth milieu of this fishing village. Along the same lines, her tone is too elegant, too finely drawn to make for convincing characterization of Grimes' helpmate, schoolteacher though she be. Ellen is a sympathetic character, but the role needs a down-to-earth attitude, a commoner humanity, and it profits from a broader tonal base than Amara can bring to it. Too often, she seems to be picking away at the notes. Mr. Bing told all, and more than he should have, when he commented in his memoirs that he had assigned the soprano Ellen Orford (a role, in his eyes, suited to her "low-profile temperament") because Amara had been, in effect, such a good soldier that he ought to reward her with exposure in a new production.[3] According to Bing, Georg Solti, who originally had been assigned to conduct *Grimes*, left the company on hearing the news. He had his own candidate. If she was out of her element in this opera, Amara, when heard in her own repertory, remained a worthy artist, one to be prized as far more than a good soldier.

The manager (and Solti, too, no doubt) was certain that Jon Vickers was the man to portray the tortured fisherman. How right he was. Today we recognize the portrayal as one of the supreme operatic characterizations of the century. The role is ideally mated with the tenor's special gifts, its psychological construct allowing him to display the varied colors of his voice, its immense dynamic range, and, above all, his ability to enter into the soul of a tormented human being. Aside from a minor rasp here or there, the voice is in prime condition at both dynamic extremes. Any artist who undertakes the role must contend with the portrayal of Peter Pears, for whom the composer fashioned the role. A few have deemed Pears' interpretation superior, especially in subtlety, to Vickers' virtuosic conception, and we know that Britten himself, ever loyal to Pears, deplored (despised, some say) Vickers' reading. I find our tenor entirely convincing in the confessional or lyrical moments of Grimes' soliloquys; there his tone, quiet but vividly alive with its evocative head resonance, is beautiful in itself and, beyond that, profoundly moving. In the 'Now the Great Bear and Pleiades' aria, he declaims on a single note (E natural) in gentle tones that, soft as they are, seem to fill and command the entire circumference of the huge Met auditorium. He brings out the strangeness, the unfulfilled longing, of the fisherman with weird, whimpering sounds at the close of the aria. And Vickers' powerful instrument, capable of ringing *forte*s and phraseology of remarkable tensility, marks the toiler on the sea as a man among men and lends the denouement greater tragic stature. Unlike some occasions where the divide between his mezza voce and full voice seems chasmlike, on this afternoon the gap is bridged—the tenor is adept at moving from one to the other with masterly transitions.

Throughout the opera, Vickers' diction is a marvel. His rhythms are bracing. He is not afraid to take chances—that is part of this artist's mystique. He moves over the serpentine phrases of the act-two monologue as though they were his natural utterance. Its melismas are deftly handled and made one with speech. In the final scene, the character's growing madness is tellingly conveyed. When he takes up the mob's sounding of his name, his rapid reiteration of 'Grimes,' rhythmically vibrant but tonally sinking to nothingness, is haunting, while the final cadenza becomes a wail, a wounded animal's moan. The tenor was entirely aware of the enormous technical demands of the role and consciously used his command of the vocal mechanism to meet them, but always in the service of the drama. "You use a technique for a purpose," he told an interviewer.[4] In terms of pure sound, his portrayal is indeed three-dimensional with its varied play of light and shadow and, rarer yet, its complex deployment of sound in the Metropolitan space. At the final curtain, Cross tells us that Vickers is "getting quite an ovation," one of the few times where he offers an understatement.

Mourning Becomes Electra
1 April 1967

Lavinia
Evelyn Lear
Christine
Marie Collier
Adam
Sherrill Milnes
Orin
John Reardon
Ezra
John Macurdy
Conductor
Zubin Mehta

In his memoirs, Bing called the 1967 revival of Grimes "the only complete success" achieved by a modern opera during his tenure.[5] For the astute manager, "success" had to include both critical and financial rewards. One reason for the triumph may be gleaned from Britten's comments in an interview for the broadcast *Opera News* issue, where he advises young composers to "trim their sails to the wind and not be scared of writing works that people actually understand."[6] I wonder whether Marvin David Levy did any trimming when he wrote *Mourning Becomes Electra*, the final new production of the inaugural season. The opera had its world premiere on 17 March and was broadcast on 1 April. Henry Butler, since the 1961–62 season a successful Met stage director and the accomplished librettist of the new work, of necessity did trim. To compress O'Neill's New England version of the *Oresteia* trilogy from the American playwright's six-hour tragedy into an operatic libretto was a Herculean task, one well met by Butler.

When the opera comes to the airwaves we again find Mr. Cross offering tribute from critics, perhaps in an effort to ease the minds of radio listeners who were suspect of these disturbing invasions into their temple of operatic serenity. With pride, he cites the *Chicago Tribune*, which hailed the premiere as "not only a triumph for the house, but for the American operatic stage." *United Press International* went further, allowing only a slight qualification to blemish its belief that "the long awaited great American opera may now exist." Some took the easy route, for comparisons with Hofmannsthal and Strauss were obvious and inevitably invidious—Butler and Levy were found wanting.[7] Others thought the comparison not worth making: Watt (not mentioned by Cross this time) considered the work not even an opera, but rather mere background movie music.[8] Fortunately, we are far removed from the time when dissonance, bits of bitonality, and other properties of expressionistic composition are in themselves immediate turnoffs that inhibit understanding and appreciation of a new work. Conservative and avant garde have exchanged places. What was thought to be new is old and what was old is now new. The only question that need concern us is whether we would like to hear the opera again and, if so, whether it can possibly gain even limited repertory status.

Study with Otto Luening, director of Columbia University's opera program, had clinched Levy's youthful decision to become an opera composer. By the time he undertook to tame the O'Neill colossus, the still young (mid-thirties) composer had a series of successful one-act operas under his belt. His musical means are far removed from the more accommodating idiom that Britten employed in *Peter Grimes*. *The New Grove Dictionary of Opera* defines Levy's compositional stance in *Electra* as "'eased' expressionism," which would seem to make it neither fish nor fowl (no homophone puns allowed). But the emphasis is more expressionistic than easy. The orchestral resources that he exploits are enormous and conductor Zubin Mehta makes the most of them. The highly charged atmospherics with which Levy underlines O'Neill's tortured theatrics are just Mehta's meat. And the Met orchestra displays an admirable virtuosity, both in the many chamber-like soloistic moments and in ear-shattering climaxes for the entire band. Levy concocts some ravishing sonorities—he has an ear for colorful orchestral effects. Does his often disjunct idiom invariably support and illuminate character portrayal, or drive the

Evelyn Lear as Lavinia, Sherrill Milnes as Adam and Marie Collier as Christine, John Reardon as Orin in *Mourning Becomes Electra*. Photography by Louis Mélançon. Courtesy Metropolitan Opera Archives.

action in a meaningful way? No. In the first half of the opera, one wearies of certain effects that, effective in themselves, are abused by excessive repetition—the quick buildup to an orchestral explosion followed by sudden silence, for instance, is overexploited. One begins to wonder if Levy has enough arrows in his compositional quiver. Fortunately, in the second half of the opera, the composer (undoubtedly responding to the changing character of the drama) employs a more lyrical style in which continuity, both of vocal lines and in the orchestral underpinning, is a more unifying force. Even on first hearing, one recognizes the melodic threads (some of lovely contour) that bind the opera and lend significance to the characters and situations.

The vocal parts are demanding. For much of the opera, the composer presses the emotional throttle of the leading players to the floorboard, a bit too insistently for their own good, both as characters in the drama and as singers. High notes abound. Sometimes their abrupt sounding seems unmotivated by the musical line or the text. Then too, in the earlier stages of the opera the composer's desire for textual clarity results in a syllabic setting that has insufficient rhythmic variety—he doesn't seem to have an innate response to the musical characteristics of words. When he makes a move toward a set form, however, he displays an inventiveness that commands emotional response—the second-act quartet for Christine, Lavinia, Adam, and Orin is a marvelous piece, and Lavinia has some heartrending moments in the final act. Clearly, Levy has the goods to make a notable contribution to the repertory.

The Metropolitan assembled a group of superior artists well suited to the arduous tasks that the composer has posed for the members of the Mannon family and their "friends." In particular, the mother, Christine (Klytämnestra is the model), daughter Lavinia (the Electra whom mourning becomes), and son Orin (Orestes) are demanding roles that require vocal stamina and dramatic intensity. The lesser characters have their moments as well. Michalski (the servant Jed), Lilian Sukis and Ron Bottcher (friends in love with the Mannon siblings) project the text with clarity and are vocally secure, while Macurdy is effective as the Agamemnon father figure. Milnes has a good deal more to do as the ship captain Adam Brandt (Aegisthus in the Aeschylus original) and, as usual, does it very well.

Adam's shipboard aria that opens the second act ('Too weak to kill') offers him (unlike some of the other principals) the opportunity for a straightforward bit of grand song. Milnes, with his equally grand baritone—one particularly resplendent in the upper range—and repoussé interpretive stance, takes full advantage of the moment. Only a slight stiffness of phrase (due, perhaps, to Levy's above-mentioned syllabic setting) lessens its effect.

The leading female roles are taken by two sopranos who made their Met debuts in the opera's premiere. Australian Marie Collier (Christine) had a decade's experience in a wide array of roles, lyric and dramatic, Italian, French, and German, with the Covent Garden company and was particularly at home in contemporary opera (Katerina Izmaylova and Jenůfa were among her triumphs). Her soprano is a fine instrument, large, vividly colored, and employed by the artist to strong dramatic purpose. It has a component of steel (some moments in the higher range call to mind the tonal shell of Maria Caniglia, or perhaps more to the point, Dusolina Giannini); occasionally, the timbre, in combination with a quick vibrato, suggests the skittering of nails on glass, a useful and not unattractive effect. In any case, in its maturity and unlikely combination of allure and flintiness, her instrument is the ideal vehicle for mother Mannon, a woman obsessed with a forbidden love that causes her to poison her husband. The house audience recognizes her quality as a singing actress of the first rank by singling her out during the curtain calls with enthusiastic applause. Her premature and tragic death in 1971 after only three seasons with the company is a real loss.

American soprano Evelyn Lear would have a Metropolitan career of considerably longer duration. It could have been even longer were she not already in her early forties at the time of her Met debut. Her early career was spent largely in Europe, where she had been a prominent artist on the German stages (Berlin, Munich, Hamburg) and in Vienna, as well as at Covent Garden. Her voice, unlike Collier's, is a lyric instrument, but one of considerable potency and resiliency. Her timbre is singularly affecting and creates more sympathy for Lavinia than may be warranted by that lady's actions. In the opening scenes, she repeatedly demonstrates how to create character and command attention with individual phrases of lovely poignancy ('when my father comes home' in act one) or dramatic thrust, embracing to good effect the melodic morsels with which Levy has larded the score. She is adept at expressive phrasing and, indeed, a remarkable communicator, a lovely singer who fulfills all the requirements (including vaulting *pianissimo*s and the ability to match timbres of solo orchestral instruments) demanded by Lavinia's extended soliloquies in the opera's final scenes. She would be with the company for many seasons (with periodic brief absences), but her versatility perhaps prevented management from settling her in a particular repertory niche. Thus, her Met tally, though wide in range (including both Cherubino and the Countess, Octavian, and the Marschallin, plus Wozzeck's Marie and Donna Elvira), was not overlarge in number. But we will hear more from her.

American baritone John Reardon had appeared as Mandryka, Eisenstein, and Count Almaviva following his 1965 Met debut as Tomsky in *Queen of Spades* (*Pikovaya Dama*). After study with Martial Singher and Margaret Harshaw, he, like so many gifted young Americans, found an early home at the New York City Opera. His career would be notable for his participation in the premieres of many contemporary operas. From his performance as the most overtly unstable member of the Mannon clan, one can understand why he would be in demand in that regard. His lyric baritone is a heady instrument, rather tenor-like in the upper range and thus able to handle the high tessitura of his role without difficulty. Orin is in a perpetual state of anxiety, and his weakness of character and eventual mental collapse are vividly conveyed by Reardon. He has command of a wide range of vocal effects that serve his character well, but he never fails to take a phrase to its full expressive power when the occasion permits. In an afternoon of fine portrayals, his portrait of the troubled son is notable for its immense conviction and fervent emotionalism. He plays at the edge.

Audience reaction at the broadcast performance was enthusiastic; artists and creators were repeatedly summoned for lengthy curtain calls. If the opera seems overlong (at a number of moments one feels an episode is over and yet it lingers on), the need to service O'Neill is probably the culprit. Butler has done a masterly job of compression, but there may be too many dramatic nuggets left intact to be mined in one evening. Early in Levy's career he had understood that an opera libretto cannot be, indeed should not be, "a complete theatre piece." Literary complexity of "imagery" and "word combinations" was the enemy of operatic purpose: "space must be left for music to work its magic."[9] Evidently, it was a lesson not entirely learned and too soon forgot. And yet, at the curtain's fall, when one looks back upon the opera's troubled path, the epic quality of the entire journey has a cumulative effect, an impact greater than was apparent en route. The revised version of the opera that the Chicago Lyric Opera presented in its 1998–99 season, however, shows that brevity can be an admirable, even though lately learned, virtue.

In the late nineties, American opera began to take on new life. The decade-long sequence of revivals and premieres by the Chicago Lyric company provides the most prominent evidence of the trend. When the Metropolitan mounted *Mourning Becomes Electra* and *Antony and Cleopatra* in the sixties, it had ventured into unchartered waters. Management, not liking the chill that the immersion caused among its conservative public, preferred more familiar seas during the next decade or so. The Levy work was floated for a second season (five performances added to the original half dozen) but Barber's opus was permanently set adrift. A quarter century later the Met again set sail and commissioned new American works, this time in the belief that it was not only a responsibility, but a valid, even rewarding, pursuit. Let us hope that the current interest is more than a passing vogue.

Having taken the measure of the abundantly equipped new house and in the process suffered crises, both financial and organizational, the Met management emerged from the shakedown season a mite chastened but with its artistic integrity intact. A more conventional path would be trod during the next few seasons.

Teresa Zylis-Gara as the Countess in *Le Nozze di Figaro*. Photography by Louis Mélançon.
Courtesy Metropolitan Opera Archives.

CHAPTER FOUR

Mozart Crowned

The radio audience was long accustomed to Mr. Cross' endearing penchant for reminiscence. On 9 December 1967 he again struck a familiar note. In announcing *Le Nozze di Figaro* as the opening broadcast of the new season, he proudly paid homage to Texaco's twenty-seven consecutive seasons as sponsor, summoning up the memory of the moment when the oil company inaugurated what was to become the longest example of program sponsorship in radio history. Mozart's comedy was the lead opera on the earlier occasion (7 December 1940) as well. At that time, Mozart's coronation as the peerless opera composer was far from certain, at least in the minds of the paying customers. After a twenty-five-year absence, the opera had returned to the Met repertory in a triumphant production only a few months earlier. By the nineteen-sixties, however, the Viennese composer's presence in the opera house was reassuringly ubiquitous.

The contrast between discovery and acceptance is worth celebrating, but the casts (both of remarkable quality) of the two broadcasts offer an interesting symmetry. Two Italian basses, each the leading exponent of his *Fach*, anchor the performances as Figaro and Bartolo (Pinza and Baccaloni in the earlier, Siepi and Corena in the later airing). Two Italian sopranos, neither wedded to the soubrette repertory (Albanese in 1940, Mirella Freni in 1967), play Susanna, and a soprano Cherubino (Novotnà or Stratas) displaces the customary mezzo in that slot. In each performance audiences relished the opportunity to hear the Countess of Elisabeth Rethberg or Lisa Della Casa, both beloved interpreters who found themselves rather unexpectedly in the twilight of their Metropolitan careers. But I linger too long in building mere patterns of historical design. One could call the Almavivas both outsiders in terms of their birth countries, but the Australian baritone John Brownlee was a longtime Met tenant, while the 1967 newcomer, Finnish debutant Tom Krause, was destined for a too-brief Met career.

Even greater (and more regrettable) is the discrepancy between conductors. Ettore Panizza was the genuine Italian article who breathed life into the revival and set it on its triumphant Met path, while Rosenstock is the reliable caretaker of by now treasured goods. He deserves our gratitude, however, for guiding his extraordinary cast with a sure hand, if not an understanding heart. Synchrony between stage and pit is excellent. His rather metronomic drive shapes the performance and, while neatness is of value in a Mozart re-creation, minimal graph-

Le Nozze di Figaro
9 December 1967

Countess
Lisa Della Casa
Susanna
Mirella Freni
Cherubino
Teresa Stratas
Almaviva
Tom Krause
Figaro
Cesare Siepi
Bartolo
Fernando Corena
Conductor
Joseph Rosenstock

ic commentary by the orchestral forces shortchanges the composer's powers of characterization. One longs to hear the winds laugh at or sardonically mimic the foibles of Mozart's all-too-human aristocrats and servants; Rosenstock prefers to let those put-upon amorists act for themselves. Fortunately, his charges are adept enough to give the opera its due.

Oddly, the one character who falls a bit short of paying in full coin is the much-praised Siepi. Of course, he remains the Figaro of his time, in excellent voice, and pouring out ear-caressing tones in ceaseless legato no matter how ill used by his poaching master or bride to be. All Figaros should wear a happy face but the enterprising servant has moments of self-reflection that require more attention than the basso is willing to accord them on this afternoon. His 'Se vuol ballare' is far from menacing (and Krause's Count is an uncommonly aggressive predator) while 'Aprite un po' quel'occhi' is untouched by bitter disillusionment. One longs for more bite in Siepi's manner, more nuance in his song (even 'Non più andrai' trundles along, gaily as it should, but without military spit and polish). A case can be made for a Figaro more lithe of voice and many-sided of manner. But even when this artist offers a casual characterization, he retains his rank as primo basso of the company.

Corena, on the other hand, presents a sharply focused portrayal of Bartolo, and he too is in good vocal form, singing well and accurately in his aria. Like the African-bred basenji, on this afternoon the buffo refrains from barking. A nod must be given to Alvary's inimitable Antonio—the fingerprint of a gardener's green thumb lies on his honest country bumpkin. Loretta Di Franco is an idiomatic Barbarina, her lyric timbre more individual than many a young soprano assigned this "tryout" role. Nancy Williams is not perfectly cast as the doctor's future wife, for her voice is more soprano than mezzo and thus some of the built-in nonsense of the lovesick housekeeper is automatically toned down. In their one-upmanship duet, this Marcellina's tonal bulk is dwarfed by the fruity tones of Freni's Susanna. But she plays her part well enough. The new Finnish baritone, who made his Met debut in the opera's season premiere, does that and much more. Only in his early thirties, Tom Krause was based in Hamburg, having launched his international career as Escamillo at West Berlin's Deutsche Oper in 1959. That career already included appearances at Glyndebourne (another Count, this one in *Capriccio*), Bayreuth, Vienna, and La Scala. His Mozart Count is one of the better ones in broadcast history. Vocally, musically, and in terms of character portrayal, he plays on a high level. At first the voice seems rather burly, a mite crude in its formation, a krummhorn of a voice, the timbre merely the customary burr of baritones who prefer mass to tonal cultivation. But is he just shaking out the vocal cobwebs? By the time he reaches Almaviva's prime moments the tone, especially in the upper regions, has taken on a bright, bronze cast whose manly vitality well mates with the Count's designs. Many an Almaviva either lacks impact at the bottom of the range or cannot handle the few exposed high notes of the role—Krause's instrument is built to handle both, and solidly beamed in between. He and Freni contest admirably as the Count insists on an assignation (he reverses 'Crudel' and 'perchè' in the opening phrase), but corporal Rosenstock sucks the sensuousness out of the duet; under his relentless baton, the tryst sounds more like a business deal. (Of course, in a way it was.) Krause has the big guns for the aria, including a touch of the old-fashioned snarl; he is intent on using them—and without benefit of supportive small arms. His assault is unvaried, but highly effective. And when his

Mirella Freni as Susanna in *Le Nozze di Figaro*. Photography by Louis Mélançon.

richly intoned petition for pardon is heard at the opera's close, no wife, as Mozart must have known, could possibly resist the Count's entreaty. The baritone will not often be heard with the company over the next few years; the Met was unduly parsimonious in granting him a fair number of roles, performances, and seasons. Krause seems rather a Finnish Sereni and probably management felt one of that serviceable brethren met their needs.

Freni's Met appearances, too, would be fewer than desired, for she appears in only four seasons of the period covered in this chronicle. Undoubtedly, the Met would have preferred a greater commitment. Partial redress would come in the late stages of this beloved soprano's career. Actually, she had made her company debut (Mimì) in the final season at the old house and was heard as Liù in a *Turandot* broadcast during the first season at Lincoln Center. Her European entry had been as Micaela in 1955 at her hometown of Modena (now notorious as having spawned and wet-nursed both Freni and Pavarotti). Initially, motherhood enjoined a slow career pattern and it was not until 1963 (debut as Mimì under Karajan at La Scala) that her international career was truly launched. In the following season, caution again intruded after she appeared in a Zeffirelli-Karajan *Traviata* at La Scala (the debacle was foreordained when the public booed before the curtain went up). She welcomed the Met as a new theater with a new public.[1] (Unfortunately, it did not turn into a new home base.) In the following years, her progress on the international scene was unimpeded.

As heard here, a dozen years into a career that would last more than four decades, she appears, as noted, as a soubrette, a *Fach* that served her well in the first decade or so of that lengthy career traversal. Though her triumphs were certain in that category, they would be eclipsed by later ventures into the purely lyric and (with less certitude) the spinto repertories. Indeed, even on this broadcast she seems uncommonly firm voiced and round toned for the soubrette breed. That is no demerit to those who have suffered many a skinny-voiced and overly cute Susanna over the years. Still, the Met had known (and the radio audience treasured) several delectable Susannas (including Sayão, Seefried, and Raskin) of less weighty cast, so we need not disdain the type. At this stage of her career, Freni's portrayals were appreciated more for tonal beauty than musical or dramatic insights. Not that she is negligent in either regard; rather, these skills (which become more highly developed in later years) seem not to have gained her complete attention as yet. In fact, she would never quite ascend (or descend, if you prefer) into the realm of the singing actress. But when nature's gifts are so abundant, they need to be dispensed with the liberality that Freni displays on this afternoon. Tonal prodigality, even if it seems for her a necessity, is in her case a compelling responsibility. And she does enter nicely into the comic spirit of the role, although this Susanna, seemingly quite comfortable with her lot, shortchanges the conspiratorial element of the feisty servant. To hear her sing without coyness as she dresses Cherubino is refreshing (and no doubt appreciated as well by the adolescent boy). The tone and timbre remain succulent even when nimbly tracing Mozart's intricate patterns, whether in song or recitative—Freni is a delight in these latter romps. She sings her part in the letter duet without affectation, molding the line with exquisite results; Della Casa (necessity again being the controlling factor) relies on a Vienna-style artfulness in her diction. Every lover of the opera waits for the garden revelation of Susanna's love for Figaro, and Freni's song would appear to be ideally mated with the moment. And so it proves. If the aim of all art is delectation (as Poussin claimed), Freni scores a bull's-eye. The preceding recitative is lovingly limned, including an enchanting play of portamento. Still, this Susanna is no girl adrift in a helpless swoon—she knows what she is about. Rosenstock's tempo for 'Deh vieni, non tardar' is a bit slow to permit the singer to relish the rocking rhythms of the aria (and the leisurely pace may cause a slight feeling that her breath support is not as perfectly sustained as one expects from the *"piccola Tebaldi"*—the lack is miniscule, but one senses it). Yet Freni's line is so well conducted, the tone so embracingly beautiful that her artistry commands love and regard; in particular, the voice exquisitely fashions the crowning moments of the aria ('Vieni! Ti vo' la fronte incoronar di rose') as she calls for her beloved in heavenly tones. The roses belong to Freni.

Stratas' Cherubino is already known to us. Her performance is the most perfectly realized of all the excellent portrayals of this broadcast. At her every entrance she energizes the situation—she stays in touch with Rosenstock and yet performs with marvelous spontaneity, even in the classically restrained phrases of 'Voi che sapete.' In her zeal, she never disturbs the musical grammar of Mozart's careful constructs and yet manages to convey the volatility and bewilderment of the love-struck youth with unfailing specificity. Her reading of 'Non so più' is delicious, a marvel of subtle musical and dramatic nuances (a slight accelerando here, a play with words there, a *subito piano*, and, in particular, the unexpected touch of sadness she introduces as the confused youth murmurs 'E se non ho chi m'oda').

Quite surprisingly, one notes that this broadcast is not only Lisa Della Casa's final radio appearance but her last performance at the Met. Earlier I momentarily bracketed her with Rethberg; recall that the latter, one of the truly memorable purveyors of beautiful song in the Met's long history, left the company a few months before her forty-eighth birthday. Now the forty-eight-year-old Della Casa departs. How the many admirers of both artists hoped for greater company longevity! Rethberg was a Met icon for twenty years, while Della Casa is in her fifteenth consecutive season (her European career reached back as far as 1941). Her refined artistry is again evident on this afternoon, though in truth, more than a few moments betray that her voice no longer is the reliable instrument of former years. (The same could be said of Rethberg in her late Met career, including her broadcast Contessas.) 'Porgi amor' is very gingerly nursed along, dignified in phrasing and sweetly delivered, but with some decidedly wispy tones. But she manages the trying ascending phrases well and caps one with a full-voiced top note. There we hear the luscious color of her uniquely sensuous timbre, the asset that we have most treasured over the years. She gathers voice in the boudoir shenanigans, cavorting delightfully with her soprano cohorts. She and Stratas play at love with aroused appetites. A number of phrases recall her best days—smoldering embers can flame again. But ahead of her lies the difficult 'Dove sono.' The firmly voiced top A at the close of the accompanied recitative is reassuring and, for the most part, her tone is more solid than in her entrance aria. She begins the melodic reprise softly (always a nice touch as it connotes reflection) and takes the long phrases in single breaths, here drawing on the experience of a long career. Yet one feels she is saving voice and negotiating the aria rather than presenting it in full bloom. Regrettably, the previously noted flatting around C in the middle of her range is too prominent for comfort—the aria is in the key of C major—a serious blemish. But the challenging concluding phrases are well managed, except for a noticeable thinning on the final top A. In the letter duet, Freni's pitch, of course, is on the button, Della Casa's less accurate; but she still wafts some lovely phrases. Her granting of forgiveness at the opera's close is rather light, even remote. We miss Mozart's benediction there.

Cross embraces Della Casa's name with special affection at the curtain calls. I share that regard, having been in the house in 1953 at her company debut in this same role. A Swiss friend with whom I attended the performance had told me to expect something special and I was not disappointed. When the curtain went up on the second act and her beautiful presence was first seen, waves of pleasure seemed to fill the house. Later, I often heard her in opera and recital in Vienna. A rare aura of cultivated courtesy always seemed to emanate from her person and her song. Her Met tally of 174 appearances might have been larger. Of the eleven roles that she undertook, her portrayals of the Mozart and Strauss heroines were magical and are not forgotten.

In some ways, Teresa Zylis-Gara assumes the departing Swiss soprano's place on the roster. Though not her first broadcast, the 11 April 1970 airing of *Le Nozze di Figaro* provides the opportunity to measure her quality against remembrance. All the female roles are newly cast, with Rosalind Elias as Cherubino, Nedda Casei as Marcellina, and Gail Robinson as Barbarina joining the Polish soprano's Countess. The delectable Stratas returns, but this time as Susanna. Repeaters from the 1967 broadcast are Siepi, Krause, Franke, and Gabor Carelli (Curzio), with Paul Plishka's Bartolo providing another novel ingredient. Now Rosenstock's firm grip gives way to the loving caress of the benevolent Krips. His overture bustles briskly along like an exuberant fanfare, an invitation to the follies of this marriage day. In the opera proper, his deft, keenly detailed Mozart style, free of hustle, touches all participants. The performance wears a domestic face. Revolution seems remote.

Krause's Almaviva again merits high regard. His vibrant baritone gives off sparks. This Count is playing with fire, stalking Susanna with decided fervor and thrusting tones. His forthright, commanding delivery is in the George London line, and like that lamented artist, he manages to suffer Da Ponte's indignities without loss of aristocratic cachet. Legitimate anger, rather than bluster, governs his grandly voiced aria, its only blemish a debilitated close (the triplets nonexistent, tonal luster momentarily siphoned off). In marvelously trim voice, Siepi, in particular, responds to Krips' presence with a recharged portrayal of the irrepressible servant. Where in 1967 he played in a subdued, almost casual, manner, now he offers (with one notable exception) a vivid and detailed characterization, musically nuanced and dramatically alive. The threat of 'Se vuol ballare' is pinpointed in Siepi's sharp staccato darts on the initial three notes of the opening phrases, with the legato response acknowledging the symmetries of the classical style—Krips' handiwork, perhaps? In 'Non più andrai,' Siepi's dotted rhythms now are exact, and the entire aria has a musical polish that had earlier slipped away from him.

Franke's Basilio is a stout fellow, no sniveling snoop, but he relishes intrigue and gives voice to it. Unfortunately, in a few ensemble passages his tone is unattractive and stands out unduly. Plishka, too, is no regulation buffo doctor. The 'Vendetta' aria is sung rather than fooled with—his Bartolo means business in the vengeance department. And what a fine, resonant instrument this longtime Met mainstay owned in his early years. His consort, mezzo-soprano Casei, is another

Le Nozze di Figaro
11 April 1970

Countess
Teresa Zylis-Gara
Susanna
Teresa Stratas
Cherubino
Rosalind Elias
Almaviva
Tom Krause
Figaro
Cesare Siepi
Bartolo
Paul Plishka
Conductor
Josef Krips

light-voiced Marcellina, but she is a stage creature: her recitatives are pertinent, her singing in the duet both musical and flavorful. Gail Robinson, a recent recruit, sings Barberina's aria and recitatives in an attractively knowing way. She is no trial debutant but rather a soprano destined for major coloratura roles with the company.

Elias continues to enjoy management's belief in her star potential—both Cherubino and Zerlina are on her radio docket. Actually, she had first sung the page a decade before this broadcast debut portrayal. Her tensely focused tone and tautly strung line rightly suggest the adolescent's troubled state, but ultimately they overpower Mozart's musical portrait. 'Non so più' is hard-driven, needlessly so, for Mozart has sufficiently delineated the confused agitation of the youth in his eighth-note setting; thus, the other side of the coin, the wonder of waking to love, is negated. 'Voi che sapete' is handily delivered—one cannot fault Elias for professional aplomb, and her timbre is inherently attractive. But again, one looks in vain for the tonal float, the poise of line, the interplay between tension and relaxation, that bespeaks polished Mozart singing.

Stratas' Cherubino had those qualities. Her Susanna has them as well, and the role offers her a larger playground in which to romp. More than any Susanna in broadcast memory, she makes something individual and dramatically pertinent of the initial duets with Figaro. When she voices his name, she acknowledges their intimacy—a small thing, but seldom heard from Susannas. Even her 'din's and 'don's have personality. How deliciously (but without spite) she mocks Marcellina in their duet! Krips' tempo for the dressing aria is quite restrained, and thus Stratas, unlike soubrettes who pick away at the piece, utilizes varied word treatment and musical nuances to achieve a tonally more satisfying reading. Some of the nose-crinkling fun may be lost, but the scene acquires an intriguing sexual subtext. Krips' escape duet, however, is traditionally fleet. Stratas lays on seductive tone as she leads the Count into their "confusion" duet. In the sextet, this burgeoning family group seems at ease with itself—the piece meanders along in friendly fashion. Similarly, Krips, unlike conductors who relish the opera's *strepitoso* moments, prefers a mild-mannered, domestically sane treatment for the wild confusion of the second-act finale. When coupled with the relaxed tempos he employs throughout the opera, the vitality of the performance can be not sapped, but curtailed. Curiously, a similar effect obtains in the final act, where the much-anticipated arias of Figaro and Susanna fail to make their expected effect (that is, to make it in the usual way). Siepi's address to the audience about the perfidy of women, while musically nuanced and deftly done, is free of gall, the "playing to the gallery" stance decidedly minimized. Perhaps Krips thought the usual showmanship out of place. And 'Deh vieni non tardar,' while given a similarly fine reading by Stratas, somehow lacks the ultimate magic that the moment demands if the opera is to gain the full measure of humanity in its final moments. The soprano seems not quite at ease with the piece, as though she doesn't like where it lies in her voice. We know beyond a doubt that she could provide the transfiguring moment that would propel the opera onto a higher plane—that is why disappointment, perhaps quite unreasonably, touches us. Thus a slight letdown occurs before the finale begins. But there Krips picks up the momentum (Elias' vibrant tone and manner do inject a welcome tonic at this point) and the opera is brought to a joyous close with appropriately vivacious ensemble work.

And what of the new soprano, heiress to Della Casa's tiara? Zylis-Gara had made her company debut as Donna Elvira on 17 December 1968. The Polish soprano, still in her early thirties, was in her vocal prime, having only recently entered upon the international opera scene. San Francisco had welcomed her in the fall of her Met debut year, and Salzburg knew her Elvira, as did Paris. Dortmund and Düsseldorf had earlier claimed her, and Glyndebourne, Vienna, Berlin, and Mexico City all had heard her well-schooled voice. Like Joseph's coat, her voice holds many colors, and central to its appeal is the timbre itself. Its basic quality suggests a wind instrument, or better, a melding of winds with the oboe's plangent tone at its core; like fully trained masters of that instrument, she holds the peculiar plaint of the English horn in reserve. A not ungainly or unattractive graininess can make an assertive appearance on occasion. But she couples with these interesting colors a full-blown, quite lustrous timbre that is at the ready in expansive lyric moments. It may be a voice to treasure. Although she can be vivid in characterization, she deploys her voice largely in instrumental fashion, sometimes pecking away at a recitative (now and then in oddly almost infantile tone) or a phrase when we know she is annoyingly holding that vibrant lyric timbre in reserve. After a cautious beginning, her 'Porgi amor' is full toned, devoid of wobble, the clarinet's woe prominent. Neither warm nor cold, the vocalism is expertly deployed. In the second-act finale trios she allows her voice its full scope and the effect is gratifying. She and Stratas have different approaches to song so the letter duet registers lower than the best of broadcast history; Stratas does attempt a realignment by adopting Zylis-Gara's more detached syllabic treatment ('ca—pi—ra') and some lovely moments for both artists ensue. 'Dove sono' is a challenge for any artist and our soprano carefully conducts its melancholy line, acknowledging the dotted rhythms without disturbing the phrase shape. Her singing is distinguished, but does not excessive care dull the aria's wonted splendor? Unfortunately, the drag on the two top As in the concluding phrase is palpable (the notes are full-toned and of intriguingly dark color) and the cadential phrase, too, lingers on the pitch underside. It seems unlikely that pitch problems could be a permanent, even if occasional, feature of her work, since Zylis-Gara will remain a member of the company, and a broadcast favorite, for a total of sixteen seasons. Early assessment will be possible, for, as we turn to examine a pair of *Don Giovanni* broadcasts, we meet her as Donna Elvira in both performances, the first on 4 January 1969, a broadcast following quick upon her Met debut.

The opera, resplendent in the celebrated 1957 Berman mounting, continued to figure prominently in the house repertory and broadcasts throughout the sixties. Its prominence was justified not only by its production values but, as we have seen in the airing during the initial Lincoln Center season, by the superior quality of the musical re-creation. Of course, there were occasional fall-offs from excellence, broadcasts where an individual cog or two had lessened the efficiency of the smoothly running machine that Böhm had propelled in the late fifties. In 1966, for instance, occurred the unexpectedly substandard contributions of Elisabeth Schwarzkopf and Teresa Stich-Randall in the pivotal Anna and Elvira roles; Rosenstock's leadership was a known quality and thus a more likely drag on that performance. Even in what probably was the most efficiently run opera house in the world, the wheels occasionally need oiling. In 1967, the return of Böhm had supplied the proper lubricant. For the 4 January 1969 broadcast, however, Silvio

Don Giovanni
4 January 1969

Donna Anna
Martina Arroyo
Donna Elvira
Teresa Zylis-Gara
Zerlina
Rosalind Elias
Don Ottavio
Peter Schreier
Don Giovanni
Cesare Siepi
Leporello
Ezio Flagello
Masetto
Theodor Uppman
Commandant
John Macurdy
Conductor
Silvio Varviso

Varviso is in the driver's seat, and he does not seem entirely at ease at the controls of Mozart's high-powered vehicle. His command of the complexities of Mozart's masterwork is uncertain; indeed, there are a few moments when coordination between stage and pit is sadly awry. Then, too, his conception is rather ponderous for an opera buffa. Granted, Mozart's mix of the profound and the foolish is heady stuff, but Varviso's way fails to acknowledge the composer's sense of humor. The Met had favored the conductor with a surprising range of genres during the sixties: *Butterfly, Pasquale, Il Barbiere, Adriana Lecouvreur* in the expected Italian repertory, but also *Die Zauberflöte, Ariadne auf Naxos, Fledermaus*, and even *Hoffmann* and *Faust*. To be born Swiss (in their mountains multiple languages flourish) evidently ensures a cosmopolitan musicality. After this season, Varviso would not return to the company until the 1982–83 season, when *Die Walküre* would be his charge.

Siepi, Flagello, and Uppman again uphold the honors of the male contingent. None deviate from their high standard of previous broadcasts. Siepi and Flagello are so much at ease in their roles that their recitatives have not only the comfort of conversation but are highly flavored with individual touches of humor or irony. What an agreeable fellow Siepi's Giovanni is—perhaps a shade too blithe for those who believe seducers are malice prone. The basso can afford to be genial for he has so absorbed all the nuances and difficulties of the role as to make it second nature to him. Once again, he is in fine voice and the portrayal is appropriately charismatic. Flagello's instrument may have coarsened a bit, loosing a touch of its tonal rotundity, but in compensation he does an about-face from last season's portrayal, expanding his characterization to embrace not merely buffo moves, but sardonic feelings toward his master. His catalogue aria bulges with interpretive gestures (including excessive mugging in the repetitions of 'quel che fa' at the aria's close). He and Varviso have an ensemble tug of war in a few ungainly moments. Uppman, too, continues to expand his characterization, the singer's sunny disposition now buttressed by peasant anger. Elias had been heard in the 1966 broadcast. (Cross tells us that she was the first mezzo to undertake the role of Zerlina at the Met. I recall that, way back in the 1890s, the delightful Zélie de Lussan sang numerous Zerlinas. Of course, the Met Annals lists her as a soprano, but in *The New Grove Dictionary of Opera*, the redoubtable Steane, who knew Zélie well, brands her a mezzo-soprano.) Much as I admire the American mezzo, I cannot find her a satisfactory Zerlina, at least on this afternoon—she was rather more satisfactory in the earlier broadcast. Here a good deal of her singing is charmless, her tone seeming too taut, her line once again too innately tensed for the minx she plays. Those qualities are inherent in her vocal makeup and serve her well in other roles, but here they get in her way musically. The arias just don't sit comfortably in her voice. Moreover, she flirts with the pitch (sharp) in a good deal of 'Batti, batti'—a higher tessitura than is her customary vocal terrain may be the cause. The Met evidently found her a capital coquette for her extensive list includes twenty-eight encounters with tempting Giovannis.

Of the new cast members, Macurdy is an uncommonly fine Commandant. His timbre may not be so granitic as to, in itself, inspire terror when heard in a cemetery, but his concentrated delivery serves the purpose well enough. One knows from his measured pronouncements that repentance would be the preferred course. New to the airwaves is the young German tenor Peter Schreier, an artist who had already achieved some renown as a Mozart singer. He had come to the

Met in the opening Lincoln Center season to spell Gedda and Shirley as Tamino. In effect, he is a Gedda manqué. The authentic article is of such superior quality that even a lesser one has value. Schreier would have a distinguished European career but his tone was perhaps too ordinary, his style, though elegant and musicianly, too contained for the Metropolitan public to hold him close. He would not be allowed sufficient years to build regard. Truth to tell, the voice, as heard on this afternoon, is at times rather unattractive in timbre, nasal and blatant. He sings his arias with taste and a manly stance, suggesting chaste affection for his affianced in 'Dalla sua pace'—a more accurate than endearing reading. In a few of the runs of 'Il mio tesoro' he relies on aspirants to help the vocal flow, but overall he imbues the aria, at Varviso's leisurely tempo, with a rewarding measure of nobility.

As in the 1966 broadcast (but in quite a different way), the two ladies who dominate the opera are cause for consternation. Arroyo (Donna Anna) and Zylis-Gara (Donna Elvira) are both expert technicians but their portrayals of these wronged and overwrought women are curiously dispassionate. Miss Arroyo's beautiful instrument and unfailing security on high and in difficult passagework are, by this time in her Met career, familiar assets. Her reliability does not, however, make one less appreciative of those precious attributes, which are again solidly displayed in Anna's two major scenes. But must we also accept as irrevocable the soprano's neutral stance in regard to musicality and dramatic presence? From the evidence of this afternoon (one need cite only her placid, uninflected recounting to Ottavio of the attempted seduction), I am afraid that will ever be our lot. But we can take pleasure in the rich color of her middle and low voice in the opening scene of the opera, in her easy command of the vengeance aria (her very ease, of course, dilutes its message), her neatly executed scales in the mask trio (but lament her awkward way with the turns), her tonal beauty and fluent coloratura in 'Non mi dir' (well vocalized but lacking the affecting grace that the best Mozarteans bring to its poised phrases). While hoping to please, I find that I have denigrated each attribute that I intended to praise. When confronting this valuable artist, a Janus swivel invariably takes over. One wants so much more from her as complement to the prized resources that are undeniably hers.

That Zylis-Gara is an accomplished vocalist was fully apparent in her portrayal of Countess Almaviva. Elvira's brief entrance aria confirms that impression, its modest demands met with almost casual aplomb, a self-assurance that never deserts her throughout the afternoon. In addition to her technical security, one again takes pleasure in the voice's unique timbre. She has a command of fioriture—in her accommodating throat, 'Ah fuggi' is child's play. Rhythmic impetus is sometimes wanting. A bit more attention, for instance, to the sixteenth-note upbeats that articulate the aria's dramatic profile would be welcome. Rounders of rhythm (Arroyo, too, has the tendency) turn the lively into the placid. As the opera progresses, both Arroyo and Zylis-Gara reaffirm that they are at heart singers of an instrumental cast; that is, they handle their voices as fine (exceptionally fine) wind or string players would. This proclivity often produces phrases of remarkable beauty (as in the mask trio); on the flip side, textual acuity and dramatic potency are sometimes, but not always, slighted. With the hindsight provided by her entire Met career, we know that this is not really an inhibiting factor for Zylis-Gara in roles that exploit the blossoming romantic qualities of her voice. Many a broadcast audience will treasure her affecting portrayals of the great lyric heroines. We get a taste of that vocal allure in her handling of the accompanied recitative that introduces 'Mi tradì.' Rather than the grand dramatic gestures favored by some interpreters at this moment (she does acknowledge the mood change at 'mortal'), Zylis-Gara emphasizes the pathos of her situation: 'Misera Elvira' is beautifully conducted and sorrowfully sounded. The aria itself is traced to perfection, but she lays a shell of coolness on its surface. Every note is in place, even in the intricacies of the lengthy roulades (taken easily in one breath), so much in place that the curves of Mozart's phraseology are neglected. 'Perchè questi sospiri e quest'ambasce?' Elvira asks herself at the close of the introductory recitative. Sopranos may answer that question by fixing upon Elvira's agony at Giovanni's betrayal or her pitifully confused emotional state (both cited in the text). Zylis-Gara gives nary a hint of either affect, preferring only an accurate, musical response. Perhaps that is her conception of Mozart style. The roulade-laden aria (a baroque *seria* hangover) is in fact susceptible to treatment as a vehicle for vocal display. Validity lies in that corner as well if the roulades are regarded as a symbolic "topic" rather than an emotive agent. The audience rewards the soprano's polished traversal with what may be the longest applause of the afternoon.

We meet Zylis-Gara again, still haunting the streets of Seville and longing for her treacherous lover, but newly companioned on the broadcast of 20 March 1971. There we first make acquaintance with Edda Moser and Jeannette Pilou, an Anna and Zerlina worthy to be catalogued by Corena (in his seventh radio edition) if only Siepi's Giovanni could count them among his conquests. Uppman, and Gedda, too, are on hand, with Paul Plishka a new recruit as the resolute commandant. Admirable artists all, but the afternoon's highest honors belong to Krips. From the murky shadows of Varviso's conception we emerge into the Viennese conductor's enlightening domain. Here order reigns, but its ascendancy is never allowed to inhibit characterization or eviscerate the drama. The result is rather the opposite, for Krips shapes and sounds each of the familiar gestures of eighteenth-century musical rhetoric with such precision, such graphic specificity, that newfound insights are revealed and long-treasured pleasures enhanced. What an informed light he sheds upon Mozart's endlessly fascinating musical and dramatic fabric! His imprint is stamped upon every moment of the score, from the grandly sculpted overture to the slightest ornamental commentary. When Mozart, with his ineffable sense of humor, sends the violins precipitously down a scale and the low strings offer an ascending answer as Leporello tallies the seductions in Italy, Germany, France, and Turkey, Krips' strings put their heads together in conspiratorial snickers; his winds so point the staccato chordal arpeggios that underline the servant's malicious 'voi sapete quel che fa' that they are converted into wounding barbs upon Elvira's fragile psyche. And he gives equal care to the score's more tender effusions. Throughout the afternoon, he paces the opera with due regard for the classical proportions of each unit (a few surprisingly broad ritards notwithstanding), all the while integrating them into a grand design. Well along into the second act, one might suspect that his measured tread is becoming just a touch enervating, but that heretical thought is immediately routed by some perceptive turn of phrase or dynamic impetus. Ultimately, the stately progress of the supper scene gathers immense force and conjures the requisite awe before Krips injects a welcome vigor into the concluding pages of the opera proper.

Best of all, Krips evidently has thoroughly impressed his conception upon his stage partners. The cohesion between singers and orchestra is notable and all the more remarkable since the broadcast is the initial offering of the opera's run.

Don Giovanni
20 March 1971

Donna Anna
Edda Moser
Donna Elvira
Teresa Zylis-Gara
Zerlina
Jeannette Pilou
Don Ottavio
Nicolai Gedda
Don Giovanni
Cesare Siepi
Leporello
Fernando Corena
Masetto
Theodor Uppman
Commandant
Paul Plishka
Conductor
Josef Krips

Nor is mere precision the goal, for the conductor has brought about significant alterations in several familiar portrayals. After he establishes his buffo bona fides as he waits outside while Giovanni and Anna tangle, Corena, though somewhat rough-voiced in the aria, there and ever after behaves with notable musical rectitude. He sings rather than grumbles, and with no loss to his characterization. Siepi, too, profits from care from the pit. Rather than swathe each phrase with his rich sonority (as is his wont) he limits sonic breadth so that Mozart's line has a cleaner channel—but his legato remains intact. His manner, too, is toned down a notch—the geniality is less all-pervasive. One senses there may be more to this rake than lust for life and its pleasures.

Of the previously heard characterizations, Gedda's Ottavio, remembered as somewhat trenchant when heard in January 1967, is now a gentler creature. Seville's sun has warmed Sweden's son. In 'Dalla sua pace' his tone is burnished with bronze and he phrases with suavity and greater variety, both in quality of movement and in play of dynamics. In contrast to his 1967 effort, he begins the reprise with a genuine *piano* and continues in that vein until the text demands more vigorous treatment. Krips relishes the *grazioso* of Mozart's marking for 'Il mio tesoro' and Gedda responds in kind, taking up the initial phrase more graciously than in 1967. Now the piece sounds like the love song it is. Oddly, under the first long-held high F before the principal roulade Krips speeds up the orchestral patterns, but then evidently realizes that this tenor needs no assist and retains the tempo on the repeat of the phrase. (One momentary imprecision occurs between tenor and conductor as Gedda moves his fioriture along while Krips' repeated chords remain fixed—a blemish noted only as an exception to the overall exactitude of pit and stage coordination.) With his fastidious art, the Swedish tenor is clearly an audience favorite. Both arias elicit vociferous applause and at his final solo bow he is greeted like an old friend.

The bass contingent on this afternoon is augmented by a commandant whose virtue is inherent in the tonal steadiness and serious musical purpose of Paul Plishka. The bass is not new to the airwaves (his company debut as Colline occurred during the first month in the new house), but, except for a lone Sacristan, his broadcast roles have been miniscule, ranging from one of the nobles in *Lohengrin* to a monk in *La Gioconda*. That status was his general lot until he received his due in the decade of the seventies, the breakout heralded by such roles as the Commandant and the Duke in *Roméo*. Few singers include in their list both the Jailer and Sacristan in *Tosca*, Pietro and Fiesco in *Simon Boccanegra*, or a Guard and Sarastro in *Zauberflöte*. That Plishka was worthy of the elevation is evident in his sonorous voicing of the father's plaint and the avenger's commands; in the latter, this commandant at one point sounds as though he would genuinely prefer the reprobate to repent—quite a generous response toward his murderer. Having come to the company at age twenty-five (recruited from the short-lived Metropolitan National Company, a junior but worthy touring limb of the august main company), the American bass will endure for decades as a house mainstay.

Jeannette Pilou's international heritage—an Italian soprano of Greek parentage and Egyptian birth—piques interest in her and her art. Fortunately, the latter is as rewarding as the novelty of her background. She had come to the Met as Juliette in 1967. Though she would not become a permanent resident of the company, Pilou gains some prominence later in this chronicle with several broadcast portrayals of leading lyric roles. In the meantime, her Zerlina is in the traditional mode and no less appealing for that—indeed, perhaps more so, for her pleasantly timbred soprano and exquisite musical style are more satisfying than the portrayals of recent interpreters. Abetted by Krips' benign tempo and loving manner (the little orchestral trills are aural snuggles), her 'Batti, batti' is a delightful thing, full of wisps of charm and delectable nuances. (Perhaps there is a little Swiss heritage in that international background as well, for she is fond, perhaps overfond, of echo effects.) She and Uppman make an appealing couple. I particularly like the natural give and take of Siepi and Pilou in 'Là ci darem la mano,' another instance of Krips' moderating influence on Siepi's seduction technique. Edda Moser, too, would be a sometime member of the company, her visits spelled by several absent seasons over a period of decades. A 1968 debut as Wellgunde in *Rheingold* was followed by a brief hearing as Nedda the following year. After this rather odd entry for one who would be known as a Mozart specialist, she returned with higher status in this season, first singing the Queen of the Night and then undertaking her initial Met Anna on the broadcast. That she was formidable in the role is evident from her impressive Met tally over the years. And, on the evidence of the radio performance, she is indeed a superior player of this demanding heroine. In marked contrast to Arroyo's tepid repulsion of Giovanni's advances, Moser is wonderfully dramatic, agitated and full of fright, conveying all the urgency of her situation but retaining vocal poise there and in the following duet with Ottavio. Her vengeance aria is purposeful in intent and vocally accurate; she is not unwilling to spend a bit of capital in the interest of character portrayal, as in her fierce, hair-raising naming of Giovanni as the murderer of her father. The voice itself may not be overlarge but it is more than sufficient to the purpose. Its burgundy-hued timbre entices and the tone is firm and secure throughout the entire range. Both the scales of the masked trio and the intricate fioriture of 'Non mi dir' are handled with dispatch and seeming ease. Rightly, the Berlin-born soprano may be called a dramatic coloratura. She nails the top note of 'Abbastanza' in the preceding recitative with dead-on precision and, in contrast to the pervasive fiery posture she assumes throughout the opera, applies a cajoling legato and splendid tone to her loving plea to the constant Ottavio. Only in the sixteenth-note garlands of the moral does she disappoint, attacking them where a gentler taking is preferred; Gedda, on the other hand, better serves Mozart by again discarding the muscular phrasing of his earlier broadcast. Unfortunately, Moser's excellence on this afternoon is not entirely characteristic of her total career pattern.

Yet another singer, this time on the distaff side, has evidently felt the press of Krips' tutelage. Or could it be merely a recognition of the size of the house and the vocal stance preferred by American audiences that has caused Zylis-Gara to leave off her earlier note-picking ways? On this afternoon, her Donna Elvira is far more involved in the wretched woman's desperate situation than in the 1969 broadcast. Not that Zylis-Gara turns Elvira into a virago—the soprano's stage persona is not built along those lines. ('Ah, fuggi il traditor' is a quite discreet warning to the bewitched Zerlina—no wonder she doesn't heed it.) But, in addition to giving her character greater dramatic life, her vocal projection is more vivid, the dynamic range expanded and the phrasing more fluid. She seems willing to spend self. Tonally, the voice's wind coloration is in recession, and when it is present, the previously dominant oboe has miraculously turned into a clarinet. But more often than not, a warm, fluent opulence prevails. Now the opening of the quartet speaks and, though she reverts to her instrumental mode in the masked trio (it is not inapt there), her pleas to the unrepentant Giovanni at the opera's close have sufficient impact. And this time, the far-flung phrases of 'Mi tradì' are bound with streams of luscious, creamy tone. In her expert traversal of its intricate traceries that curious problem which I noted in the 1970 'Dove sono' reoccurs at a few prominent points: her pitch tends to the downside, especially when lingering at the upper E-flat. Is that particular note in her voice ill tuned, or is the rather dark coloration that she employs at those moments causing the discrepancy? (I felt a similar tug on the high A in a phrase of 'Ah, fuggi,' but that can happen to any artist in the early stages of a performance.) Earlier I cited her Met longevity as reassurance on this point, but a definitive assessment must be deferred until later broadcast hearings.

At the time of her debut, Zylis-Gara remarked with amazement to an *Opera News* interviewer that it had been a half century since a Polish soprano had appeared at the Metropolitan. She proudly called up the memory of the incomparable Marcella Sembrich, whose Met career spanned twenty-five years before her retirement with full honors in 1909. Zylis-Gara's Met career will not equal that time span, but her season tally (16) will exceed that of her compatriot. Though Sembrich is regarded as a near-paragon of the committed artist, she was not above asserting her prima donna privileges. On a famous occasion in the early 1900s, she displayed her independence by quitting a performance of *Il Flauto Magico* before the opera's close.[2] In her unpublished memoirs, Fritzi Scheff recounts the contretemps that occurred. During vociferous applause for Scheff's 'Pa-Pa-Pa' duet with Giuseppe Campanari, the conductor began the next scene for the Queen of the Night and her ladies; Sembrich (as the Queen) began to sing, but the audience demanded an encore of the duet. Offended, the diva—refusing to sing 'Der Hölle Rache'—departed not only the stage, but the opera house. No such high-jinks affect the *Zauberflöte* broadcast of 6 January 1968. Unlike manager Maurice Grau, Mr. Bing wouldn't have it.

Having launched the Chagall *Flute* in the opening season, Krips again bounced back across the Atlantic to conduct the first two performances of the 1967–68 season, but thereafter Rosenstock took over. His stewardship of the broadcast holds no surprises; one may regard that judgment as approbation or condemnation. Both would be correct. The overture is weighted more toward sobriety than jocundity and that gravity portends the performance gait. Of course, it is Uppman who supplies the afternoon's joy. His Papageno not only wears well, but remains perennially young, its artless candor as appealing as ever. The deftness of his characterization is enhanced by musical and vocal surety. At the close of the suicide vignette, for instance, he employs a darker color after Papageno's timid count of 'Drei!,' the timbre drawing a momentarily somber cloud over the birdcatcher's blithe spirit. Ruth Welting's agile soprano will be heard to advantage in future broadcasts, but her Papagena sounds vocally pinched even when released from her old woman's disguise. The Queen's trio of ladies, Pracht (delightfully piquant in tone), Love, and Casei, are again smoothly integrated, unlike Nagy and Sgarro, a mismatched pair of Men in Armor—the former plays Radamès, the latter is inaudible in their important chorale. Though they had sat out the 1967 broadcast, Franke (Monostatos) and Hines (Sarastro) are longtime airwave interpreters of these roles. They know their place and fill it well. In a felicitous exchange, Franke

Die Zauberflöte
6 January 1968

Pamina
Pilar Lorengar
Queen
Cristina Deutekom
First Lady
Mary Ellen Pracht
Tamino
Peter Schreier
Papageno
Theodor Uppman
Speaker
Morley Meredith
Sarastro
Jerome Hines
Conductor
Joseph Rosenstock

and Uppman are uproariously entertaining as they shout 'Hu!' at one another. I suppose it is difficult to make Sarastro sound other than priestly (even when aided by Rosenstock's accommodating tempos) and certainly Hines does not. But his voice and manner are well suited to high-minded pronouncements and he sings the stately hymns with firm and agreeable tone. Morley Meredith, on the other hand, surprises with a more vivid interpretation of the Sprecher than is commonly heard. He grasps the elevated intent of Mozart's newly conceived German recitative style, his tone is noble in size and coloration, and he seems genuinely involved in Tamino's plight.

Three relative newcomers to the company add interest to the performance. Lorengar (Pamina) and Schreier (Tamino) have already been introduced in our survey, but Dutch soprano Christina Deutekom (Queen of the Night) makes one of her infrequent Met appearances on the broadcast. Until a year before her Met debut (28 September 1967), the soprano had been singing small roles, but Schwarzkopf accidentally heard her vocalizing the Queen's stratospheric arias and recognized that *rara avis*, a dramatic coloratura, though one not yet having taken flight. In the second act she does not disappoint, indeed earning an extended ovation after 'Der Hölle Rache.' In that showpiece, her martial manner is apt, vocal size lending impact to what has too often been a tepid, even sweet, sounding of vengeful sentiments. The timbre may be overly bright and occasionally erratic in coloration, but the technical feats are easily dispatched, the staccatos as assured and steely as sword pricks. The top Fs are on the mark. A cause for wonder (and amusement) is her babbling of the triplet roulades—they are troublesome for many sopranos, but her 'bab-bab-bab' (could the oddity be rooted in idiosyncrasies of her native tongue?) is a grotesque solution. In a later interview Deutekom complained that Met audiences relished her 'Hölle Rache' aria but were indifferent to the beautiful 'Zum Leiden bin ich auserkoren.'[3] In that aria, however, her glassy timbre, aspirated fioriture, and erratic tempo fluctuations compromise its beauty. Deutekom would be a sometime Met member. Signed for the current season only, the soprano returned in 1973 for Elena (*I Vespri Siciliani*) and Donna Anna in the following season.

If Deutekom's timbre is somewhat showy, at least it is a recognizable aural fingerprint. Schreier's sound is nondescript if one applies the standards of leading tenors on first-rank opera stages. When he enters pursued by the serpent, his timbre is so lacking in charisma one might think Monostatos had made an unscheduled appearance. His febrile manner is partial compensation, though his agitation seems a bit over the top for a princely hero, even one who is snake-routed. The 'Bildnis' aria initially suffers from thin top notes but before long that problem is solved, and, abetted by effective interpretive touches, his sincerity registers. Over the afternoon, Schrier's musicianship and skill in characterization come to the fore and concern over the quality of his equipment recedes. In fact, the vocal registers equalize and, in isolated moments, reserves of power augment expression. He is a heart-on-the-sleeve hero, unafraid of wearing his emotions proudly. When he and Lorengar finally meet at the close of the first act their rapture is palpable. After hearing his Ottavio, I named him a Gedda manqué. In the end, management must have determined that *echt* Gedda could meet their needs. Fortunately, Schreier was well established at the Berlin Staatsoper and Salzburg and his future brought him increased regard in other operatic venues (Vienna, in particular) and as a singer of lieder.

Pilar Lorengar as Pamina in *Die Zauberflöte*. Photography by Louis Mélançon. Courtesy Metropolitan Opera Archives.

Miss Lorengar, on the other hand, will have many years to grace the Met stage—though not so many as we might wish. In marked contrast to her tenor prince, she owns an instrument whose coloration is precious booty. Add to that a beguiling presence and a winning stage manner and her worldwide popularity is readily comprehended. As Pamina, she reaffirms her aptitude for the Mozart heroines. She is a more emphatic player than Raskin—the American soprano has her own lode of feistiness, but her vocal means are not so grand as those of our Spanish heroine. Lorengar's 'Ach ich fuhl's' is hardly the traditional plaint of a damsel in distress. Classical restraint does not govern her interpretation. The trying four detached notes in the highest range issue forth as cries of anguish from her pliant throat. Only the purity of her tone burnishes the classical imperative. And yet that tone is so marvelously distinctive—simultaneously sweet and acute. In the highest range, it showers radiance upon us. Yes, occasionally she can overly squeeze a tone or a syllable, or loosen her fluttery vibrato to excess. (The vibrato, notoriously not to everyone's taste, has now been cited and we need harp upon it no more.) At the aria's close she brings the piece into dramaturgical conformity with a pathetic touch of resignation. Perhaps that is why, for once, the audience refrains from covering the heartrending postlude with applause. As she joins her lover in the trials by fire and water, Lorengar, with halo-embraced tones, claims not only her prince ('Tamino mein! O welch' ein Glück!') but her listeners, whether in the house or the home.

Lorengar and Zylis-Gara figure in many a Met Mozart production and it is the Polish soprano's Pamina that we hear on the broadcast of 17 January 1970. Abetting her are three participants from the 1967 premiere of the Chagall *Flute*. Gedda and Prey are artists well versed in their assignments but newly heard by the radio audience as Tamino and Papageno, while the broadcast also serves to introduce the Czech soprano Lucia Popp as the Queen of the Night. Augmenting interest is the presence of a new conductor, Stanislaw Skrowaczewski. Since 1960 conductor of the Minnesota Symphony, the Polish maestro had guest conducted the Cleveland, Pittsburgh, and Cincinnati orchestras but was relatively new to the opera house. His opera debut did not occur until 1969 at Santa Fe. Mr. Bing had engaged him to conduct *Eugen Onegin*, but that offering was a casualty of a prolonged labor dispute. Casts during the curtailed season were a patchwork: the *Flute* cast, for instance, during the first few weeks was of dizzying variability (in the initial week of the run Raskin, Zylis-Gara, and Edith Mathis all sang Pamina). Skrowaczewski has this performance (the third) well in hand, however. Indeed, his imprint on the score is both individual and certain. In his opening remarks, Cross defined the opera as "a wonderful hodgepodge of comedy, satire, nonsense, political forays, and high ideals," but our conductor brooks little nonsense. High ideals, however, are very much his concern. His conception—which lends a welcome unity to the performance—is spacious, the serious moments moving with a decidedly measured tread. By the opera's end, the psychological time compass may have been extended, but we know that a mind has been at work. In such an austere setting, Sarastro's solemn pieces (Hines again the hymnist) and the Armored Men's chorale lose a particle of their uniqueness, but the overall gain may be worth it. Initially, Skrowaczewski's deft fugal treatment and impetus in the overture promised a lively interpretation, but the solemn introduction, with purposeful inner voice movement, proves the more reliable forecast of the afternoon's music making. Dramatic tension is prominent in his

Die Zauberflöte
17 January 1970

Pamina
Teresa Zylis-Gara
Queen
Lucia Popp
First Lady
Jean Fenn
Tamino
Nicolai Gedda
Papageno
Hermann Prey
Speaker
Walter Cassel
Sarastro
Jerome Hines
Conductor
Stanislaw
Skrowaczewski

Nicolai Gedda as Tamino, Ruza Baldani as Third Lady, Jean Fenn as First Lady, Rosalind Elias as Second Lady, and Hermann Prey as Papageno in Marc Chagall's act one, scene three set for *Die Zauberflöte*. Photography by Louis Mélançon. Courtesy Metropolitan Opera Archives.

playbook. Still, he can run with a comic episode: Monostatos' aria is crisply fleet and Franke is able to stay the course. Occasionally, the conductor's pace places a heavy burden on a singer. Hines, for instance, wants to move ahead, while Zylis-Gara in her aria heroically remains within the circumscribed time zone set by the maestro. Regrettably, this is our only encounter with the venturesome Skrowaczewski.

For this series, the Met has abandoned the boy soprano format for the genii. In addition to Forst, the trio includes two singers first introduced in the 10 January production premiere; the inauspicious beginnings of Gail Robinson (a future broadcast Gilda) and Frederica von Stade (soon to become one of the company jewels) seem grossly disproportionate to their gifts and their future value to the Met. On the other hand, one might not expect to meet two Met stalwarts as queen's ladies, in spite of the importance of their ensemble duties in the opera: Jean Fenn (remembered for her broadcasts of Marguerite and Eva in the early sixties) and Mildred Miller (the paragon Cherubino of the 1950s) are heard as the First and Second Ladies. Fenn's voice sounds rather aggressive (Mozart's head lady is, of course, a hard-liner, but her dramatic posture need not roughen tone) and the overall ensemble is not as precise as heard from some earlier units. Still, their collective sound (winningly bright and distinctive) has merit on its own terms. Dooley was scheduled for the Sprecher but Cassel takes over and gives a convincing portrayal. High ideals are indeed this priest's province and both in manner and vocal quality the baritone fills the bill. He is in excellent voice, with no intrusion of the gruffness that sometimes marks his performances. Skrowaczewski's magisterially paced *arioso* for the speaker and Tamino allows Cassel and Gedda opportunity for a noble and affecting reading of this critical scene. They make the most of it.

Gedda had first undertaken Tamino at the Met in 1958 (he sang the broadcast that year) and his prince is as assured dramatically and musically as any tenor has a right to be. What clean-cut tones and phrases he spawns when fleeing from the serpent—immediately, one recognizes the *echt* Gedda. In the aria, the voice is bright-toned and fearless in the upper range (and the concluding leaps to 'mein' land as precisely as a settling peregrine falcon on an airborne heron). This Tamino projects a love that shines with noble purpose, perhaps a little deficient in warmth, but certainly reassuring to any forsaken maiden. (After all, at this point, Pamina is only a girl in a rotogravure.) Text, rather than mood, is his concern, and he makes of the aria an absorbing narrative. He favors a single dynamic and the timbre can be a bit blatant in the ensembles. Throughout the afternoon, the breadth of phrase he employs in the accompanied recitatives commands admiration. Schreier's characterization was more appealing and he (of necessity, considering his vocal material) relied more on nuance to make his points. Perceptive artists like Schreier and Gedda are formed and nurtured by (and sometimes eventually aggrandize) the peculiar gifts that nature has given them. On this afternoon, Gedda is both a manly prince and a princely tenor.

Prey's broadcast appearances have been few (Wolfram in 1960 and Count Almaviva in 1965) even as his Met seasons were intermittent in this decade. Hearing him as Papageno, a role for which he was justly celebrated in Europe, allows an even higher value to be placed upon his abilities. His voice and manner are so engaging, the timbre so fruity, the vocal smile so welcoming that his presence in the opera is a tonic. Single-handedly, he all but restores the opera's dramaturgical balance, which Skrowaczewski has resolutely imperiled. (Recklessly, he brings down the house with the interjection of a phrase in English: "thank you very much.") Of course, his German diction is a model of clarity and vernacular style. Satisfaction with Papageno's plebeian lot is inherent in every word and tone that Prey utters. Joy seems his natural state and laughter his reward. His comic timing is on the mark, as is evident in his cannily delayed 'Ich bleibe ledig' (I'll stay single). Di Franco's clever Papagena is reason enough for him to reverse course in that regard. The Berlin-born baritone's birdcatcher adopts a more down-to-earth posture than Uppman's charmingly fey conception offered. One plays the man-child, the other the child-man. Both are winners.

Popp's renown would eventually rest on lyric roles rather than the coloratura *Fach* where the Queen of the Night lives. Evidently Elisabeth Schwarzkopf must have discovered every prospective Mozart Queen alive in European opera houses. Popp recounts to an interviewer that, when singing a small role in Salzburg, the more experienced soprano pronounced the novice "a miracle" when she heard her audition for husband Walter Legge. The latter immediately engaged her for his *Zauberflöte* recording, that performance leading to her engagement by Bing.[4] Unlike Deutekom, Popp makes her best impression in the first-act aria. 'Der Hölle Rache,' the second-act challenge, is more shrewish than expected; rather than cultivate pure tone, the soprano prefers to court the dramatic mode (as Mozart's angry Queen should) with emphatic vocalism. A slight gargle in the lower tones surprises, but the high notes are intact and the triplets decently executed without recourse to a gimmick. 'O zittre nicht,' however, reveals the dimpled tone that we later came to relish, its purity and roundness already secure and beautifully controlled. Popp's fioriture are exact and unhurried and thus the proud Queen gains in stature. Skrowaczewski's winds intermingle some beguiling phrases to compound her affecting delivery.

Though she is Czech born, Popp's tone exhibits no Slavic traits. Perhaps her Vienna base and lengthy Cologne residency account for her timbral neutrality. Zylis-Gara's soprano, on the other hand, seems resolutely touched by her Polish heritage. Within its complex makeup (the bewitching timbre is sometimes scumbled by opacity), the forlorn is inherently dominant. Thus, she cannot project the radiant happiness that Lorengar exuberated when Pamina claims Tamino. But Zylis-Gara's pronouncement is equally assured vocally. And what she can distinctively provide is a searing delineation of grief in 'Ach ich fuhl's.' Was ever the aria's death knell more tenaciously sounded? In combination with the conductor's somber pace, the soprano's reading probes the depths. The voice's barren wind coloration with its fascinating clarinet plaint (and we know how Mozart loved the clarinet) mirrors Pamina's longing for 'Ruh' im tode,' the peace that death can provide. Beyond doubt, Zylis-Gara is the Pamina to realize her compatriot conductor's conception. (A slight thinning of her tone at one high point does not lessen the aria's impact.) Even the little 'Mann und Weib' duet wears a more composed countenance when Prey and Zylis-Gara celebrate the hallowed state. Once again, her vocalism is primarily cast in the instrumental vein. Diction plays a secondary role. At the opera's close, Pamina, in her triumph, calls in the flute to guide the lover's wandering and now the soprano's varied timbral tints enhance her amplitude of tone and breadth of phrase.

The Mozart standard continues to fly proudly at the new Met, even though cyclical change exacts its toll. The second generation of Mozarteans has ended and a third begun. Those who inaugurated the succession (Pinza, Rethberg, Steber, Sayão, Novotna, Kullman, and Baccaloni under conductors Panizza, Walter, Busch, and Reiner) gave way to the fifties generation of De los Angeles, Della Casa, Seefried, Güden, Miller, Peerce, Kunz, London, Uppman, and Siepi under Böhm, Leinsdorf, and less-expert conductors. Now the generational tide has swept most of them into memory's hold. New recruits Zylis-Gara, Lorengar, Stratas, Raskin, Krause, and Prey (under Krips) are in the grand line. And more are on the way.

Franco Corelli as Roméo in *Roméo et Juliette*. Photography by Louis Mélançon. Courtesy Metropolitan Opera Archives.

CHAPTER FIVE

Latins, Light and Heavy

Mozart, fecund amalgamator, gobbled up international styles with the gusto of a cosmopolitan gourmet. Latin appetites—I refer only to compositional traits, not bodily needs—were hardly so voracious. Italian composers were, as a group, less responsive to outside influences. True, when Donizetti worked and wrote on French terrain, he was content to do as the natives did. And Verdi's Parisian operas, of course, bore the ceremonial imprint of the Opéra's conventions. But a more judicious sprinkling of national traits cross-fertilized the Italian and French genres when composers were confined to their home grounds. Often enough, the Italians liked their opera straight, largely undiluted by foreign subtleties, and the French (at least until the invasion of the Wagnerian virus) preferred their stage libations neat. The operas of Donizetti, Bellini, Mascagni, Leoncavallo, Gounod, and Bizet, which make up this group of Metropolitan offerings, are rooted in national soil.

As noted, Donizetti was certainly not immune to the lures of the French operatic scene in his final operas. And even the earlier *L'Elisir d'Amore*, written for Milan, employed a libretto by Eugène Scribe (*Le Philtre*), its content refashioned for home tastes by Felice Romani. Notwithstanding that literary parentage, *Elisir* is a guileless child of the Italian opera buffa tradition, its pastoral setting allowing the composer to color the genre's blithe but brittle facade with sentiment. Unfortunately, the Metropolitan performance of 16 March 1968 shortchanges both blitheness and sentiment. Cleva, an unlikely nurturer of buffa frivolity, lumps through the score with scant regard for its humor and without embracing its tender charms. Tempos lag, sparkle is capped, and the heavy accents that he lays on Donizetti's simple accompaniments are stones tied to a sinking body. They weight his stage colleagues down. But Peters, Kraus, Sereni, and Corena know their business and do what they can (each in her or his own way) to enliven the afternoon.

Corena is in superior form, the voice more full bodied and easier on the ear than usual, his patter's effervescence reigned in by Cleva's methodical tempos, but his delivery still vibrant. The spirit of comedy sounds in the voice's very timbre. Sereni, more often captive of opera's villainous or at least darksome characters, might seem an odd candidate for buffo chores but Belcore was an oft-performed Met duty of his. Of course, the jilted sergeant has an overinflated idea of his importance, and bluster is his mode of communication, so subtlety (not usually

L'Elisir d'Amore
16 March 1968

Adina
Roberta Peters
Nemorino
Alfredo Kraus
Belcore
Mario Sereni
Dulcamara
Fernando Corena
Conductor
Fausto Cleva

Sereni's portion) is no prerequisite for the assignment. He is a capital Belcore, his richly colored tone and manly delivery making plausible Adina's momentary infatuation (surely this Belcore was not merely a pawn in her courting games with Nemorino). Remarkably, his command of fioriture is better than that of most lighter-voiced baritones who have played the role. Clearly, we have been underestimating the baritone's talents.

Nor should Miss Peters' considerable ability be taken for granted. The New York soprano racked up over five hundred performances with the company so her place in Met history is secure. Her worth, in my opinion, was sometimes more utilitarian than treasurable, but other light-voiced sopranos came and went at the Met with lamentable frequency and without leaving their imprint on the company. She undoubtedly had something that appealed to both the public and management, the latter not prone to sentimental attachments to spent sopranos of diminished popularity. I find the answer to her lengthy career (she is still active as I write this, though no longer at the Met) in her consummate professionalism, her knowing stage manner and charming stage presence (though it was a bit too artifice-touched for my taste), and, above all, to the astonishing security of her technique. (I feel compelled to add that artifice on the stage can be mighty attractive; I certainly have often relished it, especially in the soubrette and romantic comedy realms.)

Adina can be played as a hard-hearted minx (the aforementioned "brittle" of the genre, a foil for the tender-hearted tenor). While Peters is too astute to fall into that trap, her vocal manner at least leads her in that direction. On this afternoon, after initially succumbing to her appealing timbre in midrange, I find the voice itself less pliant than usual, smaller toned (until the opera's final moments), occasionally wiry, pinched, or excessively nasal; it seems subject to undue manipulation in order to provide linear uniformity. At times she chews the text rather than projecting it. Yet she executes every roulade with marvelous precision, their articulation as clear and clean as a Vermeer checkerboard floor. Stylistically she is at home: her cantilena can be persuasive and her recitatives are full of personality. I suppose what disturbs me most is her execution of the small embellishments that adorn Donizetti's seductive melodic line (as in 'Chiedi all'aura lusinghiera'); they are all angles rather than curves, little technical exercises rather than miniature billets-doux. She summons some moments of surprisingly full-bodied tone in her capitulation to Nemorino. Indeed the entire scene confirms her abundant gifts, acutely propelled as they are by professional know-how.

The afternoon's principal interest and abiding joy is provided by the broadcast debut of Alfredo Kraus. His stage career began as the Duke of Mantua in Cairo in 1956, and theaters in Spain and South America, as well as Covent Garden and La Scala, knew him. San Francisco and Chicago were North American ports of call. I recall a windy city *Rigoletto* in the late fifties where his dapper stage presence and stylish vocalism registered strongly. The tenor from the Canary Islands (if he were a soprano, one could not virtuously refrain from exploiting that geographic fortuity) is in his third Metropolitan season at the time of the *Elisir* broadcast. The introductory 'Quanto è bella' confirms him as the musicianly singer we will come to dote upon. Yet he knows Nemorino is no Parisian puff. Rather than filling the little piece with Bergonzian elegance, he prefers rhythmic vitality and an energized text. Clearly, this peasant is no languishing tenorino, though Kraus has the timbre

Alfredo Kraus.

and the subtle musical instincts to wend his way down that path if he should so choose. The slight nasality that infects his tone recedes as the opera progresses. Indeed, in his first duet with Adina we discover his dulcet way with a melodic line, though he is not quite willing to proffer the full boon of Schipa-like suavities—not yet. Tenors who play the sentimental fool ('Io son sempre un idiota, io non so che sospirar' [I'm but a fool and can only sigh]) must walk the line between bumpkin and lover. Caruso relished the former, Schipa and Gigli the latter. Kraus mixes the two until 'Una furtiva lagrima,' and there, of course, the game is up and love is the hands-down winner. On the way to that capstone, Kraus edges toward the lover in gradual stages—in the duet with Dulcamara (no slight suspension of time at the apex of the intoxicating 'Obbligato' phrases) his voice is entirely lubricious, but still a feisty spirit governs his delivery. Even 'Adina, credimi' in the first-act finale is more a manly plea than a blandishing suppliance (the accents are stern, though a few graceful eases cushion them). Worth noting is Sereni's dexterity in a lengthy passage of coloratura in the finale, the result exceeding even some of Kraus' efforts in that vein. 'Venti scudi' (and here Cleva is entirely earthbound) betrays the almost excessive glare of the tenor's upper voice but confirms that he has not only the elegance that the best interpreters bring to the role but also the vocal heft for the larger moments, poundage that some highly regarded portrayers have lacked. And he is a clever vocal actor—one can hear a silly smile in his tone as the village girls besiege the slightly drunk, but newly rich, peasant. An abundance of lovely tone, full-bodied climaxes, a few charming diminuendos, a well-articulated cadenza, and a sweet head tone on the final 'morir' of 'Una furtiva lagrima' guarantee a rousing response from the grateful house audience. Many a broadcast audience will relish the Spanish tenor's cultivated artistry on future Saturday afternoons.

Felicitously, that pleasure need not be delayed. Kraus again plays the Donizetti romantic tenor in the composer's comic masterpiece, *Don Pasquale*, on the broadcast of 5 December 1970. Corena is also on hand in the title role, while Tom Krause accepts demotion from Mozart count to Donizetti doctor, and Gabor Carelli performs another (this time, mock) marriage. Reri Grist as Norina provides the opportunity to consider the quality of the company's soubrette resources. Carlo Franci, new to this chronicle but not to the Met podium, takes charge from the pit. One hopes that attribution of authority will be reaffirmed by deeds, for the Italian wing needs strong, knowing stewardship.

That hope is realized. In terms of musical and theatrical conception, the performance is one of the most idiomatic of recent decades. Early in his career, Franci, a student of Fernando Previtali, preferred the symphonic realm, not moving from the stage to the pit until 1959, but thereafter he was a frequent figure in Italian theaters and in Vienna. New York made his acquaintance when he brought the Rome Opera's production of Rossini's *Otello* to the Metropolitan in 1968. Hard upon that success came his official debut with the company (*Lucia* in February 1969). As the *Pasquale* overture begins, his brilliant, no-nonsense fanfare signals the lively performance that ensues. The fanfare's vitality gives way to a nuanced orchestral tracing of Norina's melody, the execution replete with all those slight hesitations and accelerandos that augment its charm. Now we are assured that the twin poles of the buffa genre will be well served. And so it goes throughout the afternoon. Franci is a master of the musical gesture that complements, even illuminates, the stage action. His pacing is masterly. At certain moments, his tempos are exceedingly fleet, and often (as in the concluding stretta of act two) the takeoff is exhilarating. When off to the races, his charges are with him all the way. (The limited choral work, however, is occasionally less than precise.) One can only regret the traditional cuts that lop off portions, sometimes entire stanzas, of many of the set pieces. Notwithstanding that disfigurement, this comic masterwork thrives under Franci's flexible, loving hand.

Corena's Pasquale is a familiar portrayal. The basso's voice is no longer in prime condition, but then, tonal beauty was ever foreign to it. Pasquale is a role well suited to his current resources, for few lyric passages interrupt the quick patter and extensive recitatives of the part. In the latter, his basso sounds full, firm, and resolute. An experienced harrumpher, he chooses not to round off a few rough edges of the testy bachelor. In the introductory 'Un fuoco insolito,' for instance,

Don Pasquale
5 December 1970

Norina
Reri Grist
Ernesto
Alfredo Kraus
Malatesta
Tom Krause
Pasquale
Fernando Corena
Conductor
Carlo Franci

some interpreters have cherished Pasquale's longing for 'bamboli' to warm his old age; Corena's straightforward treatment neither caresses the song nor warms his audience to him. Neither is Tom Krause's voice the ideal instrument for Malatesta, the suave manipulator of the action. The tone is too blunt, the manner overly emphatic for the style—indeed 'Bella siccome un angelo,' the doctor's calling-card aria, lacks a welcoming smile, and the top tones want body (indeed, a few of them are quite chancy). Even here, however, his phrasing is pertinent, for Krause is a thorough stage artist, musically correct, and committed to character portrayal. As the opera progresses, these qualities cause the deficiency in bel canto tonal spin to seem less important. I admire the panache of his portrayal, most evident in his rhythmic exactitude and accurate delivery of the fioriture. In the long run, Krause's dramatically astute Malatesta belongs in the asset column of this performance.

If conductor Franci is the prime mover of the afternoon, tenor Kraus takes the honors among the stage participants. In contrast to Krause, his instrument is in pristine condition, its tone either full bodied or dulcet, the timbre still honeyed and this time without undue nasality. The top voice roams effortlessly. A slight squeeze facilitates that security but doesn't detract from—may even enhance—the voice's appeal. Elegant phrasing abounds; the portamentos that enfold 'cara' in his introductory aria, for instance, entice. For the most part, though, his song is forthright and manly, leavened by only a few discreet diminuendos, especially at cadences. When he negotiates the climax of 'Cercherò lontana terra' with radiant ease and assured brilliance, the audience recognizes his special worth. In many a performance of the opera an inevitable let-down occurs as struggling tenors flounder in the high tessitura of the Notturno and garden duet. Kraus makes them the high point of the afternoon. Both are sung in key (lagniappe indeed) and he sings the written tenor line with none of the usual interchanges with the soprano. (He alters only one eighth-note circlet around a high B.) To hear him negotiate with firm, lovely tone the mounting, intertwining intervals of the sixth at the duet's conclusion is to marvel at his technical command. Kraus' Metropolitan career was more spasmodic than his artistry warranted; unfortunately, absences of several seasons periodically interrupted his tenure. Still, the association would be of long duration.

Miss Grist's membership in the company would be limited, but the pleasure that she gave during the late sixties and seventies was substantial. After a debut with the Santa Fe Opera, the American soprano enjoyed several seasons in Zurich. Covent Garden, Salzburg, San Francisco, and Chicago knew her before the Metropolitan introduced her as Rosina in the final season at the old house. Having heard, and most relevantly, seen her in that role, I am aware of the infectious charm that radiated from her stage performances. The voice is small, bright, the lower octave slightly burred, the upper octave almost too brilliant. The very top tones are full toned, easy, and invariably top off a phrase or aria with unexpected luminosity (the magnificent, pinpoint E-flat and D *in alt* that crown Norina's mockery of romantic heroines are vivid examples). The timbre, which can become wearing to the ear, allows for minimal variation of tone color, but our heroine is a canny comic player, responsive to her character's moods. Norina is a laughing girl and Grist owns an infectious chuckle. And she never overplays. Her agility is of high quality. I note with particular pleasure the sometimes startling dash of her fioritura, especially in cadenzas (as at the conclusion of 'So anch'io la virtù magica'). From her throat, the melody that embroiders Pasquale's patter after Sofronia has slapped him offers subtle comfort as Grist rubs away a modicum of Norina's cruelty; and here, Corena's almost whispered 'è finita, Don Pasquale' admirably enhances the sentiment. At some moments in the afternoon (the middle of the second-act quartet is one instance) the tone turns excessively infantile and its shallow timbre becomes annoying. In the long run, the European-based soprano is probably an acquired taste, the voice not one to have universal appeal. It lacks the silvery float of a Seefried or Raskin, the shine of Sayão's radiant timbre, or the presence of Güden's pithy tone. She has her own uniqueness and the thoroughness of her schooling cannot be doubted, but before the afternoon is out, one remembers the breadth of Peters' instrument and longs for the fullness of tone that, in her best moments, enhanced her soubrette portrayals. Notwithstanding the charms of Grist's piquant voice and captivating play, her portrayals are probably best appreciated as spicy seasoning, occasional alternatives to the endless parade of mainstream soubrettes. Broadcasts of Grist's Sophie and Zerbinetta will mark future chapters. In those roles, the peculiar character of her instrument may well be consistently apt.

    When considering Metropolitan soubrettes, the name of Anna Moffo does not immediately come to mind. Violetta and Lucia were her most frequently performed roles with the company. Yet she would seem to be ideally suited for the "ina" heroines, combining several of the above-cited qualities in her instrument, particularly tonal warmth and float, with considerable agility. She did in fact sing Norina, Adina, and Rosina with the company (only a few performances each) but her star stature demanded larger vehicles and, for the better part of her career, the Metropolitan recognized that fact. We hear her in one of those prime roles, Lucia, in the 1 February 1969 broadcast of Donizetti's romantic opera. Of great moment is the presence of Franci in the pit. The broadcast, the season premiere of the opera, is notable for Gedda's first Metropolitan Edgardo and for the house debut of Renato Bruson.

    Franci, already chronicled in the 1970 *Pasquale*, is also making his house debut on this occasion. The virtues noted in that broadcast are apparent here, though in somewhat less obvious form—the musical gestures of the buffa genre are extrovert mirrors of the stage action while the swath cut by early romantic opera is both broader and often subtler. Nevertheless, Franci's lively theatrical sense and sound musical instincts are everywhere apparent in this admirably paced reading. He seems just the tonic that the Italian wing needs to imbibe on a daily basis. Unfortunately, even he evidently can do nothing about the shabby ensemble and lethargic manner of this Metropolitan chorus—but then the broadcast represents his first encounter with Kurt Adler's crowd.

    Charles Anthony's bridegroom is as assured in his tenorizing as Lord Arturo Bucklaw must have been in demanding Lucia's hand, while newcomer Rod MacWherter's tenor is equally solid in Normanno's few phrases. Giaiotti provides some of the finest song of the afternoon, his resonant bass uncommonly resonant and his phrasing suavely musical. One especially values his restraint in the more melodramatic pronouncements of the last act. We are fortunate that Bruson's debut coincides with a broadcast, for his Metropolitan appearances would be very limited. Destined to become a prime ornament of the Italian music stages for more than three decades, he is heard here as a fledgling in years (thirty-three) but fully

Lucia di Lammermoor
1 February 1969

Lucia
Anna Moffo
Edgardo
Nicolai Gedda
Enrico Ashton
Renato Bruson
Raimondo
Bonaldo Giaiotti
Conductor
Carlo Franci

formed in artistry. Though not yet a La Scala debutant, since 1961 he had perfected his craft on major Italian stages. The timbre is distinctive, in effect bifurcated, the middle and lower portion well collected and wearing that attractive sneer fondly remembered from many an old-time baritone compatriot. The distinct upper voice is slightly porous (some might call it almost spread) but it is reliable and of haunting coloration. As a debutant, il signor Bruson is intent on making his mark where and when he can, and for Enrico Ashton that is at the curtain's rise. There he provides a fine, old-style barnstorming rendition of 'Cruda, funesta smania' and 'La pietade in suo favore.' His second-act scene with Enrico's unhappy sister allows him to show a subtler side of his art, and there his well-focused tone and sympathetic line conduction make Ashton's deeds less repellent and Lucia's capitulation plausible. Unfortunately, after this season he would be a stranger to the Met public for a dozen seasons and not until the 1984 broadcast of *Don Carlo* would the radio audience again hear his idiomatic style and gusty instrument.

For assured vocalism, virtually no one is in Gedda's league, at least among tenors. He is in spectacular voice on this afternoon. When was he not? knowing advocates will ask. But today his vocal poise and spirited delivery are vibrant and secure to a degree remarkable even for him. Italophiles may decry the lack of dulcet caress in Edgardo's intimate moments or regret that the voice seems untouched by those dark shadows that can suggest inner torment. If the timbre is insistently bright, it is cast from the choicest, most resilient bronze and its shine gladdens the heart as well as the ear. All listeners will find recompense in his stylistic surety and the verve of his delivery; indeed his manner in moments of extremity is more fiery than that of most Italian tenors. That he is a formidable opponent for the Ashton clan the tenor makes clear from the moment of his entrance. There Gedda is all bristling energy and male dominance, the tone pointed and splendidly virile, though his preference for strong and repetitive accents can be wearisome. But he takes up the extended line of 'Verranno a te' with complete aplomb and brings the duet to a stunning conclusion. In the second act, Edgardo's anger at Lucia's supposed perfidy needs emphatic expression, and Gedda's rage delivers the proper charge—a red-hot 'Maledetto!' curse—in the whirlwind aftermath of the sextet. (Ensemble between Gedda and Bruson is a bit problematic in the sextet—indeed, overall this grand moment is far from the exalted episode it can be.) As for high notes, they issue from his throat with perfect equanimity, their brilliance and security seemingly as inevitable as the tolling of a bell. In the final scene, the ascending phrases that close 'Tu che a Dio spiegasti l'ali,' often trying even for the best tenors, are taken in stride, the vocal ladder readily scaled. Though he sings the introductory aria in key ('Fra poco a me ricovero' is delivered in straightforward, almost businesslike fashion), like most of his colleagues, he moves the following lament down a half-step. A few lovely head tones when he learns of Lucia's death prepare us for his heartfelt delivery of the aria. A quiet beginning and elegant line are soon augmented by marvelously full tone. He is not loath to drench a few notes with sobs (take that, Italophiles) and, though the mood is not elegiac, his pain is palpable. How odd that this lover, so distraught in the throes of death, should seem so uncaring, quite lacking in tenderness, in life. Perhaps the deficiency is inherent in Cammarano's libretto, but other tenors have told us otherwise.

I have refrained from any mention of Miss Moffo's performance until this point, dreading the report that must be made. I had approached the broadcast with the hope that a novel and skillful portrayal of this demanding role would be our happy lot. Of course, like most with knowledge of that era, I was aware that the early seventies would witness a precipitous decline in the soprano's vocalism but, in truth, I had forgotten—undoubtedly it was willful repression—that it could so devastatingly affect a performance of this early date. (In *The New Grove Dictionary of Opera*, Harold Rosenthal does not acknowledge a "vocal breakdown" until the 1974–75 season.[1]) To indicate the extent of debilitation, I note that few performances by a major artist over broadcast history have been as troubling, so strong a cause for regret and dismay, as Moffo's portrayal of Lucia. (Two performances cited in *Sign-off for the Old Met* pale in comparison, namely, Delia Rigal's Elvira in 1952 and the unfortunate 1966 rendering of that same role by the indisposed Schwarzkopf, who thereupon wisely canceled the remainder of her season.) From the first and to the end, Moffo's voice is in almost total disrepair. There is little point in detailing her deficiencies episode by episode. A general summary must include inconsistent tonal production, unsupported tones, pitch inaccuracies, at times grievously blurred or labored fioriture, lurches to hard (but admittedly sometimes secure) topmost tones at the cadence, and occasional ugly chest tones. The vocal sins are many, and her penance will be seven more seasons on the Metropolitan stage. The voice is patently sick, without a core of solid tone—and her tone once was warmly Mediterranean in timbre and floated rapturously. One wonders if she will get through the performance and, most important, why management did not interfere to prevent exposure of a singer in palpable distress. In his highly informative account of American singers, Peter G. Davis reports that Bing considered stopping the performance before the Mad Scene.[2] His concern would better have precipitated action before the second act. (And the manager continued to schedule Moffo performances until the end of his tenure three years later.) Oddly, she is marginally more successful in a few moments of the Mad Scene than in earlier portions of the opera, but the improvement is spasmodic (a few staccato passages, a brief brush of fioriture, a piercing top tone) and, in any case, they are below an acceptable standard. To the vocal deficiencies must be added an attempt to camouflage them by an overly realistic, at times almost hysterical, conception of the role. Modern sopranos have not infrequently attempted to lay psychological complexities upon bel canto song in the hope of making the unfortunate Lucia relevant to our times. In a series of performances at Central City Opera in the early sixties, we offered contrasting conceptions of the role, wherein the lovely Judith Raskin interpreted the roulades of the Mad Scene as psychologically motivated, while Marguerite Gignac, pupil of the revered Lina Pagliughi, gave the music a pristine, classic poise of line. I admit I preferred Gignac's (i.e., Pagliughi's) way. But Moffo's way on this afternoon goes beyond searching for and applying a novel conception; it is carried to such extreme lengths that it may be considered a means of getting through the performance in some outwardly believable fashion. It will not wash. The overall result is an almost complete banishment of that serenely poised musical line that is the hallmark of bel canto style. What an unhappy day this is for admirers of this once treasurable instrument, and for lovers of beautiful song. The regret is the greater for I recall witnessing a fine Lucia from Moffo at San Francisco in 1961 (the only reservation a hard shell on an occasional top note). At that time, her cantilena was gracious and her fioriture fluent.

Could it be that the precarious state of her once lovely instrument on this 1969 afternoon is a temporary indisposition? Moffo is only thirty-six years old and in her tenth Met season. Or is it in fact a harbinger of the distressing fate that will be hers in the next decade? I well recall that, at the time of the Lucia debacle, a colleague whose training ground was, like Moffo's, the Curtis Institute, laid the cause of Moffo's difficulties squarely in the lap of Eufemia Giannini-Gregory. Acccording to my friend, Madame Gregory failed to provide Moffo's naturally placed instrument with a firm foundation of breath support: "with her students, the high notes were always screamed." It came as no surprise to me when, in the mid-seventies, after the beleaguered soprano had sought help from voice resurrector Beverly Johnson, the latter baldly informed the *New York Times* that Moffo had "no breath support."[3] Undoubtedly the problem was further aggravated by the young diva undertaking a fearsome number of roles and engagements (including films and television) during her ascension to international fame. That the vocal crisis was already upon her in 1969 may be gleaned from her performance history in that season and over the next few years. After the 1 February broadcast she canceled her 5 February Lucia, reappeared on 8 February, and sang 'Senza mamma tu sei morta' at the 15 February gala. She canceled the 28 February Lucia and the management took the unusual action of replacing Donizetti's opera with *Aida*. Two June concert appearances in *Traviata* in the New York parks were fulfilled. Although she continued to make house appearances in succeeding years, Moffo, though scheduled, was absent from the Metropolitan airwaves for four consecutive seasons. That lacuna is highly unusual for an artist of such prominence. She appeared in quite a number of other performances during these seasons, but evidently the broadcast format, with the inevitable taping for future reference, was too daunting a hurdle. Fortunately, we shall have an opportunity in later chapters to review performances on both sides of the divide, Violetta (1967) and Gilda (1968) in happier times, and Nedda (1975) in the twilight of her Met career.

After this distressing experience, we turn with more than usual anticipation to a performance wherein the high standards of bel canto vocalism reign—in effect, a passage from the absurd to the sublime. The 4 April 1970 broadcast of *Norma* lives in the memory of all who heard it. If nostalgia is rimmed with regret, the cause lies in the pit. Richard Bonynge became the guardian of Sutherland's greatness and, though he fostered her ascendance, indeed, tutored her gifts, he is not always their best caretaker, at least at this stage of his career. Like most husbands of famous prima donnas who, either through management or music making, tag their wives' careers, the Australian conductor is ipso facto too easy a target. As one who greatly appreciates his exploration of the half-forgotten treasures of nineteenth-century French opera and ballet, I wish he might have transferred a portion of the élan he found in them to the broadcast performance. His reading is stodgy and the stasis already present in Romani and Bellini's design is magnified. The orchestra plays with metronomic routine and the choral work is dispiritingly shoddy. The principal drawback for the singers is Bonynge's inability to float the simple accompaniments to their glorious melodies—the repetitive patterns become overly insistent as a set piece progresses. The vivifying pulse with which a Serafin shaped this music is missing; a glaring example occurs when Bonynge badly mistimes the double climaxes of the fourth-act finale, the most heartrending moments of the entire opera. And yet, throughout the afternoon musical miracles happen onstage, so some worthwhile interchange must have occurred.

Ordassy (singing Sutherland's 1952 Covent Garden role of Clotilde) and MacWherter ably fulfill their plebeian chores. Of the principal quartet, Siepi has

Norma
4 April 1970

Norma
Joan Sutherland
Adalgisa
Marilyn Horne
Pollione
Carlo Bergonzi
Oroveso
Cesare Siepi
Conductor
Richard Bonynge

the least to do—Oroveso is one of the sit-out-and-play-cards roles. Indeed, the basso seems to have aged considerably between the open-throated splendor of his first act 'Ite sul colle, o Druidi' and his darker-toned, magisterial outburst against Roman tyranny ('Ah! del Tebro al giogo indegno') in act four. Siepi had counseled Milanov's 1954 broadcast Norma, but Bergonzi is new to the opera, having learned the role of Pollione especially for the Metropolitan's new production. A *lyrico-spinto* tenor rather than the usual *tenore robusto* (Martinelli or Del Monaco in earlier broadcasts) was certainly Bonynge's preference: "You don't want Pollione bellowing through that Act Two trio," he told *Opera News*.[4] (Bergonzi bellow?—I feel I have been remiss in allowing the two words to touch.) Rather than a general's command, our tenor utilizes crisp rhythms to animate 'Meco all'altar di Venere'; the tone is vibrant and plentiful, but clearly his intent is to voice the "love song" that Bonynge believes the aria to be. On the broadcasts, Pollione's duet with Adalgisa has never been so artfully sung. The tenor introduces coloristic changes in the lyric portion of 'Va, crudele' and begins 'Vieni in Roma' with an intimate mezza voce before providing the *slancio* of an ardent lover. As Adalgisa, Marilyn Horne echoes both moods with expert skill in her responses, adding a few brilliant flashes of fioriture in the bargain. In this scene, the two superb musicians and vocalists have considerably increased the heat quotient of the opera. Bellini followed creator Domenico Donzelli's prescription in Pollione's music by concentrating on the tenor's chest voice up to G and sparingly sprinkling in the high notes, yet Bergonzi is not loath to send out a number of splendid, full-toned top tones throughout the opera. But he never bellows—certainly not in his affecting acceptance of the sacrificial compact at the opera's close.

Lovers of beautiful singing had been anticipating Miss Horne's entry upon the Metropolitan scene for some years before her debut as Adalgisa in the production's premiere on 3 March. Finding the right vehicle for the occasion had caused some delay, for the mezzo-soprano (so called in the program) was a rare operatic plant. Trained as a soprano, like many an American in those years she had learned the operatic craft in a smaller German house (three years at Gelsenkirchen, where her repertory ranged from Tatiana and Mimì to Maria Boccanegra and Minnie). Since 1960 she had been heard in San Francisco in roles as diverse as Marzelline and Nedda, and, most courageously, as both Donizetti's and Berg's Marie—I witnessed the Berg and Leoncavallo heroines with open-mouthed pleasure. Soon the Rossini operas became her specialty and "mezzo" became her signature. Early in the sixties, she and Sutherland began their unique professional and personal relationship, fostered and reinforced through joint performances in bel canto operas throughout the world. We know that earlier Metropolitan attempts to promote a Sutherland Norma had foundered upon the casting of Adalgisa (for an aborted 1964 *Norma*, assistant manager Paul Jaretzki had informed Bing that Sutherland did not wish to contend with too grand an Adalgisa—she was a bit nervous about the proposed Simionato).[5] The delay was overlong, but the wait was worth it, for Horne's contribution is everywhere on a par with Sutherland's. If one were a betting man at the track, one couldn't lose on opting for a quinella—either artist was sure to win or place. On this afternoon, a photo finish is clearly the ticket.

Not the least of the benefits of the Sutherland/Horne connection is the perfection of their ensemble in the intricate duets—and *Norma* is in large part an ensemble opera. Adalgisa lacks a major aria, so the singer, in addition to the three duets, must make the most of the solo dramatic recitatives and *arioso*s that Bellini granted her. It is in these moments that the varied riches of Horne's vocal wealth, her musicianship, and interpretative subtlety are most strikingly displayed. At her entrance, she is not afraid to exploit the widest range of dynamics and her control over all shades of volume is cause for wonder. (She propels a lengthy *messa di voce* with an incredibly resonant crescendo, though the requisite diminuendo is far briefer.) The middle voice is refulgent, and for a few fleeting moments the name of Ponselle strangely leaps into my auditory consciousness. Of course, she occasionally exploits the baritonal chest tones that please her fans, but they are sparingly employed on this afternoon. In fact, the one criticism that might be lodged against her Adalgisa is the extent of her vocal riches, for the novitiate ought to suggest youth and innocence; Horne's tones can suggest a maturity which exceeds that implied by even Sutherland's considerable tonal wealth. The mezzo's manner is marvelously grand at times: before voicing an intimate 'Mira, o Norma,' she detonates a commanding top tone before recklessly (but cleanly) plunging to the depths. We opera lovers become unashamedly replete when we can relish the joie de vivre of vocal athleticism and at the same time acknowledge the bravura display as dramatically potent. In a few moments of her duet with Pollione, Horne shows that she could rout the general if only she would. And there a touch of that hardness that could gradually creep into her tone over the years surfaces. On the other hand, often in her duets with Sutherland the vocal coloration is exquisitely varied, the phrasing magnificently plotted and executed with consummate ease. My ears tell me (though my heart wants to reject it) that a slight downward drag on the pitch in the mid-low range occasionally infects some of the quiet moments. But both sopranos shine in these virtuoso episodes, and their vocalism, expansive or subtle, drenched with sorrow or radiantly hopeful, allows us to share the sheer delight in singing that they generously offer.

In the *Opera News* article that preceded her company debut, Horne posited some interesting future career paths.[6] She believed the soprano realm was not entirely banished (Tatiana, Mimì, and the *Wozzeck* Marie were still possibilities, she opined) and, having sung Wagner scenes (including the Immolation) in concert, she noted that Brünnhilde might be a half dozen years down the road. And she was ready to more diligently pursue the Verdi mezzo parts. Only the latter would come to pass, and that pursuit (Eboli and Amneris at the Metropolitan) would be spasmodic. When one listens to her Adalgisa, the possibility of hearing her as Norma seems quite plausible—after all, Grisi, the original Adalgisa, was also celebrated in the title part. But Horne was too intelligent a singer and too astute a career manager to allow risky diversion, however welcome to her large public they would have been.

Sutherland, too, could have chosen different paths: early on in her career the dramatic soprano repertory was within her grasp, with Wagner a definite possibility. That symmetry makes one doubly aware of the prodigious gifts that both artists possessed. Sutherland has confessed that initially she was haunted by Callas' conception of the Druid priestess, but that she eventually found her own way.[7] Indeed, she has. Her 'Casta Diva' tells us that we are in Jenny Lind territory—hearing the aria in the higher (and original) key of G contends with memories of Ponselle's grand reading in the lower key. While well negotiated (and throughout her long career, Sutherland's art never sinks below high professionalism) her vocalism of this test piece is cautious, almost small-scale, the principal melody insufficiently floated, the embellishments not as liquid or gracious as expected. Still, the preceding recitative has its own dramatic verity, and the aria's high syncopated tones speak and command. A delicious trill—she owns the patent on that ornament—ends things very nicely indeed. In the cabaletta, the voice opens up marvelously, and the fioriture are full-blooded with new ornamentation added to the second verse. Bonynge, in an effort to forestall applause within the scena and yet allow response after the cabaletta (where the march music normally continues without interruption), has unearthed an 1840 version with a formal ending to the cabaletta. No harm done, and this audience needs to reward the favorite. They do so vociferously. Of course, the lack of clean-cut declamation of the text (the vowels are excessively and indiscriminately open) smudges the opera's dramatic profile. Horne has the edge in that regard. When we hear her varied vowels and crisp consonants, we know what we are missing. But Sutherland's tone is pithy in the recitatives and rhythmic impetus provides partial compensation. The best news is that the infamous Sutherland phrase droop is banished. However plausible in *Sonnambula*, it would sully the noble priestess. Sutherland's heroine is conceived on an appropriately grand scale and the pathetic is held in reserve.

In the later acts, her portrayal gains in stature. She is magnificent upon learning of Pollione's betrayal, lacing her rage with hurt in the tone itself. One cannot claim that the tragic import of her situation has the concentrated intensity it requires. Still, the splendid high D with which she caps the second-act trio is meaningful punctuation. And the three singers, serious artists and superb vocalists, are one in their conception and execution of this grand episode. The chilling scene where Norma contemplates killing her children (in the prelude Bonynge opts for solo cello) is a high point of her performance—intimacy and expansive lyricism are the touchstones of her art. In the *arioso* she provides the full-toned, settled vocalism we longed for in 'Casta Diva,' and her dramatic recitatives with the penitent Adalgisa are well shaped and forceful. The glowing tones of 'Deh! con te li prendi' swell from a full heart. 'In mia man alfin tu sei' suffers from Bonynge's lethargic tempo and Sutherland's inadequate projection—in this emphatic confrontation between Norma and Pollione, rue is an inadequate substitute for fury. But soon Bergonzi energizes the drama and the soprano's far-ranging fioriture make their own impact, as do the pair's ringing top tones at the scene's conclusion. 'Son io,' Norma's confession of her guilt, is a lovely, heartfelt moment—as though we need any reminder that beauty of tone is in itself a powerful expressive tool. As she begins the duet ('Qual cor tradisti') a momentary and uncharacteristic rasp or two in the low voice makes one wonder if she has given too generously of herself en route to the searing emotional climax of the opera, but the opera's final moments are beautifully realized, her tone at its most attractive: 'Deh! non volerli vittime,' that celestial lament, lies well for her instrument and the singer and the song bring the opera to an eloquent conclusion.

Sutherland does give us *her* Norma, not the one so many in our time and before have prized. In that long, varied list of famous interpreters, the forthright face of her portrayal has an honorable place. In 1831, Giuditta Pasta, creator of Bellini's Amina as well as Norma, was no prize vocalist, but her dramatic abilities and musical insights were so potent that they caused Bellini to draw a portrait of immense and varied complexity. Giulia Grisi, the first Elvira (1835) and Adalgisa and also a celebrated Norma, was a high lyric soprano and an accomplished technician, but she too concentrated on "animal passion" (the description is Chorley's), the extremity of it mitigated by her personal beauty. Lind sang Norma everywhere during the forties and fifties but she was evidently temperamentally unsuited to the character's ferocity. Patti wisely stayed away from its dramatic challenges (though 'Casta Diva' was a favorite aria from early childhood). Lilli Lehmann's voice was built along more imposing lines, possessed of the volume and thrust for the Wagner heroines and yet capable of suitable agility. Until the 1980s, her Metropolitan successors were limited to Ponselle (1927), Gina Cigna (broadcast in 1937), Milanov (1944 and 1955), and Callas in her debut season of 1956. The lapse of thirteen seasons between the Callas series and Sutherland's venture indicates the enormity of the role's challenges, obstacles that, until recently, have given even the greatest prima donnas pause. Our Australian diva need not have hesitated.

Norma may represent the Etna of Italian diva roles, but in its own way Gioconda, too, has been considered a vocal heavyweight, even for dramatic sopranos. The absence of fioriture (the act-four temptation bit is easy game) lowers the bar, but orchestral mass upgrades the power demand. Still, the list of Metropolitan contenders is greater than for Norma, including not only the expected Ponselle and Milanov, but ranging from Christine Nilsson (in the Met's first season), Lillian Nordica, and Emmy Destinn on through Florence Easton, Stella Roman, and Eileen Farrell. One might not expect to add Renata Tebaldi to that formidable lineup, but a reworked voice and a new dramatic manner impelled her into new territory. Augmenting the star quality of the *La Gioconda* broadcast of 2 March 1968 are Fiorenza Cossotto (Laura), Mignon Dunn (Cieca), Bergonzi, MacNeil, and Giaiotti. Cleva is on the podium, as he had been for six of the seven broadcasts of the Bing regime.

The prospect of idiomatic performance is always intriguing. Seldom in these days do we have the opportunity to hear four Italian principals under an Italian conductor in an opera like *Gioconda*. There we may expect the native-born combatants to savor its juicy fruits with unabashed gusto. Perhaps Cleva has been too long on the American scene; from the perfunctory prelude on through a listless Dance of the Hours, routine is the order of the day for orchestra and chorus. The operatic warhorse is hand-ridden home, the maestro unwilling to apply the crop to Ponchielli's teeming score. Once again, the principals on stage protect their own interests. By means of open-throated vocalism, Giaiotti manages to elevate Alvise's devious shenanigans to a par with the opera's more endearing players. His is quite a feat since Ponchielli's third act normally represents a falling off in the vocal marathon that is the main reason we continue to cherish this barn-burning opus. Only if the company contrives a superior dance sequence to make fleet the passage of time in the Dance of the Hours can the act maintain the voltage level of the rest of the opera, but opera lovers know better than to expect terpsichorean miracles in a repertory house. Then, too, Cleva's *concertato* lumbers along *a passo di lumaca*, snail-like and as earthbound as Alvise had every reason to expect Laura's corpse to be. Mignon Dunn's Cieca has graced many a Met *Gioconda* and, especially since this fine singer by now has moved up to Laura at the house, we must be grateful for the opportunity to hear once again her sensitive molding of the obliging phrases of 'Voce di donna.' Cornell MacNeil knows that Barnaba is

La Gioconda
2 March 1968

Gioconda
Renata Tebaldi
Laura
Fiorenza Cossotto
La Cieca
Mignon Dunn
Enzo
Carlo Bergonzi
Barnaba
Cornell MacNeil
Alvise
Bonaldo Giaiotti
Conductor
Fausto Cleva

an eye-rolling vehicle with vocal equivalents. Thus, he appliqués a few macabre touches here and there to maintain his membership in the baritone snarl club. For the most part, he prefers the wily (as an interpreter) to the wooly (as a singer). Oh, at his entrance the voice is raw, excessively open, and betrays a beat, but soon his majestic instrument collects itself and robust tone envelops the grand pronouncements with which the composer favored the Inquisition's spy. And why not—after all, Barnaba is a ballad singer, though his talents lie elsewhere. The character gains stature through MacNeil's unexpectedly thoughtful, yet suitably sinister, salute to the Doge's palace ('O monumento!'). The baritone's declamation and vocal size require no puffing up to make their mark, not when he can loft a crowd-pleasing top G at the close of his credo. It is well that a similar high A-flat tops 'Ah! Pescator,' for Cleva's pedestrian tempo drains the brio from the sea ditty. Bergonzi and MacNeil provide a rollicking 'Enzo Grimaldo, Principe di Santafior,' the baritone probing his prey with imaginative readings (acting with the voice, that is), while the tenor heartily latches on to the tune with the requisite *slancio*. Obviously, all is well with the male vocal contingent.

One expects finished vocalism from Bergonzi and he doesn't disappoint. The role, new to his Metropolitan repertory this season, won't permit him the varied and polished nuances of his Verdi characterizations so he concentrates on grand vocal gestures. 'Cielo! e mar' is broadly limned, with none of its exposed hurdles sidestepped. What it lacks in the expected grace of manner is redressed by forthright phrasing and tonal splendor. The afternoon's ovation is his. Enzo's lead-off in the third-act ensemble would profit from a tenor with more brass in his horn, but in his final confrontation with Gioconda on the island of Giudeca, Bergonzi provides the elevated vocalism that is his special province.

Thus far our not-so-merry crew have performed with a just balance of interpretive decorum and vocal brilliance, and we turn with keen anticipation to our two divas for the flamboyance fillip that is so essential if *Gioconda* is to come in a winner. Fiorenza Cossotto, soon to be crowned a gallery goddess by Metropolitan aficionados, is heard in her broadcast debut. She had come to the house a few weeks earlier as Amneris. The mezzo-soprano had served rather a lengthy apprenticeship at La Scala (she was that theater's child), but over the past five seasons she had risen to be, indeed been anointed as, the successor to Simionato in the big mezzo parts. Covent Garden, the Vienna Staatsoper, and the Paris Opéra welcomed her as well, and she was at home at "La Scala West" (Chicago's own). The voice is not as plump-toned as that of her great predecessor, tending more to the Barbieri side. If it lacks the bold opulence throughout its range that was Simionato's wealth, it owns a far pleasanter top voice than the admired Barbieri could summon. What purpose would it serve to lament Castagna's velvety caress? Why wallow in regret that none can enter the hallowed territory of the almighty Stignani? At this point in Cossotto's career, the registers are well balanced and the instrument is healthy, the low voice resonant, slightly grainy, slightly touched with acid (here attractive as a piquant coloration). The upper voice possesses unexpected sweetness, an almost soprano-like squeeze of tone. Pith, rather than ripeness, is the voice's overall capital. Moreover, she is a musicianly singer. Mezzos and restraint are not always comfortable bedfellows, so Cossotto's musical conscience is doubly welcome. Of course, Lauras are expected to caterwaul their way through the beastly duet with Gioconda—she who loves with a lion's ferocity. Laura's claim is tamer and Cos-

Renata Tebaldi as La Gioconda. Photography by Louis Mélançon. Courtesy Metropolitan Opera Archives.

sotto takes that cue, not forgetting now and then (by a thrusting top tone, a laying on of brazen chest resonance) that she has friends to make in the gallery. After 'Stella del marinar' they embrace her as a prodigal daughter—the vocal type is rare and heiresses have been in short supply. Her skill is apparent in her clever negotiation of the aria's twists and turns. She and Bergonzi cozy up becomingly in their mooning duet, he adding a welcome dollop of mezza voce in the midsection and she clean and clear as Laura succumbs to human frailty and savors 'love's delight,' as the old translations have it. How satisfying to hear two like-minded artists in an intimate duet. When Laura returns to life at the opera's close, Cossotto effects the resurrection with her loveliest tones and most graceful manner.

Artistic integrity seems to be in uncommonly generous supply on this afternoon. Generosity of spirit and plenitude of voice are the hallmarks of Gioconda herself, the street singer who loves and loses with fierce determination. Tebaldi's assumption of the role at the end of the Lincoln Center inaugural season (with an initial broadcast in April 1967) generally was greeted with approval, and, in some quarters, with relief. Here was a vehicle for the soprano's later years where her newly created assets, vocal heft, and a commanding manner could be fully exploited. It was, nevertheless, an odd choice for a singer who had spent the bulk of her Metropolitan career avoiding the grander vehicles of the Verdi canon. But time and trouble had propelled her into a different vocal orbit. The new Tebaldi may be viewed in two fashions, the one contrasted with her youthful self, the other as a separate, newly met entity. Let us take the latter, more encouraging path.

The good news is that she does have a voice, an instrument that has, at least at times, remarkable correspondence with that blooming vehicle of old. The voice itself sounds healthy, the tone round and often even luxuriant in its density. Then, too, nature seems forgivingly kind when occasionally Tebaldi's gentle breath caresses tones in the midrange in the fondly remembered manner. *Ma guarda*! I am failing in my effort to hear with new ears. Try again. Obviously, this newly minted instrument is a soprano of remarkable quality. Then why has it not been trained so that, in addition to tonal wealth, ease of production in the upper register would prevent the hard scream that rims many a note in that range? Vocal discomfort causes the singer to hurry around the top curve of many a circlet to the detriment of the phrase architecture. Is not fidelity of pitch a prized virtue for any singer, newly coined or long known? We have been accustomed to hear (and even sympathetically have embraced) a palpable drag on the pitch in Tebaldi's climactic tones for many a year; we hear it today, but less forgivingly—the concluding high C of the act-four trio is a discouraging B natural. Beyond those exposed blemishes, we must repeatedly suffer woefully off-key intermediate notes within a phrase. Then too, perhaps in compensation for trouble at the top, the soprano has determined to emphasize the opposite pole. At every opportunity, chest tones, ponderous, often immense (sometimes grossly outsized in proportion to the attendant tones), are eagerly seized upon, seemingly cherished for their own sakes. Unwieldy as they often are, they augment pitch problems. Vulgarity is not a term that one willingly associates with Tebaldi's once mellifluous art, but it rears its ugly head today. The wildly cheering fans (and she has legions of them) evidently relish the larger-than-life bravura of her performance. Perhaps they would react with similar fervor even if they had not known and loved the graceful artist of yore. I wonder.

A few specifics are in order. Tebaldi approaches Zinka's ethereal high B-flat ('Enzo, come t'amo!') without fear, but the note is not quite reached, nor does the quiet tone that closes the lament over the vespers safely touch home. When Tebaldi plays the lioness in the duet with Laura, her recklessness is apposite and even thrilling in its way. But the contrast with Cossotto's art startles. The duet with Enzo has moments of beauty and the concluding top notes are fair enough. And the seductive song designed to delay Barnaba's triumph, while not entirely free from harshness, is appealing. Give her credit for her belief in Gioconda's plight here and throughout the performance—temperament is not in short supply. 'Suicidio!' (how emphatically she sounds the word!) is generally of reputable tonal quality, though the climax is hurried, the descent into chest gusty, and the final leading tone (on 'l'avel') glaringly off pitch. Is there no middle ground between Eileen Farrell's abhorrence of chest tone and Tebaldi's greedy embrace? I recall decrying the American soprano's reticence, her well-behaved artfulness, in the role: "She gives us a Vidalia onion where we want the flavor of garlic."[8] But authentic seasoning need not deaden taste. Nor is the juncture of artistry and Gioconda an oxymoron. *Slancio* is a prerequisite and welcome part of the Gioconda style and many will thank Tebaldi for her full-blooded reading. But the hyperbolic style of these Italian operas is governed by its own stylistic truth. There breadth of phrase and poise of vocalism remain viable vehicles for meaningful expression. Unexpectedly, Tebaldi offers us a nosegay of that poise and expressiveness in the final act as Gioconda instructs the reawakened Laura and the chastened Enzo. Here at last we can make a not unfriendly comparison with the younger Tebaldi, for she wraps her citation of the rosary theme and the surrounding text in some of her loveliest tones. The result is very like what I have called the "gentle susurration" that held us spellbound in former days.

While in the verismo mode (and today Tebaldi's reading propels *Gioconda* into that category), we can ingest the real thing, that slice of life that Mascagni served up as *Cavalleria Rusticana*. And, in contrast with too many past broadcasts, the composer has a soulmate on the podium. Leonard Bernstein, last heard in the house in 1964 as the alert taskmaster of Verdi's intricate *Falstaff*, takes on the unlikely chore of refurbishing Mascagni's soiled goods. His effort caused considerable consternation among critics and opera buffs—the profile he gave the opera was thought to be not only beyond the ordinary but outside the prescribed zones. But when was Bernstein ever bound by custom? The broadcast of 7 February 1970 documents his idiosyncratic but always engrossing conception. The conductor acts as sculptor, taking the composer's clay and shaping it anew—and quite in his own image. Perhaps he is merely removing the crusty overlay of tradition on the composer's design. Certainly one savors his molding of the musical shapes. You can almost feel his hand erotically embracing their broad limbs or his exuberant spirit reveling in swift jabs of rhythmic vitality. Of course, when contrasts are possible, Bernstein loves the extremes. Are certain episodes slower than the norm? Yes. But when the local color vignettes that fill the first half of the opera are so lovingly manipulated, their long melodic lines stretched with such a sure feel for their contours, the time is well spent. Are certain episodes pulled into unexpectedly jagged rhythmic convolutions? Yes. But the rhythmic disorientation he inflicts on the choral 'A casa, a casa' (suppression of accents on the downbeats) is mesmerizing. And when the commonplace paean to wine fascinates or the brief scene where Santuzza betrays Turiddu to Alfio turns into a dramatic high point of the opera, we know a creative intelligence is at work. That may be what ultimately disconcerts. Is the mind a touch too active, the intent to put a different impress upon the

Cavalleria Rusticana
7 February 1970

Santuzza
Grace Bumbry
Lola
Nedda Casei
Turiddu
Franco Corelli
Alfio
Walter Cassel
Conductor
Leonard Bernstein

score too obvious? Certainly not in Bernstein's grand, yet simple, phrasing of the Intermezzo. One has heard too many pedestrian readings of the opera not to welcome this well-studied, vivid interpretation. With Bernstein, one sometimes recognizes "the man soaring above the artist"—I can't recall where or about whom I read that illuminating phrase, but it is needed here. Too bad that the choral work is cast in the old everyday mode; the orchestral playing is on another level.

Speaking of soulmates, Zeffirelli, with whom Bernstein had collaborated on the 1964 *Falstaff*, was again on board. His mounting of the operas was one of the few scheduled new productions to reach the boards in this truncated season. (Seven were scheduled, but only the twins and *Norma* were produced.) It may be that the opportunity to work again with Zeffirelli (in some ways Bernstein's counterpart in the theatrical realm) enticed the conductor to accept this unusual assignment.

Of the principals, only Cassel's Alfio is a broadcast familiar. (Guarrera, who sang the premiere, was listed in *Opera News* but he was shifted to Tonio in the ensuing *Pagliacci*. These are the vagaries of casting in this makeshift season.) The Met veteran gives the workaday role a strong profile—he is always at his best when establishing character. A few Scarpia-like touches (the final taunting of Turiddu) are not out of place. The voice is, for him, in top form and he is on the mark in mimicking the conductor's quirky rhythmic treatment of Alfio's entrance song. I like Nedda Casei's casual way with Lola's song. She doesn't do a mini-Carmen in her brief moments on stage but rather allows her attractive voice to turn the trick. Her Lola might be just a charming girl out for an early morning walk—the conception contrasts effectively with Santuzza's frantic, hard-edged hatred.

Grace Bumbry assumed the role of the betrayed Santuzza for the first time at the Met in the premiere of the new production on 8 January 1970. While the role has traditionally been the province of sopranos, it has been coveted, won, and effectively performed by many mezzos over the years. Earlier in Met history, Margarete Matzenauer, Carmela Ponselle, and Bruna Castagna had their infrequent innings, but of late the mezzo brand has been more firmly imprinted on the wronged Sicilian. Indeed, Nell Rankin and Irene Dalis were 1960's broadcast Santuzzas. Bumbry was catapulted to international prominence when she became the first black artist to sing at Bayreuth (Venus in 1961). Her Paris Opéra debut (Amneris in 1960) led to several seasons at Basle, Covent Garden, and the Met (debut in 1965 as Eboli). The artist as person is an interesting mix of the serious—she is a Lotte Lehmann product—and the glamorous. In her, the twain do obligingly, convincingly meet. Probably she was too glamorous to remain forever in the mezzo ranks, though some beauties have been content and wise enough to do so. On the 1967 broadcast, Bumbry is at that interesting point in her career where her sights are on the soprano heroines; thus Santuzza is a suitable vehicle for her on her way to next season's assumption of Tosca. Her voice is not the plush instrument of some soprano interpreters, so the melodies at times are etched rather than enveloped with luxuriant tone. Nor does its narrow focus allow for varied tonal coloration. But the tone itself is pithy, of zesty bronze color, and retains its quality throughout the entire range (how gratifying to hear chest tones that belong to the main body of the instrument). The very top tones are tense, but certain. Occasionally they sound sharp, but that may be due in part to occasional thinning at high altitudes. Indeed, the tautness of the voice, its arrant tensility, is the defining characteristic of the instrument. The overall effect can be a bit wearing. But there is no denying the uniqueness of the instrument, and Santuzza's travails make it an appropriate vehicle for Bumbry's potent gifts. On this afternoon she performs with artistic integrity, the interpretation searing in its straight-arrow intensity. The Easter hymn commentary is rather ineffectual but 'Voi lo sapete' is both direct and telling, as well as tonally agreeable (if not quite of prima donna voluptuousness). The confrontation with Alfio shows her off at her best. There the tones are fuller, the manner impassioned, and our sympathies engaged. And she is a worthy partner for Corelli in the duet that forms the centerpiece of the opera.

The contrast in vocal manner of the two artists is notable. Bumbry is ever the linear etcher, her voice sometimes cutting as cleanly as a surgeon's scalpel, while Corelli remains the painterly colorist, swathing his phrases with great blotches of reverberant tone. The tenor is in splendid form, both vocally resplendent and dramatically vibrant. The role seems tailor made for his temperament and vocal persona. Though his Turiddu was first heard as far back as 1963, he would rack up only a dozen performances with the company. Clearly, Bernstein (and Zeffirelli in the acting department, from all reports) has imposed a distinctive conception upon the tenor. The imprint is most vividly apparent in their individual treatment of 'Viva il vino spumeggiante.' There the conductor's rhythms are subtly varied, but he and Corelli are delightfully one, with only the rapid cadential close catching the tenor unawares. His Siciliana is no languishing lyric serenade but an impassioned plea in which rhythmic variety again commands our attention. The tone may be initially a bit nasal but it remains seductive for all that, and one or two phrases are remarkable for his control of breath. In the duet with Santuzza, he phrases expansively, sends out volumes of sound, and makes certain that we know Turiddu feels no regret for his unfaithfulness. In the farewell to his mother a few moments of mezza voce provide welcome relief, but for the most part Corelli pulls out all the stops. Would we expect or want anything else from him? Even the tears in the voice seem entirely apt—and they do not compromise his masculinity. Bernstein's precipitous downward rush of strings brings the opera to a close. Cross tells us that in the curtain calls the conductor "hugs Mr. Corelli and Miss Bumbry," and well he might for the two singers have responded fully to his novel interpretation. All three deserve plaudits for making the Sicilian countryside so entertaining—if somewhat daunting—a scene.

By this time in his career hailed as conductor emeritus of the New York Philharmonic, Bernstein evidently was unwilling to add *Pagliacci* to his Met chores so that assignment fell once again to Cleva. We shall return to the 1970 twins, but first it will be instructive to look in on next season's broadcast of *Cavalleria* (13 February 1971), where we find the Italian maestro in charge of Mascagni's opus as well. There we hear the opera in its familiar guise, as though Bernstein had never placed his hot-iron brand upon it. That is not meant as a demerit for Cleva. To hear his interpretation, with all the traditional musical ploys, is like coming upon an old friend whose virtues and faults are so well known as to seem part of ourselves. No need to impress us—we would be affronted by show-off moves in this comfortable companion. Indeed, Cleva's way is musically sound and satisfying, the melodies flow with an easy gait and the climaxes grow naturally out of the musical fabric, making their expected effect without working themselves (or us) into a lather. The maestro explained it all in *Opera News*. He had known Mascagni,

Cavalleria Rusticana
13 February 1971

Santuzza
Fiorenza Cossotto
Lola
Nedda Casei
Turiddu
Enrico Di Giuseppe
Alfio
Morley Meredith
Conductor
Fausto Cleva

been conducting the work since 1918, and was perfectly willing to say that Bernstein "cannot have been entirely wrong" for he was "trying to return to Mascagni's intentions."[9] And there we have a response to that unanswered question about tradition's clutter that I posed above. Cleva puts the blame for the accretion of wrong-headed tempos on Leopoldo Mugnone, the conductor of the world premiere. Our maestro admits he was "preoccupied with *Pagliacci*" in the previous season and had not heard Bernstein's *Cavalleria* (!). Thus Cleva emerges intentionally untainted, able to lay his benign, well-manicured hand on the score.

None of the principals has been heard in these roles on earlier broadcasts. Indeed, Jean Kraft is new to the company (debut as Flora in February 1970). She would become one of the Met's prime second-tier artists, fulfilling hundreds of appearances over the next decades. Her Mamma Lucia is securely voiced and theatrically potent. Casei's Lola is much as before, perhaps a shade less vocally assured, but withal effective. Canadian baritone Morley Meredith, an old Metropolitan hand, is not often heard on the broadcasts. His Alfio fits the mold of this afternoon's *Cavalleria*, for his reading is vocally solid (though the tone itself is of common stock—that is, it is reliable but not distinctive). By the time he confronts Turiddu, he has won us to his side. Sándor Kónya was scheduled to sing the tenor lead but indisposition forced him to cancel and Enrico Di Giuseppe stepped in "at the last moment," according to Cross—who seems, like Kónya, vocally out of sorts today. The American tenor (Philadelphia was home base) had been a member of the short-lived Metropolitan National Company during the mid-fifties and thereafter was well known to New Yorkers for appearances at the city's "other" house. There his debut as Michele in Menotti's *The Saint of Bleecker Street* had marked him as a singer to watch. He had already passed his thirty-eighth birthday at the time of his house debut (Pinkerton in the initial week of the labor-dispute season, the appearance preceded by an Alfredo in the 1970 parks concerts), so he was no young novice but rather an experienced professional. That impression is sustained by his broadcast Turiddu. Contrast his offstage serenade with Corelli's dashing, luxuriant, even flagrant effort and Di Giuseppe seems a boy come to do a man's job—an unfair comparison, to be sure. In that tribute to Lola his line is both lyrical and firm, the voice is true, and his success seems assured. By the end of the afternoon his equipment seems rather less impressive, for the tone, while holding an ever-welcome Italianate core, is narrow in circumference and, in the grander moments, a mite too open for comfort—our own on the present occasion and his for future vocal well-being. Cleva's orchestra now and then overwhelms him, though the tenor gamely puts every bit of his resources, abetted by a fine stylistic sense, into Turiddu's rejection of Santuzza. His Turiddu sings of wine with the untroubled exuberance of Sicilian youth—and highly effective it is. Under Cleva's concept, the toast is part of an annual village celebration where good feeling reigns. It makes a nice contrast with the ensuing melodrama. Inevitably, his farewell is small scale, but the feel of it is exactly right and he does offer a burst of tone at the climax. The audience rewards him with a comparable burst of applause and takes him to their hearts at the curtain calls. Cross tells us that Di Giuseppe was scheduled to make his broadcast debut the following week in *Il Barbiere di Siviglia* before being pressed into service today. Therein lies the tale: Almavivas do not necessarily a Turiddu make (at least not since the long-ago days of Fernando de Lucia). His Met repertory over the years will include Ferrando, Ottavio, Ernesto,

Fiorenza Cossotto as Santuzza, Jean Kraft as Mamma Lucia, and Nedda Casei as Lola in *Cavalleria Rusticana*. Photography by Louis Mélançon. Courtesy Metropolitan Opera Archives.

Nemorino, Tonio (*Fille*), Lindoro, Alfredo, and Fenton. Those were probably the roles for which nature intended him. Pinkerton and Rodolfo are his Puccini staples with Maurizio, Riccardo, the Duke, and an occasional Faust or Werther flavoring the mix. From that list one can see that he would become a much-prized house tenor.

It is Miss Cossotto who once again lends real distinction to the afternoon. She is clearly an artist of considerable moment. The portrayal is notable for its musicality and well-thought-out characterization. Her Santuzza may be the most sympathetic Sicilian peasant girl in broadcast history. She saves her hatred for Lola with only a melodramatic curse as Turiddu's punishment. Pathos, rather than vilification, is her gambit. Her phrasing is exemplary, with subito *pianos* and gentle curves where either music or text makes plausible an interpretive subtlety. Whenever opportunity arises, she pulls back to a lighter dynamic—thus her climaxes are doubly effective. She proves that a verismo heroine can make her mark without turning into a harridan or indulging in ill-mannered histrionics. One rightly may ask if subtlety is what we really crave from a Santuzza. Not always. But then, Cossotto has in reserve arresting *fortes* and resonant chest tones and, when needed, she trots them out without disturbing the overall design of her characterization or the equanimity of her vocalism. The voice is particularly lovely in the upper octave and today even the slightly grainy texture of the lower register is minimized. 'Voi lo sapete' is touching in its narrative truth with both the climax and close dramatically puissant; the former is commanding, while chest predominates in the latter (and she doesn't need the raised interval to secure the final 'piango'). In the Easter hymn, her 'O Signor's float innocently above the choral mass. With Di Giuseppe slight-voiced and Cossotto musically pliant in the duet, the heat quotient is not as high as that generated by more full-blooded combatants, but Mascagni's intent is well realized. The mezzo's confession to Alfio takes up the dramatic slack as she molds her phrases for maximum musical and theatrical effect. Cossotto's heroine is a more interesting creature than we have usually come upon in the Sicilian countryside. One hopes Mamma Lucia follows Turiddu's directive to shelter the girl. This Santuzza is worthy of a mother's care.

    Sustained by Cleva's supple *Cavalleria*, we can return to the 1970 broadcast with renewed interest in his *Pagliacci*. Of course, the maestro has this work well in hand as well, though the overall results are perhaps inevitably a letdown after the heightened bravura of Bernstein's curtain-raiser. Again, the choral work is merely passable; after two decades as chorus master, Kurt Adler is nearing the end of his tour of duty—and none too soon. The principals as well do not show at their best. As noted, Guarrera has been posted to Tonio rather than his originally scheduled Alfio. He was always more a Silvio than Tonio, the fact confirmed by his company tallies of thirty-eight Silvios and fourteen Tonios. After twenty-two consecutive seasons, the bloom is off the voice. He must gauge his diminishing resources carefully and does so in the prologue, resorting to a good deal of pallid, unsupported tone. But he rescues a desultory reading with a fine high A-flat at the close. Thereafter, theatrical effects are often substituted for vocal brawn, with here and there a surge of the remembered quality. He was ever a resourceful man of the theater and so he is today. Beppe, a cameo that is usually allotted to tenors of limited career potential but pleasing vocal material, is assigned this time to Andrea Velis, the Met's prime character tenor. Thus, the harlequin's appealing serenade does not give us the little vocal bon-bon that the play within a play needs. On the other hand, Dominic Cossa, a new colt in the Met's baritone stable, has the requisite goods for Silvio. His assured reading of the big duet provides some of the best singing of the afternoon. Like Di Giuseppe, he is a stalwart at the City Opera. Called to action in this troubled Met season, he had made his debut only a week before the broadcast. His voice is of attractive timbre, warm of color if not large bore in size, with enough baritonal thrust for an occasional Figaro or Germont, and perfect for the journeyman assignments (Marcello, Sharpless, Lescaut, Valentin) in which he would repeatedly give pleasure over the next several years. He and Stratas propel the drama into a more satisfying phase in their extended scene (even though the usual cut continues to be made in the duet).

    Stratas had to cancel her first two outings (including the premiere) in the new production and the broadcast does not find her at the top of her form, at least in the initial stages of the opera. Her Nedda is new to the airwaves, though she had first undertaken it at the Met as early as 1963. She would continue to favor it throughout her long career, though on the evidence of today it seems an unlikely candidate for prominence in her varied repertory. Perhaps it is a momentary weakened vocal estate that causes strain on a few top notes and lends an air of unease to the Ballatella. She knows how to hate, however, and gives Tonio a

Richard Tucker as Canio in *Pagliacci*. Photography by Louis Mélançon. Courtesy Metropolitan Opera Archives.

sound vocal thrashing whenever he crosses the line. More pleasing tone warms her rapt response to Silvio's ardent pleading (though she breaks each of the 'Tutto scordiam!' phrases with a breath and takes the top note gingerly). She is a lively Colombina and a fiery, tonally commanding confessor when Canio drives her to flaunt her forbidden love.

After long and persistent persuasion from Bing, Tucker had finally agreed to undertake Canio, a role he had previously forsworn as detrimental to his vocal health. The tenor was currently celebrating his twenty-fifth consecutive season with the company and the new production was intended as homage. A better vehicle might have been found, in my opinion. Yet it was a role and reading that brought him extravagant accolades from critics and colleagues (the latter including Horne and Pavarotti). As recounted in James A. Drake's biography of the singer, it was Zeffirelli who worked a "transformation" on the tenor's acting style by discovering in his "basic nature . . . a volatile energy that could be controlled only by a hard-learned self control."[10] When the man and the clown lost that control, the result was "cataclysmic." We have only the aural cataclysm for verification, but even there the description holds up.

For a tenor in his fifty-sixth year, Tucker is in remarkable vocal shape—the top voice, in particular, never fails him. Initially, age inhibits tonal vibrancy but soon a good deal of the remembered splendor returns. Still, Canio seems to call forth in greater abundance those stylistic disfigurements that blight the lyric splendor of his song. What a grab bag of accents and sputterings he sprays onto the suspicious husband's taunts! 'Vesti la giubba' is meat for his manner and the lachrymose is fully exploited in both the recitative and aria. It is a knockout performance showing the continued robustness of Tucker's instrument. To my mind, the interpretation ultimately diminishes Canio's torment. Other tenors have satisfied their public with a large-scale reading (and Tucker is rightly intent on that) but have managed, through manly conduction of line, to suggest a nobler heart. In a few moments of the second act, vocal resonance does damp down, but he summons outbursts of tone worthy of a much younger man when the grand episodes requiring thrust and abandon come along. Though wrongly a tenor's province, Tucker's screamed 'La commedia è finita!' is deservedly his on this celebratory occasion. Certainly, it is his prerogative at this point in his career to step up to this tenor challenge, to spend his capital (and many will applaud him for so doing), but why, I wonder, would he want to subject his lyric gifts to such rough usage? Perhaps it is the shadow of Caruso's primacy in the role that a tenor of Tucker's self-concept must, before career's end, challenge and, if possible, vanquish. But remember that aforementioned Bing persuasion. To Tucker's credit, he had held out for a dozen years, resisting the offer of a 1958 new production of the opera despite the manager's supplication. In a 1957 letter to the tenor, Bing had assured him that he, with Tucker's best interests in mind, had thought deeply about the matter and believed that it would be wrong for Tucker not to take up Canio now when he was in his vocal prime.[11] After that persuasive and flattering strong-arming, Tucker's refusal is an indication of his respect for his instrument. In any case, by 1970 he was willing to add his grandstand performance of Canio to the remarkable series of assignments he had undertaken during his quarter century at the Met. His repertory was wide (ranging from Ferrando to Calàf, Lionel to Lensky, Hoffmann to Samson, Alfredo to Don Carlo, Edgardo to Chénier, Rodolfo to

Dick Johnson), his commitment indefatigable, the heart unstinting, and the vocal quality invariably on the highest level.

    For those reasons alone, it will be worthwhile to look briefly at the 1971 *Pagliacci* where Cleva's prime colleagues (Tucker, Stratas, and Cossa) are buttressed by MacNeil as Tonio. Had one wished for a convincing "before and after" demonstration, one could find no better example than the 1970 and 1971 broadcasts of *Pagliacci*. The distressing aura of the 1970 *Pagliacci* is dissipated and in its place we hear a thrilling, yet discerningly adroit, performance. Yes, Robert Schmorr's harlequin song is no better than that of Velis, but he brings some nice comic touches to his scene with Colombina. And MacNeil is slow to corral his huge instrument to cultivated behavior; raw toned and with a truck-size beat on a few sustained notes in the opening measures, his Prologue gathers force as he relishes the grand line of its phrases and sets the audience aflame with an interpolated high A-flat. That slow warm-up has often been the norm with MacNeil—one can understand it when the role is long and arduous, but Tonio's main singing chore comes even before the curtain is up. In compensation, the baritone offers a full-scale portrait of the ruffian who loves. He manages to evoke some sympathy for Tonio as he confesses his infatuation to Nedda, and in response to her ridicule he hurls a magnificently malevolent curse upon her. Thereafter Leoncavallo gives him little opportunity to shine but the baritone makes something of his share of the play (including singing the bits of coloratura in full voice). Best of all is his subtle counseling of Canio at the end of the first act—the insinuation in his well-controlled mezza voce is worthy of Verdi's Iago. MacNeil's pneumatic voice is a wonder. With remarkable ease, he moves between dynamic extremes, inflating or deflating his tone to suit the musical and dramatic context.

    Cossa repeats his fine Silvio, even raising by a notch regard for the warmth and sturdiness of his instrument and the musicality of his phrasing. I had speculated that a continuing indisposition may have blighted Stratas' 1970 Nedda and, judging from her superb portrayal in 1971, that would appear to be true. On this afternoon she is in splendid vocal form, the top voice of alluring color, fluent and full, and hers to command. The freedom of her phrasing and some nuanced vocalism enhance the Ballatella, that oddly difficult entrance aria; unhappy with Cleva's tempo, she moves him along in stages. She still approaches the 'Tutto scordiam!' phrases with discretion (beginning them with tiny tone and breathing before 'scordiam,' but effecting a marvelous crescendo on the ultimate notes); the remainder of the duet profits from her sensitive molding of phrase and lustrous tone. The soprano matches MacNeil's vivid characterization in their several encounters, introducing variety of timbre to convey her scorn, and she has plenty of voice for Nedda's death-defying confrontation with her enraged husband.

    As noted above, Cleva's tempos here and there cause the singers to look to their own comfort, but beyond that, his conception and execution of the opera is scrupulous. The cantabile in the orchestral portions of the Prologue is lovingly shaped and the more dramatic elements of the score have the requisite voltage. In general, his reading is of a more lyrical cast than that of the previous broadcast. Whatever aesthetic virus affected Tucker in his initial series as Canio, it seems to have been cured. Perhaps it merely required a bit of compartmentalization—that is, making sure that the fervor of his Zeffirelli-inspired action did not soil his best musical instincts. The remedy involved cutting by half the interpretative gestures

Pagliacci
13 February 1971

Nedda
Teresa Stratas
Canio
Richard Tucker
Tonio
Cornell MacNeil
Silvio
Dominic Cossa
Conductor
Fausto Cleva

he laid on a part that even on paper can be (in the wrong throats) a blueprint for scene chewing of monstrous proportions. (Hollywood director Barry Levinson's passing remark that realism is "just another form of stylization" is a guidepost for playing in the verismo operas in our time.[12]) On this afternoon, the happy news is that Tucker gives a performance worthy not only of his reputation, but of himself. From the first, the annoying accents and splutters are, if not entirely banished, aptly applied. And his tone is firm and lustrous throughout its range—for the time being and miraculously, age seems to have been cheated of its inevitable victory. Perhaps he felt he didn't have to work so hard now that he had proved himself with what many considered a Caruso-status performance in the premiere season. Greater repose of line governs the lyrical portions ('Un tal gioco' and the noble 'Sperai, tanto il delirio accecato m'aveva'), but he never neglects to burnish a top note or two. He is rather less impressive in the low-lying first half of 'No! Pagliaccio non son,' but this time 'Vesti la giubba' is both thrilling *and* moving. After a more contained introductory recitative, he begins the aria lyrically so the buildup to the climaxes is musically satisfying rather than merely hysterically vivid. And the twin climaxes of the piece are magnificent in their breadth and tonal grandeur. After this performance, I find no need to resort to a litany of his extensive Met service to render him homage. His performance alone will suffice.

Rivalries between tenors are a prominent part of operatic lore. That between Tucker and Corelli, both contending for Bing's favor and the public's acclaim, was evidently substantial, at least on Tucker's part.[13] The Italian repertory was essentially home base for both, while their forays into the French repertory at the Metropolitan overlapped only with *Carmen*. But even there they only touched: Tucker sang sixty Josés, while Corelli was oddly content with two. Tucker undertook a few Fausts and was happier with Hoffmann (nineteen performances); four late-career Samsons would round out his Met French portrayals. Though he devoutly wished to add Éléazar (*La Juive*) to his company tally, that dream would be unrealized at the Met. (The opportunity did come, but too late, as we shall see.) None of these roles figured in Corelli's appearances with the company. But he played two heroes of romantic cast that he made peculiarly his own during the last half decade of his Met career: Werther and Roméo. When management presented a new production of Gounod's Shakespearean opus on the second night of the 1967–68 season, it was Corelli, rather than Gedda (the Met's prime exponent of French wares), who wooed the charming Juliette of Mirella Freni. However suspect their stylistic affinity for the French genre, the Italian pair were a surefire duo, guaranteed to fill the house for an opera that had been out of repertory for two full decades. Without doubt, the soprano's appealingly childlike visage and the divo's glamorous person assured a believable stage picture, a consideration not to be taken lightly with a romance so firmly fixed in public imagination. The radio audience would hear the romantic stars, but not together. On the broadcast of 13 April 1968, it is Gedda after all who addresses Freni's 'belle enfant.' And in 1970, Corelli will serenade a Juliette with a more developed sense of Gallic style than his delightful Italian companion possessed at this early stage of her career.

With Molinari-Pradelli at the helm, the performance proceeds smoothly and with surety, albeit somewhat languidly. The conductor indulges in some broad ritards where none are marked and, more important, he seldom supplies an underlying living pulse that would allow a set piece to flower, to move along with

Roméo et Juliette
13 April 1968

Juliette
Mirella Freni
Stéphano
Marcia Baldwin
Roméo
Nicolai Gedda
Mercutio
John Reardon
Friar Laurent
John Macurdy
Conductor
Francesco Molinari-
Pradelli

panache and thus animate the often static dramaturgy of this duet opera. He works the middle ground, abjuring the vibrant surge, denying us the éclat that is essential to the opera's endowment. Of his players, Shirley Love's velvety timbre makes nurse Gertrude a less formidable caretaker, while Marcia Baldwin shows off her more bravura mezzo in Stéphano's impertinent chanson. As her opponent, Alvary is his usual wily self—that is, an old pro. Charles Anthony's Tybalt is initially metallic-toned and effortful but turns appropriately emphatic in the confrontation with Mercutio. Reardon must contend early on with the fleet Mab ballad and sits too heavily on its gossamer phrases. On this afternoon, the baritone savors tone (and his is airily attractive) rather more than the word, even though the difficult aria is all point and diction rather than sonic grandeur. In fact, wit seems in short supply today. Even the reliable Michalski comes a cropper at the close of Capulet's invitation to the dance. He runs out of gas en route and muffs the cadential high note. Before that misadventure, and in later episodes with Juliette, he offers some of the more musical and tonally blandishing phrases of the afternoon. Norman Scott's vocally blunted chastisement of Roméo is merely serviceable, but Macurdy shows his artistic mettle as he attempts to convert himself into the score's prescribed *basse-chantante* for Frère Laurent's benign pronouncements. The assignment seems odd since his timbre is of rougher hue than that of his French brethren, and his musical instincts are more attuned to the Wagnerian melos than Gallic lyric subtleties. But he is an enterprising musician and brings off his task with honor, singing in a restrained facsimile of mezza voce. In fact, he may be *too* committed to the notated quiet dynamics—there are moments when he barely surmounts Molinari-Pradelli's orchestra. More pointed diction would have aided projection. Still, for a bass to resist unloading pontifical tone is a benison.

Juliettes have come in all sizes since the Met's early seasons. The aristocratic Emma Eames, the stately Melba, the elegant Bori, the virginal Sayão—each in her own way won the audience's approbation. In size, Miss Freni would be of the Sayão mold, petite and utterly charming to the eye, but her soprano is grander than her immediate broadcast predecessor. Where the Brazilian's value measured in silver, Freni's worth must be weighed in gold. Quite naturally, she is more Verona's child than Shakespeare's or Gounod's. Throughout the long afternoon, Freni pours out an unrestrained, fluent stream of the roundest, plumpest lyric tone that one could ever hope to hear. Her fioriture in the waltz song are assured and fluent (she takes the lower alternatives at Juliette's initial entrance and seemingly owns no trill), and the top tones are as full and secure as the remainder of the voice. She rarely modulates its basic fruity timbre nor does she employ a wide dynamic range in molding her phrases. But her tone and manner are replete with warmth and love, and that, after all, is the opera's essence. In the quiet peroration at the close of the bedchamber scene, she does show us what nuances she is capable of—the moment is delicious. Of course, Juliette's grand air upon hearing of the projected marriage to Paris is cut. How one would like to hear Freni tackle its marathon length and dramatic fervor—she surely would be equal to the task. The scenes at the ball, the balcony, in Frère Laurent's cell, the bedchamber, and the tomb all contain cuts of several pages of vocal score, some quite large.

At the Met (and elsewhere) these days one does not expect to hear idiomatic French diction (there are exceptions—Gedda falls into that blessed category). We have been forced to resign ourselves to counterfeit and "school" French, but we need not accept incorrect French. Reluctantly, one must remark on the inadequacy of Freni's command of the language. Of greatest moment, and for me it is a serious fault, is her inability to master the schwa vowel—she repeatedly employs a closed vowel where the neutral sound is required. The result is decidedly curious at times as when 'je' is pronounced 'jay,' which sounds like 'j'ai' and converts the singular pronoun 'I' into 'I have'—the error plays havoc with sense. 'Douce flamme' comes out 'doucay flammay' (there are many examples that could be cited) and the result is not only regrettable from the standpoint of diction but because it affects the musical content as well. The lightness of the schwa sound is replaced by the heavier 'ay,' which frequently overweights Gounod's pliant line. When compounded by her refulgent tone the result depresses the heroine's naiveté. But our soprano's vocal splendor and the knowledge of her comeliness provide so much pleasure that chastisement does seem churlish.

Gedda's diction is of a quality that the majority of his confreres cannot touch. His vocalism is equally impeccable in terms of surety of attack, brilliance of timbre, and fervid address. The lack of softer colors in the timbre (or at least his unwillingness to employ them until death is upon him at the tomb) becomes wearing as the opera proceeds; I imagine in the house that deficiency is less troubling—one can simply revel in the brilliant vocalism. And his rhythmic sense is so alert and his musical manner so energetic that he invariably supplies the charge that the conductor cannot. His recitatives pulsate with vitality. Like Freni, he concentrates on a limited dynamic range—a crisp *forte* is the norm. We know him to be a master of *voix mixte* but regrettably he refrains from employing it except at a few discreet moments. When Roméo first contemplates Juliette, for instance, Gedda might have favored us with a dulcet head tone on the high G of 'ai-je' over Gounod's *pianissimo* accompaniment; it would be doubly welcome as contrast to the *forte* of the previous phrase. He doesn't. He does, however, come through at the close of the first-act madrigal with Freni. Still, I regret the absence of demi-teintes in his reading—the voice owns but a single color. That color, however, is of blazing hue, brass of best quality, hammered to a bracing shine, a timbre to be doubly prized on this afternoon since it permeates the lowest tones as well as the highest notes of his voice. Few tenors could deliver the balcony aria with his accuracy, splendor, and, above all, assurance. Gedda's Roméo is a bold fellow, all bristling ardor. Though the role would appear to be a perfect fit, it was not a favorite of the tenor, who (according to *Opera News*) is "now a cheerful, cherubic forty-two."[14] He is not above emptying a bucket of tears onto the forceful lines of the concerted piece that closes Gounod's act three (act two at the Met, which compresses the composer's five acts into three), but his pinpoint attack on the high C needs no assistance. (Is he throwing a gauntlet to Corelli when he holds several high notes within phrases an inordinate amount of time? Gedda is usually more musically circumspect.) The three ascending phrases that try the staying power of many a tenor and soprano ('Sois béni') are triumphantly voiced by both lovers—the surety of their technique startles and should reassure doubters of this age's vocal wealth. No mystery or wonder invades his tone as he addresses Juliette's 'tombeau,' but his declamation is admirably fervent. And Freni, too, is vibrant and dramatically involved in the final moments of the opera. One final item must be noted. Both Freni and Gedda begin as they end, that is, with the voice fully warmed up and gloriously free. More singers on the Saturday afternoon broadcasts should follow their example.

The 18 April 1970 broadcast holds not only a new Roméo and Juliette, but also Díaz (Laurent), Harvuot (Capulet), Kraft (Gertrude), and Karlsrud (the Duke)—all first-time interpreters on the broadcasts. Doubly welcome is the presence of Alain Lombard on the podium. His nationality promises stylistic verity, though caution and probity dictate that one should not automatically assume that an Italian or a Frenchman will best serve the music of his native soil. But at least when birthright and homeland art conjoin, their union shifts the odds in our favor.

Indeed, under Lombard the opera's profile is more sharply defined, its features marked by some characteristic French traits: a supple, less languid melodic line, a vibrant rhythmic sense that reflects the virtues of the language itself, a preference for animation over sentimentality. The French conductor invariably feels the pulse of the music and never allows it to slacken; postludes (that to Juliette's waltz, for instance) are often propelled with delightful pluck; the dramatic climaxes are thrusting; singular stage actions find their complement in graphic orchestral gestures. Without these qualities Gounod's music can seem a sickly thing. At the time of this broadcast, the Paris-born conductor was only twenty-nine, yet his career had included three years as chief conductor at Lyons and apprenticeships with Karajan and, as one of three assistant conductors at the New York Philharmonic in 1966–67, Bernstein. He liked the American musical scene and since 1967 had been conductor of the Greater Miami Philharmonic. He came to the Met in 1965 to conduct a single performance of Ibert's *Concerning Oracles* on a ballet evening in the old house. At the new Met he spelled Georges Prêtre in *Faust*, Molinari-Pradelli in *Roméo*, Mehta in *Carmen*, and Bonynge in *Barbiere*. The premiere of the new production of *Werther* would be his own charge in 1970–71.

Of the artists who repeat their 1968 roles, Baldwin is less agreeable, Reardon more so. The mezzo's voice is afflicted with a rasp that nullifies the pert charm of Stéphano's air. The Mab ballad, however, profits from Lombard's fleet accompaniment and Reardon's willingness to forsake overblown tone in favor of pointed diction; this time, Mab, if not quite 'plus légère que le vent' (lighter than the wind) profits from the baritone's fastidious diet. Alvary's cameo remains a delight. Of the new crew, Kraft's nurse is more in the expected crow category; as singer, Karlsrud's Duke obtains no higher rank than Scott's feeble effort; unlike Macurdy, whose Laurent, taking his cue from Gounod, seemed to have migrated to the cloisters of northern France, Díaz's priest is more Fra than Frère. Undoubtedly, his parish lies in a more southern clime. Harvuot's task is eased by a large cut in the treacherous address at the ball and thereafter he contributes a stalwart portrayal of a loving, authoritative father.

With one critical exception, the execution from the stage under Lombard is only marginally more idiomatic than that heard under Molinari-Pradelli. Indeed, "one" remains the sum total of fully satisfactory portrayals. In that regard, we have merely exchanged a hero for a heroine. Jeannette Pilou may not have been to the manor born but one would never suspect it from hearing her Juliette. In fact, at the time of her Met debut in the role (1967, as alternate to Freni) the *Times* critic made sport of her casting, citing as evidence of the whimsical ways of the Met the importation for French opera of a woman who was born in Egypt of Greek parents and was currently living in Italy.[15] He was evidently unaware that Pilou was known for her affinity for and mastery of French style, a fact that should

Roméo et Juliette
18 April 1970

Juliette
Jeannette Pilou
Stéphano
Marcia Baldwin
Roméo
Franco Corelli
Mercutio
John Reardon
Friar Laurent
Justino Díaz
Conductor
Alain Lombard

Jeanette Pilou as Juliette and Franco Corelli as Roméo in *Roméo et Juliette*. Photography by Louis Mélançon. Courtesy Metropolitan Opera Archives.

have become immediately apparent from her performance. At thirty-two years of age, the soprano's experience was extensive and broad. Milan and Vienna were her permanent bases, but most of the Italian stages, Lisbon, Brussels, and Amsterdam knew her as well. Previous to her Juliette, she had been heard in a varied repertory at the Met: Nannetta, Susanna, Micaela, Marguerite, and Nedda; Butterfly, Mimì, and (as noted in an earlier chapter) Zerlina would be added in 1970–71. The radio audience had made her acquaintance a few weeks before her scheduled broadcast debut as Juliette when she replaced Caballé in *Traviata* (21 March 1970).

Pilou's instrument is a true lyric soprano, slender in circumference but capable of colors both dulcet and bracing, a voice seemingly made for the lyric heroines of nineteenth-century French opera. At its quietest, the voice is delectably limpid (once or twice Pons' delicate tone unexpectedly came to mind); at the full, which she employs sparingly, it is enhanced by an attractive metallic hue. On this afternoon, only the concluding high C of the waltz is touched by hardness. Her fioriture (absent the trill) are adequate to Gounod's demands in the waltz song, which she sings with delicacy, floating its rhythmic charm with ease, touching the line of the dreamy middle section with slender portamentos, everywhere sounding a young girl's delight in the ball. No wonder Cross tells us at the first-act curtain bow that Pilou "looks like a little girl," reminding us that Juliette is supposed to be "around fourteen" in Shakespeare's play. Throughout the afternoon, her diction is marvelously apt, deft, and clean; the musical notes take their life from its purity.

Musicality and characterization seem indivisible—among her favored expressive devices is the introduction of a *subito piano* to reveal inner emotion. The play of light and shade is often exquisite, the line so finely drawn that its pristineness rivals the miniscule stroke of a single-hair brush upon the receptive parchment of a Florentine book of hours. Occasionally, the requisite somber timbre eludes her (as Juliette muses on 'cet amour fatal,' for instance). But, for the most part, the lengthy duets (not as lengthy as Gounod wrote them, however) are full of illuminating musical and dramatic touches on her part. And she has the staying power for this demanding role, rising to the tomb scene's theatrics with conviction and reliable tone. She told an *Opera News* reporter that Manon ("maybe my best part")[16] was on her Met schedule for 1969–70. How I would like to have heard it, but that turned out to be the make-it-up-as-you-go season of the labor dispute.

At last we have the opportunity to hear Corelli's famous portrayal of Roméo. Of course, it would have been better for us and fairer to him if he were united with Freni so the stylistic manner would not clash so glaringly as it does on this afternoon when he is paired with an idiomatic Juliette. I recall listening to the broadcast in 1970 and feeling disappointed (even angry) at the casting of Corelli and his seemingly heavy-handed portrayal. Since those days, many of us, rather than fixing on his failings, have placed a greater value upon the tenor's unique assets, especially when deployed in a role where they are requisite. Thus, I approached the rehearing of this performance with particular interest—perhaps not quite with an open mind, but certainly a receptive one. There are feasts where expectations should be set aside in order to savor the sweets that are actually set before us. And, at times, the sheer beauty of the voice does quite overwhelm one. When coupled with ardor (as in moments of the bedchamber scene) or anguish (at the tomb) his voice is a powerful expressive tool that commands response. To receptive listeners, the timbre is as highly colored and sensuously suggestive as the exotic tails of the male peacock are to its mate and, like those strikingly beautiful appendages, it can be as potent an erotic agent. Beyond that powerful enticement, one is always touched by the evident sincerity of the tenor's desire to communicate.

Still, much of the music is misrepresented in Corelli's portrayal. His attack can be faulty and the portamentos overly grand. Dynamic shading is largely foresworn and the assault on the musical line is more than it can bear. Thus, Gounod's lyrical utterance is often badly bruised. There have been stout, even heroic, Roméos in the past; France has produced a good share of them: Albert Alvarez, Agustarello Affré (called "the French Tamagno"), and Fernand Ansseau, to stay in the A category. Even Jean de Reszke, by legend the greatest Roméo of them all, mutated into a Tristan and Siegfried. But they had command of language as an ally and vocal techniques that allowed for tonal modulation. Our tenor does lend tremendous energy (and a firm high C) to the performance and sometimes his recitatives are rhythmically alert. And he is responsive to the dreamy mood of Roméo's act-two peroration where the lover wafts a kiss to the sleeping Juliette—without doubt, the volume is turned too high, but the manner is affecting. He may not be in peak vocal form—one can almost hear his confidence depart as he moves to the close of the showpiece aria. There his technique fails him, for the final note turns flat as he tries for a diminuendo—the support evaporates, and he is forced to cut the note short. It is a distressing moment for him and his many admirers. Curiously, it was precisely this diminuendo that, in reviewing the 1967 premiere, Harold C. Schonberg cited as evidence of Corelli's good intentions and a forecast of significant improvement in his performances.[17] Even on this afternoon those admirers remain his strong and vocal adherents. The Met responded to public demand by presenting him thirty-seven times in the role. Perhaps his Werther, to be heard down the road in a year or two, will be a trimmer fit.

In its renewed attention to French opera, management could not be expected to ignore the genre's prime exhibit. *Carmen* had not been heard at the Met since 1961. (Two 1965 concert performances at Lewisohn Stadium and a huge run by the Met National Company do not alter the six-year house lacuna.) Bing had withdrawn the opera following the retirement of Risë Stevens. Regina Resnik recounted to me that the manager had told her he was "tired of *Carmen* and what he really wanted to do was break the pattern of only one person singing it. So he just took it out of the repertory."[18] A new production was introduced in December 1967. This time, absence did not increase fondness, at least for the mounting by Jacques Dupont and the stage direction of Jean-Louis Barrault. Far from a welcoming embrace, ridicule and outright rejection were their portion. Mr. Bing, though, remained loyal to the chosen ones. While professing that he was willing to admit his mistakes, he noted in his memoirs that he did not consider this production to belong in that category.[19] The French team had been responsible for the 1965 *Faust*, but this time most critics were merciless in their condemnation of Dupont's unit set (an open arena symbolic of the bull ring); they liked even less the overly busy direction of the distinguished French actor-producer. The introduction of nonessential and sometimes farcical distractions in the stage action was the principal complaint. *Opera News'* editor, Frank Merkling, defended Barrault's efforts as a legitimate approach that, rather than viewing the opera as a precursor of verismo, marketed it according to the largely defunct (in America) traditions of the opéra comique.[20] Whether any attempt was made to replicate those traditions in the musical rendering is uncertain, for we are given a mixed bag on the broadcast. Zubin Mehta conducted the premiere and most of the performances and was scheduled for the radio outing, but Lombard took over. The French conductor earlier had led a couple of isolated performances of the production, but whether we hear Mehta's imprint secondhand or Lombard's own way we cannot tell. I suspect it is a bit of both, with the latter predominant. If any opéra comique manners invade the afternoon's performance (Lombard would surely have known the style—in 1983 he would actually become the music director of the Paris Opéra-Comique), they probably reside in the remarkably brisk tempos that he adopts for the lively portions of the score and the sentimental caress he places on the more lyric moments. The two modes of expression are almost never intermixed, the rhythmic pulse relentlessly maintained in the faster episodes. One entirely too audible evidence of the stage direction that comes over the ether is the uncommon amount of stomping that accompanies many moments of this ever-bewitching score (Spanish dance relies on the ear as well as the eye for its effects). Lombard's hand seems far less assured with *Carmen* than was the case with *Roméo*. Quite a few ragged edges bedevil the performance. Indeed, an unsettled quality (more apparent with the orchestra and chorus than the soloists) permeates portions of the reading, the unease perhaps caused by the conductorial double image.

With one major exception, none of the soloists had been heard in these assignments by the radio audience. The opera holds no nondescript roles, for Bizet's acute dramatic sense and deft musical imagination touches even the slightest of

---

Carmen
20 April 1968

Carmen
Grace Bumbry
Micaela
Mirella Freni
Don José
Richard Tucker
Escamillo
Justino Díaz
Conductor
Alain Lombard

the stage personages. In a satisfactory performance, each singer must possess the professional aplomb, the stylistic sensitivity, and (particularly important for the lesser players) the ability to complete the composer's colorful musico-dramatic tapestry with an assured vignette. The latter often can be achieved by projecting a critical phrase or even a single note. The new crop seems not to meet these demands as well as that remarkable crew of second-tier artists that so often peopled the smuggler's camp in the broadcasts of the fifties (Amara—in her pre-principal days—or Krall, Roggero, De Paolis or Franke, Cehanovsky). The current players (Lilian Sukis as Frasquita, Baldwin as Mercedes, Anthony as Remendado, Gene Boucher as Dancairo), capable performers all, sometimes hit their mark and at other moments do not. Of the relative newcomers, Boucher is stylistically apt, Sukis sweet-toned (but her voice seems too small scale for Frasquita's frontline position atop the ensembles, solo or choral). Of course, at Lombard's hectic pace in the quintet (and elsewhere), merely keeping up is an accomplishment in itself. On the other hand, Morley Meredith's Zuniga would stand up well in any company—he is an authoritative captain of dragoons. Ron Bottcher's Morales has promise. The voice is a good one, if not yet completely finished, and time will probably take care of a slight gaucherie in the musical manner (the colloquy with Micaela requires uncommon sophistication).

Escamillo is a role that has been passed around among voice types—its peculiar tessitura, or at least, unusual range, is the evident cause. The toreador sometimes has been sung by bass-baritones (George London and José van Dam are notable exponents), and basses (Pinza), but baritones have most frequently assumed the unwelcome chore. In recent times, Warren and Merrill have managed it more than well. The impresario's task is complicated by yet another desideratum. If a singer is to fulfill the dramatic function of the role, he must radiate stage allure. Toreadors are, or ought to be, charismatic. London and Pinza could discharge both the musical and charismatic chores. Díaz, with his dashing looks and fine bass, might be expected to be in their line, though he does not in fact attain their rank. The voice remains attractive, but on this afternoon it lacks its full complement of resonant tone or sheen. His tones sometimes are effortful, especially at full voice in the upper range (they disappear in the low reaches of the aria, but that is a common failing with most impersonators). Vocal charisma also is essential; that elusive quality may best be obtained with a liquid legato and elegant diction. Díaz does well enough by the latter but his line sounds rather too lumpy. His work in the final acts is effective and, since Lombard allows him time to make something of his portion of the final duet with Carmen, he takes advantage of the opportunity. Still, even there a liquid legato would best serve Bizet's little melodic jewel. But add to the equation Díaz's *physique du rôle* and his toreador is a worthy contender for Carmen's attention.

To hear an artist of stellar rank in a role that management, without disparagement, normally casts from its house soprano ranks is always cause for rejoicing. Micaela has claimed the attention of many such prime artists at the Met, ranging from Emma Eames and Geraldine Farrar, even Melba, on to broadcast heroines Albanese and De los Angeles. At mid-century and in the decades that followed, Miss Amara's responsive throat had a hold on the role. Freni certainly warrants inclusion in the stellar category and, as expected, her luscious soprano meets all the vocal requirements of the role. Her phrasing is not particularly distinctive

Grace Bumbry as Carmen. Photography by Louis Mélançon. Courtesy Metropolitan Opera Archives.

in the duet but her tonal loveliness dispels doubts. The aria (a bit disjunct in overall concept—Lombard's languid pace is no assist) is delivered with remarkable tonal amplitude, the voice absolutely secure throughout the entire range. The high B-flat (a bit of self-indulgence in its length) is so resplendent that one wishes contemporary custom permitted the interpolation of another at the aria's close—such grand singing really seems to demand an exuberant send-off. Even without it, the ovation is long and loud. She expertly conveys the pathos of Micaela's pleas to José in the mountain retreat—his return to his dying mother seems assured. Unfortunately, her French is again execrable. To hear an important word like 'mère' repeatedly pronounced 'meray' makes one heretically consider that the old-fashioned acceptance of occasional multilanguage performance just might be the better solution—one would not want to do without Freni's gorgeous sound in the role. Better yet would be a productive immersion in the language on the singer's part.

In a role in which many a soprano or mezzo has courted disaster and barely survived, Bumbry not only survives, but thrives. Her Carmen is uncommonly fine. She has all the assets for the role and negotiates its vocal and interpretative traps with singular aplomb; beyond that, the singer earns our gratitude for her dramatic restraint and musical integrity. She neither overplays nor burdens the music and the character with expressive tricks. No sultry slurring of line, no hip-swinging phraseology sullies her quite straightforward reading of the music. Not only is the result refreshing to the ear, but ultimately Carmen's stature is elevated in the process. In 1880, Tchaikovsky, who deemed the opera "full of sincere feeling and inspiration," wrote his loving confidante Nadezhda von Meck that he particularly appreciated what he called "le joli" in its makeup, the "piquancy and spiciness" that "flow in an unhindered stream to flatter your hearing, to excite, and to touch you at the same time."[21] Bumbry's playing seems in tune with that view of the opera. The voice is in prime condition (her vocal cords are among the most resilient and true of contemporary singers) and retains a uniformity of timbre throughout its compass. Timbral uniformity, of course, can be a liability as well as a virtue—her instrument does not command many colors or allow subtle variations of dynamics. That said, its security is ever reassuring, even in the problematic delicately poised arias of the first act. For one thing, she negotiates the break with ease—that alone is cause for rejoicing. Probably her Habanera lacks sufficient playfulness (it acquires some in the second verse) and a bit of suspect pitch invades the final moments of the Seguidilla. Her way with the overly familiar arias is not very individual, except in its well-mannered musicality. I do like her nonchalant recall of the Habanera before she escapes. She deftly negotiates the frenzied phrases of the Gypsy Song (her companions are less successful) and her quiet in the face of José's proposed departure is mesmerizing. (The only vulgarity I would charge against her portrayal is her gross voicing of the final 'L'amour' at the close of the Toreador Song.) Into the pedestrian reading of the cards by Sukis and Baldwin, Bumbry injects a grandly phrased fatality. Lombard has increased the burden of it relentless ascents by an almost ungainly slow tempo and he adheres to it without any accommodation to the singer. Over the spare orchestral chords Bumbry mounts repeatedly with firm tonal control and seriousness of purpose—a splendid achievement. Some will wish for more dramatic effects (her 'La mort's are never brutally set forth), but Carmen's integrity is well defined in this reading.

The same holds true for the mezzo's encounter with the enraged José—her manner and vocalism tell us that the despairing lover no longer figures in her scheme of life. With brilliant tone she proclaims her love for Escamillo and claims her death.

Among all these newcomers Tucker once again plays the dragoon turned smuggler and murderer. He first assumed the role at the premiere of the 1952 Guthrie/Gérard production and repeatedly had appeared in the work over the ensuing seasons, including four broadcast outings and one closed-circuit television relay. The 1967 premiere, however, had been assigned to Gedda; Pilou, rather than Freni, was the Micaela. Both Gedda and Pilou would have conformed more to Barrault's intent than Tucker and Freni. Indeed, one wonders how (and if) Tucker accommodated his virtuoso portrayal to the French director's aberrant conception—the ways of opéra comique were not his ways. But then, on this afternoon Tucker's familiar way with the role is in large part foresworn. Of his portrayal in 1960 (the last time *Carmen* had been broadcast), I wrote that his Flower Song was disfigured by "the tonal blasts and emotional crudities which are increasingly part of his style." I acknowledged his firm vocalism and sure technique in the final acts but decried his "interpretive banalities."[22] On this afternoon the firm vocalism and sure technique are remarkably intact. From the first, the voice is well oiled and obedient and remains so on through José's impassioned lament at the final curtain. What is novel for Tucker is the emotional restraint of his portrayal of the dragoon throughout the afternoon; particularly notable is the absence of those stylistic crudities that have made him an easy target over the years. They are virtually nonexistent, materializing only in quite limited amount where emotional distortion is justified. What a fine line he spins in the first-act encounter with Micaela, the tone perfectly channeled, his legato dexterously employed, and the mix of head tone lending greater charm to the timbre than usual. New interpretive touches inflect the Flower Song. An intimate phrase here and there reveals the inner heart of the man who loves, while the few sobs as he moves toward the climax occur within an appropriate framework (of course, the top note is, of necessity, *forte*). And, wonder of wonders, the final 'Je t'aime' is quietly voiced, perhaps depriving him of the ovation he richly deserves. The strenuous encounters of the smuggler's retreat are forthrightly handled with strong tone and broadly stretched phrasing—the emotional temperature burns quite hotly here, as it must, but, comparatively speaking, the bluster is not excessive. In the final confrontation with Carmen, Tucker's José regains some of his lost dignity—one hears it in the tenor's firm treatment of line and focused tone. For the bulk of the scene, self-indulgence and the expected explosiveness are held in reserve. At the end of his commanding, artistic portrayal, Tucker deserves to spend tone and heart as José grandly, sobbingly bewails his 'Carmen adorée.' Bizet scholar Winton Dean maintains that the soldier lover is the "central figure" of the opera, for it is "his fate rather than Carmen's" that is most involving for us.[23] Without implying any disparagement of Bumbry's gypsy, on this afternoon, Tucker's conception of the antihero bears Dean out.

The American tenor anchors the broadcast of the next season (15 March 1969) as well. Resnik, whose portrayal had been famous in Europe for a decade, is the new heroine and this time Mehta makes it to the podium. Raskin as Micaela is another first on the broadcasts, with Judith De Paul (Frasquita), Judith Forst (Mercedes), and Schmorr (Remendado) additions to the gypsy troupe. Boucher

Carmen
15 March 1969

Carmen
Regina Resnik
Micaela
Judith Raskin
Don José
Richard Tucker
Escamillo
Justino Díaz
Conductor
Zubin Mehta

and Meredith, both excellent in voice and character portrayal, repeat as Dancairo and Zuniga. Robert Goodloe starts the show off with a capital Morales, his diction as elegant as his very attractive baritone. Merrill was scheduled for the toreador, a role he first sang with the company in 1946, but Díaz replaces him.

Mehta's leadership stabilizes the performance. His tempos are more considerate than those of Lombard and thus the somewhat hectored atmosphere that pervaded the 1968 broadcast is avoided. The more disciplined stewardship is welcome, but the elegance and suavity that Bizet's magical score warrants are seldom evident. Once again, the choral work (especially by the men) is discouragingly mediocre. The changes in the smuggler personnel improve things in that area and Mehta's *juste* tempo allows the quintet to work its wonders. The conductor has a disconcerting habit of promoting discreet accelerandos within a well-judged tempo (evidently to prevent stasis) but the procedure is unnecessary and, moreover, inappropriate in this genre. Pragmatically, it causes momentary near-disconnects with his stage partners (near the end of the quintet and elsewhere). De Paul, new to the company in 1967, has a bright soprano with sufficient heft for the ensembles, though quick passages (as in the card scene) are marred by tonal scratches. Forst came on the Met scene a year later and, though both she and De Paul will have limited Met sojourns, she deservedly will have an extensive career with other companies in larger roles than the Met offered her.

This time Díaz' Escamillo is a superior effort. He is in remarkably fine vocal form, the tone easily produced and manly in quality. The entrance song has the appropriate panache and in the encounter with José his controlled but authoritative singing is both commanding and an appropriate foil for Tucker's excited taunts. I count his portrayal this afternoon one of the better broadcast toreadors. Raskin did not often sing Micaela (a total of seven at the Met) and, in truth, the role does not allow her the best platform for her delightful gifts—Mozart and Strauss are her comfortable habitats. She is intelligent (girls who go to Smith just are) and seeks to temper Micaela's neutral sweetness and augment her fearful courage with actorly touches. The music really doesn't need it; Bizet's melodic contours and theatrical punch are enough in themselves. That said, her timbre is inviting, her vocal skill sure, her attention to the words marked (perhaps too much for this music), so both the duet and aria flourish under her care. She turns her part of the duet into a charming narrative in which her childlike interest in relaying the mother's message is touchingly apparent. The aria, too, becomes a dramatic vignette with a strong, emotional climax (and an unattractive chest tone on the lower 'Seigneur's') and she rounds off her characterization with a fervent plea to her childhood friend.

Miss Resnik is in her twenty-fifth season with the company and enjoying the fruits of international fame as a mezzo of distinctive quality. She had thrown down the gauntlet when Bing failed to assign her the new production, but the manager acceded to her desires and she sang Carmen in the year of the premiere and gained this season's broadcast. I can well understand that she would not wish to forgo this opportunity to present her famous creation to the American public but, except for its abundant musical and dramatic authority, the portrayal is probably not a representative specimen of her acclaimed Carmen. As though at the mercy of a yo-yo's string play, one vacillates between admiration and consternation at what she offers on this afternoon. She is in poor voice. The highest reaches at the *forte* dynamic are effortful and unattractive on sustained tones, the timbre there sometimes grainy in texture, and the management of register changes, despite her obvious care, is often troublesome. In the Habanera she sounds a very mature Carmen and the contrast between overly assertive chest tones and the as yet unsettled upper voice startles—still, her imagination is ever in play and her innovative touches delight. She shows her mettle in the Seguidilla, where some lovely soft singing and elegantly molded phrasing affirm her as the artist we know her to be. She is adept at textual pointing, always divining interesting ways to convey meaning. As she dances for José at the tavern she deftly strews 'lala's and builds her response to her lover's proposed departure with a sure dramatic sense. For a good deal of the afternoon the story is the same: a flavorful and varied conception of the character (a curiously satisfying mix of hard-grained earthiness and eloquence) allied with gestures either subtle or majestic—when they come off. Sometimes an attractive top tone may be compromised by a delayed attack that refuses to sound with precision. Her finest moment is her reading of the cards. There she has the voice under sufficient control to mold melodically well-knit, expressive phrases that rise to an effective climax before gusty chest tones repeatedly mark her for death. With her large voice and even larger personality one knows the confrontation with José will be commanding and thrilling and for the most part it is. By now the voice has become somewhat more pliant and she manages some grand vocal moments (not always, as one final top note confirms). To hear an artist one admires when she is not in best form is always distressing and especially so when the opportunity to hear a famous interpretation at its peak is denied. Best to concentrate on the perceptive interpretive insights that, even under these conditions, shine through.

Tucker seems indestructible. Once again, he is in magnificent vocal shape—when was he not? His technique never fails him and his artistic aims on this afternoon remain as high and largely unpolluted as in the previous season's broadcast. The musical and vocal virtues of that performance, described in detail above, are replicated on this afternoon. There we have the essence of Tucker's career, namely, that his vocalism was consistently of prime quality.

A sure thing is no negligible factor when one considers the price of opera tickets. Tucker always gave full value. Others of the tenor breed during these decades did as well. And yet we are told that "The Era of the Tenors" is about to begin.

Plácido Domingo as Riccardo in *Un Ballo in Maschera*. Photography by Louis Mélançon. Courtesy Metropolitan Opera Archives.

CHAPTER SIX

Verdi, the Provider

Not only Mozart flourished on the Met stage in the decades of the Bing regime. There were Verdi singers as well in those days. Mr. Bing loved the Verdi canon and fortunately he had the artists to realize his desires. Having launched or reintroduced to the Met public *Nabucco, Ernani, Macbeth, Simon Boccanegra*, and *Don Carlo*, and repeatedly refurbished the more well-known operas, in 1967–68 the manager added a final tribute to the Busseto master. *Luisa Miller*, the penultimate work before the consecrated trio (*Rigoletto, Il Trovatore,* and *Traviata*), was not quite an unknown quantity to Met audiences, at least those with long memories. Its history was brief: four performances in 1929–30 and one the following season. Gatti-Casazza, too, had his Verdi singers and the wonder is that a cast of Ponselle, Telva, Lauri-Volpi, De Luca, Pasero, and Ludikar proved insufficient to win the work favor, even with that paragon of Italian maestros, Serafin, to shepherd them. But then, early Verdi was not in fashion at the time, even as it proved to be an acquired taste in later decades.

As Gatti's all-star lineup indicates, the opera requires six artists of superior quality. For the broadcast of 17 February 1968 Bing serves up five—Louise Pearl is barely adequate as Federica, the promised, but rejected, bride of Rodolfo, the lover of Luisa. In Thomas Schippers, however, the manager has a sure guide, a conductor not born to the tradition as Serafin was, but one whose experience now matches the talent revealed in his early exposure on the Met stage a dozen seasons before the new production's 8 February premiere. (In an effort to add novelty to the new mounting, designer Attilio Colonnello framed his massive nineteenth-century-style sets with tiers of boxes on the proscenium sides that were inhabited by costumed operagoers who responded to the stage action. The conceit merely proved distracting to the house audience.) The overture, well known in the concert hall, is skillfully sculpted by Schippers, the composer's unity of design matched by the conductor's singularity of purpose. The taut and brisk manner, apropos as prelude, prudently is moderated when the curtain rises. Indeed, in a performance notably fleet, Schippers manages to allow his stage colleagues a modest freedom of expression. Of particular note is the fluidity of the repeated accompaniment patterns that, if rendered without sufficient buoyancy, can turn the trivial into the tedious. Verdi has granted the conductor some grand *concertato*s and Schippers does not neglect to give them the requisite theatrical thrust. Still, the opera, for all

Luisa Miller
17 February 1968

Luisa
Montserrat Caballé
Federica
Louise Pearl
Rodolfo
Richard Tucker
Miller
Sherrill Milnes
Walter
Giorgio Tozzi
Wurm
Ezio Flagello
Conductor
Thomas Schippers

117

its melodic bloom—especially in the masterly third act—betrays its transitional status in a number of set pieces; there the *convenzione* of the time (formal traditions that often enough served Verdi well) have somewhat curtailed invention. All the more reason for that all-star cast.

Opera connoisseurs who decry the current state of Verdi singing will note with surprise Conrad L. Osborne's 1968 review comment that the *Luisa Miller* premiere (and radio) cast was "not of all-time dream-cast variety."[1] That very astute vocal critic cushioned his opinion by noting it was "as strong as one could reasonably expect." From today's vantage point, expectations of Caballé, Tucker, Milnes, Tozzi, and Flagello are, if not beyond reason, certainly whetted beyond the norm. They do not disappoint. Tozzi evidently had trouble with Count Walter's act-one aria at the premiere, but by the time of the broadcast (the third performance of the little-known work) he has both voice and music well in hand. Flagello, caught in a rather unrewarding assignment that is more difficult to bring off than it sounds, manages to convert his mellifluous voice into a sufficiently villainous barb for Wurm's evil intentions. What a rich, vibrant instrument he owns and how consistently he places its rotundity in the service of the music and action. Verdi's fascinating venture in the dialogue-like duet for the two basses is one of the more interesting episodes of this fine afternoon. Yet another is the relative success of our principals in the normally uneasy precincts of the unaccompanied quartet at the end of the second-act palace scene.

The lower-voiced singers present an interesting contrast of timbres. Tozzi, whose Schiller count is even more despicable than his retainer, Wurm, has long been cited in these pages for warmth of timbre and geniality of manner. Thus, the gap between man and character is large. The above-mentioned aria ('Il mio sangue, la vita darei'), however, is a private moment, combining pathos and fervor; there he laments his son's indifference to his wishes and the mood is quite in Tozzi's line. Luisa's father is a retired soldier and in the first act Milnes' forceful baritone and emphatic style aptly replicate Miller's fury at the supposed perfidy of Rodolfo. The young singer, in only his third Met season, is intent on staking his claim to the Verdi baritone crown, and the powerhouse manner, which will increasingly dominate his portrayals, is very much in evidence as he almost brazenly executes a full-throated ascent to a high A-flat. (The note, approached from an equally puissant leading tone, is initially a shade flat but is soon rounded to the pitch.) Throughout the opera, his tone is ever refulgent, a touch open, but growing increasingly lubricious as the afternoon lengthens. When, however, in the third act, Miller must sound a father's concern and comfort his despairing daughter, the Milnes mode cannot quite earn the sympathetic response that Verdi knew so well how to cultivate in father-and-daughter moments. The touching 'Andrem raminghi e poveri,' in which Miller forecasts their destitute and wandering future, requires a more intimate framework and demands a suave mezza voce, which the American has yet to master. (Now and then he successfully cultivates a *piano* dynamic, but a few other attempts are ineffectual.) Has he won the crown? His assets are indeed numerous. In addition to vocal riches, they include rigorous musicianship and assured dramatic projection, bounty of the kind that audiences adore. For the time being, let us salute him as heir apparent in the Verdi line.

With absolute certitude, Verdi scholar Budden claims (as did Winton Dean with *Carmen*) that the opera belongs not to the title character, but to the tenor.[2]

Montserrat Caballé as Luisa Miller. Photography by Louis Mélançon. Courtesy Metropolitan Opera Archives.

On this afternoon, Tucker (as he did with Don José) all but makes us believe he is right. Once again in marvelous vocal form, the tenor gives of voice and heart with astounding plenitude. One must note the familiar demerits: the stentorian thrust startles at his entrance; his puffy staccatos, however diligent, are oddly risible; in the musically elegant duet with Federica, the rapid cascades of notes sound almost like hiccups. And, even when he is at his best, as he is throughout most of the opera, the aggressive tenorial posture can prove wearing. That said, his self-confident vocalism is a marvel. He pours out a wealth of tone, fearlessly captures top tones, and time after time catches the heart with the sincerity of his phrasing. He delivers the lengthy and vivid dramatic recitative to 'Quando le sere al placido' as though his life depends on it. Beginning the aria with quiet resignation, Tucker lovingly nurses its melancholy phrases along but does not neglect to provide a crowd-pleasing finish. His musical manner in the ensuing cabaletta is a bit overemphatic but, not being a *tenore robusto*, he relies on those excessively clipped rhythms to make up for lack of steel in the timbre. The truth is that the tenor has the unwelcome ability to pull us in two directions at once. Crudities of style may momentarily blemish his art (excessive sobs in the aria, his habit of relying only on the consonant rather than including the vowel on short notes— 'd-sso' for 'desso,' for example). But these lapses are counterbalanced by phrases of profound nobility (as when Rodolfo swears to her father that he will marry Luisa or when he somberly gives the poisoned drink to his beloved). All in all, the debit side is far outweighed by the brilliance of his vocalism. In Verdi's Rodolfo, Tucker, at age fifty-eight, has found yet another role in which he can claim center stage, either to preen or, more often, to shine.

Poor Luisa! Must we bewail her purportedly diminished stature? Not when an artist of Miss Caballé's ability is the protagonist. With artists of longevity (and at this writing the soprano is still occasionally before the public) there is always in the ear the current sound, too often but the remains of a once beloved voice, remnants that in her case include strident *forte*s, disengaged chest and head registers, the glottal curse, the abuse of her famous *pianissimo*. One is therefore the more astonished when returning to the initial flowering of her artistry where, as on this afternoon, her vocal witchery is at its peak. Were it not that we know that such a goal is unachievable, I would venture that on this broadcast her vocalism is perfection. (Well, nigh perfection—the trill is not in her arsenal.) The faults cited above are nonexistent. Most unexpected is the unforced beauty of her high notes at the *forte* dynamic; moreover, they issue from her throat perfectly bound into the line and graded into the volume progression. Her coloratura is playful and easy—in the first act, she delightfully captures the innocence and carefree happiness of the ingénue heroine. Throughout the afternoon, the musical line flows rapturously on in the most fluid stream of tone and dynamics. She saves that ravishing *pianissimo* for poignant musical and dramatic moments and the effect is often heart-stopping. Her art is refreshingly unselfconscious at this stage of her career. When, with superb control, she suspends Luisa's quiet melody over the first-act *concertato* finale she practices ethereal magic. I recall once reading in the *Times'* science pages that a spider's filament (called a spinneret) has been proven to be stronger than steel. I am inclined to believe it upon hearing Caballé draw her slender thread of silvery tone, a splinter of shining steel in its tensility. In the second act Luisa requires a grander style and, though undoubtedly unable to command the grandeur of a

Ponselle, Caballé's 'Tu punisci' is interpretively telling; she expertly encompasses the exalted curves of its phrases. For a moment, she almost makes one believe that she is that prized rarity, a Verdi soprano. The brave, *forte* high B that ends the introductory recitative is testimony to her qualifications. In the last-act father-and-daughter scene, her delicacy subtly dilutes the triviality of the 'La tomba' melody. That perceptive musicality is again apparent when she imbues a brief moment before 'Andrem raminghi' with pregnant meaning. Both tenor and soprano offer ecstatic lyricism in the final duet (and Tucker thrusts forth 'Maledetto, maledetto il dì che nacqui' with wonderful abandon). Caballé's control over the elegiac phrases of the concluding trio is (I find I must name it, after all) perfect.

Luisa Miller was well launched in its second coming to the Metropolitan. This time, its continuance in the repertory, while still problematic, seemed at least plausible. No longer need she be regarded as merely a poor sister of the anointed three middle-period operas. In future broadcasts, Adriana Maliponte, Renata Scotto, and Katia Ricciarelli, along with Domingo and Pavarotti, would see to that. Oddly, though Moffo had recorded the opera in her prime, she was never a Met Luisa. Her voice in the house would have been slight for the role—indeed, reservations were voiced even about Caballé in that regard. We come upon the American soprano again in her signature role of Violetta in the *Traviata* broadcast of 30 December 1967. With Alexander and Sereni as her colleagues, no all-star claims will be asserted today. Chorus and orchestra under Cleva's baton have been over this ground so often that frequently they appear to be merely going through their paces. At the curtain's rise, hope for rejuvenation arises in the conductor's lively banda music but soon routine becomes oppressive. He does pump up the grand *concertato*, dragging it relentlessly along, but the crisp gambling motives are allowed to noodle desultorily and thus the scene is bereft of its dramatic spine.

Once again the Met roster includes an admirable complement of supporting artists: Nancy Williams (Flora), Di Franco (Annina), Goodloe (Douphol), Boucher (D'Obigny), and Anthony (Gastone) would be welcome at any party, whether hosted by Violetta or Flora. For a newcomer on the demimondaine scene, John Alexander's Alfredo is unexpectedly combative. His vocal and musical manners are so assertive that Violetta's hesitation about love's 'croce e delizia' would appear to be, quite apart from financial or ethical considerations, merely good common sense on her part. His instrument, firm and stout, its timbre colored by a quick vibrato and affected by a sometimes annoying nasality, is ever ready in all ranges. His musicianship is equally reliable. One misses the elegance that many tenors have found in Alfredo's music, for the vocal caress is not in this singer's makeup. Suavity may not be his forte, but novel phrasing (individual units are frequently subdivided) and varied nuances lend interest to his conception. The decorum of a southern gentleman (the fellow is Mississippi-born) does not prevent a violent denunciation of his supposedly faithless lover. Happily, a well-bred musicality prevents him from overdoing his shame in those phrases ('Ah, sì! . . . che feci!') from which tenors are prone to wring the last kernel of remorse.

Sereni is untroubled by any concern about musical subtleties. His timbre is his fortune and he dispenses its burnished burr with prodigality and unvaried brilliance throughout the afternoon. He is a stern parent, seemingly devoid of feeling for his son's distress; 'Di provenza il mar' is nuance-free and rigorously sped along. He marks its lockstep rhythms with the tenacity of a robin tugging at a ground-

La Traviata
30 December 1967

Violetta
Anna Moffo
Alfredo
John Alexander
Germont
Mario Sereni
Conductor
Fausto Cleva

Anna Moffo as Violetta in *La Traviata*.

bound worm. 'Pura siccome un angelo' is neatly laid out (he runs Cleva a tempo race and wins) and firmly voiced (no pitch problems today, though a few wayward phrases infect the third-act *concertato*), but his daughter's purity must be taken on faith—tone and manner do not reveal it. Authority he has, and shows it when he delivers his rebuke to Alfredo at Flora's party. He makes a splendid noise, manly and vibrant throughout the entire range, a voice to be enjoyed merely for itself.

If we are to find distinction in the performance, we must look to Miss Moffo. All Violettas carry the burden of the opera but its weight seems unduly heavy on this afternoon. We know her portrayal to be a memorable one but, unlike this audience, we are gifted with an unfair historical clairvoyance (the regrettable Lucia just thirteen months down the road) that precipitates concern. (Allow me this time-machine legerdemain.) A wobble does cloud a few initial phrases and a few very top tones in act one hold a touch of the scream—but then, they often did, even in her early years, as I recall from that 1960 *Lucia* which I heard in San Francisco. Occasionally, she utilizes an open, harsher tone that dilutes the remembered limpid timbral warmth. But the happy news is that as of December 1967 Moffo's instrument was still healthy, beautiful, and communicative. She plays with considerable abandon throughout the performance, indeed, occasionally deploying a wealth of sound in the middle and lower voice (including some pungent chest tones) that causes one to wonder if a portion of her future troubles might be rooted in overweighting there. But rather than dwelling on ungrateful conjecture, we might better revel in the vocal largesse that she dispenses in this broadcast.

In comparison with her 1963 broadcast portrayal, Moffo has enlarged her conception of the role: the polar extremes of happiness and despair are both more vividly explored. Having performed it so often, she has the role patently ingrained in her consciousness and set in her voice so that phrases issue from her throat with uncommon naturalness. Indeed, one might regret that a certain musical casualness blights the integrity of her portrayal—that is the price paid for the abandon, even occasional recklessness, of her performance. (Artists of the keenest perception are able to bring the opposing factors of artistic conscience and performance spontaneity into a more perfect balance.) She strews laughs, sobs, and coughs wherever plausible, even with considerable profligacy. Coupled with a bit of prima donna self-indulgence here and there, the realistic manner is thrilling and vivid, but it may impinge on the classical purity of Verdi's musical concept. (One remembers that Adelina Patti was Verdi's ideal in this role.) For a true lyric soprano she manages to bring welcome fullness to several critical peaks of the score. Her lead-in to the love theme of 'Ah fors'è lui' is remarkably grand—the entire aria benefits from her fluid phrasing and attractive tone (though the totality is diminished by an ungainly cadenza). 'Sempre libera' is fluent enough in coloratura, the string of high Cs agreeable, with the entire *scena* capped by a squeezed high E-flat. She pours out streams of warm, liquid tone in the second-act duet, her passions undimmed by Sereni's indifferent manner. A curiously woofy tone (on 'Ah') introduces 'Dite alla giovine,' but the solo phrases of farewell are well executed. 'Amami Alfredo' is vocally extended and dramatically vivid, while her light, silvery tones and affecting delivery make 'Alfredo, di questo core' the high point of the gambling scene. In her excellent last act, equilibrium between dramatic verisimilitude and musical rectitude better obtains. Her delivery of the letter is light and intimate, not at all a stage reading. In the aria, she fails to sustain the long notes of the 'della traviata' major section, but the close is lovingly intoned with appealing delicacy. Her voicing of 'Parigi, o cara' is ecstatic rather than lymphatic, the latter being the more usual musical affect. In that duet, I imagine Alexander's forthright invitation is more reassuring than comforting to the patient, but he maintains *his* artistic integrity by eschewing a brutal attack on Alfredo's descending phrases. Moffo aptly defines the contrasting moods of the remaining pages of the score: stern tones command Violetta's maid to bring her robes; a pregnant sounding of 'Ma se tornando' leads to a strongly voiced 'Gran' Dio! morir si giovine'; tragedy and pathos intermingle in a proud 'Prendi, quest'è l'immagine.' Best of all is the pure voicing of 'Se una pudica vergine.' One marvels at her ability to spin her plum-skin-smooth tone with infallible ease over the curves of its phrases. Again, she surprises with a little-girl voicing of the false return to life. Moffo's vivid portrayal has been far from routine on this afternoon. The burden did not prove to be too heavy after all.

We have now heard the last of Moffo's three broadcast portraits of Verdi's challenging heroine. When Beaton's new production had its premiere in the first season at the new Met, she was the heroine. But the opening night of the current season went to Caballé (Moffo in turn gaining the broadcast); the Spanish diva was assigned the next broadcast (21 March 1970). Fortune denies us that pleasure, however, for she canceled and, as noted earlier, Jeannette Pilou, scheduled for her broadcast debut as Juliette a few weeks later, was called to the airwaves earlier than she had anticipated. The broadcast holds uncommon interest, for in addition to the unknown quantity of the Violetta, we hear new portrayals from Bergonzi and Milnes, as well as from Jean Kraft (Flora) and Leo Goeke (Gastone). And to the names of previous *Traviata* broadcast conductors Schick, Adler, and Strasfogel we add the name of musical staff colleague Martin Rich. Though on the roster since 1955 (absent two seasons), he conducted his first Met *Traviata* at a student performance only a few days before the broadcast. Belying his status, Rich makes a brave beginning with an expressive prelude. Yes, the third-act choral episodes are dull and the more dramatic episodes of the opera only modestly sustained, but to his credit, he takes the blinkers off and allows his orchestra to breathe with his soloists, a welcome but uncommon boon among infrequent podium occupants. Alone among the partygoers, Kraft's scratchy Flora sounds vocally out of sorts. The other second-tier singers again show their quality (with Goodloe's firmly focused, warm baritone particularly impressive in Baron Douphol's authoritative comments—in student performances later in the year, he will be upgraded to Papa Germont). Goeke, new to the company this season, owns a compact tenor and he, too, will be granted occasional leading roles, including Alfredo a few years down the line. Such casting moves, admirable though they be for talented young artists, forecast the downward spiral that will afflict the company in future decades.

In the meantime, Bergonzi is the Alfredo of one's dreams. He is in excellent vocal form and abundantly displays his familiar musical virtues. With the utmost courtesy he asks Violetta if his song would please her, sounding the simple 'Vi fia grato?' with the elegance of a courtier; he then proceeds to inflect the Brindisi with delightful nuances that make its well-worn phrases seem newly discovered. His quick vibrato briefly touches 'Un dì felice,' but the swell into 'Di quell'amor' is ardent and secure, as is his second-act aria. Behold an artist in complete command of his wares! He offers a surprise in the gambling scene: where most tenors bawl

La Traviata
21 March 1970

Violetta
Jeannette Pilou
Alfredo
Carlo Bergonzi
Germontt
Sherrill Milnes
Conductor
Martin Rich

their remorse or, at best, moderate it, our tenor almost whispers it (the episode is marked 'da se'), making it a genuine "aside." The act of tenorial abnegation proves to be dramatically potent.

Few baritones who undertake Germont have been willing to show comparable humility, though the father's showpiece 'Di provenza il mar' abounds with *pianissimo* dynamic markings and *dolce* directives. Intimacy between father and son was clearly Verdi's intent. Warren and Tibbett were exceptions to the norm, but they were masters of mezza voce who, priding themselves as much upon that treasurable attribute as upon their resonant *forte*s, displayed it as a badge of merit. Young Milnes is a singer of intelligence who in spite of his predilection for the "closed-fist" mode—which, to be fair, was favored by some of the most renowned baritone practitioners from Ruffo and Amato on through Bastianini—wants to honor the composer. He offers a quiet close to the first stanza and makes selective nods to the *dolce* directives, seldom fully achieving that state but earning respect in the attempt. Not possessing a command of mezza voce, the canny American often tenders a 'tears-in-the-voice' substitute, not ineffective since it suggests the caring parent, but the dodge, when overemployed, becomes rather wearisome. Nevertheless, that ringing, vibrant upper voice, blessed with a fresh-air feel, a succulent, ripe clang, is balm to the ear. His audience knows it—and I know it. His line in the grand duet with Violetta is cleanly defined by pointed tone and dutiful phrasing. Mercifully, puffery is nowhere evident and his 'Piangi's are emblems of sympathy rather than two-note baritone bawls. He manages to differentiate between Germont's scorn for Alfredo's abuse of Violetta ('Di sprezzo degno') and a father's lament for a wayward son ('Dov'è mio figlio?'); Verdi made the distinction, so (though few do) why should not even *primo baritono*s follow his lead?

Pilou's Violetta is a delicate creature, as befits her modest instrument. As replacement for the announced Caballé, she must have felt a heavy responsibility—as though the labors of this challenging role were not sufficient in themselves. No wonder her tone is skittery and touched by a feathery flutter at the courtesan's entrance. Throughout the afternoon, her voice alternately possesses an appealing, flower-like delicacy or a rawer, open tone, occasionally distressing at key moments in the upper voice. The timbre is bright and not inappropriate for the opening act but less affecting in the more sympathetic moments later in the opera. From her broadcast Juliette, we know that her artistic instincts are sound, indeed, often imaginative and subtle. They frequently come to her aid on this afternoon. She knows how to make sense of Verdi's disjunct construct in 'Non sapete,' small-toned though the darting phrases (those little piercing wounds) are. The 'Morrò' episode surely would profit from greater dramatic thrust, as would 'Amami, Alfredo'; she prepares the outburst well enough and the pathetic cast is a plausible alternative to the preferred tragic grandeur. Reedy, almost shrewish, tone startles at Flora's party, but she limns 'Alfredo, di questo core' with slight, pearly tone. A similar fluency charms in the ethereal episodes that precede Violetta's death. A sensitive rendering of the farewell aria affirms her artistic quality (for once, a Violetta doesn't rush the sixteenths). Still, her refined manner will not satisfy those who relish the flamboyant gestures of a *grande tragédienne*. That restrained, expressive mode better suits the thoughtful stance of the first-act 'Ah fors'è lui'—there the flutelike tones of Lily Pons again come unbidden (and fleetingly) to mind. In the 'Follie!' recitatives she launches a few expert coloratura flourishes. Then, quite

surprisingly, disaster overtakes her in the intricate coloratura of 'Sempre libera.'
She feels compelled to begin the descending scale that follows the 'dee volar' sequence an octave lower (it starts on a high D-flat), but recovers for a decent roulade at the end of the first verse. But in the second verse, she takes the entire scale
an octave lower. She appears simply to have lost her nerve, and the succeeding
high Cs are harsh, the final phrase forced and unattractive. Perhaps the substitution for Caballé was too great a millstone. Pilou had not sung Violetta at the Met
since a pair of performances in her debut season three years earlier. The broadcast,
quite understandably, holds the last of her Met portrayals of a role that has de-
feated many a soprano of superior gifts. She would continue with the company
intermittently over the years not only in roles that did not tax her resources (Zerlina, Nedda) but in more demanding assignments that benefited from her stylistic
acuity (Marguerite, Mélisande). In the 1970–71 season, the Met showed its regard
by presenting her as Butterfly (five performances), its confidence not surprising if
one recalls the lovely Juliette she wafted over the airwaves a few weeks after the
Traviata adventure.

Pilou's encounter with Violetta increases one's appreciation of Moffo's triumph in the role. We meet the American soprano again in quite a different milieu,
Mantua, where an equally licentious and certainly more raucous society obtained
than in Violetta's Parisian habitats. Moffo sang Gilda in the *Rigoletto* broadcast of
7 December 1968, almost a year after her Violetta (discussed above) and only four
months before the lamentable Lucia episode. Gilda had figured in her Met repertory as early as 1961 but this is her only radio portrayal. Cleva, the company's
venerable but not inevitably discerning guardian of the Italian tradition, leads
a performance of some quality. Like many who travel life's path, his beginning
is better than his end: the prelude is nicely nuanced, its dramatic character well
programmed, and overall, he is admirably responsive to his singers when they venture an expressive distension. Unfortunately, a noticeable diminution of dynamic
tension, almost a dip into somnolence, saps the perfervid energy of the final acts.
The lineup of Bergonzi, Merrill, Michalski, and Díaz suggests an array of vocal
excellence. Add in Boucher's suave Marullo and Plishka's resonant Ceprano and it
is evident that the Met's casting coffers (at least, in the male component) remain
well stocked. Oddly, Díaz offers Monterone's curse (authoritative and vocally pungent) while Michalski's handsome bass bargains his murderous wares with count-
ing-house poise. The coupling of roles and artists (Sparafucile is usually the prime
assignment of the two) seems odd in view of Díaz's opening-night Antony at the
launching of the new Met. Actually, Díaz, Michalski, and even Giaiotti had been
playing round robin with the two assignments throughout the entire season—further confirmation of the company's low-voice riches. Shirley Love's Maddalena is
remarkably well behaved for her trade but, lacking projection, she proves to be
dramatically ineffectual in dialogue, merely adequate in the quartet.

As the Duke of Mantua, Bergonzi sustains his reputation as the prime representative of nineteenth-century Italian operatic style—style, that is, of the elegant,
as opposed to the blatant, brand. His monarch is marvelously jaunty. The opening
'Questa o quella' bristles with vitality, a joie de vivre that remains undiminished
even as the tenor savors his credo ('La donna è mobile') with carefree assurance
at the opera's end. In between, he courts Countess Ceprano with almost arrogant
certitude of conquest—and why not, when he can clothe his intent in phrases of

Rigoletto
7 December 1968

Gilda
Anna Moffo
Maddalena
Shirley Love
Duke
Carlo Bergonzi
Rigoletto
Robert Merrill
Sparafucile
Raymond Michalski
Conductor
Fausto Cleva

Carlo Bergonzi as the Duke of Mantua in *Rigoletto*. Photography by Louis Mélançon.
Courtesy Metropolitan Opera Archives.

utmost suavity. Vocally, the tenor may be just a shade off maximum form—but the difference is negligible when the maximum is at so elevated a level. That difference includes a slightly porous tone in the opening act—the blight disappears thereafter—and a minimal downward pull on two or three top tones at a few treacherous moments. Perhaps in confirmation of his vocal estate, he eschews the usually interpolated high B-flat at the end of 'Parmi veder le lagrime.' But then, the tessitura of that *scena* is incredibly testing for any tenor (even Björling approached it with compunction); Bergonzi is masterly in his traversal, his technique up to the challenge. Often the top voice has a splendid shine. He sings 'La donna è mobile' in key and, oblivious of Gilda's sacrifice, thrusts out an absolutely clean, clear high B at the final reprise. He had high notes in those days. Some will regret that his timbre is neither the most blandishing nor the most stirring of the tenor brand. But, as keeper of the flame of quality, his light burns ever brighter.

When one talks of timbre, probably no male artist on the Met roster in the mid-century decades owned a warmer, more sumptuous tonal quality than Robert Merrill. His jester has too long been a stranger in these chronicles and how satisfying to remedy that deficiency with a performance worthy of his fame. By the end of his Met career his role tally will rise to fifty-six performances. Now in his twenty-fourth Met season, the singer retains the vocal plush, the thrusting puissance of earlier decades. His topmost tones are no longer always quite confident (the high A-flat that ends the 'Vendetta' sequence is decidedly strained and he shortchanges the interpolated high notes after Gilda dies), but these are fleeting moments in an afternoon of fine vocalism. (For the record, the 'Pari siamo' top G is full-toned and secure.) To his great credit, the puffs and huffs that he often employed as substitutes for dramatic insight or merely for vocal emphasis (and which, for a voice of this plenitude, were entirely unnecessary) are in large part absent. More tonal variety would be welcome—he cannot provide a mezza voce caress to cosset his daughter in their supreme moments of intimacy. (But then few big-voiced baritones since Warren have had a reliable play of light and shade.) Merrill may grow a bit disinterested as the drama moves to its denouement, but the rewards en route are many. Upon hearing Michalski and Merrill barter souls, why should we not be content merely to revel in the beauty of their voices? In 'Cortigiani, vil razza dannata' this jester leaves no doubt that he knows how to command the big moments. He comforts the kidnapped Gilda in phrases of notable aplomb ('Solo per me l'infamia') and his 'Piangi's sound with gentle sincerity. Other baritones convey Rigoletto's cry for vengeance with more bloodthirsty intent. It may be that the American baritone's geniality inhibits him at crisis points; still, at this bloodthirsty moment, Merrill surely has a right to expect Cleva to show more spunk than the conductor offers the raging father. Not surprisingly, the maestro's measured pace in the quartet robs that inspired episode of its maximum impact.

Vocal lions like Bergonzi and Merrill are the pride of the house. Remembering her still potent Violetta of a few months earlier, dare we hope for tonal wealth from Moffo as well? Indeed, her high E-flat at the end of the third-act 'Vendetta' duet is the most full-blooded top note I have ever heard from her—no scream (unlike the other interpolated notes) but rather a velvet-swathed tone. Earlier in the act, she manages to clothe 'Tutte le feste' with a portion of her wonted warmth of timbre. In the quartet, Gilda's brief darts of phrase are attractive enough and the pathos of 'Lassù in cielo' is well realized, the timbre again of good quality (though her excessively slithered line is bad form stylistically). Her interpretive stance throughout the entire opera is open to question. Moffo's Gilda is no docile daughter untutored in the passions. The virgin-like tone and phrasing that most Gildas offer are abandoned in favor of lively and, to my mind, often excessive displays of what is thought to be veristic acting (that is, overacting where abrupt releases, distorted phrasing, and sobs supposedly connote involvement). Is the posture dictated by a desire to offer a novel conception or by vocal indisposition? Truth to tell, for a good deal of the performance, Moffo's vocal condition is decidedly substandard. From the moment when she first greets her father, the voice in its lower octave sounds sick, raw-toned, tremulous (even wobble-infected on sustained notes, which, seemingly of necessity, are often curtailed). Though she can still offer vestigial tonal beauty when operating above the staff, even there control and consistency are uncertain, the attack perilous. This is the regrettable sound and manner of the *Lucia* broadcast in embryonic form. We know that further vocal debasement lies ahead, but even without that knowledge this performance would be cause for grave concern. We can cushion the truth by taking heart from some improvement in later portions of the opera (though the stylistic abuses remain). And of course, Moffo knows how to give a performance. Professionalism sustains her in 'Caro nome,' but even there, in spite of caution, precarious moments intrude. A well-managed cadenza and a good top B save the day. The audience responds favorably to her game effort.

At the time of her Gilda and Lucia broadcasts, Moffo had been at the Met only ten seasons. As I noted earlier, though she continued to perform regularly with the company, she would not appear on the broadcasts for the next four seasons. Her absence in the curtailed 1969–70 season may have been due to the labor dispute, which caused many contracts to be altered. She was scheduled for Gilda in the 5 February 1972 broadcast, but Gail Robinson took her place; similarly, she was announced for Violetta in the 13 January 1973 broadcast but again withdrew, this time in favor of Gilda Cruz-Romo. She did reappear on the airwaves as Pamina in December 1973 and sang her final broadcast (in the unlikely role of Nedda) in January 1975. Is vocal rejuvenation in the cards, some momentary late flowering of the lovely art that so captivated her public during the decade of the sixties?

Many singers endure periods of vocal indisposition (often brief, sometimes moderate in length, but too many of career-threatening severity) brought on by the wear and tear of a thriving, full-fledged operatic career. Even the seemingly impregnable voice of Leontyne Price suffered a touch of vocal trouble early in her Met career. Withdrawal for a few months to recoup was the sage diagnosis and recovery was the reward. Thus, no fears cloud expectations when we meet her again in the 29 March 1969 broadcast of *Trovatore*. A lively afternoon seems a likely prospect with colleagues like Bumbry, McCracken, and Milnes (givers all) sporting under Mehta's exuberant baton. Interest is further whetted in that all four are heard in new broadcast assignments. At the season premiere on 6 March 1969, the new production with sets and costumes designed by Attilio Colonnello was pilloried, but the singers (the broadcast artists, except for McCracken) and conductor were roundly celebrated.

In the brief orchestral introduction, Mehta shows a happy awareness of its theatrical contrasts, an acquaintance that proves fruitful in the remainder of the score. Other conductors have better masked the organ-grinder character of the

Il Trovatore
29 March 1969

Leonora
Leontyne Price
Azucena
Grace Bumbry
Manrico
James McCracken
Di Luna
Sherrill Milnes
Ferrando
John Macurdy
Conductor
Zubin Mehta

accompaniments. Those "abstract" support figures need not be decried for they form, in Virgil Thomson's graphic phrase (though he did not specifically apply it to Verdi), an "auditory proscenium," framing within their "static structure" the stage personnel's more vibrant musical expression.[3] Under Mehta's charge, their rigor is rather too insistent, causing the "proscenium" to close in on the aural focus. He is, for instance, disposed to rapid flight in the more agitated moments of the score. Still, better alacrity than tepidity—and he does allow his singers sufficient leeway in the more reflective moments of the later acts. Mehta, who is guiding *Carmen* and *Turandot* as well this season, remains a welcome podium tenant, at least at the Met.

It may not have been he who encouraged Macurdy to discover the dynamic and rhythmic variety in Ferrando's narrative—that was hardly the Indian maestro's thing. In any case, the basso delivers it with commendable precision and vitality. In these earliest years of his career, Macurdy could sound suitably ponderous when in the German orbit, but robustly Italianate in southern repertory, the chameleon's quick change doubling his house worth.

Though the setting is new (in human inhabitants as well), Price remains the prime jewel of the performance. Unlike some of her roles, her Leonora wears a welcome vulnerability, the posture apparent in her consistent reliance on a more girlish timbre than she usually displays. In momentary retirement are the penumbral colors that sometimes (and usually favorably) shadow her song. Most satisfying is her evident desire to preserve the luster of her vocal capital by selective continence. Chest is rarely drawn into the vocal mix, and then only glancingly; at this point in her career, the lower voice projects well enough and yet retains the velvety sheen of the remainder of the voice. A shimmering flutter (more prominent than usual and not to all tastes) and gentle phrasing enhance the impression of fragility in the opera's earlier episodes. Yet even there she never neglects to certify her credentials as prima donna: the cadenza of 'Tacea la notte placida' and the ensuing cabaletta are brilliantly deployed and the capping D-flat of the trio is a trifling task for her. At the cloister she is a little careless in her effects (neglecting a *piano* dynamic or slurping an interval) but, in contrast to her debut 1961 broadcast, she has found the secret, the ebb and flow of dynamics and tempo, that allows her to bind into a sustained arc those little agitated phrases which mirror Leonora's joy at Manrico's rescue ('E deggio e posso crederlo?'). (An odd orchestral lapse occurs earlier in the scene where, to what must have been Mehta's dismay, an important clarinet tone fails to sound at a key point.) Quite amusingly, Price tosses off the Gilda-like brief insertions in the act-two closing ensemble as accurately and vapidly as any light-voiced coloratura. Her diminutive tone in the little duet before the aborted wedding is almost unbelievably (but, in the circumstances, appropriately) chaste.

Glorious is the only word for Price's 'D'amor sull-ali rosee.' When an artist reaches the home stretch, the admired continence ought to give way to, if not quite abandon, at least liberality. She fills the aria with big-hearted, ravishingly colored tone—but the dulcet phrases of the introductory recitative are floated with ethereal ease. One can catalog a few quibbles: the vibrato is sometimes overly prominent; a beloved *dolce* marking goes by the board in favor of brilliance; a slippery legato briefly smudges the line here and there; notes in the cadenza ascent are neglected in a precipitous lunge to the top note. But the glory remains and one can literally feel the swell of affection that the audience's roar offers her at the aria's close. Even in the depths of the Miserere she does not abuse her chest voice and yet her emotive stance is resolute and fervid. Price is deeply involved in Leonora's plight on this afternoon. In the final encounter with Manrico her celestial voicing of 'Prima che d'altri vivere' should guarantee admission at the heavenly gates.

Corelli had been listed for the production premiere, but Domingo took over the first three performances. Thereafter, McCracken was scheduled and assumed the burden (the term is not inapt, considering his vocal production proclivities). In the final decades of the century, Verdi singers became increasingly rare creatures. Imagine a season's roster with five great tenors capable of singing Manrico: Tucker, Bergonzi, Corelli, McCracken, and Domingo—with Flaviano Labò on the reserve list as backup. And each could bring distinctive gifts to the challenging assignment. McCracken's voice, for instance, is a blunt—but not unlovely—thing. Still, Verdi has posed harrowing feats of dexterity for his Manrico. Sometimes one feels as though the American tenor is a refugee from the gym's training room; when his voice mounts above the staff, the suggestion of vocal weightlifting all but demands an empathetic assist from the listener. But this vocal Atlas invariably manages the feat on his own. He is a singer who never stints in performance. Clearly, his vocalism is no bel canto ideal and all his song this afternoon is well muscled. But within that framework, he avoids tenorial mannerisms and respects both the music's line and the character's integrity.

The voice's timbre, vibrant and dense, has genuine appeal. In McCracken's pressurized voicing, Manrico's offstage entry is a high-protein serenade, lacking in grace, but it makes a striking calling card. By the time 'Ah sì, ben mio' rolls around, the voice is sufficiently oiled to sustain a creditable reading (if you don't mind being sprayed by multiple rolled *r*s). He sings 'Di quella pira' in key, articulates the sixteenth notes better than most colleagues, and offers stout, though brief, high Cs. (The final one may be momentarily flat before having its head raised—occasionally throughout the afternoon, mid-voice tones shade the pitch as well.) McCracken confirms that a heroic voice well serves Verdi's valiant troubadour. In the confiding episodes for mother and "son," however, the composer surely imagined a more elegant manner and a gentler tone than our tenor provides. However discreet McCracken's 'Mal reggendo' and 'Riposa, o madre' may be, the tenor's tone and muscular manner can't help but dilute the mood of familial love that Verdi has so skillfully cultivated. His blazing accusation of the sacrificial Leonora is the high point of his portrayal. Splendid in tone and strong in declamation, the denunciation is a moving, Otello-like moment.

As expected, this is an afternoon of high-powered vocalism and, in that category, Milnes occupies pride of place. His 'Un balen del suo sorriso' is a magnificent display of baritonal riches, the tone abundantly resonant and opulently colored in the upper range. He is able to sustain its fearsome phrases at a broad pace, and the deployment of voice is almost arrogantly assured. Here is a young artist taking complete control of the stage and glorying in his ripe wares (including several bold top Gs). Some will find his address rather too audacious. In this instance, any sacrifice of poetic content hardly need be regretted—perhaps the baritone determined that a few discreet sobs would be sufficient evidence of his love for Leonora. Elsewhere, the lowest tones occasionally are unattractively opened in order to gain bulk, and a narrower, less plump tone is sometimes employed to counterfeit villainy. More often, he envelopes Di Luna's grand moments in luxuriant vocalism.

An impressive, and salutary, touch is Milnes' secure propulsion of a genuine *messa di voce* at the beginning of the third act ('Ah, Leonora'). The feat provides evidence that this intelligent singer is not unacquainted with the graces of an older tradition. (As his career progressed, one always hoped—and too often, in vain—for more of these vocal blandishments.) Later in the act, his brutal attack makes Azucena's survival more perilous than usual. When, near the opera's end, Price and Milnes rocket (but with precision) through the "bargain" duet, the two gifted Americans, well schooled and musically alert though they be, serve up a rousing, old-fashioned vocal treat. The audience knows it is hearing the real thing.

Without meaning to make too much of them, I will note a few qualms about Miss Bumbry's Azucena, distractions that filter complete approval of her portrayal. Never doubt, however, that she belongs in this league. Hers is a highly individual instrument, not easily categorized. Its uniqueness resides in a singularly taut texture, as though the vocal cords were bands of finely honed metal. Are instrument and role natural partners? Azucena is a gypsy hag and Bumbry's vibrant voice, with the upper range a brilliant blade wedded to a markedly firm base, fairly reeks of youthful vigor. Bumbry is a more musicianly gypsy than we usually encounter in the mountains of Biscay. Readers may decide for themselves upon which side of the merit/debit sheet that attribute falls. Admirably, she refuses to disgorge baritonal chest tone. At best, a balanced register mix is employed, even in moments where most well-endowed mezzos love to show visceral power. (By no means do I wish to denigrate the use of a well-developed chest voice; in fact, a gear change into a distinct chest register was the usual modus operandi during Verdi's early years. Tastes change.) Nor does she drive the familiar melodies with the customary maniacal thrust. Her technique and razor-like tone are so efficient that an air of detachment begins to permeate her portrayal, hardly the traditional pose for the volatile gypsy mother. And yet, singularity of purpose can be a successful means to achieve vengeance. Questionable pitch occasionally is a matter of concern. Around A and B in mid-voice the register mix causes some uncertainty: the tuning of notes there can be on the flat side. The opening of 'Stride le vampa' is a distressing example of that failing—and the aria's close is negated by lack of a trill.

Do I admire Bumbry's musicianly intent and vocal prowess on this afternoon? Decidedly, yes. Often the upper voice is strikingly beautiful and the middle and low ranges have an appealing timbral warmth. Many early episodes in the opera benefit from her well-considered vocalism. Her restraint is particularly affecting and germane in the final scene with Manrico. There, 'Ai nostri monti' has a childlike simplicity, subtly suggesting the mother's fond remembrance of her youth. Oddly, the mezzo reenters the trio with a loud, blatantly open, and unattractive tone that momentarily ruins the poignant effect of this intimate moment. (Perhaps the singer was unduly close to a radio mike.) The result is doubly surprising since vulgarity has not been this Azucena's portion. In the long run, it seems likely that Bumbry's career path will be better served by seduction than by vituperation.

With its five-star appeal, the 1969 *Trovatore* broadcast ranks high in broadcast history. Just two years later (13 March 1971), however, the Met was able to offer the radio audience a completely different lineup, and yet one of considerable merit: Arroyo, Tucker, Sereni, Michalski, and newcomer Shirley Verrett. Mehta

Il Trovatore
13 March 1971

Leonora
Martina Arroyo
Azucena
Shirley Verrett
Manrico
Richard Tucker
Di Luna
Mario Sereni
Ferrando
Raymond Michalski
Conductor
Zubin Mehta

is the glue meant to hold the performance together, which he does admirably. Interest focuses upon Verrett since the other principals have been heard in earlier *Trovatore* broadcasts.

Mehta's way with the score, fine in his initial effort, is more rewarding here. He has marginally relaxed his proprietary grip on the opera's pulse, a heartbeat that is, of itself, rapid and intense and hardly needs further stimulation. In the score's more reflective moments, his propulsion of the repetitive accompaniment figures is less intrusive than in the premiere season. The singers are given every opportunity to revel in Verdi's expansive line, and some of them (Tucker, in particular) avail themselves of it to their own glory. And yet, Mehta does not neglect to stir the melodramatic pot where a good churn serves the composer's purpose. Miss Verrett serves him well, too, for her portrayal runs on high-voltage electricity. Rage is, in large part, Azucena's lot and the new mezzo storms with uncommon avidity. Interpretive polarities (it would be pejorative and an oversimplification to pigeonhole them as involvement and detachment) cause Verrett's and Bumbry's gypsies to live in different worlds. Oddly, Verrett owns the softer-grained instrument, but her portrayal is warrior-fierce. She may tread the fine line between scene chewing and believable commitment but manages to remain within virtue's realm. That she does so is in large part due to her keen musical instincts. Even in the gypsy's rabid moments, she gains respect and sympathy by introducing subtleties of phrase and dynamics. Undeniably, there are moments where her vocal gestures are so grand as to imperil the health of her lovely instrument. For a good deal of the opera, a rasp, often slight, sometimes insistent, in the mezzo's danger zone (the notes on the lower staff) causes discomfort—ours, more than hers, evidently, for she gives unstintingly of voice and heart until the final curtain. Perhaps because it is her broadcast debut (and her first Azucena at the house) she is intent on serving notice of her arrival on the scene. Or it may be that the full-throttle mode will prove to be her normal performance pattern. Her Metropolitan debut had occurred as Carmen in 1968, but since then she had made few appearances with the company (Eboli that same season, and a single Amneris in 1970). Juilliard trained, she was a New York City Opera alumna (debut 1958) and had appeared extensively in Europe (Cologne, Spoleto, La Scala, Covent Garden) before coming to the Met. Her personal beauty, artistic integrity, and charismatic stage presence, as well as her vocal excellence, guaranteed a major career.

Let us follow her as she travels Azucena's path. Her 'Stride le vampa' is more successful than most—the dotted rhythms that define its profile are scrupulously observed. Her narration of the child substitution ('Condotta ell'era in ceppi') brings the gypsy's horror vividly to life—through her vocal performance alone one can visualize her dramatic posture and facial expressions, the mark of a fine singing actress. She bangs on the vocal cords here, but when Verdi allows the mother a contemplative moment, Verrett allows the lyrical beauty of her instrument, especially in its upper range, full play. An affecting touch is her quiet sounding of 'Mi vendica!'. 'Giorni poveri' tells us more about this sensitive artist. Azucena's lament for her lost child is radiantly limned as Verrett in caressing tones (and with deft acknowledgment of the change from the minor to the major mode) wraps 'Qual per esso provo amore' with a mother's love. In contrast, she leaves no doubt that she is a creature of the theater as she vigorously launches 'Deh, rallentate, o barbari'—and there Mehta abets her effort by sending it along with ball-bearing velocity. In the prison scene, Verrett hauntingly intones Azucena's longing for sleep, making her weariness palpable. 'Si, la stanchezza m'opprime o figlio' reveals the innate beauty of the voice, now compact, well balanced, and velvety smooth. In Verrett and Bumbry, the Metropolitan possessed contrasting Azucenas, portrayals from two artists of uncontested merit but different in vocal makeup and performance manner. Though quite distinct, the careers of the two singers would, oddly, move along parallel tracks (but certainly not always in straight lines) over the next several decades.

Arroyo's task is difficult since Price's archetypal Leonora is still warm in the memory. While her voice owns a comparable, though individual, beauty above the staff, Arroyo's lower range is metallically rimmed, its timbre and usage often limiting expressivity in that area. And by now, we are well acquainted with the lack of dramatic conviction, a certain complacency, in her portrayals. Still, her Leonora on this afternoon is a marvelous achievement. From the first the lower voice holds a richer coloration (the cold tint of metal is not entirely dispelled, but the tone has more body). In 'Tacea la notte placida,' she traces Verdi's magical expansion of the two pivotal phrases with perceptive exactitude. (In that aria, the high D-flat that launches the cadenza is avoided—her settling for the high C is unmusical since it alters the dominant chord construct of the cadenza.) The coloratura of the cabaletta (one verse only) causes no problem, though the excitement quotient is low; Arroyo has that tendency to move rhythms toward a neutral centrality. The resourceful singer does loft an easy high D-flat at the trio's end—we knew she had it in her vocal arsenal. She cannot float the *arioso* of the cloister as Price does—her voice, for all its tonal appeal, lacks an ethereal spin—but her coloratura in the ensuing trio has more bloom than her sister diva offered. Vapidity is minimized. In the final act, her vocalism is wondrously secure and gorgeous in tone—quite the equal of Price's effort. The aria is grandly paced and sung with full tone, resonant and equalized throughout the range. Its arched phrases ('le pene') are superbly rendered (the repeat not an echo, but softer), and the cadenza is more cleanly managed without Price's abrupt lurch to the top note. Arroyo is not afraid to add chest tone to make the Miserere speak. Perhaps her finest moment occurs when she tackles the heretofore neglected cabaletta ('Tu vedrai che amor in terra'). Budden deemed it "one of Verdi's best cabalettas" and Arroyo makes believers of us.[4] The audience—perhaps honoring her conscientiousness in learning the piece and bravery in negotiating its challenges as much as her superb conquest of them—gives her a well-deserved ovation at its close. Gone is her familiar neutral stance, for the soprano provides the vocal fireworks that the cabaletta demands. The remainder of the act sustains regard, with lustrous tone (and marvelous breath control to maintain the line) enveloping 'Prima che d'altri vivere.'

Michalski's Ferrando is again a treasure, musically alert and tonally attractive. As briefly noted above, Tucker is in glorious voice. Quite amazingly for a tenor in his fifty-seventh year, he gives one of the best performances of his lengthy career. Yes, a few of the fidgety mannerisms mar the first act (sometimes one feels he is a giant bouncing ball ricocheting around the stage), but distortions are few this afternoon. His serenade is well controlled and lyrical—the voice is, as usual, fully warmed up. (A slight strain on the top note marks the only sign of age during the entire opera.) 'Mal reggendo' is straightforwardly delivered, the middle voice more richly colored than usual. Indeed, throughout the performance, Tucker's command of timbral modification and overall vocal technique remains remarkable. His cultivated reading of 'Ah si, ben mio' is the high point of an afternoon of general excellence from all executants. Dramatic gestures are confined to the few phrases where Manrico ponders impending death—many tenors prefer (wrongly) to slather the entire aria with despair. Broadly paced, liquidly voiced, appropriately romantic, the reading qualifies him as a guardian of the finest traditions of the house. Not unexpectedly, he takes 'Di quella pira' down a half-tone and, though sometimes slighting the sixteenth notes, supplies the requisite fervor and decent top Bs. In the prison scene, his beautifully colored middle voice couples well with Verrett's warm mezzo. The denunciation of Leonora is more broadly paced and ringingly intoned than one has a right to expect from a spinto (as opposed to a heroic) tenor; the declamation, arched phrasing, and overall plotting would do credit to Martinelli. One's admiration for Tucker deepens in the final years of his career.

Sereni, too, must be praised. On this broadcast he proves himself no also-ran (though I have too often placed him in that category). I judge him a Verdi baritone whom we would be proud to claim in our time. Unlike most latter-day singers (Leo Nucci, for example), Sereni does not need to manufacture vocal mass for the Verdi roles. The virility of his voice is built in. Of course, the gentler emotions are not within his compass, but then, they are largely foreign to Di Luna as well. I want to believe that he has solved the once persistent bugaboo of wayward pitch. For the most part, he has. The cadence of his aria is marginally sharp, but it may be merely the topside of his vibrato overloading the tone; still, as he awaits Leonora's entry with the nuns, lack of support causes the Count's whispered dismissal of his followers to fall woefully flat. Other than that, he matches a good deal of what Milnes so vividly offered in the 1968 broadcast. 'Il balen' holds greater tonal richness in the lower part of the voice than that of his American colleague and the entire aria (sung in key) is resonantly delivered with a superb top G to begin the quasi-cadenza. He suffers a memory lapse in the cabaletta duet of the final act but, after a brief pause, recovers nicely. Arroyo and he have a jolly time (in spite of the context) careering through the invigorating duet.

Baritones, whether villains or heroes, have frequently stimulated the Verdi melos. For me, none of his lower-voiced creations is more grandly, and affectingly, delineated than the Venetian doge. After a lapse of three seasons, *Simon Boccanegra* returned to the airwaves on 14 December 1968. There we find not only MacNeil in the place of honor, but quite unexpectedly, considering his quick elevation, Milnes in the relatively brief, but dramatically significant, role of Paolo. But then, the traitorous goldsmith had been served by such distinguished artists as Warren, Valdengo, Flagello, and Díaz in earlier broadcasts. In an *Opera News* interview, MacNeil lamented that the opera is hard to cast. Verdi, while writing difficult music for them, had shortchanged the soprano and tenor, opera's usual heavyweights. *Boccanegra*, the baritone averred, holds "no big arias. Nobody wants to sing it."[5] And yet those earlier airings were peopled with quality artists. Under Molinari-Pradelli's leadership, today's cast of Tucci, Shirley, MacNeil, and Hines has merit as well. In its current reincarnation the opera had suffered an uncommon amount of cast shuffling in the two months between the seasonal premiere (Rita Orlandi-Malaspina, Tucker, MacNeil, Ghiaurov) and the broadcast. Even though the opera was no common repertory vehicle, Milka Stojanovic and Tucci, Prevedi, Morell, and Shirley, Guarrera in the name part, Tozzi, and Giaiotti all briefly became inhabitants of fourteenth century Genoa. In spite of having to contend with revolving-door casting, Molinari-Pradelli leads a finely knit performance on the

Simon Boccanegra
14 December 1968

Maria/Amelia
Gabriella Tucci
Gabriele
George Shirley
Simon
Cornell MacNeil
Fiesco
Jerome Hines
Paolo
Sherrill Milnes
Conductor
Francesco Molinari-
Pradelli

broadcast. The conductor is more responsive to the somber and reflective moods of the opera than its political turmoil. The Chamber Council scene, noble fruit of Verdi's 1881 revision, gets off to a decidedly tepid start, but picks up as revolution threatens. Still, with the exception of that towering addition, the contemplative moments are the heart of Verdi's dark-hued work. The conductor signals his intent with a notably relaxed and flowing instrumental introduction to the prologue.

The first voice we hear (to borrow Mr. Cross' often employed phrase) is Milnes' strapping baritone; subliminally one feels that this traitorous Paolo one day *will* ascend to the doge's throne. The baritone is adept at a vocal sneer, a handy asset when devious plans, both political and amorous, are your principal concerns. The Milnes persona demands central stage and even in this middle-ground part he manages to occupy it for a scene or two, most notably in the splendid recitative that Verdi added for Paolo at the beginning of act two; the baritone rides up the ascent and over the top of its climactic phrase to splendid and rousing effect. Shirley adopts a more subtle approach in his playing of the heart-sore Gabriele. His minuscule offstage serenade has little effect, but upon entering, the voice, which melds a sturdy, yet touching, baritonal core to a brighter, pinging top, rings true. The metallic timbral overlay may not be to all tastes, but Shirley's artistic musical manners and dramatic fervor surely should be. He is technically resourceful as well. Gabriele's prime moment (and a tenor's trial by fire) occurs in the second act when he believes that his beloved has been unfaithful. Martinelli made much of the episode and, while Shirley does not have quite the goods and the Italianate *slancio* to turn the *scena* into a tour de force, he makes a brave attempt. Here the baritonal timbre lends a powerful assist, and his declamation in the introductory recitative is knowing and forceful. In the aria, he inflects the transition from anger to despair with skill (shading of dynamics and mood rather than sobs are his means) and reveals the lover's hurt affectingly in the climactic moments ('Priva di sue virtù'). Even more effective are his responses upon learning that Boccanegra, her supposed lover, is Amelia's father. There he shows that he can command a wider range of vocal colors. Gabriele's remorse is keenly felt and clearly revealed.

Hines is well mated with the role of Fiesco. The afternoon contains one of his finest portrayals. For much of the opera, the granitic patriarch operates on a single expressive level. In a role where sympathetic response and subtleties of vocal modification are limited, Hines shines. His principal assets (impressive tone and breadth of manner) become the fodder for effective dramatic characterization. Verdi wanted a basso profondo for the part; Hines is not quite in that line, but his rock-solid technique turns the trick well enough. Though the basso is in his twenty-third Metropolitan season, he remains at the top of his form: the voice's sturdy, rich timbre is intact. Of course, 'Il lacerato spirito' calls for something more in the way of expressive interpretation than he is willing to give—volume and expression are hardly altered when Fiesco turns from reviling Simon to naming the blessed Virgin ('E tu, Vergin, soffristi'). He begins the aria with some sensitivity, however, and one must admire the covered tone he employs in the concluding 'Prega' section. I like best of all his work in the final act. There Fiesco's initial implacability is splendidly rendered, and when the old man's hatred mutates into sorrow he finds an honorable and traditional way to indicate his change of heart. The entire scene is quite moving for, in addition to Hines' sterling effort, MacNeil's portrayal of the dying doge strikes home.

Cornell MacNeil as Simon Boccanegra. Photography by Louis Mélançon. Courtesy Metropolitan Opera Archives.

Occasionally MacNeil's voice is a bit raw toned (indeed, his cloudy initial few notes are a shocking contrast to Milnes' straight-arrow tones), but throughout the afternoon he plays with utmost integrity. His portrayal, vocally, musically, and dramatically, tarries on a high level. The voice is huge and sometimes the singer takes considerable time before gaining full control of vibrato or polishing the tone to beauty. Happily, the delay is relatively brief on this afternoon. To hear his instrument in juxtaposition with Milnes' in the later stages of the opera allows one to appreciate the older artist's tonal density, particularly in the lower range. One might say that Milnes' voice is constructed as an inverted pyramid, while MacNeil's is columnar in design, as wide and rich at the bottom as at the top. (But remember, a column can be hollow as well as fully packed.) In addition, MacNeil's control over a wide range of dynamics and a usually reliable mezza voce provide the makings of a superior Boccanegra. Already at the close of the prologue, we hear him manipulating vocal colors to excellent effect as he narrates the tale of his daughter's disappearance and his vain search for her. The recognition duet with Amelia is sympathetically rendered, the voice fully mastered now. The inner quietude of the father's final 'Figlia!' is scrupulously observed in a fair sounding of this trying moment, even though the higher tone is touched with falsetto and the note at the bottom of the octave drop seems very slightly below pitch. The intent deserves respect.

Verdi's hero is both father and doge. The one must speak in loving, dulcet tones, the other rage against his enemies and subdue the warring populace of his domain. MacNeil fulfills the double duty admirably. In the Council Chamber his declamation is grandly, crisply, articulated. Unfortunately, he chooses not to color his tone with love at the touching moment when the doge's heart overflows as Amelia tells him of her grief at Gabriele's plight. The vocal and dramatic high point of the role ('Plebe! Patrizi!') is splendidly realized, though here again one wants a bit more warmth at 'Piango su voi'; its climactic phrases ('E vo gridano: pace!') are fearlessly and abundantly sounded. Others have been more imaginative at denouncing Paolo, but MacNeil's snarled command for the traitor to repeat the curse is hair-raising. Similarly, when Paolo's poison begins to course through Simon's veins, our doge's song would profit from more varied nuances but the overall design is effective and lovingly charted. Hines and MacNeil, owners of two of the Met's grandest low voices, initially play with such breadth and dignity in their reconciliation scene that the episode calls to mind the confrontation between Philip and the Grand Inquisitor. At the other end of the spectrum, the baritone's command of mezza voce enhances many a phrase during the last two acts. The doge's death scene is sympathetically limned.

The knowledge that Tucci's Met career will suffer a precipitous decline at some point before her departure from the company in December 1972 lends particular interest (and concern) to her vocal estate four years before that lamentable termination. Happily, as Amelia she continues to demonstrate the admirable form that has given so much pleasure since her company debut in 1960. The voice remains in excellent condition and her skillful deployment of its peculiar resources is notable. She is mistress of the nineteenth-century Italian style, adept at declamation, shapes phrases with sculptural clarity at pivotal dramatic moments, and imbues them with poise and lineal clarity in romantic or reflective episodes. The voice's modest size and relatively nonabsorbent tonal texture compel her to etch the line rather than wrap it in opulence à la Tebaldi or Price. But her technical know-how is impressive and readily apparent on this afternoon. She can, for example, troll through Amelia's opening aria, a trying and rather unrewarding piece, with aplomb and bring off its ungainly climax without mishap. Indeed, it is a superior effort. One would prefer a more dulcet tone for 'Vieni a mirar la cerula,' but her delivery cannot be faulted. (In general, the duets of Tucci and Shirley, for all their artistry, give off a slight chill—their timbres are compatibly cool.) Her trill at the close of the father–daughter recognition duet is no better than most: cleanly prepared and exited, but in between a delicate, but fuzzy, oscillation. In the Council Chamber scene Verdi's demands really require greater vocal heft than Tucci can command. Is she, however, commanding? Yes, for she doesn't stint. Her top tones invariably are cleanly struck and well supported, so the impact is often greater than their vocal poundage. Luster can inhabit her tone, as she demonstrates with a glowing *mezzo piano* high B-flat ('Un ciel d'amor non ha') when in the second act Amelia calms her lover's fears. In the face of her father's threat upon Gabriele's life, she thrusts a knife-edged protest into the dialogue, again demonstrating her aptitude for sculptured phrasing. A few shrewish phrases surface in the dramatic turmoil of that act. Like many sopranos (not including Milanov, who correctly detached them), Tucci executes the isolated notes of the final act ensemble in a continuous line; she does achieve a satisfactory effect by placing an initial press on each note. When MacNeil, after authoritatively naming Gabriele as his successor, applies a heavenly mezza voce to his final utterance of his daughter's name, his caress of 'Maria' encapsulates the high-minded mood with which Verdi invested the entire opera.

In my chronology of Verdi operas broadcast from 1967–68 through 1970–71, *Un Ballo in Maschera*, according to date of composition, should be next in line. But Verdi's 1881 revision of his 1857 *Boccanegra* has altered the game plan. The majesty of the Chamber Council scene gives me license to call into immediate play his *Don Carlo* of the 1880s. Twenty years after Bing's prime managerial coup, namely, the reintroduction of the grand opera to the American public, the work has now all but become a repertory staple. It was performed in 1968–69 but had not been broadcast since 1965. Despite the scheduling chaos inflicted by the difficult labor negotiations, management assembled a cast for the 14 February 1970 broadcast (Corelli, Kabaivanska, Bumbry, Merrill, Tozzi, and Michalski) worthy of its predecessors. Kurt Adler, hardly the expected pilot for this epic work, is on the podium. Yet the longtime chorus master had conducted both the 1955 and 1964 broadcasts, his assignments probably prompted by the choral dominance of the auto-da-fé scene. On this afternoon, his is a caretaker's effort. He moves each episode along at a no-nonsense pace; indeed, some portions of the score seem inordinately hurried, though his tempos are well within the zones of the metronome markings. The discrepancy between literalness and musical result is due to his failure to shape individual phrases with distinction and to maintain an overall dynamic pulse. All is in order, but the grand scope of the work, its somber overlay, are both slighted. The numerous cuts (a second verse here, a middle section there, a portion of the auto-da-fé chorus) are detrimental as well, particularly since the Met continues to offer the four-act 1884 La Scala version of the score.

Perhaps it was management's difficulty in launching the season that causes the suspicion of a hastily thrown-together performance to suggest itself. (A settle-

Don Carlo
14 February 1970

Elisabetta
Raina Kabaivanska
Eboli
Grace Bumbry
Carlo
Franco Corelli
Rodrigo
Robert Merrill
Philip
Giorgio Tozzi
Inquisitor
Raymond Michalski
Conductor
Kurt Adler

ment with the unions had been reached on 13 December 1969, but throughout the month of February *Opera News* was still unable to list complete casts for the Met's calendar of performances.) Of course, with artists of this cast's quality we are assured some spectacular vocalism. Merrill's voice is a marvel and it remains in fine working order. Glorious is the only word for its timbral warmth and solidity throughout the entire range. He and Corelli have a field day with the friendship duet; their tonal effulgence and decibel count is amazing (never mind that Verdi hoped his multiple *piano* markings would restrain lung power). When Rodrigo hears Carlo confess his love for Elisabetta, the Infante's stepmother, Merrill expels an extravagantly outsized gust of air ('Giusto' in 'Giusto ciel!'), the tone puffed up to blowfish rank—a savory moment, if you can treasure the ridiculous. Merrill is the only member of the cast who participated in the 1950 premiere. Is it too-long acquaintance that makes him neglect to provide minimal insights into Posa's character? The pivotal duet with his king fares well enough, for there straight-forward delivery and firm tone plead the Flemish cause with conviction. But the romanza ('Carlo ch'è il sol il nostro amore') and especially the prison *scena*, both sung with admirable security and tonal warmth, are devoid of the noble sensibil-ity that makes Rodrigo so appealing a figure in the drama. Merrill's song is all foreground. In 'Per me giunto' Adler initially adopts a fleet pace, but Merrill man-ages to quicken the tempo, dragging the subservient conductor along with him. One often wearies of the death-throe agonies that some artists lay upon their final stage moments, but this baritone patently refuses to even so much as acknowledge Rodrigo's mortal wound. He goes hale and hearty to his maker, who, abiding by a code of forgiveness, would undoubtedly cherish the baritone for his vocal generos-ity and (fortunately for us) longevity.

Tozzi had sung Philip in the 1964 broadcast where his benign vocalism and manner somewhat undermined his portrayal of the cruel, but troubled, king. This time, the bass has toughened his stance and stiffened his voice, so that the mon-arch's stature rivals his rank. In the process, his instrument is roughened, but the result is hardly disaffecting. He sends Countess Aremberg back to France with appropriate harshness, berates his queen with hateful hurt, rejects the Flemish deputation with disdain, and, when confronted with his son's rebellion, thunders with the authority of one who, to steal a familiar phrase, must be obeyed. The monarch's troubles, however, are no laughing matter. Thus, Verdi shows us the in-ner man in Philip's monologue, carefully marking it 'come trasognato'; Tozzi can-not achieve that dreamlike reverie, failing, for instance, to summon a mezza voce for the repetitions of 'Dormirò sol.' He settles for a theatrical reading, commend-ably grand in the climaxes with a splendid top E on 'amor' and occasionally almost hysterical (he is the very image of a broken man when crying 'No! quel cor chiuso è a me'). Tozzi should have been able to claim no contest in the confrontation with the cardinal, thus negating the king's celebrated acknowledgment that the state must always give way before the altar, for, in place of the usual black-toned bass, management offers Michalski's beautiful, almost baritonal, instrument. (This is the Bayonne, New Jersey, singer's only Grand Inquisitor—Macurdy had sung the 10 February premiere.) The awe-inspiring cardinal ought to exhale tones bleak and boreal, his pronouncements propelled on winds out of the north. But warmer climes inform Michalski's timbre—he is no child of Boreas. Still, he is so canny a performer, so fine a musician that, at least over the airwaves (for his height was slight and the voice not overlarge), his Inquisitor is an intriguing creature. With utmost care, he plots each episode, achieving maximum effect by gradations of volume and color; unlike many an artist of greater resources on this afternoon, he takes his cues from Verdi's markings, to which he diligently adheres. In the final terrible moments of the confrontation, the composer's brass momentarily bests him, and we recall longingly the sepulchral horror that some interpreters have conjured in this scene.

Glamor roles are Bumbry's by right, warranted both by her person and her voice. The latter is almost brazenly vibrant and she wields its thrust with uncommon surety. Varied tonal colorations and subtle nuances are not readily summoned by such a voice, but she has other, more spectacular assets. Eboli is a footlight character and the American mezzo is at home there—her accomplishments warrant prominent display. The Veil Song, for instance, bane of many a fine interpreter of the role, is delivered with complete aplomb, the melismatic figurations rapidly articulated with greater accuracy than most interpreters offer, the high reiterations deftly done, with only the lowest triplet in the pseudo-cadenza slighted. And a grateful nod is owed to Judith Forst, who joins Bumbry in the refrains—for once, the page is a worthy partner to the princess. (On the other hand, Edmond Karlsrud's firm-voiced Friar is perhaps too efficient for that mysterious figure.) Bumbry's lighthearted manner lends unwonted elegance to Eboli's colloquy with Rodrigo. Her rhythmic vitality turns the garden scene trio into a lively thing, but more suavity in her interlude with the deluded Carlo would be welcome (on Corelli's part as well). She can be a touch businesslike at times, as when she finally tumbles to Carlo's love for his queen. Her bands-of-steel instrument is made for 'O don fatale.' The pyrotechnics of the outer sections of the aria are fired off with startling accuracy and brio. My regard lessens at the central section, though it is neatly intoned; she does leave off bravado, but cannot clothe the prayer in the soft velvet it deserves. Top notes are firm, but the final pair fly sharp. In her assured traversals of Eboli's contrasting arias, Bumbry brings the princess' split vocal personality into better alignment than most interpreters of this taxing role.

Kabaivanska, of Bulgarian birth but long resident on Italian stages, performs with notable artistry as the sorrowful queen. She lacks the luxurious vocal resources that many Elisabettas have owned. (At the Met, broadcast interpreters have included Rigal, Steber, Rysanek, Arroyo, and Caballé.) She is a soprano in the Tucci, or the young Scotto, vein. Nature may not have been prodigal in stocking her voice with genomic complexity but her instrument has all the core genes. The circumference of her tone is rather narrow, its timbre not entirely welcoming. For some, those may be considerable demerits, but they become insignificant in the face of her musicality and vocal skill. The voice is ever firm, her articulation of text and command of its meaning is acute, and her interpretive insights are often profound. Like Michalski, she achieves many an impressive moment by merely following Verdi's directives, often trusting a quiet *piano* marking to marvelous effect. Her reserved sounding of the pair of 'Signor's that close the court duet with Carlo is touchingly intimate. Adler's hurried pace dilutes the pathos of 'Non pianger, mia compagna' (one verse only), but she brings it home with an ethereal *pianissimo* on the concluding phrase's apex. Sometimes her vocal character (in particular, her otherworldly soft high notes) calls to mind the curious, but magical, art of Magda Olivero. Elisabetta's precipitous entry into the king's cabinet requires more vocal heft than she can muster, but she and Bumbry, their voices separated by an octave, accurately sing the tricky parallel lines of the quartet; Kabaivanska's half-step descents are tuned with intervallic exactitude. Her response to Eboli's confession of adultery is royal indeed—how subtly she suggests the distance now imposed between them. Verdi treats his queen parsimoniously until the final act, but there he makes amends in a big way. Kabaivanska delivers a magisterial 'Tu che le vanità.' Her control of the difficult piece is complete. Is it not heartening to hear an artist of musical integrity and dramatic subtlety who knows to the nth degree her capabilities, understands her voice's weaknesses as well as its strengths, and cagily manipulates the former and proudly exploits the latter to the full in challenging moments? She sculpts the opening phrases with authority, and floats the contrasted arched phrases ('s'ancor si piange in cielo') with ease, capping them with angelic *pianissimo*s. The middle-section reverie on her homeland is a touch less effective, but no less thoughtfully plotted; and the climactic 'il pianto mio porta al trono del Signor' is spaciously declaimed with an unexpected plenitude of voice. The concluding low phrase, cruelly set by Verdi in the soprano *passaggio*, is tonally scratchy, but unlike many a soprano in this troublesome moment, Kabaivanska knows how to control it. After eleven consecutive seasons (but a limited number of performances), the soprano is absent from the Met after the 1972–73 season. Regrettably, we hear her no more on the broadcasts until 1979 when she returns to sing Tatiana in *Eugen Onegin*.

Now let us all praise Franco Corelli! The opera is hardly a tenor vehicle, but on this afternoon Corelli fills the role with such abundant, glorious tone that he deserves our salutations. Nor is his musical honesty and dramatic commitment of inferior quality. Of course, he will spend tone where the composer asks for containment—that blemish we must simply accept (and willingly, in the face of his other assets). And a few moments of ensemble intransigence (mostly where he and Merrill go their own ways at cadences) are wretched sores on their superb vocalism. He does offer a few of his patented *diminuendo*s, but I value more the sweep and molded curve of his phrasing. When Corelli as lover pleads his cause, he surely should conquer. But opera devotees know that justice is not often on the side of lovers. From the first, he is in splendid, free voice. On this afternoon we seldom hear that intrusive (and frequently deplored) scoop between intervals—he vaults to high notes with uncommon assurance. The tenor appears to be fully aware of his exalted vocal state on this afternoon, for he sings with confident abandon in the most difficult passages. At the end of the court duet with Elisabetta he tops the concluding phrase with a brilliant, and tonally luxuriant, high B-flat (the note increasing in amplitude and vibrancy—an effect remarkable even for him). The duet at the cloister of St. Just is so woefully cut in these Met performances that neither soprano nor tenor has an opportunity to weave the spell that the opera's conclusion demands. Still, Kabaivanska molds 'I fior del paradiso a lui sorrideranno!' so exquisitely that paradise is sure to smile on this Carlo—and deservedly so, for Corelli phrases as expertly as she does. Her quiet, elegant manner (the tone a shade more metallic than earlier, but fragrant on a *pianissimo* high B) is apposite for the situation, and the tenor, while naturally more assertive, is noble and relatively circumspect in their sacrificial farewell. I count this outing as one of Corelli's finest performances. It serves to all but eradicate the surprise I experienced upon reading in an essay by Leinsdorf (who certainly did not suffer tenor fools in any way) his startling citation of "those two wonderful singers, Rosa Ponselle and Franco Corelli," a coupling of our man with the vocal paragon of an earlier age.[6] The broadcast of *Don Carlo* demonstrates that, even when plagued by labor troubles, the Met management can people its offerings with a half dozen artists of the first rank.

Our musical (and undoubtedly mental) health will be refreshed if we turn from the dolorous saga of the Spanish court and, crossing the channel, hasten to the airy forests of Windsor, there to savor the comic miracle of Verdi's old age. Zeffirelli's production of *Falstaff* had been a triumph at its 1964 premiere with Colzani, Tucci, Raskin, Elias, Resnik, Alva, and Sereni. The following season Bernstein's magical wand gave way to Rosenstock's dutiful hand, but the cast was more or less intact (Miller for Elias), though that season's radio audience heard Geraint Evans' Falstaff and Shirley's Fenton. On our broadcast of 16 December 1967 Raskin (Nannetta), Miller (Meg), and Alva (Fenton) hold the fort, along with the tried and true Velis, Scott, and Mariano Caruso. The first opportunity to hear the experienced Guarrera and Barbieri in their signature roles of Ford and Quickly is welcome, as is the broadcast debut of Phyllis Curtin as Alice Ford. (The season had also held the Mistress Fords of Kabaivanska and Lorengar.) Unfortunately, the podium has been rented out to Bruno Amaducci, who though conducting his tenth (and final) Falstaff with the company, contents himself with beating time. The broadcast may be the end of the run, but it sounds decidedly unrehearsed. Evidently deeming speed a conductor's only virtue, the Trieste conductor galumphs through the score at a Toscanini pace while supplying little, if any, of that titan's witchery. Amaducci soon is dispatched to his home theater in Graz. But a masterwork that deserves to be placed in the most practiced and responsive hands has suffered grievous damage. Provoked by a "bad" 1899 *Falstaff* performance, Verdi himself reckoned that the "calamity of the prima donna" of his younger days was preferable to the current "tyranny of the conductors."[7] Add incompetence to time-beater tyranny and Verdi's preferred abuse is the hands-down choice.

The character roles are well done, with Velis's sure-footed Bardolfo outdistancing his crony Scott's Pistola and Caruso's physician. Miller's instrument lacks its former delectable sheen, but she provides able support. Barbieri by now has half an instrument at her service, and it is the better half (at least for Quickly's duties). Her 'Reverenza's have the requisite chesty thrust, and she plays with genuine comic spirit. Nor does she allow a singer's gluttony to trick her into excesses in a part that Verdi himself had furbished with sufficient opportunities for display. At this stage of her career, she treats her upper voice gingerly—her tone always narrowed as it ascends—but knows how to manage it without embarrassment. Verdi sets the action a-boil in the basket scene of the second act and Barbieri (brandishing her description of the visit to Falstaff) and Guarrera (anchoring the scrappy finale) do the heavy lifting. Even more than Quickly's traditional boffo lines, I like best the mezzo's quiet, subtle turning of 'Amor, ama il mistero' where Quickly must convince the basket case Falstaff that the Herne Oak disguise is essential. The Falstaff appearances marked the Italian mezzo's return to the company following a ten-year absence. In later years, the revenant, an old-Met Amneris and Eboli, would execute many a delectable character turn at the new Met.

Guarrera, now in his twentieth season with the company, had taken on the role of Ford in the first month of the Zeffirelli production. More than any other

Falstaff
16 December 1967
Alice
Phyllis Curtin
Nannetta
Judith Raskin
Quickly
Fedora Barbieri
Fenton
Luigi Alva
Falstaff
Ezio Flagello
Ford
Frank Guarrera
Conductor
Bruno Amaducci

stage participant (although Barbieri and Raskin are in the running as well), he seems at home in the skin of his character. Not an iota of Verdi's intricate musical realization of Boito's text escapes his notice. And he is in good vocal form, the tone far from plump, but pleasant, and the vocal gestures abundant; in particular, he jousts with Falstaff in their second-act duet with uncommon finesse. His moves are so often light of foot. One instance of his skill is the unction, the secret delight of his succulent pretasting of his extravagant hopes for Falstaff's conquest of Alice ('chiedo che conquistiate Alice!'). Of course, if one hopes for a grand, luscious voicing of Ford's blockbuster aria, disappointment inevitably sets in. Experience and artistry will out, however. Guarrera acts out the text, utilizing key words for realistic effects—and it works. Ford's frenzy at the prospect of being cuckolded leaps out of the airwaves. Moreover, his top notes are secure. Alva's instrument, too, is short of sensuous appeal and, more than a jealous husband, a young lover really should stock Cupid's quiver with dulcet tone. Confidence can, in part, take its place and Alva has that in abundance. Suiting the action to his instrument's character, Alva forswears the languid pose, and portrays a spunky suitor (but one whose traversal of the *passaggio* thins into falsetto in the aria's curved ascent).

Raskin is a delectable Nannetta, her phrases neatly nuanced and traced with piquant, lucent tone. (A momentary reminiscence of Elisabeth Schumann's feathery manner unwillingly is summoned.) One or two top tones wear a slightly harder edge than in her earlier broadcasts, but her charm, vocal and dramatic, is intact. Every utterance is sugarcoated, but the result seems so natural that the soubrette's cotton candy excess is avoided. Indeed, she sends off 'Sul fil d'un soffio etesio' with a joyous thrust, rather than a wispy reticence. Lovely as it is, I wonder if more serenity (that is, less nuance) at the aria's close might suit the mood better. Probably Raskin's keen musical intelligence can't go that route. This is the last time we will hear her on the broadcasts (she would remain with the company until 1972). Early death would claim this delightful artist in 1984.

American soprano Curtin had been more a fixture, and a bright one, at the New York City Opera than the Met. There she had shone in roles as disparate as Violetta, Cressida, and Salome, and she also had an important creator credit as Carlisle Floyd's *Susannah*. Prominent European stages enjoyed her company. She had appeared in the old house for a pair of Fiordiligis in 1961, but reappeared only now in the 1966–67 season as Mistress Ford. The role of the frolicsome wife does not show off her best qualities (pictorially, it probably did). Much of Alice's music skitters along at a fast pace and Curtin's tone, like that of many clear-voiced sopranos, turns a touch acrid when bouncing over Verdi's fleet lines. Of course, she is meticulous in her reading of the part—seldom have Alice's pointed staccatos been more faithfully clipped or precisely pitched. If Verdi wants her to *portamento la voce*, she dutifully carries the tone to the next phrase (an obligation not always observed by Alices of greater repute). She executes the flourish up to the high B ('la giuliva brigata' in act three) with aplomb and exactitude. Yet the overall impression of her portrayal is not quite prepossessing. Even 'Gaje comari di Vindsor,' where most Alices manage to project the allure that makes the character a plausible target for seduction, is deficient in charm. After all, Alice is a merry wife, not a spiteful spouse. Curtin does find ways to animate her character with a number of zestful touches. An odd, but highly effective, one is the barbed aural slap she applies to Ford in act three as she cautions him against his ferocious jealousy ('Quella mania feroce'). Verdi marked the first portion *forte*, but thereafter asks for *leggero pianissimo* in most of the phrase—Curtin chooses to maintain the ferocity and drive home the message. We always knew this American soprano had a mind of her own.

Flagello's Falstaff was not an unknown quantity, for he had undertaken the leading role back in the 1964 run. The physiognomy of the part suited him, although as a true bass, and moreover, one of the *cantante* tribe, he might be expected to find its range and sprightliness a challenge. The range is no problem. Oh, yes, he fudges on the mezza voce high F-sharp ('Martino'), interrupting its flow with a few 'hee-hee's, but thereafter manages a fine high G and clears the remaining high hurdles with ease. During the first act, he does appear somewhat discomfited by Amaducci's heavy foot on the accelerator, and, in truth, he is more concerned with getting the notes out than creating a character. Decidedly, more variety of volume and nuance is needed if we are to recognize the knight's curious mix of comic spirit and inherent integrity. In particular, one expected he would better relish the few legato phrases that flavor the part. Still, the honor monologue is well done, large and succulent of tone and sufficiently grand of spirit. There, and in the remaining acts, the full beauty of the voice, its warm, round poundage, is a thing to be appreciated for itself. That he can color tone to suit the text is apparent in his subtle molding of the phrase in which he assures Fontana/Ford that he shall soon possess Alice ('la moglie di Ford possederete'). But he neglects too many of the interpretive touches that Verdi has provided. The composer surely wanted not just Falstaff's paunch, but his character as well, to be filled out. While the bulk of 'T'imagino fregata del mio stemma,' well stocked as it is with filigree and even a frequently ignored trill, probably has never been better sung, or more richly voiced, on the broadcasts since Warren's palmy days, Verdi's *dolciss. con grazia* instruction for 'Ogni più bel gioiel mi nuoce' goes by the board. 'Quand'ero paggio' is game enough, without fully honoring the composer's *leggerissimo* marking. The monologue that opens act three brings Flagello into home territory and he roams it with security, dispensing opulent tone at will. We ought to feel for the humiliated Falstaff at this moment; Flagello can't make us do that, but we do rejoice in the knight's elemental hedonism, just as this basso cherishes his fat instrument. It is gratifying to hear the role really sung for a change, although, in the end, we don't know Falstaff as well as we would like.

The Verdi operas' chronology has dictated the order of this chapter thus far. For its close, however, I turn back to a middle-period opera in which the composer contrived a novel blend of light and dark, in contrast to the unrelieved somber palette of *Don Carlo* and *Falstaff*'s uninhibited caprice. One never knows whether one will land in Boston or Sweden when the curtain goes up on *Un Ballo in Maschera*. The gloom quotient varies with the terrain. Met productions during the mid-century decades forswore Boston in favor of Scribe's original libretto setting. Of course, it is French musical manners that leaven the political intrigue (and the Italian romantic grandeur) of this inherently buoyant work. Not that buoyancy receives its due on the broadcast of 30 January 1971. But cause for celebration remains, for the broadcast introduces us to the young Plácido Domingo, who would figure so largely in the Met's plans for several decades. A peculiar satisfaction accrues from ending a chapter with a beginning, especially one that is so auspicious.

Molinari-Pradelli had conducted the seasonal première and all performances until the broadcast. Though listed in *Opera News*, he is replaced by Cleva. Strange

Un Ballo in Maschera
30 January 1971
Amelia
Martina Arroyo
Oscar
Roberta Peters
Ulrica
Mignon Dunn
Riccardo
Plácido Domingo
Renato
Robert Merrill
Sam
Paul Plishka
Conductor
Francesco Molinari-Pradelli

METROPOLITAN OPERA

SEASON 1970 — 1971   **LINCOLN CENTER PLAZA**

Saturday Afternoon, January 30, 1971, at 2:00

SUBSCRIPTION PERFORMANCE

GIUSEPPE VERDI

Un Ballo in Maschera

Opera in three acts   Libretto by Antonio Somma
After Scribe's play, "Gustave III, or Le bal masqué"
Conductor: Fausto Cleva
Production by Günther Rennert
Sets and costumes designed by Ita Maximowna
Supervisory Designer: Wolfgang Roth
Stage Director: Henry Butler

Gustaf III, King of Sweden (Riccardo)	Placido Domingo
Captain Anckarström (Renato)	Robert Merrill
Amelia, his wife	Martina Arroyo
Count de Horn (Samuel)	Paul Plishka
Count Warting (Tom)	Andrij Dobriansky
Ulrica Arfvidsson, a fortune teller	Mignon Dunn
Oscar, the King's page	Roberta Peters
Christiano (Silvano)	Russell Christopher
The Chief Justice	Leo Goeke
Amelia's servant	Gabor Carelli

Choreographed by Thomas Andrew
Maralyn Miles, Jeremy Ives, Jacques Cesbron and Corps de Ballet
Chorus Master: Kurt Adler
Musical Preparation: Louise Sherman

This production of UN BALLO IN MASCHERA *was made
possible by a generous and deeply appreciated gift
from Mrs. John D. Rockefeller, Jr.*

KNABE PIANO USED EXCLUSIVELY

*The audience is respectfully, but urgently, requested
not to interrupt the music with applause*

THIS PERFORMANCE WILL END AT APPROXIMATELY 5:10

Program for broadcast of *Un Ballo in Maschera* on 30 January 1971.

as it seems, that long-term maestro had never conducted the opera at the Met. Whether for that reason or due to a preference for lyricism over dramatic vitality, Cleva's presentation is governed by excessive caution. Hence, the work's essential and much-anticipated élan is in short supply. (To be fair, the caution may be merely Molinari-Pradelli's residue.) Still, lyricism in itself is a virtue, and Cleva has under his charge a group of singers worthy of Verdi's craftsmanship. Consider the wealth of the casting riches of the Met in that era. Three quality performances of the maestro's more demanding works received broadcast performances with only a single duplication of principals: *Boccanegra* with Tucci, Shirley, MacNeil, Milnes, and Hines; *Don Carlo* with Kabaivanska, Bumbry, Corelli, Merrill, and Tozzi; and *Ballo* with Arroyo, Peters, Dunn, Domingo, Merrill, and Plishka. Moreover, between the premiere and the broadcast, the *Ballo* ranks had included Caballé, Grist, Dalis, Chookasian, Rankin, Bergonzi, Tucker, Franco Tagliavini, Sereni, and Milnes. O happy days!

The *Ballo* crew provides a felicitous mix of characterizations old and new. Peters and Merrill have played Oscar and Renato in many an earlier broadcast. The soprano is not only tried but always true in this chipper role and so she is today. As the page is buoyancy purveyor number one, the role requires the crispest delivery of his/her music and Peters nimbly skitters over its blithe terrain, her coloratura ever on the mark. All Oscars tend to sound alike, as though they have just sharpened their voices on a whetstone; not so Peters, whose warmly timbred middle voice makes her page a welcome presence. In the forties, Warren had squatter's rights on Renato (four broadcasts), but after an unfortunate episode with Josef Metternich, the airwaves received with gratitude six consecutive Merrill turns with the role. Today's broadcast brings the tally to a week's compass—a remarkable testimony to the satisfaction he often provided in the role. On a few of those broadcasts I have decried his insensitive treatment of the unhappy husband's 'dolcezze perdute,' but on that front there is good news today. Even for one who invariably has command of his luxuriantly seasoned instrument, the baritone is in particularly fine voice. And stylistic crudities (those aggravating huffs and puffs that served as substitutes for tones) once again are banished. The top notes are as secure and broadly beamed as in his palmier days. And he has expanded his interpretive palette: dialogues with Oscar are fleet and pointed; castigations of Amelia have a nasty overlay on that inherently warm tone. Could it be that, in this, the last decade of his Met career, the baritone's latent competitive genes have been stimulated by poachers MacNeil and Milnes? Whatever the cause of this late-blooming artistry, it has a salutary result on his performance and is gratifying to his listeners. The demanding recitative that precedes 'Eri tu' is grandly voiced and dramatically potent. In the aria, he can be a bit negligent of rhythmic niceties and he *will* move the piece along at the expense of expansive phrasing. But grandeur resides in his tone itself so the moment speaks powerfully. As for the 'dolcezze perdute,' the sufferings of Renato's sweet loss are signaled by a welcome (doubly so, since infrequent in his arsenal) diminuendo at the end of the preceding section. One cannot say that Merrill applies a gentle caress to the husband's longings, but he acknowledges the mood change and the previously bruised phrases at least emerge unmaimed—a capital improvement. A rousing finish brings him reward from his public, even as he has rewarded them with his prize vocal gift.

Although by no means so familiar as our Oscar and Renato, Dunn's Ulrica had been heard on the 1966 broadcast and her secure reading of this troublesome role is again much appreciated. Her voice owns a Castagna-like timbre, its density, napped surface, and warmth consistent throughout an extensive range. Thus, she can negotiate the highs and lows of 'Re dell'abisso' with ease and to equal effect. Dunn is probably the most cultivated seeress who ever told a fortune—but let us not hold her musicality against her. After all, Ulrica's clientele includes the court's own. Plishka's Samuel is a new broadcast characterization and he, along with brother conspirator Andrij Dobriansky, dispatches its minimal, but strategic, tasks effectively. He may be a bit short on irony, but, like Dunn, he is musically alert. Specifically, he crushes a mean acciaccatura, essential for the aristocratic nonchalance of 'Ve' se di notte.'

Arroyo has been applauded in many Verdi roles, but her Amelia is new to the airwaves (it had entered her Met repertory in 1968). She, too, is in marvelous vocal form. Indeed, the voice is fully matured, entirely secure throughout its range and owning sufficient puissance to meet the challenges of this notably heavy soprano role. She has that tendency to sing notes rather than phrases when moving in the lower range. Words, either for their rhythmic patterns or self-contained musical sounds, do not usually command her interest; thus her singing can seem too objective to summon response. Character portrayal suffers as well. Having litanied deficiencies, I revel in the sheer beauty of her vocalism—especially in the upper range. Such perfect control of that terrifying region guarantees a listener's comfort; and her fluent tone, soft or loud, exquisitely colored and confidently poised, deserves to be prized without wringing of critical hands. Almost no other soprano in broadcast history has negotiated the heath aria with comparable security and vocal richness. A touch of terror in the middle section is a boon—elsewhere she seems as unconcerned with Amelia's desperate condition and the gibbet-haunted heath as she is untroubled by the technical difficulties of this voice-breaking aria. To her credit (and it is a distinction rarely assigned to her soprano colleagues), she negotiates the treacherous high C magisterially and without sham. Cleva hampers the singers in the grand duet—the ecstasy level hovers below the boiling point (though Domingo works diligently to raise it). But both soprano and tenor fill it with beautiful vocalism. At the scene's end, she suspends a few of her willowy *pianissimo*s *in alt* over the charged dialogue of husband and conspirators and thereby receives our attention and gains our gratitude. The Met performs Verdi's act two and the third-act opening scene without intermission; thus Amelia's aria follows hard upon the soprano's strenuous duty on the heath. Arroyo's 'Morrò, ma prima in grazia' suffers from a lack of innerness, of concentrated mood, so that what should be the emotional climax of the role is slighted. Unlike many Met sopranos of old, Arroyo does sing the cadenza—and very well, of course.

Mr. Domingo's career is so well known that only a few descriptive phrases of its pre-Met stages are here recounted. Born in Madrid in 1941, he came to Mexico in 1950, made his debut as a baritone in a 1957 zarzuela, and after a tenor conversion (Alfredo in 1961) performed in Dallas, and thereafter spent three years with the Israeli National Opera. The New York City Opera claimed him in 1965 and the road to the Met was open before him. A preliminary concert appearance with Met forces at Lewisohn Stadium in 1966 preceded his 1968 house debut as Maurizio. How instructive to note that in that concert offering he sang both Turiddu and Canio, a prophetic indication of his legendary endurance capacity and repertory breadth. Indeed, the tenor's indefatigable quest after new roles and repertory stylistic challenges in the coming period of his "all-purposeness" calls to mind Berlioz's purported comment on the still young Saint-Saëns, namely, that the only thing he lacked was inexperience. Riccardo is not Domingo's broadcast debut—he had appeared as Cavaradossi in 1969 and Calàf in 1970, both of which we will explore in the Puccini chapter that follows. I think it not amiss to first take his measure, to feel his youthful pulse, in the testing role of Riccardo. Will he be up to its manifold challenges at this early stage of his career?

Though hardly in the first blush of youth (he had turned thirty a week before the broadcast), Domingo offers a leaner tone than is in the collective ear at, say, the millennium. Its compact makeup, its pointed focus, allow him to move with alacrity over the varied terrain that Verdi's monarch so joyously and infectiously inhabits. The timbre is recognizably his, but its glint is stronger, its surface marginally less supple, less responsive to the touch, as it were (few dollops of that radiant softness that he has in reserve). From the first his has been an archetypal voice, an instrument whose pivotal possibilities will allow expansion into repertory realms that would be denied to tenors of greater timbral individuality. It is a question of centrality, rather than neutrality, of timbre. And his command of the instrument is superb; vocal technique is his cunning accomplice, as it would be in sustaining a long, and in some ways punishing, career path. High notes are his, though they do not quite have that tenorial ping, that thrust or bloom, that sets auditors ablaze. Throughout this lengthy role, whether moving high or low, turning agile or dramatic, acting frivolous or romantic, Domingo meets all challenges head on and never falters. As for musicianship, he is a conductor's dream.

Though often justly accused of purveying musical and character generalities, he is quite specific in suggesting Riccardo's varied moods. His interpretive choices are apt and his response to situation is acute. He applies an elegant swagger to the introductory 'La rivedrà nell'estasi,' molding its phrases to fine effect, and he is rhythmically exact in the infectious stretta that concludes the first scene. Is Domingo as monarch actually having fun? Not entirely. A touch of the serious, the need to be "correct" lingers in frolicsome moments. One senses it in the delicious sailor's canzone at Ulrica's den; still, his reading holds some light touches as well and is as fleet as Cleva's relaxed hand will allow. The bulk of the piece lies within the staff and there Domingo's instrument is most potent, its timbre warmer and more enveloping than when flying high. He adds a long, rather nervous laugh to the orchestral introduction to the quintet and fills its measures with realistic scoffing—this monarch is highly amused and this tenor is scrupulously exact. In Domingo's reading, the king's personality is sharply etched. The tenor's musicality must be particularly prized in the concluding moments of the canzone: he subtly alters tone and volume to mark harmonic changes; his accommodating diminuendo at the cadence enhances ensemble blend and signals the artistic integrity that we will value over the decades.

Ideally, the duet demands a tenor with more steel in the timbre than Domingo possesses; those grandly arched phrases are heroic and his voice is a touch slender for this serious iron pumping. Nevertheless, he is an ardent lover, his rhythmic impulses are vivid, and, like a billiards shark, he knows how to apply enough English to a note sequence so that the raging vitality of the duet hits home. At its close, he and Arroyo send up a brief (and on his part, taut but secure) high C as modest evidence of their passion. Alone in the king's cabinet, Domingo confirms his stature with a vibrant voicing of 'Ma se m'è forza perderti,' an aria that has caused tenors of even greater resources not only regret, but reason for omission. He draws a grand line in several dramatic phrases of the opening recitative, but here and there also allows timbral pith to mellow into a softer caress. No reticence mars his heart's outpouring as he renounces Amelia. Unlike Bergonzi, he does observe the diminuendo at 'come se fosse l'ultima,' thereby reinforcing Verdi's modulation. The peroration phrase is confidently thrown out. At the ball, one hoped to hear more suppliance in the tone, a Gigli-like sweetness, to complement Riccardo's generosity toward his enemies. Domingo's well-studied farewell is marked by a discreet efficiency. In a markedly accomplished portrayal, this royal tenor takes even death in his stride.

Probably management and audience were not quite aware that a new era had begun. The publicity machines had not yet moved into high gear. Pavarotti, though on hand in 1968–69 and 1971–72, would not come to the broadcast series until 1973. In the meantime, Domingo, while staking a valid claim, was hardly the only candidate in the tenor sweepstakes. Corelli, Bergonzi, Gedda, McCracken, and Vickers were in their prime, Kónya was still on the scene, Kraus had entered the fray, and Tucker was enjoying autumnal fair weather. No need to limit the number of tenor princes, let alone enthrone a king.

Plácido Domingo as Cavaradossi in *Tosca*. Photography by James Heffernan. Courtesy Metropolitan Opera Archives.

CHAPTER SEVEN

Puccini—The Real Thing

From the first, Plácido Domingo seemed fated to be the minute man of opera. His house debut had occurred with less than an hour's notice when Corelli canceled his appearance as Maurizio in *Adriana Lecouvreur* at 7:20 P.M. on 28 September 1968, four days before Domingo's scheduled Met debut in the same role. Uncharacteristically, the normally colleague-friendly tenor told Bing that he believed "Corelli has canceled on purpose" in the hope that the new tenor would be "tired from having sung three operas [*Tabarro* and *Pagliacci* at the City Center and a Met *Turandot* rehearsal] in the last seventy-two hours."[1] Similar circumstances affected his broadcast debut. This time Corelli's father was ill and understandably he had absented himself from *Trovatore* rehearsals and canceled his appearance in the broadcast *Tosca* of 15 February 1969. Kónya was scheduled to replace him, but at the last moment he canceled. A few minutes before the broadcast, Domingo happened to be in Bing's office discussing taking over Corelli's *Trovatore* appearances later in the season when Kónya's indisposition was reported to the general manager. Domingo immediately was pressed into service.[2] By now the tenor wore not only the minute man's rescue hat, but was clearly Bing's man of the hour.

An almost new slate complements Nilsson's second broadcast Tosca. In addition to Domingo, Dooley sings Scarpia, and Plishka is the Sacristan, with fresh radio assignments for Sgarro (Angelotti), Goodloe (Jailer), Kris Kalfayan (Shepherd), and conductor George Schick. Velis, happy in his built-in timbral servility, repeats his Spoletta.

Any young tenor, whether precipitously thrust onstage or not, would find partnering Nilsson a formidable task, and in a few climactic moments where their two voices join (notably, the third-act unison celebration of triumph), the soprano blankets Domingo's respectable effort. "Effortful" describes a few other moments as well where Puccini has clothed his painter in heroic vocal garb. In the church, Domingo prepares the top note of Cavaradossi's baleful description of Scarpia with an upward slide (but not before the lower regions' dark timbre is skillfully employed); similarly, the Marengo victory cries, while firm and securely maintained, demand not only his sound technique, but a grander tonal base. We learn early that this tenor is performance committed, willing to spend a bit of his vocal capital when demands exceed nature's bounty. Not without reason have tenors of a more robust cast found Cavaradossi a congenial role. And yet the painter is

Tosca
15 February 1969

Tosca
Birgit Nilsson
Cavaradossi
Plácido Domingo
Scarpia
William Dooley
Sacristan
Paul Plishka
Conductor
George Schick

153

a dreamer, as an artist should be, and the composer has emphasized that posture when his hero muses on the stars and, later, as he lovingly apostrophizes the gentle hands of the murderess. At this stage of his career, Domingo falls between two stools, not necessarily an unwelcome landing site, as his lengthy career demonstrates. I noted in recounting the *Ballo* broadcast that he is a centrist tenor and one who serves both modes exceedingly well without quite filling either to the brim. On the plus side, that centrality has the virtue of limiting the danger of a spillover into vulgarity. Any pangs of regret over Corelli's absence must have evaporated when Domingo asked for his painting tools, so beautifully colored is his tone and redolent his diction. One is immediately struck by the velvety caress that he applies to the opening phrases of 'Recondita armonia.' The voice, owning an initial nasal blend, shaves off density as the altitude increases. But, unlike the rather tight top notes of his later career, this high B-flat blooms, cherishing a slight vibrato. In Cavaradossi's difficult duet peroration, after luxuriantly molding the 'quegli occhi' opening, he adapts his placement to travel the climactic circle with delightfully free, heady tone. If the dreamy opening mood of 'E lucevan le stelle' eludes him (too heavily accented), he does sing softly and the assist from an atmospheric clarinet solo helps. One splendidly controlled long phrase ratifies his command of breath, even as the usual sobbed close confirms his membership in the tenor union. 'O dolci mani' is excessively wordy (and here 'dolci' should govern the mood), but again his instinct (more properly, his musicianship) is sound as he moves between the dynamic extremes. These few quibbles cannot diminish the tenor's achievement in his broadcast debut. When he launches the soaring phrases that close the church duet, he leaves no doubt of present accomplishment and future stature. Further confirmation of Domingo's willingness to serve as the opera world's workhorse comes when Cross announces that (as previously scheduled) the tenor will sing the first act of *Butterfly* in the gala benefit that evening. In his memoir, Domingo tells us that during the *Tosca* second-act offstage torture scene, Bing (so often described as aloof) held a glass of water for him.[3] Could there be more positive evidence of a manager's gratitude? I offer mine as well.

Plishka performs the Sacristan's duties with appropriate devotion and fine tone. He is too solid a singer and responsible an artist to need to rely on the traditional buffo tricks that he employs (that vocal hiccup is overly obvious). Sgarro, impressed into service for the scheduled Harvuot, fails to give Angelotti either the anguish of the escaped prisoner or the firm thrust of tone that would make his revolutionary creed believable. Boy soprano Kris Kalfayan delivers an evocative shepherd's chant, a neat feat for a twelve-year-old on the grand stage.

As Scarpia, William Dooley delivers the most fully conceived and masterfully executed characterization of the afternoon. If his vocal size is a notch below the norm for the role (so critics would have us believe in similar assignments), that limitation is of no moment in the radio format. Met management evidently did not accept the validity of that stricture for they cast him repeatedly in roles demanding major vocal resources: Mandryka, Amonasro, the *Hoffmann* villains, the Dutchman, and even a single, and quite arbitrary, Grand Inquisitor. The explanation for this seemingly odd roster of commanding roles lies in Dooley's sterling abilities as a singing actor. In commenting on his earlier broadcasts, I have noted with particular pleasure the airy freshness of his Gerhard Hüsch–like timbre. On this afternoon, maturity (or is it merely recognition of the role's requirements) allows him, when needed, to call up a darker, burlier (and thus less heady) timbre; its deadened resonance well suggests the bully component in Scarpia's makeup. But what an illuminating array of vocal colors (including delectable head tone where warranted) and textual inflections he summons to paint a full portrait of the Roman police chief. The brute's volatility is the preeminent feature of his multifaceted characterization. And brute his Scarpia is, though he can turn on the charm, the aristocratic posture, the flâneur's composed detachment, at will. Even there, mockery lurks just below the surface.

Dooley makes a stunning entrance into Sant'Andrea della Valle (the composer has marked it 'con autorità'), bellowing his chastisement of the mischief makers in tones both pompous and reeking of sham horror. Throughout the afternoon, one can define his body stance, his facial expressions, from voice and text alone. Occasionally, his facility traps him into excess, as when he magnifies a pause between syllables ('cada—vere,' twisting the second half with a vocal sneer) or utters a shuddering 'Ebbene' as he awaits Tosca's capitulation. The vocal challenges are well met, with moments of appetizingly lyrical legato; in truth, it cannot match Warren's remembered unction as, for instance, Scarpia deplores the interruption of his little supper. A last meal ought to be savored, and Dooley not only makes a meal of the entire role but savors it to the hilt, a hilt whose blade, in Tosca's hand, quite opportunely, does him in.

Miss Nilsson wields her knife with the fervor of one to whom warrior deeds are second nature. Tosca had been an early entry (1962) on her Met list and the management rewarded her company fealty with a new production of the opera (premiere 4 October 1968). The role, coveted by sopranos of varied stripes, has proved impervious to their sometimes unidiomatic assaults. Our Swedish soprano holds in spades a prime requisite for the Roman diva's second-act shenanigans, that is, vocal size. For the more lyrical, intimate moments, she must refine her instrument down to a narrower compass with occasional loss of timbral character. My overall impression is of a handsome woman wearing an unflattering garment. And the color of the raiment is wrong for her. One could, if one wanted to indulge in that kind of thing, consider Tosca's timbral color to be florid, and though Nilsson wears a red gown in Scarpia's chambers, her vocal complexion is considerably cooler. Shining blue and silver, her natural aural hues, are becoming to her—after all, they are the colors of the Swedish flag. Of course, she is an artist of great integrity, intent on serving the composer. Often she succeeds. 'Vissi d'arte' is quite beguiling, sung for the most part in attractive, quiet tones that enhance the introspective mood; by this time in the opera the voice's character, though still contained, is silkier and lovely to hear. Far from a grand or emotive reading, the aria is tenderly delivered and the usual theatrics avoided in the closing phrase. At the curtain call, Cross rather inelegantly describes her as having sung the aria while "lying flat on her stomach on the floor." Somehow, it seemed more glamorous when Jeritza did it. Fortunately, the audience recognizes Nilsson's quality and gives her a thunderous, lengthy response.

The remaining focal moments of the role are less satisfying. For one thing, Schick hurries her through many a phrase, especially in the church duet. (In general, the conductor moves the opera along, hardly bothering to linger over a succulent Puccini curve. One can perhaps be grateful for his eschewal of the Grand Guignol effects on which some conductors have overdosed. Yet he seems to have little concern for motivic shape or atmospheric aura, failing to reveal to us the "mobile, kaleidoscopic" milieu in which the composer himself gloried and to which a somewhat reluctant critic reacted favorably at the 1900 premiere of the opera.[4] The 1968–69 season will be the last of his eleven seasons with the company.) A few Nilsson solutions to technically difficult passages attract attention. In the duet test phrase ('le voce delle cose'), the top two-note slurs are circumvented with what comes off as almost a yapping laugh. And, as the duet's final moments demonstrate, coquetry is not her forte. (But don't we know how delightfully playful she can be in real life!) Sometimes her tone sounds downright scratchy in the middle and mid-low voice. On the other hand, a number of phrases ('inebbr'il cor,' for one, and the weeping exit phrase after Scarpia's taunt, for another) are beautifully shaped and tonally coddled. In contrast, her employment of chest voice is effective as she encourages Scarpia's demise. (She observes the composer's setting of 'E avanti a lui tremava tutta Roma,' singing it in a low partial chest mix monotone.) What a sense of release Nilsson must feel as she allows her heroic voice greater sway when describing the murder to her lover. Quite unnecessarily, she robs the knife-plunging phrase of its grandeur by hurrying the ascent, but a long-held top note and chesty close make up the difference. In response to Cavaradossi's sweet praise, Nilsson offers quiet, but somewhat glassy, tone and, while her manner is commendably affectionate, the slithery legato proves disaffecting. Too often she neglects the word's own music. As to pitch, only at the tail end of the unison conclusion to the lovers' duet does she sharp a bit; Domingo saves the day by rigorously adhering to the pitch. Elsewhere, she is on the mark throughout the entire performance. An unusual feature of her interpretation is the added little scream that she vouchsafes after 'Avanti a Dio!'. Could it be that all her fearless play on the *Walküre*'s rocky ridges was insufficient on-the-job training to alleviate concern over the leap from Sant'Angelo's ramparts? Quite unlikely, for a brave Swedish farm girl.

The opportunity to hear a great artist in roles outside her Fach is always intriguing—more than that, welcome. One admires Nilsson's venturesomeness and often savors her honorable survival in a foreign realm. A benefice of her Tosca is the primal thrill of a singer equipped to triumphantly scale the heights and surmount orchestral surges; often those moments have caused discomfort to more idiomatic interpreters, but when Nilsson sings, the barriers are down. In evaluating a Nilsson performance one must remember that, even as Dooley is helped by the microphone's magnanimity, what is his gain is Nilsson's loss. In the theater, her voice (as I and so many of her devotees have remarked) was a far more satisfying, indeed, electrifying, instrument than either recordings or radio were able to capture. But it is only the radio broadcast with which we here must contend and, most often, relish.

Moving ahead a year, we can enjoy Nilsson and Domingo once again, this time in *Turandot*, an opera where her renown is unquestioned. The challenge of Calàf may not mate quite so well with our Spaniard's youthful talent and lyrical bent. Amara's Liù holds more than promise, for the role admirably suits her gifts. Add in Giaiotti's familiar Timur and Uppman's Ping and the afternoon (21 February 1970) welcomes us. Chorus master Kurt Adler had conducted the 1962 broadcast and returns to shepherd his charges through the opera's thicket of massed forces. And for the most part, he makes a decent job of it, though he fails to give

Turandot
21 February 1970
Turandot
Birgit Nilsson
Liù
Lucine Amara
Calàf
Plácido Domingo
Ping
Theodor Uppman
Timur
Giaiotti
Conductor
Kurt Adler

its often craggy contours a distinctive musical character. The emphasis in the first act is primarily choral and Adler's group performs with adequate tonal impact and greater precision than was sometimes the case during his lengthy tenure. He prefers to keep the opera moving along, rather than strive for Mitropoulos-like cumulative effects—Puccini has probably built in sufficient grandeur to permit the work to be merely played rather than puffed. A slight loosening of tension affects the other two acts, but the principals take up the slack in no uncertain manner.

Corelli has seemed the made-to-order Calàf since he knocked the role out of the ballpark in the 1961 premiere and repeated the feat in three broadcasts. Yet the composer was evidently of two minds about his single-minded prince, for he had approached both sweet-toned Beniamino Gigli and leathery-lunged Giacomo Lauri-Volpi before the La Scala premiere.[5] Animosity between Met manager Gatti-Casazza and Toscanini prevented both Met tenors from undertaking the role, so Miguel Fleta, a tenor tending more toward the Corelli mode, gained the prize. Domingo, heard here in his second season, would rarely sing the role during the first half of his Met career (only three performances in his initial fifteen seasons) but would take it up again during the mid-eighties. The role holds moments where stout lungs are indeed the prime requisite; Domingo is ever game in that department, but visceral thrills à la Corelli are not really his province. Nevertheless, on this afternoon, except for the first-act close and a few orchestrally mighty phrases in the final act, he more than holds his own. And ardor is his valuable aid. More to the point than weight of voice is the remarkable beauty of the voice during these early years. At the curtain's rise, the mere sound of the voice, dark and velvety, is enough to qualify him as a winner, riddles or no riddles. His top notes throughout the afternoon are easily attained and beautifully colored (even the high Bs are free from strain). He is responsive to textual meanings and musical subtleties, offering a few delectable diminuendos at suitable moments without drawing undue attention to them (Corelli's much-cited and welcome feats in that area can seem designed to provoke awe). Calàf's unaccompanied riddle solutions are firmly, even brilliantly delivered. When the prince offers Turandot his life if she can divine his name before dawn ('e all'alba morirò'), the tenor exquisitely softens his voice and executes one of those diminuendos; the brittle mood of the opera is altered as Domingo provides a touching, human moment (and in this opera humanity is in short supply). 'Nessun dorma' is an exemplary example of Domingo's ability to combine musical sensitivity and vocal beauty to marvelous effect; the contrast between a luxuriant 'sulla tua bocca lo dirò' and the intimate 'splenderà' is particularly striking. An unusual (for him) almost silvery timbre on the concluding high note surprises and pleases. The love duet holds a few similarly affecting moments: he sounds like love itself when he utters 'Mio fiore mattutino!' and softly caresses 'tuo manto d'argento.' Without slighting the role's inherent grandeur, Domingo makes memorable the intimate moments of Calàf's quest. At the bows, Cross this time confirms the Spaniard's ascendancy at the Met by correctly stressing the first syllable of Plácido. The tenor has arrived.

Of the remaining male members of the cast, Goodloe impresses with a firmly-voiced Mandarin; Giaiotti, a perennial broadcast Timur, is modestly involved in Liù's precarious life passage; and Robert Schmorr's dutifully quavery rendition of the Emperor's lines gives old age a bad name. Tenors Velis and Anthony are in the character mode for Pang and Pong, Anthony's distinctive twang in the higher regions by now becoming a bit disconcerting. Uppman, in an unusual casting gambit, lends stature to Ping. He forthrightly projects the weightier pronouncements; more important, his sympathetic timbre and tonal modification enhance the Grand Chancellor's little song where Ping longs for his home in Honan. Quite unexpectedly, I found Miss Amara's Liù a bit disappointing. As noted above, the role would seem to be tailored to her particular instrument and artistry, but initially and at a few critical moments later in the opera, the voice sounds small and—one hates to say it—a bit whiny. One of her loveliest resources is the float of exquisite head tone in the mid and upper range and often it may be so characterized here; yet it strikes me as overemployed, to the point of robbing the character of essential simplicity. Still, it remains an effective device to suggest pathos, and Liù lives in that realm. 'Signore, ascolta!' begins in lovely fashion and ends with the requisite floated *pianissimo* (an effective dramatic crescendo brings the note to a precipitous halt before descending into tears that turn into coughlike sobs). The death scene holds other attractive vocal effects and demonstrates her notable technical skill. The tragic and pathetic are appropriately limned and initially 'Tu che di gel sei cinta' profits from a welcome fullness of tone.

Nilsson has made the opera her own and on this afternoon, her fifth broadcast of the role, she demonstrates more persuasively than ever her right of dominion. I don't know that I have ever heard her in more resplendent voice. Of course, the voice is always resplendent, but today an unusual tonal depth throughout the entire range adds colors and warmth, indeed, a new dimension to the familiar brilliance of her instrument. The role's notorious difficulties are nonexistent for her. She revels in the high tessitura, not only striking all notes with her customary accuracy and with that characteristically keen shine, but giving them remarkable density and opulence. The middle and low voice are handled with equal surety. Interpretively, her command is convincing. As Turandot swears (after Calàf has solved the riddles) that she will never be his, the soprano utters 'No, no, non sarò tua' in tones marvelously colored and controlled, her manner vocally and dramatically resolute and yet oddly touching as she half recognizes her banishment. When the ice princess repeats 'L'amore' after Liù tells Turandot it is love that sustains her in the face of death, Nilsson, in a subtle interpretive insight, manages to suggest wonder, as though the princess had never heard the word before. The Alfano love duet (offered at the Met in aborted form) is apt fodder for her abilities and she sends out reams of glorious, solid tone, but does not neglect to sound a delicate diminuendo when telling Calàf that she has discovered the secret of his name ('So il tuo nome!'). Though grandeur is ever her portion, Nilsson, like Domingo, knows that now and then intimacy becomes her.

Management, in between Nilsson's fourth and fifth *Turandot* broadcasts, had the temerity to offer the radio public another artist in the title role. On the broadcast of 22 March 1969, German soprano Marion Lippert has the unenviable task of posing Turandot's riddles. The Met evidently felt a new lineup in the principal roles was in order, for in addition to Lippert, we hear McCracken's heroic prince, along with Arroyo as Liù and Guarrera as Ping. Giaiotti, Velis, and Anthony are in their familiar places. Mehta, who had conducted the 1966 broadcast, returns to recharge the opera's high-powered dramaturgy. And he does just that. The 1970 Adler and 1969 Mehta broadcasts exist in different worlds. The Indian sends off the opening execution motive with dispatch and right off we know we are in

Turandot
22 March 1969

Turandot
Marion Lippert
Liù
Martina Arroyo
Calàf
James McCracken
Ping
Frank Guarrera
Timur
Bonaldo Giaiotti
Conductor
Zubin Mehta

for a hectic ride. The conductor has a firm hand on the reins, however, at least those that control the orchestra—the choral attacks are often decidedly sloppy, especially in the first act. Nevertheless, the choristers are propelled along with unabated fervor—the quiet episode of the tardy moon and the Prince of Persia's cortège is less atmospheric than Adler's. Mehta takes to heart their cries of 'Fuggi, fuggi' when they advise Calàf to fly away before Turandot discovers his name—the pace is fleet indeed. When the spirit grabs him, he can't resist hotdogging in the end zone: ceremonial moments (the terminal episodes of each act, for instance) are milked for their grandeur—nothing inappropriate in that. Mehta's brio is infectious as he provides an exciting afternoon at the opera.

Mehta's brisk manner adds vitality to the antics of Ping, Pang, and Pong, who perform with dexterity and rhythmic élan. Guarrera, again theatrically astute, discharges Ping's varied tasks with a character actor's faithful devotion to verisimilitude. Often, that includes adopting the narrow tonal makeup of his tenor comrades (and this time, Anthony's tone is attractive). He always remains within the dramatic framework and his diction animates many a phrase. Ping's homeland lament is less effective from Guarrera's throat; Uppman's winning manner and more fragrant tones have the edge there.

In a number of ways, McCracken is well suited to the role of Calàf. Unlike Domingo, he has no choice but to occupy only one stool, decidedly the one marked *robusto*. Fortunately, Calàf's major challenges lie in that area. Of course, the American tenor shines in the final pages of the score as the prince celebrates his victory and revels in his love. There and in other magisterial passages, McCracken's instrument, with its broad compass, its trumpeting thrust, is a worthy combatant when he must contest with Mehta's generous orchestral outbursts. The tenor's vocal brawn, his rhythmic energy couple well with the conductor's resolute conception. He solves the riddles with tonal solidity and evident confidence in his answers. 'Vincerò' is McCracken's watchword not only in 'Nessun dorma,' but throughout the entire opera. But beyond those expected triumphs, he must be praised for voicing the low-lying opening section of 'Non piangere, Liù' with such appealing, resonant warmth. He is in exceptional vocal form, the voice freer at the top than in some of his broadcasts. Try as he will, however, he is unable to wreathe the unknown prince in an aura of romance, that elusive radiance that would add luster to his heroic stance. Eager McCracken is, even ardent, and his concern for Liù is palpable. And he, too, modifies 'splenderà' in 'Nessun dorma' (not as magically as Domingo, but with a tender embrace); still, the mystery of the aria's opening moments, its atmospheric mood, escapes him. When the aria moves into high gear, McCracken does, too, and he caps the piece with an open-throated top note (the final tonic is quite brief). I admire the straightforward honesty of his lovemaking.

The Calàfs of McCracken and Domingo provide a study in contrasts, but Arroyo's and Amara's faithful slave girls are mirror images of one another. Their conceptions of the role are poles apart. Of course, Arroyo is more appropriately a Verdi soprano than a Puccini specialist (though Butterfly was in her Met repertory). Amara delighted in Puccinian pathos while her sister soprano is content to play it straight. Her 'Signore, ascolta!' holds not so much as a single sigh. The body of her tone is welcome in the aria's initial low lying phrases and everywhere her vocalism is resplendent (that commendation also applies to her third-act scene). Delicious Puccinian curves are not fully exploited, nor is Liù's heartbreak when she laments 'si spezza il cuor!' The closing top tone is not quite a *pianissimo*, but the ensuing crescendo is effective before Arroyo allows herself one, possibly two, quiet sobs. In this act and in Liù's lengthy death scene, such vocal assurance and radiant song must be admired simply for itself. In act three, her rebuffs to the soldiers are not very convincing and the introductory aria is rather matter-of-factly intoned. But I have seldom heard a more consummate delivery of the trying final phrase ('Ah! come offerta suprema del mio amore!'). There her control of the *piano* dynamic is a wonder—a treasurable moment. 'Tu che di gel sei cinta' is similarly assured, with a particularly lovely tracing of 'Prima di questa aurora.' Liù was new to Arroyo's list this season. Perhaps for that reason her interpretive gestures are minimal. When the crowd apostrophizes Liù as the epitome of 'bontà,' 'dolcezza,' and 'poesia,' we realize what we have missed in the soprano's reading. Nevertheless, Arroyo's song is glorious. And cannot 'bontà' be defined as "generosity"? Arroyo certainly qualifies in that regard.

When Domingo was called to the Met the day of his unscheduled debut in *Adriana Lecouvreur* he had been pressed into service for a rehearsal of *Turandot*. The rehearsal was necessary because Nilsson was not feeling well and Marion Lippert, who was covering the role, might be called upon to substitute for the great diva. Miss Lippert had arrived in America unheralded, though some rehearsal scuttlebutt by Met personnel had surfaced. Her debut as *Turandot* on 3 October 1968 received markedly positive reviews, as was duly noted in her introductory interview in the broadcast issue of *Opera News*.[6] Munich born and still resident in that city, the soprano ("in her thirties") had been active in lesser German companies since her 1956 debut as Aida in Hagen. Cologne knew her before she became a member of the Stuttgart Opera in 1962. The European capitals were familiar with her work. That her abilities were formidable is evident from the list of her five favorite roles: Lady Macbeth, Abigaille, Tosca, Turandot, and the *Siegfried* Brünnhilde. Any soprano who uses Abigaille's arias as warm-up exercises must be either foolhardy or extraordinarily confident of her powers. Lippert is in the latter category. To those accustomed to the secure, bladelike thrust of Nilsson's instrument in Turandot's entrance aria, the initial impression of Lippert's voice may be a bit of a letdown. One suspects a hint of tremulousness lurks in her fluid tone and that a touch of acidity stains its seemingly whitish timbre. But concerns evaporate as she moves through the role. The voice is quite beautiful, not overly dense but obviously of ample size (the tone is often pillowed by a soft warmth) and yet capable of *pianissimo*s, high and low, of appealing delicacy. The timbre is constant throughout the range. The tessitura is readily handled—Lippert is entirely at ease in the many altitudinous phrases of the role. Her legato is markedly liquid; probably her Teutonic heritage makes her slight the vibrant Italian consonants—occasionally, one feels she is skating on ice. Despite all these encomiums, I find the voice takes some getting used to. I did. Dramatically, her Turandot is patently younger, more vulnerable, more feminine if you will, than that of her Swedish colleague, the difference inherent in the tone quality and musical manner. (Most often, Nilsson sculpts phrases and Lippert molds them, each mode valid and tailored to vocal character.) In many phrases of the second act (and certainly by the opera's end), the voice sheds its hint of cold whiteness; now it rather reflects the warmth of antique ivory. The difference is not so great as to conflict with Turandot's birthright, that icy demeanor adopted as

tribute to her violated ancestor, Princess Lou-Ling. Indeed, an occasional patch of
glassy tone prevents Lippert's Turandot from becoming too sympathetic. And her
voicing of the critical 'Amor' (Calàf's name) at the opera's end is less satisfying than
Nilsson's—for one thing, she omits the "m" when taking the high note.

We hear Lippert no more on the broadcasts, though she returned in the next
season, adding Senta, the Marschallin, and Verdi's Elisabetta to her list—clearly,
she was an artist of substance. A few performances in the 1973–74 season followed. I note that Lippert, in her *Opera News* interview, made clear that she enjoyed a life away from the stage with her engineer husband in their Munich home.
She also mentioned that mountains were a favorite refuge of hers. She scaled a few
in her broadcast debut.

Despite the importation of new sopranos, management peopled the airwaves
with old favorites. Miss Nilsson continued to reign supreme in her field, and
Tebaldi, though transformed, maintained a large measure of her primacy. We hear
her as Manon Lescaut on the broadcast of 23 March 1968. Of particular interest is
whether her retrained instrument and more dramatic manner will match up with
this Puccini heroine, a favorite of her palmier days. The Gioconda posture will not
do for the minxlike Manon. Joining her are John Alexander, who, Cross tells us,
"stepped in at the last moment" for the scheduled Tucker as Des Grieux, Guarrera, and Michalski, with Molinari-Pradelli on the podium.

The conductor's stewardship of the febrile score is the real thing. The bustle
of the introductory student scene is more than sprightly with chorus and orchestra
alert and accurate. (There, Charles Anthony is a capital Edmondo, engaging in
manner and singing with appealing tone and sparkling diction. His performance
reminds us that he was not always comprimario fodder, though he excels in that
métier.) Still, it is the more pensive and tragic moments that enthrall. Molinari-
Pradelli is able to apply an overall lyrical arc to the opera, quite a feat for this
notoriously episodic work. In particular, the diffuse wharf scene profits from his
architectural concept. He shapes the intermezzo with care, forswearing the hyper-
tonic in favor of the pathetic with affecting results.

Boucher (Ship's Captain), Goodloe (Sergeant), and Nagy (Lamplighter) again
confirm the vocal wealth of the company's roster while Velis shows his skill at character delineation. Taking his cue from the libretto, he plays the Dancing Master
not as the usual mincing fop, but as a professional who believes in his craft ('E cosa
seria il ballo!'). Baldwin, however, fails to uphold the honor of the comprimario
ranks. Her madrigal is a turgid offering, and the messy ensemble of her supporting singers suggests that Geronte's musicians are underpaid. Michalski's playing
of that "elderly Parisian gallant" (as *Opera News* describes him) converts him into
a more well-mannered gent than most operatic roués have portrayed. Indeed, the
inherent beauty of Michalski's instrument inevitably lowers the menace quotient
in all his roles. His lover is a gentleman of the old school, courteous and quite
enchanted with his conquest until deception opens his eyes. At that moment,
Michalski momentarily exposes the brutality that underlies the elegant pretense
of the *ancien régime*. Guarrera, in these later stages of his career, has less voice with
which to fill those phrases where Puccini allowed his Lescaut to soar, but the baritone knows how to make the most of his wares. He doesn't miss a trick in bringing
to life the charm and the perfidy of Manon's wily, witty cousin. He even convinces
us that Sergeant Lescaut is a worthy friend of the deluded Des Grieux.

Manon Lescaut
23 March 1968
Manon
Renata Tebaldi
Des Grieux
John Alexander
Edmondo
Charles Anthony
Lescaut
Frank Guarrera
Geronte
Raymond Michalski
Conductor
Francesco Molinari-
Pradelli

John Alexander. Photography by James Abresch.

In that grand and taxing role, Alexander plays with complete assurance and vocal security. Though a last-minute replacement, he was no stranger to the Met production, having first sung Des Grieux in 1965. And the Met continued to cast him in the role over the years. He best reveals his quality in the opening-act arias, applying charming nuances of volume and rhythm to the lighthearted phrases of 'Tra voi, belle,' and drawing with sureness and frankness the expansive line of 'Donna non vidi mai.' At first, his vibrato flutters a bit and, later on, excessively pressurized tone in the upper range can abrade the ear. Oddly, he makes little effect in the pivotal second-act duet, seeming overparted—but then, many a fine tenor would be hard pressed to hold his own against Tebaldi's hefty instrument. Sorrow, rather than anger, marks his 'Ah! Manon, mi tradisce,' a convincing, if not necessarily crowd-pleasing, reading of this affecting moment. He is an astute musician and interpreter, knowing how best to capitalize on his merits. In the tenor's explosive outburst at the harbor, Alexander shrewdly plots the aria's progress, setting it up with a dramatic recitative, but eschewing the fiery near-madness of the distraught lover; he confines the maniac to the final phrases, preferring to allow sincerity to certify his desperation. Here, as elsewhere on this afternoon, his potent and brightly colored upper range serves him well. In the final act, ardor and despair are appropriately summoned as Manon expires. That air of persistent earnestness that permeates Alexander's confident expertise robs his chevalier of some of his appeal. Still, though not quite top drawer, his Des Grieux is a more than brave effort.

Only two weeks before this broadcast, Tebaldi had presented her gusty Gioconda to the radio public. The near-vulgarity of that portrayal is uncharacteristic of her music making. As heard on this broadcast, her Manon Lescaut in fact preserves many of the virtues of her earlier, more supple—and, for my taste, more appealing—vocal manner. The diva is in splendid vocal form, particularly considering the travails that the sixties have brought upon her. From the first we take heart in her vocal well-being. In the undemanding phrases at the inn, the voice, while annealed by a slightly disconcerting flinty rim, is employed with assurance and security. Throughout the afternoon, when she wishes (and fortunately, the wish is often favored), she deploys that pearly, rose-on-the-lips tone that for me always has been her most endearing attribute. Manon at her toilette has many attractions, not the least of which is the delightful portamento that accompanies her application of the beauty patches ('Ed ora . . . un nèo!'). Her assurance does not extend to the very top notes, for she seldom lingers there. In fact, the entire 'In quelle trine morbide,' an aria that in the old days she sang at a snail's pace, taking every opportunity to display the velvety caress of her tones, is hurried along quite mercilessly. (Oddly, her insecurities seem to have inclined her to embrace musical virtues. I prefer the old volupté.) Still, the aria is no embarrassment and in the dancing episode she is quite wonderful, handling the ornaments and graces of the faux-eighteenth-century idiom with ease and charm. Again, the pearly tone is much in evidence (and an occasional hard top note as well). To hear Tebaldi, in the duet, voluminously intone the unaccompanied 'Non m'ami più' phrases makes one marvel again at the splendor of her instrument. True, when she allows her voice full rein ('Son forse della Manon d'un giorno meno piacente e bella?') her Manon, always a hearty girl in earlier incarnations, seems rather a bold piece. (That posture is enhanced in the later acts, where outsized chest tones anchor an occasional phrase.) But when, in the quiet close of the duet, she ravishingly intones 'Labbra dolci a baciare!' on a single pitch, who could resist her blandishments? More than most, this tenor and soprano respect the *dolcissimo* of the final 'soffrir,' he with a falsetto, she with a lovely *piano*. 'Sola, perduta, abbandonata!' allows Tebaldi to employ her polar vocal manners to maximum effect. She varies its tragic cast by lightening her voice in the middle section while elsewhere painting Manon's despair with the grand gestures of a dramatic soprano. The pathos of the heroine's final moments calls forth an abundance of cushiony soft tones, affectingly delivered. No doubt about it, Tebaldi can still deliver a performance. Oddly, audience response, while generous, seems not quite so delirious as in earlier years. On this afternoon she deserved their heartiest commendation.

The week following *Manon Lescaut* brought yet another Puccini opera to the airwaves and one whose heroine, in the person of Teresa Stratas, was a marked contrast to Tebaldi's outsized courtesan. On the 30 March 1968 performance of *Madama Butterfly*, Stratas, diminutive in stature and modest of vocal size, offered her only broadcast of the geisha wife. Lamberto Gardelli's other charges were Morell, Casei, and Uppman. Gardelli was currently at the Met for a three-season span, his *Butterfly* broadcast preceded by a 1967 *Rigoletto* radio debut. His reading has a classicist's poise, a posture that may seem antithetical to the verismo genre but marries well with Puccini's careful craftsmanship, particularly those delicate orchestral effects that make the score an enchanting aural experience. A few climaxes (the postlude to the ship sighting, for instance) may lack the preferred emotional tug, but the rewards of his nuanced, well-proportioned interpretation are considerable. For the most part, he is considerate of his heroine's lyric resources.

Except for Stratas, the cast is familiar from earlier broadcasts. Velis' Goro is appropriately oily and adept at salesmanship, the nasality of his instrument not overly pronounced. Boucher's wedding ceremony and Scott's denunciation of the frightened bride are believable cameos. Casei, her voice liquid and full toned, offers a Suzuki more feminine, less subservient than the usual handmaiden. She makes Suzuki's concern for Butterfly's plight tangible. Uppman's consul is entirely sympathetic, both in tone and manner, and he is in excellent vocal form. The voice appears to have gained in baritonal weight, thereby lending pith to Sharpless' cautionary pronouncements, yet it retains the heady resonance that makes audible his concern for Butterfly's plight.

At the final curtain, Cross, perhaps feeling the need to separate Pinkerton's callous behavior from the impersonator, assures us that Morell is a bona fide married man with four children ("all of them girls"). But, rejecting the interpretive mode favored by some singers later in the century, this navy lieutenant is as well behaved as his superiors could wish. Though deemed to have been in "mediocre voice" by the *Times'* critic at the season premiere five days before the broadcast, here the tenor offers indisputable evidence of his merit.[7] In the past I have deemed his timbre a shade nondescript for major-league tenorizing, but on this afternoon I hear marginally greater fullness in the lower octave and, most rewarding, a new-found ping and timbral brightness in the upper voice. His sureness of attack on top notes and their secure sustentation are attributes that tenors of greater repute might envy. Moreover, his phrasing is expansive in the best Puccini tradition, and his characterization, quite impassioned, is informed by intelligent touches (a powerful denunciation of the Bonze). Nowadays, tenors of Di Stefano suavity, Björling

Madama Butterfly
30 March 1968

Cio-Cio-San
Teresa Stratas
Suzuki
Nedda Casei
Pinkerton
Barry Morell
Sharpless
Theodor Uppman
Conductor
Lamberto Gardelli

Teresa Stratas as Cio-Cio-San in *Madama Butterfly*. Photography by Louis Mélançon.
Courtesy Metropolitan Opera Archives.

amplitude, or Bergonzi polish are loath to undertake Pinkerton's limited chores. Thus Morell's quality performance is doubly welcome. He cannot match in full measure each of those tenors' attributes, but the satisfying mix of them that he offers is a viable alternative.

Stratas' Butterfly was seldom heard at the Met or elsewhere. In terms of a believable stage representation, she was, of course, an ideal interpreter, but the role's stringent vocal demands (especially when Puccini looses his climactic orchestral sonorities) wisely dictated a frugal performance diet. After all, a Cherubino and a Gretel (her other Met appearances this season) seldom undertake the geisha's more formidable chores. The role does have a double image, apparent even in its earliest performances. At the ill-fated La Scala premiere (17 February 1904) the exquisite Rosina Storchio (a Linda, Norina, and Manon) played the part with, as Puccini wrote her a few days later, "refined and delicate understanding."[8] Yet the opera's second performance (at Brescia on 24 May 1904) featured the imposing soprano Salomea Krusceniski, "an Aida voice," as Phillips-Matz termed her—indeed, and more to the point, a Gioconda voice and eventually an instrument capable of handling Salome, Elektra, and Brünnhilde.[9] The interpretive duality continued in early Metropolitan history when Geraldine Farrar and Emmy Destinn offered contrasting representations of the heroine. Miss Stratas is more likely in the Storchio/Farrar line. While she had sung a concert performance at Lewisohn Stadium in the summer of 1966, the 25 March 1968 season premiere inaugurated her initial Met stage appearances. She apparently gave serious consideration to Butterfly as a staple in her repertory, for she had followed the Lewisohn Stadium reading with a series with the San Francisco Opera in the fall of 1966.

Even though denied the charms of her stage portrayal, the broadcast performance has much to recommend it. The liquid flow of her tone and its seductive warmth are powerful assets, both aural and interpretive. She is, as we know, an artist of original insights and committed dramatic representation. Yet, few novel touches distinguish her reading—no harm there, for she fills the role with the traditional nuances (including even an occasional pinched tone to simulate the purported Oriental mode—few sopranos can resist squeezing 'picciol'). Her second act is more successful than the opening one. Oddly, her characterization seems not quite to hold together there, as though she had not yet fully assimilated the role. Perhaps she was a bit preoccupied by vocal concerns; she does not attempt either the concluding top tone of the entrance (a common omission among aging divas, though unexpected in novitiates) or, more surprisingly, that of the duet. Puccini provided optional endings, of course, but the act conclusion seems oddly incomplete if the tenor is left hanging to finish by himself (and Stratas only briefly touches her note). Yet the soprano has offered some full-blooded singing in between those slights. She highlights Butterfly's integrity in her meaningful recounting of the geisha's religious conversion and is emphatic in her fear of rejection (the 'rinnegata's are replete with anxiety). In the duet, the child bride in all her volatility is touchingly exposed, but the soprano fills the more expansive phrases with lyric fullness of tone, even resorting to chest voice to launch the 'Dolce notte' sequence.

A bewitching *pianissimo* on the opening note of 'Un bel dì vedremo' seems to suggest Butterfly's fragile hopes (in contrast to the determined belief of most interpreters). Realistic questioning marks 'Che dira?' and a quick 'e un po' propels her into the more dramatic final phrases. Again, her concluding note (the two syllables not clearly articulated) is hardly calculated to arouse audience passion. Devotees forswear interrupting the postlude but provide sufficient acclaim at its close. Silken tones mirror Butterfly's pleasure in her colloquy with Sharpless. Stratas prefers a broad rejection (as opposed to the suggested sorrow) of his insinuation that Pinkerton might not return. She has a bit of hard going (lyric Butterflys do at this point) when the forsaken bride declaims her preference for death over a return to geishahood. Here Gardelli, refusing to heighten the tension, provides no dramatic assist. Her careful management of resources and his restraint combine to make the normally potent episode anticlimactic. One novel touch is the vulgar tone she applies to her son's name ('Trouble,' in English) while his rechristening as 'Joy' is hardly jubilant. After the tiniest-toned 'bianca's to describe the ship's arrival, she manages a triumphant, full-toned traversal of the 'Abraham Lincoln' episode. After this manifestation of womanhood, Stratas reverts to a childlike posture for the flower duet, treating the scattering of flowers as a lark, quickly skirting the top curves but filling the duet with satiny legato. The unaccompanied, single-phrase peroration is lovely, but slightly rushed and marred by an unlikely number of rolled "r"s in 'primo.' How charmingly she provides the peepholes before the humming chorus (one of the better readings) works its magic. The third-act lullaby is tenderly voiced, its soft close ensured by early retreat offstage. Stoicism marks her acceptance of Kate Pinkerton—the pathos of this and similar moments is minimized. A very quiet, decidedly unstagey speaking of the dagger inscription precedes the demanding farewell aria, a piece that tries her resources. Her phrasing has sufficient tensility, if not quite the requisite breadth—she is compelled to move off the climax before Gardelli does, while the voice is now more pointedly, and less attractively, focused. The conductor, again eschewing tragic impact, maintains his measured stance in the postlude. Dare we consider the aura of resignation Oriental?

I confess to some ambivalence about Stratas' portrayal. Its stop-and-go progress, the slight air of vocal caution (which often, however, is cast off, allowing beauty and conviction to triumph), the lack of a unified conception—all lessen the effect of the parts. Of interest is the young soprano's cancellation, following the broadcast, of her next appearance in the role (2 April). Thereafter it passed to a scheduled series of divas (Radmila Bakocevic, Kirsten, Arroyo, and Lorengar) before Stratas undertook a single performance on the spring tour. When next on the broadcasts (17 April 1971) we embrace the geisha, Spanish soprano Lorengar wears the bridal kimono with Shirley, Miller, and Guarrera performing under Franci. (Arroyo—an Aida voice for sure—and Alexander under Molinari-Pradelli had offered an intermediate radio reading.)

Unlike Gardelli, Franci, already introduced as steward of Moffo's unfortunate Lucia and the 1970 *Pasquale*, treads a traditional interpretive path. Shunning Gardelli's classical poise, Franci's way, though well worn, holds its own virtues, of which a more dramatic framework is the most notable. His introductory contrapuntal web, heavily accented, churns dynamically; the third-act prelude surges, its contrasts vividly etched; the detached notes of the dagger theme, played after Butterfly reads the fateful inscription, become jagged knife cuts. Yet the conductor respects the opera's architecture, both overall and in individual components (the pizzicato chords underpinning the humming chorus, for instance, are placed

Madama Butterfly
17 April 1971

Cio-Cio-San
Pilar Lorengar
Suzuki
Mildred Miller
Pinkerton
George Shirley
Sharpless
Frank Guarrera
Conductor
Carlo Franci

with exceptional precision). He never neglects its multiple lyric charms either. Like Gardelli, whom he followed in the Italian repertory at the Met, Franci regrettably would be a short-term Met resident.

The broadcast is short of assets. Franci's contribution is in that column, but some of the singing crew must be placed on the debit side. Comprimario characterizations (Karlsrud, Boucher, Christopher) are hardly vivid. Schmorr's Goro is refreshingly free of nasality, but compensatory character touches are not explored. Of the principals, Guarrera and Miller, both reputable artists, are nearing the end of their Met tether. After a slow start, the mezzo has a few creditable episodes, not the least being her discreet voicing of the flower duet, where the match with Lorengar, both in weight of voice and timbre, is apposite. Guarrera is patently indisposed, virtually out of voice here and there. Put in the best light, Sharpless' ineffectual efforts to avoid the catastrophe find an aural complement in the baritone's pallid tones. On the other hand, Shirley's stout-voiced Pinkerton has its merits, but some of the sheen has worn off the bronze metal of his instrument. Always dark hued, now the voice's baritonal character has all but usurped the timbre. High and low, all the notes are conquered, but the weightlifting seems heavy at times. Yet his phrasing reaffirms him as a sensitive artist (love inhabits his manner, if not invariably his tone, in the duet) and an occasional flash of the former timbral brightness in the upper octave is reassuring. And he thrusts a splendid high note to close the love duet, thereby raising the performance asset count.

In spite of the above demerits, the performance remains one to treasure, for Lorengar proves a most satisfying heroine. The role appears to hold no vocal terrors for her. The soprano's American renown was Mozart-based so her command of the verismo idiom is surprising—and entirely convincing. She may be the most joyous Butterfly ever heard on the airwaves. Despite the trials and tribulations suffered by the child-wife, the soprano radiates an unquenchable optimism. And yet the voice's beauty in and of itself can be heartrending—and no Butterfly can succeed without rending the heart. Lustrous in the extreme, its luminosity cushioned by a mellow roundness, her timbre is one of the loveliest of the soprano breed. Excessive vibrato occasionally has neutralized its charm, but on this afternoon the sometimes recalcitrant flutter is under perfect control. The voice is in prime condition—a stunning high D-flat caps her entrance, and she triumphantly joins Shirley on high at the act's end. (Indeed, her top notes are so much at her command that she is prone to hold a few of them overlong—in the second act, Miller must announce the cannon shot while Lorengar tarries.) In addition to its nimbused timbre, Lorengar's soprano is a healthy lyric and thus Puccini's orchestral splendors seldom trouble her. (She occupies that happy middle ground between Storchio's fragility and Krusceniski's heft.) Particularly welcome is the seeming spontaneity of her utterance. Whether capricious, pathetic, or tragic, the heroine's moods come vividly to life. Though stylistically knowing, she does not overburden her portrayal with interpretive miniaturisms (no squeezed 'picciol' for her). This geisha girl's outlook is too openhearted for small thoughts.

A few specific moments may be cited. In the duet, her 'rinnegata's are replete with the terror of rejection and contrast well with 'e felice' (which holds an appropriate crescendo). The vault to 'bambino' is tidily executed. 'Un bel dì' (with the requisite quiet initial attack) holds subtle gradations of tone and volume, and the sense of a narrative (as opposed to an aria) is admirably cultivated. Forced by Sharpless to contemplate Pinkerton's dereliction, she conjures a moment of touching intimacy, her wee tones oddly suggesting the enormity of her fears. In contrast, she has plenty of tone for the demanding histrionics of Butterfly's revelation of her child; the dramatic posture is so vivid that the audience applauds in midcourse, as well as at the end. One would prefer to hear a *pianissimo* on the high B at the lullaby's close, but at least the note is secure. Vocal pungency, a high comfort level in the upper third of her range, and dramatic commitment ensure a convincing farewell to her child.

Of Lorengar's sixteen Metropolitan roles, Butterfly tied with Elvira in number of performances (thirteen), with Pamina (twenty), Countess (nineteen), and Elsa (fifteen) predictably in the lead. The excellence of her reading would seem to have dictated more. But then, perhaps she was lucky to have been allotted any. Della Casa, her Met predecessor in their particular *Fach*, hankered after Butterfly, but was awarded nary a one. We, too, are lucky, for we have a lovely souvenir of Lorengar's portrayal.

In the mid-century decades (that is, in ante-Zeffirelli mountings) management considered *La Bohème*, hardy perennial though it be, an opera worthy of care. The roles of Rodolfo and Mimì repeatedly were cast from prime stock, as is evident from two broadcasts that featured alliterative couplings of Tebaldi/Tucker (24 January 1970) and Kirsten/Kónya (6 March 1971). Though head rhyme need not indicate artistic affinities, the pairs prove to be well matched in musical manner and vocal size.

Cleva had been custodian of many a *Bohème* performance, but familiarity has not diluted his evident love for the score's charms. He achieves an agreeable balance between Toscanini tautness and lyrical flowering. Of particular note is his considerate response to the peculiar needs of his singers. Several Americans are safely (and quite appropriately) in the interpretive mainstream: Boucher (Schaunard), Walker (Marcello), and Clarice Carson (Musetta). To hold the attention, Schaunard's 'pappagallo' narrative requires a more thrusting tone than Boucher's mellow baritone provides—this parrot's death scene seems overlong. The young artist is more successful in later acts, especially when directing the garret dance. Walker's fine instrument, on the other hand, is more imposing than in earlier outings. Its characteristic American timbre, well focused, candid, and touched with virility, is particularly appealing in roles where friendship matters. Marcello ranks high in that department and Walker serves him well. Indeed, he is more alive in his scenes with Rodolfo than when he must deal with Mimì's problems—the baritone seems marginally less committed when acting as diva psychiatrist. A major plus of his reading is his musicianly conduct in the fourth-act duet; wonder of wonders, he and Tucker obtain a more precise ensemble in its wandering phrases than most garret roommates in broadcast history. They also honor Puccini's request for a quiet close.

Carson, new to this chronicle, is an uncommonly fine Musetta. Too often have ears been tried and sensibilities offended by futile attempts to move the seconda donna into prime position. The Montreal soprano needs no tricks to hold attention and gain regard. Interest in her is piqued when we learn that she was a pupil of Pauline Donalda, a prima donna of the first decades of the century —one of those remote voices from the past whose names in themselves conjure an aura of operatic performance quite removed, not only in time, but in demeanor, from the more

La Bohème
24 January 1970
Mimì
Renata Tebaldi
Musetta
Clarice Carson
Rodolfo
Richard Tucker
Marcello
William Walker
Colline
Cesare Siepi
Conductor
Fausto Cleva

proper practice of today. Carson's voice has size, an equalized production, clean intonation, and a bright timbre, and her artistic instincts are sound. She treats the waltz song with respect, Cleva providing an unhurried pace that allows her to apply a few musical subtleties. Its only demerit is a slightly slurred arpeggio run-up to the final top note. The voice's plangency allows her to dominate the second-act ensemble in a way off limits to most Musettas; not surprisingly, her repertory includes roles as diverse as Constanze, Elsa, and Lady Macbeth. In seven widely spaced seasons, the Met made little use of her. (*Annals* addicts should not be deceived by the inclusion of thirty-two Violettas in her Met tally. Carson initially was a member of the Met's short-lived touring National Company. Her debut with the parent company occurred as the *Zauberflöte* First Lady in 1967.) In addition to the two leads, management prodigality extended to the bass roles. Siepi often took on, and made something special of, the modest chores of Colline on broadcasts, but it is uncommon to hear the Benoit/Alcindoro assignment split among performers as expert as Plishka and Corena. The latter admonishes his rebellious Musetta with welcome authority and sturdy tone, while Plishka has the greater opportunity and takes full advantage of it. He has not yet been pigeonholed as a buffo specialist (that is far in his future) and his characterization profits from being a landlord of flesh (veritably) and blood, and less a comic turn. He sprinkles a few wheezes and squeaks here and there but is not loath to display his resonant tones and hearty disposition. This Benoit, a shade younger than the usual landlord, might well handle both a wife and a mistress. The final commendatory word on basses must go to Siepi for his sonorous, truthful rendering of Colline's farewell to his coat.

Previously I noted that the current season marked Tucker's twenty-fifth anniversary with the company, and on this afternoon Francis Robinson offers a "Biography in Music" intermission tribute to him. Normally reserved for retired or deceased artists, the salute is welcome but premature—Tucker is in no need of either a career prop or an inopportune toss into the waste bin of history. Indeed, in the opera itself he may be intent on proving that age has not withered his resources. His opening 'Nei cieli bigi' confirms they are both plentiful and secure. That time might have dulled those few stylistic vulgarities that have long scarred his portrayals would be too much to hope for. In fact, they (staccato syllabic treatment, puffy accents) are not overly prominent on this afternoon and, oddly, their very familiarity warrants more a smile than a frown. From the tenor's garret behavior, one might think his poet a manic-depressive: in the opening act Tucker's cocky hero preens, but he turns lachrymose in the fourth act, a natural character progress. Still, the extremes are pushed at both interpretive ends. He all but explodes after Mimì's death. Best to regard his excesses as evidence of a wholehearted commitment to his work, a trait never doubted. When Tucker voices his despair at Mimì's illness ('Invan, invan nascondo la mia vera tortura') in expansive, tortured phrases, feeling and art are meaningfully wedded. He takes 'Che gelida manina' a half-tone down, breathes between 'Talor' and 'dal mio forziere,' and gets off a good high B before a not leisurely descent. He does observe (if only momentarily) the *dolce* marking at the opening of the duet with Marcello and phrases artfully thereafter. Throughout the afternoon, his control of his instrument, his technical know-how, the enduring security in his top voice, his conduct of line when lyricism is all—these are properties that command respect and admiration. They would be remarkable in a tenor half his age.

Whereas Tucker was ready off the mark, our prima donna is slow to gain her form. Indeed, from her voicing of 'Mi chiamano Mimì' one fears that Tebaldi's instrument, this time betraying the hard usage of her Gioconda manner, may be irreparably damaged. That instrument may have been reconstituted, but vocal blemishes, like cicatrixes left over from the healing process, can still mar the once unflawed surface of her voice. Notes above the staff appear to be palpably threatening to her and, even later in the afternoon, she seldom lingers there. She adopts a distressingly hasty tempo for her narrative, and the mix of slurred intervals and acidulous *forte* tone ('il profumo d'un fior') is unsettling. At critical points ('il primo bacio dell'aprile è mio!') she avoids initial consonants. A few dulcet quieter moments are reassuring. And indeed, before long, evidences of the beloved diva's tonal magic peep through, their frequency gradually increasing until in the final two acts we come reasonably close to the Tebaldi of her early years. In the duet, 'Vi starò vicina!' is delightfully purled, and she is able to reach the heights of the final B, both artists (for Tucker takes the note with her) relinquishing it after a few beats, as though it were an enemy to be thrust off at first opportunity. "They just kissed each other," Cross tells us at their first-act bows, an acknowledgment perhaps of the cohorts' gratitude at reaching safe harbor. The little 'honey' aria at the Cafe Momus holds a touch of that slight meow that occasionally can sour her tone, but 'più del miele' is grandly and opulently voiced. At the toll gate, she throws a phrase or two into chest voice (Gioconda will out), and in these full-blooded moments the upper register can turn hard, but the density of tone, its voluminousness, is quite thrilling. Except for a disappointingly curtailed 'senza rancor,' the farewell is a beguiling thing, delivered for the most part with a gentle flow of her loveliest tone and capped by strong climaxes. The distance between her *piano* and *fortissimo* may be more than the little aria can bear, but we can savor each extreme. In the concluding solo phrases of the quartet, one hoped for greater breadth of phrasing as an aural complement for Mimì's hope that love might last forever. Tebaldi's now supple throat and seemingly full heart allow her to limn Mimì's final moments with Rodolfo in angelic tones to touching effect. She does drop the text entirely at 'la mia vita' and, in what for me is a critical blemish, inexplicably chooses to use greatly altered pitches rather than Puccini's prescribed monotone on a single pitch for the heroine's quiet escape into death. But elsewhere in this scene, in tone and manner, she is her old, best self. Could one ask for more?

A quite different ambience obtains in the 6 March 1971 broadcast of the opera. In place of the occasionally scrappy air of the Tucker–Tebaldi encounter, Kirsten and Kónya offer a more conventional, lyrical treatment of the pathetic romance. Colette Boky, Sereni, and Hines, plus Goodloe (Schaunard), Richard Best (Benoit), and Velis (Alcindoro) are Cleva's newest charges. Like the 1970 offering in honor of Tucker, the occasion has its celebratory aspect, for it commemorates Kirsten's twenty-fifth anniversary with the company.

Mimì had been her debut role (1 December 1945) and continued as one of the staples in her repertory (forty performances with the Met company). At the final curtain, Cross notes that the celebrant throughout her career was "acclaimed for her vivid stage personality," and while the little seamstress is hardly a vehicle to showcase that aspect of her art, the role does permit the diva to certify the still-vernal quality of her voice. Her technical security and the prudent husbanding of her instrument's assets over the years provide aural dividends in this final decade

La Bohème
6 March 1971
Mimì
Dorothy Kirsten
Musetta
Colette Boky
Rodolfo
Sándor Kónya
Marcello
Mario Sereni
Colline
Jerome Hines
Conductor
Fausto Cleva

of her long association with the company. Indeed, her broadcast Mimì can seem a rebuke to those would-be divas who invade the operatic stage with inadequate technical grounding and recklessly spend their capital in the springtime of their careers. Critics often rail, in the abstract, about sixty-year-old Mimìs. Kirsten actually fills that bill (we now know her birth year was 1910), but the characterization (in vocal terms) is almost girlish. The narrow focus of the voice and a slight interpretive reticence foster that illusion. (Lyric voices do seem best mated with the character, though in support of spinto Tebaldi's long association with Mimì, one recalls that in the early flush of the opera's success Puccini proclaimed Gemma Bellincioni "l'ideale di Mimì."[10] A few years earlier she had created Santuzza. So much for pigeonhole notions of casting.) In truth, Kirsten's instrument on this afternoon seems less attractive tonally in the lower range (more nasality than of yore) and some of the bloom is off the fondly remembered honeyed tone in the mid-upper range, always her primal possession. The very top tones were always rather circumspect, indeed slender in circumference, and so they remain—but their quite remarkable pinpoint accuracy is constant as well. The purity of the high C that concludes the duet provides signal confirmation of that precision. Unlike Tebaldi, Kirsten manages the troubling climaxes of her narrative with aplomb—she always honored her audience by entering with flexed voice. Never mind that an overcast Paris sky momentarily lessens the sun's radiance in this Mimì's garret room. But the soprano knows where the role's expressive nodules surface and invariably acknowledges them—she makes her points without overplaying her hand. At the Tollgate, she doesn't counterfeit physical weakness, but her distress is apparent. A vocally tasteful and dramatically touching 'Addio' is her finest moment, with the too-often forsworn lengthy *fermata* on the penultimate tone neatly negotiated. Line expansion has never been her forte, as one notes in the phrases of longing near the quartet's close—even so, they are cannily managed. Her career-long distortion of certain vowel sounds is again apparent in the death scene (to the point that a few seem like outright mispronunciations—'grazia' for 'grazie,' for instance), but, more to the point, she has left off the infantile tone that marred her earlier broadcast of the act. It still lurks around the corners, but for the most part an affecting sweetness of tone and manner dominates. Joy, rather than regret, inhabits Mimì's memories of the lovers' meeting. Her illness seems forgotten and she sinks effortlessly into a final sleep—a novel conception without death's vocal pallor. It works.

In honor of the occasion, Mr. Bing awards her "a lovely silver bowl," but even a radio farewell is out of the question. The longtime manager will not be on hand when another Puccini heroine (Butterfly), one more in tune with her "vivid stage personality," graces that occasion a few years down the broadcast road.

According to Cross, a fund of information on this afternoon, the broadcast holds yet another honoree: Hines is celebrating *his* twenty-fifth season with the company. His was a continuous record—Kirsten had been absent for four seasons during the quarter-century period. (You who do the math—*pace*. In fixing these anniversary celebrations, some juggling of debut date and actual season tally often occurs: in this instance, Kirsten's December 1945 entry collides with Hines' 21 November 1946 debut.) The stalwart of the company bass contingent offers sonority aplenty (marginally thicker than his customary tone) and, along with Sereni's resonant Marcello, anchors the shenanigans of the Bohemians. His coat song, gruff and lacking in sentimentality (no harm there) until the final phrases, seems more appropriate for one of the aged priests in his large repertory than a youthful philosopher. This is not his time for the limelight and we will wait for one of his signature roles to commend him. Sereni can receive his due now. His painter, robust in voice and hearty in manner, is the perfect foil for Kónya's romantic poet. He flaunts his baritonal bluster most engagingly—the tone is burly and entirely attractive. Vocal bulk is essential for the reprise of the waltz melody and he dispenses it liberally. Yet his conduct of line in the last-act duet manages to be both considerate and purposeful. The "other" baritone role (Schaunard) is passed along to Robert Goodloe, one more in that seemingly endless string of young Americans whose musicianship and appealing timbres guarantee them their too-brief moments in the sun. This one omits a phrase in the hurly-burly shaming of Benoit but has the vocal pith to better drive home the parrot narrative than can be done with compatriot Boucher's suaver instrument. The comic duo is less well served. Velis is a fine character tenor, but his assumption of Alcindoro seems ill advised (the logic seems to be that De Paolis did it and he is his successor). The nasal tenor tone merely proves annoying. Best's Benoit is vocally undermanned and, perhaps for that reason, relies excessively on buffo tricks.

Musettas come and go with even greater frequency than Schaunards, but today's candidate deserves a long tenure. Boky's warmhearted girl warrants more than an 'assai buona' from Mimì. Vivacious rather than forward, spunky rather than shrewish, the young Canadian soprano fills the maligned waltz song with lovely tone and fluent phrasing. For once, Musetta seems happy in the ascent to the top B—Boky, a Queen of the Night at her Met debut, lives in that high terrain. But the low-lying prayer at Mimì's deathbed is nicely poised too. The Met evidently thought well of her, having already awarded her Gilda, Olympia, and Juliette (and the latter will be heard in a 1973 broadcast).

When Kónya last aired his Rodolfo he was woefully out of voice. He offers full recompense on this afternoon. It takes a moment or so to get used to his vocal mannerisms (sometimes he sounds as though he coddles a lightbulb in his mouth) and the timbre is so lubricious that it can cloy. But that timbre is his glory—a Gigli-like honeyed sweetness dwells there, paprika-sprinkled though it be. In the first act, the top tones are gingerly taken (a hurried rush over the top B of the narrative), but as the opera progresses, they become more assured even as the crutch of the sob is all but eschewed. When he wraps a Puccini phrase in an expansive embrace all is well. And he enters into the character with realistic fervor, savoring love with abandon, decrying Mimì's illness with genuine remorse. Indeed, his lament at the Barrière d'Enfer is the emotional climax of the performance. The third-act quartet is particularly well done by all participants. A good deal of the credit goes to Boky and Sereni, who are dramatically alive but do not split our eardrums with their quarrel. The tenor opens the duet with Marcello with ravishing tone (paprika or no) and love and longing inhabit his phrasing. Like most *Bohème* pairings, he and Sereni begin better than they end—a slight blemish. Cleva, who "worked with Puccini as a young man" (Cross again), offers no surprises, but, like his charges onstage, does not transgress. Those few words hardly seem sufficient tribute for a conductor who has honorably served the Met for twenty-five seasons. He deserves more. This is his final broadcast. Death will call him a few months later. The total of his performances with the company (957 in both houses and on tour) is an impressive achievement, a monument to an association that began as far back as 1938.

La Fanciulla del West
14 March 1970

Minnie
Renata Tebaldi
Wowkle
Frederica von Stade
Dick Johnson
Sándor Kónya
Jack Rance
Anselmo Colzani
Jake
John Macurdy
Conductor
Jan Behr

Stepping back a year to the broadcast of *La Fanciulla del West* (14 March 1970), we encounter Kónya again, this time disguised as Ramerrez. Where we might have expected to meet celebrant Kirsten in a repeat of her idiomatic Minnie, we enjoy yet another role/diva contrast. Tebaldi pulls a Greeley and goes West. There Sheriff Colzani and a host of Met miners cosset her while conductor Jan Behr minds the store. *The Girl of the Golden West* was in and out of the repertory during the sixties as management tried to turn its prize premiere (1910) into a staple. (Yet another attempt would be made in the Levine era, the maestro claiming that Puccini's *Fanciulla* was "in a sense his most remarkable opera."[11]) This time Tebaldi was the bait and her public swallowed it with unmitigated glee. Of the season's seven outings, five were her allotment. The broadcast captures her final Met performance of the role. A just mix of her Gioconda and Manon manners may be expected to produce a portrayal satisfying to all her admirers.

Banditry would seem to be no proper pursuit for the era's chaste Lohengrin, but the Met evidently believed that Puccini and Kónya were a viable combination. The tenor makes a fair meal of the role, with the better qualities of Dick Johnson very much to the fore. He bursts into the Polka saloon, begins to pour out that fund of molasses-dipped tone, and signals immediately that this bandit's vocation is stealing hearts rather than miners' gold. We learn as well, and to our regret, that high notes will not top off the afternoon's pleasures (Tebaldi already having served notice of her familiar deficiency in that area). Kónya's actually improve in the later acts. His phrasing, musical and at times expansive, affirms the core of rectitude in Johnson's makeup. The second-act defense is honorably made and potently delivered, though as happens when he aims for the big effect, a yawning gulp sometimes limits tonal thrust. He chooses not to exploit the latent bathos of the hanging scene, delivering 'Ch'ella mi creda' in a straightforward fashion that lends credibility to the denouement's histrionics.

Jan Behr, who had conducted Kirsten's final *Fanciulla* broadcast (1966) as replacement for Cleva, performs the same function for Tebaldi. With this heroine, he is able to exhibit the opera's large-frame torso to the full, while dutifully savoring Puccini's atmospheric orchestration and harmonic pungency. The male cameos are sung with assurance—many of these Met stalwarts have been with the production since its 1961 incarnation. As Wells Fargo agent Ashby, newcomer Plishka is particularly strong of voice and manner, while Franke (Nick, the bartender), Harvuot (the sympathetic Sonora), and Velis (Joe) are very much at home in this Western milieu. This time, Macurdy's grainy timbre and unbending manner dilute the sentiment of minstrel Jake Wallace's song, thereby shortchanging one of the composer's carefully plotted nostalgic touches. Destined to become one of the Met's beloved artists, the twenty-four-year-old Frederica von Stade does what she can to minimize the embarrassments that the composer contrived for Minnie's Indian maid (her multiple 'Ugh's are delivered *sotto voce*). Sun and moon gods receive their tribute as the mezzo's plangent low register effectively projects Wowkle's lullaby. Colzani, Jack Rance in both previous broadcasts, again proves his company worth. We know him to be a master of characterization (certainly he is a sheriff not to be trifled with) and on this afternoon he is in particularly good voice. The first-act narrative of his youth allows him to evoke a modicum of sympathy for his wretched beginnings and Colzani takes full advantage of it, achieving a grand climax at its close. He all but dominates the exchanges with

Renata Tebaldi as Minnie in *La Fanciulla del West*. Photography by Louis Mélançon.
Courtesy Metropolitan Opera Archives.

Minnie in their cabin confrontations. Burned by desire, the baritone slavers lust upon his phrases, crying 'Son tutto della sete di te arso e distrutto'—a wonderfully melodramatic, but true, exposure of self.

Miss Tebaldi perhaps enjoys the opera's melodramatics a shade more than is good for her, though certainly not for her public. At the 11 February season premiere, the *Times* critic found her "adorable," deeming her characterization both sweet and prim.[12] Photographs of the diva as Minnie go far to confirm those appellations, but based solely on the audible portion of her portrayal, Tebaldi's Minnie comes off as a boisterous hoyden, overbold and a bit hard-shelled. At the beginning of our new millennium, a highly regarded Met intermission commentator rightly named Tebaldi as a candidate for the "Singers' Hall of Fame," stating, in summary, that she "sang like a man."[13] Why that should be an encomium, I am not at all sure, but I understand what he meant and it is possible that he might very well cite her *Fanciulla* broadcast in support of his claim. One need not quarrel unduly with the diva's vocal estate. In fact, the voice (as opposed to its employment) is in quite remarkable condition, that is, if one considers its basic texture, which is incredibly solid, grandly effulgent, and wobble free. Of course, we no longer expect the very top notes to be full approximations of pitch; on this afternoon, a few, in the later stages of the opera, are—others decidedly are not. Indeed, that terribly exposed high C in the first-act aria is merely a secure B. Nevertheless, she sends them out with considerable sangfroid, no matter their waywardness, while often curtailing their length. Of greater importance is the application (either by need or choice) of a cutting edge, a rim of hardness, to tones at dynamics louder than *mezzo piano*. When she chooses to exhale her signature susurrus, that gently murmuring *piano* tone, she is indeed adorable; the soprano obviously still has it at her command, at least when singing in the lower octave. Regrettably, she seldom lingers in that mode. A critical case in point is her third-act plea to the miners to save Johnson, the most affecting moment of the opera. She begins with lovely, quiet tone ('E anche tu lo vorrai, Joe') but within a few measures reverts to her harsher timbre, thereafter moving in and out of the two modes. The spell is broken. Even the repeated single-pitch 'addio's that provide an evocative close to the opera bear that touch of cutting tone that robs the moment of an ethereal fade-away. Throughout the afternoon, her phrasing, overall and in the treatment of notes within the phrase, can seem a bit casual, even haphazard. Her portamentos are grand, if a dab slurpy. Then, too, at a few critical moments she employs that guttural, outsized chest tone that turns the melodramatic into the ridiculous. The audience clearly relishes these turns (the applause and cheering as she blatantly plays her aces is expected and, indeed, demanded). But for the sake of the opera and verisimilitude it might be better to underplay these moments. Reconsidering that hoped-for appropriate mix, I find the tilt toward the Gioconda manner disappointing. The core of Minnie, brave and spirited though she be, is her sheltered tenderness in a harsh environment, her longing for and discovery of love. Tebaldi doesn't quite reveal it. Her fans fill the gap by offering their love in abundance.

The above, overburdened with strictures, is one way to consider her performance, especially if you long for what might have been. And yet the opera's scenario is, for many, a kick—delectable camp whose enjoyment is made respectable by Puccini's inventive, explorative score. Why not approach it on two levels? Tebaldi—horse-riding, card-playing, pistol-packin', in manner and vocalism reveling in the histrionics of the role—is undoubtedly a treat. And we in turn can revel in the sheer grandeur of her vocalism, imperfect though it may be. Its idiomatic flavor should be treasured. Even a full-bodied wine that has moved beyond its maturation point may be imbibed with relish, if the stock is prime and the consumption limited. Better excess than the sterile heroines that the Met served up in its revivals during the last decade of the century. And Tebaldi has her share of delectable moments. In 'Laggiù nel Soledad' she describes Minnie's mother's little feet with playful charm ('aveva un bel piedino'); in the Polka love duet, her brief narrative ('Io non son che una povera fanciulla') with its dulcet play of tone is exquisite; and her parlando is invariably delivered in a rich, utterly convincing cascade of text. In the second-act aria, she manages the garlands of tripping phrases better than many a light-voiced soprano. Above all, one should never fail to appreciate the boon of a voice voluminous enough to fill a house of Met-sized enormity—and to fill it with timbral opulence as well. Minnie must own an instrument of Destinn-like proportions to effectively succor the wounded Johnson, to confess her love, and determine to save him. Our diva has the goods, the Gioconda goods, one could say, and has them in spades.

Tebaldi was absent from the airwaves during the next season but returned for a final broadcast in an uncharacteristic ensemble role, Mistress Ford in *Falstaff* (1972). In a way, her Minnie is the last of the Tebaldi we have known and loved. When she stands alone onstage at the close of *Fanciulla*'s first act, she softly and affectingly muses on Johnson's tribute: 'Un viso d'angelo!'. For the radio audience, at that moment, the diva undoubtedly was the 'voce d'angelo!'. After all, that will be her legacy—the authorized biography proclaims it.

How unjust that in the heavenly hierarchy they say even angels are ranked.

Thomas Stewart as Amfortas in *Parsifal*. Photography by Louis Mélançon. Courtesy Metropolitan Opera Archives.

CHAPTER EIGHT

Wagner on Life Support

During the final four seasons of Bing's tenure, the committed Wagnerian's thirst was barely slaked. Eight performances of six operas made up the radio diet—in the heyday of Wagner performance in the thirties that number could be heard in a single season. The grander music dramas (*Tristan, Siegfried, Götterdämmerung*) remained off limits due to a dirth of tenors. Actually, *Tristan* had figured in the opening season at the new Met but discretion kept it off the airwaves. Besides, Nilsson (who sang Turandot and Elektra in the first two broadcast outings of that season) had ended her sojourn in mid-December. During the next four seasons, management once again relied upon the composer's lyric vein (*Lohengrin* and *Parsifal*) and, perhaps believing there was safety in numbers, the ensemble pieces (*Meistersinger* and *Rheingold*). Even a taste of the *Ring*, where Nilsson could shine, was permissible since Vickers continued to make *Walküre* viable.

Under these circumstances, *Der Fliegende Holländer* was also a likely candidate to assuage the cravings of Wagnerians. Because its musical physiognomy looked backward as much as forward, the opera could be mounted with reasonable chance of success, particularly if a soprano and baritone of charismatic personal and vocal means were on hand.

The opera's Met history, though glorious, was spotty. During the company's first decade (when for seven years the Met performed its entire repertory in German), the revered Anton Seidl introduced it (1889) with the legendary Theodore Reichmann (Dutchman) and Emil Fischer (Daland). The opera was repeated in the next season and Seidl offered a single performance (in Italian) in 1892, this time with a Frenchman (Jean Lassalle) as the protagonist and Emma Albani as Senta, and with Edouard de Reszke as her father. Milka Ternina's Senta was reason enough for a revival in 1899, with the young Schumann-Heink her spinning partner and Andreas Dippel as Erik, all under Emil Paur's baton. The following year the American bass-baritone David Bispham assumed the title role under the podium care of the young Walter Damrosch. After a hiatus of several years, Anton Van Rooy lent his magisterial bass-baritone to the Dutchman's woes. Thereafter the opera fell out of repertory until the brilliant Wagnerian epoch of the 1930s required further fodder for its grand complement of singers. Now Friedrich Schorr and the beauteous Maria Jeritza struck sparks under Artur Bodanzky's flame-tipped baton. In 1937 Flagstad led a dream cast of Schorr, Kullman, List, and

Der Fliegende Holländer
27 January 1968

Senta
Leonie Rysanek
Mary
Nancy Williams
Erik
Ticho Parly
Dutchman
Cornell MacNeil
Daland
Giorgio Tozzi
Conductor
Berislav Klobucar

Thorborg, with Maison replacing the American tenor in 1939. Bing made a game effort to reintroduce the opera during his first season (Hotter, Varnay, Svanholm, and Harshaw) but not even Reiner's incandescence could do the trick. That magic was reserved for the 1960s, when London and Rysanek began their acclaimed partnership. Schippers led the initial charge, but Böhm later took up the reins.

London's forced retirement ended that memorable union, but Rysanek found a worthy successor in the unlikely MacNeil. We hear them on the broadcast of 27 January 1968, where a new helmsman whets the appetite as well. The Yugoslav conductor, Berislav Klobucar, arrived with a quarter century's experience, including fifteen years on the roster of the Vienna Staatsoper and appearances at Stockholm, Milan, Buenos Aires, and Bayreuth. Since 1960 he had served as general director at Graz. With that background, more was expected than he delivered. Of course, he has his forces well in hand; the broadcast performance (fourth in the run) is well integrated and capably executed. In his conception, the opera's antecedents seem more prominent than auguries of the composer's future path. The *Volk* element is prominent; where *pesante* is suggested, accents are pounded home. These sailors wear heavy boots. Even the spinners are a hearty group; the facile charm of the episode is minimized as Senta's jovial friends work diligently at their task. (The male chorus, prominent participant, performs robustly and admirably, to better effect than its female counterpart.) In the end, under Klobucar, one becomes overly conscious of the opera's constituents parts. Its stylistic inconsistencies jangle and, with its scaffolding exposed, the ribbed seams show more than usual, an effect augmented by management's preference for the three-act, rather than single-unit, format. Intriguingly, Klobucar has charge of the season's *Lohengrin* and (as deputy for Karajan) *Walküre*, both to be broadcast in the month ahead.

The broadcast personnel are a fetching mix of the new and the familiar. In addition to the conductor, Ticho Parly makes a radio debut as Erik, while MacNeil and Nancy Williams are fresh broadcast interpreters of the Dutchman and Mary. The mezzo's soprano-like timbre, a far cry from the usual dark-toned, dour housekeeper of Daland's establishment, adds a welcome brightness to the spinning scene. Parly, Copenhagen born but largely American trained, was at the time of the broadcast a credible candidate among Wagner tenors. He had done his apprenticeship in the lesser German houses (Aachen, Wuppertal) before moving on to Bayreuth, where he started as Vogelgesang but later made the chasmlike leap to Siegmund (1966) and Siegfried (1968). Covent Garden and Paris had taken him up as well in the major Wagner assignments. His Met debut made possible the 1966–67 run of *Tristan und Isolde* and management brought him back for Aegisth and Erik the following season. Stout voiced, even leathery toned in the old Kurt Baum tradition, he has the notes and heft for the Wagner corpus, but little of the magic. Erik's apprehensive recounting of his dream benefits from his baritonal timbre, but his granitic vocalism bruises both arias (especially the gentle love song of the final act). Heroic tenors being in short supply, this one, an interesting actor and possessed of an attractive stage presence, was allotted his moment in the Met sun. When buying Wagnerian tenors impresarios have been forced to adopt the resigned attitude of one of Trollope's hunting men. When judging horses—so Maxwell avers in *Can You Forgive Her?*—one should never expect a "perfect animal"; he liked "em to see . . . to have four legs and . . . a little wind."[1] If so, they will do. Parly, who through no fault of his own was deficient in number of legs, had more than a little wind and did do—for two seasons. He would continue to appear with favor in other venues, but the Met evidently felt the *Tristan* debt had been paid in full.

Another tenor, of lesser repute but longer tenure, would also leave the company after this season. William Olvis, the departee, is heard as the Steersman. Ping-ponging between comprimario and leading roles, he never realized the promise of his vocal and personal equipment. Yet the sound of genuine Jugendheldentenor metal rings in his voicing of the Steersman's song. Though he was preoccupied primarily with the Italian repertory during his seven Met seasons, could he have been an incubating mini-Melchior? An echo of the Dane's tenorial squeeze lurks in his song. The steersman's captain is sung by Tozzi, who had appeared in three of the previous four broadcasts of the opera. His 1963 Daland had seemed short of timbral monumentality, that black sound which reveals the greed behind the genial manner of Senta's father. Geniality he had then, and has now, in abundance, and on this afternoon the body of the voice, robust and firm, is entirely sufficient for the role's demands. And when he sings his jolly ditties (amazing to apply that term to Wagner), Tozzi brings the feel of the folk milieu—Nicolai's beer hall, Weber's black forest—engagingly into focus. In prime vocal condition, his portrayal, both vocally and interpretively, is the finest of the afternoon.

Those words need not denigrate MacNeil's achievement as the Dutchman, his first Metropolitan essay in a Wagner role. He makes a splendid baptismal effort, successful by any standard. After a decade as the Met's major Verdi baritone (I do not forget Merrill's a priori claim), MacNeil's assets are well known: an instrument of remarkable size with an aural complement of a reliable mezza voce, interpretive intelligence, and musical rectitude. Even with instruments of size, there remains a question as to whether the Italian method, with its suave resonance, will allow the voice to cut through or surmount the Wagnerian orchestral mass. MacNeil succeeds in that regard, aided by his idiomatic treatment of the Wagner text. He has absorbed the secrets of Germanic declamation and allows articulation to do its portion of the songster's task. The voice may be a bit open-toned or an occasional beat can weight a full-voiced sustained note, but these minor blemishes recede as the opera progresses. From his throat and out of his thought Vanderdecken's introductory monologue emerges in varied accents and extremes of volume (a pensive beginning, a rousing, full-voiced conclusion). In achieving these admirable ends, Italianate legato plays a telling part. It comes impressively to the fore in the lengthy unaccompanied passage that opens the second-act duet with Senta, where his control of the softer dynamic is both technically sure and dramatically potent. MacNeil almost playfully sends along the operetta-like waltz tune when he bargains with Daland over Senta's hand. At several unexpected moments throughout the afternoon, his caress of a phrase illuminates the Dutchman's longing and makes more poignant his fate. His most impressive moments, however, occur at the opera's end, where he looses a passionate tirade of denunciation at Senta's supposed betrayal. Before taking again to the sea, he grandly names himself the condemned Flying Dutchman. On this afternoon, belief and commitment ensure MacNeil's triumph.

Rysanek, heroine of the three earlier broadcasts of the sixties, has long been acclaimed as the Senta of the modern era. (Oddly, *The New Grove Dictionary of*

Opera does not include her when naming five noted Sentas of the last century.) Judging from this broadcast portrayal, the beloved soprano seems intent upon maintaining her familiar tortoise-and-hare modus operandi. Her auditors may despair as she leaves the gate but once again she proves that a slow starter can win the race. I doubt that she is in her best vocal form; a couple of catches on sustained tones in the ballad suggest the care with which she must employ her wares. But she conquers for all that.

Her beginning is woeful indeed. Senta's ballad, the focal point of the drama, is ill served by the mewling, sickly tones that she imposes upon its initial verses. Gradually obnubilation recedes, the dormant instrument gains in fiber and force, the wondrous shine of the upper octave asserts itself, and Senta comes alive. In her responses to Erik, she exposes the mystical, driven aspects of her fixation upon the Dutchman. Even in the low-lying opening phrases of her duet with the forlorn captain, the voice responds, enabling her to convincingly sound its trancelike mood. And, when Senta soars, our heroine allows her full flight (a few sharp notes confirm her abandon). Few moments in the opera house are as exhilarating as Rysanek's impassioned proclamation at the opera's end that Senta is faithful unto death. Whatever has gone before fades almost to nothingness as the soprano's exuberant delivery and pungent, silvery thrust of tone revive doubters' spirits and provoke the house into its own abandoned response at her curtain call. Heretically, I long for a first-rate traversal of that all-important second-act ballad.

I'm glad she has another go at it. Surrounded by different associates (Chookasian, Dooley, Kónya, Shirley, and Macurdy), Rysanek again offers her Senta on the *Holländer* broadcast of 31 January 1970. This time she has her beloved mentor, Karl Böhm, to succor her. The invigorating wind that courses through the introductory pages of the overture signals the contrast between Klobucar's down-to-earth reading and the Austrian maestro's more freewheeling conception. The Dutchman's ship now travels on rougher seas, precipitously pursuing its path to the Norwegian coast. Once there, Böhm's winds, the instruments this time, blow a more introspective "redemption" theme. And so it goes throughout the afternoon, each theme or choral episode keenly articulated, its specific character enhanced. The Norwegian sailors rollick more merrily (no peasant boots for them), Böhm's maidens better enjoy their sewing (their lightly sung song is gracefully floated), the warring choruses of the final act are neatly juxtaposed, and there Daland's crew and maidens seem a remarkably civilized folk. In most ways, the opera wears a more human face, the diabolical surfacing when the need arises. In those moments, Böhm's orchestra does crackle and burst into fire. Probably Klobucar's forces were more consistently marshaled, better ordered. With Böhm, some imprecision between solo instruments and orchestral choirs momentarily catches the ear (as do an uncommon number of horn bobbles), and, truth to tell, in the final act the chorus has a tendency to lead rather than follow. But the 1970 performance's cleanly etched musico-dramatic profile is a decided plus.

The stage participants offer both less and more. Shirley is a fine Steersman. His song initially holds a touch of effort but the voice is pleasant, the manner less stentorian than Olvis preferred. Characteristically, he provides some novel musicianly touches, rounding off his song with sweet, lyrical tones. Clearly, this sailor loves his 'Mädel.' Mary profits from Chookasian's stouter sound in the lower range—she probably kept house better than most interpreters. Kónya seems to

Der Fliegende Holländer
31 January 1970

Senta
Leonie Rysanek
Mary
Lili Chookasian
Erik
Sándor Kónya
Dutchman
William Dooley
Daland
John Macurdy
Conductor
Karl Böhm

William Dooley as the Dutchman in *Der Fliegende Holländer*. Photography by Louis Mélançon. Courtesy Metropolitan Opera Archives.

have wandered into the Wagnerian terrain from another landscape. His tenor mannerisms, anachronistic style, and tonal unction remind me of similar (but apt for operetta) efforts by tenors whom I heard on many an evening at the Vienna Volksoper during the fifties. The refinement that distinguished his Lohengrin has been cast off, but then Wagner's pure knight was the epitome of containment while Senta's discarded lover is a blob of desperation. At least, so he seems when Kónya plays him as a heart-on-his-sleeve tenor. (I continue to wonder what Vickers would have made of the character had we had his promised Erik in the 1963 broadcast. Perhaps he would have exposed the "melancholy" that Wagner prescribed for his tenor.) Marginal gain adheres to Erik's lyrical arias, though even there the sob, splutter, and emotive wash Kónya visits upon them is stylistically strange and aurally trying. The crack on the top tone at the close of the third-act aria confirms that his voice is not always the reliable instrument of the sixties.

Dooley and Macurdy are new broadcast interpreters. The bass is a disappointment as Daland. He always operates at an acceptable level and does so on this afternoon, but the portrait he paints of the old sea captain lacks individuality. We miss Tozzi's cozy geniality and the new bass offers nothing distinctive as alternative; this parent is neither stern not accommodating. And the voice lacks its usual weighty presence. (But then, the tape preservation is tubby, its aural ambience dull.)

Over the years, the Dutchman's woes have issued most successfully from bass-baritone throats. Van Rooy, Schorr, Hotter, and London were all celebrated interpreters of that low-anchored breed. As we have seen, a big-voiced, wide-ranging baritone of the MacNeil type can make it work. As we have heard, Dooley's baritone is smaller-bored. It has its own blandishments, but they are not quite those that complement Wagner's wandering Dutchman. In the opening monologue, Dooley does all that art can do. Buttressed by years on the German stages, he makes a fair thing of it. He has the style, if not in his blood, in his veins. Meaningful articulation of text and subtle gradations of tone are his sustaining friends. And when he can linger in the upper octave, the fresh bloom of his baritone pleases—whether that is apt grist for a Dutchman's mill is another matter. Sometimes the voice does not seem as firmly grounded as on other broadcasts. But he can float the waltz tune with sweetness and does so without cheapening the moment. Elsewhere, lack of vocal size proves fatal—and our baritone cannot hide when Böhm unleashes the orchestral mass. (The conductor, while not inconsiderate of his stage colleagues, is hardly chary with volume at climactic moments.) The second act proves most troublesome. The great duet, along with Senta's ballad the heart of the opera, suffers from the pallid voicing of his portion. He is at odds with the composer since major sections of the duet, including the all-important opening solo, lie too low for his baritone. His lyricism and musicality are welcome but the voice simply does not speak sufficiently. Occasionally it seems as though Dooley has reboarded his upstage ship while Senta on land (and at the footlights) outshines him. Fortunately, redemption is his in the closing moments of the opera. There Wagner's higher tessitura (and his own splendid declamation, forceful manner, and a lyrical touch or two) allows his seasoned artistry to make its mark.

In the right throat, Senta is indeed a center-stage role. And, in or out of voice, Rysanek is mistress of that sacred territory. The good news is that the soprano is in far better voice than in her 1968 portrayal. The vocalized phrase with which she enters signals her vocal health. Of course, there are some tones in the lower octave that wear that familiar sickly cast, but at least they are less hollow and fewer in number. Thus, she is able to deliver a quite serviceable ballad—and more than that, in its sweeping conclusion. "Serviceable" is not intended to be demeaning but, ideally, one longs for cleaner, more precise intonation in the multiple repetitions of the fifth and fourth intervals. I have felt their bracing tonic, like a cool wind off the sea, when Flagstad and Nilsson voiced them. In the final verse, Böhm slows down several key phrases, thereby allowing the soprano to muse effectively. In the remainder of the opera, Rysanek's instrument wears that unique shine that stirs her admirers to fits of adulation. We hear its magical glow in the silvery thread of tone she spins when repeating a bit of the ballad just before the Dutchman enters. The ghostly tone with which she answers the Dutchman's opening gambit is an effective interpretive stroke. More often, the effulgence of the upper voice blazes forth in unfettered splendor. She dominates the duet to Wagner's disadvantage but her own glory. And, in their brilliance, their extravagant generosity, her sacrificial pronouncements at the opera's curtain are, if possible, even more amazing than in the 1968 broadcast.

Returning to that season's Wagneriana, I take up the more familiar *Lohengrin*, broadcast on 10 February 1968 with an unusual assemblage of principals surrounding swan knight Kónya. Arroyo (Elsa) and Milnes (Herald) cross over from the Italian to the German side, while Ludmila Dvoráková's Ortrud frets the oft-heard Telramund of Cassel to the discomfort of Macurdy's King Henry. Here is our promised opportunity to gage the breadth of Klobucar's abilities. He does show us a new face, but not necessarily an ingratiating one.

In contrast to his earthbound *Holländer*, in *Lohengrin* Klobucar serves up opera on wheels. The opening prelude is properly ethereal, but thereafter the conductor's motor runs in overdrive. His way would have warmed the heart of Edward Ziegler, Johnson's right-hand man, who informed the newly arrived Erich Leinsdorf that "we in America do not go for slow tempi."[2] With Klobucar, even the old Bodanzky accelerando is back in style. The final scenes of the second act fly along and excitement is cultivated, in this instance, to good effect. Occasionally, the singers' interpretive gestures are necessarily matter of fact, and in more than one phrase, his charges are hard pressed to meaningfully negotiate a portion of swiftly moving text. The exuberance of the third-act prelude is converted into a vulgar gloss. Klobucar's fluent delivery will have merit for those who find the opera's panoply and old-fashioned chivalry a bit shopworn, but his no-nonsense stance all but plucks the romance out of this *Romantische Oper*, a period gem. If Wieland Wagner's gigantic swan did have feathers, he would be denuded before the opera's end.

The male principals all have been heard on earlier broadcasts. Kónya's knight remains worthy of acclaim, but his tenor is hardly as succulent as in his palmy days. The honey of his remembered mezza voce is seldom heard and the top voice is often effortful, occasionally unreliable. At his initial entry, he applies an odd, darkly covered tone to the swan farewell—the third-act reprise is far more attractive. Some expansive phrases of the second act are firmly intoned, but the heroics of its finale try his instrument more than expected; several high As are precarious ventures. In order to provide the requisite climax at 'In deiner Hand,' he resorts to emotional overkill, a posture that diminishes the knight's stature. More of his old

Lohengrin
10 February 1968

Elsa
Martina Arroyo
Ortrud
Ludmila Dvoráková
Lohengrin
Sándor Kónya
Telramund
Walter Cassel
Herald
Sherrill Milnes
King Henry
John Macurdy
Conductor
Berislav Klobucar

form surfaces in the demanding third act. There, cuts in the love duet and final scene come to his aid. (A few odd cuts in the earlier acts, including a lengthy one in the act-two ensemble finale also deface the performance.) In the final act, the tenor's molasses tone begins to flow. In combination with a few stagey theatrics at climactic moments, the timbre, as previously noted, can prove cloying now and then. Still, Kónya's affecting phrasing in the lengthy duet is more nuanced than Arroyo's—this Lohengrin is obviously more in love than his Elsa. Stalwart, assured voicing of the scene's final moments affirm Kónya's stature in the role. When considering the 1967 broadcast I noted that greater declamatory thrust would improve his liquid delivery of 'In fernem Land.' This time, his declamation is markedly emphatic (the conclusion, in particular, is rhythmically strong and highly effective) with a resultant sacrifice of maximum tonal beauty—not quite a clear case of "be careful what you wish for," but close. The remainder of the act is quite splendid, with a strong legato and healthy tone much in evidence. His command of both scenes of the final act continues to warrant admiration, though his manner is more stringently tenorial than ever.

The three Americans of the male contingent more than prove their mettle. Their vocal wares and convincing portrayals satisfy. Cassel, with a dozen years experience as the wretched Brabantine count, is in remarkably fresh voice, the gruff bluster of earlier performances largely abandoned in favor of headier tone. His interpretive insights (predominantly anguished, but quietly atmospheric at 'Du wilde Seherin!') remain valid. He has the stamina to thunder Telramund's second-act challenges, while his quiet, rapid, and insidious final attempt to disturb Elsa's trust is villainy of the most enjoyable sort. In this earlier venture into the Wagner realm Macurdy is a splendid king, his declamation authoritative and his interpretive stance idiomatic; the voice, in prime condition, owns a more appealing texture than it sometimes possesses. At the 22 January premiere, the Herald had been allotted to Ron Bottcher (a baritone normally of the comprimario rank) but the broadcasts tend to bring out the big guns. Milnes' baritone definitely is prime weaponry, as he confirms with his every utterance. A few of the subtleties of his 1967 Herald have fallen by the wayside (Klobucar's pace perhaps the cause), but his keen diction and clean-cut, yet tonally effulgent, pronouncements cannot be faulted.

Dvoráková, Czech born and a habitué of the East Berlin Staatsoper, is in her third Met season, although this is her broadcast debut. A Wagner specialist, she had appeared at Covent Garden, Bayreuth, and in Buenos Aires as well. After her Met debut as Fidelio at the old Met, the slim and attractive diva had taken over Isolde from Nilsson in the new house. Obviously, management considered her a worthy contender. Her individual conception of Ortrud shows her to be a thoughtful singing actress. While most portrayers of Telramund's malignant consort like to posture, vocally and interpretively, as evil incarnate, this soprano prefers to rely upon her sexual wiles rather than Ortrud's skill at casting spells. Thus, her intimate, caressing dialogue with her distraught husband is both intriguing and effective, at least until the higher ranges of the role must be claimed and the full-blooded passages brazened forth. For a certified Isolde and Brünnhilde, she seems oddly overparted in 'Entweihte Götter!' as well as in the raging final episode of the opera (but those measures can try even the most assured vocalists). Then, too, the tone at full voice can turn gummy or, in contrast, it occasionally acquires a whistle-sharp shrewishness. Moreover, the slithery approach to high tones is annoying. Still, some of her interpretive touches are fascinating, revealing the sorceress in a new and, considering her calling, quite logical light. Many nuances, some quite subtle (her seductive exchanges with Elsa, for instance), authenticate her claim to the Wagnerian melos. Her Ortrud is secretive, wrapped in a palpable aura of mystery, quite the opposite of Ludwig's thrillingly vocalized, up-front portrayal. In her introductory *Opera News* interview, the Czech soprano voiced her desire to negotiate an extension of her three-year Met contract, but management evidently did not see it her way.[3] Some downright odd moments (including portamento slides and hooty top notes) as Ortrud fulminates in the final scenes of acts two and three explain their caution. Dvořáková's European career was probably founded more on her stage persona than her vocal abilities

Dvořáková's Ortrud is an anomaly, but Arroyo's appearance as the naive princess of Brabant is greater cause for wonder. Her vocal capabilities are hardly in doubt, although the suitability of her timbre and the viability of her style (or rather the absence of the latter) are questionable. Of course, operatic history has recognized legitimate Verdi sopranos who have excelled as the Wagner heroines. Frida Leider is the prime example, although certainly Johanna Gadski and our Nilsson would qualify as well. Yet, they and their ilk, unlike Arroyo, have usually approached the task from an opposite pole, that is from the north rather than the south, moving (at least, in terms of maximum success) from the Germanic repertory to the Italian. (American Rose Bampton provides an obligatory exception.) The metallic timbre of Arroyo's instrument all but disqualifies her for the role of the angelic Elsa. Purity and sweetness of tone, emblematic of a chaste state, have been the hallmark of many a legendary Brabant princess, with Tiana Lemnitz of old and Elisabeth Grümmer of late exemplars of that brand. Still, *Lohengrin* broadcasts have profited from the orchestral splendor of Flagstad's organ or the warmth of Traubel's outsized instrument. In those cases, however, we heard stylistically idiomatic portrayals that aided believability. Then, too, Elsa has some challenging moments where a healthy soprano is more than welcome, almost essential. For that reason, Elisabeth Rethberg, prized for her silken timbre and potent vocal thrust, was an ideal Brabantine.

Miss Arroyo's introductory 'Mein armer Bruder' (marked "dreamily, to herself") is as devoid of inner musing as a court clerk's summons. Nor can she evoke our sympathy in the several sections of 'Einsam in trüben Tagen,' though, to her credit, she strives to remove the darker resonances from her low and middle voice. Her tone is cold and occasionally harsh, with a rasp or two to make one wonder at her vocal condition. Concern proves to be unwarranted. When celebrating her savior's triumph, she sails jubilantly along, the easy play of her top voice reassuring. 'Euch Lüften' is tonally a welcome improvement; indeed, her earnest attempt at girlish purity is marginally successful, although love's transport remains remote. And she wafts some beguiling tone at the close of the women's duet. Once again, we must acknowledge, indeed, be grateful for, a voice blessed with overall good health, an infallible top range, an instrument carefully nurtured and buttressed by technical know-how. The later confrontations with Ortrud offer Arroyo the opportunity to display those assets in several firmly delivered, quite thrilling, passages. But how one longs for a touch of sweetness and a prescribed *piano* at 'soll meine Liebe steh'n!'. In a few moments of the third-act love duet, the metallic plangency of Arroyo's chest voice startles, the effect out of place in this milieu. She confidently voices a good portion of the lengthy duet, seemingly on a vocal treadmill, for nuance is in short supply. Arroyo and Kónya do manage to bring the scene to a stirring dramatic conclusion—this Elsa has not suffered as a conflicted Verdi heroine for naught. Before achieving Metropolitan stardom, Arroyo had dutifully served as Woglinde, Ortlinde, even the Forest Bird, but she tarried little in German opera after her return as Aida in 1965. Four Elsas were the sum of her appearances as a major-league Met Wagnerian.

Die Walküre
24 February 1968

Sieglinde
Leonie Rysanek
Brünnhilde
Birgit Nilsson
Fricka
Christa Ludwig
Siegmund
Jon Vickers
Wotan
Thomas Stewart
Hunding
Karl Ridderbusch
Conductor
Berislav Klobucar

Klobucar conducted his final broadcast on 24 February 1968 when a starry *Walküre* cast included Nilsson, Rysanek, Ludwig, Vickers, Stewart, and radio debutant Karl Ridderbusch. The 21 November 1967 premiere of the new production by Schneider-Siemssen had been conducted and staged by Herbert von Karajan. The occasion marked the initial effort of a projected complete Karajan *Ring* cycle at the Met. The legendary maestro was in fact scheduled for a second series of three performances in February, including the broadcast. Before the act-one curtain Cross informed the radio audience that Karajan was "unfortunately stricken with influenza and still in Europe" and that Klobucar had "graciously accepted" conducting duties for the series. Fortunately, the substitute conductor was no stranger to Karajan's ways—Vienna and Salzburg were joint venues—and he had conducted *Ring* cycles at Bayreuth. The more celebrated maestro's imprint upon the performance is probably too deep to determine whether the reading is three parts Karajan, one part Klobucar or the reverse. Remembering the Yugoslav's somewhat stolid treatment of *Holländer* and uncongenial *Lohengrin*, the more lyrical traversal of *Walküre* is likely inherited. Karajan had made clear that he viewed the opera as a chamber work, a drama that required an intimate caress. Although the microphone tends to move dynamic levels to a more neutral center, its omnipresence cannot prevent some of the more discreet orchestral passages from receding almost into oblivion. Still, the performance holds many magical moments, the conception cohesive and the opera's artistic posture wonderfully poised. At the final curtain, the placid repetitions of the motive suggestive of Brünnhilde's sleep are symbolic of the mentor's reflective view of the opera. The distribution of responsibility may be conjectural, but throughout the afternoon Klobucar's competence, evident in the orderly and precise management of his forces in the pit and onstage, is never in doubt.

Competence is hardly the word one would apply to describe the stage participants. They are not only starry in reputation but celestial in execution. The Wälsung siblings reign over the first act and Vickers and Rysanek confirm their legitimacy in these signature roles. As noted, the soprano has begun to discover the means to stabilize her vocal production in the mid and low ranges. The bugaboo that has blighted her radiance during her first decade with the company is not completely routed, but the improvement is so great as to be cause for celebration. A slightly overblown quality now hovers over the lower octave range, but tonal focus has been stabilized and control of dynamics and nuance facilitated. The betterment is indeed opportune since Sieglinde's music, in particular her narrative of Wotan's visit ('Der Männer Sippe'), lies low; though some cloudy, indeed hollow, notes occur, the soprano is a good storyteller. When, near the act's end, Wagner elevates Sieglinde's emotions, he raises her song as well; at home in the higher tessitura, Rysanek rides triumphantly on the music's wings. The tormented moments of the second act are ideal for her temperament and she makes every one of them, whether quiet pathos or raging terror, count. One can sense the madness that all but overtakes the distraught wife. Not content with her famous (or infamous) first-act scream, she proffers to her approving public yet another, this one descending the full extent of her range, its overall character rather like a whinny. The soprano confirms her aptitude for the big moment in her grand, measured laying on of tone at 'O hehrstes Wunder!'. This time, perhaps under Karajan's tutelage, she gives the eighth notes their due—indeed the conductor has prescribed a noble, almost stately pace for this redemptive episode. Rysanek can, and does, handle it with vocal composure.

No reservations need be expressed about our tenor's vocal state or his interpretive stance. He is in marvelous vocal form with the mannerisms that annoy even some of his most ardent admirers entirely in abeyance. At his entrance, Siegmund's character is defined by Vickers' virility of tone and utterance—no weak sighs of weariness escape this hero. Rhythmic vitality and clean textual articulation animate his lines, their vibrant play often unexpectedly inflecting phrases in which legato and tonal color are the more dominant expressive tools. The timbral focus is quite collected, its nasal content a bit more prominent than usual. In combination with his tendency toward vowel clarity (the *e* vowel sometimes grates in its glaring, unmodulated purity), the voice's plangency augments the determined impetuosity of Wotan's mortal son. His narrative is straightforwardly propelled, the baritonal underpinning of the voice always complementing the steadfast manner. With Vickers, the actual presence of a big voice resonating throughout the grand space of the opera house is, even over the radio, vividly apparent. Yet he never neglects to nurture a moment of inner contemplation, making plain Siegmund's melancholy life. He draws out the 'Wälse' pair to Melchiorian lengths, and his tonal wealth as well is comparable to that of the revered Dane. The tenor takes full advantage of the leisurely gait of this 'Winterstürme' (Karajan's way, again); the more melodic phrases are caressed and expanded, while his diction is less stippled than he sometimes favored. No vocal caution is needed at the capture of the sword or other rhapsodic moments. How skillfully he builds the scene's climactic phrase sequence. When, in the second act, he voices 'Geliebter,' he chooses a pointed falsetto that momentarily startles—a fragrant head tone would better enhance the moment. But his numinous responses to Brünnhilde's questions, artfully molded in their upward climb and skillfully modulated from baritonal bronze into tenor gold, confirm not only Siegmund's nobility but the tenor's integrity.

Hunding and Fricka have less opportunity for character development. In particular, Hunding sounds a single note and, indeed, perhaps Wagner has told us all we need to know of him in that graphic chordal motive that the brass trumpets. We have become accustomed to Hundings who relentlessly belch their tonal brutality upon the sibling pair. Ridderbusch's husband is a more civilized foe. That moderation, too, may be part of Karajan's domestic drama concept. In any case, the German bass, a Bayreuth regular and new to the company this season, possesses a voice of attractive timbre, its clean focus and timbral warmth perhaps a shade too Hans Sachs–like for the rough-hewn huntsman. But vocal size and forceful declamation allow him to drive home his murderous intent before trundling off for a good night's sleep. Ludwig's instrument is so comfortably warm and round, and of such unassailable security, that her Fricka never risks turning into the more fa-

miliar shrewish spouse. ("Always a woman and not as a fury" is her advice on how
to play the goddess.[4]) Its size, however, and her dramatic puissance ensure that she
will be a formidable combatant in the marital wars. Like Vickers, she is an artist
in full command of her considerable powers, of which tonal opulence throughout
the range is the sovereign mark. Her musical rectitude matches her vocal wealth.
That her Fricka, uttering a final phrase to Wotan's waiting daughter, will exit with
dignity intact is a foregone conclusion.

With the father-and-daughter duo, the matter of vocal size raises its problematic head rather more emphatically. Miss Nilsson's Brünnhilde is so well equipped
in that regard that one expects, or at least hopes, the gene was inherited from the
paternal parent. That hope is denied today. Stewart, ever honorable and steadfast
in his portrayal, is deficient in vocal power. At least, critics of the premiere had
so judged him. (Stewart had sung the premiere and most performances and was
called into service for the broadcast; Walter Berry had been scheduled in *Opera News*.) Vocal size is of less importance over the airwaves unless juxtaposition
with a vocal titan overemphasizes differences of wattage. An intelligent artist can
simulate rage by means of rhythmic energy and textual bite, and Stewart often
successfully does on this occasion. He is in fact a middle-of-the-road god. His
Wotan, no matter the character's hirsute appendages, is clean-shaven in character
and of voice. The timbre, lean but healthy and of prepossessing coloration, serves
the more reflective moments well and buffs up adequately for the emphatic episodes. To his credit, unlike run-of-the-mill present-day baritones who too often
overinflate tone to counterfeit power and thereby rob their voices of prized timbral
individuality, Stewart refuses to be trapped into overloading his instrument. He
is a dink-and-dunk Wotan, one who, like an NFL quarterback, eschews big-play
mentality in favor of more cautious, small-scale efforts; the latter do, however,
get the job done. Stewart, at least over the radio, has his winning ways. Indeed,
his attractions, in particular as to vocal quality and interpretive zeal, are considerable. He is in thorough command of the lengthy role, possessing idiomatic diction
and interpretive gestures; no sign of vocal wear and tear surfaces. (I regard the
slight tentativeness in the final phrase of the farewell as too momentary to count.
More important, the lack of a tender caress at that point—and earlier in the farewell—and the substitution of emotive accents, even a slight sob, seem stylistically
inept. They violate the nobility of this Olympian peroration.) The overall impression of his Wotan may be somewhat equivocal, but I find myself often taken with
his interpretive insights, whether innately suited to the moment or, as needed,
vocal subterfuges. And his belief in the text and situation is ever apparent. It may
be that his attributes are more in tune with Karajan's human conception of the
drama than the commanding weapons of some more godlike interpreters, past
and present.

Like Vickers' Siegmund and Ludwig's Fricka, Nilsson's Brünnhilde may be
praised without qualification. I do not recall ever having been as impressed with
the beauty of her voice and the expressive potency of her interpretation as on this
occasion. In the past, while never disputing her greatness, I have noted reservations in regard to intonation, word-pointing, and variety of tone coloration. None
of these factors inhibit her portrayal on this afternoon. The voice itself, from top
to bottom, is perfectly poised, equalized, and employed with absolute certainty.
Most welcome is the copper-tinged coloration of the lower voice, now possessing

a remarkable density that, when coupled with the familiar sword thrusts of the upper voice, make the instrument rank with those of the greatest Wagnerians of whom we have aural record. And on this afternoon her communicative powers are equally potent.

The warrior cry ('Hojotoho!') is predictably dispatched with brilliance and unconcern for its dangers; the portamentos of the octave leaps are surprisingly broad, their scope unexpected. The increased tonal weight of her voice in the lower regions especially benefits the *Todesverkündigung* episode. There Brünnhilde's questions are splendidly declaimed, the body and color of the voice enhancing the momentous nature of the announcement of impending death. Conductorial pacing of the scene is notably measured and both Nilsson and Vickers have the means, vocal and artistic, to turn to maximum effect its mesmerizing ritualistic tread. Theirs is a noble effort that makes the tenor's quiet farewell to Sieglinde doubly touching. (No matter how intimate his vocal gestures, over the airwaves or in the house, the tenor manages to hold the audience in thrall with the powerful projection of his thought.) Miss Nilsson reaches similar musical and dramatic heights in her colloquy with Brünnhilde's fearsome father in the final act. Her molding of the troublesome sequence of phrase units in which Brünnhilde asks her father if her betrayal was so shameful ('War es so schmählich') may be the most successful—as to security and beauty of tone—and the most communicative of any that have gone before in our broadcast survey. That icy brilliance that has served her so well at other operatic moments is completely banished on this afternoon. She offers in its place vocal artistry that expresses a combination of the godlike and the womanly, perfectly capturing the heroine's future *Ring* state. And she can provide the touchingly intimate gesture, as when she reminds her father of Siegfried's birth and the sword fragments. I find her treatment of the role's final, expansive phrases a slight recession into a less sympathetic vocalism and style. The difference is marginal; in size and grandeur the episode remains thrilling (although oddly, she sharps quite noticeably on her final note—the only pitch blemish of the afternoon). If you are a glutton for grandeur, call up Nilsson's stirring pleadings with her sisters (an uncommonly fine warrior group, especially in the mezzo contingent) at the beginning of the final act. There 'Fort denn eile' is imposingly thrust out, its tempo again more stately than under most conductors; of course, the pace suits her spacious song just fine. And she adds a novel touch by lightening her tone as she names Sieglinde's child 'Siegfried.'

The Swedish soprano was, to put it mildly, not overfond of being under Karajan's yoke. Bing, in his memoirs, recounts her initial reluctance to be part of the projected Karajan *Ring* at the Met, in part because of the conductor's purported overtures to other sopranos for the role of Brünnhilde. For Bing, the cycle was unthinkable without his prize Wagnerian and in the end he gained both soprano and conductor. But there is more to the story. Crespin tells us that Karajan wanted her, his Salzburg Brünnhilde, for the Met performances. Both Nilsson and Crespin eventually were signed but contretemps during rehearsals resulted in each soprano being paid for the other's performances as well as her own during the initial season of the new production.[5] We have the opportunity to hear both sopranos and conductor together on the *Walküre* broadcast of 1 March 1969—their single broadcast encounter. Vickers repeats his Siegmund but an arresting group of new interpreters fills the remaining roles: Crespin (familiar, but new as Sieglinde), Martti

Die Walküre
1 March 1969

Sieglinde
Régine Crespin
Brünnhilde
Birgit Nilsson
Fricka
Josephine Veasey
Siegmund
Jon Vickers
Wotan
Theo Adam
Hunding
Martti Talvela
Conductor
Herbert von Karajan

Talvela (Hunding), Josephine Veasey (Fricka), and Theo Adam (Wotan); the latter appears in place of the scheduled Stewart, even as Crespin replaces the scheduled Gundula Janowitz.

The ruckus kicked up in the press at the premiere over Karajan's conception of the score now seems more a teapot tempest than a cause célèbre. Yes, it differs from the grandly scaled interpretations that the years have favored, but proportionality, that is, the conductor's judicious weighting and balancing of disparate elements, usually keeps it within the bounds of generally accepted interpretive standards. Above all, it can serve as a Solti antidote for those to whom excess causes greater abdominal distress than Karajan's mild-mannered draught. On the broadcast, Wagner's climaxes, even allowing for the microphone's leveling influence, continue to stir the pulses; but ultimately the magic lies in the proportions. Karajan does relish the interpretive plateau, where an accompaniment sequence is held in absolute equilibrium—he seldom favors the *Steigerung* that holds most Wagnerians in thrall. Still, rapture prolonged, though different, may be as potent as rapture spent. In compensation, the maestro offers a marvelously flexible play of motives, fluidity in transitions, an often irresistible tracery of string shimmer—the fire music, for instance, positively glows. And there was more of Klobucar in the 1968 broadcast than suspected. Karajan's storm music, less craggy but filled with startling accents, moves at a quicker pace than that of his substitute. Conversely, lyrical moments (the first-act love sequence) are more gently disposed. No one can deny, however, that Karajan's delicately etched sword motive seldom has a cutting edge. Detractors can take comfort in that paradox.

In his memoirs, Bing averred that Nilsson felt "somewhat out of place" in the maestro's chamber music concept of the opera.[6] The soprano was never one to hide her light (and what a blinding light it is) and thus reticence does not affect her portrayal on this afternoon. I am inclined to rate this reading as marginally less spellbinding than that of the 1968 broadcast. Her vocal control is equally assured, but the interpretive spectrum is somewhat more contained, and the marvelous warmth of tone that made the earlier portrayal so welcoming is not always in evidence. The plaint that can insinuate itself into her tone surfaces a bit too often. This time, she markets a piercing beauty rather than an enveloping embrace. Still, several moments of quietude and introspection again delight (especially in the last-act father–daughter colloquy). Carolyn Abbate has told us, and most persuasively, that Brünnhilde is possessed of a "unique listening ear."[7] With her godfather—as well as in her earlier questioning of Siegmund—Nilsson manages to suggest by subtle expressive means that she is indeed a good listener. But overall, she is preoccupied with vocal brilliance. If that is her intent, she fulfills it spectacularly. What remains most memorable about a Nilsson performance, in addition to her incredible stamina, is the absolute confidence of her vocalism and, though seemingly touched by a strong dose of risk (at least it would be for others), its triumphant poise. A few moments of shrillness cannot dilute her achievement.

Vickers more or less replicates his 1968 portrayal. If anything, it is even more vividly limned. He lives every phrase he breathes. And he is again in superior vocal form. Karajan's way allows him greater opportunity for coloristic effects and subtle nuances. In the *Todesverkündigung*, both artists' posture is slightly less noble (but similarly affecting) under this maestro's quieting hand, while Siegmund's farewell to his beloved is infinitely touching as the tenor's half-voice tones play over Karajan's softly glowing orchestral fabric.

Any tenor ought to be able to summon regret at leaving a Sieglinde so enticing as Crespin's. A delicious femininity pervades each phrase she lays upon the
distraught stranger on her hearth. The delicacy of her multicolored vocal tints is
aurally enticing, a kind of reverse voluptuousness. This Sieglinde is a seductress
without portfolio. According to Mary Garden, French singers are "apt to get their
voices in their noses instead of in their throats."[8] No danger of that misplacement
with our soprano. Garden's complaint rested on those damnable French vowels,
but Crespin knows how to handle them. Her tone is anything but in her nose.
When she exploits the density and roundness of her voice in the middle and low
ranges, security of placement allows her rewarding interpretive freedom. (One
must contrast her control, and its resultant expressivity, with that of the interpretively perfervid but, in these vocal regions, technically precarious, Rysanek. The
gods apportion their gifts with abundant charity but are reluctant to surrender
the totality of their booty to any given favorite. Crespin was sometimes vulnerable
at the opposite end of the range.) A particular subtlety (it likely bears Karajan's
imprint) is Crespin's exquisite matching of movement and velvety tone with the
clarinet as they purl what is often called the motive of Sieglinde's Pity. At the
other end of the spectrum, the wealth of tone, with its warming density, that she
applies to Sieglinde's cry asking Siegmund to remain is equally compelling. After
Hunding's departure, the extensive love scene enables the singer to reveal the
breadth of her instrument, at full voice weighted toward the clarinet's chalumeau
timbre. Occasionally, in the first act, one senses (rather than discovers) a slight discomfort as she lingers on high, but even there on this afternoon the voice, though
it cannot match Rysanek's revelry in stratospheric notes and silvery aplomb, is
richly colored, grand in circumference, and flavorful in utterance. Karajan does
not allow his soprano to surge and soar in 'Du bist der Lenz.' Some may feel that
a wisp of stolidity, whether due to Karajan's control or her intent, hovers over her
portion of the love sequence. Perhaps we are expected to surmise that Hunding's
abusive treatment has repressed his wife's emotional responses. Crespin makes up
for the sister's inhibition with her triumphant naming of Siegmund. Even more
resplendent is her huge-voiced sounding of 'O hehrstes Wunder!' in the opera's
climactic moment. (In her wonderful memoir, Crespin tells us that Nilsson offered
her a "bravo" during the thunderous applause that greeted their peroration.)[9] In
between, she demonstrates her skill at vocal acting, portraying Sieglinde's second-
act distress not as incipient madness but rather extreme distress. Though a creature tried beyond endurance, this screamless Sieglinde's self-knowledge remains
intact. And so does the diva's. Crespin has in fact given us her own catalogue of
her "main vocal assets . . . charm, sensuality, nobility, and a proud lyricism."[10] All
vivify her Metropolitan Sieglinde.

An abusive husband looms large on this afternoon, for Martti Talvela is enormous in both frame and voice. New to the company this season, he signaled his
gifts in an October debut as the Grand Inquisitor. Appearances as Fasolt and
Hunding confirmed his value, but it would not be until the mid-seventies that
Boris Godunov and other demanding roles revealed the full scope of his abilities.
His Hunding is oddly housed in Karajan's subdued environment and, indeed, the
conductor's cozy rendering of the husband's menacing motive (no belching brass
for him) does seem to contradict Wagner's dramatic plan. (Yet how engagingly the
rhythmically quick and blandishing brass choir, deft as ballerinas on tiptoe, sounds
the manifold repetitions of the motive.) Whether instructed or not, Talvela plays

with restraint throughout the bulk of his scene. While the voice's size registers, its timbre (like Frick's grand instrument appropriately black but, in the Finn's case, devoid of any dampening straightness of tone) is enlivened by a fruity resonance that does, after all, allow him accommodation within Karajan's domestic drama. And at his exit, Talvela, undoubtedly aided by his monumental physique, provides the necessary harsh fillip of vocal menace as warning to the incipient lovers.

While Talvela will shine as one of the company's genuine stars in future years, the other two newcomers, though artists of merit, are destined for shorter tenures. London-born mezzo Josephine Veasey's timbre is striking and her vocalism can be either thrusting or poised. Most notable is the dramatic intensity of her playing. Indeed, her portrayal of Wotan's wife, while closer to the norm than Ludwig's conception, is excessively emphatic and, in its unrelieved agitation and anger, often scratchy of tone. No wonder Wotan seeks comfort in other arms. In the final moments of her scene, Veasey, who would have a distinguished career in other theaters, demonstrates that she does know how to sing.

Theo Adam would rack up a few more Met seasons than his stage wife, but his impact upon the company was similarly limited. That he was considered a real player in the Wagnerian sweepstakes is apparent from his debut assignment of Hans Sachs a few weeks before the *Walküre* broadcast. Anchored at the Berlin Staatsoper since 1957, he had been heard as well in Salzburg (Ochs, Wozzeck) and Covent Garden (Wotan). The Met *Annals* lists him as a bass, *The New Grove Dictionary of Opera* as a bass-baritone. The confusion of nomenclature is germane since the German recruit's instrument easily encompasses the wide range of Wotan's lengthy expositions (a bass-baritone's aptitude) but lacks the dark hue of the typical bass. Nor is the vocal mass entirely adequate to the role's demands—although that deficiency is only occasionally apparent over the airwaves. More disappointing is the timbral ordinariness, the tones attractive enough for journeyman roles but hardly divine. Nor does imagination, musical or dramatic, provide a compensatory virtue. Having positioned Adam in seeming mediocrity, one must applaud his resourcefulness, his stamina, his overall command of the strenuous role. Particularly welcome, in view of Stewart's deficiency in this regard, is the size and solidity of his low range; his narrative is superior to the American artist's simply because of the vocal ease of his projection in the nether region. Clarity of diction is yet another plus. He is at his best when berating his recalcitrant daughters in the final act; the voice blooms both in color and size, and the upper range momentarily takes on an invigorating baritonal resonance. Here, and in the ensuing confrontation with Brünnhilde, he again outperforms Stewart. His reading of the farewell confirms his experience, but is rather raw toned and emotionally sterile (to his credit, he does avoid Stewart's excesses). Gratefully, I settle upon the way Karajan's strings enchantingly encircle the vocal line with their triplets and note the conductor's affinity for legato descending chords. Unlike many a Met Wotan of recent seasons, Adam has sufficient voice at the opera's close to summon Loge in strong, assertive tones. Still, the dispensers of vocal godhood have not seen fit to anoint this Wotan, no matter his status among operatic deities.

To Bing's mind, Karajan's brief Met visitation was "unquestionably the outstanding artistic phenomenon" of his later years with the Met. He thought that the maestro inspired both fear and respect within the company.[11] Bing's descriptive words are pertinent. I recall meeting Karajan—if an unobservant nod and a muttered word or two can be so described—in 1959 at Carnegie Hall. On short notice, management had called to ask me to play for a rising and greatly gifted young Canadian bass-baritone who was to audition for the maestro. Karajan entered late into the empty hall, wearing an aesthetically telling short black cape. A few questions and words of approval followed performances of Iago's Credo and other similar items. (The young singer, James Milligan by name, was greatly acclaimed at his 1961 Bayreuth debut as the *Siegfried* Wanderer, but his early death in November 1961 at age thirty-three robbed Wagnerians of a worthy and much-needed candidate for Heldenbariton primacy over the bleak decades ahead.) Karajan was often an elusive creature and even Bing could not get the conductor comfortably in his sights. Rather surprisingly, he offered as reason that "he [Karajan] is very shy and I am very shy."[12] Fortunately for those of us who relished his wit and spirit, the Met manager was never shy in his public dealings, particularly when tangling with critics, whether in the press, on the artists' roster, or of other repute.

Like many, Bing deemed Karajan's *Walküre* a touch small-scale for the American public, but he felt the maestro's *Rheingold* of appropriate stature.[13] The broadcast of 22 February 1969 confirms that judgment. Of the *Walküre* crew, Adam (Wotan) and Talvela (Fasolt) are the only holdovers. (Veasey was to have sung Fricka but canceled, so Anna Reynolds, already scheduled for Flosshilde, sings both parts, except when Shirley Love briefly stands in as the latter in scene four, where both characters are onstage simultaneously.) Karajan had produced each of his *Ring* operas at Salzburg before toting them to the Met. For *Rheingold*, he brought over a number of his Salzburg artists, some of them evidently not to Bing's liking. The Europeans' comfort level in the Karajan orbit tells in their equable performances, but their welcome idiomatic style proved insufficient to guarantee substantial or important Met careers. Mixed in with the foreign contingent are a group of Met stalwarts (including Verdi specialist Milnes, on hand to wield Donner's hammer with impeccable aim) who know how to operate on home ground.

The maestro has the Met orchestra operating like a well-oiled machine, with only an occasional horn bobble to prick the illusion of perfect harmony. While the decibel scale is fully equal to Wagner's intent (as Mr. Bing opined), even in the composer's quite waspish prologue to the trilogy Karajan's control is so absolute and his abhorrence of sharp edges so manifest that the opera glides forth on ball bearings. The manner suits the Rhinemaidens' song to perfection and adjusts comfortably enough to the machinations of giants and Nibelungs. Motives are molded with deceptive ease, transitions are masterly, and when orchestral torrents are called for, Karajan momentarily opens the sluice gates. The succulence of the maestro's instrumental play, from the plump low brass (their dragon theme makes one love the beast) on up to the swirling high strings, must be relished. And he is kind to his singers, who in turn offer character portrayals of convincing theatricality and penetrating musical insight.

Onstage, the unlikely stars of the afternoon are the giant and the dwarf. The incongruous pairing is warranted by their superior contribution to the afternoon's quality: on the one hand, Talvela's magisterial grandeur becomes Fasolt, while Zoltán Kelemen gains pride of place for the overall excellence of his Alberich. The Finnish bass' tones are distinguished not only by their size (sufficient in themselves

Das Rheingold
22 February 1969

Freia
Simone Mangelsdorff
Fricka
Anna Reynolds
Erda
Lili Chookasian
Loge
Gerhard Stolze
Mime
Andrea Velis
Wotan
Theo Adam
Alberich
Zoltán Kelemen
Conductor
Herbert von Karajan

to sham menace) but by their overtone complexity: this time, the rich bouquet issuing from his throat is placed in the service of a genuinely loathsome character. But when Fasolt laments the contemplated loss of Freia, the giant's voice all but weeps—a neat, humanizing touch for the monster who will shortly strike his brother dead. Ridderbusch, as the luckless sibling, has merits of his own, including attractive tone and a lieder-like delivery of a few of Fafner's contemplative phrases. Together, the brothers make a study in contrasts. The real find of the afternoon is Kelemen's chameleon portrayal of the Nibelung. A Karajan favorite and a Bayreuth regular, the Hungarian baritone was at home on most stages in northern Europe. His skill as a singing actor is patent from first to last—no character trait escapes his probing mind, no phrase is untouched by some imaginative vocal effect. Best of all, the voice has substantial size and the singing method is sound—in several welcome moments he even allows its timbral appeal to surface. Not surprisingly, this Alberich will tread the world stages as Falstaff, Osmin, and Baron Ochs, credits that few Nibelungs can claim. But the Met will hear little of him.

Nor will Gerhard Stolze (Loge) return for more than a few seasons. Like Kelemen, the German tenor was at home at Bayreuth and on other German stages, but, in contrast to his colleague, his vocal equipment is far less malleable. Abetted by *Cabaret*-like intonations—though no "willkommen" escapes the gods' own master of ceremonies' lips—his timbre possesses seemingly undiluted blatancy. Its bright point cuts in the extreme, and the tone occasionally is sour enough to curdle mother's milk. Thus the tenor plays on a single string, but what a master he is at manipulating that bit of catgut. One can practically taste the slippery sibilants when he tells Alberich to 'slip on home.' His characterization of Loge is unfailingly assured, the fire god's volatility, acuity, spitefulness, and any other character trait one can imagine as appropriate to the wily manipulator of the gods ruthlessly exposed. Time was when Loge was a glamor part—Maison, Svanholm, and Vinay were in that line. Not so today's player, although Stolze's Loge indeed does give off a bright light, his strident declamation illuminating every phrase. The portrayal, however it wears on the senses, does hold a peculiar fascination. The ears' receptivity is challenged when Stolze and Velis (an effective Mime) loose their mutual whines in the Nibelung's cave.

In addition to those named above, the Rhinemaiden trio (newcomers Liselotte Rebmann, Edda Moser, and Anna Reynolds) warrant unreserved admiration. Their song, pointed rather than gentle, is uncommonly attractive and pure-toned, particularly that of Rebmann's Woglinde. Moser is already familiar from her 1971 broadcast Anna but is heard here in her first Met season. The distinctive timbre of her middle voice surfaces even in this ensemble. As earlier noted, Reynolds, initially heard as Flosshilde and a most attractive artist, gains a more important role on this afternoon. She capably undertakes Fricka's chores. We expect to hear a more emphatic utterance and beefier tone from Wotan's spouse (something more of the Branzell, Thorborg, Harshaw, or Dalis stripe) than the charming British mezzo can summon. But she is a sensitive artist through and through and, both in dramatic conception and musical execution, she, unlike Veasey, proves a Fricka whose fetching vocalism and pliant nature might be expected to keep Wotan on the heavenly hearth. Lili Chookasian, she of the resonant contralto, offers a similarly appealing portrayal. Her Erda may not shake the rafters with its grandeur,

Sándor Kónya as Parsifal. Photography by Louis Mélançon. Courtesy Metropolitan Opera Archives.

but the voice is a healthy vehicle, the tone free of wobble and mercifully not overblown (no Clara Butt boom for her). Her sensitive delivery radiates repose, a quality that Wotan would be wise to cultivate.

Though he figures last in my enumeration of artists, Theo Adam is neither least nor best. At his entrance, the tone is again disturbingly commonplace. Oddly, in the prologue's closing pages, it reassumes that same slightly grainy, worn-out quality—'Abendlich strahlt' deserves something finer if Wotan's christening of Valhalla is to fulfill its purifying dramaturgical function. In between these marks, the voice blooms intermittently, frequently resonating on high with life-giving color; often enough Adam summons sufficient power to authenticate the god's right to govern. Still, on this afternoon, the scenes where Kelemen and Stolze contest register the most strongly, while, at the opera's close, it is Karajan's overall conception that remains in the memory.

After years of justifiable reluctance, Bing had been willing to ignore Karajan's Nazi associations and allow him the run of the house. Were the rewards of the maestro's tenure sufficient to assuage the manager's concerns? Yes—and no. In his memoirs, Bing is rather noncommittal about it all. Handling Karajan, notwithstanding the undeniable aesthetic rewards that Bing treasured, was a trying chore for even so adept an artist juggler as our ever-game impresario.

Parsifal
3 April 1971
Kundry
Irene Dalis
Parsifal
Sándor Kónya
Amfortas
Thomas Stewart
Klingsor
Morley Meredith
Gurnemanz
Cesare Siepi
Titurel
John Macurdy
Conductor
Leopold Ludwig

From the Olympians we turn to the saints, an elevation only if mores are taken into account. Another German maestro, Leopold Ludwig, like Karajan destined for limited Met service, joined the company early in the 1970–71 season. Placed in charge of the new Robert O'Hearn production of *Parsifal*, the longtime intendant of the Hamburg Staatsoper guided a cast including Christa Ludwig as Kundry and the debutant Helge Brilioth as Parsifal. The maestro returned to conduct the broadcast on 3 April 1971 with the "home team" duo of Dalis and Kónya in the leading roles and premiere veterans Stewart (Amfortas), Macurdy (Titurel), and Meredith (Klingsor). A feature of the broadcast (as it was at the premiere) is the appearance of Siepi as Gurnemanz, a role that he would perform nine times with the company. Kónya and Meredith had appeared in the last broadcast of the opera (1966) but the others are new radio interpreters.

The Austrian conductor, whose credits included stints as principal conductor at the Vienna and Berlin houses, as well as appearances at Glyndebourne and San Francisco, had first conducted the opera in 1937. Thus his acquaintance with Wagner's "festival play" was certifiably long and his reading may be assumed to be thoroughly considered. He held that the monumental work permitted "a wider variety of approach" than the composer's other operas, a view perhaps offered in defense of his somewhat novel conception.[14] Disputants might designate his reading as bland, while adherents probably would prefer to characterize its prevailing placidity as serene. Under Ludwig's benign leadership, the operatic plane is leveled. The orchestral fabric, its sonority as uniform and cushiony as the nap of a Kirman carpet, moves on in a seemingly timeless flow, an interpretive stance not inconsistent with the spirituality of the opera's outer acts. Virtuosity, whether affecting dynamics, tempo, or phrasing, is clearly not the maestro's intent; indeed, some opportunities along that line (especially in the second act, where serenity seems out of place) are insufficiently acknowledged. Obviously, the maestro, buttressed by experience, charts his preferred course and does so with surety and inherent belief. And mercifully, he does not allow the opera's closing pages to languish. Avoiding pomposity and with evident elation, he welcomes Montsalvat's salvation with open arms.

In those final pages, Kónya acquits himself well. His aptitude for the expansive phrase, molded with a liquid legato, and his tonal sheen complement Parsifal's elevated sentiments as he heals Amfortas' wound and accepts the leadership of the Grail brotherhood. He is equally impressive in his lovingly intoned reflections as the Good Friday Music casts its spell. But the tenor is a better third-act celebrant than a second-act youth tormented by desire. More steel in the tone, more bite in the declamation is necessary to make Parsifal's struggle and triumph convincing. Though they cannot gain the guileless fool's embrace, the Flowermaidens (with Gail Robinson proffering graceful song and von Stade's unique timbre surfacing here and there) merit reward for the attempt. Of the assorted knights and esquires, Rod MacWherter and Leo Goeke are solid participants in the question-and-answer interchanges with Gurnemanz.

Wagner has provided Amfortas with two pivotal scenes, strategically placed near the opening and the close of the opera. They are among the most affecting, indeed troubling, moments in all opera and require an artist of distinctive vocal timbre and searching interpretive gifts. On this afternoon, Stewart cannot qualify on either count. The timbre, attractive enough on its own terms, lacks the heady resonance of a Schlusnus or the emotion-laden angst of a London, either of which can in and of itself aurally personify the troubled ruler's torment. Stewart is ever the able and conscientious artist and resolutely works at his task, but his portrayal is limited not only by the voice's seeming impassibility but by its modest proportions.

Probably the orchestra is the ultimate star of any *Parsifal* performance, but Kundry runs it a close second. Dalis had been the first American Kundry on Bayreuth's hallowed stage in 1961 and that same year brought her temptress to the Metropolitan. Her thorough knowledge of the part and sure execution of it make her Kundry a significant contribution to broadcast portrayals of the role. Over the years many of Kundry's prominent interpreters have been sopranos: Nordica and Fremstad in the early years and Leider, Flagstad, Varnay, Mödl, and Crespin in our own time. The high tessitura in the closing pages of the second act perhaps dictates their supremacy. The dichotomy of the role's vocal requirements is confirmed by the cast of the original 1882 Bayreuth productions, where the role was two parts soprano (Amalie Materna and Therese Malten), one part mezzo (Marianne Brandt). (Margarete Matzenauer solved the riddle by changing her nomenclature, variously citing herself as mezzo-soprano or soprano.) In *Grove*, the role is categorized as "mezzo-soprano" and, of late, many of that ilk have braved its challenges and more than a few have conquered. Dalis surely belongs among the conquerors. Her broadcast portrayal is made memorable by the sensuous quality of her middle and upper voice. When, in Klingsor's magic garden, she first calls Parsifal's name and confronts him as temptress, she startles with the sheer beauty of her voice and her interpretive subtlety. The luscious timbre, with its seductive shimmer, contains its own magic, surely enough to win any or all but the 'reine Thor.' Her flexible phrasing and command of text bespeak a singer who inhabits her character to the fullest, achieving a fusion of musical and dramatic elements. The voice is less puissant in its lowest regions but she has managed to unite the chest voice to the upper range without noticeable break—no weakness demands subterfuge in that area. And the tessitura (with particular reference to those trying moments at the opera's close) is handled with marvelous security and tonal beauty. A singular instance of her dedication is her assured negotiation of the fearsome leap at 'lachte'—both the upper and lower tones are struck with pinpoint accuracy. No realistic baggage is piled on—she allows Wagner's huge, discordant interval to speak for itself. Other mezzos have voices of greater brilliance and wider tonal density (Christa Ludwig, the premiere Kundry, for one) but Miss Dalis owns a singular combination of vocal and interpretive gifts. When the redoubtable Cosima Liszt Wagner considered the several Kundrys of the Bayreuth premiere, she averred that Marianne Brandt would be capable of singing the role "well."[15] The devoted Cosima's conviction comes from her husband, who, fresh from working with Brandt, assured her that "everything about Kundry is costume—her ugliness, her beauty—all of it a mask." No costume assists Dalis in conquering her radio audience. With voice and art alone she succeeds in removing Kundry's mask.

As noted, the novel feature of the performance is Siepi's Gurnemanz. The great basso deserves nothing but praise for undertaking, in his twenty-first season with the company, this touchstone role of the German repertory, a category where his Met forays were limited to a single Fernando and four appearances as Sarastro. If the result, when measured against the memorable interpretations of artists rooted in the traditions of Wagnerian performance (Weber, Hotter, and Frick come to mind), is not entirely successful, the rewards are yet substantial. Most notably, they include the application of songlike legato to the old Knight's obbligato phrases in the Good Friday Music sequence and the uniquely sonorous riches of his instrument. That riverine flow of tone, bank full, may also be considered, in this *Fach*, a modest demerit. A more brusque tone (pithier than the Italian's grand but soft-grained resonance), one that permits an individualized pointing up of the text, is desirable in Gurnemanz's lengthy narrations. Siepi's German diction is adequate and far more correct than most Italian artists manage; we frequently understand the text, though it is hardly so flavorfully articulated as the speech of the best Wagnerians. (Not unexpectedly, one hears a bit more of the preferred clean articulation and tonal aptness in American Macurdy's brief pronouncements as Titurel.) More to the point is the warm humanity with which Siepi's sound and manner illuminate the elevated character of Gurnemanz. In the end, we must be content with the knowledge that Giovanni's doublet is a snugger fit for his dashing figure than the hermit's capacious robes.

The Met's Wagner history was too illustrious to allow the composer's heritage to pass, even momentarily, from the New York scene. The life support that Bing provided for the more manageable works proved efficacious. Still, several of the music dramas continued to elude the manager's grasp. Most regrettably, Metropolitan audiences would not taste the full fruits of the god's progress over Karajan's rainbow bridge. Of the planned Karajan *Ring*, only *Rheingold* and *Walküre* journeyed from Salzburg to New York. The labor strike that curtailed the 1969–70 season necessitated many alterations in plans and Karajan purportedly was no longer available when the project was later reinstituted. Though the Austrian maestro's *Siegfried* and *Götterdämmerung* would be forever lost to him, the manager, full of hope, soldiered on. He scheduled a new production of *Tristan* for his final season with the company.

After all, he still had Nilsson.

Geraint Evans as Wozzeck. Photography by Louis Mélançon. Courtesy Metropolitan Opera Archives.

CHAPTER NINE

Loners

Night after night, Mozart, Verdi, Wagner, and Puccini will fill the house and coffers of most opera companies, but often enough a work of unique character has crept into the repertory and found a comfortable niche among the bread-and-butter works. A classic myth (Gluck's *Orfeo ed Euridice*), a bit of period frou-frou (Flotow's *Martha*), an early-nineteenth-century rescue drama (*Fidelio*), commedia dell'arte on the half-shell (*Ariadne auf Naxos* by Strauss), and Berg's musically complex and dramatically wrenching *Wozzeck* all figured in the Met repertory from 1967 through 1971. I take them up not in the above birth chronology, but rather in the order of Met performance, the sequence serving to lead us from early days (the 1967–68 season) in the new house on to Mr. Bing's final opening night.

Flotow's romantic comic opera, polyglot in dramatic and musical antecedents, had been much favored by early Met audiences, but had not been heard for more than three decades when Bing reintroduced it in the 1960–61 season. Despite quality casting (De los Angeles and Tucker as Martha and Lionel), the new production found little favor and was retired after a strenuous tour workout. The manager, alert to the need for champagne evenings during the holiday season, tried again, this time opting to offer the opera's fragile charms on New Year's Eve, 1967. The broadcast of 3 February 1968 lacks the star power of the 1961 broadcast, but its singers are representative of what one would expect to encounter in prime companies throughout America. Jean Fenn and John Alexander (stepping in "at the last moment" once again, this time for the indisposed Kónya) are the leads, with Donald Gramm as Plunkett and Plishka as the Sheriff. Elias and Alvary re-create their 1961 roles as Nancy and Tristram. On the podium, as he had been for many recent Met champagne evenings, was Czech-born (but now Broadway's own) Franz Allers. One might expect that innumerable evenings spent in the company of *My Fair Lady* would guarantee the requisite accommodating touch for this slight fare. But Allers, like Verchi in 1961, applies a hard finish to the score. He drives its tempos with rigid insistence and applies cloglike accents to the accompaniment chords—the melodies hardly have room to breath, let alone bloom. Even so affecting an episode as the 'Goodnight' quartet fails to cast its spell. Perhaps Allers doesn't trust the opera's innate charm to connect with modern audiences. Liveliness is preferable to stodginess and Allers does keep the opera on the move. Mr. Bing's hoped-for champagne turns out to be merely a mild cream sherry—still slightly intoxicating, but alas, no bubbles.

Martha
3 February 1968

Lady Harriet
Jean Fenn
Nancy
Rosalind Elias
Lionel
John Alexander
Plunkett
Donald Gramm
Tristram
Lorenzo Alvary
Conductor
Franz Allers

No translator was listed for the 1961 mounting; text changes during re-hearsals were so numerous that evidently no one was willing to take credit for the resulting mishmash. For the current broadcast, the translation of George Meade is employed. Fenn is largely unintelligible, but the others deliver the English words with clarity. Not the least of these is Alvary, whose comic talents remain evident in his slightly accented, but precise, diction, while Plishka is equally effective as a forceful Sheriff who enunciates the terms of the servant—master contract with authority. Elias saves her clarity for when it counts, interjecting a telling comment at critical moments. In the earlier broadcast, she had overplayed her comic hand, the novel text and Tozzi's cloddish Plunkett the encouraging culprits. (The original *m* in Plumkett is moved up to *n* at the Met.) With the elegant Gramm as her cohort, she is more restrained. The new manner, while welcome, dilutes her dramatic effectiveness, but her Nancy remains sufficiently saucy. Notwithstanding a bit of off-pitch singing in her opening phrases, she performs (especially in a few phrases of coloratura) with her customary assurance. Gramm is an artist of considerable address and is not ashamed to swathe Plunkett with his cultivated artistry. He refuses to put on the manured boots of Tozzi's farmer (whose individuality of characterization and bonhomie, no matter their excesses, had to be savored). Deftness and attractive tone are Gramm's preferred weapons. One would not expect him to be at home in a beer garden and he is not; the brew he serves up in the beer aria is decidedly light. But it goes down neatly.

Kónya undoubtedly would have applied a honeyed slurp in the best Mittel-European operetta manner to Lionel's expansive melodies. Measured by that yardstick, Alexander's farmer comes off as a nice enough chap, but probably overly serious for the genre. Nor does he offer the grand line, the bel canto suavity of Tucker's hero, whose high-tension vocalism was modeled on the Caruso manner. Still, Alexander is ever the reliable vocalist and the committed interpreter, virtues that sustained a long and honorable Metropolitan career. His disappointed lover, obviously heartsick at Martha's harsh treatment of him, bristles with indignation. Alexander's passionate utterance would not be out of place in Edgardo's tomb scene, where the stakes are decidedly higher. He applies a narrative thrust to 'In my dream' ('Ach, so fromm'), turning it into a miniature drama, its heart-on-sleeve emotion thus augmenting character. But the result is musically a disservice—he carves the familiar aria into more than the allotted brief phrase units so that the piece looses melodic continuity. One can always count on him to provide stout climaxes, which he does wherever needed.

Miss Fenn hardly looms large in the annals of opera, but her Met career was far from negligible. Marguerite, Manon, and Eva are not insubstantial credits for the Queen's Maid of Honor turned servant. The Illinois-born soprano, trim of figure and lovely of face, undoubtedly was a Martha to give comfort to any eyes, sore or well. Nor is the ear ill treated, for her vocalism cannot be faulted. The role is bedecked with little flights of coloratura that she handily dispatches (one sticky hairpin scale the exception). Her top notes, readily reached and devoid of acidity, are on the mark. Those valuable attributes enable her to roam confidently through the varied emotions and over the vocal obstacles of her final aria. (No point in naming acts—the Met converts the four-act work into two large units.) There, regret is touchingly conveyed, and she ripples unconcernedly through the closing roulades. The voice, which in earlier broadcasts lacked individuality in the middle range, seems to have matured agreeably, the timbre in that area gaining in body and taking on an attractive amber glow. Her Lady Harriet is a spunky creature, one who might well relish the Richmond Fair adventure. Where I fault Fenn is for her reading of 'The Last Rose of Summer,' that beguiling chestnut which Flotow purloined from Irish folk song stock. At this point, the opera should stand still, suspended in sympathetic reflection. To mitigate her caste consciousness, the heroine must show us her worth, draw us to her, a heartfelt voicing of her aria momentarily making the opera's fairytale love story ring true. Fenn's delivery is deft, the phrases quite decorously etched, but one wants something more, a tonal radiance that amplifies the text's forlorn sentiment. When both 'Die letzte Rose' and 'Ach, so fromm' are downgraded, the opera's musical and emotional nodes are insufficiently burnished.

The leap from the charming artifice of Flotow's make-believe world to the fright-laden nightmares of *Wozzeck* almost causes vertigo to set in. The disorder is not inappropriate, for even Berg's Captain, when taunting the simple soldier, remarks that he is made 'quite dizzy from this man.' Note that the Met continued to present the opera in English translation. After Bing's brave introduction of the masterwork in 1959, he provided a repeat broadcast in 1961, confirmation that he meant business when he introduced the work into the Met repertory. He produced it again in the 1964–65 season, but unfortunately there was no broadcast to solidify the manager's spadework with the greater American public. Thus eight years had elapsed before the radio audience again felt the cumulative power of the Viennese composer's compressed version of Büchner's remarkable drama.

The venerable Böhm, like Berg an Austrian native, had charge of all previous productions, but this time Colin Davis, product of Britain's cooler clime, is on the podium. The maestro, still in his early forties, had triumphed in his Met debut the previous season; *Peter Grimes*, yet another twentieth-century work but one with a more traditional patrimony, was the vehicle. Davis is certainly not timid about allowing the opera's climaxes their full impact—Berlioz, after all, was not only his daily bread, but his meat. Berg would hardly be well served if those searing moments (especially the single-tone crescendo that marks the stabbing of Marie) failed to receive their due. Upon first hearing *Wozzeck*, Arnold Schoenberg had written to Berg, his erstwhile pupil, that there were things he didn't "find good" (i.e., "the fact that almost every scene builds to a great orchestral *fff*"). He thought a change there "might be necessary."[1] Judging from his emphases, Davis would not have agreed. The conductor inexorably realizes the gradual accretion of intensity in the symphonically conceived second act. And yet the dominant impression one gains from Davis' stewardship is his concern for the finer details of Berg's intricate structural forms, the compact vessels into which the composer ladled the drama's disturbing and passionate affects. He allows us to hear the incredible beauty of Berg's orchestral fabric, its ethereal chamber music effects, the colorful play of solo instruments. In this conductor's concept, few jagged contours interrupt the orchestral flow. Yet the horror quotient not only survives, but thrives. And the lyrical, curvaceous phrasing Davis applies to the final interlude drives home the composer's personal response to Wozzeck's heart-wrenching fate.

The work is almost entirely newly cast, with only Franke's maniacal Captain and Anthony's assured Andres heard in previous broadcasts. Franke's flights into falsetto are as weirdly disturbing as ever, and his stout, piercing tones are like body blows, mercilessly flaying the wretched Wozzeck. He gives a virtuoso performance.

Wozzeck
12 April 1969
Marie
Evelyn Lear
Margret
Louise Pearl
Drum Major
Robert Nagy
Captain
Paul Franke
Wozzeck
Geraint Evans
Doctor
Donald Gramm
Conductor
Colin Davis

Nagy, who had edged into the 1965 production, has the commanding timbre and brutish manner to turn the Drum Major into a natural-born bully. Gramm had earned squatter's rights to the Doctor in the 1965 run and his characterization of the sadistic physician is a performance jewel. The American bass, long featured at the rival New York company, was a singer whose fastidious and elegant artistry was highly regarded on the concert platform as well. Applying those qualities to Wozzeck's prime torturer would seem to be a hard sell—certainly it is a far cry from Karl Dönch's traditional grotesquerie in the 1959 broadcast. Gramm perhaps understood that Franke had cornered the expressionistic market on this afternoon and, in part for that reason, often chooses a different characterization route; on occasion, his sane delivery and dexterous play are doubly chilling in this weird milieu. He can be emphatic as well, and his bass, light grained and now and then heady in timbre, moves with sure-footed authority over the spiky terrain of Berg's phrases. Oddly, a few idiosyncratic moments escape his notice—he offers no trill at the end of the 'Immortal' sequence, for instance. A highlight of the performance is the second-act exchange between Gramm and Franke, where the Doctor diagnoses the Captain's fatal illness, a case certain to guarantee his fame. Gramm's glee is deliciously outrageous. The scene's morbidity seeps into the airwaves as the clarity of their diction drives it home. Indeed, most of the cast are successful in projecting the text.

Evelyn Lear, heroine of the 1967 premiere of *Mourning Becomes Electra*, again proves her right to the Metropolitan stage. She is a marvelous actress with the voice, and, unlike some who excel in that regard, her vocal equipment is as estimable as her artistry. (Eventually, the top range will be curtailed.) Her confident, richly intoned singing of the lullaby is immensely affecting. The voice's timbre, fruity and suggestive, considerably enhances the episode. Sorrow, indeed tragedy, seems to live within its compass. (It comes as no surprise that Lear, expert musician that she is, will make a specialty of Berg's Lulu as well. One rejoices at the comfortable, easy assurance of all cast members in this once-forbidding vocal idiom. Louise Pearl, playing Marie's friend Margret, is one of them.) Unfortunately, Marie's other pivotal moment, the reading of the Bible to her child, is marginally blunted by our inability to understand the all-important text; the composer, as well as the singer, is complicit in the misdemeanor. Still, the poignancy of the scene, its allegorical significance, is abundantly clear from Lear's nuanced reading and passionate delivery. The voice's voluptuousness makes Marie's identification with Mary Magdalene seem entirely plausible, even as that affinity foretells, even dictates, her submission to the Drum Major's blatant physicality.

Geraint Evans' Wozzeck is a deservedly famous interpretation. Still, as Berg's everyman, the Welsh baritone must remake his image, so apt for Falstaff and other comic chaps. The tone, while not overly large, has such substance, is so darkly colored and resonant, that it seems rather too self-possessed, almost too important, for the put-upon Wozzeck. Hermann Uhde, the earlier broadcast protagonist, was able to counterfeit a shrinking vocal nature to suit the dramatic pose. Evans has a harder job of it, but succeeds by emphasizing a certain rough commonality in his timbre. If Uhde's Wozzeck was a blob, Evans' antihero is a lump of a man. Wozzeck, no matter his lowly station, must gain and hold the center of the drama, a difficult task considering the vivid, distorted characters who surround him. Evans conquers through a masterly application of vocal gruffness and, occasionally, even a seeming mental detachment on Wozzeck's part. But when the big moments come—the stabbing of Marie, Wozzeck's apostrophe to the moon and subsequent drowning—he readily moves into, and occupies to the full, a larger frame. At home there, his Wozzeck acquires tragic stature. Berg might have appreciated his vocal prowess for, as he wrote to Schoenberg, "given a real singing voice, these apparently unsingable melodies are singable after all."[2]

In the second decade of the last century, Berg had molded Büchner's fragments into a satisfactory libretto for an insidiously provocative, revolutionary work. A little earlier in the decade, Richard Strauss and his Viennese colleague, Hofmannsthal, were hard at work as well, doing what they did best—that is, tussling with literary conceits and coming up with a work substantially removed from the original concept. Both in size and design, *Ariadne auf Naxos*, in which the tragic and comic contest and finally intertwine, was born a hybrid but mutated into a delightful opera with prologue. Molière's *Le bourgeois gentilhomme* was eventually shorn from the original play/opera carcass and replaced with an evocative portrait of pre-performance backstage life. Introduced to the Met public in the 1962–63 season, *Ariadne* reappeared the following year, but the production lay dormant until the 1970 revival. The broadcast of 28 March 1970 enlists only a few cast members from the Met premiere and 1963 broadcast: Rysanek (Ariadne), Uppman (Harlequin), Velis (Scaramuccio), Anthony (Brighella), and Meredith (Major-domo). The large contingent of new radio interpreters includes Lear (Composer), King (Bacchus), Grist (Zerbinetta), Dooley (Music Master), and the nymph trio (Pracht, Love, and Clements), as well as less prominent participants MacWherter (Officer), Schmorr (Dancing Master), Christopher (Wigmaker), and Sgarro (Lackey). Böhm once again has charge of the polyglot affair at the Viennese *parvenu*'s mansion. A lively afternoon is ensured.

The Austrian maestro, friend of Strauss and his distinguished interpreter throughout his own life span, conducts a fluid performance, one in which languors are anathema. In the introductory measures of the prologue, the strings are unable to provide a clean-cut etching of the composer's swift, arched lines; occasionally the thrill of the climax (rewarding in itself) causes the conductor to swamp a singer or two. But the Strauss terrain is clearly terra firma for Böhm. He is not as lucky as his heritage warrants in the contrasting ensembles of nymphs and clowns. The former sound bottom-heavy and overly lugubrious in their opening lament, but make up for it with a smooth, tonally glossy closing paean. In the male contingent, Anthony's pungent timbre and top note delinquency prevent unanimity in the commedia antics, while Plishka's solid work lacks comic esprit. Uppman remains a fine Harlequin, especially in the later scenes, though his 'Lieben, Hassen, Hoffen, Zagen' is thicker toned and less heady than remembered from the 1963 premiere season. (The disparity makes sense when one reads in the broadcast issue of *Opera News* that the original Billy Budd was singing Amfortas with the National Symphony that week.) As the Dancing Master (a lively character even though not a unionized member of the *commedia* troupe), Schmorr's singing is adequate, but one would expect that the character's profession would be reflected in a more pointed line delivery. On the other hand, the aural sneer that Meredith lays on the spoken instructions of the officious Major-domo is marvelously acute; one can almost see his raised eyebrow and distasteful nostril lift as he informs the company of the simultaneous presentation of the operas, *seria* and *buffa*.

Ariadne auf Naxos
28 March 1970

Ariadne
Leonie Rysanek
Zerbinetta
Reri Grist
Composer
Evelyn Lear
Bacchus
James King
Music Master
William Dooley
Harlequin
Theodor Uppman
Conductor
Karl Böhm

The principals uniformly provide good value. As the Music Master, Dooley again impresses with his idiomatic style, strong characterization, and vibrantly colored baritone. Miss Lear's Composer is a complete joy. Mezzos have first call on the role, their timbral density usually compensating for any difficulties they might encounter in the difficult tessitura of the 'Musik' tribute. Our soprano, however, owns just the right instrument for the young musician. Her distinctive timbre is erotically tinged and carries its evocative aura throughout the entire range. She is a superb musician, adept at applying a variety of nuance, a play of colors within a single phrase, shading its contours for maximum meaning, all with a naturalness that belies the complexity of her musico-dramatic conception. Transported by the naive musician's idealism or ultimate despair, she deploys her voice with soprano innocence or, contrarily, allows it to burgeon with passionate intensity. Her crescendos seem to pull one along with them. She and Grist are an endearing pair in their duet, the two highly individual voices interweaving to charming effect. Lear pours out tone at its conclusion and sweeps into the Composer's aria with comparable assurance. There Böhm's orchestral splendor momentarily overwhelms her soprano; the conductor pays his debt to Strauss in full, but more concern for the singer's capacities might have made the moment even more affecting. Her top shines out radiantly at the aria's conclusion and thereafter Zerbinetta's betrayal provokes a grand, despairing outburst from Lear at the curtain's fall.

Ariadne gains the opera's title, but an accomplished Zerbinetta can steal the thunder away from the abandoned heroine. That would seem hard to do when Rysanek turns on the full splendor of her high-octane soprano in the opera's closing pages. Grist, however, all but succeeds in purloining glory on this afternoon. Her portrayal is incredibly deft, assured in manner and fleet in vocal execution. The voice, seemingly too childlike to undertake adult music-making chores, has amazing tensility; its taut, vinegar-tinged tone (that liquid can be an agreeable condiment when discerningly employed) cuts through orchestral forces as easily as a skewer penetrates tender lamb. The nasality of the lower octave allows her to operate as an equal partner in her fellow comedians' capers—it comes as no surprise that this minx outmaneuvers the four of them. The timbre in itself is a tease. Her charm captivates not only her cohorts but her entire audience—the house goes wild after her romp through Strauss' coloratura showpiece. Beyond her gift for comic portraiture, Grist can convert her tone, both in mid-voice and especially *in alt*, from piquant nasality to an attractively smooth silver-white sheen, a metamorphosis that enables her to trace Strauss' melodies with beguiling charm. And she does so with utmost care; in the prologue, her tones, like seductive, embracing arms, weave 'Ein Augenblick ist wenig' round the Composer's uncomprehending hurt. Her 'Grossmächtige Prinzessin!' may not be the most cuttingly brilliant one will ever hear, but it is astonishingly nonchalant, its naturalness matched only by its poise. From her throat, Zerbinetta's dizzy pyrotechnics come forth as native speech rather than coloratura soprano technique. The voice appears to gain in body as the monster aria progresses, the high E maintains its color, and we can heartily agree with the prompter's inserted "Bravo!" after Strauss' private joke of a coda once again confounds the audience.

Of course, Miss Rysanek has her own innings, though as usual she is at her best after the seventh-inning stretch. Ariadne's initial lament lies painfully low for the soprano's cloudy lower voice; she cannot make much effect there, though

Leonie Rysanek as Ariadne in *Ariadne auf Naxos*. Photography by Louis Mélançon. Courtesy Metropolitan Opera Archives.

the improved stability in that underbrush is apparent and commendable. (Over time, with favorite singers, we sometimes learn not just to live with, but to almost take comfort in an apparent vocal disability—its familiarity becomes oddly reassuring.) Even in these early pages, the soprano, when moving in and out of the upper range, is able to work her wiles, offering gorgeous tone in Ariadne's far-flung phrases. One delectable moment, quite distinct from her usual thrusting radiance, is the air of quiet innocence she wafts when singing of her childhood ('Sie atmet leicht, sie geht so leicht'). Still, one would be hard put to maintain that she always has on call the gambit of resources to completely hold our interest in this lengthy double aria. The grand duet with Bacchus is quite another story. There she reveals a varied sequence of vocal and interpretive modes that confirm her stature as a singing actress of the first order. As she moves from girlish purity, maintained with appealing intimacy at the *piano* dynamic, to enveloping allure, she justifies her titular claim. In particular, I admire the quiet, contained vocalism with which she begins the final peroration, thereafter guiding its winding melodic stream through progressive stages before achieving a sublime, full-voiced climax. She does indeed live in the high growth. In these moments, she gives the lie to her grandly amusing parody of a prima donna in the backstage prologue. There, however, one would not wish to forgo her burlesqued, hooted phrases or the gaping stupefaction with which the future tragic princess utters 'Was ist das?'

James King's gifts were apparent in the Met's triumphant performances of *Die Frau ohne Schatten*, and he reaffirms them on this afternoon. King makes a specialty of surmounting the tortuous trials that Strauss visited on his tenors. On this afternoon, his firmly anchored, manly instrument handles the composer's jagged melodic profiles with accuracy, is unfailingly assured in the relentless tessitura, even conquers Bacchus' notorious acclivities, and penetrates the orchestral mass with assertive, even majestic, tones. His phrasing is hardly imaginative—he often moves note by note and word by word rather than forming melodies with a shaping legato—but his vocal security and the combination of tenorial brilliance and baritonal coloration make him a valued addition to the operatic scene of these decades. Bacchus' noble concluding oration is uttered with stunning grandeur, the tenor confirming through tone and manner that, as Hofmannsthal asserts and Strauss ratifies, he is heaven sent.

Beethoven's *Fidelio* had received an investiture in 1960, but the bicentennial of the composer's 16 December birth dictated yet another new mounting a decade later. The broadcast followed hard on its heels (2 January 1971). Though she sang the role infrequently with the company, Madame Nilsson's brave heroine had dominated the three broadcasts of the sixties, while Rysanek, a more frequent Leonore at the Met and an often-heard interpreter in the composer's hometown, gained only this single airing. Böhm was the constant guide for both sopranos, with Vickers' stunning Florestan the only cast familiar. Judith Blegen and Murray Dickie are the ingénues—he plays at it, she is one to the life. Berry (Pizarro), Tozzi (Rocco), and Macurdy (Fernando) are each dark of tone, but as characters they shade from night to day, from black to bright.

The much-honored Böhm is clearly the hero of the afternoon with the house audience. His fervid reading of the *Leonore* Overture No. 3 reaps a huge ovation. I find his way with the opera a touch hysterical. Perhaps he is responding to Boris Aronson's striking pseudo-expressionistic sets. In any case, the maestro is forever

Fidelio
2 January 1971

Leonore
Leonie Rysanek
Marzelline
Judith Blegen
Florestan
Jon Vickers
Jaquino
Murray Dickie
Pizarro
Walter Berry
Rocco
Giorgio Tozzi
Fernando
John Macurdy
Conductor
Karl Böhm

whipping up the climaxes, turning his forces into noisemakers; they, in turn, are occasionally guilty of faulty attacks. The librettist's adaptation of Bouilly's rescue play contains a goodly share of stock horror elements and on this afternoon the interpretive stance tilts rather more in their favor than toward the opera's classical posture. Still, a conductor with so long an acquaintance with the score will not fail to honor many of his fellow Austrians' reposeful inspirations—even his crowd-pleasing overture has some considered moments of serene music making.

Blegen and Dickie are an excellent pair, dramatically in the picture and musically alert. The Glasgow-born tenor, *Kammersänger* at the Vienna Staatsoper, is a more mature-sounding Jaquino than the Met has favored, but his stout vocalizing has a down-to-earth decisiveness that suits the keeper of the prison keys. The American soprano had made her debut as Papagena the previous season and, when Edith Mathis was indisposed at the *Fidelio* premiere, stepped in with the assurance that would characterize her substantial Met career. She was hardly ill prepared for the assignment. Holding degrees in both voice and violin from the Curtis Institute was not her only credit; Spoleto (Mélisande), Nuremberg, and Vienna already were acquainted with her talents. Her musicianship is impeccable. Thus, Marzelline's lead-off in the canon quartet and her aria, both requiring pinpoint accuracy, are expertly negotiated and musically charming into the bargain. Nuances often inform her phrasing. The timbre is lovely in itself and her tones, while slight in size, are skillfully manipulated for maximum effect. They can take on a pinched, peaked quality when she applies too much pressure. Some soubrettes easily float tone (the best of the Germans do—Mathis qualifies there); others prefer pointed tone to make their mark. At this time, Blegen belongs to the latter breed, but time may prove that to be a youthful necessity rather than permanent predisposition. In any case, the soprano, adept at creating character, is a decided asset on this afternoon. Her Marzelline is a spunky creature, who most likely will prove quite a handful for the prosaic Jaquino.

Of the prison's permanent residents, Rocco is especially well served by Tozzi's convivial warden. When the American basso sings of the benefits of gold to a happy home, he is definitely more concerned with family values than greed. Tozzi, who had sung Fernando in the 1960 broadcast, is new to his prison chores, adding the role to his repertory for this production. It proves a snug fit. In fact, the singer appears to be enjoying something of a vocal rejuvenation during this period. The voice is well anchored and vibrant in tone, and his interpretive touches have that naturalness that has always characterized his best work. As Don Fernando, Macurdy has the task, thankless vocally but conscience-buttressing, of playing deus ex machina for the wretched Florestan and his fellow prisoners. The bass' manner is rather earthbound for the noble minister of state (no feathery clouds could hold him), and vocally his tone lacks the Tozzi brand of human warmth that can in itself define his character's function in the drama. As a vocalist, Macurdy is sturdy—he ever was—and he makes Fernando the very picture of a reliable civil servant. On the other hand, Walter Berry, known to us as an affable Ochs and the most humane of husbands (Barak), takes to villainy as though it were his life's work. Powerful of voice, he throws out 'Ha' welch' ein Augenblick!' with notable audacity, and when he is plotting Florestan's death with the hapless Rocco his intelligence provides a few subtle touches which suggest that he could get away with the crime. His Pizarro employs a stealthy vocal slither to show us how he will steal into the dungeon ('in den Kerher schleichen'); he demonstrates the fatal blow ('ein Stoss!') with a bruising thrust of tone, and then provides a sinister echo of the word when it comes around again. Here and elsewhere, Berry is the complete artist. He and Tozzi are at the top of their form in their lengthy duet.

Vickers' Florestan is one of the great characterizations of the age. In an earlier broadcast of the opera, he was not in best voice and, perhaps as a result, some erratic vocalism and interpretive gestures surfaced. On this afternoon, the voice, powerful, intense, golden in its upper range, is in prime condition and exaggerated effects are forsworn. Its manly beauty is intact. On occasion, Vickers' initial 'Gott' has been a long-drawn cry of pain, quite wonderful in its way; today Vickers addresses his creator in straightforward fashion. His characterization proves to be as powerful as ever, but he seems more concerned with molding musical phrases into expressive shapes, allowing their pristine contours to represent Florestan's emotions. His control of tone, massive as it often is, is expert, and sometimes he operates at both ends of the volume spectrum—the opening of the ecstatic section of his aria is quietly intoned to marvelous effect. Where needed, frenzy takes over. As he thanks Leonore for the crust of bread, the tonal resonance is headier than we often hear from him, its bright sheen quite affecting. Both tenor and soprano handle the troublesome jangle of 'O namenlose Freude' with complete assurance; accurately and with abandon, they shoot its ascending phrases like arrows of joy into the aural ether.

Miss Rysanek shines there and elsewhere. Much of the role lies in that part of the voice where her gifts are abundant. Thus, her portrayal is a grand success. I need not belabor the good news that portions of her sometimes recalcitrant instrument have been stabilized and, while they never quite match the refulgence and certainty of her upper octave, they are better able to accommodate her characterful interpretive gestures. Several phrases of 'Komm Hoffnung' are bothered by the remembered clotted tone, but overall she negotiates the fearsome aria's challenges with honor. (The aspiration of the quick ascending scales is a bit of a surprise, however.) The entire dramatic compass of the aria is thoroughly explored, and when Rysanek moves into high gear, crowning the ecstatic phrases with her blazing top tones, our elation is as full as her spirit is generous. Leonore's spoken dialogue is delivered in natural, unforced tones, entirely convincing in their aptness. She is not one to neglect a theatrical thrust, however, and drives a good one home when she excitedly cries, 'Ich habe Muth!,' thereby confirming that Leonore has the courage to view the chained prisoner. Her musical cries of the same phrase are equally assertive. Of course, 'Kill first his wife,' is superbly projected, as exciting as the trumpet call that signals Florestan's deliverance. In the final scene, she looses a few fleeting sharp pitches over the lively closing ensemble, but her exuberance is certainly not misplaced. A singular feature of her portrayal is the assurance with which she traverses the ascending scales to those lengthy topmost tones, the latter the bane of many an otherwise gifted Leonore. Faulty or effortful execution of these technical hurdles—the apexes hardly crowning glories—has often dashed our hopes, but Rysanek's radiant tones provide the longed-for transfiguration. This afternoon at the opera holds an uncommon number of satisfactions. A superior group of artists has seen to that.

Tales of marital love are not as common in opera as the law of averages would prescribe. The demands of the genre favor conflict over felicity. Striking a blow for conjugality in its 1970–71 season, Bing not only offered the new production of

Orfeo ed Euridice
9 January 1971

Orfeo
Grace Bumbry
Euridice
Gabriella Tucci
Amor
Roberta Peters
Spirit
Mary Ellen Pracht
Conductor
Richard Bonynge

Fidelio, thus restoring the union of Leonore and Florestan, but preceded it with a September mounting of Gluck's *Orfeo ed Euridice*. This was a plucky move on the part of the manager; over its long history, the company had had little luck with the hallowed reform work. But then, Bing always liked to beat the odds. He had no Toscanini, whose 1909 stewardship had earned Krehbiel's admiration for his "reverential" treatment of the score.[3] Louise Homer's plummy contralto and noble bearing gained equal praise. Thorborg's mid-thirties impersonation was highly regarded, Stevens' gallant effort of the fifties less so. At least Monteux's benign shepherding of the American mezzo's effort could be appreciated. Kerstin Meyer's pedestrian portrayal in the 1962 broadcast could hardly have buoyed the manager's spirits, even with Jean Morel's knowledgeable guidance from the podium. Still, the opera's musical worth and historical importance had earned it inclusion in sixteen Met seasons previous to the 1970 mounting.

At the 1970 premiere, Gérard's gaudy settings and, especially, Milko Sparemblek's hyperactive staging and choreography were considered eyesores but, as heard on the broadcast of 9 January 1971, aural pleasure is provided by Bumbry and Tucci in the leading roles with Peters (Amore) and Pracht (Blessed Spirit) worthy aids to love. However, Gluck's transcendent score, at the Met basically a blend of the Italian and French versions (Berlioz's revision), had been irresponsibly delivered into Richard Bonynge's unresponsive hands. The Australian conductor, known for his scholarly ways, restored the original contralto keys and added a few touches based on his own research. Despite his loving sponsorship of neglected French ballet scores—which, though the genres are disparate, might predicate some affinity for the style of Gluck's French-influenced work—at this early juncture in his conducting career Bonynge cannot prevent the composer's heavenly simplicity from turning into the commonplace. The string textures are thick, all important choral episodes plod, and the rhythmic vitality of the score is ill articulated. The brief overture, with its ragged beginning and tubby progress, sets the mode for the entire performance. Bonynge is a knowing cosmopolite, as was composer Gluck, but there is little meeting of the minds on this afternoon.

Fortunately, the stage offers its own rewards. Both Peters and Pracht suffer from poor stage placement so the radio microphones do not capture the full bloom of their deft vocalism. Pracht owns the more girlish instrument, its light, silvery timbre complementing her chore as the Blessed Spirit. Peters' Amore is the more prominent role and her charm and professional assurance are supremely evident in every note and phrase. Her mid-voice warmth well serves the bulk of Amore's music. Tucci continues to prove her right to the Met stage—no sign of vocal deterioration mars her Euridice. (Of course, the role is vocally not overly demanding: the heights are avoided and the virtuoso requirements of Tucci's assignments in the nineteenth-century Italian repertory are forsworn.) Her appealing timbre, its light metallic tinge rimming a core warmth, is surprisingly apt for the genre—in her tones, classic coolness and romantic passion seem inextricably bound. Beyond tonal beauty, she brings a much-needed dramatic punch to the opera's denouement, applying the tasteful expressive devices of Italian opera in an effort to make us care for Euridice—and succeeding in the attempt. The wife's happy reunion with her husband, the seeming rejection, and final deliverance—Tucci brings all these situations to life, makes their emotions palpable, and, moreover, does so without treading on either Gluck's or Calzabigi's reform toes.

Ultimately, the opera's success rests in the throat and heart of its Orfeo. Miss Bumbry's voice is a good vehicle for the role. Orfeo's music dwells uncommonly long, indeed, quite persistently, in the lower range of a mezzo. There the St. Louis native has cultivated a healthy chest voice blend, one that, though carried quite high, glides easily into the more mellifluous middle range—and she can turn on a gleaming thrust of high notes when needed. Thus she has the notes readily on call and sounds them in a timbre suited to a hero's posture—the tone is darkly colored in its lower octave. On this afternoon, she plays with considerable repose, possibly too much in the early acts; after all, grief at the death of one's wife is a grand emotion, no matter the operatic venue. It seems she is intent on preserving the classic virtues of not violating stylistic constraints. She certainly never does.

Her portrayal would profit from a more varied articulation of the text, a heightened declamatory style in the more dramatic moments (as when Orfeo resolves to go to Hades in search of his beloved) and a lapidarian elegance in the poignant ones. The mezzo's wonder at the beauty of the Elysian Fields, for instance, is rather matter-of-fact, though perhaps she recognizes that their beauty is defiled on this afternoon by Bonynge's carelessly applied orchestral pictorialisms. Bumbry inadequately distinguishes between melody and recitative—her buttery legato better serves the arias than the expository episodes. But far better her contained manner than a show-off extroversion. I note also a slight, but recurrent, tendency to flat in the area from F to B-flat (on the staff), the discrepancy due to a problematic register mix at this transitional point. It affects a few phrases in the arias of the first and second acts, but 'Che farò' is free of that momentary disturbance. What a wealth of luxuriant tone she applies to that test piece! Bonynge's overly stately tromp is no help, but Bumbry conquers nevertheless. Elsewhere in the final act, she and Tucci play together with gratifying animation and tonal beauty. We are fortunate that Bumbry's instrument mates so well with her task. In the long run, the voice's timbral wealth, its confident employment and security, cause the few strictures noted above to recede. A resolute authority and an innate dignity are the hallmarks of her performance. Her physical appearance, too, would aid illusion, although it would seem almost impossible to hide this Venus' allure in classic tunics. Gérard's solution is some offbeat, and fetching, costumes—the *Opera News* photos of Bumbry do intrigue. If only the aural setting cradling her portrayal were more satisfying. Perhaps because it is placed in the orchestra pit, the chorus, along with Orfeo a prime presence in the opera, fails to make its points with sufficient force. The grandeur of Orfeo's friends' grief, the terror inspired by the Furies' frenzy—these emotions are muted.

Four successful productions out of five attempts was a good percentage in the impresario game. Bing knew that. Still in control of the Met turf and with his customary confidence, the manager now moved into his last season with the company. He probably felt that he had a secure grasp on the final prize, an honorable legacy.

Renata Scotto as Adina in *L'Elisir d'Amore*. Photography by Louis Mélançon. Courtesy Metropolitan Opera Archives.

CHAPTER TEN

Bing Enters the Home Stretch

In the first volume of his published memoirs, Bing opined that when he left the company at the end of the 1971–72 season, the Metropolitan was "a going concern."[1] Specifically he was referring to its financial condition, but it is likely that he thought the artistic realm enjoyed a comparable healthy state. Well aware that the managerial problems of the seventies were quite different from those he had tackled when he first came to assess the company in 1949, Sir Rudolf had no doubt that it was time for him to go. With the honesty that ever characterized his public statements, he was quite willing to admit that he was no longer "fascinated" by the duties of his position.[2] He had fought the good fight (I believe that), and he could cheerfully assert that he had "a great deal of just fun" in doing it.[3]

The artistic well-being of the company (at least as regards its all-important aural component) may be most readily gauged by a review of Bing's final season of broadcasts. Seventeen operas, several more than space has normally allowed me to consider, will be covered, omitting only three broadcasts: *Rigoletto* (aired with a largely familiar cast), *Fidelio*—a less-than-inspiring reading—and *La Fille du Régiment*. The latter was one of the season's hits, but its quality was considerably diminished when broadcast—no Pavarotti!

In several ways, the season serves as a retrospective of the Bing reign. His magisterial production of *Don Carlo* had opened his first season and it fulfills that same function on his twenty-second opening night. In addition, Verdi's epic drama will be the final opera he offers on the Saturday afternoon that brings Bing's broadcast series to an end. The manager's regard for the Verdi canon, a cornerstone of his regime, is also evident in the airing of four additional works by the Roncole-born composer. The manager's insistence on new productions is as strong as ever: *Der Freischütz, Tristan, Pelléas, Fille,* and *Otello* were this year's beneficiaries. All will be heard on the broadcasts. Successful past productions are again trotted out: the O'Hearn/Merrill efforts, ranging from *Elisir* to *Meistersinger*, are featured. And the Gérard production of *Così Fan Tutte*, a triumph of the manager's second season and still viable two decades after its premiere presentation, enjoys a revival. Like *Don Carlo*, the Mozart opera may be said to owe its current popularity to Bing's reintroduction of the work to the American public after a three-season Met run in the 1920s had failed to earn it a deserved place in the repertory. Six broadcasts in the fifties and sixties had consolidated regard for the opera. It has been absent from the airwaves since 1965 when the 22 January 1972 broadcast brings new radio interpreters in Zylis-Gara (Fiordiligi), Stratas (Despina), and Berry (Alfonso), as well as the broadcast debut of Pietro Bottazzo (Ferrando). Elias' Dorabella and Uppman's Guglielmo are characterizations familiar from the 1962 and 1965 broadcasts.

Così Fan Tutte
22 January 1972

Fiordiligi
Teresa Zylis-Gara
Dorabella
Rosalind Elias
Despina
Teresa Stratas
Ferrando
Pietro Bottazzo
Guglielmo
Theodor Uppman
Alfonso
Walter Berry
Conductor
John Pritchard

Whereas the earlier outings had felt the rather turgid embrace of Fritz Stiedry and Rosenstock, this time Mozart's effervescent score was ceded to another radio debutant, John Pritchard. A British Isles native, the fifty-year-old conductor had a long association with Glyndebourne (his tenure in fact overlapping Bing's final years there) and had officiated in Vienna, Buenos Aires, and at Covent Garden, where he led several premieres of Britten and Tippett operas. His American debut occurred at the Chicago Lyric Opera in 1969 (*Il Barbiere di Siviglia*). Pritchard had a reputation as something of a Mozart specialist. That he has definite ideas on the Mozartean performance mode is evident in his assertive stance relative to his stage colleagues. His decided preference for fast tempos occasionally sends them careering through ensemble passages in headlong fashion. The opening scene is propelled with breathtaking rapidity—musical oxygen is all but eaten up by the conductor's heady progress. Nor do phrasing niceties, either as orchestral commentary or as accommodation to a singer's preference, always surface as often as one would hope. In general, however, the performance is well charted and a number of the more reflective moments gain their due. (Oddly, the little orchestral march and its choral companion are never quite aligned.) The performance, while somewhat disjunct overall, has rhythmic vitality and a modest buoyancy, a sure gain over the weightier interpretations of Pritchard's predecessors.

Onstage Zylis-Gara and Stratas, not unexpectedly, earn the major honors. The Polish soprano is in her element as Fiordiligi, delivering a performance worthy to be classed with the much-admired portrayal of Steber. The terrors of 'Come scoglio' are welcome challenges for her. Her command of fioritura is exemplary—nothing sticks in her throat. Indeed, the fluency of her passagework, its lovely liquidity, is a treat, the afternoon's bon-bon. Her very lowest notes (those the wicked Mozart inserted to show off—or mock—creator Ferrarese's extreme range) lack body, but they are never mere ugly chest tones. And she is able to move out of them to exquisite top tones without the crutch of a disfiguring squawk, which many a Fiordiligi has found essential. Admittedly, her indignation is hardly assertive; it will come as no surprise that this 'scoglio,' this rock of righteousness, is rather easily dislodged by the opera's end. Throughout the afternoon, the varied aspects of her timbre—now light and sunny, there veiled by an inviting, even seductive, musk—add interest to her vocalism. The contrasting aria ('Per pietà') lingers overlong in the lowest portion of her voice for maximum beauty to flourish, but her careful management of tone and phrase provides further evidence of her conscientious artistry. And when she emerges unscathed from its confines into the fleet allegro moderato, unalloyed pleasure is our reward. Though Zylis-Gara enters into the fun, she remains above the farce. (Steber, in contrast, engagingly allowed her sense of humor full play.) Her portrayal has an innate dignity, never consciously imposed but rather a welcome overlay of repose that allows her character a humanity beyond that of Da Ponte's other *Così* creations. Everywhere the relaxed ease of her vocalism complements Fiordiligi's personality, providing an effective contrast to Dorabella's rather manic behavior. Zylis-Gara's portion of their several duets is vocalism of high order, quite delectable to the ear. A bit of suspect intonation on her part momentarily blemishes the beginning of the duet 'Prenderò quel brunettino,' which Elias introduces with delightful verve. The latter is an accomplished and committed participant in the opera's high-jinks. Unfortunately, the role, its dramatic character already sufficiently volatile as conceived by Da Ponte and realized by Mozart, seems to call forth from the gifted mezzo vocalism of excessive aggressiveness. Her firmly focused voice, its tautness normally an asset, too frequently turns wiry and becomes less attractive than usual, with occasional pitch discrepancies as well. The "heartbeat" duet with Guglielmo ('Il core vi dono') is curiously lacking in coy playfulness on both artists' part; Pritchard may be at fault, as well. Elias' intensity, on the other hand, proves an effective tool for Mozart's purpose as he guys *seria* heroines and causes Dorabella to ostentatiously parade her grief at the loss of her lover ('Smanie implacabili'). At a more constrained level, the mezzo's work is considerably more attractive and she manages the high tessitura of 'E amore un ladroncello' quite well.

Stratas' personation of Despina is a complete delight both as to characterization and vocalism. From the moment of her entrance, as Despina protests her servile duties, all the while sampling her ladies' chocolate, the soprano is personality personified. All the tricks of the stock *commedia* servant's trade, each dexterously exploited, seem more agreeable when she plays them—her tone, even though soubrette-inclined, is invitingly smooth, ductile, and as tasty as the chocolate she has filched. Stratas' pixilated servant is clearly the audience favorite. Her partner in plotting, Alfonso, receives a novel treatment from that gentleman vocalist, Walter Berry. The old bachelor, instigator of the intrigue, is often impersonated by a singer whose tone in itself conveys the cynicism that motivates Alfonso's actions. That mode adds another layer of meaning to the dramatic (and musical) texture of the opera. Berry is all accommodating courtesy (the Viennese brand), the refined instructor of naive youth. His lessons are not meant to cause permanent harm. When Cross tells us at the final curtain that Guglielmo returns to Fiordiligi and Ferrando to Dorabella, Berry's conception seems plausible—it was all in fun. Of course, his vocalism is as elegant as his manner; a single reservation concerns his excessive restraint when tracing the bass line of 'Soave sia il vento,' a modesty that dilutes the impact of that divine trio. Uppman is adept at assuming the guise of Mozart's guileless characters—his Papageno and Masetto, as well as his Guglielmo, are testimony of that attractive ability. On this afternoon his portrayal, not surprisingly, is a shade weightier in manner and tone than remembered, the voice's makeup a bit looser. But his instrument's timbral warmth is intact and, if his comedic thrust is a touch muted, he plays with complete confidence. He blusters when necessary—his brand of bluster always makes a character more appealing—but if Mozart allows a legato phrase its head (as when Guglielmo bids a temporary farewell to Fiordiligi or, returning as an Albanian, courts Dorabella), Uppman takes it to his heart. His elegance enhances the Albanians' little serenade, though his complex timbre and Bottazzo's narrow tone are ill matched. In Guglielmo's big solo moment ('Donne mie, la fate a tanti!') he adopts an effective buffo posture, even resorting to a useful baritone snarl here and there, demonstrating that woman's purported perfidy can sour the humor of, even drive to distraction, the most genial of men.

Signor Bottazzo, too, may be a genial gentleman but his voice cannot convince us of his right to the Metropolitan stage. The tenor from Padua was brought over for the entire run of *Così* and his familiarity with the role is evident in the ease of his fioriture, his adept recitatives, his well-modeled phrasing. It is the voice itself that denies him acceptance. Mozart has gifted Ferrando with some exquisite moments, episodes where tonal beauty is requisite, its soothing balm providing relief from the farce, the brittle milieu, of other episodes. Bottazzo's timbre is often nasal, excessively open—inherently unattractive. (Quite surprisingly, a *New York Times* critic noted at Bottazzo's debut that the voice reminded him, both in its usage and its admittedly less rich texture, of the young Richard Tucker's instrument and manner.[4] The American tenor, whose luscious voicing of this part in four broadcasts of the fifties remains vivid, could have sued for punitive damages.) Fortunately for the new recruit, Ferrando's more dramatic, and difficult, arias are cut. A critical demerit is the tenor's evident need to employ a pseudo-falsetto in the uppermost regions of his range. Moreover, on several important top tones even the management of the falsetto dissolves with a resultant crack (both the final note of 'Un' aura amorosa' and the climax of the 'Fra gli amplessi' duet, the emotional peak of the opera, are despoiled, the first by a gargle, the second by a squeak). The tenor is an accomplished musician (*Opera News* names him a Rossini specialist) and well acquainted with bel canto style. Clearly, he wants to do the right thing—and tonal appeal is somewhat enhanced (an exercise in relativism on my part) in portions of the second act. But the Met was not his theater. A single repetition of *Così* four days after the broadcast marked his final appearance at the house.

Staying with the comic breed, more uniform pleasure awaits us for, though we cannot claim Donizetti as another Mozart (a man who "spoke music as others speak words"), his buffa operas deserve our regard and respect as masterworks of a slighter genre than the Viennese master parlayed.[5] In this instance, the 19 February broadcast of *L'Elisir d'Amore*, the Met honors the Italian composer and itself with a performance worthy of both.

'O Gioia!' cries Nemorino, feeling the heady effects of Dulcamara's spurious elixir. Though lacking Bordeau to lift my spirits, upon hearing this performance, I echoed his cry of joy. Seldom has Donizetti's comic gem received so artistically unimpeachable and forthrightly endearing a reading as Scotto, Bergonzi, Sereni, and Corena provide under the empathic guidance of conductor Carlo Franci. The idiom is mother's milk to these artists, steeped as they are in the elegant ways of mid-nineteenth-century Italian opera. Though Swiss born, Corena qualifies, while American Loretta Di Franco's name gives her honorary status in the Italian cadre, even as her sweet-toned and charming Giannetta confirms her as a worthy partner of her more celebrated colleagues. Franci's well-judged leadership is an artful blend of light-handed control and beneficent regard for the peculiar talents of his artist singers. The composer's musical gestures, whether energizing or languishing elements, are graphically realized by Franci's pliant hand. Buenos Aires born but Italian trained, he knows when to apply the whip to a buffa tempo and when to allow the reins to slacken so that we may relish the singers' stylistic subtleties (a talent rare at the time, and increasingly elusive in later decades). With unobtrusive skill, he adjusts his beat to the rubatos that Scotto and Bergonzi so bewitchingly apply to Donizetti's melodies. The maestro's way tips the delicate balance between the buffa genre's brittle exterior and its responsive inner heart toward the life-sustaining warmth of the latter. I prefer his more human embrace to Schippers' taut 1966 broadcast reading.

L'Elisir d'Amore
19 February 1972

Adina
Renata Scotto
Nemorino
Carlo Bergonzi
Belcore
Mario Sereni
Dulcamara
Fernando Corena
Conductor
Carlo Franci

Sereni and Corena again offer their professional and well-seasoned impersonations of Belcore and Dulcamara. Donizetti was less generous to the cocky military man than to the dominant trio, but the portrait of the sergeant is nevertheless acute. Sereni, in appearance and vocal manner well equipped for the task, makes much of the role's limited opportunities. When on his own, he bristles with the requisite vocal strut, and yet he plays within the ensemble with unexpected restraint. Corena, in contrast to his more contained impersonations in earlier broadcasts, shows his true colors as the flamboyant quack doctor. He is in excellent voice, the top notes firm and his patter articulated with uncommon clarity. Franci's easy tempos are helpful in that regard, and though they may check virtuosity a bit, they cannot curtail Corena's high spirits. His sales pitch in 'Udite, o rustici' is guaranteed to reap rewards from a responsive clientele, both on- and offstage. In their barcarole, he and Scotto rely on the force of their personalities rather than off-putting vocal tricks—this time the insouciant piece travels on light feet. 'Quanto amore' calls for a more imposing manner and grander vocalism and they readily supply it. There the basso commits the afternoon's only breach of comradely good breeding (if the soprano doesn't mind—unlikely, in this case—one would not call it trespassing). Scotto takes up a melodic reprise and Corena puffs out several decidedly suggestive grunts and growls. But then, Dulcamaras must be allowed to peddle, in addition to their phony medicines, their legitimate buffo wares, though they be but good-humored ribaldries.

The soprano, strangely absent from the airwaves since the 1967 repeat of her 1966 broadcast debut as Butterfly, is an adorable Adina. Her flower-petal artistry, beguilingly delicate and yet immense in impact, is vastly appealing. As to tone, her singing is quite ravishing, only one or two wiry top notes momentary distractions; on a few other occasions, she cagily ensures that modest number by lightly spinning tone after a pointed attack in the upper regions. Let all sopranos know their imperfections and so astutely (and attractively) minimize them. In her introductory aria, she shows her stage mettle by immediately placing before us a maiden whose mockery of Isolde's plight is so captivating as to give even a besotted Tristan pause. This *civetta* needs no love potions to corral her admirers with her coquettish ways. Notable on this broadcast is the firm core of the voice, the timbre glinting with varied colors, ranging from an instrumental plaint (a wind, perhaps just a touch of the English horn) to heart-piercing, pointed thrusts of tone, with a welcoming, but never pallid, sheen occupying the dominant territory in between the extremes. The instrument is employed, with unfailing discrimination, for musical expression and character painting. This is operatic portraiture of immense skill; if it be judged a mite artful, the genre easily, even willingly, bears the charge without shame or regret. Scotto's tone is focused with pin-point accuracy and ever an obedient tool for her microscopic art. She traces melodic curves and buffa curlicues with an etcher's skill, the expansion and contraction of the line quite mesmerizing. It will be well to acknowledge here that her tenor is equally proficient at line conduction, his instrument necessarily blunter by virtue of its tonal density, but, by that same token, even more astonishing in its vitality and in the scope and grandeur of phrase modeling. The duets of Scotto and Bergonzi, artists well mated in tonal weight and, above all, in their stylistic affinities, provide performance peaks. For the most part, Bergonzi eschews the well-remembered (and magical) Tagliavini tonal whisk; our tenor's vibrant tone betrays a fuller heart. He

Carlo Bergonzi as Nemorino in *L'Elisir d'Amore*. Photography by Louis Mélançon.
Courtesy Metropolitan Opera Archives.

and his stage partner treasure portamentos, diminuendos, rubatos, all the graces of period style; better yet, they execute them to perfection, filling 'Chiedi all' aura lusinghiera' with elegance and 'Esulti pur la barbara' with brio. A lovingly executed cadenza *a due* at the close of the latter profits from their command of *mezza voce*. Scotto is able to articulate her dotted rhythms (the composer's emblems of Adina's independent spirit) with accuracy and yet avoid the scratchy shrewishness that most soubrettes apply to these vocally trying figures.

Nemorino's spirits are not confined to Dulcamara's wine—as Bergonzi imbibes, confidence radiates from him. His comic touches are genuine, deft, and delightfully naïve. (On this afternoon, the tenor's little sibilant lisp is prominent; it seems merely to be an extension of Nemorino's peasant status, a token of his appealing innocence.) In his three all-important solo episodes, Bergonzi takes command of the stage. Indeed, at his entrance he seems intent on signaling that the opera belongs to him. Why should he wait for 'Una furtiva lagrima' to establish ownership? His tenorial grandstanding all but transforms the slight 'Quanto è bella' into a *Chénier romanza*. No matter—the splendor of his singing admirably conveys the lover's stupefaction as he views the charms of his indifferent Adina. Has Nemorino's plight ever been worn so heart-on-sleeve? Bergonzi's magnificent cadenza, replete with full-blooded tone and technical mastery, rouses the audience to vociferous enthusiasm. He has staked his claim to the afternoon's honors and the palm is his. At the crux of the act-one finale, a more serious tone invades the tenor's song as he pours into 'Adina, credemi' his art's considerable bounty. He begins quietly, allowing the phrases to gain in vocal amplitude until feeling and tone spill out as one. At a climactic point he rather astonishingly binds together two phrases, thereby fixing attention and augmenting admiration. Of course, 'Una furtiva lagrima' holds similar delights. Except for mezza voce initial phrases, his reading, animated by variously colored timbres and charming portamentos, is more expansive than in the 1966 broadcast. After a lengthy *forte* tone on the penultimate note, he attempts a not entirely successful diminuendo and all but runs out of breath (and momentarily flats!) on the final note. So much glory has gone before, not only in the aria but throughout the afternoon, that nothing can deter the audience's approbation.

Miss Scotto, too, wins their hearts for her engagingly nuanced 'Prendi, per me sei libero.' The aria and ensuing fireworks are notable for pencil-point clarity of line and silvery glint of tone, the latter occasionally made fervent by a touch of bracing acidity before reclaiming either its dewdrop freshness or its plaintive yearning. Her fioriture are seldom idle displays of technique; they seem quite natural reflections of feeling. The rapture of the lovers on stage can hardly exceed the contentment of their admiring audience, whether in the house or at home. Cries of 'O Gioia!' all around.

Could the gifted Franci have achieved this happy union of music and drama without the aid of a Scotto and Bergonzi? Regrettably, we cannot know, for he leaves the Met at the season's close. Mr. Bing offered yet another Donizetti comedy during his final season, a performance now celebrated as legendary. Sutherland and Pavarotti made *La Fille du Régiment* a hit, but when broadcast time arrived, the tenor had given way to Enrico Di Giuseppe. The opera contains Pavarotti's breakthrough portrayal and thus I hold off appraisal until next season's double-threat broadcast with diva and divo.

In German romantic opera, a genre not devoid of lighthearted episodes, a homely folk element, quite removed from the artifices of opera buffa's commedia dell'arte *topici*, takes over. A more reflective, even somber, cast pervades Weber's *Der Freischütz*, where the composer mixed folk episodes, lyrical romance, and supernatural effects to concoct a down-home brew, one that allows the genre greater scope than the simpler (though equally meaningful) buffa format permitted. The Met's new mounting, the first in forty-three years, was roundly trashed in the press. Set designer and stage director Rudolf Heinrich, a Felsenstein associate who "wished to escape from the not-necessary romantic feeling" of the opera, evidently succeeded admirably, at least in that regard. He cited his "cleverness" in making "a kind of collage" in which nature was not imitated but rather suggested.[6] The production was retired after a single season. The musical presentation that the broadcast preserves, however, while not ideal, makes a strong case for Weber's *Romantische Oper*—as though that were necessary for those who, though long denied a stage performance, have treasured its melodic bounty and orchestral wonders. On the broadcast of 15 April 1972, Edith Mathis and Gerd Feldhoff join familiars Lorengar, Kónya, and Macurdy under Leopold Ludwig in the first Met radio presentation of the opera. Although the broadcast occurs near the end of Bing's tenure, the new production premiered during the second week of the season. Even at this late date, we are able to hear the opera with the premiere cast intact, yet another sign of Bing's managerial expertise.

After breathing the rarefied air of last season's saintly *Parsifal*, Ludwig makes a right-angle turn, wrestling now with librettist Friedrich Kind's forces of evil. The conductor has his charges well in hand, and the ensemble is neat; chorus, orchestra, and principals are well-behaved. (The male choristers are marginally more adept at hunting and beering than the spinners and bridesmaids at discharging their homely duties. Probably the nature of the tasks tilts enjoyment to the male side.) Obviously, Ludwig feels at home with the colorful score. Yet, in the end, his broadly gauged reading seems rather prosaic. All that order robs us of the full complement of rustic joy that the folk episodes can give off and deprives us of the knee-hugging shudder that the supernatural effects should provoke. His musical gestures are seldom strongly limned. His silences do not speak. In the all-important Wolf's Glen scene, terror is tepidly summoned as the orchestral effects are dutifully, rather than startlingly, sounded. The lack is performance-wounding, since Weber himself named "the rule of demonic powers" (Max's 'finstre Mächte') as depicted in the orchestral colorations he so successfully contrived as the "principal character of the opera."[7] Sometimes his accompaniment figures march insistently rather than cushion his singers' attempts at character development. An honorable reading, certainly, but hardly probing, and less than fulfilling for Weber's imaginative score.

That score warranted a more welcoming reception than Metropolitan audiences had given it during the company's lengthy history. *Freischütz* has never been a regular fixture at the Met. Even in the 1880s, though the company was German through and through, it had received only a few performances in a single season. Partial redress came in 1910 (the pattern of lengthy interims between revivals was set early) when Gadski's Agathe added a touch of vocal glamor—but Hermann Jadlowker's Max and Robert Blass' Kaspar did not. Bella Alten's Ännchen, Otto Goritz's Ottokar, and Herbert Witherspoon's Hermit were positive elements, as was Alfred Hertz's leadership. A later outing that season featured Emmy Destinn and Karl Jörn. A few performances sufficed to satisfy audience interest. In the twenties, the work seemed to gain a foothold, figuring in four different seasons. The star quotient increased considerably in 1924 when Rethberg's radiant Agathe was endangered by the powerful Kaspar of charismatic Michael Bohnen. The supporting complement was of prime quality as well with Queena Mario, Gustav Schützendorf (Ottokar), and Léon Rothier (Hermit); Kurt Taucher supplied a decent Max. In an effort to assuage audience discomfort with spoken dialogue (in a foreign language, for some) conductor Bodanzky composed recitatives to replace it—the transgression was to become a habit with him. It was a vain effort, though Gatti-Casazza's astute packing of the work with first-rank artists momentarily turned the tide. The opera was retained in the repertory for a few more seasons (1925, 1926, and 1929). Maria Muller and Rudolf Laubenthal were alternate romantic leads. And there the six-season *Freischütz* saga ended until Bing took up the challenge in his final season.

Clearly, the current management understood that if the work was to have a fair chance of success with the American audience, it required singers well versed in the idiom. Kónya, though Hungarian, was German trained, and, at least in his younger days, had exactly the voice for freeshooter Max. The role has its heroic moments but its lyrical episodes are even more critical. The period's anointed Lohengrin ought to prove ideal for this assignment. Unfortunately, the tenor's best days are behind him, but he can still manage a fair Max. Immeasurably helped by the role's low tessitura, he is in good voice for the radio performance. A touch of his characteristic gargle and a hint of uncertain pitch affect the opening of Max's grand scene ('Durch die Wälder'), but he soon moves into more solid form. The lyricism of an Anders or Wittrisch is not quite his to command, but he serves Weber and Kind well enough. As luck would have it, on this occasion his nemesis (Kaspar) is cut to size. While theatrically effective in his supernatural ventures, Feldhoff is merely mortal in discharging his vocal chores. In the contest between good and evil, the playing field for once is even. His instrument is of normal size, its timbre agreeable, and the tone well focused. The German baritone, a permanent member of the Deutsche Oper, Berlin, frequented the principal stages of his homeland, including Bayreuth, as well as Vienna. His experience tells. A committed and sincere interpreter, in order to make his effects he must hurl his attractive tones at the notes, pounding heavy accents and snarling where the voice cannot project the requisite evil on its own. (Frick had a built-in stock of that commodity.) That said, Feldhoff's portrayal merits approval. His strong, heart-in-throat declamation in the Wolf's Glen takes up Ludwig's theatrical slack. And a singer who can handily negotiate the descending and ascending scale passage ('die Rache') at the end of his aria ('Schweig, schweig') with clarity and ease is a good man to have on the roster. The Met did not think so. After his Kasper stint, he was allowed to pursue his European career, and did so with notable success into the early nineties, especially at his Berlin base. In today's opera, of course, Max eventually triumphs and in his later scenes Kónya's instrument does prove remarkably sturdy. He puts out a good deal of stout tone in a comfortable middle range, declaiming with appropriate fervor in moments of stress (of which there are a good many for poor misguided Max).

In this production, spoken dialogue is cut to a minimum and the first scene of the final act is omitted. In the smaller roles, Karlsrud's healthy bass adds stature to Cuno, while Dobriansky's homespun vocalism suits Kilian, a man of the people. Oddly, the Met casts Prince Ottokar with a tenor rather than the expected baritone. MacWherter has a heroic voice (of sufficient size so that he really needn't hector it as he is wont to do) and thus can adequately discharge his limited chores. Macurdy, in the brief but important role of the Hermit, admirably fulfills his dramatic function at the opera's close when he grants Max a reprieve. His voice has never sounded better; indeed richness of tone prevails in the upper range and the timbre is more appealing than usual. He convincingly assumes the appropriate hermit manner, a blend of beneficence and solemnity (or pomposity, if you will).

Reservations fall away when dealing with the *Freischütz* distaff side. Edith Mathis, in her third Met season but making her broadcast debut, plays Ännchen with delightful verve and admirable musicianship. Indeed, her pithy performance all but negates her status as *seconda donna* to Lorengar's more sedate Agathe. Of course, Weber himself built in the contrast, but Mathis takes advantage of every opportunity to put herself forward in the best possible light. Pert damsels can become trying and overstay their welcome, but Mathis' vivacity and charm, vocal and interpretive, never pale. Swiss-born but resident in Germany, where Berlin and Hamburg were her prime stages, the young soprano first appeared as Pamina at the Met, with Marzelline following in the next season. Sophie and Zerlina are in her Met future, though regrettably that will be a limited one. Her instrument is healthy enough so as not to be tainted by the soubrette brand. On this afternoon, the lower range is slightly shadowed (you may regard that as a positive or a negative according to taste), a coloration one does not expect in a soprano of this type. But the voice blooms into brightness in her secure top range. Thus she is able to cloak her ghost tale in appropriately suggestive colors, enhancing believability and deftly blending the character's blithe personality into the darker mood of the opera. In their opening duet, Mathis and Lorengar trace its interweaving vocal lines with easy assurance.

By this time, the Spanish soprano seems entirely comfortable on the Met stage. Perhaps for that reason, her vibrato is reasonably corralled and no longer discomfiting to those who are captivated by the voice's luscious timbre and the singer's enchanting personality. As frequently happens with this artist, some inner excitement can rob her sustained singing of ultimate repose—the second-act aria, lovely as it is in many ways, is touched by a bit of seeming unease. She does not offer the gently floating song of a Lemnitz (a standard for many in this music), but then that lovely singer's perpetual sweetness can sicken. Lorengar's Agathe is saved from excessive propriety (theatrically deadly) by a slightly assertive manner, her liveliness enhanced by the healthy glow of her vitamin-fed tone. She lightens her voice for the opening of 'Leise, leise,' and the varied moods of the lengthy aria are well defined, though not pushed to the extremes. That means she is modestly serene in the prayer and quite rapturous in the hope-drenched conclusion, where her passagework is poised and clean. The secure, shining top voice is her crown and she wears it becomingly, constantly pouring forth a blend of bright, yet reassuringly round, tone. When it soars, it invariably lifts listeners' spirits. And the voice's diamond-point clarity enhances critical lines in the ensembles. The arched contours of 'Und ob die Wolke' are well sustained and lovingly phrased without affectation. Some may feel that the hint of tensility that is a singular component of the voice's makeup robs her appeal to heaven of ultimate ethereality. I find Lorengar's way with the music not only sufficiently celestial, but also endearingly direct. Hers is an accessible God.

Rescue operas cannot count on the supernatural to solve their plot entanglements. The troubles of their characters will not be remedied by a magic bullet. Couples like Leonore and Florestan live in the real world and Beethoven intended them to struggle on their own and earn their triumph. The opera had political ramifications at the time of its composition and does so today, oppressed as it is with symbolic significance laid on by events of the mid-twentieth century. Thus the work carries a double burden. It may be that on the shoulders of Hans Wallat (who oversees the broadcast of 11 March 1972 with Anja Silja, Blegen, Helge Brilioth, Leo Goeke, Dooley, Macurdy, and Plishka) the burden is so heavy it all but sucks the lifeblood out of the opera. The conductor's conception is as serious a reading of the score as the broadcasts have yet presented. The Austrian was currently musical director of the Bremen Philharmonic and had conducted at Bayreuth. In the broadcast, he gives us two *Leonore* No. 3 overtures. At least, he treats the *Fidelio* overture as though its unpretentious classical design were as grand as the more famous piece that the composer wrote for a later performance. Strong contrasts, emphatic accents, solemnity, and dramatic thrust are all set forth with a heavy hand. Upon hearing the grander overture (played as usual after the dungeon scene, but mercifully not quite joined at its final tone), I find that I was wrong in the preliminary assessment. His stately traversal of the real No. 3 makes the curtain-raiser, relatively speaking, a veritable romp. The conductor controls his forces well enough, but before the monumental offering has run its course, time has come to a standstill. One can respect the nobility of his conception but dearly want to get on with the opera and share in the newly united couple's happiness. By this time in the afternoon, we have had enough lugubriousness, a dangerous mood to court. Occasionally, Wallat's *Fidelio* tends toward a horror show, so lovingly does he slaver over its moments of *Schrecklichkeit*. His reading owes much to the honorable Austro-German tradition of serious music making, and thus a number of episodes throughout the afternoon are quite affecting in that regard. The spaciousness of his overall conception—and he adheres to it at all costs—is often imposing when considered in itself. Individual components also can be effective; other episodes seem in danger of dying on the vine. He takes the canon quartet, for instance, at so slow a pace, and nurses it so tenderly, that one despairs of following its thematic threads. Nevertheless, the singers, perhaps encouraged by the unhurried movement, sing with a gracious fluency and succulent tone.

Wallat carries the serious tread of his *Fidelio* overture into the opening scene of Marzelline and Jaquino, thereby diluting the momentary lightness that sets the stage for the drama to follow. His moderate pace does allow Blegen and Goeke to project their voices and the text with welcome clarity. But both singers, sounding in perfect vocal health, give evidence that they would prefer a sprightlier tempo the better to demonstrate their characters' youthful impulsiveness. We know Blegen's excellent Marzelline from the previous year's broadcast and on this afternoon she sings with greater tonal fullness than her narrow voice normally encompasses, even in a fluent bit of fioritura in her aria. But Goeke's bright tones and clean line are a pleasant surprise. The voice has more body than those of many light-voiced tenors and his assurance makes Jaquino an uncommonly attractive fellow. Marzelline had better hold on to him.

As her father, Macurdy takes a step forward in establishing himself as a bass of the first rank. Over the many years of his career, he would remain a house bass, content to be available for the entire season. But his vocalism, musicianship, and

Fidelio
11 March 1972

Leonore
Anja Silja
Marzelline
Judith Blegen
Florestan
Helge Brilioth
Jaquino
Leo Goeke
Pizarro
William Dooley
Rocco
John Macurdy
Fernando
Paul Plishka
Conductor
Hans Wallat

interpretive qualities are on a high level and could have guaranteed him a wider career path. Like the best house artists, he is as reliable in what he offers as nature permits humans to be. In splendid voice, he sings with rock-bottom security, his instrument now capable of varied timbres to suit the text and mood: heady as Rocco enters in the canon quartet; honest and upright when dealing with his daughter's whims; solidly businesslike when he hankers after gold (assuredly it will come to him, so firm is his voicing of the aria); haunted as he reacts to Pizarro's murder plan; darkly sonorous in the dungeon scene—but lightly deployed there when fear is upon him; a touch rustic when explaining his actions to the ambassador. Here is an artist at work. He and Dooley make something special of their duet as Pizarro tries to enlist the jailer in his murderous plan. By now one expects Dooley to deliver an idiomatic performance, so well grounded is he in the interpretive practice of the Germanic stages. But he always has something individual to contribute as well. He doesn't play Pizarro as a monster. In his dialogue he sounds like everyman, a good ploy. Of course, Beethoven requires that he reveal himself as villain in 'Ha! Welch' ein Augenblick!' and there the baritone's voice, especially in the upper regions, is both beautiful and terrible, the mood greatly aided by Wallat's intense *sforzando*s and vivid orchestral strokes. Castel's unexpectedly somber tones are effective in the first prisoner's lament, while Christopher's warning (he is number two) combines to good purpose with the fear and gentle wonder that Wallat cultivates in this choral episode. The choristers' 'Leise, leise' as they depart is heartrending in its quietude. The chorus shines as well at the opera's close, exuberantly sharing in Leonore's triumph and welcoming Fernando's timely arrival. Plishka's plushy voice has cordiality built into its smiling Slavic tone. Surely tyrants could not survive in the face of such benignity as this vocal ambassador offers.

Along with Wallat and Silja, Helge Brilioth is making his broadcast debut. He had followed the familiar career path trod by Wagnerian tenors since the beginning of the last century, that is, in 1960 he began as a baritone until conversion led to a 1965 tenor debut as Don José. Bayreuth and Covent Garden soon knew his Siegmund and Salzburg his Siegfried. He had come to the Met as Parsifal in 1970 and taken on the role of Florestan a year later. It may be that the voice does not carry well in the vast spaces of the Met. But over the air, his timbre is attractive, the tone solid and free of the wheezes and sneezes of many tenors in this repertory. Of course, with Vickers' revelatory interpretation still fresh in memory, the young Swede is hard put to compete in terms of creating character. In fact, he does little in that regard. But he emits a solid 'Gott' to introduce his solo *scena*, conducts the line of 'In des Lebens Frühlingstagen' forthrightly (seemingly untouched by sorrow or regret), handles 'Und spür ich nicht Linde' with bright, firm tone until the tessitura at the aria's end closes in on him and robs him of vocal ease. The desperation apparent in those few measures is, quite without intention, his sole recognition of Florestan's plight. He is more on track when he thanks Leonore for the crust of bread with expansive phrasing and tonal pith. The joyful (but contained, at Wallat's tempo) thrusts of 'O namenlose Freude!' are recognizably what Beethoven wrote, not always the case with tenors in these frenetic moments. In the noisy finale of the act, Brilioth provides further evidence of his voice's compact makeup and the seriousness of his intent.

Miss Silja is known for her creative approach to her roles. The accolade has more to do with her stage presence and interpretive insight than her vocal attributes. Since her 1955 debut (Rosina), the Berlin-born soprano had been performing a wide variety of roles in an astonishing number of genres. Among her characterizations, primarily on German stages, were the Queen of the Night (Aix-en-Provence), Marie in *Wozzeck*, Desdemona, Salome, and Cassandra (Covent Garden) but, beginning in the 1960s, her most memorable association was with Wieland Wagner at Bayreuth and other German houses. Her Wagnerian heroines ranged from Elsa to Isolde. The voice was a narrow one for such heavy tasks but her repute as a singing actress was no fabrication. Indeed, *Opera News* had the temerity to note that she was often called the German Callas, a designation damning in the eyes of many and sacrilegious in the hearts of the Greek-American diva's worshippers. Not much in that regard can be affirmed on this afternoon.

Silja's Leonore is an unexpectedly modest maid, dutiful, almost serene as she assists Rocco in quotidian chores. The voice is sufficiently disciplined to agreeably discharge its replicating part in the canon quartet. When the notes are staffbound, her timbre has an unusual cast to it, for it sounds both round and hollow at the same time, if such a thing be possible. It holds no bloom, but the coloration appeals much as a sepia engraving (lovely in itself) might distinguish itself from a color print. Above the staff, it often loses fullness, turning white and, occasionally, harsh. On this afternoon, once past a few introductory passages, neither wobble nor bleat disfigure the tone. The lack of vibrato lends clarity to her conduct of line even as it robs her tone of splendor.

Leonore's big aria is remarkably contained for a singer with a reputation for stage magic. In its way, her reading is quite wonderful. Her cry of 'Abscheulicher!' would hardly frighten Pizarro if he heard it (even as the critical 'Tödt erst sein Weib!' later will fail to galvanize her listeners), but her cantilena in the 'Hoffnung' section is most touching. The modest coloratura and upward scale are neatly handled, nothing special vocally (the top B thins), but within her interpretive format they are just and appealing. (Oddly, one wants to cosset this Leonore. Callas, in her varied repertory, frequently did not solicit that response—I think she rather often sought to avoid it.) Later in the aria, the subdued phrase 'die Liebe, die Liebe wird's erreichen' is lovingly shaped. The sense of inner quiet that Silja subtly projects throughout the entire episode does sustain her repute as a stage magician. She doesn't turn tiger in the ensuing *agitato* section ('Ich folg' dem innern Triebe')—persistence rather than bravery will sustain this wife in her noble endeavor. Within the agitated section, the 'und süsse Trost dir bringen' phrase is a moment of endearing calm, in Silja's throat an intimate confession intended only for her imprisoned husband. Now Beethoven's horns begin to chug diligently along and Silja's voice, forced into emphatic utterance, turns shrewish. It whitens at the top and thus deprives us of the opportunity to share in the thrill of her hoped-for triumph. In the dungeon she and Macurdy often sing with commendable restraint but when she is not awed by her grave-digging task her tones are marginally fuller, even acquiring—may I say—a modest bloom. It flowers again in a few moments on the meadow when, at Fernando's command—and movingly—she sets free her husband.

Soon upon the trumpet call's reprieve, Leonore relishes her victory, intertwining her voice with Florestan's in a rapturous musical union. There the soprano's voice proves sufficient (except for a thin little flip-up) to satisfy the feverish demands of 'O namenlose Freude.' Consider that, in the duet, a single radiant calling of her husband's name is Silja's most abandoned exposure of self during the entire afternoon. It may be a brilliant, but overly subtle, plotting of her character's trajectory to triumph. Somehow, I had expected more.

Fidelio and *Der Freischütz* were pivotal elements in the development of German opera. The former has long been an everyday event for most opera houses but, as noted above, Weber's romantic Singspiel is seldom heard outside Teutonic borders. How different the history of Weber's opera from the seasonal recurrence of yet another German opera of the folk genre, but one with international appeal. Humperdinck's *Märchenspiel*, *Hänsel und Gretel*, had first been heard at the Met in 1905, a dozen years after its Weimar premiere. From its Met debut on through the 1971 broadcast it had popped up in twenty-eight seasons, and it held a warm spot in the hearts of radio listeners as the inaugural performance (1931) of the broadcast series. The fairytale opus is a natural for the Christmas day broadcast of 1971 (a forty-year anniversary to the day), which features the 1967 O'Hearn/Merrill production with Stratas and Elias playing the truant children and Chookasian and Walker their neglectful parents. Franz Allers conducts. With an eye to the children in the audience, the Met, like most American companies, performs the opera in English translation.

Stratas has stated her belief that *Hansel and Gretel* is definitely an opera for grown-ups.[8] I am prepared to take her word for it. The Wagnerian forces that Humperdinck employed and the strenuous vocal demands on Gretel are reasons enough for her regard (and ours as well); she felt the work's uplifting story made it appealing to adults, who find the triumph of good over evil refreshing in a depressing world. She might have gotten an argument from the Brothers Grimm if they were still around. Certainly, Schonberg, the *Times'* critic, did not see it that way in his curmudgeonly review of the premiere, railing against the sentimentality and spurious religiosity of a glitzy production that illustrated the gross failings of the Metropolitan itself.[9] In the end, his complaint was more against management's ostrich-head-in-the-sand attitude toward repertory than against Humperdinck's popular opus. After all, the Met always needed a seasonal cheerer-upper and it got more than its money's worth from the O'Hearn effort. The production survived for decades.

The Met orchestra bears the major burden of the afternoon's music making and that experienced body deals handily with the composer's polyphonic complexities and Wagnerian corpulence. A horn bobble at the very opening of the prelude signals trouble but fortunately embouchures firm up and mellow is the word from the pit. Franz Allers, the Met's chief purveyor of holiday spirits, recognizes where his responsibility lies and bartends with dispatch. The only performance novelty is a Witch in drag. When it was first heard in 1967, master character artist Karl Dönch had taken the role but by now Met regular Velis wears the robes of Rosina Dainty-mouth. As usual, he is capable, but scary he is not. Horror is in short supply. Except for interjecting liberal doses of expertly disaffecting cackles, he sings for the most part in his normal voice. Perhaps we should be grateful to him for his restraint. We can be sure that Dorothee Manski, the first broadcast Witch, knew how to give size to the part—she was a Met Brünnhilde. Sandman Raeschelle Potter (sounding appropriately mezzo-like, but listed as a soprano) and Dewfairy Di Franco (hurried by Allers and swamped by his swelling sonorities) adequately perform their gracious chores without elevating their walk-on status.

Chookasian has trouble articulating the text, but more to the point, her broadly based contralto tells us that we need not worry about child abuse. Surely

Hansel and Gretel
25 December 1971

Gretel
Teresa Stratas
Hansel
Rosalind Elias
Gertrud
Lili Chookasian
Peter
William Walker
Witch
Andrea Velis
Conductor
Franz Allers

those resonant tones, solid and secure, confirm that an inherent good nature hides beneath her anger and nagging. Throughout its wide range, the voice is in excellent condition. I always think that a forest-dwelling broomsman should be burly of tone and swaggering in manner. Walker, owner of a fine all-American baritone, sounds as though he has come straight from the office, hardly stopping for a tipple at a neighborhood bar. All right, grant that father Peter on this day is a successful salesman—he has sold his brooms at a high price. Good humored we want Peter to be, and Walker certainly is that. It would seem likely that the children have inherited their pristine diction from their father; Walker is top notch in that regard. Except for a few final phrases where the tessitura momentarily threatens, his singing is quite attractive.

Elias is entirely at ease as the mischievous Hansel. Her wobble-free instrument with its arrow-keen tone never fails her. Some mezzos with a heartier mix of chest tone are able to suggest the boy more than her timbre allows, but her impish conduct makes up the difference. Gretel is the more demanding role and interest in the afternoon's offering is piqued by curiosity as to what light Stratas' fertile artistic imagination will shine upon the child. Before the curtain, trepidation is aroused. Cross tells us that the soprano is "indisposed really today, but has consented to begin the performance" in order not to "disappoint" the broadcast audience. (Is that "really" prescient, a forecast of Stratas' penchant for cancellations?) Fortunately, his hope that she will be able "to get through the entire performance" is realized. Moreover, as so often happens in cases of announced indisposition, her portrayal gives little or no indication of vocal infirmity or a depletion of energy. (I suppose that freedom from full responsibility allows for a game effort.) The soprano's tone is not of the shimmering Germanic soubrette variety that we often hear in the role—its silken sheen is darker and rounder. In Stratas' case, that means Hansel's sister is touched by tomboy ways—no namby-pamby docility from her. The manner is appealing. But why should a singer negate her best qualities in order to mimic childish tone, a posture that Stratas allows a shade too much prominence in the opening act? Of course, the answer is that she is a singing actress and Gretel is a child—but still, adults playing at being children sound like adults playing at being children. Better to allow us to enjoy the music. And, more often than not, Stratas does get around to doing just that. Brother and sister sing the prayer with affecting simplicity; Hansel's part tends to sound like a monotone, but Stratas' lovely tones aptly convey the message. The aria goes well enough, considering the circumstances—the opening portion in particular is tellingly sung. A difficult piece with coloratura flourishes that are hardly child's play (Stratas slides up and down some of the scalework), this aria alone would be reason for concern when indisposed. Elsewhere, the role doesn't offer the soprano many opportunities to work her subtle brand of magic, but she searches out a few phrases to imbue with meaning beyond the genre's expected scope. As she questions the liberated gingerbread children at the opera's denouement, her poignant delivery adds another dimension to the fairytale.

At the Met in 1931, operagoers in the house, unlike the radio audience, heard a performance of *Pagliacci*, as well as the introductory *Hänsel und Gretel*. By the seventies, Humperdinck's minor masterwork was considered sufficient fare on its own. Despite its Wagnerian idiom, the opera is relatively brief. Still, redoubtable Wagnerian Ernest Newman felt that "in many ways *Hänsel und Gretel* reminds us of Wagner's *Meistersinger*."[11] That masterwork is indeed a meal in itself

Die Meistersinger
15 January 1972
Eva
Pilar Lorengar
Magdalene
Shirley Love
Walther
James King
David
Loren Driscoll
Hans Sachs
Theo Adam
Kothner
Donald Gramm
Beckmesser
Benno Kusche
Pogner
Ezio Flagello
Conductor
Thomas Schippers

and the Met serves up a fine repast on the broadcast of 15 January 1972. Theo Adam heads a cast including Lorengar, Love, King, Driscoll, Gramm, and Flagello under Schippers' baton. Newcomer Benno Kusche (Beckmesser) adds further interest to the lineup.

Though his posthumous reputation is not anchored in Wagner, during his Wunderkind days at the Met Schippers had been entrusted with *Der Fliegende Holländer* and *Lohengrin*. Bayreuth had certified his Wagnerian credentials in 1963 by placing the new production of *Meistersinger* in his charge, and by the time of the Met broadcast we may assume that his interpretation of the massive opera's inner workings had profited from additional fermentation. The conductor's view of the opera is remarkably sunny. From the sprightly gait of the overture, we gather that his tradesmen are a genial group, devoid of pomposity and quite content with their lot. The maestro likes to keep things moving and does so with notable sangfroid throughout the afternoon. The journey is pleasant because the flow is so fluent; the orchestra plays at the top of its current form for him. His winds sparkle at the lift of the second-act curtain and, enhancing Wagner's marking (*Gemächlich*), he sets them dancing as they sound the Johannistag motive. Subtleties of the opera's philosophical stance—its weighty overtones—are hardly an up-front concern, but the lacunae are partially filled by an expressive Vorspiel and several thoughtful episodes in the third act.

The general air of well-being is augmented by a group of bright-timbred singers who cast a concentrated light. Chief among them is Theo Adam, whose Sachs served as his calling card in 1969. He would not often be heard at the Met, though his success merited greater exposure. The voice, secure throughout its entire range, is shiny-faced, uncommonly so for a bass. In fact, the timbre in the upper range suggests the Nordic baritonal brilliance of Ingvar Wixell, while the lower range holds some of the point, even a touch of the rawness, of James Morris' fine instrument. (The latter sounded the few notes of Hans Schwarz in this broadcast, long before he himself would become a distinguished Wagnerian.) Though inherently attractive, the voice is robbed of maximum expression by its monochromatic character and his preference for singing full voice no matter the dynamic marking. The cost to the cobbler's reflective monologues is considerable. When he breaks into the introspective orchestral lead-in to the war monologue with a blatant 'Wahn,' the mood dissipates. He deserves credit for the stab he makes at mezza voce for 'Ein Kobold,' and the welcome and effective head tone at 'Gott weiss' indicates that he might do more if he would. Overall, the youthful timbre and lively manner subconsciously limit our perception of the purported depth of the poet's wisdom. Sachs' gravitas suffers. I feel certain this cobbler doesn't for a moment believe he would be a King Marke in the making. He might rather have taken Eva up on her offer. Adam's distinction is more apparent in the third act, where his instrument's heady resonance is increasingly attractive. There he positively radiates good humor and assurance when instructing Stolzing in the mysteries of the mastersinger's art. Community service is obviously his thing, as the Nürnbergers know very well and demonstrate at the opera's close. It would be wrong not to value the artist's easy and thorough command of the notes and the wonderful clarity of his diction. Above all, let us be grateful for his staying power; his instrument remains potent and alive to the very end of this long and difficult role. The customary Met cuts (including a verse of the 'Jerum' episode, a snatch of Sachs' instruction of Walther, and a major portion of the cobbler's final address on the Masters' art) are in effect, but he would have had no need of them. Other cuts (a portion of Beckmesser's second-act serenade, the final verse of Walther's practice lied, two eliminations in the last-act scene with Sachs and Beckmesser, including the final stanza of his audition) are evidently intended to retain audience attention by avoiding repetitive episodes.

Sachs' colleagues are summoned to order by Donald Gramm's Kothner, an entirely satisfying portrayal. One would have to hark back to the days when Herbert Janssen played second fiddle to Friedrich Schorr's Sachs (an embarrassment of riches) to hear the baker's role so well sung—even the coloratura bits (except for the tricky triplets) are expertly negotiated. Though Gramm's voice retains its customary plangency (another bright timbre), it holds unexpected depth today while his comfort with the language, his idiomatic style, are exemplary. A Stravinsky protégé, Wyoming-born Loren Driscoll had been heard on Broadway (Freddy in *My Fair Lady*), at Glyndebourne (Ferrando), and in Santa Fe, and was resident, since 1963, in Berlin. Contemporary scores were his meat. New to the airwaves but not to the role of David at the Met, Driscoll, too, owns a voice of distinctive timbre. He is one of those tenors whose upper notes mix in the soprano hue. But it is oddly husky lower down. The result can be disaffecting, yet his portrait of the mischievous apprentice holds a peculiar charm—David's episodes seem less obtrusive as Driscoll easily integrates them into the dramatic action. At the other end of the spectrum is old hand Harvuot's sturdy Nightwatchman, whose call, while not magical, proclaims him a guardian of the people's peace in whom one could believe. Flagello's Pogner is familiar from several broadcasts. I kept checking the *Annals* to make sure it was really the American bass, whose tones are normally so plump, that I was hearing. In counterfeiting the manner of the weighty German basses, the singer effects what he must have regarded as a necessary transformation. But how one misses those rolling, resonant sounds of yore. In act one, his goldsmith is a stodgy, woolly-voiced guild member, but he undergoes yet another transformation in the second-act interlude with his daughter. Nuances and timbral glow again begin to penetrate his tones. But then, Lorengar could warm any father's heart.

German bass-baritone Benno Kusche's justly famous portrayal of Beckmesser was secured by the Met solely for this season's *Meistersinger* series. Now in the fourth decade of a distinguished career, he was based in Munich but frequented the stages of Salzburg, Berlin, Covent Garden, and Glyndebourne, among others. His thorough command of the difficult role is evident throughout the entire afternoon. Initially, his Beckmesser seems at most a compendium of those sniveling, mean-spirited effects that the years have made all too familiar, the difference being that Kusche's jabs and thrusts are more expert than usual. With deadly aim, he spits out the text and strikes his human targets. However much on the mark, the portrayal seems one-dimensional. All that changes in the later stages of the opera, however, when he allows the unfortunate town clerk to reveal some measure of his own needs, his unsatisfied desires. His tone, while betraying a few traces of age, warms and his song is sincere. Recognizing human frailty, Adam treats him, though caught red-handed in thievery, with respect. And so must we.

In so male-dominated an opera, Magdalene and Eva must fight for their place in that sun which Schippers worships. Shirley Love's companion to Pogner's daughter calls to mind some interpretations of yore where 'die Alte' had not yet become converted into 'die Andre.' The aging process may be attributed to her

Pilar Lorengar as Eva in *Die Meistersinger*. Photography by Louis Mélançon. Courtesy Metropolitan Opera Archives.

dark mezzo tone. It is clouded a bit by the chill within St. Katherine's Church but, upon escaping to the midsummer air, proves effective enough. (In reality, St. Katherine's was a small church, but O'Hearn's set, like most stage cathedrals, is vast, so undoubtedly there were drafts.) Driscoll's David is singularly youthful, so the age difference really might have mattered if the apprentice were not so taken with the motherly comforts his Lene provided. As expected, Lorengar's Evchen is a fetching creature. Feisty beyond the norm (agitation being a built-in component of the singer's instrument and stage temperament), the maiden early on makes clear she will have none of Beckmesser's mooning; in Sachs' workshop she turns her fire on the benign, and to her mind, recalcitrant, shoemaker. Stolzing will have his hands full with this young wife. Her tone is a bit scratchy in the church (praying evidently has not improved her humor) but soon it takes on its customary embracing blush, becoming quite mellow in the critical moments of the third act. The voice has sufficient body in the lower range to anchor the give and take of the several dialogues with her lover knight and counselor cobbler. The round core of her middle voice soothes, even as the top voice glories in ecstatic release. The latter asset turns her passionate outburst ('O Sachs! Mein Freund!') into an episode of singular abandon, the thrilling ascents causing a responsive tingle in the listener. Eva's claim that Sachs' generosity has made her 'edel, frei und kühn' (brave, free, and true) is reaffirmed by Lorengar's song. Occasionally, she delights in effecting a sudden change of mood by employing, for example, a *subito piano*, one of many douceurs that in turn stimulate a responsive sigh of appreciation on our part. Her limning of the all-important opening of the quintet, while not quite suspending time in the Elisabeth Schumann manner, is heartwarming and steadily intoned. Sometimes, in the intricate mazes of this mammoth opera, Eva comes off as a cipher, merely a nice girl who serves as a pawn for the guild's entertainment. Not Lorengar, as her knight surely will discover.

Happily for future wedded bliss, her Stolzing is no weak, lily-livered lyric tenor. On the other hand, though his knight makes the mastersinger roster, King is no poet, so marital problems could arise on that score. Yet he is ardent in the church and even more so when promoting elopement. His tenor, a straight-arrow voice if ever there was one, is so commanding that his heroic stature may well be enough to satisfy any girl. The voice is certainly a strong one, unusually consistent in its glabrous tonal makeup, and the timbre, so manly, so clean-cut (and so unvaried), has its own appeal. With King, what you hear is what you get. And that means he will triumph in the first act, where Walther is both firm and fierce, pig-headed and (with this tenor) uncommonly defiant. Lyricism and legato are not King's strong suits. When Sachs takes on the job of teaching him musical manners, his pupil is tractable, but the learning has not been fully absorbed by the time he must deliver the Preislied. There we must take comfort, as in the earlier trial runs of the act, in King's ability to climb fearlessly up the scale to stentorian top notes, which even an occasional bit of effort cannot deflect. Unlike most contestants in more lamentable readings, he neither falters nor grunts or gargles tone in the treacherous tessitura of the recurrent prize song. Too bad that the young couple will move out of the neighborhood—Sachs has more to teach them both.

The Wagner dearth at the Met, while not quenched, was mitigated in Bing's final season by the inclusion of *Meistersinger, Parsifal* (not broadcast), and *Tristan*, the latter in a new production for Nilsson, the undisputed queen of the Wagne-

Tristan und Isolde
18 December 1971

Isolde
Birgit Nilsson
Brangäne
Irene Dalis
Tristan
Jess Thomas
Kurwenal
William Dooley
Marke
Giorgio Tozzi
Conductor
Erich Leinsdorf

rian realm. Joining her on the broadcast of 18 December 1971 are Jess Thomas (Tristan), Dooley (Kurvenal), and Tozzi (Marke), all new portrayals for the radio audience, plus Dalis as Brängane. Conductor Leinsdorf, survivor of the Met's Wagner heyday in the thirties and forties, returns to the company after an absence of five seasons. The seminal work had not been heard by radio listeners for eight seasons, though 1966–67 contained house performances.

New York operagoers were agog at the rhapsodic production that Günther Schneider-Siemssen provided for the opera. With the use of projection techniques and almost cinematic procedures, he achieved in space the magical evocation of timeless ecstasy that Wagner had painted in sound. With stage director August Everding's compliance, the German-born, Austrian resident artist captured the lovers' escape from reality by literally sending them aloft; in the second-act love duet they floated high above the stage before returning to the harsh world of Melot's revenge. Lacking Schneider-Siemssen's pyrotechnics, the performance heard by the radio audience may not be quite as emotionally shattering as that which those in the house experienced, but the aural component holds many satisfactions of its own. Conductor Leinsdorf sees to that. His direction is a model of integrity. Of course, we hope for a bit more than rectitude when *Tristan und Isolde* is on the boards.

Almost three decades had elapsed since Leinsdorf had led three broadcasts of *Tristan* (1940–43) with casts of memorable splendor, including Flagstad or Traubel, Thorborg, Melchior, Huehn, and List or Kipnis. For most of the sixties, he had been at the helm of the prestigious Boston Symphony. We may be grateful that the opera house once again claimed him, for his judicious musicality is, as ever, a welcome complement to the more flamboyant ministrations of some of his colleagues. His brand of thorough professionalism and technical know-how is a tonic easy to swallow. He runs a tight ship, and his acute sense of just proportions guarantees the orchestral crew and stage passengers safe harbor at the final curtain. His treatment of the prelude is emblematic of his way with the entire opera. In the approach to the *Tristan* chord, he propels the marked crescendos with intensity but allows the crowning motive (desire, if you will) unexpected equanimity. Thereafter, his thrusting phrases, not quite explicitly sexual (the orgiastic was never his preserve), climb to an effective climax, one that emanates naturally from the total fabric of the prelude. Similarly, the rushing string ascents at the opening of the second act are well set out musically, only modestly suggesting Isolde's impatience as she awaits her lover. The mating of just proportions and emotional turbulence may not be to everyone's taste for this rapturous score, but this musical sophisticate has his own code, an honorable one, and abides by it to the satisfaction of many.

The meticulous conductor must have become spasmodic when Goeke, the elegant lyric tenor who would have a career of decent proportions in leading roles, jumped the gun by half a measure with his sailor's song. Cautioned to begin again, he does so and expresses longing for his Irish maiden in sweet tones and meaningful phrases. The tenor's youthful timbre and optimistic outlook signal that this recruit has not been before the mast long enough to become hardened by a sailor's cruel life. Dooley as Kurvenal is a bit of an oxymoron. Commendable artist that he is, the American baritone might be categorized as a lieder singer caught playing at being bluff and hardy—and bringing it off with unexpected panache. Clean runs are hardly essential to put over Kurvenal's taunting song, but they are a welcome novelty. Dooley, quite surprisingly, rises to the more imposing challenges of the third act. His tone is secure on high, retaining its beauty even at the *forte* dynamic, and his phrasing is alternatively emphatic and devout. Dooley's heart lives in his prismatic tone, and when Tristan's faithful liege, at his wounded master's side, permits himself a rush of feeling, the baritone finds himself once again on artistic home ground.

Dalis is too often positioned in some remote area of Schneider-Siemssen's design for maximum aural effect. Brangäne's warning, for instance, should emanate from an invisible source, but audibility is strained; in the house, the effect was probably mesmeric. Too frequent breaths in that critical episode rob her cautionary phrases of ultimate ethereal float, but the individual tones are worthy. Their unforced beauty is enhanced by an occasional enticing *morendo* effect. The San Jose native's oft-broadcast Brangäne betrays its familiar virtues today: the voice remains solid over the entire range and her style is idiomatic. Her conspiratorial delivery of the handmaiden's suspicions regarding Melot are only one evidence of her dramatic perceptivity. Rod MacWherter's Melot, wretched confidant of both Marke and Tristan, trumpets such stout tone that one surmises he could be a Tristan in the making. Such hopes seldom prove warranted—stamina often being the disqualifying agent. In the forties, for instance, Emery Darcy, a frequent Met Melot, tested the waters with Siegmund and Parsifal, but his career in the big time proved to be short-lived.

Over the years, Tozzi's appealing instrument has not been as reliable as in his earliest days, but on this afternoon the voice is well focused and full toned, and his delivery is assured. This Marke is no mournful whiner after the fashion of some basses, but rather a man sounding young enough to regret losing a prospective wife even more than a trusted friend. A few moments of suspect pitch in the unaccompanied phrases at the end of Marke's lament cannot detract from the considerable impact of his peroration. Leinsdorf helps by sending along the king's woeful plaint at a fleet pace. At one point ('Die Tristan sich zum Schild erkor') Tozzi's anger spills over, and the bitterness gives Marke a stronger profile than that of the kindly old man who discovers that, even among loyal friends, medieval hormones must be reckoned with.

Without artists of equal stature and stamina in the title roles, *Tristan und Isolde* can come off as an orchestral feast that, while remarkable in itself, is a torso without a face. Jess Thomas is a hero who deserves to be honored on his American hearth, but the salutation is awarded as much for valor as for achievement. Like most tenors who venture into the Heldentenor arena during this fallow period, he is valued most for enabling us to hear Nilsson's pivotal Isolde. Not that his artistic sensibilities are without merit—he knows how a Tristan should sound and act. Then, too, his stage presence—tall and handsome—is a welcome enticement for ticket holders inured to the optical blight of portly heroes. His bald timbre is not inherently attractive. Deficient in enriching overtones, the voice dutifully encompasses the notes (no mean achievement in this opera) but without the density, the vitality, or, above all, the emotional charge to enhance his carefully molded phrases. Quite often (in a good deal of the love duet), his sensitivity warms us to his music making. When note accuracy in fleet passages is required, he can supply it—the delirium after imbibing the love draught and a few moments in

Birgit Nilsson as Isolde and Regina Resnik as Brangäne in *Tristan und Isolde*.

the act-two love duet profit from this skill. Still, even in the latter episode, his principal virtue lies in his not despoiling Nilsson's more appealing song. Stalwart he is, and he wrestles bravely with the hero's third-act dementia. If, as for most tenors, the ordeal is troublesome for him, many moments are equally trying to his auditors—the voice simply lacks sufficient variety of coloration to vivify the wounded hero's successive flights of hope and lapses into despair. *Pis aller.* In Tristan's final moments, some top notes, not unexpectedly, must be finessed. And yet, at two climactic moments—as Tristan curses the fatal love potion ('verflucht sei, furchtbarer Trank!') and when he believes Isolde's ship to have gone down ('Verloren!')—the tenor manages some genuinely grand, tragic utterances. The wounded man's agony becomes real and acute. At the least, Thomas convinces us of the gravity of Tristan's wounds and his febrile mental state. And his deft and sensuous breathing of Isolde's name as death claims Tristan notches up his credibility. But validation has been a long time coming.

Mr. Cross prefaced his plot description with a reminder that Nilsson's sensational 1959 Met debut—he notes that it was famously accorded front-page treatment in New York newspapers—occurred twelve years ago to the day of our broadcast. Since that red-letter day, Miss Nilsson's admirers have become legion and their devotion does not allow them to suffer detractors gladly. Having heard her frequently in Vienna several years before her arrival in New York, I count myself a longtime admirer. Who can resist the blazing brilliance of her instrument on high, her integrity in performance, and, above all, her sensitive cajoling of vocal and musical niceties from a voice not inherently designed for them. To speak of growth in expression and characterization in an artist of the Swedish diva's accomplishments seems the height of condescension. Yet if one recalls her excellent Isolde broadcasts of the early and mid-sixties, a responsive listener will be struck by the heightened artistry of this 1971 airing.

From the first, nuances proliferate. Let me name a few: in only her second phrase, the delectable *piano* caress she imparts to 'du'; the pin-point darts and enlivening rhythmic energy of Isolde's angry outbursts, beginning at 'Entartet Geschlecht'; her rich, darkly colored voicing of 'Mir erkoren' and forceful shaping of the entire sequence ending 'Todgeweihtes Herz,' the latter word almost a groan of pain; a lovely portamento on 'Augen' in that significant phrase 'er sah mir in die Augen' and the emotional turmoil she lays on 'jammerte mich' in the next phrase; her sardonic mimicking of Tristan's intent to make her Marke's bride; the broadsword of tone and breadth of manner she deploys when cursing Tristan ('Fluch deinem Haupt!'); the grandeur with which she cites her mother's death draught, a phrase that culminates in a striking plunge into chest voice ('gab sie den Todestrank'), perhaps her most telling utterance. Well, the list is endless and I will weary you if I continue to cite her virtues. No need to worry that a few items on the downside will balance the scales. The 'gold'ne Schale' (the goblet that will contain the fateful drink) could be caressed with greater warmth. While occasionally a touch of honey does soften the diamantine surface of her timbre ('dein Eh'gemahl zu sein'), the very act reminds us of the more fragrant nectar offered by other Isoldes. (And yet Lilli Lehmann's Isolde, considered a paragon by some critics, was thought to be overly austere, indeed almost a harridan, by others. No honey at all flowed from her lips to her auditors' ears.) If Nilsson neglects to honor Wagner's *zart* marking when citing Frau Minne's 'Zaubers Macht' to Brangäne, she has saved her tenderness for the lover himself. Her cultivated, feminine tones becomingly grace the major portion of the love duet, and there Leinsdorf wafts a soft cushion of support, his flow of gentle, yet intoxicating, sonorities atmospherically apposite for Schneider-Siemssen's space journey. The second half of the duet does lose some potency as Thomas' voice wearies and its tonal core dissipates. Nilsson goes gamely, but a shade less intriguingly, on, her tone now touched by a cooler breath. She accurately traces the concluding rush of phrases with remarkable fluency. Thomas' invitation to Isolde to join him in exile, while insufficiently poetic, is one of his best moments—his tone is marginally more, shall we say, inviting. At the act's close, Nilsson's response fails to enhance the poignancy of their fate (the cool breath again). Her Liebestod and the arrival at Tristan's death bed, however, restore the opera's transfiguring mood, abetted by Thomas' aptly colored, otherworldly, voicing of her name. From the moment Isolde touches Kareol's shore and tenderly greets her lover, Nilsson's sound and expression are suffused with a beguiling intimacy. Can this be the era's most commanding Brünnhilde? The Walküre's battle cry is indeed remote. This time Nilsson's rendering of Isolde's supernal farewell reveals her consummate artistry at its fullest. Its overall cast is quite magical, the tone in its inner moments of utmost purity, delicate in its caress, yet blending effortlessly into a bronze coloration for the grander moments. Her legato is exemplary, the artful shaping of phrases now molded into a satisfying, expressive unity. Best of all, she offers perhaps the lightest, most sweetly touched 'Lust' of broadcast history.

Too often, upon lengthy acquaintance, an artist's peculiar greatness becomes taken for granted and we begin to lament the inevitable chinks in what (in Nilsson's case) is virtually inviolable armor. Does Sutherland's mushy diction, for instance, limit expression to the extent that her amazing technical prowess (and with an instrument of remarkable amplitude for her *Fach*) should be ignored? Hardly. That Nilsson's timbre is not always ingratiating in no way prevents us from realizing our good fortune at having a voice so capable of dominating the Wagnerian orchestral mass and sending aloft, and with unfailing accuracy, tones of heart-piercing splendor. Deficiencies may—indeed should—be noted. To cite them cannot defile these supreme artists. Having done so, we return to contemplate their greatness, often their uniqueness. Nilsson was a beacon shining into what was, at that time, a Wagnerian wasteland. Without minimizing her capabilities in other genres, including her Italian roles, Mr. Bing might well lament, as he did in a 1964 epistle to associates Herman and Jaretzki, that he was unable to mount the Wagnerian operas with the frequency that her remarkable aptitude for those epic works warranted.[11] During the six Bing seasons at Lincoln Center, the soprano was heard in ten broadcasts including two Elektras, three Turandots, two Toscas (each portrayal valuable in itself), but only two *Walküre* Brünnhildes and one Isolde. (The diva canceled a scheduled airing of her Lady Macbeth.) Nor would future years bring the flood of Wagnerian performances that was fervently desired by so many; not, at least, until *Ring* fervor gripped the entire country in the nineties. All the more reason to be grateful for Nilsson's superb portrayal of Isolde on the 1971 broadcast.

The soprano deservedly had made her mark as Strauss' tormented pair of heroines, but when Salome next haunted the Baptist's cistern, the more likely Rysanek dispensed with veils of limited number. Absent from the airwaves since

Salome
18 March 1972

Salome
Leonie Rysanek
Herodias
Irene Dalis
Herod
Gerhard Stolze
Narraboth
Rod MacWherter
Jokanaan
Thomas Stewart
First Nazarene
John Macurdy
Conductor
Karl Böhm

the 1965 broadcast, the opera is virtually newly cast on the broadcast of 18 March 1972. In addition to the charismatic Austrian soprano, who in this season is singing her first series of Met Salomes, the radio audience is introduced to Stewart's Jokanaan, Stolze's Herod, MacWherter's Narraboth (a step up for him), and Macurdy's Nazarene. Dalis (Herodias) and Böhm, ever the composer's advocate—and our soprano's, as well—gladly return to the fray.

Now in his seventy-seventh year, the conductor has become something of a monument for the appreciative Met audience. He in turn delivers a performance monumental in its sonic grandeur and rapture. His control over Strauss' tempestuous orchestra is sure (the brass blow with welcome security and tonal warmth), frequently mesmerizing in its precise exploitation of timbral color, and occasionally even subtle in its restraint (as in the orchestral peroration that distends Salome's triumph at the opera's close). His version of the dance, replete with alternating hesitations and slight surges, is hypnotically slow, its vulgarity astutely minimized. Even at that, it remains, as most forbidden fruit does, a treat—if you go in for that sort of thing. One could say that Böhm's virtuoso orchestra is the afternoon's star. Strauss probably would not mind.

If control is dominant in the pit, it does not inhibit Böhm's stage cohorts. They inhabit Wilde's dysfunctional creatures with unabashed abandon. Their vocalism and interpretive gestures are flamboyant enough to stimulate even jaded operagoers. Foremost in flamboyance is Gerhard Stolze, whose tenor, whether piercingly bright or grotesquely shadowed, holds a maniacal nervosity that makes Herod's dementia seem a natural state. Like his Loge, his besotted Tetrarch is a fully realized portrait, each carefully considered phrase delivered with an assurance verging on bravado. In its totality, the interpretation assaults the ear and causes nerve ends to bristle—just the result a mad monarch would be expected to produce. As his consort, Dalis is equally effective. One series of vulgar, chesty laughs is marvelously callous. While convincing in depicting Herodias' hysteria, the mezzo cannot fully disguise the health of her instrument; its secure intonation is always a boon, for she is a practiced Straussian who invariably travels the composer's tricky terrain with confidence.

Macurdy, too, brings a welcome solidity to the First Nazarene's pronouncements, while the tenorial Jews are uncommonly clean and clear in their theological arguments. Anthony stands out, but Velis and Franke's distinctive timbres count as well. MacWherter—as we know, a tenor of more heroic proportions—delivers Narraboth's phrases with force and belief. One has often heard young Syrians whose instruments are of a lyric cast, their tonal sweetness imbuing the soldier's longing and resultant suicide with greater pathos. MacWherter's captain of the guard, though vocally admirable, is so commanding that his poetic description of Salome's feet as 'little white doves' seems foreign to the soldier's temperament. On the other hand, I am sure I read somewhere that strong men are helpless when confronted with wily women. No wonder Godfrey Ben-David's page, though possessing a contralto's wealth of tone, is unsuccessful in her caveats.

As John the Baptist, Thomas Stewart offers one of his most successful portrayals. The voice is well focused, fetching in timbre, and well up to the considerable demands of the role. Cistern resonance aids him in the understage pronouncements, but he turns his own manly tone to good account in his encounter with Salome. By this time we understand that his instrument's density is not overly grand, nor is its coloration awe inspiring (and all prophets should inspire awe). But its pointed focus suggests a fanatic's zeal, a trait that his emphatic delivery augments. His rejection of Salome's kiss is replete with repulsion—the masterly repetition of 'Niemals' thrillingly mirrors his disgust.

Miss Rysanek had triumphed when singing her initial Salome in Munich in the summer of 1971. The role seems tailor made for her altitudinous soprano and extrovert stage manner. Waiting more than two decades into her career to claim the Strauss temptress seems almost unduly cautious on her part. (Would that more artists were similarly discreet in their repertory choices.) The soprano may be expected to offer a finished portrayal, however recent the role assumption. Her Salome, though not quite as overwhelming as anticipated, is a worthy addition to her gallery of memorable Strauss portraits. The Judean princess calls forth many of her best performance qualities. The hazy character of her lower octave is put to good use in suggesting the young princess' weird anatomical fixation on Jokanaan—ghostly shadings suit the young woman's psychopathic state. Veiled or not, that portion of the soprano's unique instrument has by now been well stabilized—the greater solidity enables her to make some of her more potent effects in that region, something that would not have been possible in the early sixties. Unfortunately, some ungainly sharping on high notes marginally detracts from the visceral thrill of her vocalism in the scene with Jokanaan. Other sopranos may be more assertive at punctuating the opening marcato notes of 'Ich will deinen Mund' and its sister phrases—her instrument is rather soft grained for emphatic reiteration—but few can trace their subsequent path with comparable tonal glory. Nevertheless, a bit of unexpected strain surfaces now and then in that elevated territory where her ease and splendor have normally been supreme. Probably the blemish is merely an afternoon's momentary impurity. In the aggregate, the voice meets the strenuous demands of the role head on and conquers. In early scenes, seductive nuances enrich her encounters with Narraboth and Jokanaan; I particularly relish her exquisite taking of a soft note on high in the latter episode. Her skill as a singing actress is evident in the varied shapes and nuances that she applies to Salome's oft-repeated requests to Herod. Even more impressive is her fervid depiction of the princess' ravings when she hovers over the cistern as Jokanaan's head is severed. The final soliloquy holds some of her most assured vocalism (notwithstanding a little patch of suspect intonation at an intermediate climax). The voice's elasticity, propelled by the singer's teeming vitality, never fails to amaze. She chooses to underplay a few dramatic moments, notably when citing the 'bitter taste' of the prophet's lips, while the ensuing recall of her 'kiss' phrases are quietly (and most effectively) sounded as though in a trance. When needed, a touch of innocence can invade her silvery tone. More often she spends voice and emotion throughout the lengthy scene with the thrilling liberality we have come to expect from her.

I suspect that Rysanek was not in her best vocal condition for the *Salome* broadcast, but she leaves no doubt that she merits inclusion in the grand sequence of Metropolitan interpreters of Strauss' princess of Judea, a succession that embraces Fremstad, Lawrence, Welitch, Varnay, Goltz, Borkh, and Nilsson. The memory of Nilsson's 1965 broadcast, her singing marked by timbral brilliance and fearless negotiation of Strauss' treacherous line, remains strong and vivid. Rysanek offers a softer radiance, a bewitching femininity. Both top voices thrill: the one blazes, the other shines. Their characterizations, the one commanding, the other hypnotic, are well formed and satisfy. No need to choose between them. Only a desert-island challenge would make me, quite unexpectedly, take Nilsson.

Salome, though unsuccessful in gaining Jokannaan's interest, may be said to have acquired his capital. And she had other admirers in Narraboth and Herod, though their fixation led to no good, at least for them. Temptresses figure large in opera and rightly exert uncommon fascination upon both their active stage lovers and a watchful audience. During the first intermission of the 8 January broadcast of *Samson et Dalila*, Francis Robinson trots out a succession of major-league operatic seductresses and their prime interpreters. In his ever-stimulating *Biographies in Music*, the Met's assistant manager and first-class raconteur explores in words and with recordings the vagaries of what he says sociologists used to call "the unadjusted girl." Robinson lingers over the charms of the Salomes of Strauss (Ljuba Welitch) and Massenet (Maria Jeritza), of Thaïs (Mary Garden), Manon (Bori), Manon Lescaut (Margherita Sheridan), Carmen (Geraldine Farrar), and Lulu (Evelyn Lear). He places Kundry at the tail end of his survey of femmes fatales and he can't resist recounting that when Carl Van Vechten brought Fremstad (the first Met Salome at the beginning of the century) to hear Flagstad's Kundry, the older diva summed up the Norwegian soprano's portrayal with a whispered "Wie mütterlich!" Even the immortal Olive could not apply a pejorative "How motherly!" to Grace Bumbry's ravishing Dalila.[12]

Saint-Saëns' opera had not been heard by the radio audience since the O'Hearn/Merrill production was launched in 1964 (Dalis and Thomas were the broadcast title pair). With Bumbry on the scene, her physical and vocal glamor quite naturally dictated a revival. At the 10 December 1971 seasonal premiere, Tucker had taken on the heroic chores of Samson for the first time, but on the 1972 broadcast it is McCracken who succumbs to Bumbry's allure. Bacquier (High Priest) and Macurdy (Old Hebrew), holdovers from the 1964 broadcast, are joined by Plishka (Abimélech) under the leadership of Marseilles-born Serge Baudo. A product of the Paris Conservatoire with credits including the Aix-en-Provence Festival, the Paris Opéra, and La Scala (*Pelléas*), Baudo, currently director of the Orchestre de Lyon, had come to the Met in 1971 for *Les Contes d'Hoffmann*. His command of French style is perhaps a given—and the expectation is fulfilled—but beyond that, he manages to make *Samson* a genuine theatrical experience, a novel result if one takes the opera's oft-cited oratorio patrimony as gospel. (That slur is at best a half-truth.) In any case, Baudo all but disproves the charge. The New York critics were forever decrying the opera's musical crassness, but in Baudo's hands, Saint-Saëns' biblical epic has its musical charms as well as theatrical validity—all this, of course, within the parameters that Saint-Saëns' facility allows. With the notable exception of the temple duet of Dalila and the High Priest (where Baudo pulls a reversal, taking it at a moderate, square tempo and, in the process, rubbing off some of its customary cheap gloss), the conductor's pace is fleet. Orchestral colors are assiduously, and often subtly, cultivated. When passion flowers, as it must in the hothouse second act, its tumult is unabashedly embraced by the French maestro.

The stage participants, without exception a fine group, profit as well from Baudo's knowing ways. The title roles command the bulk of our attention but American basses Plishka and Macurdy each contribute worthy vignettes. The former's voice sounds uncommonly secure, well-focused, and tonally attractive, a far

Samson et Dalila
8 January 1972

Dalila
Grace Bumbry
Samson
James McCracken
High Priest
Gabriel Bacquier
Old Hebrew
John Macurdy
Conductor
Serge Baudo

cry from the looser, more Slavic-timbred instrument that we still heard with plea-sure at the beginning of the twenty-first century. With admirable musicianship, he partners the brass in their unison phrases with complete fidelity of rhythm and pitch. Macurdy's voice in the upper octave has taken on a more becoming color, while his seriousness of purpose suits the Old Hebrew's limited dramatic function. In the trio for Dalila, Samson, and the Old Hebrew ('Je viens célébrer la victoire') all three artists conduct their vocal lines with a precision that lends a stronger profile than usual to the attractive piece. (Only Macurdy's final solo phrase, an important moment that profits from an elegant curve, recalls the occasionally tur-gid vocalism of his earlier years.) Bacquier, of course, is supreme in his assignment. Whenever the French baritone dons priestly robes, whether the habit clothes de-monic deceit or saintly virtues, he wears them with practiced ease. If pushed to the limit (as in a few opening gambits where bluster is Saint-Saëns' prescription for the priest's curse) his voice can lose some definition, but that minor blemish is soon remedied. Declamation receives its due (and in French opera that is substan-tial), and when, in his second-act encounter with Dalila, cunning is the priest's tool, Bacquier gives it aural life. The baritone's declamatory vigor in the hate duet of the final act ('Il faut, pour assouvir ma haine') suggests an exhilarating delight in rancor, his resolute delivery allowing us to savor it as well.

When two artists with high-powered voices such as Bumbry and McCracken possess are joined (opposed might be the better term in this opera), they immedi-ately cause the stage temperature to rise. It seldom abates thereafter. One wishes, in fact, for a few more musical niceties *en route* but, that minor reservation aside, the two singers contribute vivid portrayals. McCracken enters with voice ready, willing, and able either to rebuke or inspire the oppressed Israelites. In prime con-dition, the voice seems to take on a more appealing color in French roles—gleams of brightness illumine the upper octave and the shudder that his pressurized pro-duction sometimes summons is marginalized. The result is gratifying, especially since the baritonal solidity of the lower voice remains intact, its thrust and power augmenting belief in Samson's heroic deeds. An approving nod must also be given to his clean French diction. The second act belongs to Dalila and if the tenor can manage a decent high B-flat at the end of 'Mon coeur,' he is all but home free. McCracken can and does. He supplements it with a grandly voiced 'Trahison' after his entrapment is complete. At the gristmill, our hero is somewhat less effective. He drenches his tones with self-pity (the text perhaps dictates it) but the result diminishes Samson's stature. A nobler stance with tears of subtle color within the voice rather than auditory drops would ultimately be more convincing. Vocally he is up to any and all of Samson's feats and, happily, the lamented noble stance returns as he asks God to lend him inspiration (i.e., brute strength) so that he can bring down the temple of Dagon on the Philistines. All in all, a crashingly good finale for an afternoon of superior vocalism.

Miss Bumbry's share in the quality music making is predominant, as it should be for all Dalilas, but seldom has been in recent years. She is in magnificent vocal estate and performs with assurance and pithy projection. I cannot say that her portrayal is replete with vocal or interpretive subtleties. Those attributes may or may not be absolutely requisite for a Dalila—after all, her principal charge is to exude stage allure and radiate vocal glamor, both of which the American soprano discharges with dispatch and to gratifying effect. (Her attractive person assuredly would have taken care of the former need and we have the taped evidence for the latter.) More specifically, in order to lend legitimacy to the need for a revival of this period relic, a Dalila must be able to deliver her several arias with luxuriant tone and commanding purpose. Again, Bumbry qualifies. I do find her voicing of the "hit" tune ('Mon coeur s'ouvre à ta voix') the least satisfying episode of her portrayal. Not that it is ill done—in fact, it rates high enough among recent broadcast readings. But the overall effect is a bit heavy-breathed, in the old silent movie meaning of the term. It is a difficult piece. Traversing those downward phrases with seductive and grand tone too often calls forth the contralto curse of tubby tone. Bumbry stops short of that, but the directional move is toward grandiosity. (And it need not have been. Oddly, and greatly to her credit, I heard her recently—in the late nineties—deliver a beautifully poised, elegant rendition of the aria that was not only testimony to her musicality but to the longevity of her voice's well-being.)

Having discharged that caveat, I can revel in the many beauties of her performance. The rich, pungent tones, so perfectly focused and beautifully colored, with which she launches 'Je viens célébrer la victoire' are complemented by stylistic restraint that is becoming not only to her but to the composer's intent. The registers are intelligently handled. She moves from her plangent chest voice into a resonant middle voice and on up into a secure, more soprano-like top voice without disturbance of the musical line or tonal quality. Only an occasional sudden large leap from a chest tone to a high note startles by the tensility and acuity of the upper tone. Here it should be noted that the mezzo is by this time well into her soprano transformation. Bing had offered her a Tosca during the schedule displacement of the labor strike season and Bumbry grasped the opportunity to try her wings in the soprano terrain at the Met. (The progress had begun earlier at Salzburg with Lady Macbeth and more recently as Salome at Covent Garden.) Thereafter, the soprano goal became her career focus, to the consternation of some of her many admirers and the gratification of others. No point in expressing regret—her star status was preordained and the soprano repertory seemed the obvious route to greater glory.

Throughout the afternoon, her top voice is reliable and alternately exquisitely colored or pointedly thrusting. The instrument is indeed a remarkable one. I admire the poised fluidity of her phrasing in the often overly static 'Printemps qui commence.' (Baudo helps here, as elsewhere, by never allowing the music's pulse to lag.) Bumbry's self-possession, her confidence in her vocal allure, in moments like this is formidable. No wonder, when the act-one curtain falls at the aria's end, that Samson (as the old-time plot descriptions so deliciously put it) "writhes in amorous expectation." I should like to have seen McCracken pull that off—the American tenor never did anything by halves. When, at the beginning of the second act, Dalila calls upon love to aid her seduction of Samson ('Amour! viens aider ma faiblesse!') the mezzo's delivery thrills; her command is complete—is it also a bit businesslike?—as though an affirmative response were never in doubt. A clean, lovely high B-flat and ascending scale confirm her right to that certitude. When she reaches the aria's nadir, a treacherous vocal descent often trying for artists whose claim to a sepulchral register is greater than hers, Bumbry marches untroubled into the depths; only the final A-flat loses maximum tonal vibrancy. A few phrases of fioritura in her scenes with the High Priest provide evidence of her technical expertise. Occasionally, one feels that her proficient handling of the voice is overly manipulative, a bit offhand even, but then she dispels that notion by momentarily summoning more delicate colors and lightening the voice's resolute pressure. One realizes what varied vocalism is at her call if she would choose to exploit those qualities more fully. The voice's brilliance is unassailable, but now and then the glare is rather insistent.

In the *Opera News* broadcast issue, Bumbry, intent upon her soprano quest, opines that if it were not for contracts currently in force she would have removed Dalila from her repertory. She notes that Vickers convinced her to take on the Met production—he thought it marvelous. Thus we have her quite wonderful portrayal of one of opera's most captivating 'unadjusted girls.' Is it possible that her in-progress vocal transformation will produce comparably satisfying results?

Gounod's Marguerite, heroine of our next French opera, is evidently a well-adjusted (in the sense of ordinariness) young maiden—at least if we take her entrance line at face value. She rejects Faust's offer of assistance at the Kermesse with bourgeois complacency, disclaiming his compliments on her beauty and social rank. Of course, her poise is merely put on and her reluctance to enjoy his company will prove short-lived. Zylis-Gara treads Marguerite's downward path on the broadcast of 28 February 1972, her person and virtue pursued by Domingo and Tozzi and repudiated by Sereni. A feature of the performance is our first glimpse of Von Stade in a prominent role (Siebel). All of these artists are heard in initial broadcast portrayals.

Lombard was scheduled to conduct the broadcast but gave way to Martin Rich, who had first led the opera with the company in the parks concert performances in June 1971. A couple of regular-season performances preceded his broadcast assumption. Rich is an old Metropolitan hand, having been affiliated with the company since 1954. We may assume his thorough acquaintance with the production since he had been responsible for its musical preparation for Lombard. Still, over his nearly two-decade Met career, his status was hardly that of best man, let alone bridegroom; he warranted no career notice in either *Opera News* or the Met's own *Opera Encyclopedia*. Barring a few ragged alignments of chorus and orchestra in the Kermesse, his reading proceeds without mishap (though Tozzi runs him a race in a few key moments where the bass obviously prefers a faster tempo). Interpretively, caution is Rich's byword. A glaze of staidness overlays the performance. A case in point is his treatment of the ballet music in the Walpurgis Nacht scene. From the standpoint of enablement, his concern for the dancers is functionally apt, but the lockstep movement he applies to the dance music minimizes its elegance and engaging sweep of phrase. The Kermesse dances are better served and the music of the soldier's return is deftly propelled, the entire episode wearing its hearty plebeian spirit lightly and precisely. The male chorus performs well throughout the afternoon. As usual, the Met format reverses Gounod's intent, placing the church scene before the soldier's return, and omits Marguerite's grand aria in the latter scene. In general, Rich makes the appropriate musical moves without ever allowing us to breathe the refined perfume of Gounod's lyrical score.

The performance, however, holds a number of aural rewards (as well as one disastrous portrayal). Let us begin with a high point—or rather a mezzo point. Von Stade's Siebel is quite out of the ordinary. Her French is idiomatic and cleanly articulated, the textual definition lending, as it should, character to both indi-

Faust
26 February 1972

Marguerite
Teresa Zylis-Gara
Siebel
Frederica von Stade
Faust
Plácido Domingo
Valentin
Mario Sereni
Méphistophélès
Giorgio Tozzi
Conductor
Martin Rich

vidual tones and, even more importantly, phrasing. Delightful nuances (gentle portamentos and varied colors) abound in a fluent 'Faites-lui mes aveux.' She sings it in key. Management, during her initial decade with the company, could not always reward her talent with assignments that would assure an ascending career path (her vocal type demands a special repertory), but her increasing prominence on the international opera scene is signaled by this polished portrayal.

In contrast to Von Stade's cultivated style, Sereni's bluff manner originates on another musical planet. He is a known quantity and will enjoy an uninterrupted Met tenure of almost three decades. Longevity should be a guarantee of a certain quality of performance and in his case the wish has generally been fulfilled—provided one does not set the level too high, that is, up there with a Tibbett or a Warren. Unlike our mezzo novitiate, the baritone's capital resides in his stout instrument rather than in his art. Thus, it comes as no surprise that he will bellow his way through the Kermesse aria at maximum, unvaried volume and scoop up to a few top tones at its close. His assurance is brazen and complete, and probably deserved. After all, Valentin's aria comes early in the afternoon's entertainment and throats must be lubricated one way or another—but preferably in the dressing room. His French is quite acceptable, far better than many Italian singers have offered over the years. Sereni's voice gains a cleaner focus when Marguerite's brother and his fellow soldiers confront Satan with their swords poised as crosses. And in Valentin's death scene the baritone demonstrates why he has been and will remain a Metropolitan fixture. His reading is not subtle, but it strikes home with its honesty—the heartfelt response of a valiant soldier, an offended brother. Now his tone is all burnished bronze, a really glorious, well-channeled outpouring of dignified song. He eschews the usual vocal weakening unto death preferred by the singing actor—perhaps it is beyond his vocal method—and delivers his final lines (in effect, that he dies as a soldier, upright to the end) with defiance, an original and telling touch.

Tozzi, like Sereni, is a veteran of the Met operatic wars, and a bit closer to quitting the battlefield. Cross informs us that he is in his eighteenth season. Only three more remain on his string and his performance this afternoon tells us why. On earlier broadcasts, Tozzi has offered portrayals that merited approval, sometimes modest and often much more than that, though suspect intonation has affected some of his readings. On this afternoon, suspicion turns to certitude and is all-pervasive. Moreover, the overall conception is so crude, so overbearing that one repeatedly cringes at the basso's vulgarities. (To her credit, Batyah Godfrey retains her composure in the quartet.) I imagine his intent is to present Méphistophélès as a larger-than-life fellow, with a big-hearted enthusiasm for his job, despicable though it be to us. Undoubtedly Satan did enjoy his work. But in assuming that posture, Tozzi feels compelled to shout streams of raucous laughter, to raise pitches at will, and in general deny Gounod's devil his due—that is, the elegance of phrase that the composer allotted him. In another age, Plançon and Journet paid the debt in full. Tozzi's serenade is the most ear-offending episode of his performance—it sounds like an early example of polytonality. The basso is clearly not in best voice on this broadcast—it fails him occasionally and is generally considerably looser in focus than usual. Perhaps it is vocal condition that drives him to overplay his hand. Let us hope for better things from this deserving artist in his few remaining seasons.

In taking on Marguerite, Zylis-Gara, now in her fourth Met season, continues her exploration of the lyric repertory. The Gounod heroine and Desdemona (heard later in an April airing) are new Met undertakings for her. Clearly, she is intent on escaping from her Mozartean pigeonhole; her affinity for that elevated category has been evident in earlier broadcasts of the Countess, Donna Elvira, Pamina, and Fiordiligi (the latter also a new Met assumption). With Marguerite, the balance between pristine vocalism and the singing actor's talent is tipped toward the former. The Polish soprano may be expected to realize its gratifying opportunities for beautiful song with vocal ease and tasteful musicality. And she does, to our delight. It would be churlish to ask for more. Some sopranos have made Marguerite's jewels shine more brightly. There, if report can be believed, an earlier crop of Marguerites, which included Melba, Eames, and Suzanne Adams, excelled. A few interpreters (Calvé was one) have made the hackles rise as our heroine experienced Satan's taunts in the church scene. And some with hearty instruments have proved their stamina (the role demands that) by earning salvation with a rousing trumpeting of 'Anges pur, anges radieux!'. (How I would love to have been present when Nordica, with her Isolde voice, sent forth that passage into the old Met.) A chosen few have possessed the stylistic elegance to elevate the opera's charms to a higher realm of musical quality—De los Angeles achieved that elusive goal. Zylis-Gara does not quite match any of these feats, but her portrayal to a degree embraces them all (no mean feat) and conveys such a general air of excellence that we take her to our hearts. Probably, it is the De los Angeles mode that provides the closest parallel. Beyond that, Zylis-Gara has her own peculiar virtues. Her beguilingly smoky timbre in mid-voice lends a discreet remoteness, a suggestive medieval aura, to the Thulé ballad. The episode is often dull and trying for even capable Marguerites. Bon vivant and vocal aficionado Reynaldo Hahn would probably have approved of Zylis-Gara's way with it, especially in the introductory recitative. Tired of "thin-voiced" Marguerites who were consistently "inaudible" at that point, Hahn encouraged more than mixed tone on the reiterated low E; he singled out Yvonne Gall for her treatment of the questioning phrase.[13] Zylis-Gara doesn't pressure her chest voice but she does employ, like Gall, a "well-supported, distinctive timbre" that would likely warrant Hahn's commendation.[14] Our soprano's jewel song purls along quite comfortably, charming in its coquetry, its fluency capped by a confident, clean high B. In the garden duet, Zylis-Gara is appropriately girlish, even shy; Domingo evidently recognizes the character trait, for a considerate gentilesse infects his manner and tone—at least until desire takes hold. One can't say that Zylis-Gara excels at creating mood. This Marguerite evidently does not have strong feelings about her parents, for instance, nor does she frighten easily—her plea to Faust to leave her seems more likely to ensure his continued presence. But her apostrophe at the window is loveliness itself. Such accomplished vocalism is always welcome. (In the interest of "warm-up" fairness, I should note that she finesses the leap to the top tone in her entrance phrase, emitting a coo instead of the text.) In the church scene she displays coolness under fire (the furies' taunts) until her tones sail out confidently over the chorus in Marguerite's appeal for mercy. And her allotment of stamina proves quite sufficient to meet the role's varied challenges, as her effortless ascents in the prison trio confirm. There her gentle remembrance of Faust's courtship (a touch of suspect intonation notwithstanding) is fluidly intoned as though in a trance. The fascinating mix of wind timbres that her voice holds is markedly (and charmingly) deployed.

Domingo offers comparable vocal excellence and, as suits his character, a greater drive and pressing ardor. One of the pleasures of hearing early performances by an artist of remarkable career duration is the opportunity to discover him in roles that were abandoned (or at least absent from the broadcasts) by midcareer. The afternoon holds the tenor's only Met broadcast Faust. All his familiar merits are on display. His tone, brighter and without any dull overlay, is compact, in the earlier scenes a bit more nasal than we later came to know, but warming considerably with an inviting caress in the mask for the more intimate moments of the garden scene duet. There an occasional seductive glow in mid-voice forecasts the certain capture of his stage quarry. And his ardor is catching: conductor Rich senses the tenor's excitement in the concluding section of the duet and whips up the orchestra accordingly. Domingo's attack on top tones is not always impeccable, but once upon the note he makes a splendid sound, secure and brightly colored. 'Salut! demeure' is delivered with the skill and assurance of the star tenor he will become, the high B this time neatly taken (as is the exuberant concluding B of the prison trio). Of course, he is everywhere musically observant and dramatically diligent. True, he makes little attempt at characterizing the old philosopher in his cell, but his 'Merveille!' (as the vision of Marguerite appears) is full of wonder and finished off with a delectable, quiet portamento. At the other end of the spectrum, his stoutly trumpeted, sonorous commands at the end of the Walpurgis Nacht scene certify his tenor credentials, while his confident negotiation of the low-lying phrases as he comes upon the imprisoned Marguerite (moments where many interpreters can only offer sickly tone) impressively reveals the baritonal underpinnings of his instrument. An Otello may indeed be in the making and perhaps his future assumption of that demanding assignment need not have startled us or seemed a rash, unwise decision. Continuing with hindsight, one can discern an occasional slight drag or tightness on notes in the mid-upper range and also suspect a generic interpretive stance, both as to musical reading and characterization. But that is perhaps merely time instructing us. In the seventies, only delight at our good fortune filled our thoughts. Solo bows after the final curtain confirm that the "Mexican tenor from Madrid" is already the marked favorite of this opera crowd.

Still, the tenor who reaped the larger share of the glory (at least from the audience) in those days was the tenor of the romantic persona and vibrant throat, Franco Corelli. Those qualities having been deemed appropriate to Roméo (and who but a diehard seeker after idiomatic style would quibble with that judgment), they were applied to yet another French hero who suffered from love's delight or, more likely in this case, its pain. On the broadcast of 4 March 1972, Massenet's Werther allows Corelli to moon over Elias' Charlotte, while Boky (Sophie) and Cossa (Albert) are decorum's champions. The vehicle had been mounted for Corelli and broadcast (with Elias, Robinson, and Reardon) in the previous season, those performances marking the opera's reappearance after a lapse of six decades. Around the turn of the century, stylistic authenticity evidently was more prized: Eames and Jean de Reszke, both creatures of the Paris Opéra, headlined the initial offerings in 1894 and 1897, while the 1909 production featured Farrar and Edmond Clément with Dinh Gilly and Alma Gluck as support. Mancinelli, a conductor of sensibility, guided the nineteenth-century outings while

Werther
4 March 1972

Charlotte
Rosalind Elias
Sophie
Colette Boky
Werther
Franco Corelli
Albert
Dominic Cossa
Bailiff
Donald Gramm
Conductor
Jan Behr

a lesser light, Egisto Tango, was entrusted with the later revival. Upon hearing the United States premiere in 1894, Krehbiel of the *Tribune* found merit in its "lyric charm" and "masterly scoring," deeming the opera a "work of importance," though "not great."[14] The redoubtable Henderson opined in the *Times* that the opera had "no genuine depth," laying the fault to a deficiency of tragic passion on M. Massenet's part.[15] Still, the immortal Jean triumphed, as expected. I imagine Corelli can be counted on to remedy the passion deficiency.

Though Lombard had guided the premiere and *Opera News* again had him listed for this broadcast, he was replaced by Behr. Massenet's unusually somber (for him) but delectable orchestral palette is somewhat stolidly replicated by the maestro—greater pointing up of its piquant combinations would add spice to the drama's downhill course. The result is a rather staid reading, hardly what best benefits a Massenet opera in performance. Only occasionally (a few moments in the tempestuous third act) does Behr urge Massenet's orchestral fires to burn at melting temperature. But he knows how to hold a performance together and maintains a fluent continuity, while allowing the singers space and air to fan the emotional flames on their own.

In the second half of the twentieth century, management might as well have posted placards in the lobby warning audiences to abandon hope all ye who enter hoping to hear idiomatic French style. No one expected it and hardly anyone got it. Few may have wanted it, or at least known what they were missing. And yet several of this afternoon's singers show that Americans can cultivate that elusive idiom to good effect. Right off, Donald Gramm's nuanced phrasing and elegant French diction are prudently applied to the good-hearted Bailiff, a man of seemingly bluffer disposition and earthier appetites than Gramm's refined art conveys. (The gruffer Corena alternated in the role.) No matter, the basso's stylistic acuity is welcome; after all, though Charlotte's father frequents the inn, he is a good family man who teaches his children a Christmas carol as early as July. One only regrets that the Bailiff quits the scene so soon. His cronies supply the earthy touch. Best's Johann sounds reassuringly plebeian while Anthony, the comprimario's point man, displays a liveliness, an invigorating spunk uncommon even for him. The tenor's voice in this career period is at its peak.

Montreal-born Colette Boky may be expected to add to the authenticity quotient and she doesn't disappoint. The easy, natural flow of her singing, its spontaneity, its tripping textual fluency embellish the adolescent sister's blithe airs. Her upper voice is brightly colored (without being harsh) but the lower octave is less attractive, the tone there slightly veiled or lacking in point. Stylistic credibility is further enhanced by Cossa's unexpectedly idiomatic diction and his voice's timbral aptness for French opera. Moreover, he manages to make something interesting of dull Albert, creating a character who develops as the opera progresses. In act one, Charlotte's future husband returns after a long absence, eager for reunion with his fiancée; there Cossa sings with a concentrated head resonance and employs cultivated phrasing that both suits the lover's mood and complements the Massenet idiom. Albert comforts the lovesick Werther in act two and now Cossa's voice takes on greater depth of tone, his manner reflecting his maturity. As he questions Charlotte after her tumultuous scene with Werther in the third act, the baritone allows virility and a hint of menace to invade his tones. An interesting portrait and ably sung as well.

As Charlotte, Elias is heard in her most prominent broadcast role to date. Her Dorabella, Hansel, Zerlina, and, of course, her creation of Erika in *Vanessa* have marked the upward path of her career, each confirming how far she has progressed since her 1954 debut as Grimgerde. And, in spite of the "bread and butter" stigma, Charlotte is more of a glamor part, something to gladden any mezzo's heart. Never mind that Henderson felt Charlotte was an incomplete character; he succinctly downsized her importance, writing that the only thing we learn about her is that she doesn't have "the courage of her convictions."[16] I doubt her slate is that blank, but, convictions aside, Elias does reveal her own courage in the vocal realm. She tackles the role's several demanding episodes with fearless abandon. Her instrument is a secure one, wobble free, most attractive in its narrow focus and slightly erotic coloration—erotic not in the sense of warmth or sultriness, but rather in its concentrated, pithy fruitiness, hardly luscious as a peach but pungent as a pomegranate berry. As noted in earlier roles, she has a tendency to overextend herself in the grander moments (and Charlotte's third act is full of them), giving way to palpable excitement, sounding at the full extent of her resources and occasionally beyond them. One admires her dramatic flamboyance, her commitment, at the same time wishing she could more cagily align her moderate-sized instrument with her interpretive design. (The amazing, and consoling, aftermath is that the voice does not seem to suffer from her strenuous efforts—invariably, she turns up at her next broadcast with the instrument in pink condition.) On this afternoon, her chest voice holds a more inviting coloration than usual, while the upper voice often (when not pushed to the limit, that is) thrusts forth bursts of radiant tone. To be specific about clearing those third-act hurdles, I would award her a silver medal, but not the gold. For maximum effect, the lengthy letter scene, Charlotte's grandest moment, requires a keen demarcation of its many mood changes; the mezzo fails to exploit the contrasts as effectively as she might. Still, a few sections are beautifully vocalized—I particularly like her loving, expansive treatment of the letter beginning 'Tu m'as dit: à Noël.' And the final pages are equally poised and tonally attractive. Unfortunately the aria's opening and closing words are less effectively handled: the composer marks an initial sounding of Werther's name *songeant*, but Elias' manner is hardly dreamlike, and the chilling final 'tu frémiras,' marked *pianissimo*, is spoiled by poor control of chest tone—she dissolves in tears as a cover. Ineffectual chest tone similarly mars the close of the Air des larmes. Its melancholy cast would be better conveyed by greater restraint—the score is replete with *pianissimo* markings, but Elias eschews pathos, playing at fever pitch throughout. The full-bodied climax is effective, however. Of course, she is up against a high-powered competitor in the confrontation scene, and there she gives her all, acquitting herself honorably—quite thrillingly, in a few moments. When she can linger in her upper range the voice's focused sensuality owns a distinctive allure. At the side of her dying lover, her manner is quite understandably distraught (Massenet is unkind to Charlotte in that regard), but the top notes are beautifully formed and comfortably voiced, while a few seductively colored phrases reveal a more sensitive musicality.

With Corelli, we leave off considerations of idiomatic performance, though repeated outings in the French repertory appear to have improved his French pronunciation. 'Rien de trop' is the watchword of French culture but judiciousness is hardly a trait one associates with Corelli's art. In Elias' case, she has difficulty in wedding her modest instrument to an overly assertive manner, but our Italian tenor has no problem in that area. There can be no question but that Corelli's grand instrument is fully equipped to execute his expansive conceptions. Then, too, one must remember that the title role was created at the Vienna premiere by Ernest Van Dyck, a Parsifal, Lohengrin, and Tannhäuser and, later in life, a Siegmund and Siegfried. The Belgian tenor excelled, however, in the French romantic repertory as well, so the voice must have been many-sided. The role of Werther does contain both dramatic and lyric episodes. The entrance air, in which Werther expounds the beauties of nature, should reveal the poet's sensitive side; Corelli is ill equipped for the duty. Romance is his province, but it is of the heart-on-sleeve variety, rhapsodic philosophic musing falling outside its orbit. The beauty of his voice, its luxuriant sensuality, always counts for something in moments like this, but the result is too weighty of tone and heavy handed in phrasing. In the celebrated moonlight episode, its delicate accompaniment simplicity itself, the tenor tries for a few pastel effects (the intent must be recognized) but soon resorts to blatant assault. He cannot play the languid poet; as forecast, all his passion is unfurled. And, for the most part, he operates on this level throughout the afternoon. It is best simply to enjoy the voice's amazing vibrancy, its invigorating thrust in the upper range, its almost baritonal wealth in the lower octave, the whole leavened with an occasional lengthy diminuendo.

The two grand arias of the second act ('J'aurais sur ma poitrine' and 'Lorsque l'enfant revient d'un voyage') are better suited to his outsized gifts. He allows them full play. When Werther confronts Charlotte after his long absence, Corelli adopts an aggressive stance and barbed tone—he means business in his pursuit of her. The opera's showcase tune ('Pourquoi me reveiller') receives the expected star treatment. The lead-in recitatives are delivered with emphatic, tragic grandeur, and though he admirably coddles the aria's opening phrases (his delivery aptly suggesting that he is quietly reading Ossian's verse) and elegantly molds the aria's final note, early on he moves into high gear. In fact, his vocal churning comes perilously close to shouting at times, to the evident delight of his militantly vocal fans. They shout in return. A few episodes show us what he can achieve when he applies his talents to more substantial musico-dramatic purpose. When, in act two, he accepts Charlotte's verdict of exile, the tenor acknowledges his fate by employing a darker tone, a more somber manner, effectively showing off the varied colors of his instrument. And in Werther's drawn-out death scene (a difficult act for any tenor to pull off) Corelli does play with a measure of restraint. He offers reflective declamation, doles out a few "acting-with-the-voice" touches as death approaches, and sets his tones aglow with a soft, but enveloping, splendor.

In 1894, Krehbiel had felt that the opera could "appeal to fine musical sensibilities."[16] The 1972 broadcast performance, though it has its own rewards and demonstrates that the opera deserves a place in the repertory, does not achieve that end. In future decades, Massenet's evocative score will return to public favor with multiple complete recordings featuring the world's foremost tenors (Kraus, Domingo, Carreras, and Alagna among them). Familiarity of a homelier kind further prompts my own regard for the opera. My wife and I have long had a large nineteenth-century metal bread box in our kitchen whose sides contain prints of episodes from Goethe's novels. The front door contains my preferred scene, a reproduction of the painting by Kaulbach showing Lotte "dressed for a ball, awaiting Werther," who arrives "to find her in the midst of her young brothers and sisters, cutting bread"—clearly a fit subject for everyday viewing in an old farmhouse kitchen and an indulgent reason for me to welcome the opera's resurgence. A later broadcast with Crespin and Kraus raises the ante; perhaps Krehbiel's optimistic regard for our sensibilities will prove warranted.

Love triangles are the stuff of operas, old and new. The indiscreet wife, the suspicious husband, the lover friend are the familiar pawns whose entanglements inevitably lead to a tragic denouement. Charlotte, Albert, and Werther or, traveling back in time, Mélisande, Golaud, and brother Pelléas fit the mold. But beyond numeric makeup and sharing a foregone fate, these assorted couplings inhabit different worlds. Massenet's crew thrashes wildly about as his orchestra pulsates, while, for much of his opera, Debussy's buttoned-down ménage moves with the discretion that the composer's subtle score prescribes. Of course, when Golaud's jealousy bursts the bounds of civility, the result is more world-shaking than Massenet ever could have imagined. The 29 January 1972 broadcast of *Pelléas et Mélisande* shows us why. Except for return appearances by Tozzi as Arkel and Harvuot as the Physician, the participants are new radio interpreters of their parts: Blegen (Mélisande), Chookasian (Geneviève), Stewart (Golaud), with Barry McDaniel making his broadcast debut as Pelléas. Conductor Colin Davis returns to place his singular imprint on this ever-fresh score.

House audiences benefited from the new production of the opera by Desmond Heeley, with stage direction by Paul-Émile Deiber; both of their efforts were generally well received. No matter how effective the opera's mise-en-scène, *Pelléas* remains a conductor's opera. The radio audience has heard some distinguished readings from the podium: Monteux (1954) and Ansermet (1962) lead the pack, with Morel (1960) also deserving a nod. Earlier efforts were not uniformly pleasing. In the thirties, Louis Hasselmans had guided Bori, Johnson, and Pinza in their famous interpretations, while the unlikely Emil Cooper husbanded the 1945 broadcast with a starry cast including Sayão, Singher, Tibbett, and Kipnis. Davis was already renowned as a champion of Berlioz' exuberant works, a French operatic mode far removed from the etched precision of Debussy's music making. And Maeterlinck's text is more notable for what it leaves unsaid than for what his characters concretely reveal; but then come the raw-boned scenes of the opera's original fourth act, episodes from which Davis seemingly takes his cue. (The Met telescopes the numerous scenes into three acts, the first including Debussy's acts one and two, with the fifth act standing alone as broadcast act three.) As expected, Davis' way with the score is less diaphanous than those of Monteux or Ansermet; their readings, vibrant with coloristic touches that reveled in Debussy's orchestral palette, favored transparent textures and judicious pointing up of Maeterlinck's elusive dramatic substance. Davis' control of his orchestral forces is equally assured, but the emphases have changed. We hear the difference in the opening measures of the opera (marked moderato molto) where a lugubrious atmosphere is immediately summoned as a heavier tread weights the spare octave theme. The conductor's explicit expressivity governs the entire opera, progressing step by step until emotion spills over in the dramatic episodes of Golaud's physical abuse of Mélisande and the long-delayed lovers' confession of their consuming passion. The excitement that Davis foments in these scenes is both terrifying and exhilarating—the release of dramatic energy is startling and thrilling to hear. The maestro

Pelléas et Mélisande
29 January 1972

Mélisande
Judith Blegen
Geneviève
Lili Chookasian
Pelléas
Barry McDaniel
Golaud
Thomas Stewart
Arkel
Giorgio Tozzi
Conductor
Colin Davis

#2555

Colin Davis. Courtesy Metropolitan Opera Archives.

has other arrows in his conductorial quiver. He fondly draws lyrical lines from his pit companions (and occasionally from the singers as well, Arkel being the favored recipient of his largesse). The score sings in unexpected, and enchanting, ways. The Englishman's way may differ from that of his French colleagues, whose orchestral colors emerged as captivating entities in themselves, but he is scrupulous, even masterly, in his control and guidance of his forces. The conception is whole and fully realized. Light feet evidently are not as essential as one thought for roaming the bleak caves, the shadowed castle rooms, the subterranean vaults, and the misty terraces of Allemonde.

More than most operas, *Pelléas* demands care in matching artist and role. Chookasian's voice, dark and deep, is ill suited to Geneviève's brief but mood-setting task of reading Golaud's letter. A thick legato weights her reading; her French diction lacks point and is devoid of illuminating tints. She is more effective in the scene with Mélisande, where her upper voice is more brightly colored. As opposed to previous Met practice that utilized a soprano in the role, management has assigned Yniold to a young member of the children's chorus, Adam Klein. The child's scene with the rock and the sheep, often omitted, is included in this performance and there the young artist seems a bit overwhelmed by the responsibility for what is (except for the shepherd's single line) a solo scene. He is game, but the symbolic overtones of the boy's play are not revealed. On the other hand, his clear voice and fine French are a decided boon in the tower scene when Golaud causes him to spy on Mélisande and Pelléas. His frequent, brief answers to Golaud's probing questions are on the mark and his piping tones, irrepressibly optimistic, effectively contrast his innocence with the father's devious pursuit. The episode, always a frightening experience in the theater, gains in verisimilitude, and our repugnance at the father's exploitation of his son is heightened by the child's guileless responses and his emergent distress.

Much of the humanity of the drama, its philosophical depth (if depth there be) rests on Arkel's shoulders. Happily, Tozzi, heard here a month before his unfortunate tussle with Méphistophélès, gives a fine account of himself. The *Faust* encounter may have been an aberration, after all. Ideally, one wants to hear a weightier voice with a darker coloration in the part (Kipnis brought something special in that regard—never mind his Russianized French). Tozzi's bass is decidedly light and even slightly porous in the lowest phrases of the role, but in compensation, his timbre, particularly in the mid- and upper-voice, owns a kindly cast that complements the old king's function in the drama. Debussy has gifted Arkel with some moving phrases and Tozzi takes full advantage of them. If you happen to believe that the solemn pronouncements that Maeterlinck has put into Arkel's mouth are a bit obvious you may be comforted by the American basso's defter touch, a vocal and interpretive sounding that makes his old king's summary phrases seem like natural effusions.

The role of young Pelléas is best served by a singer who can handle the many high-lying phrases of the fountain love scene, but whose baritonal heft in the lower voice easily penetrates Debussy's orchestral web. The gain in manly substance is welcome as well. Radio debutant Barry McDaniel does not quite fill the bill, but he is a reasonable facsimile of the baryton-Martin type. Like many gifted Americans of the fifties, the Kansas-born, Juilliard-trained baritone was a Fulbright scholarship winner and did journeyman service in lesser German houses

until 1961, when he became a member of the Berlin Deutsche Oper. Coming after
an eighteen-year stint with German companies, his Met debut seemed to him "another beginning."[17] The voice, while well schooled, owns no commanding beauty
at either end of its range. In particular, the lower notes lack color and are often inadequately projected through Davis' orchestral texture—at least, that is how they
come over the airwaves. *Opera News* notes that McDaniel has earned his highest
critical acclaim as a lieder singer, one who prefers "emotional involvement" rather
than an "intellectual approach," to use his words.[18] His talent for word-pointing,
phrase-shaping characterization—in short, the observant musicality of the lieder
singer—is evident in his portrait of Pelléas. Although he employs falsetto for the
two climactic notes of the fountain love scene, he wraps the ensuing phrase in a
seductive legato and ably handles the strenuous tessitura of the entire episode.
There, and often in his wooing, McDaniel's manner is uncommonly aggressive
and assured. His ecstatic responses when Mélisande's hair engulfs him in the tower
scene are similarly affecting—at his entrance, his exuberant 'Moi, moi, et moi!'
seems the epitome of youthful bravura. True, some of the poetry of these scenes
goes by the board since the baritone lacks an airy head range. But in these pivotal
episodes, he leaves no doubt that the young lover is uncontrollably swept along by
his repressed passion for Mélisande. His way—call it "emotional involvement"—
meshes with Davis' overt orchestral play. But the hoped-for American beginning
proved to be just that, an introduction without issue. Following this debut season,
the erstwhile Midwesterner returned to his West Berlin home to continue his successful European career.

In the numerous roles that she assumed during her lengthy Met sojourn,
Judith Blegen perpetuated an image of the eternal ingénue, the unspoiled *jeune
fille*. That posture can suit the external pose of Mélisande, and so it does in the
soprano's expert voicing of the part. The heroine's allure, her enveloping mystery—"that 'nothing' that Mélisande is made of," as the composer described her to
Ernest Chausson—these suggestive properties mate less perfectly with the Blegen
voice and persona.[19] Illusion is in short supply. Having said that, one can appreciate her portrayal on its own terms. It is finely etched and deftly voiced in tones of
delightful purity, the text uttered in expert French. Over the years, it has become
increasingly difficult for Mélisandes to sound convincing when pettishly crying 'Ne
me touchez pas!' or 'Je ne suis pas heureuse!' Blegen is more believable than most.
When she is discovered, distraught and alone in the forest, she nimbly conveys
the maiden's volatility and skittishness. Throughout the afternoon, phrase after
phrase is placed with unerring certainty, a valuable attribute for, while the other
characters have speeches of some length, Mélisande is content to utter only a few
words at a time. The little tower song is glowingly delivered. And there are some
illuminating dramatic touches. When Mélisande misleads Golaud as to where she
lost her wedding ring, Blegen manages to convince us that, at that moment, this
strange creature whose eyes never close might really believe her story. Her stance
is dramatically more valid than exposing Mélisande as a practiced liar. When the
young wife espies her husband watching in the obscurity surrounding the tower,
her whispered 'C'est Golaud!' is a hand well underplayed. At the fountain in the
park, when Pelléas suggests that she does not seem happy in his love, Blegen utters 'Si; je suis heureuse, mais je suis triste' with infinite sadness, as though sensing
the tragedy to come. She projects these subtleties with a sure touch. Still, it is the

pinpoint placement of each phrase and, above all, the fresh beauty of her tones that linger at the opera's close. Mélisande is more than that—but who can say with certainty just what she is.

With relief, we turn to Golaud—we know who he is. Or at least we can be sure he is one of two things, either a brute of a husband who in the end is more concerned with his own peace of mind than his wife's approaching death or an honorable man made miserable by his uncontrollable suspicions. Both behavioral patterns are explicit in the text. Only a great singing actor can entirely reconcile them. Initially, Stewart seems unlikely to achieve that end. When he discovers Mélisande in the forest, he comes off as a man with a hard shell; his tone is overpointed—a hint of menace lurks in it. Stewart has tipped his hand at first meeting. But we want to feel some measure of warmth for this hunter who takes obvious pride in being a 'prince' (one can almost see the baritone's chest expand as the word spills from his mouth), but one who equivocates as any man might when his gray hairs are noted by the young beauty. ('Quelques-uns, près des tempes'—a few, near the temples, he responds.) Stewart's prince is a man's man, seemingly without a scrap of poetry in his makeup. But in Debussy's second act, a denser tone warms the voice and a dollop of sensitivity surfaces as Golaud attempts to understand his wife's unhappiness: the baritone allows a breath of tenderness to escape as he takes his wife's 'petites mains,' and his instrument opens up nicely ('La joie') as he tries to explain that life's path is not always joyous. When he discovers she has lost her ring, Stewart's about-face is startlingly abrupt—with businesslike acumen he questions her in sharp phrasal jabs. The artist has begun to unfold a telling portrait. And it grows with each succeeding scene, although not always in a straight line. We do expect a more subterranean sonority when Golaud threatens Pelléas in the vaults. Stewart's tone thins in the lower regions—undoubtedly, oxygen is in short supply in the bowels of medieval castles. Nor does his voice hold many colors—menace is maintained too long on one level—but he makes his points with a variety of nuances of rhythm, of accent, of articulation. In the hair-pulling scene and at Mélisande's deathbed, the baritone finally exposes Golaud's tortured soul. Agitation approaching madness consumes him. His cries of 'Absalon' are both grand and wretched; as though in a trance, he repeats 'c'est l'usage' to ghostly effect. Now, when Golaud is physically beaten down and emotionally spent, the singing actor stands tall before us. Quite unexpectedly, he calls up a telling vocal color as, in a poignant head voice, the husband begs for his dying wife's pardon. On and on the husband's jealousy and guilt drive him as he torments Mélisande to the end. Debussy would have approved of Stewart's extremity. For a 1906 revival of the opera, he had encouraged Hector Dufranne to "exaggerate, even, Golaud's poignant misery . . . to get over clearly all that he regrets not [having] said and done . . . and all the happiness which is lost to him for ever."[20] Stewart is a master of Golaud's mood swings. But it is Tozzi's heartfelt peroration that helps to appease *our* anguish.

Not until 1980 would Colin Davis be knighted, but almost a decade earlier his *Pelléas* confirmed his right to an elevated position among his musical peers. At the close of act four on this broadcast afternoon, a gallery rat's shouted "Viva Boulez!" pierced the airwaves. Evidently, Davis' way was not to everyone's taste. It would probably not have been to Debussy's either. The composer, in excoriating conductor Henri Busser's interpretation of the score, wrote André Messager (who had led the 1902 premiere) that he alone infused the opera with the requisite "tender delicacy."[21] A steady diet of Davis' protein *Pelléas* might be overfilling. Still, add in his earlier *Peter Grimes* and *Wozzeck* and it would appear that Bing, troubled throughout his reign by conductor inadequacy, had in his final years gained a podium treasure. The departing manager's successors, however, would not have the comfort of Davis' name on the Met roster. He had recently been named music director of the Royal Opera. One cannot help but wonder how the Met would have fared, how many crises it might have been spared, had Davis been granted comparable rank at our national house.

But the time of Bing's departure is not quite upon us. The manager's final bows are reserved for his beloved Verdi.

Sherrill Milnes as Iago in *Otello*. Photography by Louis Mélançon. Courtesy Metropolitan Opera Archives.

CHAPTER ELEVEN

Tutto È Finito: Bing and Verdi

Bing's preference for the Verdi canon resulted in a regime-long reexamination of familiar masterworks and a courageous exploration of the often hidden wealth of lesser-known works. The host of new productions of the Verdi corpus would be a prodigal gift the departing impresario bequeathed to those who followed him in the manager's chair. The value of that heritage is evident in the five Verdi operas that buttressed the 1971–72 radio schedule. Verdi both opened (*Luisa Miller*) and closed (*Don Carlo*) the broadcast season, with intervening airings of *La Forza del Destino*, *Otello*, and *Falstaff*.

Bing had brought forth the little-known *Luisa Miller* in the 1967–68 season, offering a broadcast with Caballé, Pearl, Tucker, Milnes, Tozzi, and Flagello. The work is newly cast for the 11 December 1971 broadcast with MacNeil as Miller, Alexander as Rodolfo, and Mignon Dunn (Federica), Giaiotti (Walter), and Plishka (Wurm) in supporting parts. In the title role we hear Adriana Maliponte, a soprano new to the airwaves and the Met. Where Schippers had once stood, another American is positioned. Twenty-eight-year-old James Levine now invades the Metropolitan; current and future regimes are thus neatly, if as yet unsuspectingly, conjoined.

Cincinnati-born and a piano prodigy, the new maestro was a Juilliard product. There Rosina Lhevinne, embodiment of the nineteenth-century Russian piano tradition, had guided his studies, while the respected Jean Morel tutored him in conducting. Max Rudolf and Fausto Cleva were later mentors. Undoubtedly, his strongest formative influence was a six-year association (as assistant conductor) with George Szell during the final years of Szell's tenure with the Cleveland Orchestra. But opera had been very much a part of his life during his formative years. At nineteen, he had led *The Pearl Fishers* at Aspen, and during his Cleveland sojourn he conducted staged performances for the Cleveland Institute of Music (*Figaro*, *Falstaff*, *Pelléas*) and concert readings for Cleveland Concert Associates (*Don Giovanni*, *Fidelio*, *Don Carlo*, *Die Zauberflöte*). The gifted tyro evidently was unfazed by the most demanding works of the repertory. Upon Szell's death in 1970, young Levine set out to try his wings on his own. They would carry him far. The San Francisco Opera heard his *Tosca* a year before Levine joined the Met for performances of the same opera during a special June festival adjunct to the 1970–71 season. After the death of maestro Cleva in August 1971, the Met en-

Luisa Miller
11 December 1971

Luisa
Adriana Maliponte
Federica
Mignon Dunn
Rodolfo
John Alexander
Miller
Cornell MacNeil
Walter
Bonaldo Giaiotti
Wurm
Paul Plishka
Conductor
James Levine

261

trusted Levine with the revival of *Luisa Miller* (season premiere on 15 October 1971). Within two years he would be named principal conductor for the company. The wings tryout proved to be breathtakingly brief.

Once again, the broadcasts confirm their documentary importance by capturing an artist at the very beginning of what will be a brilliant career. Levine's shepherding of the early Verdi work is both masterly and masterful. But shepherding is too modest a term; rather, he takes hold of the opera with hands, ears, and heart and molds it into a sinewy, yet pliant, musical and dramatic shape. The neglected Verdi work gains a brawny spine under his baton. He sets his sights on his arrival points and takes us along, occasionally rather precipitately. And what an invigorating ride it is. The first measures of the overture put us on alert. The reading is notable both for its structural coherence and pointing of detail. Verdi's crisp little chords, nestled under the opening theme, are rhythmically alive and propel the thematic line onward; integration between melody and accompaniment is complete. When the clarinet takes over the theme, Levine allows it to sing—the change is slight, but the intent is clear. Here is good news for singers: the Verdi line will be allowed to expand where warranted. Count that another important facet of Levine's musical posture. The overture's concluding measures are a bit hard-driven—yet another angle added to the conductor's interpretive profile. The clarity of conception and vitality of execution are remarkable, as they continue to be throughout the afternoon. Yet another Levine virtue surfaces in arias with a repetitive accompaniment figure (whether simple or fussy), a feature prominent in Italian operas of the first half of the nineteenth century. Many conductors, well equipped in other ways, belabor the iteration until the set piece bogs down under the figure's cumulative weight. Levine invariably discovers an appropriate shape and nuance for the figure itself, be it insistent or relaxed, and deftly sends it along, thus providing uninhibiting support for the singer's flexible phrases. *Luisa Miller*'s final act is recognized as one of the more notable creations of Verdi's early years. Levine's commanding conception enhances what the composer has wrought as he draws the act's varied elements into a cohesive musical and dramatic entity.

The Met had long lacked a conductor of the Italian repertory who combined an impeccable ear for detail with the ability to shape formal structures, small or large, for maximum musical and dramaturgical effect. Mr. Bing had found one in Levine. And, of greatest importance for the future, his repertory range (which can only be imaged at this point) will be all inclusive.

His charges perform with superb assurance. Has his tutelage already taken hold? Dunn has little to do as Federica, but her warm, solid voice is always a pleasure to hear. Levine takes her duet with Rodolfo at a decidedly slow pace—it makes sense and adds character to the rather facile music that Verdi cagily provided for the disaffected couple. Alexander can't come close to equaling the recorded Bergonzi's deft manipulation of Rodolfo's skittering phrases, but Dunn anchors the piece well enough. Verdi asked for two top-notch basses (though, to an impresario's despair, he underemploys them) and the Met has them at hand. Giaiotti has the bigger part (Count Walter). His black-toned instrument is in prime condition with none of the cavernous resonance that sometimes limits appreciation of his skilled performances. Plishka's superb instrument is almost baritonal in its bright, firmly collected timbre, and he plays with the assurance of the veteran we know he will become. The two singers make a capital moment of the singular duet where they recount the murder of the Count's cousin. Both vocally and dramatically, their rousing portrayals fulfill Verdi's intent; those good old-fashioned horror effects are meant to be enjoyed.

MacNeil, grand Verdi baritone of the sixties, is not as satisfying a Miller as his earlier portrayals of the composer's father figures would lead one to expect. Initially, the voice sounds rather coarse, and the progress of phrase is laborious. The voice's tonal density is huge and the lifting is not without effort—a few hoarse notes at the conclusion of the act-one cabaletta ('Ah fu giusto il mio sospetto') tell us that time and/or indisposition have worked their will. The instrument, however, and the artist, for that matter, remain impressive. His voice limbers up as the afternoon goes on and the fondly remembered, plush tone of old frequently reasserts itself. But momentary regressions occur as well. The 'Andrem raminghi' duet (one of Verdi's more touching episodes) would profit from a warmer tone than MacNeil now can summon, but the baritone knows his business and everywhere conducts the Verdi line with assurance.

Tucker, remembered from the 1968 broadcast, had sung this season's premiere as well. Alexander is not up to the Tucker standard but, as usual, his diligent adherence to the score, forthright delivery, and assertive dramatic stance must be acknowledged. I know the voice well (Central City days) and do not recall that in younger years its rather blatant coloration and nasality were so insistently present. Fortunately, they recede considerably as the opera moves to its denouement. The tenor ascends to his top notes with complete confidence. And some phrases are so expansively shaped and tonally solid that they serve Verdi well: the critical act-one phrase 'Son io tuo sposo' (marked *grandioso*) is nobly voiced. But too often he resorts to overaccentuation of the text, punching at a word here and there, chewing up the musical line. The vice affects the opera's most famous episode, 'Quando le sere al placido.' After an appropriately vivid dramatic recitative (Levine gives him marvelous assists there), Alexander breaks up the expansive line into small segments and vitiates the mood of reflection that is the aria's hallmark. Moreover, he imbues Rodolfo with a repellent self-pity. We are used to tenorial lachrymation, but this is not the moment for self-indulgence. I'm afraid this afternoon is one of the occasions where the singer is stylistically a bit bumptious. The cabaletta better shows his strengths. And the third act offers retribution. There Alexander makes a strong showing, purposefully confronting Luisa with the offensive letter and stoutly facing his fate.

Miss Maliponte had been introduced to the Met public as Mimì in March of the previous season and makes her radio debut on this occasion. Luisa is her second Met assignment. Micaela, Pamina, Juliette, Euridice, Marguerite, Violetta, Maria Boccanegra, and Liù will follow shortly. Her debut broadcast confirms her right to the prominence which that repertory list indicates. At home in both the Italian and French repertory due to formative years in her native Italy and residence in Alsace as a teenager and conservatory student, Maliponte had made her debut in *Bohème* at the Teatro Nuovo in Milan in 1958. Moving to Paris in 1962, she sang frequently at both the Comique and Opéra. La Scala finally beckoned in 1970 (Manon). Previous to her Met debut, she had appeared in many American cities, Chicago, Philadelphia, and New Orleans among them. Her assured, cultivated Italian operatic style and obvious thorough preparation of the role make her Luisa one of the more accomplished performances of recent broadcast seasons.

Adriana Maliponte as Luisa Miller. Photography by Louis Mélançon. Courtesy Metropolitan Opera Archives.

Not that the role is ideal for her instrument. After all, Rosa Ponselle had been the first Met Luisa back in the twenties. During the course of the opera, the lighthearted ingénue of act one is transformed into a tragic heroine in the final two acts. Maliponte's instrument is slender, finely tuned, and delicately colored. But her technique is firmly grounded, her phrasing stylistically acute; she knows exactly what is required of her and, to the best of her ability, delivers it. The timbre (woodwind, mostly flute mixed with just a hint of reed to firm it up) is distinctive and delicious, pearly in its uppermost regions. The voice's circumference may be narrow, but it holds a nugget of solidity at its core (like the nut in its shell) that prevents harshness. Sometimes, especially in the lower regions, its marmoreal gleam can be both intriguing and distancing. Her fioriture are entirely adequate for the role. She may lack the dash of a Sutherland or the flair of a Caballé, but at critical dramatic nodes she strikes with determination and confidence, turning a roulade or executing a cadenza with poise and accuracy. Invariably, her attack, whether light or hearty, is quick and certain. Strongly in her favor is her ability to trace a melodic line with appealing cameo-like precision. When, with pointed but limpid tone, she initiates a phrase on high and moves delicately down the phrase ladder (a shape Verdi frequently allows his heroine's music), she is vastly appealing, both as singer and unhappy maiden. I note one possible danger sign. Occasionally her tone is so pure that it sounds as though she is blowing into a hollow reed; a living recorder tone is not necessarily the best communication tool in the opera house.

'Tu puniscimi, o Signore,' the heroine's grand second-act lament, tries her resources to the fullest—the prima donna showcase demands greater breadth of phrase and size of voice than our soprano's intaglio-forged song can offer. She throws in a few chest tones (good ones), tellingly acts with the voice, puts her faith in rhythmic play and perfectly placed top tones, plays for pathos whenever possible, and achieves an audience triumph. Miss Maliponte is a gifted and sincere artist. Dexterous upward scales in the ensuing cabaletta are yet another item in her technical arsenal. One of the most moving moments in the opera occurs during the third-act father–daughter duet when Luisa lightly etches repeated notes over her father's reprise of the main melody. The haunting effect is partially negated when Maliponte fails to honor Verdi's request to be "scarcely audible" (*dolciss: appena sensibile*). A few heartrending moments ('Padre ricevi l'estremo addio') in the final scene with Rodolfo provide the capstone for a lovely portrait and a welcome debut from an artist whose artistry promises much for the future.

Soon enough, the entire Verdi canon will fall to Levine's charge. The *Luisa Miller* broadcast authenticates his claim to that vast legacy. On the broadcast of 12 February 1972, it is Michelangelo Veltri, however, who contends with the composer's diffuse but fascinating *La Forza del Destino*. The cast is enticing: Price (Leonora), Bergonzi (Alvaro), Siepi (Guardiano), and Corena (Melitone), with Casei tackling Preziosilla and Kostas Paskalis making a broadcast debut as Carlo.

Veltri, though not cast in the Levine mold, is a worthy contender. In his early forties at the time of his Met debut (*Rigoletto*, November 1971), the maestro had conducted widely in his native Argentina before taking up residence in Europe in 1970. There his career would be wide-ranging, while the Metropolitan would benefit from his knowing art only in sporadic visits during the coming decades. His affinity for the Verdi style is apparent in this well-conceived, securely executed

La Forza del Destino
12 February 1972

Leonora
Leontyne Price
Preziosilla
Nedda Casei
Don Alvaro
Carlo Bergonzi
Don Carlo
Kostas Paskalis
Padre Guardiano
Cesare Siepi
Fra Melitone
Fernando Corena
Conductor
Michelangelo Veltri

performance. Those who prefer whiplash Verdi will not be happy with his considerate tempos—supple phrasing and nuanced musicality take preference over tautness of line and rhythmic vitality. The overture is played after the opening scene. Under Veltri's accommodating baton, singers and orchestra maintain a cordial relationship throughout the afternoon. The performance, however, is rife with the usual Met cuts—this time not even a trace of the Hornachuelos inn scene remains. The score's scope is severely diluted as Verdi's majestic epic is compressed into a drama of thwarted love and vengeance.

The lesser parts are only marginally well served. As Trabuco, Schmorr attempts to convert his passable tenor into a buffo character tool (complete with a vendor's whine), but his efforts fall short of the goal. Casei's Preziosilla is hardly the vivandière of Verdi's conception, but then at the Met the role is so truncated (not even the 'Rataplan' is included) that the deficiency cannot be held against her. In the little aria allowed her ('Venite all'indovina'), she cagily substitutes lighthearted vocal charm for gypsy swagger—it almost works, especially when topped off by her fleet ascending scale. As the Marquis of Calatrava, Edmond Karlsrud is solid toned and suitably parental, his attractive bass well projected (though he unaccountably omits a key phrase, probably driving the prompter to distraction). Melitone, of course, is a principal part (or so Verdi intended—the role is designated *primo baritono brillante*). Corena, his friar familiar from four earlier broadcasts, upholds his *primo* rank, though his vocalism is neither baritonal nor *brillante*. Yet he justifies inclusion in the leading role quintet, for he manages to dominate his scenes. As Melitone discovers the distraught Leonora, the Swiss-born bass immediately exposes the friar's testy nature. His churlish bouts with the camp followers and pleading beggars are skillfully plotted and, granting the roughness of his production, confidently intoned. On this afternoon, the voice, even in the upper range, retains its potency.

Siepi, sole survivor of the 1952 *Forza* premiere, is in his penultimate Met season, but upon hearing him deliver Padre Guardiano's expansive song with such rich sonority and plastic phrasing, one would never believe the end is in sight. Time seems not to have touched his grand instrument and only to have further deepened the cultivated musicianship that he has brought to his parts over the years. A noble abnegation of self is the father superior's lot, the measured dispensation of tonal splendor his assignment. Siepi scores on both counts. In his duets with Leonora he offers magisterial comfort and, in opposing mood, he and Corena, old hands at the Met, turn their modest duet into a gem of character contrast. The Greek baritone Kostas Paskalis, new to the airwaves, is a singer of considerable experience and repute. His 1958 debut (Renato) in Vienna inaugurated a two-decade relationship at the Staatsoper. Stints at Glyndebourne, Salzburg, La Scala, and Covent Garden were outreach assignments and American houses had welcomed him. He came to the old Met in 1965 (debut as the *Forza* Carlo), but during four widely spaced seasons over the next decade he would make only seventeen appearances with the company. His equipment and delivery warranted greater Metropolitan exposure. The voice is in the Bastianini line, that is, it owns a burly resonance, in its upper octave sometimes suggesting the ripeness of 1940s baritone Alexander Sved's monumental instrument. Bastianini's tonal beauty is not entirely matched by the newcomer: this baritone must fabricate his lowest notes with unattractive open tone. But the body of the voice is sturdy and has considerable impact. In short, it is exactly the kind of thrusting weapon to make villainy a marketable commodity. A few diminuendos here and there and circumspection in the 'Solenne in quest'ora' duet suggest that Paskalis is no musical or collegial blackguard. He is a powerhouse in the confrontational duets, however, his vibrant tones making the airwaves quiver with theatrical excitement. Carlo's big solo scene is trying for even well-equipped baritones. There, Verdi's far-ranging line embellishments often have proved too difficult for big-voiced singers, the vocal type that the brother's trenchant character demands. Our debutant handles the extended scene better than most of his contemporaries. No baritonal grunts mar 'Urna fatale.' Indeed, his sensitivity in regard to dynamics and tone colorations is reassuring, while the spiraling line at midpoint is handily, if hardly gracefully, negotiated. He sings Verdi's cadenza (with words added) capably. Only the underside of the pitch in the final cadential tones limits appreciation (and he cagily manipulates his resonance in order to lift the heavy tonal weight to relative safety by the note's end). The traditional cut in the cabaletta aids survival, while a rousing interpolated high note at its close provokes audience regard. Verdi's Ford in this season's upcoming broadcast of *Falstaff* is another Paskalis assignment. It may prove to be just his ticket.

Vocal virtuosity is de rigueur for the artists who undertake Don Alvaro and Leonora. Verdi's swift-paced rhetoric, its dramatic puissance and expansive emotional course demand singers capable of thrusting vocal gestures and dilated phrasing. Bergonzi and Price fit the mold. If shored up by belief in the romantic melodrama that Piave fashioned from the Duke of Rivas' play, their efforts will reap certain triumph.

Bergonzi is the Verdi stylist of his generation and we are fortunate to have this live documentation of Alvaro, his only broadcast appearance in the role. In vocal weight, he is more in the Tucker than the Corelli line; the American was the oft-heard interpreter in the fifties, while Corelli's plangently intoned Alvaro enlivened the airwaves in the sixties. Only a hint of a drag on a few of Bergonzi's topmost notes (a tug that in future years will become insistent) infects the overly critical ear. Worthy of note, however, is the tenor's splendid, open-throated high B in Alvaro's solo peroration at the close of the 'O tradimento! Sleale!' duet. Everywhere, his command of line, modulation of tone, and musical manners are balm for the too-often roughed-up sensibilities of those who love discerning artistry. Not that this Italian is deficient in tenorial swagger when self-effacement would be a curse—he merely prefers to savor a grandstand stance as an occasional garnish rather than the core of his art. Both he and Price begin the performance with colors already flying, converting the agitation of their act-one duet into dramatic and vocal gold. Throughout the long afternoon, they give full value. Would a bit more steel in the tenor's tone, a touch more fire in the heat of battle be welcome? Perhaps, but less may be more in this case. Two vintage Bergonzi episodes command particular attention. As it issues from his flexible throat, Alvaro's *scena* ('La vita è inferno . . . O tu che in seno'), always a testing piece for spinto tenors, is notable for vocal control, musical refinement, and revelation of inner feeling. The voice is everywhere free (the upward sixths neatly vaulted) and variously colored, with a few phrases spectacularly bound together, the bridge enhancing the broad arcs of Verdi's line, the spatial grandeur of his thought. The mood is serious and devoid of sentimentality (the initial 'succorrimi' is sung *dolcissimo*, as marked). In the pivotal 'Solenne in quest'ora' duet with Alvaro, Bergonzi scorns sobs, employs his magical legato, and maintains a resonant mezza voce until the reprise of 'Or muoio tranquillo' draws forth a skillfully sculpted crescendo. How well he understands the composer's affective design.

The role of Alvaro has had its share of broadcast celebrants, each adopting his own interpretive posture for the Incan prince. Before Bergonzi, Corelli was the tenor most recently heard by the radio audience in the part. The two tenors operate on distinctly different wavelengths: Bergonzi is ever the poet/priest, Corelli the warrior/lover. Eugène Delacroix's words wherein he contrasted his artistic credo with that of the poet Alfred de Musset help to define each singer's chosen métier. Musset (like Bergonzi) handled his instrument (a pen, in the poet's case) like an engraver who "cuts grooves into the hearts of men," while the painter (and Corelli) preferred "gaping wounds and the bright color of blood."[1] Tucker, who sang the role most often, favored a more centrist approach, but Vickers, our next radio Alvaro, will, as usual, follow his idiosyncratic muse.

Price's place in the forefront of the broadcast succession of celebrated Leonoras (Rethberg, Roman, Milanov, Tebaldi, Farrell, and Tucci) is secure. Her command of the role is complete. None of its fearful vocal hurdles endanger tonal beauty or challenge her technique. Were it not the height of ingratitude, one might suggest that it all seems almost too easy for her. A case in point is the lack of a sense of desperation, of the heroine's struggle with fate, in her practiced, tonally luminous reading of 'Pace, pace, mio Dio!'. Price is, in her person and in her art, a creature of such radiance that the aria's pervasive aura of *dolor*—a Muzio property by right—seems, at least on this occasion, beyond her reach. I wish she had applied her delectable *pianissimo* to the high B-flat of 'Invan la pace quest'alma.' Verdi called for it and we long to savor its caress. The Mississippian's soprano is definitely of the spinto variety rather than a genuine dramatic soprano—one recognizes that when she must surmount the full orchestra's tumult with her 'Maledezione's. Her spinto legitimacy, however, superbly equips her for the bulk of the role. She pours out her silvery top notes and glides smoothly down into a suggestive mid-voice before settling lightly on those ghostly lowest tones, the latter only occasionally reinforced by chest resonance. Hers is a remarkable instrument and its easy employment, her palpable confidence in her ability to negotiate any challenge, and the comfort she radiates as she revels in its sensuous beauty—this bounty is generously conveyed to her listeners, allowing them a peculiar and rare pleasure. Miss Price owns assets available to few operatic artists. Would that she had been willing (or more likely, thought it advisable) to share her treasure more frequently with admirers of her operatic artistry. Mr. Bing never could bring himself to accept her "silly theory" that she would be overexposed if she trod the Metropolitan boards too frequently.[2]

Having noted a slight aloofness in her reading of 'Pace, pace,' I quickly affirm that throughout all the turmoil of the initial act (the Met's act one includes the convent scene), Price is completely involved dramatically and musically, perhaps more than in any performance yet heard in her broadcast history. With her father, she is touchingly filial, suppliant, full of remorse over the deception of her imminent flight with Alvaro. With her lover, her rhythmically assertive and tonally vibrant protestations of 't'amo' expose the heroine's passionate nature. Alone at the church, she plays with extraordinary abandon, the flamboyance of her delivery thrilling in its dangerous exposure of self; yet vocal control is complete, her tones coursing up and down the widely ranging phrases like the unfurling coils of a whip. Within the tumult, however, she launches 'non m'abbandonar, pietà di me' in serene, pleading tones, tasting the hope of succor. Again, I miss the *pianissississimo* that Verdi calls for at 'm'assistimi' when Leonora, in calm resignation awaits the father superior's coming. Kudos must be awarded for her mastery of the two-octave ascent to high B ('Nè terribile l'ascolto . . . la sua figlia maledir') as Leonora fiercely pleads with Guardiano. Upon hearing the padre refuse to shelter her, the soprano assumes a strenuously dramatic stance, causing a welcome expenditure of precious vocal capital. At midcareer, Price well knows how to make a role her own property. For the ethereal 'La Vergine degli angeli' she lofts a healthy *mezzo forte* (rather than Verdi's *sottovoce, pianissimo*) over the male chorus' cushiony support, seemingly willing to forgo celestial repose for earthly reward; probably her theatrical sense told her the audience would better appreciate her song at that volume level. In any case, when means and ends are as positively aligned as they are in Price's portrayal, the rewards are immense.

One remembers with gratitude the grand quartet of principals who anchored the Berman production when it was first unveiled in the early 1950s. On many a broadcast, Milanov (one of a kind), Tucker, Warren, and Siepi filled the airwaves with their resplendent song. Price, Bergonzi, and Siepi (still in prime form) measure up to the remembered greatness. Though Paskalis cannot duplicate Warren's bel canto reading, he places his own fiery brand upon the role of Leonora's malignant brother. After more than two decades at the Metropolitan helm, Mr. Bing can continue to be proud of his Verdians.

The *Otello* broadcast of 8 April 1972 provides further affirmation of the manager's Verdi vocal coffers. Zylis-Gara, McCracken, Di Giuseppe, Milnes, and Plishka thrive in Böhm's rare excursion onto Italian terrain. His interest may have been spurred by the prospect of a new Zeffirelli production (costumes by Peter Hall), the first since the unveiling of Berman's 1963 production with Tucci, McCracken, and Merrill under Solti's galvanizing baton. The American tenor had starred in all three broadcasts since that date until the opera departed the repertory in 1967. In that year's broadcast, Mehta's exuberant, high-powered style dominated. Our Austrian maestro may be expected to offer something quite different from his famous predecessors. He does. But the opening storm music is appropriately driven (*tutta forza* in the orchestra markedly observed) with full-scale allotments of agitation and fear from the shore-bound crowds. The 'Vittoria' chorus is a joyful sprint and even 'Fuoco di gioia!' enjoys a companionable swing—the choral members respond to Böhm's dynamic leadership with admirable precision. The reins of the spirited drinking song are tautly held, with order in Verdi's carefully plotted inebriant chaos expertly maintained. Before the premiere, Böhm was spotted in a New York record store tracking down Toscanini's NBC Orchestra broadcast (1947) of the opera.[5] Memory refreshment was evidently the only object, for Böhm's acquaintance with the opera in Europe was long and frequent, beginning in Graz in 1921, with repetitions in Dresden and Vienna. Still, the Toscanini mode may be divined in these opening scenes, though more likely Verdi's markings are the inspiration. With Desdemona's entrance, a sea change in Böhm's conception occurs. Thereafter, a bit of Viennese rounding-off of edges takes place and a more objective stance obtains. When Iago quizzes Cassio about the handkerchief, the

Otello
8 April 1972

Desdemona
Teresa Zylis-Gara
Otello
James McCracken
Cassio
Enrico Di Giuseppe
Iago
Sherrill Milnes
Lodovico
Paul Plishka
Conductor
Karl Böhm

bouncing orchestral motive is cleansed of its insouciant jauntiness in favor of an elegant suavity. Climaxes are only occasionally pushed to the limit and the obvious in-your-face moments are notched down a degree in tempo and volume (markedly so in the Credo and vengeance duet). A certain neutrality settles over the performance, though Verdi's vibrancy will out even within this framework.

Adding to the cool tenor of the afternoon are the tonal characteristics and interpretive predilections of the three principals. Miss Zylis-Gara's timbre, fascinating as it is, lacks Italianate warmth. But her tones uniquely mate with Verdi's wintry wind ensemble in Desdemona's fourth-act *scena*, a union that may be relished for its aesthetic subtlety. Bleakness is apt for Desdemona's 'Salce' plaints, but a more caressing tone would have allowed Barbara's lament to touch the heart. The soprano ignores Verdi's directive (*troncando*) to break off the high note when the fearful wife suspects someone is at her bed-chamber door, and other theatrical moments ('Esterrefatta fiso' and the opening of the *concertato*—'A terra! sì, nel livido fango'—after Otello throws his wife to the ground) are similarly downplayed. Both of her intimate scenes with Otello seem to me insufficiently nuanced and lacking ingratiating warmth as Desdemona tries to cajole her husband into forgiving Cassio. Zylis-Gara is on firmer ground when she can allow her sizable tone to embrace an expansive curve of phrase: 'E un dì sul mio sorriso' in the *concertato* all but makes up for the earlier dramatic deficiency. And the Ave Maria, sealed by an ethereal 'Amen' ascent, is expertly voiced. Indeed, one can apply that approbation to most of the soprano's careful work on this afternoon. Many a broadly paced phrase on high satisfies, from her loving tracing of Desdemona's lines in the first-act duet on through the challenging climb of 'le amare stille del mio dolor' in the *concertato*. She handily negotiates the latter phrase without a break, safely rounding the phrase's crest with crowning top notes. In the remarkable succession of broadcast Desdemonas that began with Rethberg, Caniglia, Roman, and Albanese and continued with Steber, Tebaldi, De los Angeles, Rysanek, Tucci, and Caballé, Zylis-Gara is undoubtedly the most passive victim of spousal abuse. Perhaps Vickers' Moor will summon a more varied response. Next season's broadcast will provide that opportunity.

McCracken and Milnes are not generally celebrated for the subtlety of their portrayals. Both are power performers, that is they prefer to demand their auditors' attention, to take them by force, rather than win them over with blandishments of tone or character. Their take-no-prisoners style can be relished for its own sake in many an opera. Otello demands something more. Major portions of the opera do profit from the thrusting grandeur of their vocalism and the extrovert conviction of their interpretations. Indeed, McCracken's eminence in the role has been in large part due to precisely those attributes. The role of Otello requires vocal muscle, no doubt about it, and the American tenor has a corner on that market. His splendid, poised articulation of Otello's entrance 'Esultate!' demonstrates the singular density and tensility of his instrument. Many a moment throughout the afternoon reconfirms that judgment, for the tenor is in remarkably fine vocal form. Time after time, and often in phrases where either the high tessitura or isolated top tones sorely try other interpreters, he surmounts the difficulties with surety and tonal pith. But on this afternoon he does offer something more. In an earlier appraisal of his Moor, I decried his tendency to play at too high a dramatic pitch, to diminish Otello's character and flatten his musical profile by prolonged dwelling on a single dynamic and emotional level. Today, no such charge need be made. Happily, the tenor has altered his conception in favor of a more subtle dramatic stance and a rewardingly pliant musicality. He modulates his tones and calms his person to good effect, all in the service of Verdi's directives, and does so without significant loss of vocal pungency. The peaks stand out more vividly from the varied terrain over which they tower. He signals the new posture in the love duet by sensitively intoning the passage beginning 'Venga la morte!'; the fearsome final notes are safely negotiated as well. Each monologue benefits from his increased care. In particular, he no longer resorts to repeated pitch alterations in the opening phrases of 'Dio! mi potevi scagliar'—only 'd'angoscie' is singled out (and appropriately) for dramatic emphasis. (Oddly, in that monologue several prime phrases are less effective than in his 1967 broadcast: multiple breaths mar the magical ascents of 'volere del ciel' and 'quel sorriso, quel raggio.' It seems we can't have everything.) The death scene appropriately is the climax of his portrayal. 'Niun mi tema' is nobly declaimed, its tone clean and pure; rather remarkably, he honors Verdi's *pianissimo* at 'Or morendo'—a stunning and heartrending effect. Clearly, this voice has more colors in it than we had imagined and than he has been wont to show us. McCracken's portrayal on this broadcast is not only testimony to his growth as an artist but a welcome caution against dropping singers into preordained slots.

Milnes added Iago to his repertory for this series of Met performances—the broadcast is the fourth in the run. We have evidence from other radio outings that the young American is capable of varied, intelligent portrayals, at least when he believes that goal is worthy enough to outbid a natural inclination to "wow" an audience with his healthy baritone wares. On this afternoon, the voice, characteristically focused with a somewhat narrow circumference (an advantage in penetrating orchestral mass), often exhales a fruity bouquet. Occasionally, in the mid-voice his tones call to mind Warren's timbre. (Later in his career, the great baritone's widow would allow that Milnes' voice most resembled her husband's instrument. I had not thought so until a modest similarity surfaced in this performance.) The care with which Milnes has prepared Iago (in his autobiography he brands him "an enormously intelligent psychotic") is apparent in his portrayal and reaffirms his own intelligence.[4] The surety of his performance, its tonal ebullience and rhythmic alacrity, the attention to dynamics and courting of textual nuance ensure a triumph in one of opera's most difficult parts.

Still, I doubt that this performance represents the final measure of his Iago. Fine as it is, a certain studied quality—a desire to get everything right, rather than to live within the character itself—is apparent at some points, most notably in fast passages, where Böhm gives no quarter. Certain phrases might well be tossed off with more aplomb—"thrown away," to use theatrical parlance. Then, too, while he cultivates a mezza voce, sometimes with telling effect, the technique (especially in the extensive phrases of 'Era la notte') is not quite of bel canto quality—but all honor to Milnes for the attempt. There and in similar moments, he fails to bring word and tone into perfect equilibrium so that a genuinely suave legato obtains. His delivery of the tripping phrases of the drinking song (including the descending 'beva' scales and flip up to the concluding top note), however, is singularly assured and rhythmically precise; the result is one of the finest broadcast renderings of this tricky ensemble piece. (In the drinking scene, Enrico Di Giuseppe's Cassio

disappoints as he jousts musically with Iago. Although the young American will
be heard in many prominent roles with the company, on this afternoon the voice
unexpectedly sounds small, lacks color, and is rather pinched in timbre. Later
and larger efforts will allow a continuing appraisal. On the other hand, Plishka's
Lodovico and Love's Emilia register on the plus side.) Milnes' Credo is more than
commendable, but probably not quite top drawer; low notes lack body, nuances
are insufficiently varied, and a few theatrical touches seem overdone. Baritone
and tenor both acquit themselves with distinction in 'Sì, pel ciel.' In sum, Milnes'
Iago is emphatically a creation to be reckoned with, as future broadcasts may be
expected to confirm.

Otello was Bing's final obeisance to Verdi, the last in the lengthy list of new
productions of the composer's works. Zeffirelli's stage pictures and direction found
favor, but Böhm's "debut with Italian opera at the Met" (as Cross put it) received
a mixed reception from the press. The broadcast performance provides evidence of
its musical rewards. Somewhat fearlessly, Bing assigned the revival of Zeffirelli's
triumphant 1964 production of *Falstaff*, an opera whose intricate construct challenges any conductor, to a house debutant, Christoph von Dohnányi. The 1 April
1972 broadcast also features the return of Tito Gobbi to the radio series. Joining
him are Peters (Nannetta), Joann Grillo (Meg), Resnik (Quickly), Alva (Fenton),
Paskalis (Ford), and, most notably, Tebaldi in her final radio appearance.

Gobbi dominates the afternoon, though not always in the most reassuring
way. His knight is a magnificent creature, huge not only in stage avoirdupois, but
in vocal weight and extrovert bluster. The Italian baritone plays at so lusty a pitch,
conveys so palpable a sense of Falstaff's self-satisfaction, that the jolly libertine's
ego fairly bursts through the radio ether. The outsize portrait, its glorious swagger, must of course, be appreciated for its own sake. At times, Gobbi seems to be
not only commanding the stage but taking over the podium. One critic of the premiere performance accused Dohnányi of having his nose in the pit (I paraphrase)
when the singers needed his attention.[5] On this afternoon, Gobbi all but reaches
over the footlights, grasps the debutant conductor by the nose, and pulls him
along on the singer's exuberant romp. Indeed, the German conductor's way with
the score is a bit sedate. It lacks sparkle. Yet by this time in the run (the seventh
performance), things move along without major mishap (though the women's
ensembles in act one are hardly models of clarity). Dohnányi possessed substantial
credentials. At the time of his 25 February 1972 Met debut, the forty-two-year-
old conductor was a well-seasoned opera practitioner, having come up through
the time-tested system of provincial German stages: Lübeck, Kassel, and, more
importantly, Frankfurt. Berlin and Salzburg already knew him as well. While an
air of excessive care permeates his reading, some evocative orchestral effects (especially in his fluid treatment of the Windsor forest fairy episode) have the requisite
charm. And his fugue is fleet and accurate, no mean accomplishment. A pair of
Rosenkavalier performances in the next season would better show his quality. Eventually, he will attain musical heights in his much-acclaimed stewardship of the
Cleveland Orchestra.

I have put my own nose into the score and find that our baritone knight,
while rendering unto Shakespeare his portion, again serves Verdi less well. As
the merry wives attempt to thrust the bewildered suitor into the laundry basket,
Tebaldi, indulging in a humorous bit of audience courting, thrusts out an exor-
bitantly chesty 'è troppo grosso'; this knight is not only 'too fat'—the baritone's

portrayal may be a shade gross for even this old reprobate. One can readily ignore the woefully flat top note at 'San Martino' in the opening scene, but why try a blatant *forte*, when Verdi requested mezza voce (which most interpreters fudge with falsetto)? Indeed, throughout the afternoon, Gobbi repeatedly ignores Verdi's call for varied dynamics; the quieter ones are entirely abjured—yet we know the baritone has employed a magical mezza voce in the past. Legato phrases that should charm are foresworn in favor of stout declamation of the text. Of course, that superb textual articulation can be savored on its own terms. Gobbi's portrayal thrives as a theatrical creation, larger than life, but one hoped for the full complement from this operatic paragon. Still, When Falstaff and Ford meet, Gobbi demonstrates that musical and theatrical excellence can live in happy union. His voice blooms (at the top as well) and virtuoso treatment of phrases abounds: 'Se lo porti all'inferno con Menelao suo avolo!,' for instance, bristles flamboyantly and is expertly molded as well. And his 'Quand'ero paggio' is deft enough. In the end, the great singer reaffirms his stature in his realistic, touching reading of 'Mondo ladro,' where Falstaff, bruised in body and soul, muses on his fate. There the complete artist is once again before us. Hark back to Milnes' Iago, where scrupulous adherence to the score rather inhibited (at least in his initial encounters with the role) complete identification with the character. And remember Flagello's 1967 broadcast Falstaff—though singing with sumptuous tone, he committed some of the same musical sins as Gobbi but failed to show us the man. Gobbi truly inhabits Falstaff's skin. He shoulders the knight's weight and makes us share his greedy lust for life. Can there be a golden mean?

Falstaff's companions occasionally overplay their parts. While Best's Pistola operates within a modest frame, Franke's Dr. Cajus is markedly stentorian in the opening scene (he is more credible in a later scene). As Bardolfo, Velis manages to score comic points in a nasal plaint—at least his vocal clarity is welcome. He is a holdover from the Bernstein premiere, as are Resnik and Alva. The mezzo-soprano's booming chest voice is a boon to Quickly's comic utterances; she delivers them as robustly as in her prime. For most of the afternoon she manages, though with obvious care, to manipulate the register gears satisfactorily. Occasionally splintered tones (even a momentary weakness of voice) intrude, but they cannot vitiate what is a justly famous characterization. When two master actors like Resnik and Gobbi, old pros at the comic game, joust at the Garter Inn, the airwaves crackle with theatrical vitality. Alva's instrument has seen its best days. His timbre has never been the most beguiling and Fenton's principal chore, that is, to play the lover and wrap 'Dal labbro il canto' in dulcet folds, is further short-changed in this broadcast. Yet, he knows how to negotiate the aria's pitfalls and does so with honor. His partner at kiss stealing, Peters, on the other hand, is in top form and contributes an engaging portrayal of Nannetta. At times the voice takes on an attractive sheen and her technical skill is everywhere apparent—evidence a neat *messa di voce* on her first high A-flat. Her timbre is a shade dark (and mature) for the young minx, and some of the exquisite shine of 'Sul fil d'un soffio etesio' cannot be summoned. Timbral changes (warmth in the lower range, thinness at the very top) are apparent as she traverses its ascending phrases. But all that skill can do, she does. The result is a masterful exhibition of a singer's cultivated artistry. Overall, I find her Nannetta delightful, one of her most satisfying broadcast portrayals. Grillo, too, makes a positive contribution with a more impressive instrument than the Met management has often allowed Meg Page.

Renata Tebaldi as Alice in *Falstaff*. Photography by Louis Mélançon.

As Ford, Koskalis is once again in good voice, his burly instrument able to rage convincingly at his wife's suspected perfidy. He is unwilling (or unable) to infuse the opening of "E sogno? o realtà?' with the desirable quiet mystification, but thereafter fills its demanding phrases with vibrant tone, capping the aria with a powerful high G at its close. Verdi's show-stopping intent is fulfilled (even though the show never stops—no applause interrupts the composer's dramatic continuity). The Greek baritone and Gobbi are both in fine fettle (the two timbres not unlike) in their comic encounter. A special nod of approval must be given to Kostalis' liquid traversal of the rapid coils of 'madrigale.'

Tebaldi's Mistress Ford proves to be a formidable combatant when treating with both husband and prospective seducer. She is a game player in all the shenanigans that the merry wives undertake. Her tone, for the most part healthy and certainly sizable, is a determined mix of two parts late-career steel and one part early-career velvet. The result remains an effective vehicle for operatic expression, since the voice's core is still intact—no wobbly or weak tones lessen its impact. When she voices an exuberant 't'amo,' fond old memories are reawakened. She cannot loft a *dolcissimo* 'e il viso tuo su me risplenderà,' and the bewitching moment is thereby downgraded. Nor can she supply a trill on 'mio marito' in the opera's denouement. Still, an occasional rasp in mid-voice or edgy tone in the upper range cannot limit appreciation of her goodhearted play in the second-act farce. And the bulk of the role is well intoned, its lively gambits invariably executed with decided theatrical flair. In particular, I find it exhilarating to hear so full-bodied a voice in feisty Alicia's pronouncements. Her final lines are pithily thrown out, an affirmation of Tebaldi's continued stature on the Metropolitan stage. When, in the heat of the fugue, she executes the staccato ascent of 'tutto nel mondo è burla' and tops it off with a comfortable high B-flat, she serves notice that, though retirement is imminent, that decision will be her choice.

In this, her final Met broadcast, the soprano found herself in an unlikely situation: a participant in an ensemble opera. (She had sung the role elsewhere.) To hear her so handily discharge her obligations in that venue makes her broadcast portrayal of Mistress Ford doubly worthwhile. Still, the diva was accustomed to occupying center stage, commanding the spotlight in no uncertain terms. Few Metropolitan stars, at least in the later decades of the house chronicle, have had so legitimate a claim to the limelight. Over the years, there had been performances where its probing rays were unkind to her troubled vocal condition. Fortunately, she was unwilling to succumb to those travails and returned in the early sixties with a voice toughened by a new technique that enabled her to satisfy audiences for another decade. Not many artists have maintained their standing with so large and enamored a public for so long, continuing to reap its seemingly boundless affection. Though she was known to be willful, her person and stage manner, as well as her song, inspired love. The voice itself undoubtedly was an important one, possessing both lyrical and dramatic components; its circumference was noble, yet, in her best days, it possessed a dulcet, almost tactile, caress that was all but unrivaled among contemporary sopranos. Tonal wealth, whether susurrant or assertive, was the voice's intoxicating cargo. Her portrayals of Desdemona, Mimì, Tosca, Manon Lescaut, Adriana, Maddalena, the *Forza* Leonora, Maria Boccanegra, and Minnie were compounded of a rare blend of command and submission. That was their singular appeal and one that set her apart from most of her colleagues during her seventeen Metropolitan seasons. The soprano would return for a pair of appearances as Desdemona (the role of her 1955 debut) in January 1973. In a way, her departure from the company may be said to represent, in words that have often been abused by misapplication, the end of an era.

The end of an era does in fact occur on the occasion of the final broadcast of the Bing regime on 22 April 1972. Having entered with *Don Carlo* in 1950, the general manager ("perhaps for sentimental reasons," he admitted) chose to offer Verdi's epic drama as his final gift to the radio public. Where Rigal, Barbieri, Björling, Merrill, Siepi, and Hines had once trod (with Stiedry at the helm), now Caballé, Bumbry, Corelli, Milnes, Siepi, and Macurdy perform under Molinari-Pradelli's baton on a similarly historic occasion. Siepi and Amara (who warbles the Celestial Voice, the role of her 1950 debut) neatly bind the two events together.

The broadcast performance, distinguished in many ways, has at its heart an enfeebling element and, regrettably in view of the celebratory nature of the occa-

Don Carlo
22 April 1972
Elisabetta
Montserrat Caballé
Eboli
Grace Bumbry
Carlo
Franco Corelli
Rodrigo
Sherrill Milnes
Philip
Cesare Siepi
Inquisitor
John Macurdy
Conductor
Francesco Molinari-Pradelli

Cesare Siepi as Philip II in *Don Carlo*. Photography by Sedge LeBlang. Courtesy Metropolitan Opera Archives.

sion, it is one that has plagued the Bing management throughout its tenure. Conductors, particularly for the Italian repertory, have been the questionable factor in a number of performances throughout the years, the Achilles heel in Bing's generally elevated performance standards. Molinari-Pradelli's leadership is disappointingly limp. The Met has always utilized the 1884 La Scala edition in which the original French version is shorn of the Fontainebleau act and significantly altered by other revisions. Even so, the opera is long and somber in tone and, more than most, profits from an energizing dramatic thrust. (A few additional internal cuts are made in the cloister garden duet of Elisabetta and Carlo, Rodrigo's first aria, the auto-da-fé, and the act-five love duet, among others; they seem gratuitous on the Met's part.) The more reposeful portions of the opera benefit from the Italian conductor's fluid lyricism, but the auto-da-fé lacks fire (!), the entry music of the enraged queen into her husband's cabinet is pallid, and in many similar moments the dynamic pulse of the drama slackens.

Several stage participants help turn the tide with their vibrant portrayals. Surprisingly, Siepi is not one of them. The revered bass sings gloriously, his tone as plush as ever. But he is a somnolent monarch, seemingly unable to rouse himself to command or to anger in degree sufficient to make his Philip the focal player in the drama as Verdi intended. His characterization lacks a strong theatrical profile. Not only in the more dramatic episodes, but in the secret musing of his chamber, the husband's despondency, his deep regret at his wife's indifference, are not fully explored through imaginative variations of dynamics or textual nuance. On this afternoon, the bass, a potent performer when in churchly garb (Guardiano) or in zestful mood (Figaro and Giovanni), evidently finds dour and mean-spirited traits unwelcome intruders on his equable disposition. The role's considerable vocal difficulties are readily conquered and provoke audience response. A superbly deployed instrument and secure song are potent operatic tools. The two-octave phrase that closes the scene with the Grand Inquisitor, for instance, has the requisite grandeur. Perhaps a conductor of different propensities would have inspired the grand singer to greater effort.

While nothing can entirely suppress the enormity of Verdi's achievement in the fearsome confrontation between crown and church, the encounter suffers from lack of bite in the tones of both Siepi and Macurdy (at least for the major portion of the scene). Its macabre sobriety is veiled. Molinari-Pradelli's all-purpose manner further dilutes the scene's potency. Often he fails to make audible Verdi's orchestral tone painting—the composer's graphic representation of the dragging entrance gait of the aged, blind churchman, to give a single example, is muted. Macurdy's adherence to the composer's markings must be praised and his astute plotting of the scene's progress, that is, the gradual crescendo that climaxes with the Inquisitor's domination of the subjugated monarch, affirms his keen preparation of all his roles. I have never heard the American bass sing with more beautiful tone or greater musical sensitivity. Whether that is what one wants from the hoary Grand Inquisitor is another matter.

The opera thrives in a number of other portrayals. From the moment of his entry into the cloister of St. Just, Corelli, his brilliant tenor and outsized emotions in complementary embrace, brings a much-needed vibrancy to the stage action. If, throughout the afternoon, his remarkable vocal potency occasionally swamps the musical line, or his fondness for elongated top tones endangers phrase shape, his vital presence and unique voice, the tone pulsating with life, begets belief. He is in his best vocal form. The top notes are securely attained—a lunge occasionally may be the means, but no scoops compromise the assault. Everywhere the tenor gives his all. That all is considerable, for his vocal endowment is so generous, so caloric that one wonders if at birth he was allotted more than the basic twenty amino acids, those building blocks of life. His dramatic gestures inevitably are sweeping in their breadth. How ardent, and yet how musically responsible, is his delirious lovemaking in the garden duet! And he can act with the voice—witness his altered tones, drenched with weariness and despair, in the prison-cell colloquy with the Marquis of Posa. As that noble character, Milnes contributes one of his finest broadcast portrayals. He, too, is in remarkable vocal form. In their initial meeting at St. Just, the two singers parade their magnificent instruments with unashamed ostentation. Their friendship duet occasions full-blooded bursts of tone; they, like most interpreters, ignore the *piano* directive, but the ensemble is more precise than we usually hear. In the long run, however, the baritone is the more disciplined artist. He offers a fully rounded characterization and (with an exception now and then, as noted above) he follows Verdi's markings to an unusual degree. His song is both agreeable and informing. In the cloister gardens, suavity permeates his exchanges with queen and princess (and a baritone trill is a novelty). A few distractions may be noted: an odd tendency now and then for the core of a high note, after a solid attack, to recede and turn cloudy or hollow, even a shade flat; a patch of slight pitch deviation in the prison scene. These are evidently vocal mannerisms rather than musical indiscretions. In the pivotal scene with Philip (and here Siepi's vocal and interpretive play may be commended), Milnes' phrases are either resonantly commanding or subtly inflected; at the close, a quiet, insinuating 'Ei fu Neron!' honors Verdi's intent. His control of the *piano* dynamic in the agile phrases at the close of the cabinet quartet is impressive—few baritones would venture so precarious an exposure. Rodrigo's prison *scena* is nobly delivered with consistently rich tone; the baritone's theatrical surety all but compensates for the lack of a mezza voce caress in the 'estremo spiro' section.

Miss Bumbry, too, owns an impressive instrument and her command of it is equally assured. She is also in the enviable position of being able to fulfill both the disparate soprano and mezzo facets of this difficult role. As noted, during the early seventies, her Metropolitan repertory aptly included Dalila, Eboli, Tosca, and Salome. (When Verdi was confronted with a change of artists midway through composing the work—Rosine Bloch, a contralto, gave way to Pauline Gueymard-Lauters, a soprano "of wide extension"—he ended by settling a hybrid vocal character on Eboli.[6] Bumbry is his ally.) Her broadcast portrayal is potent with the vocal allure that an Eboli must command. The Veil Song's curious vocal acrobatics are handily executed with notable ease in the cadenza's high flicks and similar comfort in its low, twisting turns—only her slightly gulped triplets are less clearly executed. As the page Theobald, Von Stade again demonstrates her affinity for trouser parts with her pert pronouncements and deft partnership in the Veil Song. In Eboli's showpiece aria ('O don fatale,' sung in key with a clean, glittering high C-flat) Bumbry, to our delectation, flaunts her bold instrument and confident manner. She roams over its wide-ranging phrases as though they were home ground, while her bronze timbre, the vermilion hue included in a balanced mix that eschews ungainly chest tones, quietly embraces 'O mia Regina'; the concluding portion (delivered with appropriate *slancio*) is enlivened by rhythmic alacrity. A similar vitality would have better propelled the court garden scene trios for Eboli, Carlo, and Rodrigo if only the conductor had applied more spine to their febrile phrases.

Caballé had been scheduled to open Bing's final season. She canceled and the honor went to Arroyo, who with Domingo and Merrill (yet another veteran of the 1950 production) formed an impressive alternative to the radio trio. On the broadcast, the Spanish soprano sings with notable sensitivity and musicality, her luminous instrument in prime estate. At all dynamic levels, hearty or dulcet, her vocalism is agreeable to the ear, indeed, often ravishing in timbral content. 'Non pianger, mia compagna' is an ideal vehicle for her soft-grained tones. Her fluent shaping of its reposeful phrases is a model of vocal art, the line discreetly drawn, the *pianissimo*s lovingly poised. In her duets with Carlo, she performs with dignity, providing heartfelt, if appropriately muted, responses to his more violent protestations. In the last act, that flower of a phrase, 'I fior del paradiso a lui sorrideranno!,' is voiced with delicious fluency and subtly molded in a single breath. 'Ma lassù ci vedremo in un mondo migliore' wears an exquisite, celestial suavity—heaven realized on earth for her lucky listeners. Elisabetta's grand aria ('Tu che le vanità') has proven to be problematic for most sopranos. On the one hand, its architectural scope profits from steel in the voice, a capacity enjoyed by several lamented Italian sopranos, but Caballé is no member of that sisterhood. The *pianissimo* arcs of its phrases and the queen's nostalgic remembrance of Fontainebleau, however, require a gossamer sheen. Caballé, of course, supplies the latter attribute with ease (the means almost incorporeal), and since at this point in her career her vocal control is all encompassing, she is able to summon more than adequate sweep for the grander moments. How cagily she negotiates the difficult final cadence, precariously placed as it is in the soprano *passaggio*; as heard on several earlier broadcasts, a number of reputable sopranos have been brought to grief due to faulty technical control at that point. Our singer knows her instrument. The audience awards her the most vociferous, longest ovation of an afternoon replete with fine vocalism.

Once again, Mr. Bing can take pride in his superb Verdians. As he takes leave of the operatic scene, he leaves behind a Verdi treasure chest, a repertory far richer than he had found when he came to American shores. In plotting his final season, he thought it would be "a nice idea to close the circle" with *Don Carlo*.[7] Now the circle is closed.

Program for gala performance honoring Sir Rudolf Bing, 22 April 1972. Title page (left) and Part I (right, autographed by Richard Bonynge, Plácido Domingo, Sherrill Milnes, Anna Moffo, Luciano Pavarotti, Roberta Peters, Paul Plishka, Ruggero Raimondi, Thomas Stewart, Teresa Stratas, Joan Sutherland).

CHAPTER TWELVE

A Tribute to Bing

'Die Frist ist um.' The Dutchman's words are sung by Thomas Stewart, one of the leading Metropolitan artists who offer vocal tributes to Rudolf Bing during the first intermission of the April 1972 *Don Carlo*.[1] 'The time is up'—Mr. Bing obligingly translates the phrase from *Der Fliegende Holländer* for interviewer Cyril Ritchard and the radio audience. Indeed, it is. Rysanek, the most celebrated Senta of her generation, follows her colleague, singing an additional fragment of the opera, which Bing again translates: 'Well do I know you. Well do I know your fate. I knew you the first time I saw you. Now the end of your suffering has come.' Though denying that he has "really" suffered, the manager is grateful to Leonie for "being glad at my deliverance."

In more somber mood, during the second intermission the manager affirms that he is "pleased to be through with management responsibilities." He remarks that 'I had a wonderful time. . . . I'm sad to leave, but I think I made the right decision . . . after twenty-two years I don't think I had much new to offer." What he had offered during his lengthy tenure (only Gatti-Casazza held the reins longer than he) was worthy of tribute. Most notably, he had jolted the Metropolitan out of its comfortable ways, drastically improved production values, and led the company to its new and technologically up-to-date home at Lincoln Center. On that same intermission, Anthony A. Bliss, longtime Met board member who in a few years would become the new gray eminence of Metropolitan management, recalls how Bing, relatively unknown to Americans, "burst upon the operatic scene with a driving force that carried the Metropolitan into the greatest period of activity in its history." He acknowledged that Bing's tenure had not been a "placid" one, that he "enjoyed more than his share of controversy, but he rode through the stormiest moments with courage and conviction and, above all, with an unfailing sense of humor." Fair enough.

Ritchard, collaborator in many a new Met production, teases his friend as he inquires whether Bing enjoys "tiffs with prima donnas." The manager maintains there were not that many tiffs, that he did not have "bad relationships with the company," rather he "made friends" and will remember them "with pleasure and gratitude." When his friendly interlocutor asks if Bing would call himself a prima donna, the manager denies the charge in mock affronted tones: "Certainly not! I am mild, mellow, and old, none of which applies to prima donnas—certainly not the ones I've known." The Bing wit is alive and well.

His prima donnas offer more tributes, which the manager engagingly accepts. 'Abscheulicher!' sings Régine Crespin, in the guise of Beethoven's Fidelio. 'You ghastly creature. You fiend! You monster!' Mr. Bing relishes the words and the Gallic irony of the French soprano. 'What are your plans?' her Leonore wants to know and Ritchard wants us to know that Madame Crespin is "a darling person"—her comments are well meant. Bing agrees. Sutherland (Violetta's 'Felice siate!'), Pavarotti ('Addio, Rudolf, fa core'— Mignon's name replaced by Bing's), Price, and Peters provide more conventional (and agreeable) tributes. Horne (singing Norma's 'In mia man, alfin tu sei') is jubilant at finally having Bing in the palm of her hand, and in response he gamely avers he is glad to be there. One can hear in Bing's tones the special affection he has for "beloved Renata" and the afternoon's tenor lead, Corelli, "with whom I've enjoyed a particularly happy association." Evidently, he didn't mind all that tenor hand-holding.

Over the years, Bing has garnered tribute from others besides these amicable artists. But not all singers were so obliging. Gedda, for instance, was of two minds. Writing in his memoirs, he acknowledged that he owed his Met career to Bing and he liked to sing at the house because "the atmosphere among colleagues was always so friendly and open."[2] The latter may reflect an American milieu. But Gedda felt that Bing's "amateurishness and lack of judgment caused the theatre to decline."[3] He repeats the oft-heard claim that Bing did not "understand voices," that he too frequently cast artists in "inappropriate parts." The tenor's judgment becomes suspect when he adds that Bing had no "visual sense." Yes, there have been dissenters, but Bing generally has been acclaimed as one of the great opera impresarios of his century. And justifiably so. I never met Mr. Bing, but I did once make contact with him. In 1953, the New York City Opera opened its fall season with *La Cenerentola*. I was the guest of the excellent American tenor, David Lloyd, who was singing Ramiro in the opening-night performance. My seat was in the fifth or sixth row of the orchestra, where some notable musical figures were lodged. I arrived just before curtain after a contretemps with my capricious landlady, who for some unfathomable reason had threatened a rent increase (she relented, with apologies). Entering hurriedly into my row, I passed by a set of bigwigs, among whom was Bing. In my haste, I stepped on his foot, he grimaced, I mumbled a quiet "Sorry" and moved on. I hope that I have not stepped on him in this study of his Met stewardship. One misstep can be forgiven, but two, to fall back on Bracknellian parlance, would seem like "carelessness."

The major accomplishments of Bing's tenure are universally accepted. He transformed the production values of the company by bringing in major talents from the legitimate theater to design and oversee new productions, the number of which grew over the years. Seasonal length expanded greatly and with it the sum of performances. He enlarged the repertory, though generally along conservative lines. Even in the sixties, one is not surprised to discover an impresario downgrading the Handel corpus (Bing damned "that sort of thing" as "oratorio, not opera"), a body of work that today we find so enticing.[4] Few in earlier days divined that the dramatic truth of the music could be translated into imaginative staging in that purportedly static genre. But for a responsive manager to hold that *Les Troyens* is "one hell of a bore" requires more charity than many have at their disposal. Give him credit for the courage of his convictions. In a more positive vein, Bing was eventually able to realize the dream of a new, well-equipped opera house, a triumph that had eluded his predecessors for decades. Early on, he eradicated the despicable color line that had prevented black artists from joining the company. (At the close of the final *Don Carlo* intermission, Marian Anderson offered 'Auld Lang Syne' as her tribute, its honored placement signifying the importance of that breakthrough.) Administrative competence in all departments became the norm. Vicissitude or ill-judged actions might affect the artistic quality of performances or the legitimacy of new productions (the pluses and minuses of both components have been noted in this chronology), but management under Bing and his administrative team was without doubt efficient. And the company, even in the last years of his reign, included some magnificent artists, as the roster of the 22 April evening gala for the departing manager confirms.

Nearly three decades after the farewell *Don Carlo* broadcast, another Met general manager offered his own appraisal of Bing and his regime. On that occasion, Joseph Volpe, heading the Met at the turn of the new century, spoke with unusual candor.[5] The view from the throne is always worth hearing. Volpe, who had joined the company in 1964, had learned firsthand that Bing was always "in charge"; anytime something happened, he was on the scene. He speculates that Bing may have employed a "good spy system." The younger man became aware that the tart-tongued Bing was Janus-faced, that is, he could be charming, could win you over when he wanted to, but, conversely, there were times when he remained aloof, times when he should not, indeed must not, be approached. According to Volpe, one of Bing's most important attributes was that he was "never afraid to make a decision." He relates how Bing had given him a philosophic approach to decision making, advising that the "easy" part is making the decision (though he admitted it might be "hard" to make a correct decision). In any case, if you erred, you simply made "another decision." No problem—evidently for Bing and certainly for Volpe, as he himself maintains. The new man marvels that an administrator, no matter how resolute, could micromanage so massive an undertaking as the Lincoln Center project while continuing to run the company at the old Met. Volpe says that Bing believed he had to be "cautious" when planning new productions of repertory staples—the Met audience expected conventional productions in that area. But he did establish what Volpe calls "production value," in contrast to "the stand-and-sing" type of performance.

The millennium manager then proceeds to decry the administrative structure that the Met adopted after Bing departed, that is, the appointment of an executive director, with the division of responsibility among several parties (i.e., Bliss, Dexter, Levine). Volpe remembers that Bing surrounded himself with a bevy of "great musicians" and relied "heavily" on their expertise. At the same time, he avers that the earlier manager was very chary of allowing anyone to have much "authority." Control remained in his hands. When his interlocutor reminds him that Bing had no artistic director, Volpe salutes his artistic director, James Levine, whose coming to the Met in 1971 would prove to be one of the most important Bing legacies. He notes that Levine is a partner ("the finest partner one could have"); despite that productive union, he maintains that Bing and he employed the same administrative structure. He believes that Bing fathered a type of Met governance that would serve the company "long into the future." The new man and his rough-edged manner are a world apart from the elegant, witty Bing. Nevertheless, with goodwill, one can imagine that an oracle has spoken. In a parting shot, Volpe can't resist opining that, though later in the Bing era there were still "highlight" performances, as regards the "night after night" record "the artistic level [is] somewhat higher" in the Volpe regime. No doubt some longtime broadcast listeners will believe that oracles had better quit while they are ahead.

I return to the farewell *Don Carlo* broadcast to find Ritchard asking Bing for a phrase that "sums up your feeling on leaving the Met." The manager, who often figuratively donned the clown's costume when confronted with difficulties, suggests Canio's 'La commedia è finita.' But life's comedy was not entirely over for the retiring impresario. The company's financial problems and struggles with labor unions that marred the last half decade of his management were considerable burdens, but they would be dwarfed during the final years of his life by unexpected trials in the form of illness and press ridicule.

But as he comes to the end of his twenty-two Metropolitan years, all is well. Birgit Nilsson has chosen for her vocal intermission tribute a few lines from the *Götterdämmerung* Immolation Scene. Bing, again the translator, tells us that Nilsson's Brünnhilde, upon viewing Siegfried's dead body, sings: 'More sincerely than he, no one swore an oath. More faithfully no one kept contracts. More purely than he, no one loved.' The manager, in sportive mood, cannot resist wondering how the Swedish soprano knows about "his way of loving," but he is happy to learn that "she feels I kept my contracts." With noticeable pride, he adds, "I think I did." That badge of honor is the tribute Bing most relishes. And deserves.

Luciano Pavarotti as the Duke of Mantua in *Rigoletto*. Photography by Louis Mélançon. Courtesy Metropolitan Opera Archives.

CHAPTER THIRTEEN

Anchors of the New Regime

Long tenures inevitably produce a desire for change. Bing knew it, the Met board knew it, and both acted upon it.

As Bing's successor, the board selected Goeran Gentele, a prominent Swedish opera stage director whose innovative ideas were admired (and occasionally decried) by Europeans. At the time of his appointment, he was director of the Stockholm Opera, having succeeded Set Svanholm in the post. Fate intervened and the chosen one (then in his mid-fifties) was killed in an automobile accident in Sardinia on 18 July 1972. Management and company were thrown into shock, not only by the necessary change in plans but because Gentele's affable disposition had endeared him to many during his yearlong residency in New York as he prepared to take up the managerial reins. (His appointment had been announced as early as 9 December 1970.) George S. Moore, president of the Opera Association, paid him extravagant tribute. "The company reacted like a thirsting field to water" to Gentele's presence, Moore wrote, claiming that the new man had boosted "the morale of the place" incredibly, everywhere "captivating" all who met him.[1] (In what seems a gratuitous slight, Moore referred to Sir Rudolf as "our capable and distinguished general manager"—"distinguished" may refer to his knighthood but "capable" was totally inadequate to describe the departed manager's authoritative, wide-ranging abilities.) During his observation year, Gentele had developed a long-range plan of repertory and new productions for seasons 1973–74 through 1975–76. Moore averred that Gentele's newly designated team of Schuyler G. Chapin (appointed assistant manager and senior assistant), Rafael Kubelik (named the Met's first official music director), and James Levine (promoted to principal conductor) would carry out his program. To that end, in a move that would prove baneful, Chapin was named acting general manager.

Dashed hopes and crushed spirits were opportunely channeled toward turning the opening night into a tribute to the lamented manager. Bing had scheduled *Tannhäuser* for that notoriously social occasion, but the new man had early divined that Wagner's weighty opus was hardly digestible fare for socialites. More important, it would not allow him to demonstrate his producing know-how. *Carmen* became the ticket. And, following the pattern he had established in Stockholm, Gentele had original ideas for the new production. Though seemingly the most familiar of scores, the opera would be revealed in what was proclaimed to be the

Carmen
10 March 1973

Carmen
Marilyn Horne
Micaela
Lucine Amara
Don José
James McCracken
Escamillo
Tom Krause
Conductor
Henry Lewis

287

"original" version, which reflected Bizet's thwarted intent. Most important was the substitution of spoken dialogue for the illicit composed recitatives of Ernest Guiraud, the latter almost universally employed throughout the world and, since the late nineteenth century, at the Met. The stage action would thus be accentuated, dramatic continuity purportedly heightened by the interjections of speech. With some alterations, Fritz Oeser's *Kritische Neuausgabe nach den Quellen* (published in 1964) was the edition utilized. Oeser had discovered the 1875 conducting score and orchestral parts, which contained many alterations made during the rehearsal period for the opera's Paris premiere in that year. The inclusion of several previously eliminated *mélodrame*s (spoken text over orchestral music), the expansion of the men's address to the cigarette girls, the opening up of the third-act duel, all add to the opera's impact at several key points and there are other credible additions to the score. But the inevitable tension between Oeser's musicological "authenticity" and theatrical verisimilitude invalidates some aspects of the Met production. In fact, the highly regarded Bizet scholar Winton Dean described the Oeser edition as "perhaps the most corrupt score of any major masterpiece published in modern times," rightly naming Oeser's additions and changes "arbitrary" and unfaithful to Bizet's true design.[2] Dean noted that the first American production of the opera with dialogue occurred at Central City, Colorado, in July 1953. I well remember José praying before an altar in the final act as Bizet's Agnus Dei was interpolated into the score, one of stage director Herbert Graf's "inspirations," which brought down the wrath of the purists on his venerable head and on our company as well. Dean called it "nonsensical."[3] Graf's pioneering effort to restore spoken dialogue was otherwise praiseworthy.

The Met's "authentic" revision had its adherents. The *New York Times* and *Opera News* heralded Oeser's work and, hence, the Met production as revelatory, while Boris Goldovsky, in the broadcast's first intermission, proclaimed the superiority of the new look over the corrupt version of yore. For my money, corruption seems endemic to both the old and the new.

The presence of Leonard Bernstein on the podium for the premiere lent additional stature to the occasion. "Production conceived by Goeran Gentele" appeared on both the program and the broadcast *Opera News* listing, but Bodo Igesz was credited as stage director. He based his treatment on Gentele's notes, as well as discussions with him and others acquainted with the late manager's ideas. Necessarily, he discarded some Gentele plans (a fourth-act ballet, for instance) and made cuts in the dialogue. Sets by Josef Svoboda were modestly innovative, the conductor's treatment of the score considerably more novel. At the 19 September 1972 premiere Bernstein's slow tempos startled audiences and critics, but many of the latter deemed the conception so thoroughly thought through that all could be forgiven in the name of originality and consistency. After all, Bernstein would not be Bernstein if his Peck's bad boy willfulness were not allowed to surface. Of course, there is always more to Bernstein than that appealing trait. In spite of considerable press kudos, however, a vocal minority cried sacrilege. After the initial run of six performances, the grand seigneur departed, allowing Henry Lewis (at the time Marilyn Horne's husband) to shoulder the considerable responsibility of the 10 March 1973 broadcast and numerous house and tour performances. The forty-year-old Los Angeles native had earned his spurs conducting the U.S. 7th Army Symphony Orchestra in Europe. Music director of the Los Angeles Opera from 1965 to 1968, he then took on the leadership of the New Jersey Symphony. *La Bohème* in October 1972 served as his Met debut. For the most part, and quite understandably, he maintains the Bernstein conception (the latter is preserved on commercial recordings made at the time of the new production) and conducts a well-ordered, expertly controlled performance. The broad ritards (within an already inert pace) in the major choral pieces can try patience; perhaps the remarkable slowdown at the end of what in former years had been thought to be a jaunty ensemble (the smugglers sing as they leave the mountain retreat before Micaela enters) is intended to suggest their weariness. Preconceptions are best abandoned, but here and there, they die hard. What a treat to hear the bassoon's saucy nose-flips in the act-two entr'acte, and again as the instrument perfectly mimics Carmen's final 'lalala.' The insouciant aura of the opéra comique momentarily invades the opera's measured progress. Lewis' effort occasionally comes off as a bit staid, rather more constrained than the older maestro's; though Bernstein's way has its pompous, even turgid moments (the opening bull-ring music, for instance), overall his reading sounds more fluent. His ability to shape phrases with flexibility lends a sense of movement to the opera as a whole and suggests that adjusting to his conception might be easier than the broadcast indicates. Obviously, the Bernstein brand without the man diminishes the product. A more comprehensive, and fairer, assessment of Lewis' abilities can be made in later broadcasts when he is on his own.

Opera house routine never infects this well-rehearsed performance. Of the opening night cast, Maliponte's Micaela, Baldwin's Mercédes, and Gibbs' Morales have given way to the broadcast's Amara, Love, and Boucher. Horne's first Met go at Carmen is tracked by McCracken's José, and sustained by Boky (Frasquita), Gramm (Zuniga), Velis (Remendado), and Christopher (Dancaïro). Boucher and Gramm are expert players, vocally adept and stylistically knowing. Boky and Baldwin lend attractive voices to the card trio, though in some ensembles with chorus the former's top notes (important to firm up the musical profile of the big set pieces) are a bit skittish—oddly so for a soprano whose appearances with the company include Juliette, Gilda, and other leading roles. The spoken dialogue allows Velis to contribute a personality turn as a hyperactive smuggler. The quintet, pulled back a notch (Minnie Hawk, legendary Carmen of the opera's first decades, could vouch for the restrained tempo as an authentic read), now seems less a musical tour de force than a vehicle to propel the dramatic action. Both purposes are well served by this crew. Under the new order, Lillas Pastia provides Paul Franke with a nonsinging role as an annoyingly boisterous innkeeper.

Of the major players, Tom Krause has the notes (high and low) and vocal size for a role that has tried the resources of many a fine baritone. On the other hand, his timbre is a touch raw. Lengthy performance practice has dictated that vocal brawn shall be Escamillo's portion and the German baritone eats his with a vengeance—a single nuance in the little fourth-act duet is all the variety he can find in the music. The composer served up more than that, in particular dictating that the refrain of the infamous toreador song be approached with a lengthy diminuendo and the ensuing couplets sung *piano avec fatuité*; moreover, he prescribed—anathema to burly baritones—a *pianissimo* ending. The curse of vulgarity would thus be, at the least, altered and the toreador's character transparently exposed if Bizet's directives were honored. Let us be grateful to Krause for covering the notes so bravely—he is one up on most interpreters in that regard. Miss Amara had sung countless Micaelas during her two-decade duty with the company and it seems a bit odd to find her familiar peasant girl mingling with this new crowd and in an unusual venue. (The broadcast edition of *Opera News* listed the role as "to be announced.") Commenting on the use of spoken dialogue, she opined (and I think rightly so, in this instance) that without the recitative before Micaela's aria the audience could not know that she was "frightened by the smugglers."[4] To embark on the aria immediately upon entry seemed unduly abrupt. However, the middle section of the piece can convey fear if the singer can provide sufficient rhythmic thrust. Though Amara had been appearing in parts like Aida, both Leonoras, Desdemona, and Ariadne for years, her Micaela is about as virginal of tone (occasionally, even excessively demure) as when first met in the 1952 broadcast under Reiner. (Now, there was a worthy alternative to the Bernstein concept—he balanced the opera on a ballerina's point and execution was fleet.) Still, the Amara voice has a delectable sheen when at its best and her routine is reassuring; a few lovely portamentos in the duet with José and steady control of the concluding 'Seigneur' of the aria testify to her expert technique. Lewis (read Bernstein) takes the more conventional set pieces (Micaela's aria, the flower song, and the first-act duet) at traditional speeds—evidently experimentation has its limits. More likely, sentiment was to be minimized.

McCracken's healthy voice adds substantially to the burly vocal quotient of the afternoon. He is in splendid form and, if one cottons to his pressurized, high-relief vocalism, his antihero is both creditable and impressive. He had been singing José at the Met since 1966 and confessed that when confronted with Gentele's concept, he found it difficult to accept the young soldier as a killer type ("I just couldn't find the element of cruelty in the score," he astutely observed).[5] Of course, his bulky tone and lack of phrase nuance in themselves reinforce the idea of contained violence, no matter his intent. Conscientious he is, managing the quiet close to the Micaela duet well enough with a bit of vocal subterfuge. He turns the flower song into a narrative, not a bad mode if lyricism isn't your meat; the baritonal underpinning of his instrument reinforces his sincerity, but musical subtleties are few. At the premiere, his *pianissimo* ascent (falsetto?) to the top tone in the flower song was commended by critics as the genuine article—it is famously so marked but seldom achieved. McCracken avers that Bernstein had "flipped" at his rehearsal trial run, saying the effect was "exactly" what Bizet wanted. But Lewis brusquely (and truthfully, in view of the nature of the tenor's instrument and person) told him the effect "just isn't you."[6] On the broadcast we get "you," as McCracken hastens up the stepwise ascent to a *forte* top tone. Elsewhere, he plays a bit over the top. Tone and text often burst forth impetuously—it suits Gentele/Igesz's violence-prone man, I suppose. Act four contains McCracken's best efforts, for there he does an about-face and performs with absolute control of voice and character (the director had banished the traditional "stalking" actions that had accompanied suggestive phrases in the orchestra). Sobs, too, are mercifully foresworn and José is allowed to quit the scene with his dignity intact. The tenor intones the final passages with vocal surety and nobility of phrase.

Sopranos of all ilks have played Carmen, many to their regret, some gaining modest approval, and a hallowed few in triumph. It was foreordained that Marilyn Horne would try to capture the gypsy coronet. Though it sits a bit uneasily on her

Marilyn Horne as Carmen. Photography by Louis Mélançon. Courtesy Metropolitan Opera Archives.

head, she demonstrates her right to wear it. Her reading is admirably conceived, thoroughly studied, well schooled, and occasionally a bit overcalculated in execution. To hear Bizet's elegant phases sung with such exactitude of rhythm, equality of tone, and ease of phrase is immensely gratifying. Too often in the interest of "characterization" the music is sluttishly rendered, slurred and slurped, musical shapes pulled apart in a misguided attempt to suggest sexual potency. The California-bred Horne is too intelligent for all that nonsense. Her mastery of vocal technique, the unruffled tenor of her instrument, the ability to confidently project tone in all ranges and at varied dynamic levels, permit her to choose her interpretive weapons with precision and purposeful intent. The timbre may not be innately seductive—all Carmens ought to be—but her artistry is. Faithful she is to Bizet, reasonably so to Meilhac and Halévy, but with hardly a nod in Merimée's direction. The latter's contribution was Gentele's expressed focus for the new production—did he forget that the composer is always the dramatist?—but it simply is not in Horne's makeup to play the ruthless manipulator. Good humor will have to do—and often enough it suffices, though in some moments of dialogue she sounds incorrigibly American ('these cords, these cords,' she cries before José allows her to escape). There, and repeatedly in her rowdy hoyden's play at the inn, one can't resist a smile, either of genuine mirth or regret. Of course, she is a prisoner of Bernstein's pace in all the set pieces, but how ably (and with praiseworthy aplomb) her musicality inhabits his space. Have the Habanera and Seguidilla ever been so judiciously rendered in a Met broadcast? Both honor the composer, acknowledge the text, and are intoxicatingly discreet. To hear a singer embrace the initial 'L'amour' of the Habanera with a quiet caress is delicious reward. In the Seguidilla, she deftly touches the isolated bottom D (which initiates several successive phrases) with the pinpoint drop of an antique metal stenciler. Many similar small, but telling, nuances inform her readings of these overfamiliar arias. Only an occasional exaggerated boom of chest voice (the requisite conciliatory bone tossed to her many fans) disturbs the musical landscape. Carmen is, after all, no toney princess—a touch of vulgarity suits the girl. Horne manages the difficult gypsy song without the usual mezzo gargles (the contained introductory tempo is an immeasurable aid). Here, as elsewhere, the little written ornaments are cleanly etched. She mimics the trumpet's retreat with rhythmic precision while betraying a withering scorn for José's attack of conscience. The card aria (the *pianissimo* designation of the score is seldom honored in performance) is delivered with lovely, almost delicate, fluency, as though in a reverie. Unlike many a Carmen, she need not hold the voice in a vise to counterfeit the uniform upward traversal prescribed by Bizet—equality is built into her voice construct. Except for the appropriately grand 'la mort's that precede and end the aria, the easy flow of tone is hardly touched by chest voice. For the final act confrontation her tone takes on a steelier cast and a few theatrical touches enlarge the compass of her portrayal. She fiercely trumpets her love for Escamillo to José—the top tones are brilliant and here luscious in timbre. At the end, as Carmen throws back the ring, virtually commanding her death, Horne snarls with bitter disdain (rather too obviously for the well-adjusted, home-grown girl that she is). Still, throughout the denouement, a marked step-up in dramatic urgency adds another dimension to her portrayal. Is Horne the *authentique* Carmen of one's dreams? Probably not. Like most portrayals of the role, her gypsy is an adumbration. But the musical rewards are immense.

Though the principals are expert performers, most of them do not seem ideally suited to their roles. It is Donald Gramm (though his Zuniga is only a cameo even when the role is enlarged by the Oeser format) who provides the afternoon's missing ingredient: idiomatic style in word, tone, and phrase; elegance; the je ne sais quoi of French opera. After a *Carmen* repeat next season, a new heroine, French-born and Opéra-schooled Régine Crespin, will play the femme fatale in the 1976 broadcast. Will she be the real thing?

A month after her *Carmen* broadcast foray, the estimable Horne doffs her gypsy disguise and returns to the airwaves as her true self, the Rossini mezzo coloratura heroine. Her supremacy in that field encourages listener assurance. On the 7 April 1973 broadcast of *Il Barbiere di Siviglia* she is joined by Di Giuseppe, Prey, Corena, and Tozzi under Levine. During the Bing broadcast years, the opera had passed from Erede, Rudolf, Strasfogel, and Varviso to Bonynge and Schippers until, under the new regime, Levine undertook the task. Podium promiscuity would continue over the next decade, when a pair of Johns (Pritchard and Nelson), Andrew Davis, and even the unlikely Emil Tchakarov would husband Rossini's imperishable, but frangible, masterwork. Seemingly, any imprint—or worse yet, none whatsoever—would do for *Il Barbiere*. Not unexpectedly, the young American conductor has his own ideas about the work; they both add to and diminish its character, fortunately with the weight on the positive side. His way with the overture is oddly less reassuring than expected. This orchestra is not the burnished instrument that he will skillfully fashion in later decades, nor are its members as yet entirely his obedient servants. These inhabitants of the pit seem to be feeling their way, on this afternoon not quite willing to trust Levine's restrained manner in what has normally been a mere Rossinian romp. At the curtain rise, Levine cultivates lyricism—he will search it out in every permissible orchestral phrase of the entire score. Tempos will be on the slow side, musical shenanigans curtailed, and the ironic, the caustic, the incomparable Rossini wit constrained. He adheres rigorously to his scheme throughout the afternoon and the overall proportions are decidedly just and satisfying in themselves. Soon enough, the orchestra begins to play with silken suavity and the famed crescendos are so considerately cultivated that their modest furor seems enough. We can savor unaccustomed tidbits (the deliciously fluttering flutes while Almaviva and Bartolo gabble their 'pace's and 'gioia's, for instance—now there's wit for you!). Though the stage action can lapse into slapstick (old hands Corena and Tozzi retain their prerogatives), the music, its formal construct in particular, retains its integrity. Is the reading too straight-faced? Probably so—more time would be needed to effect the necessary cross-fertilization between care and spontaneity. We, unlike the onstage players, should be allowed to enjoy Rossini's incorrigible musical levity more than Levine permits this afternoon. Nevertheless, to hear *Barbiere* free of tradition's barnacles brings a smile in itself.

Prey is the enlivening presence onstage. Whenever he appears, our spirits rise. His vocalism is not quite as expert as his breezy manner, though he is in fine vocal form on this afternoon. *Opera News* takes pains to assure its readers that though he is the first German-born singer to sing Figaro at the Met, his appearances in the role at Salzburg, San Francisco, Chicago, and Milan are guarantees of *Echtheit*—er, of legitimacy. He tackles the entrance aria with fierce abandon (sounding almost angry in its initial phrases) and wins the tussle. A bit ham-handed here and there

Il Barbiere di Siviglia
7 April 1973
Rosina
Marilyn Horne
Almaviva
Enrico Di Giuseppe
Figaro
Hermann Prey
Basilio
Giorgio Tozzi
Bartolo
Fernando Corena
Conductor
James Levine

(a falsetto high C is offered), his interpretation brews charm, insinuation, and bravado—the principal ingredient—into a crowd-pleasing mix. Forthright in tone, the timbre's manly fruitiness complements his boisterous play. The top notes are secure, though the fioriture are not uniformly clean. In the lengthy duet with Almaviva, Prey's ebullience is harnessed by Levine's judicious proportionality (the vivace portions hardly reach that carefree state), but the baritone's exuberant diction and the hint of mirth in the voice itself take up the slack. Almaviva, his partner in plotting, is a role that has had very few first-rank interpreters over the broadcast history. Valletti may claim that distinction but he stands virtually alone. Landi, Di Stefano, and Shirley each had merit, but the totality of the role escaped them. Di Giuseppe, more than most, demonstrates that he is up to the job. In spite of the wide spectrum of roles that he will eventually undertake in his career at the Met and elsewhere, the bel canto realm seems his true métier. The voice, though not luscious in the manner of Schipa and Valletti, is well collected and gains in warmth and flexibility as the opera progresses. Its Italianate timbre is a boon. Obviously, he has thoroughly studied the role so that every phrase, whether in recitative, aria, or ensemble, is given an appropriate musical and dramatic stamp. Some of the fioriture are labored, but the majority of the runs and ornaments are felicitous in sound, fluent in execution (a few are surprisingly gracious), and more accurate than most of his broadcast predecessors have offered. He plays with fervor but never overplays, even when impersonating the drunken soldier or the irritating music master. Taken altogether, Di Giuseppe turns what, for the audience, has too often been a cross to bear into felicity.

Fiorello and Berta are lesser players, but Goodloe (sounding like a budding Figaro) and Kraft lend them stature. The mezzo is awarded a prime turn with Berta's aria and makes a good thing of it, the voice sounding both solid and worthy and—in characterful manner—creaky with age. (I knew her when the latter was entirely foreign to it. A quarter century earlier as an eager college student I played the *Winterreise* song cycle for her when she visited her Midwest hometown during her Curtis Institute studies. Later an imaginative singer of character roles at the Met, she was then a sensitive lieder singer.) Of the two veteran basses, Corena is in better voice—its core is still vibrant and a few top tones can be boomed out with buffo assurance. The big cut in Bartolo's aria is a help, but he doesn't seem to need it. By this time in his career, Tozzi is seldom heard at peak form. His instrument has grown porous with age and, in Basilio's aria, Levine's very measured and (for the singer) merciless tempo tries him rather conspicuously. The tricks of the trade save him as some flagrant acting with the voice pulls him through. Calumny does seem even more insidious than usual in Levine's restraining hands; how tiny the orchestral motive sounds at inception and how the orchestral growth burgeons! Tozzi manages to capitalize on slander's mesmerizing impact and wins approval from the audience.

Of course, Miss Horne is the greater crowd pleaser (as her initial broadcast Rosina in 1971 under Schippers affirmed). She sings 'Una voce poco fa' in the written key of E (as mezzos should and do) and spins an enchanting web of lyricism and virtuosity out of its well-worn phrases. Indeed, the aria has so often been mangled by aspiring soubrettes that it has long been banished from my leisure-time listening. Horne reanimates its pleasures in full measure. The virtuosity is entirely expected. She has signaled it in the deft little trill that she applies to

Rosina's answering phrase in act one. What is so gratifying—and, I confess, a bit unexpected—is the captivating charm of her vocalism. Her drawing of line is always exceptionally firm, sometimes almost intimidating, but in this introductory aria, phrase after phrase is touched with a light, delectable tone that ingratiates and, in combination with that fluent virtuosity (including an exquisite trill), ensures triumph. She begins to ornament from the get-go and the roulades grow more elaborate as the aria progresses. No matter, the execution is so felicitous that one would not wish to forgo a note. (Only a little gargle at the final chesty cadence tells us she is, after all, human.) I have never heard Miss Horne sing with such infectious musicality. Curiously, my reaction to the lesson scene interpolation is less propitious. For a number of recent seasons, Met Rosinas had been confined (and rightly so) to Rossini's 'Contro un cor.' Horne, willing to exercise her prima donna prerogative, revives a tradition that had been blessed by coloratura sopranos from Sembrich to Pons, namely, the right to interpolate a showpiece of her choice. Perhaps because of its long history, I find the practice relatively inoffensive and, in its way, endearing. Forbidden fruit is always inviting to the taste. (One doesn't know whether to smile or cry at some of the interpolations. Sembrich, during the Met's inaugural season, sang German lieder or a Queen of the Night aria—later on she favored Strauss' 'Voce di Primavera'; Galli-Curci offered Titania's aria from *Mignon* and clinched response with 'Home Sweet Home'; Bishop's warhorse, 'Lo, Here the Gentle Lark,' figured prominently in Pons' selections, at least when she was not chirping French bon-bons.) Horne chooses 'Tanti affetti' from the composer's *La Donna del Lago* and sings it with both barrels blazing. The gun metaphor is intentional for, after some appealing lyricism in the opening section, she trots out every weapon of her formidable arsenal of fioriture. Her aim is deadly—she is the Annie Oakley of the vocal arena. Ascending and descending two-octave runs, leaps from the stratosphere to a chest netherland, motorized patterns that rattle on—the battery is impressive. The overall result seems like overkill to me, a too weighty insertion into this particular opera and at this point in the comic action. Rossini's Rosina is an enchanting creature, a volatile minx intent on getting her own way, but to tip the balance toward the grand, the formidable, in this fashion seems the wrong path for this particular diva. Her artistry and her instrument are so awesome that one would expect her to want to increase the charm quota rather than obliterate it. Of course, taken as a thing in itself, her reading is remarkable, almost stupefying. The ovation that she gains is wondrously long, vociferous, and entirely earned. (When Gail Robinson and Nedda Casei took on Rosina during this season's tour performances, they reverted to 'Contro un cor.' Prima donnas have a way with them: theirs.) Continuing in curmudgeonly mode, I might as well mention that Horne's delivery of some recitative seems gauche; her comic touch is a bit emphatic. And how did Levine allow her to utter—*in English*—'It's the list of last week's laundry' before the 'Freddo ed immobile' ensemble? Indeed, the crashing noises—for comic effect, I suppose—that stage director Cyril Ritchard introduces during that wonderful episode are antithetical to the frozen stupefaction that is the precise point of the ensemble.

Elsewhere, our diva is always mindful of the need to corral her booming chest tones (especially when isolated) and full-blooded top tones (uniformly splendid as they are) into a companionable unity with the bulk of her well-ordered instrument. Also to be guarded against is the slight, almost negligible, megaphone effect that occurs when, conscious of her skill at projection and probably in an excess of zeal, she hardens her tone. For the most part, she is successful in these endeavors on this afternoon. Indeed, my few strictures are trifling in the totality of her achievement. Such skill in cantilena and fioriture must be lauded without prejudice. To hear Horne twirl her delicious roulades around Figaro's cantus firmus in 'Dunque io son' is to experience unalloyed joy. Many other moments during the performance replicate that experience.

La Fille du Règiment
6 January 1973
Marie
Joan Sutherland
Marquise
Regina Resnik
Tonio
Luciano Pavarotti
Sulpice
Fernando Corena
Conductor
Richard Bonynge

Levine's circumspect, informed musicianship and Horne's flamboyant virtuosity provided the radio audience with an afternoon to remember. An event that proved, over time, to be even more memorable was the performance run of *La Fille du Régiment* with Sutherland and Pavarotti that began in 1972 and continued into the following season. As noted earlier, the star pairing was diluted in the 1972 broadcast, but both diva and divo are on hand for the broadcast of 6 January 1973. Bonynge again guides his wife, Corena (Sulpice), and Velis (Hortensius), with Pavarotti (Tonio), Resnik (Marquise), and Kraft (Duchesse of Crakentorp) heard in new broadcast portrayals. The opera had been out of the repertory for three decades when reintroduced in a production borrowed from Covent Garden. Earlier Met outings had utilized either the composer's Italian version (which emasculated the tenor role) or, even when performed in French, a grab bag of ingredients from the original Paris score and the Milan rewrite. This time, the management offered the real thing. With an archaeological zeal for the neglected milieu of French opéra comique and ballet (plus an ever-alert eye to his wife's vocal and comic talents), Bonynge had promoted the original French version at Covent Garden. The production and the husband-wife team came to the Met prepackaged and New York profited from the lend-lease arrangement.

Donizetti's opéra comique, slight of proportions but agreeable in content, would not seem to have the makings of a blockbuster success. Of course, the triumph had more to do with the drivers than the vehicle. Even so, the composer's "fabric of exquisite nothings" (to borrow a Saint-Simon nonoperatic phrase) always refreshes the opera lover's receptive palate.[7] On the broadcast, Bonynge's conducting is dutiful, occasionally limp in orchestral passages, but knowingly supportive of his stage charges. Donizetti (adept at disguise) packed the trio 'Tous les trois réunis' with Gallic wit and charm, but the conductor's reading shortchanges its élan. Beyond the star turns for soprano and tenor, the work offers supporting players little opportunity for solo vocal display. Where Ljuba Welitch had returned for a walk-on as the Duchesse de Crakentorp in the 1972 premiere, Kraft now performs that minuscule task. Fortunately, Corena and Resnik are such experienced theatrical personalities that they distinguish themselves as Sulpice and the Marquise with only adequate assistance from the composer. Corena, on his best behavior musically and vocally, manages his phrases with remarkable adroitness (for a buffo specialist, that is) and plays with admirable discretion in the ensembles. He delivers his 'rataplan's with the pride and assurance of a sergeant fully committed to the 21st Regiment. His Sergeant Sulpice has both heart and comic point (including a wicked mimicry of one of the prima donna's roulades). The bulk of the Marquise's part consists of spoken dialogue, but that limitation can't keep Resnik under wraps. Her portrayal of the silly, snobbish, selfish, but ultimately generous mother manqué is a full and (within the wide latitude the role allows) deft one. Her rich, fruity chest voice is her reliable ally in the solo phrases (including a careful, cagey traversal of her opening *couplets*), and it serves admirably as well to propel her dialogue, the latter delivered with utmost clarity and comic point. Hoots and howls are her principal weapons until, at the opera's denouement, the Marquise confesses to Sulpice that she is Marie's mother. In yet another demonstration of stage-worthy cunning, Resnik ranges in turn from the comic to the sympathetic, on to the serious, even the borderline tragic, before pulling us back into the stage world of the Marquise's garrulous humor—all in the space of a few minutes.

In the leading parts, Sutherland and Pavarotti are simply stupendous. No other word will do. One might note (and it would be ridiculous to do so) that the enormity of their talents all but bursts open the genre's slender framework. The effect is rather like loosing a sleek greyhound and a friendly Saint Bernard onto a playground where only poodles previously have frolicked. Who would want it otherwise? The Met has known few regiment daughters, either *figlia* or *fille*: Sembrich and Hempel played in Italian, while the inimitable Pons showed Marie's true colors. Sutherland's healthy voice and person may make Marie less a mascot than a member of the troop itself. Our diva enjoys that station. For Pons' remembered playful charm (laced with Gallic point), the Australian soprano quite rightly follows her own star and offers a full-scale bel canto assault. She strikes each note with such unfailing accuracy that one suspects she is practicing echolocation, that cryptic gift that enables bats to navigate in the dark. The vocal command (apt word for the opera's military milieu) is complete; her tones are secure in flight and anchored in repose, beautifully colored throughout the entire range. The cantilena is exquisitely fashioned, positing its own brand of wistful charm. I would count her reading of 'Il faut partir' in the first-act finale as the high point of the afternoon, so affecting is her swath of sentiment, so beguiling her conduct of line. That is not to slight the vocal fireworks that she repeatedly sets off with sparkling assurance, glazing the roulades with tonal brilliance to boot. But even in those rapid trajectories, her deft modulations of volume, her subtle transitions of tempo, her touching of brief motives with the lightest of strokes, are cherished as much as the brilliantly executed fioriture, the bewitching trills, the full-voiced high Ds and (in the final 'Salut à la France') clean E-flat *in alt*. Of course, in the lesson scene her parody of coloratura soprano antics is as astonishing as it is laugh-inducing. The audience loves her.

While Marie has always demanded diva treatment, Tonio evidently could be well enough served with stars whose light was less blinding. Thomas Salignac (Sembrich's partner) may have had honorable stature as a creature of the Opéra-Comique, but Fernando Carpi (Hempel's own) was hardly in the race. Pons' Tonio, Raoul Jobin, could cover the entire course—but ultimately was outdistanced by his Marie. (Still, the French Canadian tenor's quality counts with longtime broadcast listeners.) Pavarotti, on the other hand, seems certain to be a winner. Like Horne, he was a member of Sutherland's youthful coterie and had served as her Tonio in the London production. With additional Met performances under his belt, the tenor was comfortable with the role—and it shows. *Fille* marks his broadcast debut, though he had come to the company in 1968 as Rodolfo. Additional appearances as Edgardo and Alfredo followed after an absence during the 1969–70 season. The 1972 *Fille* premiere had gained him enormous publicity as the "tenor of the high Cs"; repute had already reached such proportions that the

Opera News broadcast issue cited him as "one of the great tenors of the century."[8] Though the early anointment seems premature, the broadcast confirms that it was not unwarranted.

Even after decades of acquaintance with his instrument, upon hearing his initial phrases I was startled by its rich, fruity resonance, its tactile density, its radiance, and blazing brilliance of color. The voice's vitality, coupled with the crisp assurance of his phrasing, is immensely invigorating. Perhaps because of the French language (or could it be merely youth profiting from hormonal stimulation?), the timbre is brighter, enjoys a higher resonance than that which future years will certify. He launches the first act duet with an all-conquering beauty of tone and raptness of phrase. That impression is doubly affirmed in the second-act aria ('Pour me rapprocher de Marie'). Here is bel canto of the finest order, the line caressed and unhurried; it is well to remember his savoring of phrase, that interpretative care, when regretting their neglect in the waning years of his career. A slight nod to mezza voce at the reprise is yet another welcome, and later too infrequent, boon. 'Pour mon âme,' with its battery of high Cs, has the essential panache. The pairs of high notes are ticked off firmly and with brilliant tone through the fourth set. The tennis term is not inappropriate, for the tenor knocks out the Cs as accurately as a court star hitting returns to his ball machine. The final held high C is sustained (match confirmed) but is touched by a few of those odd little scratches that will become familiar features of some of his uppermost notes. Pavarotti latches on to the melodic curve of the aria with winning exuberance, a thrusting openheartedness that in time will win the hearts of millions.

At the opera's end, Cross brands him a *tenore robusto*, probably more in tribute to his physique than his vocal endowment. The veteran announcer notes that Pavarotti, "full of fun as he usually is," intends to go on a diet, starting on Monday and finishing on Tuesday. Of more interest, but equally without result (at least at the Met) is the tenor's expressed desire to sing Faust and Don José—so he averred in the *Opera News* interview, noting that he believes audiences would not "accept" him in the costumes of Werther or Des Grieux.[9] (An early La Scala outing in Italian—with Freni as Manon—gives the lie to that assertion.) Concerning the notoriety of his *Fille* high Cs, Pavarotti (again in the broadcast *Opera News* issue) prophetically expressed his desire to be known not as a "tenor of the top," but rather a "tenor of line." That he will be, and gratifyingly so, for decades ahead.

A month later, a more testing assignment awaits this paragon of tenors—the Duke of Mantua in the broadcast *Rigoletto* of 10 February 1973. In contrast to Donizetti, who granted Tonio a clutch of high Cs, Verdi has swathed the entire role of the rake with bravura. As he will in so many Pavarotti ventures, Levine guides the tenor's effort, with Grist, Grillo, Wixell, Macurdy, and Morris in the lineup. Most of the principals are new to the airwaves in these roles (Grillo and Morris appeared in the 1972 broadcast under Levine). Also new to the broadcasts is the voice of Lloyd Moss, who introduces the performance. Faithful Met radio listeners who for forty-one years had heard no other tones than the cultivated ones of Milton Cross suffered shock at his absence, the first in those many decades. His wife had died two days before the broadcast and condolences were proffered.

Having tasted the American conductor's way with relatively early Verdi (*Luisa Miller*), one's expectations are whetted for his *Rigoletto*, a certified masterwork. Though only *Stiffelio* intervened between the two operas, the gain in dramaturgi-

Rigoletto
10 February 1973

Gilda
Reri Grist
Maddalena
Joann Grillo
Duke
Luciano Pavarotti
Rigoletto
Ingvar Wixell
Sparafucile
John Macurdy
Conductor
James Levine

cal power was considerable. Levine takes full advantage of the structural coherence of the opera; indeed, his greatest contribution is a religious adherence to a unifying conception for the entire work. (He retains a few brief cuts in the first act but opens up most of the customary later ones.) One could take exception to certain tempos. They sound slower than we expect, but most often they adhere to the metronome markings; it is the measured tread and consistency of application that create the mirage. His occasionally rigid marking of Verdi's varied accompaniment figures can add to the discrepancy, but there, too, one is appeased by sudden adjustments of weight and shape that suit the music's and text's changing intent. A case in point is the contrast he makes between the father's accompaniment figure for 'Ah! veglia, o donna' and his daughter's 'Quanto affeto, quali cure!'. There, the melody remains the same, but the composer has slightly adjusted the accompaniment figure for Gilda's repeat; Levine, aware of the subtlety, allows the insistent underlay of Rigoletto's tune to morph unobtrusively into a floating cushion for the young girl's song. Overall, his firm hand on the reins invigorates the almost too familiar but ever welcome score. The American's sense of proportion is seldom so controlling that it subjugates his lively theatrical instinct; he invariably applies his foot to the pedal at precisely those moments when Verdi's rhetoric demands forward propulsion. Some moments, particularly in the final two acts, possess unusual vitality; the orchestral playing is vigilant and precise: spic-and-span pizzicatos underlie phrases in Rigoletto's 'Pari siamo,' for instance. Levine's banda music must be the most well-ordered to which any Mantuan court has danced. (I wonder what Verdi would have thought of that immurement—the banda music is casual, everyday stuff.) Even the male chorus is wide awake and alert, limning 'Zitti,zitti' with commendable accuracy and deftness. Is it merely knowledge of what lies ahead for this alliance between conductor and pit colleagues that allows one to hear hints of a Levine sound and manner? "Warmth, integrity, and purpose," according to Raymond Gniewek, concertmaster for much of Levine's tenure, eventually did the trick.[10] He initially had wondered how the young batonist could possess the attributes of a great conductor ("formidable intelligence . . . awesome memory") and yet be "gentle, considerate, and patient," have "an uncanny knack of personal communication," be able to "coax, cajole, inspire" his charges, and yet maintain utmost control while providing "incredible support" in the hard patches. For Gniewek, Levine evidently had all the answers. Clearly, a love affair between conductor and orchestra was in the making.

The male contingent onstage is well stocked with sure-voiced singers. From the old days, only Harvuot is on hand. His Marullo is as steady of tone and skilled at plotting as when he first took on the role in the early fifties. Morris, a relative newcomer, makes a capital Monterone, while Macurdy, rapidly becoming Mr. Reliable at the Met, contributes a novel Sparafucile. He relies on a lazy, almost sleazy legato to convey the villainy of 'un uom di spada'; one can well believe him a man handy with a blade. He gives us a brute of a beast where Verdi's jaunty tune more often has called forth an assassin of menacing elegance.

Making his broadcast debut in the title role is Ingar Wixell, "the toast of Sweden," according to announcer Moss. Now in his early forties, he is a well-seasoned artist. The Swedish Royal Opera had been home base for a dozen years, with outlying visits to Glyndebourne and the Deutsche Opera in Berlin. Frequent performances with the San Francisco Opera since 1967 preceded his Met debut as

Rigoletto a week or two before the broadcast. His company career would not be overlarge in total performances, but his qualifications as a "Verdi baritone" guaranteed prominence over eight seasons. The voice, solid and secure throughout the entire range, is rather a curious one: a mix of a dark lower range with a bright, occasionally almost tenor-touched upper voice. A prominent vibrato lends character (and at times causes consternation). Density it has, but overall its pointed focus prevents it from applying that strenuous assault on Verdi's more theatrical moments that some old-time aficionados prefer. For me, the voice's appeal rests most engagingly in the airy upper range—often it opens up as though ballooned by a fresh, Nordic breeze. His reading of the demanding role is everywhere secure and polished. The interpretation is mainstream. Few musical subtleties inform his phrasing, though he is always correct and intelligent in his play. One looks for a more inviting tone and manner in the father–daughter duet; probably Wixell's Rigoletto has devoted more time to his jester duties at court than to developing an in-depth relationship with his charge at home. Nor is he able to fully convey the horror that Monterone's curse inflicts upon the father. The changing tempers of 'Cortigiani, vil razza dannata' are delineated, but more touched upon than embraced. (Some of the interpolated high notes are eschewed—Levine's dictates?—but a bit of baritonal ego engagingly informs the 'tu taci' transition to 'Miei signori perdono'). Mood setting is not Wixell's forte. What he does offer, however, is an entirely professional reading of a demanding role with a voice of utmost dependability and considerable tonal appeal. In later decades, where a Verdi baritone is a rara avis, he would have been a prize of considerable worth. Even in his own time, he is a decided company asset.

There are sopranos who sing coloratura and there are what are popularly known as coloratura sopranos. Turning from Sutherland's Marie to Grist's Gilda is a move from the prodigious to the Lilliputian. As our heroine trips onto the scene to welcome Rigoletto home, Grist startles with her infantile tones. Even when matched against coloratura voices of the pre-Sutherland vintage, her tones seem excessively small, metallic, even tinny. But, in addition to her piquant stage presence—a commodity regrettably denied the radio devotee—Grist is a bewitching and cunning artist, capable of providing varied sonic grains for the listener's auditory mill. Soon the tone gains its delectable hue, oboe based and silver plated, its purity an invaluable aid to her exemplary conduct of line. She will make us love her, for she works her finely honed needlepoint art with utmost circumspection. (Our Australian diva would more likely be in the employ of weavers of large-scale Renaissance tapestries.) The American's 'Caro nome' is etched with remarkable precision, her tone bell-like, the interpretation hardly exuberant but deployed with a careful, enchanting innocence appropriate to Gilda's nature. The notes are placed with the skill of a dart thrower—and the cadenza's little top flip is on the button. Genuine trills do not seem to figure in her fioritura stock, but a spray of loving portamentos provide compensatory balm. It is good to hear her fluent, accurate tracing of the final upward scale in the 'Addio' cabaletta of her duet with the Duke—so many fine Gildas merely offer a smudge there. She embroiders Rigoletto's cries of 'Piangi' with accents easily and exactly placed. One would think the 'Vendetta' duet would swallow her up, but her knife-edged, concentrated line saves her from the gasps and gulps that even the treasurable Sayão had to rely upon in her infrequent assumptions of the role. At the act's close, Grist's shimmering E-flat *in alt* provides a touch of prima donna shine as Rigoletto rages. 'Tutte le feste al tempio' and 'Lassù in cielo' (both slow-gaited under Levine's tutelage) profit from her straightforward delivery. No simpering allowed.

Allow me to get it over with straight away: I wish Pavarotti would moderate his tonal vibrancy into a lover's mezza voce and better fondle the cantabile curves of 'E il sol dell'anima.' That said, all the rest is glory. (Oh, he makes a late entry—'che importa a te?'—in the lead-in to that duet, causing a momentary mix-up, and a bit of suspect pitch infects the quiet close of the piece. But those are the common property of any live performance.) Everywhere else, the big tenor's performance fairly bursts with assurance. Lusciously colored tone, easy top notes (no high Cs this time, but ringing high Bs and B-flats), expansive phrasing, succulent diction—one could almost dance to the castanet click of his consonants—here is the singer's art in full flower. Best of all, we are allowed to savor his unabashed delight in displaying the fullness of his powers. He communicates an exuberant joy in singing, entirely devoid of that wearying staidness that frequently affected his late-career performances. The Duke's three arias are sheer delight. 'Questa o quella' has a carefree swing, the ornaments neat and the top notes confident. 'Parmi veder le lagrime' is serious business, dramatically and vocally, and Pavarotti knows it. The vocal hurdles are not only vanquished, but enveloped with full, rich tone and meaningful significance. (In the grand recitative preceding the aria, I note again the tendency—a habit that will in late career seriously infect his phrasing—to push on rhythmically where a caress is called for: he fails to observe the dolce marking at 'E dove ora sarà quell'angiol caro?'.) 'La donna è mobile' has made too many tenors sound as though they were being led to the woodshed. It is no punishment for this afternoon's rogue. He tosses it off with utmost ease. The aria's several incarnations all profit from his *leggiero* touch and insouciant manner. He has no fear of the concluding high Bs (well, yes—the attack on number three may be a bit precarious). All four principals deliver the goods in the quartet, but the grand ensemble becomes Pavarotti's ultimate triumph. (Early on, Grillo is sluggish in regard to Levine's whip-crack rhythms, but she becomes efficient in the quartet and is tonally attractive in her avoidance of chesty bellowing, the refuge of many a Maddalena.) The tenor wraps his voice around 'Bella figlia dell'amore' with lip-smacking relish for the Verdi phrase, negotiates the trying *stentato* ascent with aplomb, and affectionately slavers the repeated 'le pene's with self-satisfied portamentos. Surely any girl would feel compelled to 'consolar' his heart's pain. On this afternoon, Pavarotti's vocal mastery and rakish swagger are feel-good rewards for all who care for the singer's art.

A month later management trotted out its other prize tenor for the *Trovatore* broadcast of 17 March 1973. Pavarotti would wait to tackle his Met Manricos until late in his career, but Domingo, younger by five years than his colleague, displayed the intrepidity that will characterize his entire career by assuming the virtuoso role during his baptismal years. (He had sung his first Met Manrico in 1969.) The cast is furnished with vocal wealth: Caballé (Leonora), Cossotto (Azucena), Merrill (Luna). Cossotto's husband, Ivo Vinco, sings Ferrando. On the podium is Carlo Felice Cillario, new to the company in this first Bing-less season. *La Sonnambula*, *Norma*, and *Macbeth* were his early Met charges with *Cav* and *Pag* and *Tosca* to follow *Trovatore*—quite a full plate for the single-season debutant. The Argentine-born maestro was raised in Italy and, after early symphonic experience,

Il Trovatore
17 March 1973

Leonora
Montserrat Caballé
Azucena
Fiorenza Cossotto
Manrico
Plácido Domingo
Di Luna
Robert Merrill
Ferrando
Ivo Vinco
Conductor
Carlo Felice Cillario

conducted opera at Glyndebourne, Covent Garden, La Scala, and Chicago. Now in his late fifties, Cillario has a familiarity with the traditions of Italian opera that is apparent in his sure control over *Trovatore*'s volatile pulse. In fact, his control is occasionally so austere that volatility vanishes, the pulse all but stilled. He can launch one of Verdi's oom-pah accompaniment figures and drive it home with a plebeian insistence that denies a reassuring lift to a singer's expressive purpose. The straightjacket rhythms do enhance 'Di quella pira's square syntax, but on at least one occasion the orchestral underpinning sounds like a threshing machine. *Trovatore* is hardly a conductor's vehicle, but a podium occupant can choose to emphasize either its brute vigor or (the opportunity is seldom taken) its classical elegance. Cillario drives through the opera as though at the wheel of a Chevy pickup rather than a sleek Ferrari.

Vinco, in the fourth season of a brief tenure with the company, is the low man on this performance's totem pole. He is a journeyman bass. His Ferrando does have the virtue of sounding more like an old soldier than many of the legion of interpreters of the role. The smell of the barracks dwells in his delivery. And Verdi's rhythmical gyrations are accurately rendered. Merrill, of course, is such an old hand at Luna's villainy (seventy-three portrayals will be his Met tally) that even though age's tendrils threaten to choke his magnificent organ, they cannot depress his confident stage manner. Woolly tones, thickened by time, indeed are what he offers the unresponsive Leonora in her palace gardens. Not unexpectedly, on this afternoon he is no match for the bel canto suavity of 'Il balen del suo sorriso,' even when pitched down a half-step. A firm top tone and an influx of tonal warmth in the cadenza save the day for him. Thereafter, the voice begins to take on more than a touch of the luxuriant roundness, the inimitable Merrill plushness, remembered from his better days. Cillario unexpectedly makes a lively thing of 'Vivra! Contende il giubilo' and, as if in anticipation of Leonora's surrender, the baritone comes to life as well. This is Merrill's 501st Met performance and Cross tells us that only six other principal artists in the company's ninety-year history are members of the exclusive five hundred club: Caruso, De Luca, Martinelli, Scotti, Pinza, and, as ornament to that Italian quintet, an American beauty rose, Geraldine Farrar.

The reverse side of the age coin is heads up for Domingo. At thirty-two, he is enjoying all the blessings of tenorial youth and, more to the point, putting them to good use. I doubt that Manrico is quite his meat, however. With all the vocal wealth at his disposal, one hoped to hear the offstage serenade for once enveloped with a lover's grace. But even this troubadour's aural billet-doux is as businesslike as those most tenors are able to offer in this introductory trial; the notes are all there, though, and the vocal color carries its own welcome message. A certain not unattractive earnestness can permeate Domingo's interpretations. It does on this afternoon—he knows so well what he wants to do and sometimes allows us to hear his intent. Manrico is a challenge for even the most well-endowed tenor. The Spaniard's spinto voice provides a fertile middle ground from which to conquer the opposing testing episodes of the role—its lyrical line and its thrusting robustness. 'Mal reggendo' is phrased with musical forthrightness and as straightforwardly declaimed as any troubled mother has a right to expect from a dutiful son (though the relationship proves more than tenuous). The ultimate in expressive suavity may not be summoned, but these are worthy tenor wares.

Domingo is in top form for the third-act double-threat arias. 'Ah! sì, ben mio' provides a splendid display of his manifold virtues: vibrant tone, eloquence, carefully rounded phrases, artful technical manipulation of the tessitura, and acute diction with tonal colors varied according to textual promptings. Perhaps the voice's most valuable asset is a caressing warmth in the middle range; his instrument gains a taut, sometimes hard-edged, brilliance on the topmost notes—at this stage of his career, they are potent and secure, though a modicum of effort can peep through the compact tone. The tenor's musical rectitude is affirmed in his quiet modeling of Manrico's part in the little duet with Leonora. Few tenors can so effectively sustain a dulcet mezza voce in those encircling final phrases (a similar softness enhances the conclusion of the fourth-act trio with the dying Leonora and drowsy gypsy). Like many a colleague, he takes 'Di quella pira' down a half-step. Success is thereby ensured. Lacking a *robusto*'s vocal size and thrust, our tenor injects sufficient vitality into his effort by pinpoint rhythmic sounding of the rapid sixteenth motive; in contrast, he introduces variety (a subtlety most tenors neglect) by applying a color and mood change to the brief midsection. All tenors put their reputations on the line when attempting the interpolated high notes near the act's end. Domingo hooks on to a wonderfully clean, firm high B at the curtain (followed by the briefest sounding of the final syllable). The top B in the earlier solo rendition is firmly taken, but one hears a bit of throat roughage in its continuance. His denunciation of Leonora's supposed betrayal is overtly dramatic and well laid out. In itself, the reading is highly effective, but memory insists that the episode's tragic grandeur is a bit shortchanged. There his middle-ground instrument betrays its limits. I like better his velvety sounding of 'Riposa, o madre,' where he exploits the several colors of his lovely voice to intoxicating effect. When Domingo sheds his earnestness and relaxes his vocal production, he can be as cherishable—indeed he is—and as estimable as any tenor the world over. Taken all in all, a middle-ground Manrico may be more listener friendly than one playing at only one extreme.

By the seventies, Cossotto was enthroned as the premiere Verdi mezzo of her generation. On this afternoon, she gives a performance worthy of her status and reputation. The Italian mezzo owns in abundance the outsized vocal and dramatic attributes that the role of Azucena demands, namely, thrusting top tones, a flamboyant chest voice, a reliable (and quite lovely) mid-range where the bulk of the gypsy's narratives lies, and—the intangible that binds the components into a stageworthy whole—an exuberant temperament. In sheer density of tone, her instrument may not be as wide or deep as those of a few grand interpreters of this pivotal role, but she has compensatory attributes. Most notable of these is her fine-grained artistry, a musicality that adds subtlety to her phrasing and architectural backbone to her plotting of a set piece. Her interpretations are buttressed by a judiciousness that enables her to tread the fine line between the telling gesture and vulgar display without ever straying into the latter domain. Azucena is a great storyteller and Cossotto's aptitude for narration makes the mother's accounts of past wrongs and present longings mesmerizing. She draws one into the gypsy's plight with uncommon urgency. The terrors of 'Condotta ell'era in ceppi' are so vividly rendered that one literally participates in the character's dementia. Vocal stamina is yet another valuable aid. The high B-flat at the narrative's climax resounds bravely and, as she recounts thrusting her own son into the flames, she pounds out the marcato 'il figlio mio's with extraordinary intensity. Immediately thereafter, she honors Verdi's 'morendo' close with a discreet blending of head voice into her firm chest tones. To maintain one's vocal poise throughout this dramatically wrenching role is no uncommon feat. Azucena's introspective moments receive equal care. Maternal tenderness infects Cossotto's lovingly traced 'Giorni poveri vivea.' Pathos is given tongue (and here Cillario shapes phrases with equal nicety). 'Ai nostri monti,' too, receives the honest simplicity that it merits from Cossotto's pliant throat and responsive heart.

Caballé is, of course, water from a different well. (I wanted to write "a different kettle of fish" but prima donnas won't suffer an ichthyoidal comparison.) Her art is so individualistic, her vocalism so ethereally poised, her interpretive stance so novel, that she must be considered a law unto herself. Her bel canto stamp on a role almost invariably works to her advantage and most often to ours. (Occasionally, neither party is well—or at least fully—served.) What point is there in decrying the banishment of text at the peak of high-ranging phrases! Why bewail her tendency to enfold phrase after phrase in a moony dynamic so that even God might need a hearing aid to enjoy its heavenly glow! Better to bathe in the celestial beauty of her tone and revel in the fluid subtlety of her phrasing. With all her idiosyncrasies, she is as beguiling a singer as ever trod the Met boards. Not that the Verdi milieu allows her the best canvas for displaying her greatness. Some steel à la Cigna, some purple plushness of tone in the Milanov manner, are invaluable aids to a Verdi soprano if she values character creation as well as vocal supremacy. Yet Caballé does present us with a character of a sort, that of a Spanish aristocrat who exists apart from the outside world and is most alive when musing rhapsodically; for this Leonora to show up outside Manrico's prison tower and bewail his fate, or to even own a poison ring, wrenches the imagination. The soprano's grainy chest voice, which surfaces in the Miserere, startles and further augments the oddity of her situation. It must be said, however, that Caballe's *forte* tones in the higher range (when she chooses, in however niggardly a fashion, to deploy them) are round and firm, without a shred of harshness, and thus beautiful to hear. They add just enough punch to key dramatic moments to prevent somnolence.

Of specific rewards, Caballé offers many. 'Tacea la notte' is floated with impeccable ease. With subtle discretion, she honors both the *espansione* and *animato* of Verdi's marking at 'dolci s'udiro e flebile gli accordi d'un liuto,' before deliciously relaxing the descending curve of the two phrases. (The effect calls to mind a performance of *Les Sylphides* that I witnessed in the 1950s; as a Chopin nocturne sounded, Alicia Markova was wafted aloft by her partner and, face and body full forward, glided on high with absolute stillness and grand extension across the length of the stage. It was, for me, an unforgettable instance of time suspended.) The soprano attempts no high D-flat in her cadenza (C is the apex there) but concludes the first-act trio with that note. Trills are not always honored, but the tiny cackling motives of the cabaletta are chortled with absolute self-possession—most sopranos sound like shrews at that point. And she whips around the few curls of coloratura with the facility of a ballerina. Perhaps it is the weary women's chorus at the convent that causes her to apply the shyest, pencil-thin purl of tone to the forlorn heroine's little *arioso*—a bit more tonal bloom would be welcome. She knows how to make musical sense of Leonora's splintered phrases when Manrico arrives: 'e deggio e posso crederlo?' is artfully molded. The long-limbed phrase

Fiorenza Cossotto as Adalgisa and Montserrat Caballé as Norma in *Norma*. Photography by Louis Mélançon. Courtesy Metropolitan Opera Archives.

that crowns her happiness is equally assured. In the recitative to 'D'amor sull'ali rosee' and in the aria itself, Caballé sends along several lengthy phrases (normally broken into separate units) in a continuous train of silken tone—the result is quite breathtaking. (Here perhaps an avian image may be permitted. The breathing system of birds is extremely efficient: it's a one-way process, since the lungs refill even as a bird exhales. Caballé is a true songbird.) In spite of previous dispensations, I must regret her failure to articulate a few 'le pene's—those words must sound if Leonora's emotional pain is to be conveyed. But everywhere vocal beauties abound: exquisite portamentos; a *pianissimo* high C as she rounds the curve of a final phrase; the grand *forte* B-flat that launches a gliding descending scale in the cadenza; a concluding feathery trill leading to a tenaciously held (and increasingly pallid) tonic note. The touches of self-indulgence only affirm that we have been granted the rare pleasure of hearing a soprano from another century, from an age when prima donna whims were treasured as imaginative bounties, not as transgressions to be decried. In the duet with Luna, Caballé flies over the tricky little flourishes and, unlike some sopranos, maintains her dignity while doing so. Before the curtain's fall, the soprano's seemingly endless top note diminishes to nothingness as death comes to Leonora—an imaginative detail we can prize not only for its indulgence but, more importantly, for its truth.

Norma
17 February 1973

Norma
Montserrat Caballé
Adalgisa
Fiorenza Cossotto
Pollione
Carlo Cossutta
Oreveso
Giorgio Tozzi
Conductor
Carlo Felice Cillario

The vocal riches that Caballé and Cossotto lavished upon *Trovatore* had been applied with similar generosity a month earlier to Bellini's *Norma*. On the broadcast of 17 February 1973, Cillario again is on the podium with Tozzi lending support as Oroveso and Carlo Cossutta making his Met debut as Pollione. The seasonal premiere of the opera had gained press encomiums that rivaled the extravagant praise for the 1970 production premiere with Sutherland and Horne. Over the Met's history, management had been reluctant to mount the opera, for its challenges were formidable. But the seventies held more than a single first-string slate willing and able to contest in the hallowed precincts of Bellini's masterwork.

Maestro Cillario is more impressive on this afternoon than in his *Trovatore* effort. The overture is merely workmanlike in a sprightly way, but his orderly tread prefigures the gathering of the Druids. He loves to foment orchestral excitement and never inhibits, indeed encourages, the stage drama to flame at critical points. When a square tune, orchestral or vocal, comes along, he has a tendency to force its angular contours into rhythmic lockstep. He applies a slow crawl rather than a tidal surge to the celebrated double climaxes of the fourth-act finale—the elongation is more than Bellini's inspired buildup needs. But he grasps and, significantly, realizes in performance the architectural scope of the entire act, thereby granting the composer's imposing conception the honor it merits. (I adhere to the Met's four-act format, though Bellini intended two.)

Cossutta had been scheduled to make his debut in the premiere but canceled in favor of Alexander. No signs of indisposition are evident in his robust handling of Pollione's forthright music. Now in his fiftieth year, the Italian-born, Argentine-raised tenor was a late starter in the international arena. After early Teatro Colon outings in Buenos Aires, he was welcomed by the Chicago Lyric Opera in 1963; Covent Garden embraced him beginning in 1964, and the Deutsche Oper of Berlin and Vienna Staatsoper required his services as well. Dramatic tenors are a sufficiently rare quantity that any qualifier will be received with gratitude by managements. Cossutta qualified, but the managerial welcome proved to be perfunctory. After his single-role seasonal duties, the tenor returned to the European arena, revisiting America for another season of Polliones a half dozen years down the road. Taken on its own terms, the voice has merit. The lower range possesses baritonal heft and the upper voice (at least in the limited employment that Bellini allowed the aging Donzelli of the 1831 La Scala premiere) takes on a timbral brightness that can be exciting when the vibrato—nay, a suspect bleat—does not blemish it. He can trumpet a decent *squillo*, but, like most of his breed, he so loves the *forte* dynamic that none other commands his interest. The hint of a sob (it may be a tiny gargle) is part of the voice's makeup. The instrument is stout and its usage blunt. Yet a Roman proconsul, and one who treats women as his by right, is well enough served by Cossutta's talents. After all, a militant vocal stance comes naturally to opera's military men. 'Meco all'altar di Venere' receives a governmental stamp rather than a lover's endearment (and at best a modest amount of the deceitful lover's fear of Norma's vengeance), but the introductory recitative is delivered with commendable authority and better reveals his quality. Top notes are generally firm. Surprisingly, any little fioritura bits are cleanly dispatched. And in the fourth act, the tenor's vocal delivery and interpretive response are considerably more affecting than the earlier acts had proclaimed. His manly delivery, the voice's impressive tonal density, and its timbral richness in the mid-voice augment the crushing impact of the opera's concluding scenes. Tozzi, riding a vocal seesaw from performance to performance, is in good late-career form. He attempts to counterfeit the terrible aura of Oroveso's priestly calling, but does not quite succeed. His vocalism is entirely acceptable but ideally—that is, if the opera is not to be entirely ceded to the ladies—the role requires a more imposing vocal organ than the American bass now owns. As for the ladies, even Carlotta Ordassy's Clotilde makes a positive contribution.

Just as Norma and Adalgisa work out their differences and achieve mutual regard, our contending divas, Caballé and Cossotto, prove to be vocally friendly. In their *Trovatore* outing, the aristocrat and gypsy inhabited different realms, so the two artists' stylistic affinity and comparable vocal mastery were seldom in tandem. Also, in *Norma* Bellini and Romani dictated a role reversal for the two prima donnas. Thus Verdi's vengeful hag takes on a young girl's demeanor while the introspective Leonora becomes "a raging tigress" (to quote the words of Rosa Ponselle, whose 1954 interview concerning her Norma outings is repeated on this broadcast afternoon).[11] As Adalgisa, Cossotto's artistic integrity is evident in each phrase she utters, for she abandons every shred of Verdi's thrusting vocal gestures, of verismo gustiness, those endearing qualities that have made her the gallery's own. (One justifiable chesty descent is her only homage to her formidable patrimony.) Fortunately, in the process, her voice's tangy color is not suppressed nor its plangency blunted. But the tonal circumference is appropriately narrowed and its potency more sparingly applied. A few debits may be assigned, the most important her neglect of Bellini's prescribed *messa di voce* at 'Io l'obbliai'; she offers in its place merely volume, whereas the more seductive vocal effect would have set in flow the emotional current of the young girl's act-one duet with Pollione. But everywhere one hears in her recitatives and duets the concentrated mind, the intent to mold phrases of import, to reveal a character in conflict. Her mastery of the role's considerable demands, in particular its extensive fioriture, is impressive.

In terms of role reversal, Miss Caballé's achievement is even more remarkable. First off, let it be noted that the deity can put away his ear trumpet. One wonders if it was character definition or (unlikely as it seems) vocal predisposition that caused the soprano to treat Leonora with such circumspection as regards dynamic range and vocal emphases. Of course, Norma is a goddess capable of waging war as well as a warm-blooded woman engaged in an illicit love affair. Reticence is no part of her character. The soprano responds in kind, singing for the most part with full-throated splendor throughout the long afternoon. She is in glorious vocal form, her high *fortes* grand, free of harshness, and allied intrinsically with the totality of her instrument. At the premiere on the Monday previous to the broadcast, she evidently had pitch problems with 'Casta diva' and suffered accordingly in the press reviews. (In an interview at the time of the *Trovatore* broadcast, she acknowledged that she had not sung the aria "well," adding that "the Met means very much to me. . . . I have a special emotion here that I don't feel at other theaters," a regard that affected her singing and caused her legs to "tremble."[12]) On the broadcast she does sing the aria well, in the customary downward transposition. With only a minuscule exception, her pitch is well tuned. Perhaps with a mind to the long afternoon's demands, she performs the aria with a tone chaste enough to satisfy even the goddess of the moon she addresses. One senses a bit of constraint, a need for redemption, in her careful treatment of the long-breathed phrases and her quick sounding of their subtle ornaments. Is her concern more to emerge unscathed rather than to fully capture the evocative mystery of this famous episode? A curiosity is her treatment of the syncopated (at least, in most editions) repeated high As; she enters on the beat of the third one, not only negating the syncope, but lessening the impact of the phrase climax. Her soprano hydroplanes over the fioriture here and in the vibrantly sung cabaletta, lightly touching the notes with liquid tone, the surface flight skillfully negotiated; their expressive intent has been more apparent in other interpretations, but their ethereal beauty invokes a poetic aura of its own. The ordeal behind her, Caballé thereafter performs with considerable abandon and convincing dramatic projection. The fioriture are tonally lovely, reassuringly accurate, and mesmerizingly fleet. In the opera's later episodes, several high Cs, impressively reached within a phrase's lengthy contour, are resoundingly struck to grand effect.

The duets of the two priestesses, pivotal in any successful performance of the opera, are marvels of sensitive collaboration. Not only do Caballé's and Cossotto's minds and voices work as one, but the results, entirely eloquent, seem more natural, more the issue of deeply felt emotions than did the magnificent, but slightly more mechanized, vocalism of their immediate predecessors in these parts. (The act-two duet is performed in the higher key, the more familiar third-act episode down a step, as usual.) Cossotto's timbre is heart-piercingly touching in her confession to Norma of her love for Pollione, while, in response, Caballé moves from affection to anger to acceptance with a vocal actress's application of mood-dictated vocal colors. (That brief, but telling utterance, 'Oh rimembranza,' however, emerges from Caballé's throat as merely a mellifluous, discreet recollection rather than a release of emotions deep and divided.) The soprano's voice holds more colors than the mezzo's—the mournful plaint of her timbre is particularly affecting as Norma contemplates murdering her children. (On the other hand, the damning—only as inappropriate to Norma—epithet of "pretty" that Caballé's instrument might suggest cannot be laid upon her colleague's more pungent instrument.) As Norma awaits Adalgisa at the opening of the third act, she alternates between noble utterance and flaming rage; Caballé captures both emotions, playing with an overtly dramatic fervor than I had not imagined was within her ken. Cossotto's 'Mira, o Norma' is deliciously lemon-tinted in timbre and sensitively phrased (the plea aspect not overdone) while Caballé's sweeter fruit is applied to her portion with equally felicitous results. With exquisite delicacy the two artists signal the return of the cabaletta's tune by landing with hummingbird weight on its initial notes—any hint of vulgarity is assiduously avoided. The fioriture roll lightly out of their throats. (Some rightfully may miss the gutsy swagger of the old Milanov/Harshaw effort of the 1940s.) When, as the duet progresses, the two artists engage in that jolly volley of phrase repetitions, their give-and-take is refreshingly clean and clear.

Any Norma lives or dies by the quality of her emotional and vocal response to the demands of the final act. Caballé rises magisterially to the challenge. Her vocalism is entirely assured in these episodes. A particularly spectacular moment occurs when, expecting that Pollione will return to her, the soprano lofts a wide-ranging melisma in an uninterrupted sweep of full-voiced, radiant tone. In the final confrontation with her unrepentant lover, she deploys a healthy chest voice devoid of its customary guttural overlay. There too, the overall richness of her mid and low voice is quite unexpected and, of greater moment, it proves capable of encompassing both Norma's hurt and anger. The soprano spends her vocal capital with unwonted abandon in the climactic moments of the opera, offering some of the most vibrant singing to be heard from the Met stage in many a year. If she cannot quite make us weep at Norma's 'Qual cor tradisti' as some artists have, the vocal delineation is expert and 'Deh non volerli vittime' has the requisite punch. She opens her heart as Norma asks her father to care for her children. One only regrets that she could not have summoned the same confident, involved manner for 'Casta diva' (I grant that few Normas could equal her reading of that test piece). Even so, her Norma ranks as one of the grander achievements of broadcast history. Normally, one savors a Caballé performance not so much for its illuminating detail but for the overall poise and beauty of her vocalism. She offers more than that on this afternoon.

The bel canto realm holds challenges of a less commanding order than Norma. Still, Donizetti's Lucia is no small change even for sopranos with a solid florid technique. Unlike its limited tally of Normas, the Metropolitan chronicle contains a reassuring number of triumphant brides of Lammermoor. Madame Sembrich had played her during the Met's first season. In 1892, after the hiatus caused by the German seasons, Patti (with her own troop) came, conquered, and went away. Then the line quickened with Melba, Tetrazzini, Hempel, Barrientos, and Galli-Curci leading the parade. A few anomalies (Ellen Beach Yaw, Josephine Antoine) intruded now and then. After the multiplicity of glories earlier in the century, new Lucias took to the airwaves but broadcast brides have not been overly numerous: Pons (who had a corner on the market for a quarter of a century), Munsel, Callas, Peters, Sutherland, and Moffo. Renata Scotto, who a decade later will be an aspiring Norma, picks up the gauntlet on the broadcast of 21 April 1973. Molinari-Pradelli is on hand to guide her, Alexander, Sereni, and Plishka.

Molinari-Pradelli's view of the opera is rather more somber than that of most Italian baton wielders. The firmly sculpted introductory measures sound his credo for the afternoon, foretelling the architectural scope that he will apply to the entire score. The dramatic content of the opera (as opposed to the dominance

Lucia di Lammermoor
21 April 1973
Lucia
Renata Scotto
Edgardo
John Alexander
Ashton
Mario Sereni
Raimondo
Paul Plishka
Conductor
Francesco Molinari-
Pradelli

of singers' display, so prominent earlier in the century) is enhanced, a propensity that plays into Scotto's hands. Not all of his stage cohorts have fully absorbed the conductor's purpose, however. Imprecise, weak-kneed choral work (and a few of Scotto's individualistic phrases) lessen ensemble unanimity.

Three stalwart male voices not only add to the afternoon's vocal avoirdupois but strengthen Molinari-Pradelli's concept of the opera. The conductor's unhurried tempos allow Sereni to depict a Henry Ashton of greater substance than often met. A certain unexpected status accrues to Enrico in Sereni's full-blown but unhectored traversal of 'Cruda funeste' and its brief cabaletta. MacWherter, whose stout tenor proclaims him a liege as worthy as any Scottish laird could command, provides a strong assist. The baritone, having relished his moment in the spotlight, plays in a subdued, rather considerate, call it brotherly, fashion when promoting his sister's marriage with Bucklaw. Even when threatening her with the prospect of financial ruin for the Ravenswood house should she refuse to comply, he remains circumspect. Goeke's attractive lyric tenor makes the prospective bridegroom a man whom Lucia might actually have found congenial, if her inclinations were not so firmly fixed elsewhere. Plishka offers the most consistently assured vocalism of the afternoon. The voice, solid and attractive in tone, is alive to character as well. (In that regard, his mimicking of Lucia's words in an otherwise top-drawer 'Dalle stanze' is over the top, however.) The American bass' assets are more than enough for the brief duties Donizetti allowed Lucia's tutor cum chaplain. A fine instrument, musicality, alert intelligence that doesn't get in the way of communication—these are gifts worth nourishing, as Plishka will do over the decades.

Alexander had "stepped in at the last moment" for the scheduled Kónya (the intelligence comes from Cross at the opera's end) but one would never suspect the hasty substitution from his focused clarion tones as he bounds into the Ravenswood gardens. The American is the quintessential Boy Scout tenor—"be prepared" seems to have been his lifelong motto, as I have reason to suspect from personal acquaintance (including a long series of Edgardos in Central City). A decade's membership in the Met company has certified his reliability and, beyond that, augmented his natural assurance of manner. His Edgardo is interpretively emphatic and vocally potent. On this afternoon, his mentholated tone is more attractive than on some occasions, almost devoid of the nasality that can mitigate pleasure, and brilliant in the upper range. Indeed, unlike many a Met tenor before him, he sings the trying arias of the last act in the original key and does not falter when negotiating them. 'Fra poco a me ricovero' is deficient in line and overly accented but 'Tu che a Dio spiegasti l'ali,' taken at a slow tempo, is broadly limned with the requisite arch of phrase. He proves his mettle by handling the double ascent of the 'bell'alma' phrases with the assurance of a skyscraper wall-climber. The American tenor is nothing if not energetic both in his vocalism and stage manner. His way may not be the ideal posture for a bel canto opera, but Edgardo's early scenes are full of fustian, enough to make our tenor's assault on Donizetti's music plausible. When first coming upon Lucia at the Ravenswood tomb, Edgardo's thoughts are entirely on revenge, and Alexander's 'sangue's threaten convincingly. When modulating his tone for 'Verranno a te,' the effort causes a feel of vocal strangulation. If his launching of the sextet is oddly a bit undersized, his 'Maledetto's again confirm that action is his appropriate sphere of activity. This tenor deserves to come off the bench and often has for broadcast outings.

Miss Scotto, although she seems game enough for anything, does not attempt the harp solo that at least one nineteenth-century Lucia performed herself. But her deliciously idiosyncratic bride of Lammermoor is, at the least, intrepid and, in the aggregate, sui generis. By this time, Met audiences had heard her Butterfly (debut), Lucia, Adina, Violetta, Gilda, and Marguerite, with Amina and Mimì added during the current season. The predominance of bel canto roles (though it was her natural habitat) is surprising in view of her Phaeton-like immersion in the dramatic soprano repertory in later years. But the path to that end is prefigured in her approach to Lucia. Writing in her 1984 autobiography, Scotto proclaimed that she felt compelled to abjure "tradition" in the bel canto repertory in order to sing "the way that felt honest, satisfying."[13] She deemed the bel canto heroines to be "figures of flesh and blood" and that in portraying them "the drama and the music are inseparable." Undoubtedly our diva is an artist who recognizes the seriousness of her calling. Her hallmark qualities—thorough study of her roles and command in their realization on stage—are everywhere apparent in her portrayal of Lucia. Not a single phrase shape has not been predetermined, bent to her will; not even the placement and color of a single note is left to chance. The fruits of her diligence ripen in performance because of her complete immersion in a role. Willful she may be in interpretive matters, but assured and meaningful her song and phrasing always are. One may—and should—question the logic of her modification of dynamics within a phrase where neither text nor musical context prescribes change. Yet the phrase shapes, often uttered with the utmost delicacy of tone and manner, are savory entities in themselves and, in moments of high emotion, dramatically effective as well. Unlike many Lucias, who regard the fountain narrative as a mere entrance aria convention, Scotto summons genuine horror as she narrates Lucia's recall of an earlier Lammermoor maiden who was murdered by her Ravenswood lover. There (and in 'Quando, rapito in estasi,' as well as in isolated moments later in the opera) her fioriture can be a bit sketchy, skittering where greater note delineation is desirable. But the girl's ghost is made visible. Are those four usually decorative flip-ups to brief top tones (coloratura sopranos have delighted in the gesture) intended by Scotto to be cries of pain? They sound decidedly strange. An odd feature of the cabaletta is her treatment of the opening phrase, where the note separation and quick anticipation of the top note are intended to sound a change of mood and convey the girl's belief in her lover's constancy; Scotto's evenhanded way is restrained and less than joyful. Perhaps the fervency of the lead-in dramatic recitatives, where the diva is marvelously involved, prescribed the ensuing caution. Or is it a subtle early sounding of Lucia's instability? I wouldn't put it past her.

The voice is in prime condition and responds to her bidding. One of her most valuable resources is the ability to match the mournful cast of her tone with the plaintive timbres of the wind instruments. The oboe is her soulmate, as she proves in the subdued second-act interchange with Ashton. Everywhere she is mistress of tonal chiaroscuro, the kind of shading practiced by the old Italian painters. Her métier is the world of Caravaggio's "tenebrism," the employment of stark, realistic contrasts between light and dark hues, in preference to the more modulated tints of earlier Renaissance masters (or, in the diva's case, the more equiponderant art of her sister sopranos). With Scotto, the caveat about notes *in alt* must be repeated—they will not invariably be easily taken or easy on the ears. Occasionally one of her high notes is wiry enough to clear out an auditor's sinuses, if one had need of such a remedy. For the most part they are agreeable, often far more than that. Indeed, at moderate volume they hold a collected density that converts their suggestive colors into dramatic weapons. This diva's tracing of Lucy's madness is markedly introspective. Here Scotto's attractive, multifaceted tones are sometimes diamond-edged but more often fragile (which paradoxically can make them either delicate or intense). How lovingly she takes up 'Alfin son tua,' as though living in a dream world. The lengthy cadenza with flute is handily negotiated with firm staccatos and accurate traceries. Once again, the caveat. Alas, Scotto must resort to subterfuge to bring off the pair of high E-flats of the mad scene—if the world were not so insistent on hearing them, it would be well for her to forgo them. The first, extremely brief, ends in a howl, and the second is thin and tenuously held until she indulges in a slow glide down an octave—I imagine the ungainly effect is allied with Lucia's stage collapse. Earlier in the afternoon, the various high Ds are well negotiated and decidedly worth hearing.

All artists, if wise in the ways of their instruments and their art, attempt to convert weaknesses, vocal or interpretive, into assets. Scotto succeeds better than most in the transformation. Even when her tone all but disappears into the ether or startles with a sinewy harshness, it speaks. Scotto commands you to listen, to side with her, to experience the heroine's woes, her struggles, her joys. Idiosyncratic, even mannered—yes. But alive.

A decade down the road Scotto will take up the challenge of Lady Macbeth. That intransigent queen will require perhaps more skill at remaking a role in one's own image than even she commands. In the meantime, no such effort will be attempted by Martina Arroyo on the 3 February 1973 broadcast of *Macbeth*. Milnes will be her put-upon consort, with Franco Tagliavini (Macduff) and Ruggero Raimondi (the unfortunate Banquo) as opposing forces. Molinari-Pradelli's baton continues to wave in a Scottish orbit.

Metropolitan audiences owed their acquaintance with Verdi's early triumph to Bing's fostering of the composer's neglected progeny throughout the manager's long tenure. The opera was first heard at the Met in 1959 in the Caspar Neher/Carl Ebert re-creation of their famous 1930s Berlin production. At the time of the Met premiere, the New York press was divided in its evaluation of the production's merits (Kolodin deplored it as a "revival of a revival").[14] Bing stuck to his guns, repeatedly offering the opera (including four broadcasts) until 1964. Then it faded from the repertory. (A single 1967 performance at Newport, Rhode Island, featuring Bumbry and Paskalis was not staged.) When his successors revived the opera during the 1972–73 season, they determined that the Neher/Ebert effort was ill suited to their public and provided a drastic face-lift. Retaining only the basic set conformations, Neil Peter Jampolis used projections to alter the production design, while Bodo Igesz, gifted with a fresh cast, performed surgical repairs on the stage action. Except for a few notable exceptions in the final act, Verdi's 1865 Paris revision of the original 1847 Florence premiere was utilized.

One might expect that Molinari-Pradelli's imprint on the score would be more idiomatic than those of Leinsdorf and Rosenstock (Santi had led the last broadcast). His approach, while suitably well informed and expertly controlled, is markedly contained, almost classical in its architectural propriety. Horror is downplayed and musical brutality shunned. His witches sing, rather than cackle,

Macbeth
3 February 1973

Lady Macbeth
Martina Arroyo
Macduff
Franco Tagliavini
Macbeth
Sherrill Milnes
Banquo
Ruggero Raimondi
Conductor
Francesco Molinari-
Pradelli

Sherrill Milnes as Macbeth and Martina Arroyo as Lady Macbeth in *Macbeth*. Photography by Louis Mélançon. Courtesy Metropolitan Opera Archives.

which may be a blessing. Verdi's graphic gestures are sometimes converted into abstract symbols (again, not necessarily a bad thing). Add to Molinari-Pradelli's circumspect direction Arroyo's well-behaved Lady Macbeth and the opera's face has not only been lifted, but scrubbed clean.

The performance has definite assets. The apparitions are potent elements in the drama (Verdi saw to that), while Ordassy's Lady-in-Waiting and Karlsrud's Physician are solid participants (too solid, perhaps, for they sing rather than whisper their commentary in the sleepwalking scene). MacWherter (Malcolm) reaffirms his status as the Met's most muscular comprimario—decibels, rather than barbells, are his tools. Two first-rank Italian artists lend distinction in major, if brief, roles—brief, but important to Verdi, who prior to the opera's 1847 premiere, adjured the Florence impresario to "take particular pains" in casting the role of Macduff.[15] Franco Tagliavini's collected tenor is hardly the dulcet instrument that Ferruccio (of the same surname) lofted in his palmy days. It has its own suntanned Italianate appeal, however, and a clean, compact focus. His discreet harmonizing in the unaccompanied quartet that introduces the act-one *concertato* (an expert realization by all concerned) is particularly noteworthy—few tenors could be so accomplished at ensemble blending or would be so self-effacing. He preserves the musical integrity of 'Ah, la paterna mano,' touching its contours here and there with only minuscule tears, preferring prudent conduct of line over overt emotionalism. Neither he nor Raimondi will become Met regulars over the decades, but the basso's return visits, as well as his international status, will be the greater. Like Macduff, Banquo has limited opportunities for vocal display. But the bass' timbre carries within its substantial weight an inherent sobriety, a suggestive *misterioso* shroud that lends a hint, unsummoned, of menace, more glamorous than threatening, to his characterizations. In 'Due vaticini,' the offbeat duettino with Macbeth, Raimondi's collected bass contrasts effectively with Milnes' juicier instrument. Later in the act, Raimondi's briefest pronouncements have impact as he reacts to the murder of Duncan. When song finally becomes his allotment, 'Come dal ciel precipita' rolls off his lips with ease and import, the scent of evil evoked by its measured tread swelled by the singer's timbral suggestiveness.

Miss Arroyo, accomplished singer but sedate interpreter that she is, seems an odd choice for the bloodthirsty Lady Macbeth. Never mind Verdi's oft-quoted (and overvalued) preference for the ugly rather than the beautiful in the person and voice of his Scottish queen. Skill in acting with the voice is the essential element. (Rysanek had that, no matter how stunningly beautiful her upper voice; then too, Verdi's prescribed hollowness was often patent in the Austrian soprano's lower tones.) As a singing actress, Arroyo inevitably falls short. Her efforts at demonic rage and insinuating evil are dutiful but merely well-coached accents appliquéd to the moment. The vocal acrobatics of the role are readily overcome ('Vieni! t'affretta!' and the drinking song are technically secure) and tonally she has some glorious moments. The size of her instrument is welcome for she is able to surmount ensemble turmoil, often to thrilling effect—a case in point is her valiant high D-flat as the act-one curtain falls. Her repeated upward scale thrusts in the act-two *concertato* are splendid. Whenever the voice ascends into its shining upper octave it fairly blooms with radiant color as the singer revels in her technical security; regrettably, at each flowering of tone the queen's character dissolves into a luscious sound world remote from Verdi's (and Shakespeare's) malefic creation. 'La luce langue' suffers in that regard—horror and impetus are wanting. The soprano doesn't comprehend or is unable to execute rhythmic accents or tragic inflections with conviction. Banquo's death is 'neccessario,' the queen declaims; Verdi's marked the passage *risoluto*, but Arroyo is irresolute. Still, as the aria proceeds the unfailingly impressive upper voice, as always, saves her. At the aria's close (and the scene's end), Cross quite joyfully tells us "that was Lady Macbeth" and his joviality seems not at all out of place. Verdi's inventive 'Gran Scena del Sonnambulismo' suffers the most from Arroyo's limitations as a singing actress. Convincing immersion in the Redonesque world of slumber with its tortured remembrances of past crimes requires a concentration and sense of purpose that are apparently foreign to Arroyo's talents. Again the gorgeous top voice comes to her aid, but to what purpose? In a final rebuke to the composer, she does not attempt his prescribed *fil di voce* for the final phrase; the soprano mounts securely to a full-voiced high D-flat. The intended weird effect is entirely blunted by a prima donna's earnest song. And yet, unlike many another Lady Macbeth, Arroyo technically may well have been able to honor Verdi's request.

Writing in 1853, Verdi, in an oblique way—he was prescribing roles for Marianna Barbieri-Nini, the original Lady Macbeth—indicated the essential qualities he preferred in interpreters of his Scottish queen. Barbieri-Nini was scheduled to sing *Trovatore*, but was unhappy with Leonora's 'Tacea la notte' and requested an alternative. Verdi declined, but wrote informatively to Piave (who had relayed the soprano's request): "why is Barbieri singing that role [Leonora], if it does not suit her?"[16] If she wants to sing in *Trovatore*, let her take on Azucena, he rather astonishingly counseled, for it is "the most important role, more beautiful, more dramatic, more original" than Leonora. Unlike Barbieri-Nini, Arroyo does own a Leonora voice. Azucena would have been as foreign to her as Lady Macbeth proved to be. (A curious, but aptly coincidental, episode occurs during the quiz intermission of the *Macbeth* broadcast. In response to a question on the "miscasting" of artists, Osie Hawkins, longtime stalwart of the roster and currently stage manager, voices a quite undiplomatic, and almost unheard of—on the quiz, that is—indictment of the previous management's treatment of young singers, and retention of veteran stars in roles now unsuited to their gifts. He hopes the new team, including maestros Levine and Kubelik, will remedy the serious miscasting gaffes of the previous regime.)

In contrast to Arroyo, Milnes is well equipped to shoulder the Scottish lord's heavy chores. His conception may have a dollop too much of self-pity (the tears-in-the-voice gambit is a bit overworked) but the manner is as assured as the voice is strong. The assertive American was intent on showing that Macbeth was no "milquetoast dominated by his wife."[17] In a realistic assault on the role, "sweat [and] muscular tension" will be his weapons. On those terms, he succeeds without reservation. Milnes inhabits the character. At this prime stage of his career, he is in marvelous vocal form. It cannot be said that he honors all of Verdi's demands for *sotto voce* declamation at key dramatic points (few baritones do, and perhaps the totality of them would be impracticable in a house the size of the Met). But he does make a subservient nod to them here and there, most conscientiously after Duncan's murder (a genuine *voce soffocata* there). The baritone is adept at sounding the quick changes that make Verdi's quasi melodic recitatives powerful and expressive instruments of the drama. Varied color tints are an effective aid. Nor is he deficient when pure song is called for—he launches the act-two concerted finale with firmness of line and purposeful intent. The performance gains a stronger dramatic profile in the third act as Milnes realistically portrays the king's confused, frightened responses to the apparitions. Eager for interpretive potency, the baritone may trot out a few too many vocal gimmicks, but the cumulative effect is powerful. Oddly, the downward plunge of Macbeth's climactic phrase ('ah! che non hai tu vita') is deficient in vocal thrust, one of the rare occasions when the big-voiced baritone fails to deliver the goods. To close that act, the Met chose to retain the formal duet of the royal pair rather than employ the 1847 aria that figured in the 1959 Met premiere. The duet, 'Ora di morte e di vendetta,' is more a grand excuse for vibrant, forceful vocalism than an expression of dramatic truth. Fortunately, in Milnes and Arroyo the Met has two principals who can respond to its challenges with hearty assurance. In the final act, two episodes from the original score are inserted into the 1865 revision. The melodic 'Pietà, rispetto, amore,' allows Milnes the kind of broad cantilena in which he, a genuine Verdi baritone—the type, alas, now become hound's-tooth rare—can display his command of legato and (relatively speaking) more intimate vocal effects. Admirably, he refrains from belting its swinging phrases and eagerly envelops their welcoming curves. He almost seems to be indulgently savoring his vibrantly colored tone as it luxuriantly rolls around in his mouth. The mood of regret is well plumbed—at least until the baritone inserts a stunning high A-flat (not quite impeccably taken, but resonant thereafter). The firmly executed cadenza that precedes the divo feat is a more attractive feature, however. In yet another departure from the 1865 score, the final choral hymn is banished in favor of Macbeth's somber 'Mal per me,' thereby permitting the wretched king to depart with a surfeit of realistic death gasps.

After this single-season effort at resuscitation, the opera, too, departs the Met stage. A new production will surface in the 1982–83 season. More important Verdi, however, remained on the Met calendar. In contrast to the coming fate of *Macbeth*, Bing's final-season remounting of *Otello* will not be mothballed in the future. The 9 December 1972 broadcast demonstrates why. Jon Vickers introduces his vaunted creation of the Moor to the radio audience with Zylis-Gara repeating Desdemona and Michalski again heard as Lodovico. Quilico (Iago), Goeke (Cassio), and Kraft (Emilia) are new radio interpreters of their roles. Where Mehta and Böhm had earlier presided, the henceforth omnipresent Levine takes over the podium.

As expected, the "brilliant young" conductor (Cross does the early anointing) is unfazed by his elevation from galleys Verdi to the masterwork of his maturity. Structural plotting is clean and clear, the interpretive thread is tautly drawn, control over his forces is complete. Objectivity may govern his choices, but he is ever willing to allow dramatic momentum its head—up to a point. The reins are never dropped, nor are they loosely held. The opening act has turbulence aplenty. Some lightening of tension in the choral 'Fuoco di gioia' might better set up the rhythmic brio of the drinking episode, which Levine propels in headlong fashion. In general, he dearly loves a stringendo, and an accelerando is his heart's delight. But then, classicist that he is, he may offer redress with an overly grand allargando (the conclusion of the third act *concertato* is positively heroic). With a physician's certitude, he has his fingers on the opera's quivering pulse. The orchestral interjections between Iago's musings at the end of the Credo are contained, almost mesmer-

Otello
9 December 1972

Desdemona
Teresa Zylis-Gara
Otello
Jon Vickers
Cassio
Leo Goeke
Iago
Louis Quilico
Lodovico
Raymond Michalski
Conductor
James Levine

Teresa Zylis-Gara as Desdemona in *Otello*. Photography by Louis Mélançon.

izing in their inertia. Time is arrested and we, too, hold our breaths. At this early point in his career, Levine invariably knows when the theatrical moment must be cultivated beyond the notation of the score. However intellectually judicious his conceptions, they are constantly tweaked by his concern for affect. His assured handling of Verdi's monumental opus forecasts the musico-dramatic riches that the ensuing quarter century will hold for us.

Zylis-Gara's Desdemona remains much the same as in the previous broadcast. Eight months would be little enough time for major change to occur. One notes a slight, and welcome, increase in dramatic involvement on her part. (Is Levine the cultivating agent? We know he has a way with singers.) Resplendent tone, nobly molded arcs of phrase, and plaintive timbral colors (including a bewitchingly smoky *fumoso*) remain the admirable features of her considerable artistry. Hers is such an unusual instrument. When the English horn solo sounds its lament as Otello watches the sleeping Desdemona, its timbral resemblance to the soprano's instrument is quite uncanny. Kraft's formidable Emilia is convincingly affronted by the Moor's murder of her mistress, and Iago's tool, the put-upon Cassio, is well served by Goeke's agreeable tenor. His voice is not large, but the upper range is neat and assured. Better yet, he is alert musically and, in the placement of his phrases throughout the rapid ensembles, his aim is accurate. Michalski repeats his warmhearted, warm-toned Lodovico to good effect.

Quilico is a newcomer to the roster, having joined the company in the previous season as Golaud. The Canadian baritone was no novice, for he had appeared with the New York City Opera as early as 1953. San Francisco knew him early on and even London and Paris had experienced his assured performances in the early sixties. By the time of his Met debut he had made a mark as a Verdi baritone of quality. His broadcast Iago sustains that repute. Over the years, his Metropolitan achievements would be substantial, though his star power was never of the headline variety. (Oddly, Quilico's son, baritone Gino—seventeen years of age at the time of the *Otello* broadcast—rates more space in *The New Grove Dictionary of Opera* than his more richly endowed father.) At the Met, probably Milnes' blazing vocal light and brazen stage manner cast too great a shadow. Whereas the latter's instrument has a superficial resemblance to Warren's, Quilico's voice rests more in the Merrill line, that is, solidity of tone and innate warmth of timbre are its dominant features. Thus, his portrayal of Iago's character will not be sustained by coloristic variety, nor will musical moods be sharply contrasted. In Otello's army, Milnes (Iago in the previous broadcast) would have been spotted early on as officer material. Quilico's ensign more likely came up through the ranks. He will know how to handle his men, as his manipulation of Cassio and Roderigo confirms. In his interpretation of Iago's wiliness, in the generality of his musical moves, he comes off as more the comrade than their superior.

But Quilico knows the operatic trade as well as his Iago grasps the politics of the barracks. He looks full in the face of the role's challenges and bests most of them. His drinking song, confident and hearty, seems a natural expression of the man. In the Credo, he does manage to suggest Iago's sardonic view of life. There, and elsewhere, the top voice is reliable. With the heavy lifting of the Credo behind him, Quilico tunes his instrument to a finer bore, the tone becoming more appealing. The repetitions of 'vigilate' are quietly delivered, as marked. On the other hand, his musical ornaments (a subtle definer of Iago's slippery character) are more bluster than pinpoint accents. Iago's warning of the dangers of 'gelosia' may not be the ultimate in suggestiveness, but you get the baritone's insidious drift. However carefully he limns 'Era la notte'—and his good intentions are evident— he cannot quite invoke its magical mood. Surely one must hear a *dolcissimo* top tone on 'sogno.' In the grand duet that closes the second act, Quilico ably carries his share of the weight, as, not unexpectedly, does Vickers—and Levine's somber pace adds considerably to the avoirdupois. In the Bianca episode, few baritones can trip Iago's jousting with Cassio off the tongue as blithely as desired. Quilico does not add to their number. Still, the voice has grown increasingly attractive as the opera progresses and his professionalism is never in doubt. The role requires something more than nature has allowed him to provide, but Quilico's gifts are more than sufficient to sustain a lengthy Metropolitan career in some of the most demanding baritone roles of the repertory.

Nature has assuredly been more generous with the baritone's countryman, lavishing upon Vickers not only vocal size and an intriguing timbral quality, but, most importantly, a musical and dramatic sagacity quite unusual in his vocal category. Earlier I noted that Miss Scotto's employment of chiaroscuro called to mind Caravaggio's manner. Vickers' individualistic art, in contrast, warrants comparison with the intensely personal, deeply moving, visionary drawings and poetry of William Blake. The estimable eccentricity of both artists bespeaks their unique imaginative powers. Met tour cities had first seen Vickers' Moor in 1965 but McCracken's hold on the role had prevented a broadcast presentation until the current season. Of course, it is worth waiting for. In pristine vocal form—sometimes the brilliance of the upper voice is almost glaring—the tenor enters with an 'Esultate!' of generous breadth and ringing power. Most notable is the golden sheen of the voice; though it has satisfied many an Otello of repute, a display of mere brute strength could never be sufficient for Vickers. When quelling the drunken disturbance of his troops, our tenor reveals the Moor's lofty nature; their crassness seems to offend his sensibilities. Thus the transition to the elevated mood of the love duet is smoothed. Throughout the opera, Vickers all but avoids the crooning effects that annoy some listeners—a few *piano* moments here and there are the more affecting for their rarity. The piercing beauty of his tone in the middle and upper ranges makes the love duet a searing experience. Even the trying final phrases are sustained with remarkable assurance (notwithstanding a tiny frog on one note). Again, a golden resonance obtains. He takes his time, too, which is a novelty, since most tenors can only hope to emerge unscathed if the time values are telescoped.

The monologues display the summit of his artistry. 'Ora e per sempre addio' becomes an extended cry of pain, yet its musical and vocal character is preserved. That union defines the measure of Vickers' greatness: he is able to fuse the musical and the dramatic realms into a heightened expression without violating the integrity of either. (Human, not godlike, he remains, for he neglects the marked *dolcissimo*—which he could so easily provide—on 'che m'innamora' in the lead-in to the monologue.) The grand vocal gesture is his as well. Witness (in the third-act confrontation where he commands Desdemona to swear her innocence and thus be damned) the tonal splendor he bestows on the descending line of 'Giura e ti danna!'. A ringing high C makes audible his rage before he intones 'Dio! mi potevi scagliar' in measured accents and with note fidelity (the raised 'd'angoscie' is customary). Now the *piano* (approaching falsetto) tints are affectingly applied before he moves to a brilliant climax at 'quel raggio' (a breath before it, but the moment is stunning). He conquers the high B-flat ('gioia') at the monologue's conclusion with a fearless attack. Before the assembled court, Vickers hurls a mighty curse upon Desdemona and the suggestion of madness prepares us for the final tragedy. The circle is closed by the unearthly calm of 'Calma come la tomba,' a wrenching moment as Otello contemplates his wife's motionless body. Following the strongly intoned opening lines of 'Niun mi tema,' he moves into an inner quiet (a grand 'Gloria,' a minimal 'fu'). Much of the monologue is delivered as though in a daze—a genuine Vickers touch. Realism and illusion become one as the character consumes the singer.

Otello was the opening broadcast of the new regime. In time-honored fashion, the intermissions featured the new manager, Schuyler G. Chapin. On "Opera

News on the Air" Mrs. Belmont introduces him to the radio audience (and notes, in passing, that, while starring on Broadway in *Merely Mary Ann* back in 1905, she had rushed to the Met to hear Ternina in *Götterdämmerung*; the memory sends us back to the company's adolescence and reminds us of the Met's durability). She invokes a "new era" with "a fine musical staff, an outstanding new musical director." Gentele's brief tenure, she opines, has prompted in the house "a warm atmosphere of unity and good-will" such as she, purportedly Bing's champion, had not experienced since 1940, the year the old house was purchased. Chapin, Gentele's aid, who will carry on the "heavy responsibilities" of the company, pays elaborate tribute to the dead manager. He notes that initially he had turned down the assistant general managership, but, at his wife's insistence and upon further Gentele persuasion, changed his mind. He, Kubelik, and Gentele were to have worked as a troika—now they are two. Reassuringly, a three-year plan had been laid out before Gentele's death. "Contemporary theater" will be his watchword; American artists are to be welcomed to the roster; appearances by Danny Kaye will spark the education program; the Mini-Met will be launched for chamber performances at the Forum Theatre at Lincoln Center. The new man opines that the Met is "alive and well and flourishing"— Mrs. Belmont's "new spirit" is real. In short, he and his team are "rolling up their sleeves" and are hard at work.

In turn, during the third intermission, Chapin introduces that team, bravely calling them "the best in the world": Michael Bronson (technical administrator), William Hadley (director of finance), Charles Riecker (artistic administrator), and the seemingly irreplaceable Francis Robinson (assistant manager). After asking his subordinates to name the operatic character with whom their Metropolitan responsibilities suggest an affinity (Alberich, Lohengrin, Figaro, and the young Wotan are their choices), he rather mysteriously takes for himself the role of the shadowy Fieldmarshal in *Der Rosenkavalier*. Perhaps, in his modesty, he was prescient.

Richard Tucker as Radamès in *Aida*. Photography by Louis Mélançon. Courtesy Metropolitan Opera Archives.

CHAPTER FOURTEEN

The Old Guard

Without doubt, the future of the house lay in the throats of Sutherland, Caballé, Scotto, Nilsson, Rysanek, and Zylis-Gara, of Verrett, Bumbry, Cossotto, and Horne, of Vickers, Domingo, Pavarotti, and Milnes, with Bergonzi and Gedda still very much in the picture. And management, in the time-honored ways of higher-ups, was intent on showcasing these acquisitions, some more recent than others. Still, honor must be paid to those who for decades had upheld the finest traditions of the company, especially when the ends of their careers are in sight. Tucker, Merrill, and Kirsten, favorites for almost three decades, were now nearing the point of no return. All three were 1945 debutants, the tenor in January, the other pair in December. We still have time to praise their art and then pause to lament their leave-taking.

In addition to providing Tucker with a virtuoso role in which to display his well-seasoned talents, the 27 January 1973 broadcast of *Un Ballo in Maschera* offers some new faces. Peter Herman Adler, the guru of televised opera, temporarily departs the studio in favor of the pit, and Mexican soprano Gilda Cruz-Romo (Amelia) stakes her claim as a Verdi soprano. Gail Robinson cavorts as Oscar, Milnes is friend and foe to Riccardo, and Dalis (Ulrica) forecasts the sea change in that relationship, while Morris (Samuel) and Best (Tom) are the abetting heavies.

Though his fame will ever be rooted in his pioneering activities with the NBC Opera Company and later productions for National Educational Television, Adler was a polished product of the European training ground of provincial opera houses. He had conducted his first *Ballo* in Brno, Czechoslovakia, at age twenty-five and served as director of the Bremen Opera (1929–1932) before migrating to America. There, in addition to his television work, his credits included a near-decade as music director of the Baltimore Symphony. His professional assets are apparent in the broadcast *Ballo*. The relationship between stage and pit is rather more autocratic than usual (Tucker struggles now and then with the conductor's straightjacket rhythms) and a certain rigidity is early apparent. But then, few conductors want to take chances with the disjunct elements of the opera's tricky prelude. More troubling is Adler's heavy hand on Verdi's repetitious accompaniment figures and the hard-heeled boots of his oom-pah-pah chords. At moments, the opera's lifeblood all but coagulates as the delicious play of the composer's pseudo-French elegance is suppressed. The Bohemian-born Adler oddly lacks what the

Un Ballo in Maschera
27 January 1973

Amelia
Gilda Cruz-Romo
Oscar
Gail Robinson
Ulrica
Irene Dalis
Riccardo
Richard Tucker
Renato
Sherrill Milnes
Sam
James Morris
Conductor
Peter Herman Adler

323

American Levine possesses in such abundance, namely, the ability to establish a buoyant pulse that allows singers the freedom to float their song in seemingly spontaneous fashion. And yet, paradoxically, when not constrained by a set rhythmic pattern, Adler is often indulgent to his singers' wishes, allowing them broad tenutos and sufficient leeway for a few time-honored nuances. Still, Adler's heavy ritards, his excessive pointing up of a phrase's climax, are a bit obvious for this fleet-footed opera. But when Italianate grandeur is Verdi's goal, it receives its due. The love duet has the requisite sweep; indeed, the musical gestures are more exultant than most conductors allow. At this focal point in the opera's design, the composer's expansive phrases are warmly embraced by the conductor—rapture and abandon are unleashed and singers and audience rejoice. The broad swath of the Meyerbeerian oath scene is exactly Adler's meat and the final act as well is architecturally well laid out. The complex musical mix of *Ballo* may not be quite the right vehicle for Adler's abilities. After a season's absence, he will return to put Puccini's more accommodating *Manon Lescaut* through its paces. In the end, his brief Met tenure is more likely management's courteous acknowledgment of his important role as an operatic Pied Piper rather than any consideration of him as a significant player in the company's activities.

Of the stage participants, only Miss Dalis (quite uncharacteristically) disappoints. The role of Ulrica, its murky depths troublesome to most mezzos, does not play to her strengths. She, too, is nearing the end of her Met career (three seasons remain of her allotted nineteen) and, while the Met continues to schedule her as Amneris and Azucena, the prime occasions and assignments are now given to Bumbry and Cossotto. In addition, she is probably not in good voice on this afternoon. The aria is decidedly underpowered; it provokes a solitary (and quite unusual from the well-behaved Met audience) boo from high up in the house. When Ulrica is permitted to quit the vocal cellar, Dalis is on more agreeable terrain. A single appearance as Zita in the 1975 *Gianni Schicchi* will bring to a close her prominent and distinguished broadcast career. The voice was rather a singular instrument, especially beautiful in the upper regions, and her artistic integrity was impeccable. Her value to the house, spanning as she did with equal command the Italian and German repertories, was significant. At the other end of the vocal spectrum, Robinson soars with the greatest of ease on the trapeze bar phrases of the quintet. Her bright, attractive tone and perky rhythms make Oscar's couplets doubly welcome amidst librettist Somma's conspiratorial gloom. Best's ordinary bass handily supplies the latter quality, while Morris' sonorous instrument elevates Samuel's moments to limelight status.

Like many a Met baritone before him, Milnes finds Renato a gratifying assignment. His auditors, as well, can take pleasure in his conception of the role for he displays a wider range of vocal character and musical thought than his two-fisted (or lion-hearted, if you prefer) interpretive stance sometimes has allowed. Renato is not by nature a villain, and Milnes, unlike some predecessors, acknowledges that seemingly obvious quality in his portrayal. In spite of its martial gait, 'Alla vita che t'arride' expresses the minister's genuine concern for the safety of his monarch; most baritones are content to belch tone and act the heroic protector in its grateful phrases. Milnes finds the right balance between concern and warning, introducing a few musical subtleties of volume and timbre, and thereby making Renato a more sympathetic character whose third-act pain seems plau-

Irene Dalis as Eboli in *Don Carlo*. Photography by Louis Mélançon. Courtesy Metropolitan Opera Archives.

sible. Throughout the afternoon, his top notes are often attractively covered rather than openly thrust forth. When encouraging the king to flee before the assassins arrive on the heath, Milnes again relaxes his up-front stance in favor of beautiful vocalism. The ploy works, for when, in their home, the duped husband confronts his wife, Milnes' big-voiced threats and hostile stance are even more dramatically effective than usual. Now the baritonal brawn is tellingly employed, and undoubtedly, the house audience is overjoyed at hearing the meaty voice ricocheting throughout the auditorium in the recitative and opening portions of 'Eri tu.' In the oath scene, 'Dunque l'onta di tutti sol una' is rhythmically compelling as well as tonally vivid. The baritone is not above a few grotesque melodramatic touches when he triumphantly names himself as the assassin, and his hollow 'morte' as the curtain falls is small Guignol. But earlier he has neatly rounded off his portrayal of the unhappy husband. The 'dolcezze perdute' of the middle section of 'Eri tu' are quietly and sympathetically sounded and given a velvety caress; the result may not quite match up to the De Luca brand of suavity, but it will do as a commendable auditory likeness of Renato's sweet, lamented memories. Even Milnes' tendency to overdo the sob at peak dramatic moments (in this case, the final curtain) cannot dampen enthusiasm for his portrayal.

Cruz-Romo had come to the company as Maddalena in Cleveland on the 1970 tour, appeared later that season as Nedda in the parks concert performances, and made her house debut in December of the same year as Butterfly. This early spectrum of roles indicates both the character of her instrument (a mix of lyric and dramatic qualities) and her utility to the management. She had the look of a prima donna as well, generous of figure with a striking, chiseled profile, its strong features framed in a severe, but becoming, wimple-like hairstyle. Onstage she presented a handsome picture. Early on in her relatively young career she had appeared in leading roles in Mexico City and smaller ones with the Dallas Civic Opera (moving up to Tosca and Anna Bolena) before her debut at the New York City Opera (*Mefistofele*) in 1969. After winning the Metropolitan National Council Auditions, she was awarded a Met contract. Even as her Cleveland company debut had been as a replacement for Arroyo, her intended broadcast debut in this afternoon's *Ballo* had been preempted by the need to replace Moffo two weeks earlier in the radio *Traviata*. In the house, in addition to Butterfly and Nedda, she had already been heard as the *Forza* Leonora and Tosca, with Aida, the *Trovatore* Leonora, and Manon Lescaut to follow in short order. Clearly, she was a soprano of substance.

Her instrument is a fine one. Its most notable feature is the equalization of her scale throughout its substantial range; the voice owns a sure, clean top, a modest but purposeful middle voice, and substantial chest resonance. The security of the voice's placement, the absolute absence of wobble, and its attractive, Latin-hued timbre make for easy listening. At the loudest dynamic, a high tone can turn hard (but only on the rarest occasions). Normally, the voice's warmth is notable, though lushness, either in density or coloration, is seldom marketable. That lack is balanced by a neat, graphic control of line. Her musicianship is well grounded, her musical instincts (something else apart) appealing, her dramatic sense strong without being intrusively original.

All these considerable attributes are apparent in her Amelia. The arch of 'Consentimi, o signore,' lovely in itself, does not quite blaze—she saves the fire for a splendid reading of the heath aria. One of Verdi's more demanding soprano ventures, 'Ma dall'arido stelo' profits from her thorough command of its wide-ranging phrases. Both the aria and, in particular, its introductory recitative, indicate sufficient temperament for the Verdi milieu. Neither the low center of gravity of the aria's opening phrases nor the tricky progress to the high C faze Cruz-Romo (and how astute she is to momentarily lighten her voice before beginning the ascent). In quitting that C, this soprano needs no concluding squeak or dramatic fall of tone to mask technical inadequacy. At the aria's conclusion, the prompter's very audible 'Brava!' is well earned. The audience agrees and its response is long and vociferous for what is the high point of the soprano's performance. Not that the grand duet disappoints. It is merely that her instrument (and musical posture, for that manner) are not quite flamboyant enough to massage this rapturous episode into maximum frenzy. Tucker, however, takes care of that department, while Cruz-Romo's tracing of her music remains both musically refined and vocally satisfying. A bit more rhythmic bite on her part would upgrade the agitation of the heath trio with lover and husband. The ingratiating phrases of 'Morrò, ma prima in grazia' are becomingly shaped, her tone a touch edgier than earlier on, though still entirely attractive to the ear. The high attack on the cadenza startles with a momentary hardness, but overall her vocalism and artistry remain potent. Perhaps motivated by the dramatic situation, she chooses to sing the phrases in which she warns Renato of his impending murder in lighter tones than some sopranos employ. Over the next decade, the radio audience would have ample opportunity to enjoy her artistry as Manon Lescaut, Suor Angelica, and Aida (both twice), as well as Elisabetta and a repeat of her impressive Amelia.

Tucker, who in the summer of this broadcast year would celebrate his sixtieth birthday, again gives an astonishing performance. Barring a slight touch of age in his opening gambits in the throne room (where the timbre is more open than velvety), his vocalism is quite amazing in its brilliant, almost brazen, thrust of tone and its commanding authority. Could it be the burgeoning splendor, both in terms of their accomplishments and the resultant critical regard, of new recruits Domingo and Pavarotti that occasions such a display of vocal prowess and tonal abundance? Whatever the cause, the American tenor is clearly in his glory throughout the afternoon. Every gesture is distended to its fullest extent, raised to its highest power. Every challenge seems welcome and its difficulties are met head on. Is it all not a touch self-indulgent? No doubt. But then, old-time favorites, like raging bulls, must be granted the freedom of the ring. After all, how much longer will they be around to demonstrate to their successors, whippersnappers or no, what being an operatic divo is all about? In the face of such a performance, admiration, amazement, delight, and amusement (only a smidgen of the latter) are inseparably entwined in a listener's regard. At moments, one feels that Tucker is more in charge than Adler; the tenor takes hold of the opening scene stretta and propels it on to good effect. The conductor may shortchange the gentle humor of the barcarole but our Riccardo pays in full. In the quintet, Tucker's rather measured reading suits the king's incredulous mood, while his assured vocalism accents the ironic humor of the moment. (No interpolated chuckles—more power to him—as custom would dictate, but the laugh quota is belatedly achieved by a burst of mirth over the quintet's final chords.) Both the love duet and the demanding third-act aria show the tenor at the peak of his form. One can only marvel at his spendthrift vocalism. Each section of the duet is given its appropriate inflection, the grander moments flung out bravely into the house. Both singers take a long high C at its close, the soprano with ease, the tenor secure and on pitch with an effortful release. When one recalls Björling's abstention, Tucker's no-holds-barred rendition of 'Ma se m'è forza perderti' is further cause for wonder. The opening recitative benefits from lovely tone and an introspective manner, while the aria's phrases are grandly sculpted, the tone as firm as that he offered in midcareer bloom. Undoubtedly he is playing now to the house, secure in the knowledge that they will reward his veteran vocalism with unstinting approval. He deserves it. To his credit, and in a surprising moment of abnegation, he allows the king a dignified death, devoid of sobs and self-pity.

The old warrior is far from resting on his hard-won laurels. A month after the *Ballo* broadcast, Tucker is heard as Radamès in the 24 February 1973 airing of *Aida*. His Egyptian general had not been heard by the radio audience since he first assumed the role at the Met in 1965. Arroyo (Aida) and Bumbry (Amneris), participants in the 1970 broadcast of the opera, are enamored of the triumphant soldier, while MacNeil (Amonasro) and Tozzi (Ramfis) thwart his plans on the home front. Molinari-Pradelli keeps a watchful eye on all of them. Too cautionary a regard, for that matter, for his manner is too prudent for this exuberant work. Routine is the conductor's method on this afternoon. Dramatic tension and vibrant rhythms are Verdi's potent weapons, but they are not the well-versed Italian maestro's, for he invariably adopts a sedate pace, content to comfortably plod along. Fortunately, his pulse quickens when reaching the Nile and, perversely, at the tomb. It is well that the quartet of stout-voiced principals, who are alive to their responsibilities, do not intend to be denied their prerogatives.

The less prominent singers make modest contributions, as well. Shirley Love, filling in for Jeannine Altmeyer (a novice here, still in her pre-Wagnerian-heroine days), is a smooth-voiced priestess. There is something to be said for a mezzo practitioner in the temple. As the messenger, MacWherter exceeds in decibel count even the redoubtable Franke, the familiar carrier of dire tidings in many an opera. Morris and Tozzi initially offer a study in contrasts, the younger bass singing the King's lines with rhythmic exactitude and firmly focused tones, the veteran singer more casual as he runs the Ramfis course one more time. Oddly, Morris disappears after the first act—the dependable but dull Karlsrud takes over. As if experiencing release, in the later acts Tozzi warms to his task, his voice gaining in both quality and solidity.

MacNeil, of course, has a heavier load to pull. Amonasro's music is all fiery ferocity and the hearty-voiced American knows how to pour on the heat. Perhaps taking to heart Anna Russell's advice about stunning an audience at entry, the baritone throws a vocal thunderbolt with an outsized 'Suo padre.' Here and there, top tones may shake at the enormity of their burden and the now-familiar rawness of tone is apparent in initial phrases, but the authority of his utterance gives Amonasro a king's stature. What chance would any Aida have against the big-boned vocal assault that MacNeil launches against an obedient daughter after trailing her to the river's bank! There the vocal quality becomes more attractive to the ear, while the artistry (a nobly arched intoning of 'Pensa che un popolo vinto, straziato') continues to please. In her responding phrase of submission, Miss Arroyo offers a consoling nuance with a *subito piano* before 'costi' ('Oh patria quanto

Aida
24 February 1973

Aida
Martina Arroyo
Amneris
Grace Bumbry
Radamès
Richard Tucker
Amonasro
Cornell MacNeil
Ramfis
Giorgio Tozzi
Conductor
Francesco Molinari-Pradelli

mi costi!'). Consoling both to Aida—in the face of her contemplated sacrifice, that is—and to the soprano's auditors, who long for any musical or character-delineating subtlety from this vocally resplendent artist. Her paratactic phrasing can unduly inhibit appreciation. But we know only too well in our new century how grateful we should be to a singer who can perform a long and challenging role such as Aida with vocal plenitude and unblemished tonal quality. From first note to last, the soprano's voice is full, fresh, and opulent, and the vocal hurdles that Verdi posed for his heroine in this virtuoso role are handily dispatched. Too handily, probably, for the artist, little prone to utilize textual nuances, rarely evokes in us a sympathetic response to Aida's plight. (Bumbry, on the other hand, in a role, at least on the surface, of less appealing humanity, allows us to know and respond to Amneris' torment.)

Arroyo's vocalism is indeed superb throughout the afternoon. The exposed phrase that breaks forth as a ray of light from the massed ensemble of the triumphal scene is neatly controlled. 'O patria mia,' graveyard of many a gifted singer, is surely voiced, poised in its phrasing (there's musicality for you), the high C approached with confidence and scrupulously woven into the fabric of the ascending/descending phrase. The note is not screamed, as even some great Aidas are wont to do, for Arroyo cagily lightens her tone as she begins the assault and manages, if not the prescribed *piano*, at least a fruity *mezzo forte*. Earlier in the aria, we miss the mesmerizing *pianissimo*s that Verdi allotted his prima donna, for Arroyo is deficient in that area. Or at least she is reluctant to try them on this afternoon. One feels she certainly could supply them if only she would. In fact, the final duet gives evidence (but not at every opportunity) that the device is in her vocal arsenal. There, entombed with her lover, the soprano appropriately adopts a more dulcet tone and accommodating manner. The best feature of an Arroyo performance is the knowledge that we are sure to be untroubled by angst. Her vocal condition is certain to be prime, her generosity in dispensing beautiful tone unlimited. There are no cliff-hanging moments in an Arroyo portrayal. Of course, lack of danger removes a bit of the sport of operagoing. I once heard, in the long-ago past, a fellow Met standee complain that it was "no fun" hearing Björling's 'Salut demeure!' because "he always makes the high C."

As indicated above, it is Bumbry who provides the most accomplished, the most fully rounded, performance of the afternoon. By that I mean accomplished in the creation of character, in vocal certitude and allure, and, perhaps most importantly, in achieving a balance between theatrical magnetism and artistic responsibility. Though new in this chronicle, this is her third broadcast Amneris and her claim on the role is assured. (Cossotto would be the other claimant, but unfortunately, no broadcast of hers falls within the period of our survey.) A few reservations may be voiced. As sometimes happens in her performances, the vocal bands occasionally can be very tautly drawn, thus causing the voice to sound a shade glacial, not in its coloration, which always remains intriguing, but rather in inducing a kind of intrusive scratchiness. The only unsatisfying moment of that type on this afternoon occurs in the three descending phrases of act two ('Ah! vieni, amor mio'), precisely where one wants a more seductive tonal embrace, a languid phraseology. But almost without exception, the remainder of her vocalism is replete with burnished tone throughout the entire scale. The middle and low voice, all of a piece, are remarkably lustrous today, and her top voice shines with thrusting brilliance. And, despite the voice's potency, it can charm as well, and does so as Amneris seeks to beguile Aida and win her confidence. But when the princess drops her friendly pose, Bumbry snarls out a commanding 'io t'ingannava,' fully exposing Amneris' claws—the mezzo is never one to ignore the requisite theatrical gesture. In their pivotal scene together, Arroyo's top notes are her glory, but all the drama issues from Bumbry's throat.

In the confrontation with Radamès and the ensuing judgment scene, the mezzo's tone flows with unchecked ease, resolutely bronze in the mid- and lower voice and everywhere poignant in expression. Not for her the ugly growls of chest voice of some of her colleagues; Bumbry's chest voice retains the tonal fabric of the remainder of her instrument. And, in an afternoon of sometimes excessively stentorian vocalism, her recourse to a few glowing whispers, as Amneris contemplates saving her lover ('Vorrei salvarlo. E come?') and later regrets sending him to his death ('io stessa lo gettai!'), is doubly effective. On the other hand, she serves theatricality equally well when she boldly catapults the closing phrases into the house; in winging these high-flying missiles her aim is not quite perfect—a top tone may fly a bit sharp. Verdi wanted his Amneris to have a "highly developed dramatic sensibility," to be an artist who is "a mistress of the stage." A beautiful voice was "not enough," nor did "polished singing" matter much to him. He wanted his Amneris to have that quality which he could only describe as *being driven by the devil*."[1] Bumbry qualifies. In the afternoon's third intermission, tribute is paid to Lotte Lehmann on her eighty-fifth birthday; at the final curtain, Cross notes that Bumbry is a protégée of the revered soprano. On this afternoon, the pupil's performance honors both self and mentor.

The broadcast begins with two unusual announcements. In the first, Cross, returning to the booth for the first time since his wife's death, thanks the many listeners who wrote offering their condolences and wishes for his speedy return to his duties. The bond between the Saturday afternoon audience and the Metropolitan and its prime spokesman was real. The second announcement, made from the stage by acting manager Chapin, is more pertinent for the afternoon's music making. In polished tones, he cites the following day as the 100th anniversary of Caruso's birth and dedicates the *Aida* performance to his memory. He notes that the opera holds the record for most performances by the company (574 to date) and that Caruso sang sixty-four of them ("more than 10 percent," he adds, apparently for those who like statistics). Corelli had been scheduled for Radamès on this important occasion, but it is Tucker who gains the reward. Chapin significantly notes that the American tenor had "received his artistic inspiration" from the great Caruso. The substitution for Corelli probably gave Tucker secret satisfaction, for on occasion (and publicly) he had been tormented by and writhed under the impact of the Italian tenor's high-powered publicity. One wonders if his reading of the role in this broadcast was influenced by the shadowy presence of the two tenors, Caruso and Corelli, both renowned for their vocal prodigality. The thought surfaces because he plays to the gallery—his Radamès is all but overwhelmed by a reliance upon stentorian power (and his tone is considerably less blandishing at that level). Moreover, it is regrettably replete with those exaggerations of diction and style that in the past (but less frequently of late) have marred the beauty of his vocalism. The voice is all there—only the final top note of the tomb duet, taken in unison with the soprano, betrays him, and even then he knows how to handle it. Occasional signs of effort here and there are now seemingly integral to his dramatic conception of his roles.

At the outset, as he strives for Caruso power in the recitative to 'Celeste Aida,' the tone is a bit hollow and more open than remembered. Even when the reservations that I have noted are taken into account, it must be said that Tucker delivers this trying piece with more tonal security and personal comfort than most of his colleagues could manage. (For the record, the final note is *fortissimo* and solid—but with a seemingly necessary fall-off at its conclusion.) The spitfire manner continues as he woos Aida on the Nile's banks, where Verdi's rhythmic energy allows the tenor to exploit to the full his fustian style. Raised pitches and fearsome accents are called upon to counterfeit the *robusto* manner. He does too much and his Aida too little. (Once again the gods might have shown greater discrimination when distributing their favors.) Nevertheless, many moments confirm his continued control over his instrument. 'Io resto a te' is as elongated and grandly voiced as any gallery rat could desire. The final act requires a less demonstrative stance and here Tucker does accommodate to situation and to the composer's dynamic framework. Shedding general's togs for a lover's tunic can be gratifying for both a soldier and his inamorata. The calmer manner and quite gracious conduct of line are more than welcome in the face of what has gone before. Indeed, his delivery of 'Morir! si pura e bella!' is quite affecting in its sincerity and tonal character. And, unlike many of his tenor brethren, he is able to voice the repeated 'il ciel's with clarity (the word is distinctly formed) and relative ease. Let us hope that the occasion motivated Tucker's relapses earlier in the performance and that in his final radio offering (Gabriele in *Simon Boccanegra* on 19 January 1974) we will find him returned to the quality of vocalism and music making for which he will be remembered.

On the *Boccanegra* broadcast, Tucker is joined by Maliponte (Maria/Amelia), Wixell (Simon), Tozzi (Fiesco), and, as Paolo, newcomer Lawrence Shadur. Sixten Ehrling, debutant of the previous season, is the guiding force. The gloomy opera, never an audience favorite—but one of mine—had not been heard since the 1968 offering that featured Tucci, Shirley, MacNeil, Hines, and Milnes under Molinari-Pradelli's baton. Once again, we can marvel at the Metropolitan's ability to mount a Verdi opera with two completely different, but entirely viable, casts.

Despite its rather low rating in the Verdi canon by audiences worldwide, the opera had a storied history at the Metropolitan. Nine broadcasts previous to today's offering testify to the management's belief in the work. And they peopled it with their finest artists. The 1932 Met premiere enlisted Maria Müller, Martinelli, Tibbett, and Pinza under the authoritative hand of Tullio Serafin. Rethberg soon took over Amelia's chores and the magnificent quartet made memorable the broadcasts of the thirties. The 1949 revival featured the unlikely (but effective) Varnay with Tucker, Warren, Székely, and Valdengo (Paolo) under Stiedry. Milanov, Tebaldi, and Bergonzi later added their starry voices to the mix with able assists from Tozzi and Hines. And Mitropoulos had overseen the 1960 broadcast.

Ehrling had come to the house for *Peter Grimes* in February of 1973. He had conducted the broadcast of the opera during that season, but this is our first encounter with this important musician. He would be granted the enormous responsibility of the 1975 *Ring* series as well as the following season's *Meistersinger*. Swedish by birth, he had spent the last decade at the helm of the Detroit Symphony,

Simon Boccanegra
19 January 1974

Maria/Amelia
Adriana Maliponte
Gabriele
Richard Tucker
Simon
Ingvar Wixell
Fiesco
Giorgio Tozzi
Paolo
Lawrence Shadur
Conductor
Sixten Ehrling

and his early career had included a prewar apprenticeship under Böhm in Dresden. Two decades with the Swedish Royal Opera, much of that time as musical director, followed his return to his homeland in 1939. There he collaborated with Gentele; their *Ballo* was a famous, even notorious, treatment of the opera in which Swedish king Gustavus III was portrayed as a homosexual. Currently settled in New York as head of the Juilliard orchestra department, Ehrling was obviously a well-seasoned pit maestro. The *Boccanegra* broadcast confirms his operatic know-how. He casts a more benign light on the opera than the volatile, greatly cherished Mitropoulos had. Verdi's Genoese epic has always been regarded as excessively somber. But rather unexpectedly, since Swedes are thought to be dour, Ehrling's lighter touch reinforces the humanity that Boccanegra espoused without sacrificing the blood and thunder of the political struggle that is the backbone of the plot. The conductor's fluent, graceful sounding of the prologue's introduction sets the tone for the afternoon, with the pay-off coming in the elegiac pages of the final act.

The stage participants are worthy successors to their forebears, although that is not immediately apparent. In a role whose villainy had been limned by the glamorous instruments of Warren, Flagello, and Milnes, Lawrence Shadur's efforts as Paolo in the prologue seem of ordinary coin. The voice, at least initially, lacks distinction—but then villainy may be better served by common clay than luxuriant topsoil. The new baritone (filling in for Michalski) surprises by springing to life in the more demanding scenes of the Council Chamber and second act. There he summons a few outbursts of commanding tone that shed light on why management would later allow him the *Lohengrin* Herald, Jokanaan, and Monfort (*I Vespri Siciliani*). Still, his Met tenure was brief. Tozzi's Fiesco was heard in the early sixties broadcasts; but by now the portrayal is vocally a bit long in the tooth. The enamel has worn off his instrument and the hard-hearted old nobleman needs steely tones to reinforce his unyielding stance. The prologue's effectiveness in large part hinges on a grandly intoned, but moving, rendition of 'Il lacerato spirito.' Tozzi flubs the opportunity. The most affecting moments of the aria should occur when the bass takes the raised third (which sounds the change to the major key) at 'Prega, Maria, per me' with absolute pitch accuracy and apparent sensibility. Tozzi's thirds are flat and the affect goes by the board. He redeems himself in the final act, offering there a few splendid phrases that remind us of the fine artist of old. I have never felt Fiesco to be a role that played to Tozzi's best qualities, so it is unfortunate that we must say good-bye to him with this portrait. Only his Basilio in a March *Barbiere* remains of his broadcast career. He would depart the company after the following season, closing twenty-one years of more than honorable service in a wide-ranging repertory, including a number of memorable broadcast portrayals. Though it may have been a less grand assignment than many he undertook, his genial doctor in *Vanessa* lingers in the heart and the ear as a characterization that proved a perfect fit for the man and the voice.

Vigor is what Ingvar Wixell offers in abundance. The youthful Boccanegra of the prologue is thus better served than the aged, weary doge of the body of the opera. One hears little change as Wixell matures from the fiery young corsair to the commanding leader—at least, until Paolo's poison begins to take its toll. Even there, the dutiful suggestions of time's toll and death's specter seem mere overlays on a vibrantly healthy voice. This baritone's instrument holds no shadows—its Nordic light is too brilliant to allow us the full flavor, the mellowed sorrows in particular, of Verdi's conception. The overtones of pathos are simply not built into the voice. 'Il mare, il mare,' Simon quietly drones, and one ought to hear the sailor's love and longing for the sea in the tones themselves. No luck. That said, one must revel in the generous outpouring of vibrant tone throughout the range that Wixell dispenses—only a few notes at the low end are touched by dross. The heady resonance of the upper voice is a joy in itself and the baritone's delivery reeks of vocal and musical security. Surely that is enough cause for thanksgiving. The singer's forceful presence ably dominates the dramatic moments of the score. His menacing probing of the guilty Paolo is imaginative (aided in that regard by a pregnant bass clarinet), powerful, and entirely convincing. I, for one, would like a broader scale of phrase in the opening of 'Plebe! Patrizi!,' inspired product of Boito's and Verdi's 1881 revision and the supreme episode of the opera. Though sturdily vocalized, 'E vo gridando pace, e vo gridando amor!' is not quite the heartbreaking invocation that the elevated sentiment of the text warrants. On the other hand, the altered color and manner that warm 'Piango su voi sul placido' are consoling. Similarly, the not unattractive falsetto 'Figlia!' at the close of the recognition duet and the pseudo-mezza voce (it sounds more like a "marking" voice) employed to bless the lovers as death approaches ('Gran Dio, li benedici') are worthy attempts to fulfill Verdi's demands. The robust voice and confident artistry make one want to hear more portrayals from the Swedish baritone.

Miss Maliponte is an artist whose achievements deserve more acclaim than history has accorded her. The soundness of her schooling and her integrity as a performer are confirmed right off as she launches Amelia's opening aria ('Come in quest'ora bruna'). Verdi was not kind to either his heroine or Fiesco when, as with Radamès' 'Celeste Aida,' he set them a trial by fire as soon as they set foot on the stage. But Maliponte's control of her instrument is nigh perfect. Her pellucid tones are infinitely touching, though I admit that appreciation will depend to some extent on an inordinate fondness for the flute as a timbral coloration. Hers is not a rainbow voice. With loving care she negotiates the intricate coils of the entrance aria, putting a seal of approval on her effort by an expert molding of the final downward cascade of tone. In addition to my caution about the flute timbre, her low voice would benefit from more body, especially for this brave Verdi heroine; the middle section of the aria suffers from that defect. Yet, in flamboyant dramatic moments, the soprano is not unwilling to employ a touch of chest voice to good effect. Nor is she at all deficient in temperament. In Amelia's castigation of her abductor and subsequent defense of her lover, Maliponte knows how to make an operatic point, even if a top tone or two vibrates with the force of breath pushed to its limit. An artist who knows just where to expend a bit of capital—and does it expeditiously and to sound purpose—is both cagey in her plotting and considerate of her audience. Yet the soprano's vocalism is inherently instrumental in conception and execution. One of her most satisfying attributes is her unerringly accurate attack on top tones, a surety that, in combination with intonation purity, often results in effects of singular, piercing beauty. Thus can a predominantly instrumental technique achieve dramatic and affective moments of substantial impact. At the end of the Council Chamber *concertato*, a fluent trill, emerging immediately from the ensemble as Verdi prescribed, demonstrates her technical command. For a Verdi heroine, Amelia does have more than her share of docile moments, and scattered throughout the opera are numerous episodes where

Maliponte's cantabile charms. The recognition scene narrative ('Orfanella il tetto umile') and the wordless descending lament in the final trio are only two of many examples of the soprano's ability to trace a melodic line to poignant effect.

It is a pleasure to report that Tucker, in his reading of Gabriele Adorno, re-affirms his stature as an artist in the best traditions of the company. That status was momentarily interrupted, as Chapin recounted in his memoir. James Drake further augmented the tale of backstage trauma in his Tucker biography. The tenor, weary of being the "drawing card" for what he termed a "baritone's opera," wanted to be released from several performances of *Boccanegra* in order to sing *Ballo* in Florence.[2] Chapin refused and, learning that Tucker was Florence bound after the *Boccanegra* broadcast, fired him—and, after pressure from board members and opera fans, reinstated him. It happens that I was in the house for the broadcast performance and I recall that I was amazed at the beauty and pith of the tenor's vocalism. Hearing the broadcast again three decades after the original confirms my impressions of that 1974 Saturday afternoon. In superb vocal form (and when was he not?), he is on his best musicianly behavior as well. Yes, the artistry is heard in what may be an overripe stage (the gestures can be extravagant) but the fruit is still of prime quality. Nor will decay be allowed to set in.

The offstage serenade is only slightly brushed with the blemish of age, for its line is neatly sculpted without exaggeration. When he is alone with his love, his top voice has its familiar ring and the timbre wears its uniquely somber mask, a quality that could make its owner comfortable at a Renaissance ball. No Tucker reading can entirely forswear a few huffs of tone or spits of consonants, but they are decidedly minor league on this afternoon; the brief cabaletta to the act-one duet has a few, as does his plea for pardon at the end of act two ('assassin son io' was ever an inevitable hissing trap for him). Of course, it is Gabriele's grand *scena* in that act which allows Tucker to demonstrate the splendor of his instrument and his still potent command of it. Believing Amelia to be false to him, the young patrician expresses his torment with pain worthy of a wounded animal. In the thirties, Martinelli played it thus, sending out onto the airwaves a veritable vocal agony, a marvelous creation of suffering in sound. Considering his stylistic proclivities, if Tucker had allowed himself such a reading, the results would probably have been disastrous. Our tenor does not neglect to adopt a *robusto* stance when portraying the lover's jealous fury in the dramatic recitatives and in 'Sento avvampar nell'anima,' but his delivery of 'Cielo, pietoso, rendila' is conducted for the most part with almost classical restraint. This prayer for Amelia's return to his heart is a moving testament to the tenor's musical integrity. A few stentorian tones represent only his badge of membership in the tenor union. In that regard, who would wish to be denied the thrusting grandeur of his 'Pietà, gran Dio, del mio martiro!,' the monumental phrase that precipitates the prayer? When Amelia appears, Tucker begins 'Parla, in tuo cor virgineo' with wondrous quietude and Maliponte responds in kind. A momentary blemish here and there (a slightly flat attack—readily corrected—on the unison 'Padre' with Maliponte as the final curtain nears, for instance) does not detract from the quality of the tenor's performance.

Tucker would have hated to have that 'Padre' the final sound heard from his throat by the radio audience. Yet it was so destined. Though the tenor was scheduled for the 18 January 1975 broadcast of *Cavalleria Rusticana* on 8 January 1975 he unexpectedly suffered a heart attack and died as he prepared to sing a concert in Kalamazoo, Michigan. A funeral service before a "full-house" on the stage of the Metropolitan itself followed on 10 January.[3] The Met *Annals* lists an amazing 734 performances by the tenor (504 in the old Met and new Met, 230 elsewhere) over thirty-one seasons. At the time of his death, only Martinelli and Scotti had longer company tenures. Enzo was his debut role in 1945, Canio his final house performance on 3 December 1974. According to Robert Jacobson, he had suffered a "singing crisis" in the mid-sixties, but returned to form for the 1968 production of *Luisa Miller*.[4] In spite of that aberration, Tucker's career was notable for the remarkable consistency and elevated level of his vocalism. The preserved record of his Metropolitan broadcasts certifies that achievement. What remains pertinent is not the occasional obvious gaucheries of style, but rather his serious attitude to performance, his commitment to the composer and (though the two could conflict) to his "public." Add to that his respect for his instrument, his need to protect and preserve it. On the afternoon of this final broadcast, as on so many earlier ones, what most impresses is the poised, judicious arch of his phrasing, his resolute conduct, taut but fluent, of a melodic line, and a timbre somber and intriguing. Though the high-powered portrayals of roles like Canio were much hailed in the final years of his career, to me they seem less memorable than the clean-cut vocalism of earlier portrayals such as Ferrando in the early fifties, Don Alvaro (heard over several decades), and the Puccini Des Grieux. And there were others. Happily, we may add his 1974 Gabriele to that list. I find the most revealing moment of the afternoon to be his reverential tracing of Gabriel's portion of the duettino religioso, 'Eco pia del tempo antico.' Tucker may not have always been humble in life, but a becoming humility permeates his sensitive delivery of this devotional moment. The cantor is back in the temple.

Merrill was Tucker's frequent stage colleague, both in opera and in the many joint concerts they gave, and his friend in private life. He, too, would soon depart from the company that had been his operatic home for thirty-one seasons. The 1975–76 season would see his final Met stage performances (he returned for an operetta duet with Moffo at the 1983 centennial gala, thus trumping the retiree's "point of no return," which I confidently cited at the chapter's head). The broadcast of *Un Ballo in Maschera* on 6 December 1975 marks his last radio appearance. Peters' Oscar is the other familiar component of the afternoon, but Riccardo is a new radio role for Morell, a frequent broadcast tenor. Maureen Forrester makes her broadcast debut as Ulrica, while Elinor Ross (Amelia) and conductor Henry Lewis add interest to the lineup.

Lewis brings a fresh outlook to this demanding score. His way with the elegant intricacies of the initial act may be overly cautious—Verdi's varied components are not easy to blend into a fluid continuity. Thus, his care shortchanges the opera's buoyancy, but a sense of release permeates the remainder of the opera. He knows how to shape a lyric phrase for maximum effect (even act one holds a few choice examples) and extends that precious gift to larger units of the opera as well. The grand duet has the requisite *espansione*, the amplitude nevertheless not inhibiting its pell-mell course; he sends along the repetitious arpeggio accompaniment of 'Oh qual soave brivido,' for instance, with a fleetness that effectively mirrors the uncontrollable passion of the lovers. The final act, too, is well plotted for theatrical impact. The American conductor is no mere operatic caretaker. He takes

Un Ballo in Maschera
6 December 1975

Amelia
Elinor Ross
Oscar
Roberta Peters
Ulrica
Maureen Forrester
Riccardo
Barry Morell
Renato
Robert Merrill
Sam
Raymond Michalski
Conductor
Henry Lewis

charge and places his imprint upon the performance. Can he help it if a number of musical and vocal vulgarities are perpetrated onstage, crudities from which Peters, Morell, and Michalski, to their credit, are exempted?

Miss Peters, like Merrill, is celebrating an anniversary, as announcer Peter Allen reminds us. Twenty-five years at the Met is a formidable milestone, but then the singer came to the company at an early age, so, as sopranos go, she may be considered to be still in her prime. Judging from her vocal estate on this afternoon, she is. Of course, the wear of an exceptionally busy career is bound to rub the luster off a voice. Here and there, the pungent timbre is grainier than the remembered sheen of her early seasons, and one can hear a beat in sustained tones. Beyond those minor strictures, her Oscar is much as it has been for many a broadcast, that is, authoritative, firm in intent, full of sparkling staccatos, and, especially in 'Saper vorreste,' tonally attractive. In the broadcast issue of *Opera News*, the soprano laments that the Met (both in the later Bing years and currently) has not given her more roles and performances; that Rosina went to another high soprano in this anniversary season is a particular sore point.[5] Peters was able to repeat (and did) her *cri de coeur* on the occasion of a much later anniversary of her 1950 Met debut, at a time when she was still singing her inimitable Oscar in the house. Her company worth was considerable.

The Montreal-born contralto Maureen Forrester had long been an esteemed artist on the orchestral and recital circuit. Her operatic career began late and was spotty, though her stage credits, which included the New York City Opera, San Francisco, and a late-career La Scala outing as the *Pique Dame* Countess, eventually added up. It never quite took off, but that may have been by her design. The Met sojourn would be limited to two seasons. An April 1975 debut as Erda (*Rheingold*, with *Siegfried* to follow) led to this sequence of Ulricas. The role choices tell us a good deal about her vocal character. Throughout her career, she had made much of a resounding chest register and it is much in evidence this afternoon. Few Ulricas can emerge from the aria's two-tiered trials unscathed, but one might expect that if anyone could, Forrester would be the lucky one. Even this formidable singer has problems with the piece; perhaps she is just trying too hard for effect. That chest register booms emphatically forth, but the tone is heavy, aurally dead—it lacks vivifying overtones—and the emergence into the higher range is not always well negotiated. (Unfortunately, the 'E lui' section provokes mirth at her numerous moves in and out of registers.) The singer is renowned not only for the size of her instrument but rightly for her musicianship. Still, that admirable quality is bruised by crudities on this afternoon. But then, fortune-tellers are not known for behavioral niceties—a heavy hand is probably an occupational hazard. Forrester fares better in Ulrica's exchanges with Amelia and Riccardo. There vocal size and experience tell.

Morell is a known quantity and he invariably performs with admirable consistency, secure in his vocalism, ably schooled in operatic deportment, and well mannered also in his attention to the score's message. That the tenor, a Met stalwart since his 1958 debut, is unlisted in *The New Grove Dictionary of Opera* (1992), regrettable as it is, suggests a clue to the nature of his equipment. The tone, while not unattractive and notably firm in the voice's upper range, lacks an enveloping velvet. Indeed, it can seem monochromatic over a long role, and its timbral deficiency is not mitigated by density or size—though the voice is so neatly collected that it carries well in the house. Indeed, this tenor has merit and his performance standard must be applauded. By broadcast time, Riccardo had been long in his repertory, both at the Met and other houses. His familiarity with the role and the security of his technique enable him to navigate with both facility and commendable result the considerable vocal traps that Verdi planted in the king's music. In addition, the tenor has acquired a convincingly Italianate style and, more to the point, one that serves the composer, rather than the gallery. (Though lately returned to America, he had been living on the outskirts of Rome since 1968—perhaps the extended residence solidified and augmented his stylistic acuity.) Time after time, Morell's phrases are idiomatically shaped and musically expressive. Those are qualities to be cherished in a tenor. His barcarole, for instance, swaggers with a touch of the sailor's insouciance. True, his portion of the duet seems a bit underpowered when he must compete with a soprano of Ross' vocal endowment. And, while the trying third-act aria is beautifully considered and resolutely delivered (the tessitura does not trouble him), he may just be running out of voice at its close and in the final moments of the opera. Riccardo is a meal for any tenor, but, taken all in all, Morell digests it without causing discomfort either to himself or his audience.

Unlike Morell, Ross has more of the vocal assets that can guarantee admittance to the big-time opera circuit, but she is less expert in her employment of them. Early in her career, the Tampa, Florida, native had appeared with many American companies, beginning with Cincinnati (debut in 1958) and including Boston and San Francisco. A 1965 appearance at La Fenice provided a European send-off for numerous continental engagements. She came to the Met in 1970 as Turandot and throughout the seventies (for nine seasons) would appear with the company in the grand roles of the Italian repertory: Aida, Santuzza, Elisabetta, Gioconda, Lady Macbeth, Tosca, and the *Trovatore* Leonora, with even a single Donna Anna adding to her cachet. The broadcast audience had heard her Tosca in 1970 and Turandot in April 1974. From those assignments, one would assume that the Met management felt she was a candidate for stardom.

The voice itself is a notable one, big and blooming in the upper octave with a fresh-air timbre suggestive of that apple-cheeked wholesomeness which American sopranos as diverse (in merit, too) as Eileen Farrell, the lamented Susan Dunn, and Sharon Sweet have shared. Like Farrell's, hers is a voice that can swell with a welcoming generosity. Her vibrato is wide, however, and, while it lends color to the timbre, it is not always under control, as is evident during the early moments of the opera. The lower octave can be (but is not always) decidedly squawky in agitated moments; it can turn tremulous and lose body as well. She is a committed interpreter, flinging herself into Amelia's torments with passionate involvement. Add that quality to her assets of timbral glow and vocal size and you have a performer who can wake up an audience and command fervid regard. Her reading of the heath aria provokes just such a response. The blemishes and the thrills are there, fortunately not quite in equal proportions, and she builds the climax of the aria (with its troubling ascent to—in her case—a brilliant high C) with sensitivity and assurance. The pair of 'Miserere's is effectively contrasted, the cadenza is fluent, and the low close is negotiated with surprising security. In the duet, tremolo can affect a moment here and there, but she has the vocal means and grand swing of phrase to allow Verdi's rhapsodic rhetoric to thrive. Ross loves to attack a high note softly and then crescendo till the full fruit of her voice hangs free. This time, her high C—at the duet's end—betrays a bit of strain. I wish her syncopations in the agitated trio were cleaner—she offers only a pulsated legato smear. 'Morrò, ma prima in grazia' is less suited to her talents. In spite of its emotive content (before death, Amelia pleads to see her son), the aria profits from a stylized, almost serene delivery in which purity of tone allows the music to speak for itself. Such an interpretation is foreign to Ross' vocal makeup and, perhaps, her temperament. For all that, her tone is emotion-laden, her sincerity is evident—at least, she begins quietly—and, in her own way, she makes the piece work. Her cadenza, though, is not top-drawer. (The introductory cello solo is souped up; could Lewis have dictated this interpretation to coincide with Ross' proclivities, or did he just give the cellist his head?) Ross and Morell have some affecting moments at the ball, she correctly opting for discreet vocalism, he offering some marvelously expansive phrases. In the end, Ross proves to be that type of worthy performer whom every opera management loves to have at hand, but one whose star does not consistently shine brightly enough for membership in the company's premier ranks. Still, a soprano who can soar over the final *concertato*, as Ross does, honors Verdi as well as her talent.

Merrill has been reaping his due for three Met decades and the audience again rewards him on this, his last broadcast appearance. His réclame in the role is confirmed by a remarkable eight broadcast Renatos. One hopes that this final outing will call forth a superior effort. Indeed, the baritone begins well enough, the tone big, dense, and burgeoning with a goodly measure of its wonted warmth. 'Alla vita che t'arride' is reassuring, straightforward in expression, as the aria's rather square construct requires, with only a bit of strain on the top note and thickened tone in the cadenza to indicate excess age. (The baritone carries fifty-eight years at this time.) He is on his best behavior in the heath trio, and notwithstanding—or perhaps because of—a bit of his patented huffing and puffing, the ceremonial oath and its dramatic aftermath are vintage Merrill. (The warm-blooded vocalism of Michalski and more menacing tones of broadcast debutant Philip Booth add character to the Meyerbeerian ceremony; they perform deftly as well in the second-act finale, but it is Lewis who evokes the genuine article of Verdian irony.)

Merrill's reading of 'Eri tu' causes regret, as it has in the past. He declaims the introductory recitative vigorously, but without adequate regard for its rich dramatic and musical subtleties; the voice is all there, but the declamation is punched out rather than scrupulously molded. The aria proper is unduly hurried and cavalier in execution (rather like what late Pavarotti offers in tenor arias at the time of this writing). He does not even take care to give the opening words the dotted rhythm that the brass instruments have just enunciated. The first half of the aria confirms that he still has a fair measure of the vocal goods that have sustained his long career, but as he moves into the remaining portion, he phrases haphazardly and belts out tone. Of course, as of old, the 'dolcezze perdute' suffer, though he does give at least a nod to the text's dictates; he shortchanges the 'brillava' climax before soldiering on to a quick conclusion. Perhaps he felt this was the only way he could negotiate the piece. Complete vocal mastery is no longer his to command, as it had been for so many seasons. In its place, many aging artists have been able to fill in the gaps, so to speak, and offer something special in the way of interpretation. The result can often be uniquely moving. Of course, interpretive

Robert Merrill.

subtlety had never been Merrill's forte. Nevertheless, we could not but hope that he would age well.

When, in the second act, Merrill comes upon the lovers at the gallows hill and briefly utters the husband's warning, he needs only a few tones in the mid-range to demonstrate that he, among the afternoon's performing artists, is the one with a major voice, one that could withstand comparison with the great instruments of memory. In fact, each time that I hear the initial sound of his voice, I am always startled at its resonant solidity, the density of its tonal makeup, its enveloping warmth. British critics occasionally accuse their American brethren of being unfair in judging Merrill's abilities. I suspect that it is his recordings (though not all of them) that commend him so fully to them; our baritone on records was often more alert musically than he was in live performance. Unlike the veteran Tucker, who seemed compelled to always perform at his peak, Merrill, similarly or even more greatly endowed, could not, or at least did not, always deliver his musical and interpretive best. In pure vocal terms, he was far more consistent. And even in the house, some earlier broadcasts reveal how high he could score when put to the test. Moving backward in time, I cite his 1966 Renato, a 1962 Don Carlo, the 1962 and 1961 Barnabas (a role tailor made for the baritone's prodigious vocal assets and straightforward interpretive manner), a 1958 Germont, the 1953 Valentin, and the splendidly voiced Rodrigo of Bing's introductory broadcast of 1950, as well as several earlier performances from the Johnson regime that caused us to believe that equilibrium between voice and artistry could, and would, be achieved. Let his astounding tally of Met performances—788, including Met galas and concerts—testify to his company value and the ongoing regard of the American public. Why should we not accept Verdi's (and Trollope's, for that matter) dictum that audience approval is a valid criterion of excellence?

Of our three American retirees, Dorothy Kirsten would linger longest. And to good purpose. Notwithstanding a 1975 onstage farewell ceremony, it was not until a 1979 Tosca (as replacement for Rysanek) that the final curtain would fall on her Met career. Her radio performances end with the 8 March 1975 broadcast of *Manon Lescaut*. Joining her are Alexander (Des Grieux), Walker (Lescaut), the indispensable Michalski (Geronte), and Jon Garrison (Edmondo). They perform under the direction of Peter Herman Adler, he of television fame whom we met earlier in the 1972 airing of *Ballo*, where he had overseen one of Tucker's last broadcast appearances.

Adler has his own ideas about the opera, preferring, in the earlier portions of the score, a graceful fluidity rather than sparkle (act one) or romantic sweep (act two); in the later acts he adds weight to the harbor scene, at the expense of incisiveness, and draws out the already lugubrious denouement. En route, the gestures can seem guarded, the interpretive posture middle-of-the-road (Adler's measured opening scene, in particular, inhibits the spontaneous character of the students' gaiety). By the final curtain, however, the overall impact is considerable, the conception valid. The later acts indeed are quite impressive—I don't recall the roll call of prostitutes having quite the mournful sordidness that Adler here achieves. His way with the intermezzo combines the two manners effectively, its conclusion leading purposefully into the tragic mood of the opera's final half.

The male functionaries are a fine lot. Castel converts the Lamplighter's vignette into a character study, while Schmorr's Ballet Master is alternately whee-

Manon Lescaut
8 March 1975

Manon
Dorothy Kirsten
Des Grieux
John Alexander
Edmondo
Jon Garrison
Lescaut
William Walker
Geronte
Raymond Michalski
Conductor
Peter Herman Adler

dling or sycophantic, and vividly so in each case. Much of the opening scene's esprit depends on Edmondo, but too often the character comes off as a cipher. Jon Garrison remedies that defect, his every line telling of musical confidence and an alert dramatic sense. His diction is clean and idiomatic while the vocal quality of his modest-sized tenor proves consistently attractive. He will make a career in bigger parts. Kraft's voice is hardly the sound one has in one's ear for the Madrigalist's bewitching song. What art can do, she does. In fact, she dominates the little piece more than most solo madrigalists have in other broadcasts, and her cohorts make up the timbral deficiency.

Puccini has placed so heavy a burden on the two lovers that Lescaut and Geronte, especially in lesser hands, can seem mere plot facilitators. Walker and Michalski, both expert in song and action, make their brief moments count. In his early years with the company, Walker's instrument came off as merely another of those pleasant baritones that America produces in large numbers; his song was invariably attractive, but not marked by individuality or having notable expressive impact. On this afternoon, the voice has gained in heft without damage to its collected focus and, especially, its appealing timbre. Lescaut has no aria as such, but Walker makes one out of an aural sow's ear as he recounts to Manon how he saved her from life in a 'casetta augusta' with the penniless Des Grieux. Every nuance of the part is embraced with relish in his spirited playing of the heroine's ambivalent brother. Geronte is another brand of rascal entirely, and one far less to be welcomed as an acquaintance. Michalski's cultivated instrument may be a shade too fine grained to suggest the lecher, but perhaps the old roué had other attractions than his wealth—this mellifluous bass makes us think so. It does no harm to hear the role sung rather than sinisterly intoned for a change, especially when tone joins thought so advantageously as in Michalski's portrayal.

Des Grieux is a role for great tenors. Lesser lights, beware! Few would give Alexander rank in the breed's most elite, but when he performs at the top of his form, as he does on this afternoon, categorization seems not only ill-natured but ill-advised. This may be the American tenor's finest broadcast portrayal. The initial act's two arias are well contrasted and carefully plotted for overall effect; individual phrases are given distinct profiles and his high notes are tonally dense and securely anchored. Both pieces benefit from greater interpretive variety than he normally allows to infect his song. The role turns into such a high-powered vehicle in the later stages of the opera that Alexander's plangent tones (enlivened by a quick vibrato and occasional calorific overload) cannot overburden Puccini's passionate phrases. His portion of the second-act duet is effective, if not quite searing—and tenors have been known to generate considerable heat in its racing courses. The sea air of Le Havre evidently has resuscitative powers, for there Alexander plays with considerable abandon, Des Grieux's desperation made real in tones both forceful and suppliant.

Kirsten's final broadcast became hers by default. Caballé was scheduled, but nine days earlier the *New York Times* reported the Spanish soprano had been in an automobile accident and would not come to the Met until the 12 March performance. (In the end, the soprano canceled her entire season. Management evidently was having difficulty casting the opera. Price had appeared in the season premiere, but later the scheduled Teresa Kubiak did not go on; Price and Amara took on her appearances.) Announcer Peter Allen opens the broadcast with a lengthy

Dorothy Kirsten as Manon Lescaut. Photography by Louis Mélançon. Courtesy Metropolitan Opera Archives.

statement, and one quite unusual in its specificity. He informs us that Kirsten ("a major, beloved artist") will be performing her oft-repeated feat of "saving" a performance by replacing "her ailing colleague" (the oft-canceling Caballé). He assures us that she has "regularly scheduled" performances as well and that her good deed is partly motivated by her love for the role of Manon. (Longtime broadcast listeners will recall that the diva starred in the opera's revival in the final year of the Johnson regime.) Clearly, the diva's rescue missions were much appreciated by management and they were taking pains to avoid any implication that she was merely a cover artist.

We now know that, by this time in her career, Kirsten had experienced sixty-five winters and, with agreeable freshness, was about to enter her sixty-fifth spring, the tally to be confirmed by a summer birth date. Thus her heroic deed is even more admirable. Need she be offered a handicap? Only, I would say, in regard to the character of her timbre, which on this afternoon rarely reveals its familiar sweetness. The tone itself is invariably secure, devoid of wobble, and accurately deployed, indeed, sometimes on high with sharpshooting marksmanship. Those are commendable assets at any age. The upper range still holds her loveliest tones, and a few top notes on this afternoon have a fullness—occasionally even a dramatic thrust—that she did not often allow herself (and us) in her youth. But probably the soprano sets forth more of a fast-day collation than a holiday vocal feast. Too many of today's tones lack warmth and are excessively narrow, sometimes even pinched. I would have difficulty recognizing the voice in its first-act incarnation—it was so often a blandishing instrument in her younger days. But any aging soprano needs an act or two to warm up, and things improve decidedly in the second act. Her singing of 'In quelle trine morbide' is a marvel. With exquisite control, she etches its elegant phrases, the timbre initially still a bit acidulous, but gaining calescence as she goes. How well she knows her instrument, what it can do and, of even greater import, what it cannot! The latter guides her during the grand duet. Care and control can inhibit this rapturous music, but Kirsten finds a judicious balance between the imperatives of her present vocal estate and the requirements of Puccini's rhapsodic construct. Yet those imperatives are, in reality, little different from those she imposed upon her voice in earlier broadcast portrayals. Tone is always collected, even pointed, seldom voluptuous. At a few moments, she would prefer to move things along more than Adler's gracious stance permits—hers is the better medicine. When singing a few key unaccompanied phrases ('Son forse della Manon d'un giorno meno piacente e bella?' is one), she shines as any Manon should, displaying there (and, one could say, virtually everywhere else) the accumulated wealth of her experience. One demerit of that know-how is her avoidance of any text in the soaring phrase 'Pensavo a un avvenir di luce.' (Her crime may be forgiven. Imagine the number of such lapses we would be counting if Caballé were wafting her delectable tone on high.) But a touch of interpretive poverty robs 'E fascino d'amore' of love's purported magic spell. Nor is her suppliance at 'Un' altra volta ancora' (after Geronte's discovery of the lovers) quite convincing. Better to pass over a few earlier moments (an aspirated 'Lodi aurate mormorate' and an excessively doll-like 'L'ora, o Tirsi') and offer as justification a belief that Puccini was, for once, unkind to his soprano. Even so, Kirsten's splendid, velvety high C and firm cadence rescue the librettist's salute to the miracle of love.

I wish I could write more enthusiastically of her efforts when Manon suffers on the Louisiana plain. For me, her bright, metallic tone cannot conjure the desperation of 'Sola, perduta, abbandonata.' The soprano has added some credible veristic touches ('Orribilemente!' now suggests horror, unlike some earlier readings of the cry), but her skills, considerable though they are, do not seem to include the ability to evoke despair or pathos—not to the full, at any rate. Nor will the employment of a childlike tone summon heartfelt response for the dying Manon. Yet the voice never wavers in its control, even when Kirsten gives her all, which she does here and with notable success throughout the entire afternoon. Now and then, she joins Alexander in a full-throated sounding of a climactic phrase; in contrast, as death approaches, she applies to 'Mio dolce amor' a fond caress. For her artistry, her vocal mastery, her reassuring professionalism, and her longevity, Kirsten deserves more than one in return. She was mistress of her craft.

Of course, all was not over for the diva, even at the Met. She was granted the rare opportunity to say a farewell to the radio audience on the broadcast of 27 December 1975; a Tosca three days later was to have been her Met farewell. But management called upon her during the next three seasons to again "save the performance." Her Met seasons eventually added up to thirty (she was absent for several years during a Met career span from 1945 to 1979) and her appearances numbered, according to Peter Allen's count, 282 (the *Annals* lists 281), 114 of them on tour. One notes that the Lincoln Center house heard only thirty-five performances during the twelve seasons when she appeared there. Nor was the broadcast total as large as one hoped. Her nineteen radio appearances began with Louise (1948) and included Fiora, Manon Lescaut, Marguerite, Butterfly, Tosca, Mimi, Minnie, and Rosalinde. Micaela, Nedda, Juliette (how I should love to have heard that portrayal—her voice and style seemed made for French opera), Violetta, and Manon were welcome house ventures. For a major portion of her career, some aficionados were not overly enamored of her portrayals. Her famed efficiency evidently chilled their ardor. Instead, the diva enjoyed a wide public, nurtured in part by a few early film appearances and a major radio career. Today we value more highly her thorough mastery of her roles, the assurance of her vocal control, and the remarkable consistency of her portrayals. The charm of the honeyed tone that characterized the majority of her performances remains a precious memory for all who heard her. I recall, in particular, seeing a number of live performances, portrayals apart from her more familiar Puccini heroines: most notably, an informative (for me) San Francisco Fiora; that Lisa (in *Pique Dame*) which she regretted undertaking, but which she brought off with characteristic poise; and a Violetta in St. Louis (the Met on tour) where her enchanting, shining 'Alfredo, di questo core' quietly crept into the musical fabric with wondrous subtlety.

Tucker, Merrill, and Kirsten depart and with them any leftover imprint of the Johnson regime all but disappears. (Hines, the indestructible, of course remains.) In effect, Bing's mark upon the company was so strong in the intervening years that the three departing titans (especially the men) may be considered more his creatures than his predecessor's. In the mid-seventies, just what managerial force would ultimately establish itself with the authority of the Bing regime—or, for that matter, even govern with assurance—remained in doubt. But most opera watchers agreed that the Metropolitan still had, in relative abundance, major artists on its roster, singers who could assuage regrets at current losses.

Wagner and His Friends by Wilhelm Beckmann. Cosima Wagner, Richard Wagner, Franz Liszt, and Hans von Wolzogen at Wahnfried, 1882.

CHAPTER FIFTEEN

Teutonic Resuscitation

To quit the human passions of Italian opera and take up the more cerebral musings of the Teutonic genre involves considerably more enterprise than merely crossing the Dolomites. Culture shock is inevitable. But the disorientation may be cushioned by a stopover in Vienna, where the scent of the south lingers in the nostrils and Gemütlichkeit reigns. There Mozart penned his *Zauberflöte* and Strauss situated *Der Rosenkavalier*. After an astringent bath in the Munich-born composer's *Salome*, we can turn back in time to tackle the weighty Wagner corpus, the burden more easily shouldered by our agreeable detour. The body Wagnerian at the Met, insufficiently nourished during this period, continues to require life-saving measures. *Tristan und Isolde* is on the docket—passion is its watchword, proving that the Italians have no monopoly on that marketable commodity (though it's true that the redoubtable Richard did write *Tristan*'s searing middle act in Venice). A complete *Ring* will follow. An intriguing auditory voyage lies before us.

Mozart, as ever, is the most obliging of guides as we set out. *Die Zauberflöte* had long been one of the Met's superior efforts and the 1967 Chagall production added further stature to the record. The broadcast of 23 December 1972, its coffers enriched by a pride of principals either new to the airwaves or these roles, ranks near the top of the line in the radio chronicle. On this afternoon, we first come upon maestro Peter Maag, and welcome his companionship is, for his conception of the opera is not only well thought out but, *en route* and in the aggregate, endearing. Joining him as broadcast debutants are tenor Stuart Burrows (Tamino) and bass Hans Sotin (Sarastro), with Maliponte, Moser, Reardon, and Gramm offering virgin radio portrayals as Pamina, Queen of the Night, Papageno, and the Speaker.

Maag, Swiss-born and a conductor cosmopolite, is heard in his introductory season, the first of three consecutive visits, with limited Met exposure later on. *Giovanni* had been his calling card, and future years would hold an unlikely *Traviata*, the more plausible *Falstaff*, and *Norma* (no surprise there—it was on Wagner's list). Onetime assistant to the revered Ernest Ansermet and thereafter resident at Düsseldorf, general director of the Bonn Opera, and principal conductor of the Vienna Volksoper in the late sixties, Maag had been heard in Chicago as early as 1961. The opening chords of the *Flute* overture are grand, but less assertive than most conductors command. They not only usher us into the Masonic ideal, but

Die Zauberflöte
23 December 1972

Pamina
Adriana Maliponte
Queen
Edda Moser
Tamino
Stuart Burrows
Papageno
John Reardon
Sarastro
Hans Sotin
Conductor
Peter Maag

347

signal that a tender hand will be laid upon the opera's musical felicities. His spacious phrases give way to a fugato that is more gracious than the pell-mell scratching we sometimes hear. And he allows the winds to sing. The stage participants will be honored with the same courtesy and their reward is our gain as well. The Swiss conductor loves to linger over the enchanting postludes that Mozart scattered throughout the opera; ritards are anything but mere obeisances—they become to-the-floor genuflections. But his music making is loving, well ordered, and in harmony with his singers. In spite of a few momentary disconnects, it satisfies.

Several familiar characterizations still give pleasure. Franke's Monostatos, hefty enough in voice to sound the moor's wickedness, is played with such comic unction as to exempt the villain from his villainy. Di Franco's Papagena is delightfully decrepit in her old hag dialogue and pert-toned as Papageno's longed-for spouse. Pracht is comfortably at home as First Lady, her silvery tones cushioned by the warm voices and solid ensemble of Love and Casei. MacWherter's stentorian Man in Armor again overbalances Sgarro's compatriot. Priests Castel and Christopher are better matched. As negotiated by three boys, the Geniis' trios are piquantly piped; though not quite *echt* in execution, their song, tonally acute, adds color to the vocal spectrum. The spoken realm is another story. The overall level registers in the neutral zone. Maliponte's spoken words sound excessively childish for even the virginal Pamina; Burrows and Sotin are at ease with their lines; and Reardon's everyday speech defines his character.

The vocal acrobatics of the Queen of the Night are capably performed by Moser. Her voice is healthier in size and darker in timbre than those of most interpreters, a point in her favor. Dramatic verisimilitude is thereby enhanced and the pathetic temper of 'Zum Leiden bin ich auserkoren,' often the weak sister of the mother's royal offerings, receives favorable treatment. She has the high Fs, one squeak notwithstanding, and, though she warbles those troublesome triplets, her staccatos are on point. Eighteen Met outings in the role testify to her qualifications for this benighted role. In the decades ahead, often fruitless searches by management would seldom uncover a comparable winner of these coloratura sweepstakes.

As usual, a few phrases of Maliponte's flutelike tones are needed for the ear to adjust to the relative absence of vibrato. (Her ensemble with the three boys is informing and entrancing—the unity of timbre, pure, one might say even innocent, provides a unique listening experience.) Reconciliation achieved, the soprano's elegant tracing of Pamina's grateful music is one of the main treasures of the afternoon's superior vocalism. Notes in the opening phrases of 'Bei Männern' may be excessively discrete, but the vocalized descents at its close confirm both her technical command and tonal beauty. In the ensembles with Burrows and Sotin, her tones take on surprising size and density, and all to the good, for Pamina needs to show some spunk in these grander episodes. 'Ach, ich fühl's' is wonderfully assured, precise in attack, and tonally beguiling. The aria, linear and spare in Mozart's design, is expertly drawn by her instrumentally conceived vocalism. The result is far from antiseptic in overall effect, for Pamina's grief is subtly sounded, not only by the soprano's discreet treatment of the appoggiaturas, but in particular by her intervallic exactitude. In the florid coils of 'so wird Ruh im Tode sein,' for instance, the half- and whole-steps are so accurately delineated, their intonation so minutely gauged, that both the affect and the music are enriched. And here, Maag displays a finely graded control of pulse in his fluid placement of the repetitious two-chord accompaniment; that quality of movement, arsic, unhurried, yet supportive, must be reassuring to a responsive singer.

The men on stage merit acclaim as well. Gramm's Speaker, tonally ingratiating, dispenses a saintly calm that allows Mozart's pioneering *arioso* declamation unusual poignancy, especially in the lengthy exchange with Tamino. Reardon is at the opposite end of the interpretive spectrum. His Papageno is very much a man of the people. Uppman's six broadcast portrayals (with one more to come) have given his charming, subtly whimsical conception such prominence that at certain points in the opera ('Klinget, Glöckchen' is one moment) the ear must adjust to Reardon's more plebeian—but still appropriate—playing. He is Schikaneder's pawn. The vocalism is a bit matter of fact (and rather too serious in the duet with Pamina), but no doubt this birdcatcher is adept at his day job. His ensemble playing is expert, his dialogue emphatic and clean. Probably he carries his fractions a bit too far in the suicide scene. (Papagenos love to prolong the comic suspense in the countdown to the birdcatcher's threat of suicide by splintering the count as they near three.) The ploy is such a sorry, audience-massaging device. Never mind—Reardon's assured performance of this pivotal character belongs on the positive side of the ledger. Debutant Sotin, at home at the Hamburg Staatsoper, had been heard at Glyndebourne before coming to the Met. Still in his early thirties, he contributes to the overall genial tone of the afternoon with a portrayal of Sarastro that is more ingratiating than most basses, particularly those of Germanic heritage, are wont to offer. The voice is a sizable one (bung full, in fact), but to his credit, he prefers not to spend all its wealth at every opportunity. Moreover, the timbre is not overweighted with the black coloration that many of his breed proudly nurture—indeed, an attractive dab of sweetness infects the voice's upper portion, an additive that lends uniqueness to his instrument. Like the Queen of the Night's about-face, Sarastro's double image (was it really a libretto change of heart?) causes puzzlement to this day. But Sotin's sorcerer is humane from the get-go, and is none the worse for his smoothing away the priest's excessive sternness. Maag reinforces that conception by sending the hymns neatly along—lugubriousness is routed. I wonder if the touch of suspect pitch in Sotin's arias played a role in limiting his Met sojourn to a single season in the seventies. The later decades of the century would correct that neglect.

In an afternoon of multiple pleasures, I would place Burrows' Tamino at the head of the list. The Welsh tenor had begun his career with the Welsh National Opera, moved on to Covent Garden in 1967 (twenty-two seasons there certify his quality), and had appeared at San Francisco, the Vienna Staatsoper, and Salzburg before his Met baptism as Ottavio in the current season. As Tamino, he plays a prince and a prince of vocalism he is. I do not mean to slight the dramatic focus of his portrayal or his fire in recitatives—there he excels, whether dealing with the aggressive ladies of act one or confronting authority later on. And he is ardent when contemplating his beloved. But it is the beauty of the voice, its confident production (not a note is out of place throughout the entire opera), its ease in the upper regions, that are so compelling. The timbre, airy and meaty at the same time, is most attractive, holding within its generous confines an unspoiled freshness, as though the man had been born and suckled in nurturing climes. Add in responsible musicianship, notably his exemplary control of line and dynamics, and his worth registers considerably above the norm. And he is a manly tenor, not one of those simpering Mozartians who discreetly peck away at the composer's precious provender. Occasionally one hears echoes of the best German tenors of successive generations (fleeting suggestions of singers like Wittrisch and Wunderlich, to name two) in his tones. 'Dies Bildnis is bezaubernd schön' is about as securely vocalized as I have heard it, the tenor bestowing upon it not only tonal wealth and a lover's eagerness, but a reverence of thought made audible in his conduct of line. His portion of the all-important dialogue with Gramm is noble and moving; how tenderly his quiet lyricism closes the interchange. The second-act trio of Maliponte, Sotin, and Burrows is, as Mozart intended, one of the peaks of the afternoon's music making; sometimes the episode is spoiled by mismatched casting, but all three artists have legato, fluency in brief divisions, and tonal discretion at their disposal. With Maag expert at deepening affect, the opera thrives here and elsewhere. An early nineteenth-century critic called it "one continued and deep river of music."[1] It flows freely on this afternoon.

Der Rosenkavalier
14 April 1973

Marschallin
Leonie Rysanek
Sophie
Judith Blegen
Octavian
Yvonne Minton
Italian Singer
John Alexander
Faninal
Morley Meredith
Baron Ochs
Walter Berry
Conductor
Ignace Strasfogel

From Vienna north to Dresden is a sizable leap, but Strauss probably felt the distance was not as great as the ground mileage—sound is the composer's medium and thus musicians travel by air. The premiere of *Der Rosenkavalier* occurred in that northern city and even the serious Dresdenites were charmed by the opera's cozy Viennese milieu. In spirit, Strauss inhaled that southern fragrance and sprinkled it liberally over his "Mozartian" masterwork. In the broadcast of 14 April 1973, Walter Berry's Ochs is the genuine article (he had played the reprobate in the 1969 and 1970 airings) and the occasion holds a raft of new radio portrayals. Yvonne Minton undertakes the title role with Blegen as the winsome Sophie, Meredith her father, Alexander the foiled Italian singer, and Velis and Baldwin as scheming intriguers. Topping the inviting cast list is Rysanek, whose Marschallin is also a carryover from the 1969 and 1970 broadcasts. Whereas Böhm had guided the previous pair of radio performances, this occasion falls (the verb is advisedly chosen) to Ignace Strasvogel, a veteran member of the company's second-tier conductors.

Caretaker is the usual lot of the well-schooled Metropolitan staff conductor, and Strasvogel cannot escape that delimiting function on this broadcast. The orchestra players seem marginally inattentive. One notes lack of precision when solo winds add punctuation to a phrase and string melodies are sometimes casually guided. Overall, the orchestral fabric lacks definition. The performance proceeds without mishap but neither the infectious sparkle nor the luxuriant sonorities of Strauss' orchestration come into their own. Strasvogel paces the concluding trio and duet rather slowly, and his way has merit, more than much that has gone before. Yet the surly trumpet entry as Mahomet trips out is overly intrusive (and barely on time) and symptomatic of the orchestral playing on this afternoon. The conductor's honorable service in sixteen Met seasons (conducting thirty-two operas) would end with the current season.

Experienced practitioners people the stage. Velis' Valzacchi, nasal in timbre, pointed in delivery, and entirely convincing, carries the load for the Italian intriguers—Baldwin only passes muster as Annina. Anthony's clarion-toned Innkeeper enlivens the final act, where Best's Commissioner is appropriately officious, but dull-voiced. If you believe that Italian tenors should spout brilliant tone, you will find Alexander your man. He sings the trying aria to greater effect than many a

Judith Blegen as Sophie in *Der Rosenkavalier*. Photography by Louis Mélançon.
Courtesy Metropolitan Opera Archives.

more famous tenor, assertively scaling its mountainous peaks with assurance, even choosing to linger here and there on top tones that most interpreters are content to barely touch before leaping off in fright. Here is a Bacchus in the making. Meredith, too, makes something out of the ordinary of the ungrateful role of Faninal. His impressive height would have added to the force of his characterization. The voice has a touch of pomposity built into its gray timbre—the self-importance suits the bourgeois father. Even so, when Faninal bewails his daughter's behavior and later deals with the wounded Baron, Meredith mixes genuine regret with the stock fustian gestures we normally witness.

And well this father might lament his daughter's willfulness. As Blegen plays her, Sophie would be quite a handful for the most insightful of fathers to manage. Even as she awaits Count Rofrano's arrival, this young lady clearly knows her own mind—not a single simper will escape her lips the entire performance. ('Das Ganze war halt eine Farce' comes close, but at that moment Sophie's fantasy world has suddenly collapsed around her.) The voice is nigh perfect in character and usage for an ingénue soprano; beyond attractive timbre and secure placement, it is deployed with expert technical control and precision. Musicianly deportment and adept response to character further guarantee her prominence as the broadcast Sophie of choice over the next decade. The young American soprano had first taken on the role at the Met only a month before the broadcast. Some might prefer the dollop of sugar in the timbre that other singers have brought to the part; in Blegen's interpretation, a bit of the maiden's charm is suppressed. But in the long run, her minx wears well. The 'himmlische' leaps as she receives the rose are indeed heavenly, the attack exact, the tone sweet enough. She finds a delightful variety of utterance as she enumerates Octavian's names. Minton is equally assured and tonally lovely as the two singers take full advantage of the celestial spell that Strauss cast in the presentation scene. The contrast with Blegen's spunky rejection of the proposed bridegroom makes for good theater. While she glowingly delivers her portion of the trio, oddly she fails to shine in the closing duet. Perhaps it is merely distance from a microphone that makes her sound ineffectual; even if one accepts that caveat, her sign-off note thins out (and Minton's has an uncharacteristic hooty cast).

The young Australian mezzo, already a fixture at Covent Garden, makes an auspicious broadcast debut, preceded by Chicago outings in the same role a few years earlier. She owns a superb instrument, healthily bronze in cast, with a brilliant shine; the voice is not overburdened with vibrato (in fact, occasionally it can sound a bit straight or slightly wooden—but those are rare moments of high tension). Happily for her listeners, it is devoid of the pesky register breaks that plague many of her ilk. The instrument is so forthright that it seems tailor made for trouser roles; her vocal character and assertive dramatic playing make Octavian seem more mature than most interpreters of Hofmannsthal's precocious seventeen-year-old suggest (one could deem him well on the road to manhood, but that would only add to the confusion). Height and noble bearing (apparent in *Opera News* photos) add to that impression. Her sculptured delivery of Octavian's difficult opening lines is remarkably assured, clarion of timbre, interpretively alive, the phrases beautifully shaped. Immediately we understand that she will be a cavalier who can inspire both respect and love. The opera's progress reinforces that belief. Her climaxes thrill, her theatrical impact is potent; the Marschallin's 'heut oder morgen' prognostications, for instance, draw forth fervent musical and dramatic responses from Minton. And yet she can be tender, and is, to both the Marschallin ('Will Sie sich traurig machen mit Gewalt?') when the princess recounts how she stops the clocks in the night, and to Sophie, in the quiet repose of the rose presentation colloquy. She makes a charmingly touching moment of Octavian's little apology to Faninal for the "accident" to Ochs. But it is her radiant vocalism that remains favorably in the ear, notably as heard in the trio and final duet. Regrettably, Minton's Met career would be severely limited, but her European triumphs would continue for many years.

With the memory of Berry's warm, humane Barak still strong, one is not disposed to think him a likely candidate for the boorish Ochs. Most biographical notices list him as a baritone, rather than the bass-baritone (*Grove* names him so, however) usually assigned the part. But Berry is so intelligent an artist that he is bound to play to his strengths no matter the role, and so he does on this afternoon. He offers no country bumpkin, no crude roué, but rather a cousin to the Marschallin who has not entirely forsaken his aristocratic heritage. Beery bass growls are beyond the pale. He *will* sing the part—and worthwhile it is to hear Ochs thus performed. Of course, trade-offs are inevitable. We forgo at the voice's bottom what we gain at the top: a weak 'Da lieg ich' and hasty traversal—disguised by a curtain laugh—must suffice for the final low notes of the 'mit mir' waltz episode, but the firmest, heartiest high F enlivens the waltz scene and a delightful head tone cushions 'aus lauter Federbetten.' Obviously, comfort means something special to this Ochs. Throughout the afternoon, he will rely more upon interpretive touches than rough, boorish tone to bring the Baron to life. The singer allows the first version of the 'mit mir' waltz tune to bloom and the fragrance is intoxicating. No slurring, sliding, or nasal ploys for him. Yes, he might well "throw away" a few phrases in the rapid patter of the first act. But Berry's Baron is no caricature. He has backbone and he is determined. He manhandles the notary and, even when discovered in disreputable circumstances at the inn, bargains with the Marschallin in solid, earthy tones. Yet he sings his 'silberne Rose' phrase with polish, proving his right of entry into the Marschallin's boudoir. Thereafter Berry takes the often troublesome high note (usually sung falsetto) with a graceful portamento, adding an anticipatory note, before expanding the tone in an admirable demonstration of the singer's art. Oddly, though a native of the city, in diction and dramatic posture Berry is less "Wienerisch" than most who play the role. Is his Ochs a 'schlechte Kerl?' Hardly. Does he misrepresent Hofmannsthal's and Strauss' brazenly coarse character? You may think so. But it is such a pleasure to make his acquaintance. And to hear him sing.

When Berry and Rysanek discuss the uncanonical parentage of Mariandel, the two pros (the soprano likewise at home in Vienna) know how to play the game. The much-loved Leonie was so much associated with the Strauss heroines that one is tempted to give her Marschallin the same pride of place in that galaxy as her Empress, Ariadne, Chrysothemis, and Salome have earned. Yet the Princess von Werdenberg is an atypical Strauss creature, for (except for the act-three trio) she is not favored with those soaring flights of phrase that were Rysanek's playground, phrases where shimmering arcs of silvery tone were ecstatically, sometimes almost erotically, brandished to her auditors' delight. The Marschallin is a pensive creature, more given to musing than to airborne action. Moreover, a good deal of her perusing lies in the mid- and lower range, territory where our soprano must proceed with care and caution. As often noted, considerable improvement in that troublesome area has been achieved. Indeed, her full-voiced initial phrases are reassuring. Still, care and caution remain as inhibitors to an ideally realized portrayal. Whenever Strauss allows his Marschallin to dwell in the upper vocal range, Rysanek showers the glittering petals of her vocalism upon us. Even when such a critical act-one curtain phrase as 'Da drin ist die silberne Ros'n' does not quite meet expectations, its impact is retrieved when she crowns it with an exquisite top tone that is almost worth the price of the whole. The monologues suffer the most from the deficiency; too often the mid and lower tones are clouded, the overall effect murky. She is such a perceptive artist that she can command with tones of utmost quietude, and often does in the Marschallin's personal revelations. And yet that care and caution, the ever-lurking murkiness, cast an overlay of sadness, a pervasive melancholy, upon the entire characterization (even in her public moments). The pose seems more like overkill for this still-young woman. Surely, her creators wanted us to believe that there is more to the Marschallin than the frightened stopper of clocks in the night. Should our soprano not be more relaxed, less restrained, more playful when prescribing her visit to dear uncle Griefenklau and—especially—when inviting Octavian to ride beside her carriage in the Prater? One more thing. The princess is given to talk and we need to hear her words; Rysanek's vocalism is based on tone and line rather than the word—that's one reason she can soar—so here again the role does not quite fit.

That said, does she bring it off? Of course. She gives a polished performance, with many interpretive touches that touch us in turn. When she tells Quinquin 'Es ist ein Besuch,' the soprano offers not only a charming inflection but also conveys the Marschallin's relief upon learning that the intruder is not her husband. And her preoccupation with sending those glistening high tones out into the house pays dividends even when the interstices are longer than one wants. In the monologues, lovely phrases do surface, as when she remembers young Resi. And her silences tell as well. Her hauntingly intimate reading of 'Ist halt vorbei' (understatement is her weapon) confirms the dramatic actress' skill as the princess acknowledges to herself that she, as well as the Baron, must renounce what was precious to her. The trio opening is expertly controlled, not quite as tonally glowing as I believe she can deliver, but still very fine, as is the remainder of the purifying ensemble. At the bows, the audience gives her the tribute that this committed artist deserves.

At one point in the opera, the befuddled Ochs asks, 'Was ei'm Kavalier nit all's passieren kann in dieser Wienerstadt!' (What curious adventures can happen to a cavalier in this city of Vienna!). More of them await us, as we take up another broadcast *Rosenkavalier*, that of 23 February 1974. An entirely new cast of principals is on hand. Evelyn Lear is the musing Marschallin, Birgitte Fassbaender the precocious lover, and Edith Mathis the bride bait. Veteran bass Manfred Jungwirth plays the reprobate Baron, with Dooley as his prospective father-in-law and Leo Goeke the Italian singer. Best of all, Böhm is back on the podium's throne.

The appetite for adventure is whetted by the novel cast that management has provided. Seldom do we have the opportunity to hear a repertory opera stocked entirely with new portraits and, in this case, with strangers to our terrain. The prospect is both inviting and dangerous, the former because of expected pleasure,

Der Rosenkavalier
23 February 1974

Marschallin
Evelyn Lear
Sophie
Edith Mathis
Octavian
Brigitte Fassbaender
Italian Singer
Leo Goeke
Faninal
William Dooley
Baron Ochs
Manfred Jungwirth
Conductor
Karl Böhm

Evelyn Lear as the Marschallin in *Der Rosenkavalier*. Photography by James Heffernan. Courtesy Metropolitan Opera Archives.

the other for the same reason: disappointment can be great when artists known and valued only through recordings are heard firsthand. When hope is high, the odds for disheartenment increase as well.

With the return of Böhm to guide his friend Strauss' buoyant concoction we may expect pace and execution of a higher level than Strasvogel provided. No disappointment on that score need trouble us. True, as is often apparent in the maestro's late-career offerings—a summer eightieth birthday awaits him—pleasure is pitted by occasional ensemble imprecision and stylistic crudities. Exuberance can get out of hand, as it does in the second-act brawl. And he turns Ochs' exit at the opera's end into the orchestral equivalent of a bump-and-grind routine. But those are momentary aberrations. From the first notes of the *Einleitung* (instead of Strasfogel's glutinous mass, Böhm provides a clean, no-nonsense reading, one purposefully paced) on through Mahomet's curtain wave, the Austrian maestro demonstrates his thorough command of the intricate score. He is at ease with both its delicious fizzle—the fugato that opens the inn act fairly sizzles as its blithe string figurations fly on the wind—and its lyrical sentiment. The maestro's handling of the latter moods is discreet but revelatory. Time after time the orchestral commentary speaks with extraordinary perspicacity upon the stage action, augmenting the inner thoughts of the characters. A particularly felicitous characteristic of Böhm's music making is his ability to nurture a momentary expressive peak, allowing it to billow forth in a brief spilling of orchestral tone before easing it back to a safe dynamic middle ground.

Velis' flinty Valzacchi and Ordassy's fussy duenna are hardly sufficient constants to safely anchor expectation. Mildred Miller, a new broadcast Annina and now near the end of a long and, most often, felicitous Metropolitan career, has the not very agreeable task of echoing her fellow intriguer's machinations. In her time a delightful Cherubino and knowing Nicklausse, here she executes the most confident and clean delivery of that tricky roller-coaster phrase 'Die Kaiserin muss ihn mir wiedergeben!' in broadcast history. Goeke's Italian tenor, however, cannot erase memories of earlier tenor turns. The voice is merely serviceable, with noticeable strain on the topmost notes, but his legato is able enough. Perhaps we should seek comfort in verisimilitude: Goeke's singer is a more likely approximation of what a Viennese princess could command for an early-morning boudoir appearance than the star tenors of many a broadcast. That rationalization is as hard to swallow as its cause.

Dooley's Faninal, however, is cause for celebration. American though he be, his career has for long been moored in German houses, where text treatment and detailed characterization are essentials. Once again, he proves their efficacy in his detailed, fully realized portrait of Sophie's father. At first the voice seems grayer than the heady instrument of old, but he soon warms to his task and warms his voice in the process. His parvenu evidently has absorbed more graces, vocal and histrionic, than the libretto dictates, but they are nonetheless welcome.

Austrian bass Jungwirth was a latecomer to the international operatic scene. At broadcast time, he was already in his mid-fifties, his career at major venues acknowledged by a Glyndebourne appearance in 1965 and his long-delayed debut at the Vienna Staatsoper in 1967. Appearances in San Francisco (1971) preceded his Met debut as Ochs in the current season. Vast experience in his earliest years at Innsbruck, Frankfurt, and Berlin anchored these prime engagements. On this afternoon, the busy career of more than three decades seems to have worn away the shine and diluted the pith of his bass. The tone lacks vibrancy and his interpretation individuality. Berry's effervescent creation, novel to be sure, seems a far remove but, more pertinently, Jungwirth has converted the familiar arrogant rogue of other interpreters into the equivalent of a public accountant. Put more judiciously, his Ochs is a fair replica of a country squire, one oblivious of city ways, hardly a 'Kerl,' but a man who knows his own mind and is unfazed by the glitter of Viennese society. Of course, to play in such a middle-of-the-road manner has the virtue of committing few interpretive mortal sins—except for the hardly venal one of minimizing our delight. By the end of the second act (the all-important waltz scene) he seems on the verge of losing his voice; the low E and its precursors are no more puissant than Berry's baritone efforts. The intermission cures the ill, however, and he makes a commanding exit from the inn. He does make a meal of his first voicing of the 'mit mir' tune, swinging it jauntily, the voice taking on body and color. And I do like his sure handling of the upstart Octavian when the infatuated youth warns him off Sophie. There the seeds of a well-thought-out characterization are apparent in his shrewd combination of disdain for the cavalier's belligerence and amusement at the boy's sexual precocity. One could name other evidences of his long familiarity with the part. Perhaps it is only because we have become accustomed to more florid interpretations of this role that his professionalism seems minor league. His career, which includes recording the role under Solti, would seem to dictate that a more receptive appraisal could be warranted.

Miss Fassbaender, unlike Jungwirth, had made a big splash early on in her career. Just a few years in small parts at the Bavarian State Opera (beginning in 1961) had preceded appearances in major roles in Berlin, Hamburg, Salzburg, Covent Garden, Paris, La Scala, and San Francisco. Of equal note, she was the daughter of Willi Domgraf-Fassbaender, a favorite Glyndebourne baritone. Theater was in the genes. At the time of her Met debut as Octavian the week before the broadcast, the mezzo, just entering her mid-thirties and trim and agile onstage, was at the peak of her form. Her Octavian was justly famous throughout Europe. In the broadcast, she proves herself an artist of strong convictions made doubly potent in execution. Repeatedly, she demonstrates her quality, most often at key moments of the performance. Not the least of these is her authoritative delivery of Octavian's opening phrases. There the voice's security, its vibrant timbre, and, above all, the singer's passionate ardor in turn command our imagination and regard. She never sings anything without conveying a sense of complete involvement in her mission. In her treatment of text, she evidences the lieder singer's preoccupation with word inflection. It is well that she does, for despite the voice's intense coloration, the heavy mix of chest in the lower notes, always powerfully deployed, and the carrying up of that resonance high into the upper range allow for little modification of timbre, color variation, or, at least to some degree, dynamic shading. That is cause for disappointment. While her tendency to perform at full tilt most often provokes thrilling results, it can be wearing. She is able to sing softly, however, as she demonstrates in her loving voicing of the presentation episode. By the opera's end, we have heard a few hooty top tones, but overall the voice retains its luster, dark and assertive, even in the most demanding episodes. As was evident in her response to the 'heut oder Morgen' musings of the Marschallin and her open combat with the culture-deaf Ochs (she is a veritable spitfire there), it is Fassbaender's zealous playing, her complete immersion in Octavian's volatile emotions, that remains as the salient feature of her portrayal.

Sophie is a new Met role this season for Mathis, though we have met the singer herself in the 1972 broadcast of *Der Freischütz*. When considering her Ännchen, I noted that her soprano was healthy enough not to be damned with the soubrette brand. That can be a vocal asset or, in a few roles—of which Sophie is one—a debility. Indeed, Mathis' voice is touched by a darker coloration than one would expect, considering her repertory. Sophie is an ingénue role par excellence and Blegen's timbre and vocal usage, for instance, are emblematic of the girl's character. They complement the music—giddy in its heights—that Strauss penned for her. Mathis, a lovely artist and secure vocalist, brings many virtues to the role: a voice devoid of tremulousness, a warm timbre, integrity in musical matters, and skill in characterization. Nevertheless she little suggests Sophie's naiveté, her girlish inexperience. Even as she awaits, rather calmly, the arrival of her prospective bridegroom, she is an assured mistress of her fate. This maiden is more her father's true daughter than the unspoiled, demure creature one expected to meet in his 'Stadpalais.' Let us look on the bright side: her maturity might ensure a happier marriage with Octavian than we normally anticipate.

In the Viennese manner, the Swiss soprano favors portamentos—they aid her vaults to Sophie's high notes. An occasional hardness encrusts a few of those (and a bit of strain mars the inn duet's final top tone, where Fassbaender's loud ascent also dilutes the critical moment). And yet 'Ist wie ein Gruss vom Himmel,' sparked by a splendidly controlled crescendo, is a superior feat of vocalism. Everywhere she serves up a flow of honey, rather than the sweetness of sugar that can more quickly sicken the palate. Indeed, as she cottons to the young cavalier, she darts up and down her range with the unfettered freedom of—yes!—the soubrette. But the timbre never loses its inviting core of warmth. She has plenty of voice to sound Sophie's outrage at Och's boorishness—her anger flares into flames of indignation. It comes as no surprise that by career's end her Ännchen will mutate into Agathe, her Sophie burgeon into the Marschallin. Would that they were in our future too.

Perhaps the Marschallin should have put up a braver fight for her young lover. Though she herself is nearing fifty, on this afternoon Lear sounds as young, even younger, than rival Sophie. Hofmannsthal was right to have it otherwise, or we should miss all those philosophical meditations of Marie Thérèse. Now at the midpoint of her Metropolitan career, the American soprano had sung her first company Marschallin in the seasonal premiere a week before the broadcast. She was no stranger to the opera however, having sung both Sophie and Octavian (the latter at the Met in 1969). Her acquaintance with the idiom is readily apparent, the knowledge imbibed during early sojourns in German houses and sustained since 1957 by permanent residence with the Deutsche Oper Berlin. She chooses, and rightly so in view of her petite figure and relative delicacy of voice, to stress the "French flavor instead of the Prussian" in defining the princess' character.[2] In the broadcast issue of *Opera News*, Lear forthrightly describes a recent period of vocal crisis, brought on, she avers, by excessive involvement with Berg, Schoenberg, et al. She claims that her new teacher and a diligent reassessment on her part have mended all and put her voice back into prime condition. I hear a few hard top tones in the trio, but I think she is right to feel vocally rejuvenated.

Frieda Hempel as Baroness Freimann in *Der Wildschütz*.

Her Marschallin is a lovely creation, full of subtle bendings of phrase and nuances of vocal color. The voice may be a shade light for the part, but in the big moments she marshals her resources well—indeed some full-voiced phrases are quite splendid in their tonal effulgence. As to vocal size, Frieda Hempel, a favorite Marschallin of the composer in Berlin and the Met's own creator of the role, described herself in her memoirs as a lyric coloratura, as was Margarethe Siems, the original Dresden princess. Hempel maintained that Strauss, if he had wished, could easily have cast a dramatic soprano as the Marschallin: "several excellent ones [were] available in Dresden and Berlin."[3] Lear's voice may be the proper "light, lyric soprano" that Hempel says Strauss "definitely wanted." All in all, I believe she manages the double image of the role rather better than Rysanek did in her last broadcast. Lear, unlike her more celebrated colleague, astutely apportions the 'Ein halb Mal lustig, ein halb Mal traurig' division of the princess' existence (the Marschallin herself defines her character as 'half the time merry, half the time melancholy' to the undiscerning Octavian). Her tone is innately more charming, more delicate than Rysanek's and, since the tessitura—modest for the most part—does not trouble her (as it can in some other less accommodating roles), she can confidently play with the princess' conversational gambits. Their spontaneity and tonal variety are delightful to hear. Multiple examples of her skill and insights as a singing actress might be cited. I will be content with a couple from the first-act scene with Ochs: daringly but discreetly, she applies a suggestive insinuation to Octavian's name as she brings him to Ochs' attention as the favored rose bearer; she captures the prescribed amusement in her delivery of 'Aber wo Er doch ein Bräutgam ist?' Her voice, though in every way lighter than Rysanek's, has a lower center of gravity, from which the role profits. (Here one must except the opening of the trio; Lear manages it well, but her bobbed soprano requires infinite care when operating in the stratosphere. Not unexpectedly, Rysanek has the better of her in this all-important moment.) As to the critical first-act monologues, they are well contrasted. The initial one (highlighted by a straightforward 'Wie') is almost underplayed; the second, where 'die Zeit'—time with its inexorable march—enters the picture, is converted into a dramatic miniature. Some may find the latter a shade overly emotive, but I think it remains within the frame. Certainly, the 'silberne Ros'n' phrase at the act's curtain has the right bittersweet tincture. At the inn, a number of surprisingly grand bursts of tone and a magisterially royal manner halt the Baron in his tracks. But Lear's exit 'Ja, ja' is hardly given breath. She hides her hurt within herself.

The afternoon's adventure is over. Hope has been sufficiently rewarded. Disappointment, if not entirely averted, has in large part been skirted. Of the new adventurers, Jungwirth and Fassbaender will prove to be brief occupants of the Met stage. Mathis goes them better by several years, but the trio of visitors, for reasons hinted at in the above account but also because of the fullness of their European careers, ultimately did not build upon their New York beachheads. Strauss had profited by their coming, but the company owned artists capable of keeping his torch aflame. And flame it will, as we move from the elegant sport of the boudoir onto the moonlit terraces of Herod's palace. There human attractions are neither a game nor a farce (to quote the comedy's libretto), but rather a matter of life and death. In this same season, Grace Bumbry embraced Salome. On the broadcast of 5 January 1974, her preoccupation with the Baptist is variously viewed by

Salome
5 January 1974

Salome
Grace Bumbry
Herodias
Regina Resnik
Herod
Ragnar Ulfung
Narraboth
William Lewis
Jokanaan
Lawrence Shadur
First Nazarene
Raymond Michalski
Conductor
James Levine

Resnik's Herodias, Ragnar Ulfung's Herod, and William Lewis' Narraboth. Lawrence Shadur essays Jokanaan, while the intrepid Levine takes on yet another of opera's symphonically challenging ventures.

The American maestro's command of the score is, as expected, sure and complete. His objective cool oddly mates well with the work's turmoil, the weirdness and frenzy all the more mesmerizing when so carefully and considerately tended. The opera almost steals into being with the sounding of the clarinet's sinuous theme, and many passages thereafter flow with ingratiating subtlety, their antiseptic sweetness invitingly spreading over our greedy taste buds. Where passion is wanted, Levine is there as well, and Strauss' most rhapsodic phrases (in the final scene, in particular) are expansively drawn. They glow and shimmer under Levine's knowing touch. The several grand orchestral passages, however emphatic and thrilling their execution here, never burst the seams of the conductor's minutely organized, carefully layered program. How insistently, and with what efficiency, he presses the repetitions of Jokanaan's motive in the interlude that precedes Herod's entrance. The work's neuroticism has seldom seemed so easy to swallow, its hothouse atmosphere so tonic a bathe.

Batyah Godfrey's Page knows her place, while Soldiers Karlsrud and Dobriansky are dutiful as well. The quintet of Jews is appropriately voluble, the combined flinty tenor timbres of Anthony, Velis, Carelli, and Franke (anchored by Best's bass) raising a remarkable clatter in their philosophizing before Michalski's Nazarene, suavely recounting the miracles of Jesus, pours balm on their argument. Narraboth's luxuriant opening phrase ('Wie schön is die Prinzessin Salome heute Nacht!'), which should sound the erotic tone for the entire opera, lacks the requisite enchantment as uttered by William Lewis' mainstream tenor. Nevertheless, he is an imposing Syrian captain, fervent in his longing for Salome, audibly troubled and resistant in his initial refusals of her demonic wishes. Resnik's playing of Herodias is suitably macabre, the manner frenetic, the voice imposing in size, though occasionally effortful and shrill, even as the vengeful queen is herself.

Shadur's budding European career had included a year at Berne (the big German roles) and five years at Lübeck (the big Italian roles) before returning to America for his Met debut as Paolo in the current season. His Metropolitan career would be brief. The voice has size and a solid tonal core, though the timbre is of no great individuality. Jokanaan's proclamations are substantial enough, even when coming from the cistern, but their burly thrusts do not sufficiently convey the prophet's threatening austerity of person or his nobility of thought. Unfortunately, the critical curse is small-scale intimidation. When in Salome's sight (sights, as well), the voice gains in color, but the sense of otherworldly repose that should inflect his vision of a penitent Salome is not inherent in his song. I recall how Hans Hotter's Baptist made one feel that he had conversed with God. In contrast to Shadur's neutral play, the besotted Tetrarch, Salome's other foil, enters upon the scene already burdened by the overload of *Schrecklichkeit* in Ulfung's wailing tenor. The Swedish tenor is a thorough professional, a true creature of the stage—his characterizations are never bland or boring. Ulfung's lustful ruler is as pungent and malformed as ginger root. The voice is Herod's warped self personified in sound. One would think we had the all of him in his initial phrases, but the crafty player adds layer upon layer of hysteria to the man's Salome fixation until dementia floods the airwaves. Indeed, the voice has substance, and he dominates his scenes not only by his acute projection of the baser emotions but by the clarity and sureness of his vocalism.

Undoubtedly, Miss Bumbry's princess in person would be sufficient to cause the monarch to pledge both her mother's throne and his beloved white peacocks (and in that order) to his perverse stepdaughter. Vocally, too, she is a formidable contestant, not only for Jokanaan's head, but for Salome's laurels. While Welitch (Welitsch in Wien) nostalgia has not receded, and probably won't for those who recall her incandescent portrayal, memory has been assuaged by the varied, and invariably imposing, conceptions of Goltz, Borkh, Nilsson, and Rysanek—to name only the broadcast creations of recent years. Bumbry's Salome is worthy to be added to the line. Covent Garden in 1970 had heard her initial Salome under Solti's baton. Several years having solidified her elevation into the coveted soprano terrain—in mezzos' minds, divas reign with greater potency there—she certified her ascendancy by augmenting her name as well. For three seasons, the first being the current one, Grace Melzia Bumbry would be her roster nomenclature.

We may well ask—as another has before—"What's in a name?" In this instance, a voice mutation—not a change. The instrument retains throughout a good deal of its range its familiar, potent charge of vibrant color and steely firmness. The very top tones, narrower and keener in timbre, are not always easily reached. Most often they simulate a poniard's thrust—no seductive spinning of tone on high can be counted among Salome's weapons on this afternoon. The apotheosic final phrases of the score, in particular, suffer from the voice's ferric content. There are pluses, as well. Even with its narrow top extension, the voice remains compactly knitted throughout the range. When one must continually negotiate the Strauss escalator, articulating text while passing quickly in and out of depths, medians, and heights, a continuity of timbre—and one free of tremulousness at that—is a precious asset. At her entrance, Bumbry's instrument startles. Its plangency hardly seems Salome's province. One misses the sweet acidity, so apt for the young girl's willful nature, of a more compliant soprano timbre. Occasionally a phrase here and there is less graceful, less magnetic, than Salome's celebrated allure demands. Temptation seems more obvious when it comes from Bumbry's throat. Her princess of Judea is not only knowing, but known—mystery is alien to her address. But of course, the potent appeal of her burnished tones, bronzed and brassed, is never in doubt. Narraboth feels it and so do we.

She gabbles well when Strauss sets his girl to twirling the Wilde text. A bit of silver even touches the top voice in her first encounter with Jokanaan. Levine's graceful waltzes expand the momentary enchantment before the hint of a scream invades her top notes. Later the conductor's subtly controlled Dance of the Seven Veils gleams with insinuation. His way with the notorious set piece is neither bawdy nor tawdry, for he remains faithful to his overall conception, abiding within its cultivated zones. (The diva brought her own revealing costumes from the Covent Garden production and had plotted her dance moves with Arthur Mitchell of the Dance Theater of Harlem.) Bumbry's childlike tones chill when she asks for the Baptist's head as her reward; a gentle top tone, rare and welcome, complements the muted manner. Herod can't help but give in after she repeats her request, this time in splendidly trumpeted tones. The soprano's vocal steel and stamina sustain Salome's fierce intent, and her assurance effectively contrasts with Levine's fluid orchestral movement. Now the top voice frees itself and beauty touches it.

In the extended closing *scena*, Strauss sought and achieved a novel aura for his heroine, allowing her a momentary sense of release that finds expression in some of his most extended phrases. Often, Bumbry fulfills his demands, not with the lyrical bloom, or conversely, the majestic splendor of some interpreters, but with a comparable utterance in which dignity is prominent, frequently abetted by luxuriant tone. Unexpected subtleties enhance a few critical phrases. A magical moment is her quiet, low voicing—but without chesty emphasis—of Salome's musings on the mystery of love and death. Equally effective are her observations about Jokanaan's closed eyes, on her need not merely to kiss, but to bite, his mouth. These episodes are intimately played, as is her ensuing wonder over the differing tastes of blood and love. There her voice softly mirrors the text's mood. The final ecstatic phrases, while tellingly limned, lack the full measure of rapture (ideally it calls for Rysanek's silvery ecstasy) and at the climaxes the voice flips momentarily sharp, thus weakening their shattering impact. Levine's orchestral line has been expansively deployed throughout these measures. The maestro resolutely sustains its sweep as Wilde's pervasive moon illuminates the stage and Strauss' brutal orchestral blows signal Salome's death.

Wagner, too, was preoccupied with the enmeshing threads of love and death, but his Isolde and Tristan are lovers of quite another sort. Night may be their world as well, but its darkness shelters them and, at least for a while, nurtures their passion. On the broadcast of 26 January 1974, we find Leinsdorf again at the helm with Dooley repeating his faithful Kurwenal. New occupants fill the remaining roles: Dunn plays Brangäne, Lewis is Melot, Ahlstedt the Sailor, and Macurdy King Marke. Isolde and Tristan? Although the seasonal premiere had occurred on 11 January, the singers of the title roles were in doubt for some time previous to the broadcast. Therein lies a tale. At least three versions by participants in one of the most traumatic events in Metropolitan history are available.[4] The participatory trio—manager Chapin, conductor Leinsdorf, and tenor Vickers (via his biographer)—agree on most of the details, although placement of blame for the debacle is adjusted according to the narrator.

The tale begins a few years before the broadcast, when Swedish soprano Caterina Ligendza, a worthy, internationally known Isolde, was engaged for the title role, the initial performance to coincide with Vickers' first Metropolitan Tristan. A few days before rehearsals were to begin, she canceled (a habit with this diva, it seems) due to illness. Leinsdorf believed the entire series of performances should be canceled—after all, Isoldes don't grow on trees—but financial considerations made it imperative in Chapin's mind to proceed with the production. According to the manager, his concerns were not only pecuniary but altruistic. He wanted to ensure that Vickers and Nilsson, who were scheduled to sing together later in the run, would be heard by the New York audience. (The great Birgit was to return to the company for the fifth performance on 30 January.) In his dealings, Chapin thought Leinsdorf uncooperative. He believed the maestro worked behind his back with Vickers and stage manager Everding to cancel the production. He deemed Vickers difficult—in the manager's mind, par for the course. Kubelik, music director of the company, remained in Europe during the entire crisis, adding to Leinsdorf's audible disgust. Eventually, Klara Barlow, a soprano who had sung Donna Anna and Fidelio at the Met several years earlier, volunteered to take over Ligendza's performances. Chapin gratefully accepted. Leinsdorf was furious

Tristan und Isolde
26 January 1974
Isolde
Klara Barlow
Brangäne
Mignon Dunn
Tristan
Jon Vickers
Kurwenal
William Dooley
Marke
John Macurdy
Conductor
Erich Leinsdorf

Francis Robinson and Schuyler Chapin at reception following the Metropolitan premiere of *Death in Venice* on 18 October 1974. Photography by Sam Siegel.

(though—or perhaps because—he had earlier worked with Barlow) and wanted out of his contract. After participating in some rehearsals, Vickers, too, asked Chapin to release him. According to his biographer, the tenor did not wish to make his Met debut as Tristan under such adverse conditions; he headed back to his Bermuda home before the premiere.[5] Chapin recounts that Leinsdorf finally agreed to conduct when the possibility of a young replacement recommended by Nilsson (Leif Segerstam, at the house for *Bohème* performances) was bruited about.[6] By that time, Leinsdorf had unloaded to the press about what he called in his memoirs "seismographic indications" that the Met management situation was a muddle of incompetence.[7] In the end, Jess Thomas took over the premiere from the scheduled Vickers, the press lauded Barlow's initial effort, and the Canadian tenor consented to sing the broadcast. In the broadcast issue of *Opera News*, Isolde is listed as "to be announced." Miss Barlow was the eventual nominee. As Leinsdorf summed up the entire situation, "there was no one else."[8] But, above all, there was Vickers, heard in one of only two Met *Tristan* performances and his lone Met broadcast of the role.

By the time of the broadcast, the fourth performance in the seasonal run, Leinsdorf, the Met's inveterate Wagnerian, must have accepted his fate, although seeds of discontent may affect his reading. This maestro knows what he wants and gets it from his pit charges. Expert master of geometrical music making, he conducts a performance where all the score's lines, angles, curves, and triangles (the drama docs contain one—and on this afternoon, it suggests more a domestic dispute than an epochal affair) are precisely gauged, the relationships calculated for maximum equilibrium. The process may dilute the surging passion of Wagner's love fest, but a certain satisfaction, a poised certitude, always resides in mathematical proportions. The maestro supplies it, though one can almost hear the tumblers drop. And at a few moments, his orchestra exultantly flies (in regular formation, of course), as in the buildup to Tristan's second-act arrival and, predictably, at the sighting of the ship. Nor is he adverse to a bit of rafter shaking now and then, to simulate passion. He disposes of the opera with such dispatch that, by the time we, along with Isolde, arrive at Kareol, one may wonder if he just wanted to get the whole thing over with. Did he need to get out from under, so to speak, that is, wish to erase the preliminary debacle and seek refuge from Barlow's continued presence—she whom Vickers, in his recalcitrance, considered an unknown quantity?[9] Leinsdorf's attitude toward her (and, more pertinently, his view of himself) is summed up in a comment from his memoirs, where he prides himself on "managing to pilot Barlow through four Wagner evenings [*sic*] without overt mishap."[10] No one could ever call our maestro an unknown quantity, either as man or music maker.

At the first-act curtain, Ahlstedt's light-voiced sailor seems rather timid for a man who lives on the mast, one hardly destined to perturb Isolde. His tenor compatriot, however, is a commanding Melot—Lewis is adept at characterization. And Dunn, Dooley, and Macurdy are the real thing. The mezzo's dark, rich tones are as reliable as ever, though her vocalism would profit from more nuanced phrasing (especially on board the ship). She does not communicate the fullness of feeling for her mistress, which the greatest Brangänes have suggested. The later acts provide improvements in both regards. An adequate appraisal of the warning is impossible; one has no idea of how it came over in the house, for she is very closely miked. And for the radio audience, Dunn's all-too-solid tones negate the illusion of distance and the magic of the moment. Dooley is once again the experienced, expert practitioner of the singing actor's art. Not that he lacks for vocal appeal. Indeed, his instrument issues forth with convincing pride, even in the servant's moments of blustering chauvinism. The tone may lack the brawn that should be Kurwenal's pride of possession, but the baritone's robust projection and rhythmically alert phrasing do the job. On this afternoon, he utilizes fewer of the coloristic effects that would confirm the servant's love for his master—we know he has them ready to hand. And yet, the melancholy of his watch over the wounded Tristan in Brittany and the pathos of his own death speak.

Macurdy's Marke provides further evidence of his continuing growth as an artist, both in its vocal appeal and its interpretive potency. No languors trouble his monologue. The American bass moves with ease through the maze of the king's conflicting emotions. He never resorts to self-pity or relies upon lugubrious movement of phrase or tone (those favorite devices that many Markes employ to suggest the husband's age and anguish). The characterization is full and intensely moving. His voice seems more malleable than in his early Met career, touchingly delicate at 'Da kinderlos einst schwand sein Weib.' Tone color is more varied, as well. To hear head tones from a bass (a clarifying one on 'Freund') is an unexpected and enlightening pleasure. His phrasing, too, has become subtler. He shapes the section beginning 'die so herrlich hold erhaben mir die Seele musste laben' as though it were an arietta; the opening phrase is sung with the most tender legato. This king is intensely human. That he will ultimately forgive the potion-struck lovers seems certain from his interpretive stance.

Inevitably, focus was riveted on Vickers, heard in his broadcast and house debut as Tristan. The role was relatively new to him, though, previous to his New York appearances, his noble knight had been heard in Buenos Aires, Salzburg, and Orange, France. Expectations were high. On this afternoon, his reading might be characterized as splendidly idiosyncratic, idiosyncratically splendid, just plain splendid, or even, if you prefer, merely idiosyncratic. Certainly, it is enthralling. But also, at a number of points, oddly disappointing. When approaching a Vickers performance, one must remember that the tenor is a law unto himself and expect to encounter whatever he conceives that the role requires, not what an audience or critics consider to be the norm.

Overall, his conception, at least in this debut performance, seems a bit fussy. Ordinarily, he has at his call command of the entire spectrum of dynamics and, when he chooses, he can employ a gratifying legato at all volume levels. On this afternoon, he seems overly fond of the softer dynamic levels—one even wonders about audibility in the house. We desperately want to hear his heroic tones clinging and clanging over phrases that have been the bane of less endowed Tristans. For the most part, it is not to be. He is chary of employing the full power of his magnificent instrument. When he does, of course, the results *are* splendid. Then, too, patches of his "phrasing" hardly justify that appellation. In the opening act, in particular (as well as in the final act—though there, his desperate, wounded condition better justifies the disjunct treatment of text), he consistently treats syllables and tones as separate entities. Some of it is highly effective, but the device ultimately is tiresome. (Infuriated, one considers asking him—and here I modify Olivier's famous advice to the method-imprisoned Dustin Hoffman—"Why not try singing?") Add in a pervasive habit of attacking a tone softly, swelling it, and allowing it to recede before it fully blooms; the result, especially when combined with the above described note-picking, worries his wonted legato.

Enough. No more pillorying of this rightly revered artist. Consider his interpretation a lyrical embrace of his charge, welcome in itself when opposed against the strenuous and often strained manner of predecessors and successors in the role. (In Tristan's opening colloquy with Isolde, could the tenor's lightness rank as comradely courtesy on his part, a desire not to overwhelm Barlow's slighter vehicle with the grandeur of his tenor?) Appreciation need not be sparing. He can shape a key dramatic episode with surety, as he does at 'War Morold dir so werth,' for instance: he begins quietly and moves to a stunning climax before receding to nothingness at the end of 'dass du nicht dir's entfallen lässt!' The wrenching passage of isolated utterances ('Tristan's Eland') is masterfully executed with maximum variety, extending from the dreaded soft croon up to hefty cries of pain as he drinks the fateful potion. Both singers manage the intricate, intertwining phrases of the act's rapturous close with admirable clarity of line.

The lengthy second-act duet is performed with the customary Metropolitan cuts. In the demanding passage before 'O sink' hernieder, Nacht der Liebe,' our hero proves he has the requisite power for the occasional grand utterance. He molds the long phrases with greater freedom than most Wagnerians allow; the textual sense is enhanced by his liberality. Some grand portamentos, akin to slides, decorate the lead-in to the orchestral interlude that introduces the lento moderato of the duet. (There, Leinsdorf's syncopated pulses called forth to my mind an unsolicited image of buzzing bees aswarm.) How skillfully Vickers negotiates 'Niewiedererwachens wahnlos hold bewusster Wunsch' as the difficult phrase weaves in tandem with Isolde's song. Most tenors cannot adequately supply the mezza voce that should mirror the lover's dreamlike rapture in the 'Lass mich sterben!' section of the duet; Vickers, singing as though in a trance, gives it to us in full measure (almost more than we need, in fact). He does love the extremes. Now (in the portion beginning 'Dein' und mein', Isolde's Liebe?'), he begins to pour out that grand, golden tone which we have been longing to hear. Still, vestiges of the unwilling Wagnerite remain. But once again, after uttering 'So stürben wir, um ungetrennt' as if to himself, he brandishes the true *helden* manner in climactic phrases that thrill. They mark the high point of his performance thus far. And, before Melot interrupts their idyll, he sings the final frenetic phrases with a clarity, accuracy, and tonal effulgence that few tenors can have matched. The disjunct phrase manner returns in his appropriately numb responses to his king.

The hero as wretched exile is predictably the recipient of this tenor's most ardent care. His carefully conceived, somewhat muted, creation of the faithful liege and possessed lover of the early acts seems planned to heighten the wounded hero's despair. The several episodes of Tristan's delirium are plotted for maximum variety and solar plexus impact. No matter Leinsdorf's predilection, any notion of a domestic triangle is entirely routed—when Vickers suffers, world-shattering emotions come into play. Weariness, pain, longing, torment—all receive their due in an intensely naturalistic reading, one quite removed from the usual operatic posturing: he rages mightily when the demented knight accuses Kurwenal of failing to see his phantom ship; the grand cries of 'Sehnen! Sehnen!' are longing made articulate in sound; his powerful 'Verflucht sei' lays a terrible, terrifying curse upon the love potion. The phrases of the lengthy episode ending 'Wie schön bist du!' are intensely moving as they fall from Vickers' lips. In Tristan's final moments, Vickers' abandoned outbursts as the ship hoves into view contrast with and set up his ultimate 'Isolde!' The cherished name floats on an expertly controlled mix of resonances.

And what of the unknown quantity? Of course, Barlow was not quite "unknown." In addition to singing a pair of Donna Annas in the 1970–71 season, she had saved a performance of *Fidelio* when Ligendza (!) canceled. During the same period, other duties had occupied her as well: Leinsdorf tells us that Barlow had served as Nilsson's nonperforming understudy for Isolde. Evidently, the Bing regime considered her adequate Metropolitan material. His management team had been dispersed, of course, so the new crew may well have been in the dark about her abilities. Was she presumptuous to put herself forward as the savior of the Met's 1974 offerings? While Anna and Fidelio have been in the repertory of some Met Isoldes, not all Annas or Fidelios have been able to count Isolde among their repertory jewels. But Barlow had sung the role about forty times in smaller European houses, so her claim was at least legitimate. She could not have anticipated the ruckus that would occur when all the internal shenanigans of the operation became known, causing preperformance publicity, even humiliation, which she undeservedly had to endure. Standards and civility were in conflict, with Barlow caught in the middle.

At the season premiere, did the press come down on the side of civility? Or were they perhaps offended at the discourtesy of some of the participants? In any case, they credited her Isolde a worthwhile creation, apt for even the hallowed Metropolitan stage. (By this time, the Lincoln Center stage may be deemed anointed, having been trod by Nilsson, Sutherland, Price, et al.). At broadcast time, Barlow was ill with a sinus infection. In an interview with Vickers' biographer, the soprano relates that though she could sing, she couldn't talk, and that she had had cortisone injections. She wanted to cancel, but—the old refrain—there was no one else.[11] Actually, her performance has merit. In sum, it is neither as bad as it could be nor as good as it should be. The voice itself would not normally be thought of as an Isolde voice—at least to those who gauge that illusive vehicle by the standard of a Gadski, a Leider, a Flagstad, Traubel, or Nilsson, let alone such esteemed professionals as Harshaw. Size alone might be a disqualifier, although there have been too many slight-voiced Isoldes in recent times to rely on that measurement. In timbre (especially the upper octave), Barlow's soprano resembles somewhat the shaft of clean tone of future Isolde Hildegard Behrens, although it lacks the bracing purity of that artist's instrument, its accurate attack, and easy top. Her highest tones, often powerful, do shine, though the rapid vibrato that lends an erotic color to them can be excessive. Sometimes it pounds away at inopportune moments, destroying mood.

During the first act, her low tones are insignificant; 'Mir erkoren' and similar low-lying phrases require an act of imagination on the part of even the radio listener. What must it have been like in the house? The voice's narrow circumference, its rather wiry makeup, causes more than a few phrases to skitter along with hackle-raising result. Aboard ship, the cutting edge of her instrument, a very narrow blade indeed, allows the climaxes to tell—but not to tell all. Nor does she command sufficient resources of color and possess the subtlety of intent to vivify a phrase like 'Er sah mir in die Augen.' Still, Barlow has assets as an interpreter. Her sense of phrase is far from negligible, and many nuanced touches evidence her dramatic sensitivity, as well as confirm her experience in the part. Despite deficiency in the low voice, she constructs a meaningful arc for the 'tiefstes Weh' phrases and makes the moment count. Often, she allows one to believe in Isolde's conflicting emotions—a few celebrated Isoldes have failed to do that with comparable consistency. Her Isolde is a younger, more feminine-sounding Irische Kind than we normally hear (and Barlow's slim figure and blond good looks would have complemented that impression in the house). She knows what she is about, goes after things with conviction, and gives a performance. Under the circumstances, could the Metropolitan expect more from her?

Her second act is an improvement on the first. The voice sounds more relaxed; it has gained in fullness. The entire 'Frau Minne' episode is effectively sounded—her tone thrives (the tessitura lies well for her instrument) and her line is strong. The text's dictates are mirrored in her song. Something ripe in the tone, a pungency, exposes Isolde's longing for love, a perception not always apparent in readings by more grandly endowed Isoldes. The glancing high Cs are avoided (but the act-one Bs were worthy, 'preis' struck dead on, 'lacht' a bit less centered). Although its size cannot be accurately gleaned over the radio, her voice has pith and carrying power in episodes where the orchestra operates at moderate levels. One wants a more dulcet tone when she muses on 'und,' ('and' is the sweetest of words, Isolde tells us) and a softer timbral caress would enhance the lengthy introspective portion of the love duet. She does herself proud in its frenetic closing pages, meeting Vickers on his own level, as they eagerly propel the lovers' passionate vows. (Their paroxysms are probably what Hofmannsthal had in mind when, writing to Strauss in 1910, he bewailed, "Wagner's intolerable erotic screaming . . . a repulsive, barbaric, almost bestial affair this shrieking of two creatures in heat."[12]) Oddly, after coming through thus far in relative safety, she comes a cropper in the final moments of the opera. She executes all the notes but, hard upon Vickers' noble, searing sufferance, her voice sounds pinched and small as she lingers over Tristan's inert form. The tinny timbre, now markedly less appealing, simply won't do. Perhaps her indisposition caught up with her. She recovers volume for the Liebestod, indeed sings all its phrases at full tilt, neglecting dynamic subtlety and eschewing any innocent *subito piano*s. The buzz-saw vibrato in the top notes is hyperactive, precisely at those points where ethereal purity is required. The magic of Isolde's transfiguration goes unrealized.

During the bows, Cross, ever the gentleman, takes pains to let us know that in the fall Barlow is scheduled to sing at La Scala under the direction of Karl Böhm. The ordeal over, management sought to do right by Barlow, in view of her valiant service. She sang with the company during the next two seasons, her roles including Marina (seven outings during 1974–75), Amelia (twice), and a single Elektra the following year. She returned in the 1979–80 season, but as one of the girls in *Mahagonny*. She was no longer an unknown quantity, and, in the end, she proved not to be a marketable one for the Metropolitan.

Eventually, Thomas and Nilsson sang the 1973–74 season's final performances of *Tristan und Isolde*. But before that unequal pairing, the long-awaited union of Nilsson and Vickers occurred on 30 January to the feverish acclaim of an ecstatic house audience. The New York press bowed beneath their greatness.

Even the crusty Leinsdorf acknowledged that he was "glad to have been a part of it."[13] Then he and the Met parted company yet again, though not for long. The 1976–77 season would see his return to the house. By then, a new management was in place.

In the meantime, Wagner must be served. This time the Met intended to do it in grand style. The so-called Karajan *Ring* was now complete, achieved in its final stages without the maestro's commanding presence on the podium. Even his stage directions for the final two operas were executed by proxy when *Siegfried* was mounted in 1972 and *Götterdämmerung* in 1974. By the 1974–75 season, management deemed the time propitious for the presentation of a complete *Ring* cycle. The prime requisite for the venture, Nilsson, was on hand, and, while a Siegfried was still a sometime thing, it was now or never for the great diva. On alternate Saturdays of February and March, the radio audience once more was allowed to experience the ultimate in Wagner immersion. *Das Rheingold* on 15 February 1975 enlisted a mix of homegrown and imported Wagnerians, including Pracht (Freia), Dunn (Fricka), Chookasian (Erda), Dooley (Donner), Rundgren (Fasolt), and Macurdy (Fafner). Debutants Glade Peterson and Donald McIntyre were assigned Loge and Wotan, while Ulfung and Rintzler fussed and combated as the ill-matched brothers, Mime and Alberich. Gods, goddesses, and sundries all performed under Sixten Ehrling's baton. The long haul had begun.

Each broadcast is prefaced by a careful statement from announcer Peter Allen relating that the performances are based on Karajan's *Ring* productions for the Easter Festivals in Salzburg. Filling the maestro's shoes is a considerable burden for Ehrling. If the size is smaller, the quality of workmanship remains high. In particular, *Rheingold*, an opera in which plot exposition takes precedence over grand expanses of song, profits from the careful nurturing of motives and the chamber music manner that Ehrling favors. The singers' articulation of text is clearly heard and the drama prospers. His way is also kind to the voices, and some of these interpretations—new undertakings for a number of the stage participants—need tender supervision. Ehrling provides it. The Swedish maestro's thoughtfully conceived, well-proportioned interpretation serves them well. Wagner's dramaturgy and orchestral magic also flourish under his rational hand. If the interpretive walls have closed in and the volume meter's range narrowed, they nevertheless retain sufficient impact when the perspective is so consistently maintained. The afternoon flows along in a fluent stream of motivic play with nary a wearisome moment. Some scenes are dramatically vivid as well. Of note in that regard is the first mountaintop scene: when the gods and giants contend at length for Freia, their contest causes the airwaves to crackle with excitement.

Evaluation of Wagnerian singers of the seventies involves juggling the passage of time. The view is markedly different depending on whether one approaches the era with vivid memory of the glories of the 1930s and '40s or from the vantage point of the millennium's lowered horizon. If one can contrive a judicious blend of the two perspectives, standards and reality may abide the one with the other. Application of both, whether joined or discrete, will be apparent in these *Ring* discussions.

On this afternoon, the vocal standard is unexpectedly high. Voices sound in prime condition. Tones are invariably unforced and well projected, even when the inherent power of the voice (apparent over the radio and undoubtedly more so in the house) is less than overwhelming. There are no small roles in *Rheingold*, no matter the length of individual assignments. Each singer has moments of prominence, greater or lesser, and congratulations to management are in order when one is able to commend almost all performers. For the most part, some downsizing of the future inhabitants of Valhalla has occurred. Though their orbit may have shrunk, basically these gods are an attractive crew. Broadcast debutant Kolbjörn Höiseth's Froh is a lyrical, but occasionally strangulated, guardian of spring; during this single-season sojourn, the Swedish tenor would tackle both Loge and Siegmund. Donner's hammer probably is lightweight as swung by veteran Dooley. Of course, the American baritone knows how to make the most out of what he has, i.e., interpretive subtlety and idiomatic style. Indeed, at the opera's close, he dispels the mists from the mountaintop with godlike nobility, the tone lovingly laid out. He might well form a rainbow bridge worth crossing. Like most Freias, Pracht is cast more for stage allure than vocal glamor. And again like most of her predecessors, the American soprano, affectingly fearful in manner and occasionally pinched in tone, adequately delivers Freia's few lines.

Fricka's more prominent chore of wifehood is better discharged by Dunn's worthy instrument. The role may lie a shade high for her. The voice, a bit less velvety and sounding smaller in the Wagnerian milieu than in some other assignments, grants Wotan's spouse a welcome femininity. At moments, the mezzo flies with greater ease over some of Wagner's fleet phrases than a few legendary Frickas who are remembered for the magnitude of their voices and their interpretive pith. In the end, Dunn's familiar tonal wealth and expressivity touch many a brief phrase, animating a characterization of considerable variety. Wagner has given Erda but a single string to strum and one that has too often failed to gain maximum oscillation since early in the century when Schumann-Heink's voice caused vibrations of seismic proportions. Chookasian's earth mother may be no earth shaker, but her 'Weiche, Wotan, weiche!' is notable for both dignity of utterance and reliability of tone. Her voice's wobble-free depths likely would have comforted Wotan if her message ('Alles, was ist, endet') were not so dispiriting.

At the curtain's rise, the Rhinemaidens are a much jollier crew (the plot synopsis describes them as "carefree daughters of the river's spirit"). They could provide welcome diversion in any Wagner opera, but alas! like most carefree daughters, they neglect their duty. Too soon their laughing 'Walalaleia' darkens into woeful 'Wehe.' As Flosshilde, Ben-David's warm and dense tone anchors the trio and makes a proper foil for Baldwin's more pointed mezzo and livelier delivery. Weidinger's somewhat straight tone lacks either the gleam or shimmer of some Woglindes (Erna Berger's 1951 broadcast sprite spread the sweetest honey over the trios), but she is always precise. One does hope for more than childlike tone in that pregnant moment when Woglinde sings the motive of resignation ('Nur wer der Minne Macht versagt'). As if in compensation, Ehrling applies a delightful swing to their ensemble tunes.

Neither of the brother duos, Fasolt and Fafner or Mime and Alberich, would ever qualify for membership in an optimist's club. 'Wehe' is ever their lot. The giants might have some sort of home life, I imagine—at least they are not confined to underground caves. Still, the blackness of their outlook and their outsized persons ought to be reflected in their voices. Rundgren and Macurdy come close to filling the bill in that regard and interpretively they rank high. The American

bass initially characterizes Fafner as a dull tool, his sleepy, slurred vocalism an effective contrast with Fasolt's emphatic utterance. Of course, when he gives Fasolt
his comeuppance, the American bass springs to life with Iago-like craft, a neat
conception on the reliable Macurdy's part. Rundgren, yet another Swedish import, is in his vocal prime, his instrument both formidable in rage and capable of
songlike vocalism. (The *New Grove* calls him a *basso cantante*, a creature not often
found in Wagnerland. Bass-baritone was his official designation on that ground.)
When, in the final scene, he laments the loss of Freia, he almost wrings the heart.
Are giants supposed to do that? He sounds more like a hero, a man whose longing
is palpable, than a monster. But he can afford to bare his soul, for he has thun-
dered menacingly in the second scene when first bartering for Freia. He owns a
fine instrument, free in the upper range and solid as it descends, the vocal hoard
buttressed by impressive authority. Many years with the Swedish Royal Opera,
a 1970 debut in Chicago, smaller roles at Bayreuth—soon to be upgraded to
Hagen—these are a few of Rundgren's career credits. He had come to the Met as
Hagen in the 1974 *Götterdämmerung* production. After this second season, the Met
management was less than hospitable to him, as they were to another newcomer,
Marius Rintzler, debutant in the same 1974 production. He had been on the operatic scene for little more than a decade, but in addition to his first audiences in
Bucharest (he was Romanian by birth), Düsseldorf, Glyndebourne, and other European and American centers already appreciated his worth. When Alberich ogles
the Rhinemaidens and steals their gold, he plays the proper churl quite effectively,
dutifully roughening his voice. A climactic 'So verfluch ich die Liebe' gains him
the gold and seemingly motivates a sea change in his vocalism. Happy is the man
who gains wealth, no matter the means. The timbre can be most attractive; it acquires baritonal brightness in the later scenes. Still, the voice has sufficient pith to
power key moments; his curse of the ring, a mountain peak of the cycle, is cagily
plotted and resoundingly delivered. He demonstrates his skill at characterization
when playing Houdini games with Loge, craftily contesting over the Tarnhelm
before losing out as a toad. His finest moment occurs when Alberich spouts his
disdain for the gods as a race; the decibel count and breadth of phrase he summons
for 'Zaudert wohl gar? Zittre und zage' would do credit to a Wotan. He goes one
better than Rundgren, returning in 1977–78 for multiple appearances as Ochs
and Varlaam.

In other cycles, we have become accustomed to gnomes who snarl, spit, and
whine. As Alberich, Rintzler sings—whether he should or not. Ulfung, however,
takes up any slack in the character singing department with hardly any left over
for a brother gnome. Groveling and sniveling are second nature to him. So convincing is Ulfung's vocal acting that Mime's self-pity seems ingrained in the Swedish tenor's timbre. The broadcast of *Siegfried* will reveal the full range of his gifts.
Yet another tenor shines on this afternoon. Glade Peterson makes his broadcast
debut as Loge after a company debut in the role a few days earlier. The dramatic
action of *Rheingold* ought to blaze and it is Loge who must provide the spark.
Wagner's god of fire is an independent cuss, both wily and wise, Wotan's crutch
and his torment. Vocally, his line darts all over the place, leaping here and there
like flames spreading from branch to branch in a forest fire. Yet he cannot be
merely a character tenor like Ulfung—his tone must have both heft and appeal.
We don't need to take Loge to our hearts, but he should fascinate; at least modest

tonal allure is essential for him to capture and hold us in his igneous grasp. Past broadcast interpreters have included big players on the Wagner scene: René Maison, Set Svanholm, Ramon Vinay, and Karl Liebl. Peterson isn't in their league in terms of celebrity, but he qualifies as a first-rank Loge. The voice, securely placed, is not particularly individual in timbre, but it is agreeable overall and blessed with steadiness. More important, fleetness seems to be its natural mode of movement. Loge's aim must be accurate as he barks out advice and chastisement. Peterson's is. The character comes alive. A few singular moments may be noted. As he describes the need to forswear love in order to gain the ring ('doch einer übt ihn leicht, der sel'ger Lieb' entsagt'), he underlines the significance of the ring motive with insidious legato. When Loge invites Wotan to slip down the sulfur cleft to the Nibelungen lair, Peterson's 'dort schlüpfe mit mir hinein!' becomes the audible equivalent of their slithery descent. A brilliant stroke is his swift, startling shout of 'Durch raub!'; 'Steal the ring!' he cries to Wotan and the advice pierces the ether like a gunshot. Peterson's skeptical musing on the folly of the gods at the opera's end seems not only well earned, but his by right.

Of greatest moment for the future of Wagner at the Met is the company debut of Donald McIntyre on the broadcast. Still, his toil in that sometimes unproductive vineyard would not be as extensive on American shores as one might hope. Born in New Zealand and forty years old at the time of the broadcast, the singer had done yeoman's service on the British opera stages since 1959, culminating in his Covent Garden debut in 1967 (Pizarro). The same season saw the beginning of a lengthy Bayreuth tenure in the big roles of the Wagner corpus. A wide and varied repertory occupied him in the intervening years before the Met beckoned. In future seasons, he would return frequently to the company, though the number of his performances would not be overlarge.

As revealed on the broadcast, McIntyre's voice is a substantial one, well schooled and capable of strong, authoritative, well-projected declamation and song. On this afternoon, its bass-baritone timbre is lower-centered than anticipated. (The *Walküre* broadcast will set right the division between the bass and baritone components of his instrument.) Upon hearing the opening scene, one considers that the voice's slight recalcitrance may be a character touch caused by Fricka's waking him from sleep. But some heaviness of movement lingers throughout the initial mountaintop encounters. Still, the voice's weight, its dark coloration, above all, its freedom from wobble are encouraging. One hopes that tone coloration will grow more varied as the opera progresses. Those hopes are realized. Gradually, the voice warms, the quality of movement becomes easier, light invades the dark center of his tone. His top notes are wonderfully firm and powerful, unusually so for a voice possessed of solidity in the lower range. A genuine Heldenbariton may well be within our ken. True, the vocalism cannot be called mercurial—the manner may be overly serious even for the leader of the gods. I would prefer the evening sunlight to gild the tone as well as inform the text when, at the opera's end, Wotan launches 'Abendlich strahlt der sonne Auge.' In that apostrophe, a pair of splendid top notes adds markedly to the credit side of the ledger, helping to assuage disappointment in this pivotal moment.

Earlier, and oddly, the voice appears to profit from breathing the stifling air of the Nibelungen lair; its resonance becomes headier and (when the god returns to the mountaintop) converts into a more interesting vehicle for expression. His line is invariably strongly drawn, the legato firm. And he is a thoughtful interpreter. Greed invades his whispered tone as he covets Alberich's ring. Like a tonal explosion, 'Her den ring!' bursts from his lips as he tears the prize from the gnome's finger; the gesture, vocal and physical, provides an effective contrast to the breadth of line and tone that he summons as Wotan triumphantly salutes his might ('Nun halt' ich'). Nobility and pride swell in his tones as he sets Freia free. His fear of the curse ('Furchtbar nun erfind' ich des Fluches Kraft!') may be dramatically tame, but the ensuing 'Wie doch Bangen mich binder' profits from a measured pace, expressive phrasing, and bright top tones. The *Rheingold* Wotan operates at a lower temperature than the compelling father figure of *Walküre*. We must expect more from McIntyre in the latter's more febrile environment.

Das Rheingold may thrive as a team effort; *Die Walküre* requires a headliner quartet. In Nilsson and Vickers, the Met had a pair whose star power was beyond cavil. The only question that remained was whether their light, almost blinding in wattage thus far in their careers, would continue to shine as brightly as ever. Rysanek, the scheduled Sieglinde and an incontestable headliner, had canceled and would not appear with the company during the 1974–75 season. With the able Janis Martin as her broadcast replacement, the star quotient was reduced to a possible trio, whose number was not entirely verified by the prospect of McIntyre's Wotan. Dunn (Fricka) and Rundgren (Hunding) rounded out the necessary sextet of principals on the broadcast of 1 March 1975.

Ehrling's equitable stance ensures that the opening storm will be taken at face value (one can almost count the raindrops in the quarter-notes of the deliberate motivic play), but, withal, his is a meteorological event that moves expeditiously. Atmosphere and sweep in Wagner are less his concern than care over details. He melds them, however, into a conception both poised and, especially as the opera progresses, fluent—yet unhurried. When he can quietly nurse a nest of motives, he is on happy ground. I cite in that regard the transition from Wotan's narrative to the agitated entry of Sieglinde and Siegmund, and later, Brünnhilde's contemplation of the weary couple—there the horns softly, appealingly, vibrate as death motives prophesy. He may be niggardly with the composer's orchestral climaxes but, when he chooses, he allows a few of them (the episode after Brünnhilde's decision to succor the hero, and the ecstatic orchestral section at the midpoint of Wotan's farewell) to spill forth in rhapsodic freedom, their potency enhanced by the surrounding self-possessed lyricism. This may not be the grand-scale Wagner cherished by many, but, in the long run, Ehrling's cleansing action proves refreshing.

The conductor's discreet sounding of Hunding's chordal motive hardly augments the husband's brutality; this domestic maleficence would be punished in small claims court. But it does prefigure Rundgren's oddly minor-league Hunding, a surprise after his robust Fasolt. Perhaps he wants to expose the ruffian as a moral weakling, with voice to match. A coarse manner must do to counterfeit the host's threatening hospitality. Dunn fares better as Wotan's unhappy wife, a step up from her *Rheingold* portrayal. In the initial stages of Fricka's tug of war with her husband, the mezzo's phrases are brushed with the shrew's plaint, apropos dramatically but unexpected from Dunn's normally molasses-tinctured tone. A more appealing texture returns as Fricka grows more confident of her case for marital fidelity. The American mezzo's strongly delivered phrases are capped by some vibrant, utterly secure top notes. During these seasons, her Met career is deservedly

Die Walküre
1 March 1975
Sieglinde
Janis Martin
Brünnhilde
Birgit Nilsson
Fricka
Mignon Dunn
Siegmund
Jon Vickers
Wotan
Donald McIntyre
Hunding
Bengt Rundgren
Conductor
Sixten Ehrling

Sixten Ehrling. Courtesy Metropolitan Opera Archives.

flourishing at a level not quite expected from her earliest outings. Her prominence on the broadcasts verifies management's regard for her abilities. In some ways, she is an American Ludwig—the timbres and the density and lava flow of tone are not dissimilar—though Dunn's voice lacks the vivifying lights of the German singer's instrument. Dunn's assured portrayals would be improved by greater individuality in characterization.

Upon hearing McIntyre's impressive Wotan, I think it churlish not to increase the performance's star quotient to three, or at least allow the bass-baritone honorary membership along with Vickers and Nilsson. The broadcast *Rheingold* provided evidence of his merit, and his *Walküre* Wotan not only solidifies that positive impression, but adds considerably to his stature. The voice holds up extremely well under the opera's more stringent demands, and his characterization is strong, full, and believable. He shows us a god both glorying in his power and a man struggling with torment. The achromatic timbre is perhaps a bit stodgy over the long haul—it is shy of primary colors—but its solidity, its unfailing core of well-supported tone, is immensely reassuring to listeners starved for the *Heldenbariton* sound. McIntyre's voice is resonantly assured in both the high and low ranges, another gift not common to recent interpreters of his repertory. In the grand sequence of brief phrases where Wotan bewails Fricka's interference ('O heilige Schmach!'), McIntyre utilizes breadth of phrase and strength of tone as though he had borrowed Donner's hammer. Often one approaches the second-act narrative with trepidation—Anna Russell's bewilderment at Wotan's telling the whole tale again hits home. But McIntyre rings so many changes upon the god's account of his troubles that interest never flags. Textual subtleties, rhythmic variety, attempts to color the tone—many of the welcome devices of the singing actor's art enliven his storytelling. Anger, frustration, self-pity, tender intimacy are courted at will and with entirely adequate vocal means. Admiration for the singer's abilities, both vocal and interpretive, is commensurate with the episode's infamous length. In the third act, McIntrye rages fiercely at the distraught Walküren. He is less troubled than most by orchestral surges. I recall James Morris, the late-century preferred Wotan, on a Chicago Lyric Opera broadcast mimicking his coach and mentor Hans Hotter's deep tones as the latter advised him not to trouble himself about those few moments in *Walküre* when no Wotan could be heard.[14] I doubt that McIntyre gave them another thought. But from my repeated hearings of Hotter's Wotan in Vienna in the 1950s, I know that Hotter himself didn't have to worry about it. Tone just poured out of him.

McIntyre convincingly plays the disciplining parent with the disobedient Brünnhilde during her pleas for understanding. He chooses to top the chordal descent of 'In festen Schlaf' with strong tones (and gratifyingly accurate intonation) rather than cosseting them with pain-inflected regret, a not entirely inappropriate stance considering the text. (Wagner's music tells us otherwise, however.) The farewell, strongly intoned at its beginning and replete with authority in the concluding instructions to Loge, is a splendid piece of singing. It validates a portrayal that needs no apology. The voice lacks only that touch of sweetness in the tone that could tear the heart as the father muses on 'der Augen leuchtendes Paar' and 'holden Lippen' of his favorite daughter. The lack of a reliable mezza voce compels him to a novel solution for the concluding phrase of farewell proper: when he breathes 'so küsst er die Gottheit von dir!,' 'Gottheit' all but disappears into the ether before 'von dir' is granted, as though drawn from inner torment, an unexpectedly brusque utterance. The device works. Thereafter, Ehrling rhythmically propels the flame motive in so jaunty a manner that the fire seems to dance along gleefully, impervious to the curtain's fall.

Janis Martin is one of those rare creatures who escaped early Metropolitan servitude, fled to Europe, built a major career on foreign shores, and returned triumphantly to the company in major roles. During three seasons in the early sixties she moved, with commendable persistence, from an endless round of walk-ons as Flora, Inez, and Kate Pinkerton on to Siebel, Lola, and Nicklausse. After several years of European prominence (Fricka and Magdalene at Bayreuth in 1968), in the early seventies she shed her mezzo-soprano trappings and turned soprano (Tosca, Eva, Sieglinde). San Francisco knew her as a mezzo and Chicago as a soprano before her second Metropolitan debut, this time as Marie in *Wozzeck* on 7 October 1974. Nilsson, forsaking the heroic realm, had gamely undertaken Sieglinde in the premiere of the season's cycle (and for three performances later in the run), while Martin portrayed her in the 25 February performance immediately preceding the broadcast.

Unlike most conversions from the mezzo terrain, Martin's transformation seems entirely warranted and successful. The voice, of healthy size and bright color, retains its mezzo density and security in the low range. The wonder is that the soprano heights share the same confident thrust and tonal solidity. Her all-purpose timbre—its brilliance, though, giving her a leg up over many American sopranos—and a somewhat placid temperament prevent her Sieglinde from becoming the searing experience that artists as different as Lehmann, Varnay, and Rysanek have contributed to the airwaves. Still, to hear a completely frazzle-free voice in Wagner is always an occasion for celebration. Martin can be too careful when singing a pregnant motive in tandem with an orchestral instrument, but many moments of vocal splendor enliven her portrayal ('So bleibe hier!' in the first scene is one early instance). And how gratifying it is to hear both the low-lying initial half (richness of utterance there) and the soaring final portion of 'Der Männer Sippe' delivered with equal surety of voice. But her storytelling is more recitation from rote than living experience. She does name Siegmund with commendable assurance. Sieglinde's second-act madness ought to inspire both sympathy and terror; Martin's competent way is too measured to achieve a resonating response in us, but her third act holds a surprise of considerable magnitude. In reply to Nilsson's blazing announcement of the hero Sieglinde is to bring forth, Martin summons a correspondingly splendid utterance in turn, filling 'Du hehrstes Wunder!' with full-blooded, brilliant, well-colored tone; her mutated soprano is entirely at ease in the high tessitura, the rhythms of the expansive phrase measured out with exactitude, its pace unhurried, its thrust potent indeed. I had not thought the voice capable of so compelling a summation. One might expect that the Metropolitan would make room in many future seasons for its novice turned protagonist, but during the seventies the company limited Martin's soprano sojourn to a period comparable in length to that of her earlier mezzo residence. Her gifts warranted more than they allowed her (which included Kundry and, in 1977, another broadcast Sieglinde). Her career flourished in other venues, both European and American.

Unlike the principals described above, Nilsson and Vickers by now have become avatars, that status earned both by the grand expanse of their careers and in these particular roles. Their quality has been authenticated in six *Walküre* broadcasts dating from 1960 on through 1972. The current broadcast contains their final assumption of Brünnhilde and Siegmund for the radio audience. Other roles would maintain their preeminence with both the house and radio public, but signature roles such as these do not vanish from the airwaves without enormous regret on the part of the artists' admirers.

On this afternoon, the tenor gives what may be the performance of his life. Banished are any reservations we might have regarding idiosyncratic interpretation; none of the vocal vagaries that plagued his broadcast Tristan of the previous year interfere with our appreciation of his gifts. Mannerisms are nonexistent. Except where he acknowledges the text's call for restraint (and even there he never croons, but employs a resonant mezza voce), he sings with full-toned splendor, allowing the vibrant strength of his grand instrument to ring forth in phrase after phrase, often magnificent in their span. Of course, he varies tone and volume to shape the phrase and illuminate the text, but the overall impression is one of heroic and unfettered vocalism and strength of character. He would not be Vickers if he did not at some moment take us into the very heart of his being, and he does so in that harrowing communion where Siegmund bends over the sleeping Sieglinde immediately before he goes to his death. In a ravishing mezza voce he coddles her, the mood of intimacy magically sustained in tones wonderfully quiet and encircled by the loveliest of head tones at 'Und Friede dich erfreu'!' Immediately he springs up and flies into combat, a hero incarnate in tone and manner. One could cite individual glories of his performance, but then all would need to be mentioned. (I should note that, as often happens early on in a Vickers performance, some of his vowel sounds are so far forward and touched with nasality that their pointed thrusts can offend.) As to glories, I will be content to note only a few: the directness and rhythmic alacrity of the first-act narrative, the vivid telling enhanced by a splendid arc of phrase and tone at 'Nächtiges Dunkel, deckte mein Aug'; the easy flow of his love song celebrating spring (the entire duet sequence and the act's fiery close somewhat harnessed by the conductor's restraint) and the thrilling power of his sword embrace; and, in the second act, the pregnant tonal fullness of 'Grüsst mich in Walhall Froh eine Frau.' Did the tenor ever unfold a more nobly luxuriant phrase? Probably so. There have been so many of them—and more to come.

Vickers was still on the favorable side of fifty in years, but Nilsson was now in her mid-fifties and manager Goeran Gentele's statement that one "couldn't count on Birgit forever" has a more creditable ring now than it did in 1972 when he made the comment to Leinsdorf as they discussed the hiring of Ligendza for the ill-fated Isolde sequence of 1974.[15] The illustrious Birgit would go on singing for almost another decade, but her Metropolitan career was interrupted by a four-year hiatus after the current season and appearances thereafter were sparse. To have documentation of a Nilsson complete *Ring* cycle in live performance, even from this late stage in her career, is welcome bounty. Though included with regret, the phrase "late stage" is worth mentioning, for, truth to tell, we hear, for almost the first time, a few signs of erosion in, and an increase of surface rime on, the soprano's amazing instrument. Far from being a voice in disrepair, the fearless blade is now and then merely harsher in timbre, the familiar brilliance touched occasionally by shrillness in the uppermost notes (always her prime asset); intonation problems (more prominent early on in her Met career, then all but vanquished) now return. When the two limitations unite, as they do in Brünnhilde's final towering utterance, they momentarily bring the peerless soprano (forever that in her era's memory) onto earthly terrain. But only momentarily, for the bulk of her third act has much of the remembered splendor of tone and a gratifying flush of belief in the heroic maid's trials. Portions of the second act are less satisfying, though her questioning of Siegmund is impressive, both for its authority and the compact blend of tone (barring a brief touch of an intrusive whine) of the middle and low voice. And as she agrees to succor him in battle, she soars in fettle fine.

When Brünnhilde, with the exhausted Sieglinde in tow, greets her sister warriors, Nilsson sounds like a singer released. Now we hear the shining thrust of tone, poured out in all its glory, that has given her such preeminence in the Wagner realm. 'Fort denn, eile' is equally memorable for its interpretive fervor and tonal amplitude. She throws in a Rysanek scream (a good one too) in the face of her father's chastisement. The disjunct phrases of 'War es so schmählich' are shaped into a convincing arc, Brünnhilde's wretchedness exposed. 'O sag, Vater!' and the ensuing phrases are fervently pleaded, some of her tones darkly colored and all lovely to hear. Except for that brief final section ('Auf dein Gebot'), all of the searing scene between father and daughter not only carries evidence of her continuing vocal puissance, but confirms the growth in expressive potency that her performances since the early years of her Metropolitan career document.

One deft Nilsson touch in that lengthy father–daughter scene is uniquely appealing. The soprano plays with the text and notes of 'Du zeugtest ein edles Geschlecht,' lightly tossing it off as she taunts Wotan with the prospect of the hero who is to come. In the 15 March broadcast of *Siegfried*, we come upon that innocent early, but regrettably the valiance of Sieglinde's son, that stout heart that Brünnhilde assured her father would vindicate him, will lie more in the imagination than the reality. Nilsson and McIntyre are the holdovers from *Walküre*, with Ulfung (Mime), Rintzler (Alberich), Macurdy (Fafner), and Chookasian (Erda) familiar from *Rheingold*. Betsy Norden pipes as the Forest Bird while Siegfried's lot, unlucky both in Wagner's drama and often in performance, falls to Jess Thomas. Ehrling, of course, remains on the podium. Usually, *Siegfried* causes more apprehension and requires greater care than the other operas of the cycle. The reasons are many, but foremost are the long sequences for male voices alone and the difficulty of the title role. Nowhere would management's determination to mount the cycle be more open to debate than in performances of this mammoth opera.

Thus Ehrling's task is a lofty one. He seems to prefer not to soar, however, and therefore membership in the top rank of Wagner conductors lies beyond his reach. Though he is loath to circle the dizzying heights of the composer's imagination, he nevertheless operates in his own comfortable range with certainty of intent and execution. As in *Rheingold*, the opportunities for chamber music play are frequent in *Siegfried*, and Ehrling cherishes that circumspect mode; he takes full advantage of them, granting the solo instruments preeminence. The conductor infuses the opera's more spirited moments with just enough lively seasoning to drag a few rather slackly drawn episodes into renewed life. He knows where the dramatic situation needs a jolt and delivers it. Overall, one cannot quarrel with his pacing—at least, if one accepts his rather introspective stance.

Modesty infects the opera itself. Wagner provided two offstage turns, each at the extreme of the vocal spectrum. Betsy Norden chirps the Forest Bird's calls with commendable élan. Her timbre, spot clean, as though unsullied by the world's

Siegfried
15 March 1975

Brünnhilde
Birgit Nilsson
Forest Bird
Betsy Norden
Erda
Lili Chookasian
Siegfried
Jess Thomas
Mime
Ragnar Ulfung
Wanderer
Donald McIntyre
Alberich
Marius Rintzler
Fafner
John Macurdy
Conductor
Sixten Ehrling

ways, suits her task. Even through the horn, Macurdy's bass can't equal the tuba's cumbersome growl, but he gives a good imitation of a sleepy dragon and delivers a pertinent death warning to Siegfried. Chookasian, blessed with natural density and breadth of tone in the lower vocal region, again proves that she is a natural for Erda. The goddess' vaunted wisdom seems to lurk in the bosomy depth of the American contralto's solid tones. When she ascends momentarily into the upper range, the singer's vocalism is equally comfortable—even though flying in musical space seems an unlikely pursuit for an earth mother.

During the first two acts of the opera, one might well wonder why Wagner did not call the opera *Mime*; perhaps the composer should have allowed him equal billing with his willful "child." An altered title makes sense on this afternoon, for Ulfung's Mime sometimes dwarfs Siegfried's heroic efforts. The two tenors are well matched in vocal size. Indeed, the Swedish tenor's timbre is so uncompromisingly pointed that earache can set in before Siegfried commits functional "patricide." Mime's skin fits Ulfung as though he had been born into it; instrument and style are perfectly in tune with the Nibelung's self-concept. He need not rely upon a tiresome whine to suggest the dwarf's perpetual complaint—his preferred weapon is a resonant tonal *épée*, invariably thrust home with deadly accuracy. No wonder Siegfried can't stand him. The audience loves him, however, and loudly cheers him in the curtain calls. And why not? Such expert villainy, such careful plotting (a bit of light-toned dreaming as he muses on a sleep draught for Siegfried), and so many sneers so craftily doled out deserve reward. Rightly so, since Wagner made sure he didn't receive any—no ring for him. Nor for brother Alberich. The brief scene between the brothers plays like black comedy as Ulfung and Rintzler joust in a show of one-upmanship. In general, for dramatic verisimilitude, the most powerful Nibelung really ought to be more formidably repugnant than Rintzler suggests in this episode of the cycle. Try as he will to make his voice snarl and thunder—and it can, to a considerable extent—his instrument is blessed as much with tonal sweetness as brawn. The timbre is markedly attractive and his technical aplomb is notable, but those are not the expected prerequisites for conveying Alberich's evil designs. As Rintzler and McIntyre join forces when the kings of the dwarfs and the gods lock horns at Fafner's cave, their resonant voices provide unalloyed pleasure—hardly Wagner's intent.

The Wanderer, most urbane and equably tempered of the gods either in or out of disguise, cannot offer McIntyre the mood changes that made his *Walküre* so vivid a characterization. Wagner allowed him, however, ample opportunity for broadly declaimed song and the New Zealand–born bass-baritone clearly is at ease with that assignment. At each appearance of the god, he pours out reams of firmly centered tone, commanding in sonority and decisive in purpose. He is particularly good at pointing up a climax, whether musical or, more often, those dictated by situation; Wotan's power is often inherent in his thrusting tone and purposeful phrasing. In the scene where the Wanderer tests Mime with the three riddles (each emphatically intoned by McIntyre), the baritone proves adept at buttering up the Nibelung—his suave legato enhances 'Walhall heisst ihr Saal.' Even more impressive is the searing session with Erda. At its end, as Wotan foresees his fall from power, McIntyre's noble phrasing and expansive tone bring his *Ring* portrayals to an imposing climax. His entry into the Metropolitan company was not merely welcome. It was essential. Even in that benighted era, worthy Wagnerian gods were in short supply.

John McIntyre as the Wanderer in *Siegfried*. Photography by James Heffernan.
Courtesy Metropolitan Opera Archives.

The dearth of qualified members for the Heldentenor Fach has, over the centuries, been an impresario's prime headache. In particular, casting the role of Siegfried causes managerial migraine. Any tenor who tackles that assignment has the odds stacked against him. Those gifted with a voice of the requisite power and contrasting tonal qualities are frequently vanquished by the brutal length of the role. Thomas, who figured in the previous season's new production of the opera, probably never qualified in regard to vocal heft or tonal appeal. At this season's premiere (5 March), the *Times* critic trashed both the performance and, specifically, Thomas.[16] Reviewing the broadcast performance, his *Times* colleague found our stalwart much improved.[17] Whether improved or not, the American tenor deserves kudos, not only for bravery under fire, but for delivering a performance notable for stamina (his voice holds up to the very end, something most recent Siegfrieds cannot claim), note fidelity (normally that would be a given, but times have changed), and response to situation and text. True, the timbre is hardly blandishing. But he is in excellent late-career vocal form. A beat infects his bleak tones during the opening scene, but gradually the voice—one cannot say warms, for the timbre remains inherently dry—opens up. It takes on frequent touches of brighter color. Like Conan Doyle's accommodating dog (in *The Adventure of Silver Blaze*), he barks not. Compact, collected tone must suffice, for vocal glamor is not within his compass. The forging song (the first stanza mercifully cut) gains no reflected heat from the forge's fire; neither sufficient power nor abandoned joy in youth's prowess inform it. Still, it is correct—most of the notes are in place. Hardly a shred of velvet caress can Thomas summon in the intimate moments when the forest murmurs—the orchestra must supply all of nature's wonder. But he knows what he ought to do, and does it when he effectively shapes 'So starb meine Mutter an mir?'. (Imagine what Vickers, the reluctant Wagnerian, might do with that phrase!) Top notes are for the most part secure, though not always free of strain; one of them ('Lust,' as Siegfried describes his heart's cravings to the craven Mime) actually glows. And a few attractive head tones (in 'Nach lieben Gesellen,' as the hero prepares to blow his horn) stand out amid the second-act desert of sere tone. He sets the mood for the discovery of Brünnhilde well enough with a tender sounding of 'Selige Oede auf sonniger Höh!' and follows it with some aptly colored full-voice phrases as he surveys the forbidden rock. The surprise (and for the audience, amused delight) of 'Das is kein Mann' is appropriately abrupt and unashamedly fierce. Of course, the duet belongs to Nilsson, and nothing Thomas can do—though even here, his stamina counts for something—could alter that certainty. Throughout the long afternoon, the tenor has rendered honorable service.

Not only the duet, but the afternoon's prize belongs to the soprano. Did the *Walküre* broadcast appear to signal some diminution in her resources? We need not have worried. Here is the redoubtable Nilsson in prime form, contributing one of her finest broadcast performances. She makes one agree with Wagner's assessment, made in a letter to his friend Anton Pusinelli, that the "awakening of Brünnhilde" was his "most beautiful thing!"[18] It is as Nilsson sings it. The voice is full and secure from the moment when Brünnhilde hails the sun and continues its free flight until the final curtain. It grows in richness and surety as the duet gains speed. Her timbre on this afternoon is a unique blend of winds, quite different from the honed, cutting singular brilliance of her earlier seasons. Probably it represents a natural progression of depth gained as career years have grown in number. Complementing the voice's effulgence is a notable sensitivity to mood and text. The reflective mood of the middle portion of the duet holds many phrases of pensive tenderness. When Brünnhilde notes that Siegfried has also waked her faithful steed, Grane, the soprano folds 'Mit mir hat ihn Siegfried erweckt' into a delightfully fond embrace; one might suspect that memories of the Swedish farm girl's youth rumble in the soprano's subconscious. As the heroic maid notes that the Walküre's shield and helmet will protect her no more, the little *frisson* she applies to 'Er birgt mich nicht' is interpretive gold. 'Trauriges dunkel' warrants darker coloration than she supplies, but her girlish play of light tone and easy manner (including a delectable *subito piano*) turn Brünnhilde's praise of Siegfried and subsequent pleading to leave her undisturbed into unadulterated pleasure. Is she playing the coquette, engaging in unlikely flirtation? I hope so. Aided by Ehrling's considerate pace, she throws out floods of superb tone in the final pages of the opera. Naturally, Thomas' tones are swamped by their splendor. Better to have half a loaf than none. When she looses a splendid high C to summon the curtain's fall, Miss Nilsson's enthronement in the Valhalla of Wagner singers is once again assured. Of course, coronation was never in doubt.

Götterdämmerung, the final opera of the cycle, looms. Both its imposing length and blatantly operatic propensities can be of some concern to the opera lover. And we will swallow a double dose, for it will be well, before wrapping up the 1975 cycle, to look in on the broadcast (23 March 1974) of the previous season, when the opera was newly mounted. Rintzler and Rundgren appear as Alberich and Hagen in both broadcasts, as do Rankin (Gutrune) and Dooley (Gunther). In the earlier performance, Rita Hunter is Brünnhilde, Dunn plays Waltraute, and Helge Brilioth Siegfried, in contrast to the complete 1975 cycle where Nilsson, Anna Reynolds, and Thomas perform those roles. Differences occur in the Norns and Rhinemaidens as well. Most important, Rafael Kubelik, at the time music director of the company, conducts the 1974 airing.

The Czech-born maestro had conducted the broadcast of *Les Troyens* the previous week. That monster work and *Götterdämmerung* were his two mammoth charges during his introductory season. The broadcast performance possesses a dynamism beyond the ordinary, its exuberant gait quite removed from either Leinsdorf's or Ehrlings's considered (and distinctly individual) pace. When Kubelik's evident love for the grand climax is coupled with the propulsive pace he sets, the combination makes for an exciting afternoon at the opera, the fervor consistently maintained even though almost six hours' time at the listening post are involved. The most famous orchestral passages (Siegfried's Rhine Journey and the Funeral March) are consecrated in the maestro's flamboyant reading of their graphic phrases. The funeral progress, in particular, profits from not only the expected dramatic thrust, but also the conductor's ability to draw forth phrases of marked tenderness in the more reflective passages. The brass do double duty in this opera and Kubelik allows them a free hand to hurl out their majestic tones. Their glowing sonorities are, for the most part, welcome. Kubelik's control of his forces, both those in the pit and onstage, is everywhere secure and entirely rewarding. He was scheduled to conduct the 1975 complete *Ring* cycle, but his dissatisfaction with certain administrative and artistic decisions (plus his absence during the *Tristan* debacle) brought, at his request, an end to his directorship and conductor responsibilities after a single season. A conductor at home in both the concert hall and the opera house (Brno, Glyndebourne, Sadler's Wells) and music director at Covent Garden for three years in the late fifties, he had been expected to contribute much

Die Götterdämmerung
23 March 1974

Brünnhilde
Rita Hunter
Gutrune
Nell Rankin
Waltraute
Mignon Dunn
Siegfried
Helge Brilioth
Gunther
William Dooley
Alberich
Marius Rintzler
Hagen
Bengt Rundgren
Conductor
Rafael Kubelik

to company stability, both behind the desk and on the podium. His premature and regrettable departure was yet another indication of administrative distress.

When dealing in threes, Kubelik's disinclination to dawdle has mixed results. The Norns' weaving of the rope of destiny is facilitated, but the Rhinemaidens' play loses some of its customary graceful sway. In the former able trio, Dunn is the livelier interpreter, Rankin's top voice shines, and Godfrey's darker, slightly blousy tones seem appropriate for the oldest Norn. The conductor's frequent out-sized climaxes cover their vocal efforts now and then until the rope break removes them from the scene. By the opening of the third act, Godfrey has shed gloom in favor of frolicking in the Rhine; she adds her fuzzy warmth to giggling girls Baldwin and Pracht. Their blend pleases, even when the soprano slights Woglinde's high B-flat as their flirtation with Siegfried ends. Rankin, too, does double duty. Gutrune, a broadcast first for the Alabama-born mezzo, is most often assigned to sopranos, but Rankin's upper range is her prime comfort zone and she handles the assignment with aplomb. Actually, patches of scratchy tone are more likely to invade phrases in her middle voice. The Gibichung sister and brother are ungrateful roles, but Rankin and Dooley are old hands whose interpretive skill keeps them in the picture no matter how limited their opportunities. Gunther is such a weakling that even Dooley's imagination must work overtime to keep the chieftain's vital signs functioning. The baritone's aptitude for declamation based on the rhythms of the text helps and when songlike phrases occur—as in Gunther's act-one greeting of Siegfried—his appealing timbre does the rest. He and Brilioth, both sensitive artists, perform like lieder singers in their discussion of future brides—a captivating moment and a respite from the highly charged theatrics of the opera.

Unlike the Gibichungs, Waltraute is granted a limelight episode with her narrative. Dunn, no longer concerned with weaving, makes the most of her opportunity. Ideally, one wants Brünnhilde's Valkyrie sister to ladle out grander tones than the American mezzo supplies. But her voice is so firmly anchored and its basic coloration so inviting that she qualifies as an able executant. Her interpretive skills appear to be growing at a rate commensurate with her increasing prominence. Hers is an emotional reading, alive with belief in Waltraute's mission and well calculated to fix attention. More body of tone in the lower range would better serve the daughter's recall of Wotan's prophetic words about the return of the ring. She is at her best in her moving description of her father's gloom ('So—sitzt er, sagt kein Wort'); the quiet mood flatters her instrument and feeds her interpretive instincts. Still, when Waltraute closes by vehemently urging Brünnhilde to give up the ring, Dunn rises to the challenge with a grandly scaled plea.

Of all the crisscrossing familial relationships in the cycle, the father-and-son unit of Alberich and Hagen may be the strangest. Rintzler and Rundgren are again on hand. The former's rich vocalism dilutes the malevolence of the gnome's grubby power grab, but his actor's craft restores it with interpretive touches of considerable power. Rintzler easily dominates their act-two scene and exits the cycle adjuring Hagen to be trusty and true, a seeming impossibility, but one made vivid by the bass' coloristic quick-changes. Unfortunately, Rundgren continues the downward slide from his impressive Fasolt to a middling Hunding and, here, a small-change Hagen. The fault lies more in his instrument than in his art. Evil must live in the singer's tones if the villainous Hagen is to fulfill his function in the drama. Rundgren's voice is too light for the task and the deficiency is not redressed by the timbral blackness that would signify in sound Hagen's vengeful depravity.

His European repute is sustained, however, by insightful touches of characterization and a few musical subtleties. Give him credit for the seductive vocalism that leads Gunther to agree to Hagen's abduction of the maiden on her rock.

With their nemesis of less than fearsome stature, the hero and heroine are guaranteed an eminence even greater than Wagner allotted them. Our Siegfried, Swedish tenor Helge Brilioth, will be remembered for his 1972 Florestan. Parsifal, Aegisth, Siegmund, Tristan, and the *Siegfried* hero had already profited from his sensitive artistry before his first *Götterdämmerung* Siegfried a few days before the broadcast. From that list of roles, one might imagine that the voice is of the rare Heldentenor breed. That hope is not rewarded. He had made his Met debut as Parsifal and that lyric youth better defines his vocal wealth (or lack thereof). Nevertheless, he is an artist of quality and the voice is most attractive in timbre. He does not push it beyond its limits even in a role like Siegfried, where the opportunities are many and not easily avoided. His timbre marries a bit of the lyric balm of Windgassen with the grainy solidity of compatriot Svanholm. His legato is commendable, his phrasing more than that. Whether drawing a phrase with breadth or nurturing it with a delicate caress (or even occasionally sending it flying with playful rhythmic emphasis), his musicality all but overcomes regret at the deficiency of heroic thrust. Of course, his best qualities come to the fore in the scene with the Rhinemaidens. How unusual to have a Siegfried one can actually like! And later in the third act, his touching narrative of the hero's youth is full of expressive tints; lovely head tones at 'da lauscht' ich wieder dem wonnigen Laller' contrast effectively with the darker color he summons when telling of Mime's vile purposes. (He exploited the latter color as well when counterfeiting Gunther's voice as he wooed Brünnhilde.) The tenor remembers Siegfried's encounter with the Forest Bird in phrases as nimbly executed as those by the soprano songstress. Most affecting is his farewell to Brünnhilde. In short, at least over the radio, his portrayal is far more satisfying to hear than those of many more celebrated and long-lasting tenors of the Wagner Fach.

The announcement that Rita Hunter, a broadcast debutant, would replace the scheduled Nilsson as Brünnhilde must have caused a good deal of despondent breast-beating in both house and home. I had pounded on mine a few times back then, but by the final curtain, breast soothed, I was considerably elated at the quality of the English soprano's portrayal. Hearing her performance a quarter century later not only reinforces regard but enhances it. The lowered horizon of our expectations in this postmillennial era, mentioned earlier, may play a role in this upgrade, but I doubt it. As heard on the broadcast, Miss Hunter's Brünnhilde would elicit kudos in most of the Met Wagnerian eras of the last century. Let her be a Gadski to Nordica's or Fremstad's primacy, a Lawrence to Flagstad's glory, a more than honorable status. Hunter's pre-Met experience had largely been with British companies, where her Wagner singing (often in English) attracted attention from 1970 on. She came to the Met in 1972 as the *Walküre* Brünnhilde (her first in German), acquired Santuzza the following season, and, following Nilsson's triumph in the premiere of the *Götterdämmerung* production on 8 March, sang, as scheduled, in the third presentation of the opera. The Swedish soprano had appeared with her arm in a sling (the result of a painful fall during a rehearsal) at the premiere, but Cross tells us her radio cancellation was due to the flu.

Hunter has her voice well in hand, even as the lovers emerge from their trysting cave. Initially, its timbre has a slight metallic overlay, the mid-low range not so ringing as to invariably penetrate Kubelik's hearty band. But soon, both its size and consistency throughout the entire range (including a productive, but not coarse, blending of chest where necessary) reassure the listener. Top-voice *fortes* can either be insistently brilliant or warmly rounded (the latter outnumbering the former as the opera progresses). She alters timbre and dynamics to suit the text (early on signaling an interpretive gift by applying a flush of color to 'an Liebe reich, doch ledig der Kraft'). Placidity seems foreign to her temperament, routine routed by alert rhythms and spurts of tone and shooting movement. A rapturous 'O heilige Götter' prepares one for her blazing, on-the-mark high C at the duet's close. A more neutral coloration in the colloquy with Waltraute momentarily dims expectation, but not for long. Her delicate trill and finely colored tones as she tells her sister of her happiness with Siegfried are unusual attributes for any Wagnerian dramatic soprano. Breadth of tone and an actor's skill inform her terror at "Gunther"'s penetration of her supposedly secure space. Her oath on the spear is fiercer and more brilliant than the tenor's—a feature familiar to opera lovers of late. An emotional peak both for Hunter and her listeners occurs when Brünnhilde tries to understand Siegfried's betrayal ('Welches Unhold's List liegt hier verhohlen?'). The commanding manner is affirmed by clean high B-flats before shame overcomes the trusting wife—the soprano's splendid tones and affective expression are quite moving. Perhaps the loveliest moment of the afternoon is her delivery of the long, winding phrase beginning 'Sein Mannes-Gemahl bin ich' when she tells Gutrune that Brünnhilde was Siegfried's 'Eheweib'; her expansive upward thrust on 'Eide' before pulling back to a *subito piano* demonstrates both her interpretive sensitivity and technical skill.

Authority, vocal puissance, and stamina are the principal virtues of her immolation scene. I find the more interior, introspective moments less affecting. 'Alles! Alles!' is ordinary gruel. But the 'Ruhe' pair are embraced with the softest velvet—an affecting moment indeed (I wonder if they could be heard in the house). Best of all is her spirited delivery of the final section, beginning with her summons to Grane: her involvement is palpable, excitement runs high, the high Bs are superb, and the final phrase ('Selig grüsst dich dein Weib!') is broadly declaimed to maximum effect. Hunter would come a cropper with her Met Norma in 1975 (she sang Italian roles frequently in England); she returned for Aida in 1976 and would be heard as the *Walküre* warrior maid on a 1977 broadcast before the company saw the last of her. As a worthy Wagnerian, she has her adherents to this day. One reason for their regard may be that Hunter's Brünnhilde seems a natural outpouring of self. For some dissidents, Nilsson's portrayals can come off as remote, perhaps even a trifle calculated, as though shooting off comets of tone were essential to satisfy audience expectations. Of course, that is the price even the most conscientious of artists (and Miss Nilsson is certainly that) pays when converted into an icon. Icons are icons because of their uniqueness and must deliver their singularity.

The Swedish diva may be counted upon to do so in the 29 March 1975 broadcast of *Götterdämmerung* that rounds off the complete radio cycle. Other aspects of the performance are not so certain. This time it is Thomas who tackles Siegfried, and newcomer Anna Reynolds, after being released from threading rope as the Second Norn, tells Waltraute's narrative. Christine Weidinger is a new swimmer in the *Götterdämmerung* Rhine. Rintzler and Rundgren reappear as gnome and villain, and Dooley and Rankin repeat their brother-and-sister act, all under the guidance of Ehrling.

Die Götterdämmerung
29 March 1975

Brünnhilde
Birgit Nilsson
Gutrune
Nell Rankin
Waltraute
Anna Reynolds
Siegfried
Jess Thomas
Gunther
William Dooley
Alberich
Marius Rintzler
Hagen
Bengt Rundgren
Conductor
Sixten Ehrling

Ehrling's orchestra can, and often does, create a different sound world from Kubelik's more vibrant sonorities. The latter's dynamic stance is more exciting, but Ehrling's mellow and less frenzied posture throughout the afternoon may, in the long run, offer a more satisfying reading of Wagner's fecund score. The Swedish conductor loves to linger over details and they speak clearly under his careful tutelage. But more often, he moves rapidly over major portions of the score and brings the long opera to its rhapsodic close earlier than his Czech colleague. Time as measured by tempos (that is, chronological time) is hardly the issue in determining the pace of a performance. Ehrling's reading, more relaxed and smaller scaled, moves at a more leisurely pace (or so it seems) but time passes more quickly—it is the quality of movement, not minutes spent, that count. His brass are always more considerate than Kubelik's. The Funeral March is a case in point. Both interpretations have sufficient vibrancy; if I were to characterize them, I would say Ehrling's differs from Kubelik's in that the one suggests a private, though appropriately grand, tribute and the other a state funeral. Both are ceremonial in nature, but they play to diverse audiences.

Ehrling's Norns mirror his way. As a group, they are more contained than Kubelik's, as though their centuries of weaving have subdued them. The three singers are impressive in their somber ministrations and splendid in their measured song. Chookasian, new member of the sisterhood, sets the tone with her firm, deep tones and noble phrasing. What a fine artist she is! New also is Anna Reynolds, possessor of a bright mezzo and, like Chookasian, sensitive to her mission. Rankin continues to loft top tones of delectable color in the upper range. With the conductor's aid, the three singers' languorous song suggests a world in which time stands still. Not for long, of course. The Rhinemaidens, carefree at the beginning of the cycle, remain hopeful for the return of the ring at its end. Their joyful ripples in triple time are neatly executed by Baldwin and Godfrey, with the added Weidinger's Woglinde preserving sisterly accord. The blend remains agreeable. One small false entry need not disturb the maidens' evident self-satisfaction. Rankin's Gutrune and Dooley's Gunther fall on the profit side of the ledger, both in vocalism and interpretation, just as they did in the 1974 broadcast. Rintzler (Alberich) is equally impressive as he quizzes his son. His voice is vibrantly alive, even though his final adjuration to Hagen, when he asks his offspring to be true to him, is less varied, and thus, less compelling, than in 1974. Rundgren again plays at Hagen; he is gifted at portraiture but the black heart of the role is colored a middling gray. This time round, I suspect he may be running a little short of voice by the opera's end. He must have made an effect in the house, for the audience gives him favorable response, somewhat less only to that awarded Thomas and Nilsson.

In addition to her Norn duties, Reynolds also has the key responsibility of Waltraute's narrative. The English mezzo had appeared at the Met as Flosshilde in 1968 and returns, after a considerable lapse of time, to sing Fricka and Waltraute in this season's cycle. She is an expert Wagnerian with credits at Glyndebourne, Aix-en-Provence, La Scala, Salzburg, and Rome. Her voice is not overly large and bears more of a soprano cast than the instruments of most interpreters of the disturbed warrior sister. Its texture can be slightly grainy and hold an edge; nevertheless, it is an attractive instrument that does her bidding with admirable results. Subtlety rather than fervor (as opposed to Dunn's 1974 interpretation) is the key to Reynolds' narrative. Authority, evocative diction, and interpretive conviction balance a lack of tonal depth in a few key moments of the lengthy episode. Her sensitive artistry has undoubted merit, but her Met performances will be minuscule in number.

Thomas as Siegfried does not inspire tribute. Honor, perhaps, but even there I find the tenor's *Götterdämmerung* hero less admirable than his *Siegfried* mate. He is in comparable voice, but on this afternoon, his declamation seems dominated by excessive accents and gruff consonants. If only he would sing! He constantly separates words and syllables, abjuring legato, so that the sense of phrase is often negated. Few indeed are the legato phrases that he ventures to offer. His tones, firm enough, seem engaged in an unremitting struggle to escape from his throat. The little exchange with Gunther (where Brilioth contrived a charming moment) passes by without a nod to its possibilities. The lighthearted exchange with the Rhinemaidens is equally bereft of charm. Emphatic declamation is his crutch. Even Siegfried's pivotal narrative when he tells of his youth and gradually regains memory of Brünnhilde receives no poet's touch. Faithful he is in notes and text, and fervent at times. In its lower regions, the voice has a more attractive, baritonal cast and now and then he shows that he can mold a phrase to good effect; 'Der Mutter Erde lass' das ein Labsal sein!' and 'Seit Frauen ich singen hörte,' the one following hard upon the other in the third act, are examples of such workmanlike care. And the voice seems as strong when he begins his final greeting to Brünnhilde as when he left her on her prologue rock.

Not unexpectedly, it will be left to Miss Nilsson to do the vocal honors. And, as ever, she is prepared to deliver. True, in the opening duet, her voice is not heard at its most blandishing. The tone, full and secure even in the mid-low and lower voice, is infected now and then by a grainy texture and (heretical assumption) a touch of whine. Subtlety in interpretation, however, is the bartered gain when age requires warm-up time, as it does here. We value her ease in the part and the confidence of her utterance, even in these initial stages. The timbre warms at 'Ihn geiz' ich als einziges Gut.' At the prologue's end, breadth of tone and manner seem more her concern than Brünnhilde's rapture, the latter a requisite since 'O heilige Götter' is marked *in grosser Ergriffenheit*. The first act proper finds her in full possession of her remarkable powers, the voice solid in the low register and possessing a round core of tone as it moves upward. The long passage beginning 'So wagtest du, Brünnhilde' profits from these attributes, but even more valuable is the variety of phrasing and dynamics that she employs. 'So zur seligsten schuf mich die Strafe' is exquisitely shaped and particularly lovely in tone. I don't hear the hoped-for trill. 'Denn selig aus ihm leuchtet mir Siegfried's Liebe' is anointed by the grandest Nilsson manner. A neat interpretive touch is the string of rolled *r*s she applies to 'Schrecklicher'—the disguised (and hence loathsome) Siegfried is her target. The absent Wotan, too, feels her ire as she unloads a fearsome amount of tone when remembering his punishment of her ('Wotan! ergrimmter, grausamer Gott!'). When the long first act ends, it goes out with a whimper—at least, Nilsson's pathetic final phrase 'Was könntest du wehren, elendes Weib?' marvelously reflects Brünnhilde's helpless state.

In the second act, her tendency to sharp surfaces when she thrusts forth the stunning pair of accusations ('Betrug!' and 'Verrath!') against Siegfried. But now we are in the imperious presence of the indubitable icon, and Nilsson casts an uncommonly bright light, as an icon ought. 'Dem Manne dort bin ich vermäht' on high is struck with almost unbelievable power and accuracy. The outsized theatricality of the moment—undoubtedly shattering in the house—penetrates the airwaves as well. A delicate turn as she exits from what should be a trill is welcome for itself. Of course, her oath on the spear is the real thing. Bewailing her fate, her 'Jammer's are as enormous and weighty as pieces of granite crane-lifted from a quarry. Still, one might question pitch here and the tone can be a little acidulous. But the earlier 'Nothung' passage was superbly vocalized and free from any taint.

Taken all in all, her vocalism as the *Siegfried* Brünnhilde was more consistently true and satisfying. But then, the challenges of the *Götterdämmerung* maid are greater. And one must keep in mind when listening to a voice such as Nilsson's that electronic reproduction does not flatter it. Her instrument loved space, and the more of it the better. The Metropolitan's gigantic auditorium complemented both her voluminous tone and bold expressive manner—its expanse of air allowed the voice to bloom. And Brünnhilde's Immolation is its proper sphere. She invested it with a unique combination of tenderness and heroic brilliance. More than the allowed tipping of pitch (the allotment is permitted because of the icon stature) affects the 'Fliegt heim, ihr Raben!' section. The defect becomes particularly troubling as Brünnhilde prepares to leap into the fire (but that prospect would make anyone nervous), beginning at 'Lockt dich zu ihm die lachende Lohe?'. That reservation aside, her generosity is manifold, and we are, as we have been throughout her career, the fortunate beneficiaries. Initially, the tone at full volume is round and devoid of impurities, the way we like to think of the Nilsson voice. The quiet phrases of the 'Wie Sonne lauter' section are ably drawn and imaginatively inflected. Her light-voiced 'Alles! Alles!' subtly betrays Brünnhilde's newly gained understanding, while the long-drawn 'Ruhe!' holds several color changes. Of course, the Grane portion, even with pitch problems, brings forth all the shafts of grand, brilliant tone that have made her so beloved a Wagnerian. The audience tumult that greets her at her solo bow confirms their immense regard and loyalty. Were they aware that she would absent herself from their company at the close of this season? Infighting with the Internal Revenue Service over taxes caused her to avoid the United States until the 1979–80 season. Thereafter, little Met service would remain to her. For the radio audience, only a 1980 Elektra and, as a parting favor, the *Tristan* love duet with Vickers on the final broadcast of the 1980–81 season would be our portion. After the 1981–82 season (and a 1983 centennial gala turn), Nilsson, one of the Metropolitan's greatest luminaries, would depart. Gustave Flaubert once opined to his friend Ivan Turgenev that "the Alps are out of proportion with our beings. They are too big to be useful to us."[19] Miss Nilsson's soprano was indeed Alpine. But she made good use of it.

During Nilsson's self-dictated absence, Wagner in performance would inevitably lose a good deal of its luster. Gods and goddesses went into hiding. Repertory choices revolved around *Meistersinger* (1975–1977) with *Lohengrin* and *Walküre* added in 1976–77; *Tannhäuser* played in 1977–1979 and *Fliegende Holländer* was performed in 1978–79. Even when our diva returned in 1979–80, she sang no Wagner; only *Lohengrin* and *Parsifal* were on the docket. Once again, voices of mere humans, often agreeable enough, had begun to inhabit the Wagner operas, whether mundane or heroic, at the Met.

Marilyn Horne as Isabella in *L'Italiana in Algeri*. Photography by James Heffernan. Courtesy Metropolitan Opera Archives.

CHAPTER SIXTEEN

Comic Adventures

Over the centuries, the comic muse beckoned so alluringly that not even Wagner could resist her blandishments. His *Meistersinger* will top off a cosmopolitan group of operas that includes a novelty, Rossini's *L'Italiana in Algeri*, Donizetti's familiar *L'Elisir d'Amore*, Verdi's magisterial *Falstaff*, and Offenbach's *Les Contes d'Hoffmann*. The mixed-genre *Don Giovanni* allows us to enter the comic milieu with a somewhat more solemn gait.

Management assembled a starry cast for the premiere of *Don Giovanni* on 25 March 1974, a benefit for the Metropolitan Opera Guild production fund, and the radio audience is favored with the same notable assemblage in the broadcast of 13 April. Levine, whose prominence in company plans increases from season to season, gains this plum assignment, guiding Price and Zylis-Gara in broadcast repeats of Anna and Elvira. The remainder of the cast consists of portrayals new to the radio audience: Stratas (Zerlina), Burrows (Ottavio), Berry (Leporello), Morris (Commandant), and Michalski (Masetto). All fall within the mesmerizing orbit of the new Don Giovanni, Sherrill Milnes.

The opera holds its share of shadows. Levine signals his spacious conception in the forceful opening chords of the overture. They seem rather too portentous upon first hearing, but when their chordal mates introduce the Commandant's presence in the churchyard scene, the maestro's interpretive construct becomes clear. Already, the orchestra has taken on some of the Levine characteristics that we will come to know so well. If primary accents seem overly insistent in the overture and Leporello's pacing *arietta* at the curtain rise, they, and a corresponding sense of correctness, are soon smoothed away. Indeed, the balance between control and freedom is deftly achieved, the one often giving way to the other in unexpected ways. One becomes increasingly taken, as the opera progresses, with the conductor's sense of continuity, that is, chordal or melodic traction, often sustained as it is by a more vigorous legato than normally heard in Mozart. The modus operandi provides a comfortable cushion for the singers' song. In contrast, the many orchestral commentaries between the singers' phrases are enhanced with purposeful nuances, also more individual than we may anticipate. One moment in Anna's recitative to the vengeance aria particularly intrigued me: as she tells of twisting and writhing to escape Giovanni's grasp ('torcermi e piegarmi'), Levine's exaggerated syncopated chords replicate her struggle to marvelous effect. In short,

Don Giovanni
13 April 1974

Donna Anna
Leontyne Price
Donna Elvira
Teresa Zylis-Gara
Zerlina
Teresa Stratas
Don Ottavio
Stuart Burrows
Don Giovanni
Sherrill Milnes
Leporello
Walter Berry
Masetto
Raymond Michalski
Commandant
James Morris
Conductor
James Levine

the gifted American offers the kind of imaginative, yet purposefully controlled, interpretation that, at his best, he would repeatedly provide.

Melding so many vivid artist personalities, all intent on displaying their wares, into a cohesive whole is Levine's major accomplishment. One can find in their portrayals reflections of his comprehensive understanding of the vocal art. Surprising expressive touches abound in their work, making their characterizations lively and fruitful. Sometimes the conductor allows them (or perhaps has instigated) astonishing freedom. Burrows 'Dalla sua pace' is a case in point. Levine's pace is entirely unhurried, and the Welsh tenor makes good use of the sedate progress. When he approaches the reprise of the opening section, he molds 'e non ho bene, s'ella non l'ha' in the most leisurely manner, as though time (and Levine) had no schedule to keep. No lockstep hampers the singer's expressive intent. The orchestra participates in the emotional flux as well—even the two-note instrumental interjections that follow 'morte mi dà' in the opening section are given a life of their own. Levine's perspective on the opera is a roomy one and his musical gestures are sufficiently expansive to comfortably furnish it.

In an earlier book, I hailed Miss Price's 1963 broadcast Donna Anna as one of the memorable portrayals of broadcast history. More than a decade later, the salutation needs no revision. Her remarkable throat seems to do her bidding at will. Ease in the upper voice is entirely unfettered and the lower octave retains its focus, the hollow rasp that affects late-career performances nowhere apparent. Her vengeance scene is a marvel of vocal plenitude and dramatic force. She rages well—and without harm to her instrument. In her accompanied recitative, one of Mozart's most vivid creations, she is alert to every nuance. I like particularly how she begins her account of Giovanni's assault. As though terror is still alive within her and she can hardly speak of its horror, Price tells the tale in soft, yet vivid, tones, achieving a touching intimacy, drawing us in to her struggle before her anguish bursts forth in violent phrases. Thrilling expanses of phrase and tone in the aria proper maintain the tension and garner her the greatest ovation of the afternoon. Levine has a penchant for broadening (beyond a simple ritard) the final measures of a set piece and makes a lengthy slowdown here—too much, to my mind—but his prima donna handles it with ease. The tonal beauty of Price and Zylis-Gara (aided by Burrows' gentlemanly support) turns the mask trio into a feast of vocalism. Price's descending scales are not as well articulated as those on the way up, but still credible. Her fluent line and the Polish soprano's instrumentally conceived movement provide perhaps more contrast than is stylistically ideal, but they both excel at what they do. 'Non mi dir' benefits from the Mississippi diva's supple soprano and control of line, although, in contrast to her 1963 effort, she now slows down not just the staccatos, but the entire lengthy fioritura section. (Elsewhere in the opera, she manipulates Mozart's decorative coloratura in tempo and with clarity.) Some sopranos have managed to convey more of Anna's resignation and sorrow in this test piece; Price cannot manage the full complement, but her vocalism contains within itself an adequate message. Not only Anna's grand moments profit from her musicianly interest: her vocal line in the sextet is drawn with utmost care in silken tones, full, well colored, yet discreetly blended with her colleagues' efforts.

Zylis-Gara, too, is in exemplary vocal form and has added some interesting interpretive features to her portrayal. Her tone seems richer than ever on this afternoon, its complex wind hue haunting in itself and her expert management of it throughout the range entirely commendable. She plays the role straight rather than as a parody of a *seria* heroine. Thus, her two first-act arias, while admirable, lack that touch of peculiarity that makes Elvira an intriguing stage creature. Nevertheless, her recitatives are splendidly varied and her portions of the many ensembles vocal tonics. She traces the opening of the quartet ('Non ti fidar'), for instance, with exquisite delicacy, and few sopranos can execute the two-note slurs of 'che mi dice di quel traditore cento cose' with the confident clarity and expressive design of this lovely artist. The intricate roulades of 'Mi tradì' are easy work for her (the longest patch of fioritura is taken in one breath), and if the piece comes off more as an instrumental concerto than a moment of self-discovery, Mozart's convoluted workings are simultaneously cause, blame, and bouquet.

Zerlina's function in the drama is more circumscribed, but her duet with Giovanni and two arias provide any budding lyric soprano with plentiful opportunities to make her mark. Stratas does so with both enormous charm and evocative vocalism. Her tone is innately so delectable that she has no need to resort to soubrette coyness to put over the twin pieces. She avoids it with the crafty sensibility that would guide her throughout her long career. (Even the revered Sayão, a Zerlina with impeccable credentials, evidently felt the need to employ it, quite knowingly, in 'Vedrai, carino' and its introductory recitative.) The coiling phrases of 'Batti, batti' flow forth with unfailing grace in Stratas' charming rendition; she doesn't pick at the notes but sends them along in a stream of purled tone. The little roulades are thrown off in full voice with no loss of tonal bloom. She seems a bit less comfortable in the 'Pace, pace' conclusion of the aria; Levine prefers not to hurry it and she perhaps would be more at ease with a livelier gait. A more rapid vibrato gives 'Vedrai, carino' a touch of eroticism, the voice holding overtones (note the warmth in her mid-low voice at 'Sentito battere') that convert the aria into something more inviting than a mere comic soothing of Masetto's aches and pains.

The sequence of Uppman's ten broadcast wedding grooms, novel in their blitheness and high-spirited anger, now gives way to Michalski's more conventional Masetto. The bass is happy with Mozart's low tessitura, but has to hurry to keep up with Levine's rapid beat in the introductory duet. His portrayal of the young clod is in line with our and Da Ponte's expectations. Morris, at this point in his career a stripling bass, can offer only a yeoman of the guard where an authoritative Commendatore is wanted. His self-effacing voicing of the father's death throes in the first-act trio robs one of Mozart's most affecting moments of its pathos. In the churchyard, the invitation to his murderer is undermanned, but he summons more tonal metal for the supper confrontation. Berry does not try to visit upon Leporello the character reversal that he succeeded in so agreeably imposing upon Baron Ochs—Giovanni's servant cannot be upgraded either in class or vocal character. His instrument, too, is not overweighted with basso profundity, but he plays in an appropriately plebeian, if hardly earthy, style. 'Madamina' is a wonder of artful vocalism and character portrayal. His catalog recitation trips along with the Berry light touch discriminately applied to Mozart's patter, while his vocal ease allows the andante con moto movement to fall more agreeably on the ear than the effortful execution of most recent Leporellos. If, in the process, Mozart is better served than Da Ponte, that can't be all bad. The radio audience, at least, profits from Berry's preference. His invitation to the masked intruders is politeness itself, and he makes no stab at mimicking Milnes' voice when the servant dons the master's cloak. Most interpreters relish the opportunity to parrot their colleagues' vocal idiosyncrasies. When it comes to addressing the statue, however, Berry knows where his responsibility lies. The servant's fear is real and strongly conveyed by the singer.

Burrows had a reputation as one of the great Ottavios. He more than lives up to advance notice. Initially, when supporting his beloved's grief and terror, his tone is rather dull in color, but when it comes his turn to sing, the voice takes on a heady mix, tenor capital is spent freely, text articulation and phrasing are pointed and varied. As noted above, 'Dalla sua pace' becomes an expression of self, not merely a tenorial exercise. His reading of 'Il mio tesoro' is simply splendid. Connoisseurs of fine singing will immediately want to know how he delivers the longest fioritura sequence. How many breaths does he need? How clean is the note articulation? One only is the inhale number (and he has plenty of breath to spare, even sounding the final *r* of 'tornar' at the roulade's end), and each note is sung with confidence and admirable clarity. He is musically and dramatically astute, everywhere seeking variety of mood and movement. Many a manly phrase takes the curse off Ottavio's effeteness. His singing is equally accomplished in the vaudeville. When, in their duet portion, he and Price combine their voices in coloratura rapport, their compact coupling suggests the eventual union of Ottavio and Anna might actually come to pass.

Milnes' seducer may not be all he should or can be, but the baritone is a possible contender for Siepi's relinquished Giovanni crown. Several episodes of his portrayal are of superior quality. The vocal suavity and cultivated expression that he lavishes on 'Là ci darem la mano' result in one of the more musicianly interpretations of that deceptively simple duet in broadcast history. (Pinza's mellow cello vocalism is, of course, sui generis.) In the duet, Milnes' singing is light-years removed from his familiar brawny Verdi baritone posture. His legato liquidity ensures that Giovanni's suit will be irresistible—and Stratas' enticing response makes his seductive intent entirely reasonable. The serenade is equally superb, its supple phrases elegantly vocalized, the baritone's airy tones discreetly maintained within the bounds of the slight frame that the composer fashioned. I deem the champagne aria a disappointment. Milnes surely has the goods to fire off the bauble with the requisite panache. But the result on this afternoon is more dutiful than effervescent, and details like the little trill and the flourish before the reprise are cloudy at best. Elsewhere, he sometimes resorts to a narrow, nasty tone to convey the nobleman's mean-spiritedness—occasionally it seems employed to facilitate delivery of fleet passages of notes and text. But overall, the voice's baritonal resonance, predominately rich, yet heady, is a welcome relief from the surfeit of basso depths that of late has weighed down the lighthearted intriguer. Musically and dramatically pertinent details invariably enliven his recitatives and mark his ensemble work. This seducer seems preoccupied by the matter at hand rather than concerned about any of those larger philosophical issues that have troubled commentators for decades. In the final scene, he is properly dismissive of Elvira's concern and defiant to the end. Although some have decried it, Milnes' Giovanni, as broadcast, adds a welcome feather to his more trenchant repertory cap.

Few companies in the world could put on a *Don Giovanni* of comparable vocal excellence. A slighter challenge, but one that holds its own vicissitudes, is

L'Italiana in Algeri
8 December 1973

Isabella
Marilyn Horne
Elvira
Christine Weidinger
Lindoro
Luigi Alva
Taddeo
Theodor Uppman
Mustafà
Fernando Corena
Conductor
Gabor Ötvös

Rossini's *L'Italiana in Algeri*, newly mounted by the Metropolitan in fall 1973. In essence, the work was a complete novelty for the Metropolitan public, its sunny tomfoolery previously having been enjoyed on only four occasions in the 1919–20 season. At that time, Gabriella Besanzoni played Isabella with Charles Hackett as Lindoro and Giuseppe De Luca (Taddeo), Adamo Didur (Mustafà), and Marie Sundelius (Elvira) in the cast. Gennaro Papi conducted. Obviously, the presence of Marilyn Horne, our very own Rossini guru, motivated the new production; the impulse was entirely welcome, both for the composer's intoxicating manner and the singer's bountiful gifts. The broadcast of 8 December 1973 offers Alva (Lindoro), Uppman (Taddeo), Corena (Mustafà), and Weidinger (Elvira) in support of Horne's Isabella. Gabor Ötvös leads pit and stage charges.

"Leads" turns out to be a misnomer, for rather than sending his stage cohorts rollicking along the foible-strewn path that Rossini laid out, Ötvös lays heavy hands on them, weighting them down in their antic pursuits. Like the handler of a prize racehorse, a conductor of opera buffa must hold the reins lightly for most of the course, controlling the pace, yes, but taking care not to throttle his charges' spirits, while encouraging an exhilarating release as the finish line nears. Sometimes Ötvös does just the reverse. After plodding along with a Clydesdale tread, he puts the brakes on when an aria or ensemble reaches its climax. Conversely, he may set a rapid pace but adhere rigidly to it—no sparkling wit infiltrates its steady progress. To his credit, he guides a mishap-free performance; indeed it has a well-studied, thoroughly rehearsed feel (it ought to, since the broadcast is the seventh performance of a long run). Perhaps the Hungarian conductor's temperament is simply not sympathetic to the lighthearted ways of opera buffa. Chapin, having served the previous year in an acting capacity, by the time of this first broadcast of the 1973–74 season was enthroned as general manager of the company. He wrote in his memoirs, where numerous apologias are recorded, that he and others were opposed to naming Ötvös to shepherd the new mounting of *Italiana*, but Kubelik insisted that he was the man for the job.[1] *Turandot* was his other assignment in this, his second and last season; therein may lie the answer to his puzzling reading. The massive Puccini spectacle and blithe Rossini comedy are polar opposites and the stylistic mileage between the poles was too great for Ötvös to travel.

Corena, heard late in his career, is in good vocal form. The voice retains its characteristic bluff resonance—it still can boom effectively. Pitches are reasonably centered, and, though his coloratura has long been makeshift, on this afternoon his dodges are astutely designed to minimize both his and our discomfort. (He and Alva must rely excessively upon aspirants to clear the fioritura hurdles that Rossini so generously placed in their paths.) 'Già d'insolito ardore' is Corena's most effective attempt at song. Elsewhere, he proves that his Mustafà merits induction into the Pappataci order; since silence is one of the requisites for membership, that may be a left-handed compliment. In the aggregate, his impersonation is rather contained, hardly as dominant a force in the performance as expected from so experienced a buffo practitioner. Uppman as a buffo baritone is a novelty. True, he has been a worthy Guglielmo and a memorable Papageno, but the former is only a near-relative (and more than twice removed at that) of the buffo model, while the Mozart birdcatcher, a role that suits the California-born singer's stage personality, has a much lighter touch than Rossini allowed Taddeo. Playing the fall guy, which Isabella's machinations make of her erstwhile suitor, is hardly the posture that will allow Uppman to capitalize on his more endearing vocal and dramatic qualities. Still, he provides a fair representation of the buffo breed. Initially, the voice lacks the full measure of its remembered baritonal buzz, but soon the familiar resonance returns to enliven the disappointed lover's song. He blusters convincingly whenever called upon to rant and, characteristically, manages to inject a few moments of sympathetic introspection into the tangle of Taddeo's perpetual writhing. Rossini contrived a tiny center-stage turn for Haly, Mustafà's captain of the guard, and Boucher makes it count. Weidinger's consort of the Bey is a disappointment. Her top notes in the ensembles (a prime reason for Elvira's presence in the vocal mix) are edgy, and her inability to negotiate the introductory flourishes of the onomatopoeic first-act finale with adequate tone and clarity robs the ensemble of a zany liftoff.

Alva at one time probably delivered Lindoro's fleet music with as much security as any tenorino could provide in his era. The Peruvian tenor, though now at the crepuscular stage, remains an able representative of the Rossini light-voiced romantic lead. That said, his entrance aria ('Languir per una bella') immediately betrays his several liabilities: his top notes whiten, aspirants accumulate, and the timbre is afflicted with excessive nasality. There are moments even later in the opera when his instrument has warmed to its task, when the sounds he produces can be as annoying as the signals sent by a circling wasp. (Several French horn bobbles in the lovely introduction to the aria make it even more difficult for the singer to redress the charm deficit.) In spite of these reservations, it must be noted that he is comfortable with the bel canto style and entirely assured in tackling the role's vocal difficulties. Add to that a lively dramatic presence and his contribution to the afternoon's success is not negligible. Having chosen to sing Rossini's original aria rather than the more imposing one that he fashioned for the Milan production, Alva launches 'Oh come il cor di giubilo' with considerable panache and a vocal nonchalance that allows us fleetingly to savor another century's art. Even here, his timbre is rather too insistently open. Still, the top voice takes on more color as he begins the wonderful trio, and his rhythmic éclat and neat coloratura contrast effectively with Uppman's and Corena's solid support. The three singers rock on with contagious vitality.

Miss Horne is in glorious vocal form—she invariably was, and not only in her early years. My wife and I were in the house for the performance (30 November) just preceding this broadcast. I can still see the singer making her entrance, nattily outfitted in what appeared to be a nineteenth-century couturier's idea of a businesswoman's attire: fashionable suit and perky hat. The diva seemed to be everyone's conception of a feminist in the making, which Isabella pretty much proves to be. What a take-charge manner Horne radiated from beginning to end of the performance, just as she does on this broadcast afternoon. She is not a natural comedienne. That must be said, though it may come as a surprise to many who know and love her jovial, unaffected offstage persona. Thus some of Rossini's wit goes by the board, a sacrifice we can afford to make in view of the rewards of her vocalism and her commitment to the highest standards of performance. Right off, 'Cruda sorte!' receives the benefit of her rich embrace of the lower depths, the latter always a favored playground for the Horne voice. She immediately proceeds to establish her credentials in fioriture with a glorious run up and down the length of her range. How the top voice opens out in generous splendor! Her credentials are never in doubt for the rest of the afternoon. And the soft caress of tone that she applies to the aria's middle section (the atmospheric change prompted by thoughts of her beloved Lindoro) indicates that her attention will not be confined to fireworks on this afternoon. The ultimate in velvet-swathed tone, the kind that might suggest a swooning and mooning liquidity, is not hers to offer. (For that matter, any "-ooning" would probably not be in this all-American girl's line.) The substitute (that is, her considerate phrasing and carefully modulated dynamics) does very nicely indeed. 'O che muso' is hardly the comic send-up it can be, but after all, Miss Horne is there to sing and to fire off shots of coloratura with a marksmanship that William Tell might well envy. 'Per lui che adoro' (and here the Met prefers the flute obbligato of the 1814 Milan revival, rather than the original cello version) offers a change of pace; the love song, an essay in subterfuge, profits from the singer's thorough knowledge of the vocal art, a command evident in her management of resonance and registers. A mid-voice trill of subtle intimacy enhances both the singer's reputation and the aria's mood. Still, a metallic tint on some tones occasionally blights Isabella's ardor. It touches a few moments of 'Pensa alla patria' as well. As might be expected, that grand *scena* is the high point of her performance. In the spacious recitative and rondo Isabella rallies the Italian servants to her cause in typical *opera seria* fashion—the lovers' escape is her intent. Now Horne is in her element. After all, she would prove adept at playing generals—the voice is well supplied with brass; entire armies, let alone mild-mannered servants, could hardly fail to respond to her broadly declaimed injunctions and resolute thrusts of coloratura. Several double-octave jumps, beloved by her fans, have their familiar accuracy. Greatly to her credit, she does not overdo the athletic feat, nor does she allow her chest voice its full boom, preferring to allow, in its place, her top voice its full bloom. Recall that Oscar Wilde's young suitor accused his beloved of being "quite perfect" (a charge we might level at Miss Horne), but the *Importance of Being Earnest* heroine demurred, fearing "that would leave no room for development." Our prima donna enjoys just that danger.

Even in its premiere season, *L'Italiana in Algeri* earned a measure of success, due in large part to Horne's assured portrayal of the Italian girl. A happy ending awaited the opera during the next decade or so as it passed, always with the indispensable Horne, through the hands of a series of conductors like Henry Lewis, Nicola Rescigno, and, in 1985, Levine himself. In each revival, their guidance upgraded performance quality and increased regard for Rossini's comic craft. Another bel canto landmark, *L'Elisir d'Amore*, required no such careful nurturing for repertory inclusion. Its success reached back into the Caruso era; it had thrived under Tagliavini's dulcet tones in the mid-fifties, and became a repertory staple with Pavarotti's prince of clowns later in the century. Joining him in the 6 April 1974 broadcast are Blegen (Adina), Reardon (Belcore), and Flagello (Dulcamara). An old and esteemed friend from an earlier Metropolitan era, Max Rudolf, is at the helm.

Rudolf's return is doubly welcome, not only for old time's sake, but for his masterly demonstration of how to give an opera buffa its due. At first, in the little theme and variations prelude, the interplay of solo instruments seems a bit rickety and their tone scratchy, but by the time the action begins, all is trim, as pit and stage fizz along together. Even in the opening chorus, the buffa spirit asserts itself. As the soloists take their various turns, most often pattering along, they

L'Elisir d'Amore
6 April 1974
Adina
Judith Blegen
Nemorino
Luciano Pavarotti
Belcore
John Reardon
Dulcamara
Ezio Flagello
Conductor
Max Rudolf

undoubtedly relish the soothing cushion of orchestral support under them. The accompaniment figures flow by in supple order, now ebbing, now gently pressing on. Rudolf, with deft exactitude, highlights the exquisite melodic orchestral flourishes, giving them a blithe profile, but he never impedes the rhythmic flow of the larger musical unit. The conductor's sense of pacing is everywhere acute. How fruitfully he allows the *concertato* climaxes of the first-act finale to expand at their peaks—one senses the rush of feeling Donizetti injected into this grand moment; thereafter, the conductor subtly quickens the pace, a rhythmic rustle in the accompaniment sending on the finale to a curtain escape. Rudolf's performance again calls to mind my mythical racehorse. But this time the beast is controlled by expert pacing and given his head when jockey Rudolf sights the finish line. With our maestro, the play of energy is intoxicating, but the volume never descends into mere noise. Every set piece benefits from his loving care, whether he chooses to momentarily expose unexpected spasms of feeling or, more prominently, to invigorate the performance through rhythmic flexibility.

Not only the orchestra responds to Rudolf's experienced hand. Longtime chorus master Adler's departure goes unlamented, for David Stivender's choral provender proves to be of superior quality. Di Franco's Giannetta is piquant and pleasant as she and the peasant girls chat. Reardon's homegrown instrument provides relief from the more stentorian Italian (or Italianate) voices that, while enhancing the macho pose of Belcore, have sometimes made rather a hash of his music. His voice is light at the bottom and the timbre can be excessively dry. But, equally often, it can have a breezy bloom in the upper range that makes Belcore's bluster easy to take. Most welcome is his clarity in fioriture, the bane of most interpreters of the role. Even he cannot cleanly articulate the quick coils of coloratura at the end of 'Venti scudi,' but everywhere else his flourishes are neatly done. A fine musician, he senses the rhetorical import of each phrase he sings. After Nemorino's outburst ('Adina, credemi'), Belcore's scorn for the deflated lover is forcefully expressed, and in the duet with Nemorino, Reardon's voice burgeons, the tone gaining in quality and density.

Flagello, equipped with a lover's tonal balm but Falstaff's figure, is always a bit of an anomaly in his buffo roles. He never allows his character's comic status to dominate his vocalism ('Io son ricco' is delivered straight); usually (as in this case) he fills out the character in more general ways. Most often, they are sufficient to make clear his function in the action. I find it a pleasure to hear the music presented in so attractive a fashion, the tone warm, the pitches well centered, the notes sounding where they ought to be and all done without unduly depressing the comic spirit of the interpretation. I imagine the voice is just a little less luxuriant than it was in earlier days. And I would savor a grander swing for the big tune at the end of 'Udite, o rustici!,' but elsewhere in his entrance aria the patter is fleet and distinct. Where needed, his manner is commanding. I would buy Flagello's elixir. He and Pavarotti are adept in the 'obbligato' passages of their duet and, in his session with the troubled Adina ('Oh quanto amore!'), the sham doctor acquires medical veracity. Dulcamara may be a quack, but the warmth and ampleness of this doctor's instrument surely have therapeutic value.

Blegen had come to the house as a sprightly Papagena in 1970, and her roles in the next year or so had remained of the ingénue variety. Marzelline, Ännchen, Sophie (*Werther*), Amore, and the Forest Bird had been her lot, the novice gradually acquiring status with an occasional Zerlina and Nannetta. By 1972, the fey Mélisande, as we have seen, was deemed suited to her vocal character and diminutive person. Strauss' Sophie, added in 1973, turned out to be an ideal mating of artist and role. Adina, acquired only a few weeks (25 February) before the broadcast—though she had sung it in San Francisco earlier—appeared to be the next logical step in her elevation to prominence within the company. (Full status would be achieved when she was assigned Juliette in the fall of the current year.) Adina, while it may be classified as lying in soubrette territory, is nevertheless deceptive in its requirements. This young landowner is hardly an ingénue, though she relishes and exploits the qualities associated with a young flirt. But beyond that, her music demands extensive coloratura technique and, above all, exquisite control of the bel canto line. For an audience's maximum enjoyment, as well as for the projection of character, the latter attribute (that is, bel canto phrasing) profits from a timbre that encompasses both beguiling tone and mettlesome point. Of these several qualities, Blegen has to her credit quite sufficient coloratura technique (she is ever accurate and clear in this regard), and her tone has adequate point to it—though, since it lacks body, it is perhaps less than mettlesome. Still, she knows how to (and, more to the point, is willing to) go after things when challenged. A demerit is the voice's lack of a genuinely alluring timbre, a soothing, captivating tone that can linger on and luxuriate over the spiraling phrases of 'Chiedi all'aura lusinghiera,' for instance; that sympathetic timbre should give the lie to Adina's harsh treatment of Nemorino and let us know that she will have him by curtain time. What will serve Sophie more than well—as Blegen's finely etched tone deliciously did—will not suffice for the bel canto heroines. Blegen's tone, in a commendable search for projection and body, is placed far forward, so much so that its narrow core can sometimes hold the suggestion of complaint. Still, she is such a knowledgeable technician that she often manages to coax forth decidedly attractive tones and satisfying music making. Her top voice is secure and the most flavorfully colored part of her instrument—that asset is a boon for any soprano. Moreover, she is a splendid musician, and knows how to create a character (she works a neat mood change when she sympathetically tells Nemorino that, while he is good, it's simply no go for the two of them). Two moments seem misjudged on her part. 'Io son ricco' undergoes a role reversal, with Blegen offering pinched tones and a mincing manner while her Dulcamara sings forthrightly. Who has the corner on the comedy market in this opera? Then, too, the opening of the more serious duet with the doctor is disappointing: 'Oh quanto amore!' can cause us to quiver with delight when given full value. Blegen makes little of it. Still, she rises to the final moments of the opera, sending off Adina's coloratura flourishes with a virtuoso's command. I like her spunk. (It came to her aid in the fast section of the Dulcamara duet as well.) And the audience admires it, too. At the first-act curtain, Cross had described Blegen as a "sweet little Adina." She probably would have hated that description, but he was not far off the mark. Of course, three decades earlier, we both had heard Sayão in the part and that is a hard standard to be up against. Management thought well of Blegen's portrayal. Adina would be one of the soprano's most frequent roles with the company, her numerous appearances including three broadcasts and a television showing in 1981.

In her *Opera News* remarks about the opera, Blegen notes that she will be singing it this season with both Carreras and Pavarotti. The riches of some decades make one long to pull a reverse Jules Verne and journey backward in time. Not surprisingly, it would be the Italian rather than the Spaniard who would become the favored interpreter of this prize tenor role during the next decades. On this afternoon, the first of his many broadcasts of the role, the not-yet-quite-a-superstar tenor's performance is a complete joy from start to finish. The voice is vibrantly colored and secure in every way. Most treasurable in his portrayal is the degree of his involvement, both in terms of musical expression and character delineation. Writing as I am after the millennium, when the tenor's reputation is being impugned by his own frequently tired, blasé impersonations, I value these early portrayals not only for their quality, but for their rehabilitative impact. They leave no doubt that here was a tenor.

Right off, 'Quanto è bella' signals the high standard of his interpretation. Every phrase is marked not only by the expected vocal allure, but with a multitude of nuances, rhetorically fitting both as expression and as character clues. His legato flows with an ease that even his vibrant diction does not curtail. When he takes up Nemorino's portion of the 'Chiedi' duet, he favors it with loving phrasing; his way is naturally quite different from the Schipa type, with its honeyed toffee pull, but it is equally—and, for many, I don't doubt, more—impressive for its richness of timbre and artful shaping of phrase. And he handles the decorative elements expeditiously. (Later, though, in the 'Esulti pur la barbara' duet, his descending scales are mere stabs.) When first approaching Dulcamara about his troubles, Pavarotti strikes a sympathetic pose that is quite touching. Later in that encounter, I find his attempts at mezza voce less than the real thing—the very soft tone sometimes disintegrates into a thin wisp of falsetto. His recitatives are ever alive with rhythmic impulse and pungent in meaning. He takes hold of the finale ('Adina, credemi') just as any Nemorino ought, voice and person fairly bursting with pain and love—a magnificent outpouring of heartfelt song. Flagello deftly covers an early entry by the tenor in their colloquy at the beginning of act two. At the close of 'Venti scudi', his top C is a little grainy, but solid enough. He delivers the fast flourishes of 'Dell'elisir mirabile' with commendable élan. 'Una furtiva lagrima' is a triumph from start to finish. The brief head tone on the introductory 'una'—that coo not always on a tenor's agenda these days—is welcome; thereafter he applies a gentle caress to the first phrases before expertly expanding the climactic tone in the time-honored manner. At the cadence of the first stanza, he again employs the imperfect tonal wisp earlier described. The second stanza is remarkable for the heart-on-sleeve emotion that Pavarotti injects into the bel canto line. It makes for a strong contrast, but I find it a bit overdone—though preferable to tenorial boredom, certainly. The classic proportions of this exquisitely formed aria are slightly disturbed by his urgency. At the close, 'morire' (the 're' syllable is sung) is gloriously full, with the *e* vowel held much longer than the brief *i*; traditional head tone graces the repeat. The cadenza is cleanly articulated, each note heard, and resolutely shaped. To his credit, he attempts a *messa di voce* at the cadence, offering a slight crescendo and a longer, attractive diminuendo before landing on a soft tonic note—there an active vibrato all but takes over. The tenor's reading of the testing aria is one of the finest of the many Pavarotti performances to be heard over the decades. One feels rather like the nineteenth-century critic who, upon hearing a tenor excel as Lionel in *Martha*, thought that any listener would "wish that his entire being were one enormous ear."[2] On this afternoon,

Pavarotti's Nemorino is notable for its remarkably generous outpouring of song and heart in a portrayal worthy of a superstar.

Superstars take cover when *Falstaff* is on the docket. The ensemble opera *par excellence*, it requires a team spirit that most often brooks little grandstanding from its cast members. For the broadcast of 5 April 1975, management assembled a virtually new crew of Windsorites, including Lear (Alice), Benita Valente (Nannetta), Douglas Ahlstedt (Fenton), MacNeil (Falstaff), and Stewart (Ford). Barbieri's Quickly and Grillo's Meg Page had been heard in earlier broadcasts. Levine is on the podium. He may be just the man for this quicksilver opera. He has the conducting technique to harness its difficulties and the drive to send it spinning homeward toward the philosophical fugue.

The maestro, musically mature beyond his years and opera wise almost beyond belief, does drive the opera on at a few critical moments so that we feel that extra spurt of adrenalin to which we are entitled when a comic opera is on the boards. But he treats the opera's innards with utmost care, one might even say a gentle hand, so that each musical gesture in the orchestra complements either textual thrust or the stage action. Levine grants the opera more of a human face than most of his fellow pit men allow. Grace and elegance achieve equal status with the score's justly celebrated wit and spirited fleetness—not that he slights those essentials. He delights in Verdi's orchestral virtuosity but holds the tricky large-scale vocal ensembles in a just, though necessarily taut, equilibrium. In them, he generally prefers clarity and transparency over speed, and the musical gain from the steady gait miraculously restores the velocity quotient in the meters of our minds. The *fortissimo* chord outbursts that punctuate the opening scene clue us immediately to Levine's judicious scale for the opera—no blatant blasts for shock value are tolerated. Nor is he bound by a rigid time clock—his second hand is an accommodating one. Singers have time to make their musical points—they may be caressingly lyrical or outrageously comic, as the need arises—and Levine often offers them an interpretive assist in his lead-ins. The chords that introduce 'Va, vecchio John,' for instance, are replete with the knight's proud strut, and if they are perhaps excessively weighty in time and tone, he has a Falstaff whose vocal strut is comparably assured. Levine insistently lays a profound musical and dramatic sensibility upon the opera's treasures but his moves usually have the requisite momentum to keep the farce alive and well. Only in the final scene, where Falstaff is taunted by one and all, does his way seem too tame for the situation. By that time, we are eager to be pushed along to the denouement, and a touch of ferocity would help send us on our merry way. The fugue is fast, fleet, and clean. His singers know (or he has taught them) always to sing the second half of the theme as lightly as possible so that a sunny light pierces the grand ensemble's mad flight. A few short descending lyric phrases are voiced with obliging legato, offering the ear yet another anchor in the fugue's folly.

In the opening scene, Franke seems intent on setting the volume control beyond the red zone. His phrases are fearfully strident. But then, Verdi has marked Cajus' lines repeatedly with *gridando*, *sempre in furia*, and *scoppiando*, so the experienced tenor is only following the composer's lead. He does seem to take the markings excessively to heart. Best's dull-toned Pistola is a good foil for the outraged doctor, and Velis' pinpoint Bardolfo is appropriately assertive and clean-toned to comic effect. For once, Meg Page becomes a positive force in the opera—so of-

Falstaff
5 April 1975
Alice
Evelyn Lear
Nannetta
Benita Valente
Dame Quickly
Fedora Barbieri
Fenton
Douglas Ahlstedt
Falstaff
Cornell MacNeil
Ford
Thomas Stewart
Conductor
James Levine

ten, we hardly know she is there. Grillo's voice has just the right fruity acidity to make Meg's phrases count. Her contribution adds up to more than the sum of her lines. From the chaste tones of Ahlstedt and Valente, Fenton and Nannetta would seem to be the youngest, most virginal players yet heard on the broadcasts in these roles. They are definitely creatures of the English forests rather than Verdi's southern clime. Their lovers' passion, a teenage thing, may be thermostatically controlled, but their vocalism is charming and assured. Ahlstedt's tone, while basically attractive, cannot entirely escape the light tenor's white timbral blight, but he is able to introduce a touch of manly firmness into its cool surface as needed. Its pointed nib proves valuable in the ensembles, where Fenton's legato line often helps to focus the quality of movement; unlike many Fentons, whose tones get lost in these frenetic moments, Ahlstedt's lover can be heard. His characterization is adept, both in subtle musical touches and dramatic perception; the role is brief and yet the American singer fills in Fenton's character for us. 'Dal labbro il canto' begins a bit sheepishly, gathers force, and finishes in fine form. 'Bocca baciata non perde ventura' deserves more of mouthwatering desire and velvet tonal enticement than he can muster, but the climactic phrase ('e innamorando l'aer antelucano') is neatly spun on a single breath and lovingly shaped with a crescendo and diminuendo—a fine demonstration of the singer's musicality and technical resourcefulness. Miss Valente's instrument has more to recommend it. It must be one of the sweetest sopranos to ever sound over the airwaves. The mid-voice, slightly grainy—attractively so—in texture, is a sugar-sprinkled confection; when the singer escapes from the staff, the tone takes on ethereal purity. Nannetta's suspended top notes float with unworldly innocence and immaculate poise. The two lovers make more of an effect with their first-act duet than in the second-act imbroglio. Valente's exquisite 'Sul fil d'un soffio etesio' delights with its appealing vocal texture and musical restraint, both dictated by the text: her song floats on the slightest thread of breath. Levine sets up the magical scene with a loving exploitation of the composer's orchestral nature-painting. The varied figures glisten and coil deliciously. And Valente responds in vocal kind. Her technical resources are such that the line of many phrases need not be broken by catch breaths, and she is able both to observe the portamento at 'cifre i fior' and execute a 'morendo' on the final note. Some may find her tone too childlike. The timbre of Raskin (a superb broadcast Nannetta) was very like in sweetness, but its tonal mix included a pinch of erotic suggestiveness. Still, Miss Valente's instrument has its own charms, and they are considerable.

MacNeil, like any long-surviving Verdi baritone, undoubtedly deserved his shot at Falstaff, and, luckily, the Met gave him the opportunity. But Stewart, admirable Wagnerian that he is, would not seem to possess the thrusting, brawny tone that we expect to hear in the distraught Ford's aria. He is so intelligent an artist and committed an interpreter that we may be sure he will provide deft touches of characterization and vocalism. His Ford is not quite the bumbling, frustrated dupe that many have made of Alice's confused mate. He plots convincingly, meets Falstaff on his home ground with plentiful assurance, and lets us know that he is no man to be trifled with, let alone a husband to be cuckolded. Musically, he is always honorable. True, his 'madrigale' flourish is more an effort than a pleasure—*leggerissimo* is beyond his ken. He injects a slight snarl into his timbre to better collect resonance and increase the voice's potency, and the maneuver works well for him throughout most of the opera. The monologue poses a problem—the voice is not comfortable at its very top. He shortchanges the high G-flat at 'Ma non mi sfuggirai!' and cannot quite reach the crest of the all-important concluding phrase ('nel fondo del mio cor'); the G is anemic and a mite short of pitch. He covers the moment as best he can, and aims for a strong finish, sounding a long, manly tonic note. But the damage is done. The aria is the only star turn of the afternoon and he has muffed it. That may be an intemperate view when an artist has given so fully of himself in every way throughout the afternoon, including a good deal of the monologue. Quite true. Still, that moment is a salient one in Verdi's careful plotting of the score's profile—he has strategically placed it at the midpoint of the opera. Levine does all he can to elevate the episode, vigorously pacing it for maximum impact, his graphic orchestral strokes adding dramatic punch wherever possible. He is fully aware of the importance of driving this moment home and intends to do so, whether the baritone can or not.

Whatever the holes in her technique and however uneven the condition of her instrument, Barbieri has just the vocal meat that Stewart does not. She lays it on a bit overgenerously, but then who would want to do without all the chesty bravura that she doles out with unashamed boldness? The galumphing (a Lewis Carroll–coined compliment) manner is familiar from an earlier broadcast, but on this afternoon the singer manages a better register blend and the tone in the upper range is occasionally full and attractive rather than merely simulated (although there are evidences of the latter as well). Her 'Reverenza's and 'Povera donna's resound like the pummeling jabs of a jackhammer on a New York pavement. Verdi meant them to be enjoyed. (I wish she would honor the dotted rhythm he noted at the end of 'povera'—it adds a little swagger to her fake concern.) Here and there, the aging Italian mezzo (remember, she came to the Met with Bing in 1950) plays with a touch more restraint than she sometimes exhibits. Perhaps Levine's notorious cosseting of singers, coupled with his expert counsel, was a leavening influence. In any case, the mezzo not only puts her best foot forward in her solo moments, but she is a bulwark in the ensembles, trumpeting forth with complete confidence, anchoring them without hobbling their lively flight.

Miss Lear's voice occasionally comes over the air as a bit light for the role. That said, her Alice Ford is an entrancing creature. The American soprano offers some of the loveliest, most elegant phrases to be heard in many a season in this or any opera. The voice is at its most beguiling, discreetly sensuous of timbre, the tone flowing like liquid white gold. The phrases that conclude Falstaff's love letter ('Facciamo il paio . . . e il viso tuo su me risplenderà') are magically voiced, their shapes elegance personified, the tone exquisitely purled. (A real trill would have put the full seal of approval on them.) And when spunk is Alice's ticket, that quality is supplied in quantity by Lear. In more exuberant moments, Alice's phrases effortlessly flow from her accommodating throat. Gaiety is inherent in her manner and tone as she summons the wives to their merriment ('Gaje comari di Vindsor!'). With consummate control, she executes 'Poi ci smaschereremo' (introduced with a masterly portamento), the flash up to the high B accomplished with aplomb. At such a moment, mischief is inherent in the tone itself. And her subtle artistry is not confined to Alice's prominent solos. Many perceptive touches animate her conception. A notable one is her taunting of Falstaff in the final scene as she unmasks; her 'Vi siete fatto muto?' is languorously suggestive. Lear's Mistress

Ford is more of a worldly creature than we expect to find at home or in the forest. The contrast with her offspring's chaste manner is striking—how could so knowing a mother have such a dove for a daughter? No matter. To make Alice Ford's acquaintance in the form and voice of Miss Lear is as exhilarating as suffering a schoolboy's first crush.

MacNeil, now in his early fifties, is no longer quite the baritone force that he was in his earlier days. He still has more than a decade's devoted service to the company ahead of him, however, and on this afternoon his instrument is a responsive one. His control over it is remarkably constant, and his intelligence, both musical and dramatic, works overtime to create a character worthy of the master's multifaceted creation. The beat that has disfigured some of his late-career performances is nowhere in evidence, nor is tonal rawness at all prominent. He places his still pungent resources at the service of the composer, adhering far more than many an interpreter to the score's directives. Dynamic variety, engaging phraseology, contrasting qualities of movement, deft portamentos, firm legato (sometimes allied with a skillfully executed *dolcissimo* as at 'e il suo desir' in the opening scene)—all the devices of a singing actor's art are employed with a surety of touch that commands admiration. When roistering with his blustering cohorts at the Garter Inn at the curtain's rise, MacNeil immediately lets us know that, though the wily knight may not be an honest man, he, the artist, is. 'Quest'è il mio regno' he proudly claims in grand tones, the top F well focused and gloriously full. 'Immenso Falstaff,' Bardolfo and Pistola name him. MacNeil's rogue fills the bill. Sir John's self-satisfaction and the baritone's honor will increase as the afternoon progresses. Levine's micromanagement of the opening scene—well matched with MacNeil's artful playing—may dilute Falstaff's earthiness, but, remember—as the baritone does—the man is a knight, and, moreover, one who consorts with princes.

MacNeil, always fond of the singing line and not shy about displaying the grandeur of his instrument, nevertheless is not afraid to roughen his tone, even growl a bit (a wonderfully gruff 'Ladri' in the honor monologue) in the service of character portrayal. That duty does not prevent him from capping his railings about honor with a brilliant top G, proving that his resonant top voice can still function. (But the requisite mezza voce on the high F-sharp at 'San Martino' is beyond his skill. He compromises with a keenly focused note, the tonal mix as heady as a lyric baritone might offer. It works well enough. Most baritones are content merely to circumvent the difficulty with an overly cute falsetto.) MacNeil can be as nimble as the fat knight when he was 'sottile,' lightening his tone at any given moment. Suiting the voice to the image, he does so in his recall of his youthful days as a 'slender' page. In contrast, when, in the wake of Quickly's visit, Falstaff cries, 'Alice è mia!,' the singer's greedy anticipation sounds as lascivious as the mouthing of a lusting Jupiter in pursuit of Antiope. Later, as Falstaff quits the mystified Ford and goes to prepare himself for his amorous adventure, MacNeil lofts an unctuous 'Vado a farmi bello'; we can almost see Falstaff swell with self-regard (the baritone all but smacks his lips over that 'bello'). As the now humiliated Falstaff salutes the wonders of wine, Levine's orchestra shivers and shimmers, the trills magnifying sonorously; 'il buono vino' rebuilds the knight's confidence, inflates his ego, and the singer matches the orchestra's brilliance as he savors the drink. Throughout the afternoon the American baritone delivers a virtuoso performance of a rogue big in heart, enormous in craft. The singer, too, qualifies in those regards—though he is anything but a rogue. At a time when younger baritones are invading his turf, MacNeil proves that, in terms of vocal endowment, discerning musicality, and depth of character portrayal, he remains an artist of considerable value to the company. Not many big Verdi baritones could launch the fugue with comparable dexterity.

The brutal beating that Amaducci dealt Verdi's comic masterwork in the 1967 broadcast demanded a powerful antidote. Levine provides it in his nuanced, glowing reading of the mercurial score. He has bound up the composer's wounds and delivered *Falstaff* whole and hearty to us once again. We, hale as well, now may press on to new adventures, refreshed and ready for the fantastic concoction that Offenbach made of *Les Contes d'Hoffmann*. The broadcast of 2 February 1974 offers precious booty, for Sutherland undertakes all the heroines. Management's bounty is not unlimited, however. Harry Theyard assumes the title role, while Stewart sings the villains, Huguette Tourangeau is the trousered Nicklausse, and Velis is the downstairs man of many guises. Bonynge, of course, is on the podium.

The production is, in fact, Bonynge's baby, having been imported from the Seattle Opera. There, in 1971, the conductor, joined by Bliss Hebert and Allen Charles Klein as stage director and designer, respectively, attempted to return to the composer's original concept of the opera. That well-intentioned goal, however, is a task that has befuddled conductors and musicologists ever since the opera's first public performance in 1881. (Offenbach had died four months before the premiere.) The conductor utilizes the "original" spoken dialogue rather than the composed Guiraud recitatives but, dramatic effectiveness winning out over scholarship, retains the time-honored order of the acts. Thus, Hoffmann stops off in Venice before proceeding to Munich. In particular, Bonynge's epilogue caused the New York critics fits of near-apoplexy. Abjuring the long-familiar construct of the end piece, he reformulated it, prefacing the action with a replaying of the minuet and an orchestral version of the barcarolle—rather like a tour of Offenbach's greatest hits. After a bit of the more familiar epilogue, he leapt (this was the bête noire of the critics) into a version of the notorious non-Offenbachian septet, the latter normally included in the Giulietta act. In an intermission interview on the broadcast, Bonynge bristles at the idea that he has offered a "new version" or even a "version" of the opera.[3] He avers, with incontrovertible certainty, that he has simply done what Offenbach intended. In particular, the placement of the ensemble, reduced to a "quartet," is valid, for he maintains that Offenbach originally included a quartet in the epilogue. Commenting on the roughhouse treatment to which the opera has been subjected over the years, he closes off discussion by noting that "everybody's had a go at it." Adopting a tempest-in-a-teapot attitude, he dismisses criticism of his refashioning or restoration (take your choice) with a shrug: "I've had my little go!"

Beyond the controversy over the "original" text of the opera, the conductor has had to bear the onus of being a prima donna's husband before he became her pit guardian. In that regard at least, on this afternoon the monkey is off his back. Bonynge is entirely conversant with the style of nineteenth-century French opera and dance, having made a detailed study of its practices and scores. Thus, his pacing has the requisite panache and—in the opposite corner—his timbral sense includes a love of sensuous sound. Grotesquerie is a front-and-center component

Les Contes d'Hoffmann
2 February 1974

*Olympia, Giulietta,
Antonia, Stella*
Joan Sutherland
Nicklausse
Huguette Tourangeau
Hoffmann
Harry Theyard
Servants
Andrea Velis
*Lindorf, Coppelius,
Dappertutto, Dr. Miracle*
Thomas Stewart
Conductor
Richard Bonynge

Joan Sutherland as Olympia in *Les Contes d'Hoffmann*. Photography by Louis Mélançon. Courtesy Metropolitan Opera Archives.

of the opera's makeup and Bonynge knows how to serve it up; the solo wind instruments, especially in their lower regions, are often wonderfully suggestive of E. T. A. Hoffmann's weird world. The conductor sends several set pieces rollicking on their way in a manner that Offenbach might well have approved.

Multiple roles are the order of the day. Interpretive distinction is seldom evenly distributed among their several charges when artists spread their wares over disparate characters; but the deficiency surfaces only if the composer has given each character a distinctive musical profile. Yet, as Bonynge points out in his radio interview, a single thread unites the four baritone roles, even as it does the four character tenor roles. The former are representations of evil, while the latter are the agents of the action. Velis adopts a single tonal quality—and a most annoying one it is—for Andrès, Cochenille, and Pitichinaccio. Surely, his pinched soprano whines and incessant cackles would raise the hackles of even those who savor the prominence of the grotesque in Barbier's and Carré's drama. Velis' (or Mr. Hebert's) conception is over the edge—and I do mean edge. (According to old opera hand Quaintance Eaton, Bonynge tried to tone down the comprimario's "hamming."[4] Judging from the broadcast, he was unsuccessful in the endeavor.) Frantz gets the full fuddy-duddy treatment and his song remains the usual trial when Velis "la-la"s his way through it. Franke, a veteran of earlier broadcasts, remains a forceful interpreter of the deluded inventor, Spalanzani, while Anthony, his commitment and bright timbre always positive elements in any opera, helps to animate the tavern roistering. Morris' agitated concern for daughter Antonia is dramatically telling, and, when singing is called for, he displays some of the tonal appeal and vocal suavity that soon would guarantee larger assignments. Miss Tourangeau, a Bonynge/Sutherland protégée, makes her broadcast debut as Nicklausse. Her instrument is an unusual one, its dark, dusky timbre striking as a sonority, but just a touch ungainly in usage. The timbre, constant in color throughout its range, confirms that she will be at home in trousers. Nicklausse does not yet have restored to him the couplets that later productions will allow him, but the mezzo deserves them. Quite naturally, she puts to shame the French accents of most of her confreres—especially in her lengthy spoken speeches, including those of the Muse. Her sangfroid is so obvious and her poise so convincing that I thought Hoffmann surely would have followed her advice.

Stewart's gallery of portraits is much easier to take than Velis' irksome portrayals. While their unifying evil intent is well signaled by him, the four villains offer a singing actor like the American baritone an interpretive challenge that he is eager to accommodate. He works hard at differentiating them by means of varied tone quality and, especially in the spoken dialogue, changing pace and altered speech mannerisms. Luther's villainy profits from the narrow snarl that the baritone likes to employ in his lower range to compensate for lack of depth. Coppélius' speech is oppressive in intent and more weirdly suggestive. The tessitura is high enough so that Stewart's healthy upper register speaks in the 'J'ai des yeux' aria. Dappertutto's suave deceitfulness demands elegance and a sure vocal touch—as does his aria. Stewart does well enough on both counts. His voice, a trifle short at both ends of the range, dictates the transposition (a full tone down) of 'Scintille diamant'; the lower key does minimize its diamantine coldness. One misses the timbral glaciation that Martial Singher applied so effectively to the aria in the forties. The transposition does allow our baritone to achieve a comfortable close (the F-sharp is solid and large enough to acquire a tail-end wobble). The ascending phrases that precede the closing lift are measured out in masterly fashion by Stewart, his tone at its most attractive. Dr. Miracle's music profits as well from the baritone's solid vocalism—it lies well for his instrument. He doesn't lay on the villainy too thick—perhaps the relative normality of Antonia's home cautioned against excess. But we know this physician is up to no good. Bonynge propels the trio along at a precipitous gait, Sutherland at full voice enjoying the trip, with Stewart and Cynthia Munzer tagging along. The mother's phrases demand a more substantial voice than the mezzo can offer.

Alexander was scheduled as the broadcast hero but, in a reversal of fortune, he had "a lapse of the flu," according to Cross. Newcomer Harry Theyard takes over the role. The November premiere of the Met production had featured Domingo in the title role. Thus we are twice removed from the best the Met had to offer in this lengthy, demanding assignment. Theyard had sung the role at his house debut on 17 January. A member of the Met's touring National Company (1966 debut in Indianapolis as Alfredo), the New Orleans–born tenor comes off as an experienced, committed artist. His broadcast performance is doubly commendable since he was pressed into service after having sung the Puccini Des Grieux the evening before. The voice has considerable thrust and intensity, though its size cannot be accurately gauged on this afternoon—in their duets, Sutherland's grand tone tends to dominate. (Oddly, and purely in terms of an evocative timbre, I found myself thinking of Corelli here and there, if only in a minimal way. *Opera News* tells us that Theyard describes himself as a spinto; he would, in fact, sing a couple Don Alvaros in the next Met season. To move from Alfredo to Alvaro in eight seasons is to travel a long distance on a precariously rocky road.) He gets off a few brilliant top notes that would do credit to any tenor—and the audience knows it and shows it. His verve makes the budding poet seem just the kind of impetuous fellow who could become involved in a succession of eerie amorous adventures.

Theyard's tone has point and an agreeable vibrancy that mates well with the French operatic idiom and language. His French is good and his phrasing musically attuned, particularly effective in the romantic moments of the opera. There his ardor is alive and insistent. In addition to his heart, he wears vitality on his sleeve: the Kleinzach episode is rhythmically alert and tonally thrusting. The Chant Bacchique, in particular, benefits from his fresh-air timbre. Even when the tone is occasionally touched by granularity or nasality, its core remains attractive. Considering his own adventure of the previous evening, the voice holds up amazingly well, seeming to tire only a bit in the rising phrases of Hoffmann's strenuous address to Giulietta ('O Dieu! de quelle ivresse'). But the tenor has saved up enough for a strong finish in the epilogue. There his tones, touched by a silvery glint, ring out with the confidence of a job well done. We will meet him again, and soon enough, in the unexpected venue of a Rossini *opera seria*.

To undertake all four heroines has become rather more commonplace in the later decades of the century, but at the time of this production only Vina Bovy and Anna Moffo had performed the feat at the Metropolitan. Most exponents who make the attempt inevitably belong to the "coloratura soprano" breed—Olympia's high-wire act makes that a necessity. The sheer size of Sutherland's instrument, however, means that the tonal amplitude required for Antonia and Giulietta will be more than adequately supplied. Few singers have made much of the Venetian courtesan, and the Australian soprano is no exception. The fault lies as much with the composer as the interpreter. Offenbach failed (or didn't have time) to do much beyond allowing the courtesan to fill a costume—and it was a gorgeous one as seen in the current *Opera News*. The soprano speaks her lines in suggestively vamplike low tones and tries her hand at a few dramatic effects as Dappertutto bids her seek Hoffmann's reflection. In the duet, she doesn't stint on tone—and it is glorious in the upper range—all but dwarfing her tenor when rising above the staff. Her voice projects less clearly in mid-voice. For the radio audience, the barcarole is a complete fizzle—the vocal parts can hardly be heard. Antonia's aria ('Elle a fui, la tourterelle') doesn't quite come off. The climaxes are wonderfully pungent, but elsewhere the line is not cleanly drawn nor is the text articulated so that the distinctive sounds of the French language add to the music's poignancy. Only in this single piece do I hear the famous Sutherland phrase droop—pathos is thereby evoked, but the contours of Offenbach's languid line adequately supply that in themselves. A sweet tartness of timbre (the French ideal) would better bring the lovely piece, as well as the character, into focus. That said, her singing of the remainder of Antonia's music is thrilling. Sutherland's healthy tones are propelled with such obvious joy that the heroine's need to sing is made abundantly real. The diva's tone is as rich, round, and secure as ever heard from her—now even the mid-low voice is free of either veiled or grainy texture. The trio calls forth her best efforts. She tosses off Antonia's feverish phrases with abandon, the girl's ecstatic release fully conveyed by Sutherland's rapt vocalism. On this afternoon, the soprano's topmost notes (D-flat to E-flat) may betray a bit of effort, but their size makes the lifting worthwhile. How fitting that this heroine should succumb on a Sutherland trill. They have always been to die for.

Of course, a major reason for undertaking the assignment is the show-stopping pyrotechnics of Olympia's aria in the opening act. There Sutherland is again stupendous. Bonynge takes the piece at a fast clip and his wife's virtuosity, almost brazenly accomplished, makes the aria anything but the doll's plaything that most miniature-voiced sopranos have offered. The entire arsenal of coloratura technical devices is executed with amazing fleetness, accuracy, and—greatly to the diva's credit—a piquant charm. Particularly notable are her glittering staccatos and enchanting echo effects. In rehearsal, the conductor cautioned her not to "press on the trill," claiming it had "a rattle in it."[5] Unlike his unavailing attempt with Velis, Bonynge's words to his wife took. One can't know whether it was husbandly concern or conductorial tyranny but no rattle is heard over the airwaves. All the roulades tumble out at a head-spinning pace. (At one point, where the flourishes repeatedly romp up and down, the image of Bea Lillie gaily, madly swinging her long loop of pearls around her neck flew into my mind.) The end result is intoxicating, so exhilarating that one almost wishes the opera would end at the first-act curtain.

I was in the house for the 1973 premiere of this production. Visually it was worth seeing—the costumes were treats for the eyes. Beyond Sutherland's virtuosity, what I most remember is the initial sound of Domingo's voice as it softly pervaded the huge auditorium. Its dulcet caress was transporting. Even while acknowledging Theyard's quality and achievement, I know what we miss by Domingo's absence on this afternoon. Nevertheless, Bonynge's "little go," as heard on the broadcast, can stand as one of the Met's worthwhile performances.

Die Meistersinger
17 April 1976

Eva
Arlene Saunders
Magdalene
Marcia Baldwin
Walther
Jean Cox
David
Kenneth Riegel
Hans Sachs
Thomas Stewart
Kothner
Theodor Uppman
Beckmesser
Günther Leib
Pogner
John Macurdy
Conductor
Sixten Ehrling

Les Contes d'Hoffmann is the odd man out in this comic survey. Its fantastic format is unique. Opera buffa, on the other hand, is a daughter of tradition and progenitor of a happy and numerous family. The genre works its merry wiles within small frames, but *in piccolo* won't do for Wagner. He could hardly be expected to forfeit grandeur even when contesting with the comic muse. *Die Meistersinger von Nürnberg* is painted on a broad canvas, but the composer's touch is so deft that time spent with the guilds is unalloyed joy. The broadcast of 17 April 1976 is largely a homegrown affair, at least within the proscenium. Stewart takes center stage as Sachs with brave assists from newcomers Arlene Saunders (Eva), Jean Cox (Walther), Kenneth Riegel (David), and Günther Leib (the interloper, as Beckmesser). The large cast also offers Baldwin (Magdalene), Uppman (Kothner), and Macurdy (Pogner), as well as a host of fine voices for members of the guild, including Anthony, Castel, Garrison, Schmorr, Goodloe, Thompson, Booth, and Karlsrud. The strands of the drama are neatly gathered together by Ehrling. If, in act one, the performance sometimes seems small-bore (remember mere humans now populate Wagner at the Met), in later acts the reading gathers force as Wagner's magic works its will. At curtain's fall, we emerge content once again to have lingered long in sixteenth-century Nürnberg.

The Swiss conductor is up to his old ways, demystifying Wagner, taking the load off his back, putting a spring in his step. What better opera to receive the full-body treatment than *Meistersinger*, a piece so formidable in length, so blithe in spirit. Having brought in the *Ring* whole during the previous season, Ehrling well understands the difference between the heavens and the earth, between twisted gods and homely burghers. After his lightweight Vorspiel, devoid of pompous emphases, we are not surprised to meet a happy crew of *meister*s, self-satisfied tradesmen no doubt, but hardly crotchety. Even Beckmesser seems to have a lighter side to his thievery. The conductor's control over detail is as keen as ever, and the orchestra, in fine fettle despite it being the rump of the season, responds to his careful leadership with commendable tact. For Ehrling, 'die heil'ge deutsche Kunst' sits on no pedestal—he prefers to embrace it with good-humored ease, rather than bow down before it.

Most Beckmessers offer familiar wares. Debutant Günther Leib is no exception. Familiar or not, his bag of tricks is more agreeable than most. Born in Gotha, in the former German Democratic Republic, and since 1957 with the Dresden State Opera, Leib has a long acquaintance with Beckmesser and it shows in his thoughtful, detailed characterization. Happily, when first met, he chooses to sing in a soft, unassuming manner. He is listed on the Met roster as a bass, but hardly sounds like one. Eventually, of course, the nasal whine comes into play—the town clerk's temperament seems to require it, and his smallness of spirit sustains it. But Leib makes the grouse easier to take than most; for one thing, he believes *his* prize song should be delivered as a serious effort to win Eva. And he and Stewart are absolutely charming when they duel over who owns the text of Walther's prize song. With subtle artistry, the Dresden visitor suggests the changing suspicions that flit into Beckmesser's mind as Sachs offers him the song. He can't (and shouldn't) believe his good fortune as Stewart big-heartedly leads him on. His punishment does seem severe after such agreeable game playing.

Aside from the Dresden import, American talent holds center stage. Pennsylvania-born Kenneth Riegel came to the company in 1973 (Iopas in *Les Troyens*) and had been heard by the radio audience in that role and as Jaquino a few months before the *Meistersinger* broadcast. He may well be the finest David in our broadcast survey. His tone is pointed and bright, not unattractive in timbre. All the notes are there. The most prominent feature of his portrayal is his happy outlook, his unfailing vitality, his unquenchable pixiness. This apprentice is what is popularly referred to as a "live wire." He all but bests Stewart in some of their scenes together, so spic-and-span is his vocalism, so vital his chatter. In some performances Davids can get on one's nerves, but appreciation for Riegel is constant and acute. Not surprisingly, the tenor would soon move up to Tamino, and eventually his Hoffmann would figure largely in the company's plans. For the time being, he at least deserves to win his Lene, and Baldwin sounds young enough and strong enough not only to deserve him, but to have the spunk to handle him. Some of the American talent has given pleasure for decades. It might seem odd to find Mozartian Uppman in the Wagner milieu, but he is at home with the idiom; as Kothner calls the roll, he sputters consonants to the manor born, the characterization aided by age now having touched his buoyant instrument. Philip Booth's Night Watchman is clearly a rustic, his intentionally crusty tones a far cry from the elegance that some artists have felt appropriate for this evocative moment. As Pogner, Macurdy continues to expand his galaxy of subtle character portraits. He sings well, too. When he discusses the contest rules with Beckmesser, Macurdy adopts an understanding manner and light tones; they continue to decorate 'Das schöne Fest'—the manner suits Wagner's gently loping line in that extended segment. He shies at a few top notes early on, but soon his voice takes on both breadth and vigor. Eva benefits by his kindly counsel in their colloquy—his mezza voce 'Eitelkeit' surely would invite any daughter's confidence. When he thinks on the celebratory events of the morrow, pride and affection for Eva ('dass du den Preis') all but burst his tones.

Stewart, by this time a devoted and persistent toiler in Wagnerian fields, views Sachs as the "high point of his long Met career," or so announcer Allen tells us at the curtain calls. One understands his regard for the assignment, and yet his voice is not the ideal instrument for the role. He is a baritone, and a lyric one at that, whereas Sachs benefits most from a bass-baritone's weightier tending. Stewart's voice, with its relatively narrow focus and a tendency to disappear in the lower range, denies Sachs a good measure of his presence, both in its authoritative and kindly aspects. His interpretation lacks the girth of tone, the corpulence of spirit, the sheer avoirdupois that makes Sachs the natural leader of the mastersingers. Early on, nasality and the familiar snarl are employed to aid projection. Oddly, where he might take advantage of his instrument's lyric quality, he seldom chooses to do so; many moments marked *piano* are ignored. The 'Flieder' monologue suffers from this defect, and the 'Kobold' section of the heartier 'Wahn' monologue is bereft of enchantment; in the latter, his sounding of 'Johannisnacht' (marked *zart*) is a full-voiced pronouncement, where it ought to come off as a mere breath of air. He is a better cobbler than a philosopher, crying 'Jerum' as though he not only enjoys aggravating Beckmesser with his marks, but finds release in singing his exuberant song. One interpretive novelty catches the attention. He goes all emotional when citing to Eva the Tristan and Isolde legend; sobs almost spill into the quotation and out of his voice. Stewart's manly stage presence would have made the temptation for this Sachs to gain Eva as wife entirely logical. With him, we are made to feel that, by taking the nobler path, Sachs is giving up something he valued.

Of course, having been a Bayreuth regular for a decade and a half, the American baritone has the Wagner melos in his blood. No matter if it doesn't consistently run at full force and ruddle his philosopher cobbler; he *will* give a performance. He can summon tone, reasonably rich and decidedly attractive, in the upper half of his voice, and is experienced enough to know when and where to apply it. Even the first act here and there enjoys a touch of his bounty, and he paces himself so carefully that the third act finds him dispensing wisdom and tone, in equal amounts, with considerable largesse. The usual cuts aid endurance, but even so, one must commend him for arriving at the meadow in happy vocal estate. In broadcast history, Schorr had been the model Sachs, with Schöffler and Edelmann as worthy successors. Despite their respective merits, more recent claimants—Tozzi, Adam, Stewart, Ridderbusch—have been unable to place their signature upon the multifaceted character. As of this date, I continue to live in hope. Bryn Terfel may be the man. Or will it be René Pape?

Jean Cox, a native of Gadsden, Alabama, had traveled to Europe as a Fulbright fellow in 1952 and soon made a career for himself in a raft of European houses. For most of his sojourn he performed on the German stages, beginning with Kiel and Brunswick, before adopting Mannheim as his home base. Bayreuth early claimed him and by the late sixties that holy of holies had heard his Lohengrin, Parsifal, and Walther, with Siegfried on deck early in the next decade. In America, Chicago (1964–73) became his favored haunt. Now, at age fifty-four, he arrived at the Metropolitan, which most regarded as the American operatic temple. One hears why the German repertory became his playground, for his timbre has that combination of mead and ring (though neither in ultimate measure) that is the province of the best German tenors. Discreet echoes of forebears as diverse as Dane Helge Rosvaenge and American Charles Kullman steal into my mind as I listen. Initially, his tone is lightly uttered, soft at its core, at least until he moves to the top register, where an ungainly twang sometimes surfaces. His Gs and As are quite open and not always attractive to hear. That may spell trouble for the Prize Song, where those pitches abound. But the top notes grow marginally more acceptable as the opera progresses. By the time of Walther's disastrous trial song, his voice has taken on recognizable tenorial authority, in spite of that occasional "wow" on high. In the third act, he is cagey about handling the several versions of the Prize Song itself: he sings the initial one rather casually, as though Walther is thinking on his feet as the lines come to him. It's a good ploy, for it saves heft and bloom for the real contest, where he supplies them with reasonable success. When was the last time we heard a 'Morgentlich leuchte' that really merited the prize? After all, it is Eva's hand that is at stake. This knight is only a winner by default. Probably if Cox had come to the house in his forties rather than his mid-fifties, he would have provided greater pleasure than he can offer on this afternoon.

From the sound of Arlene Saunders' Eva, her Nürnberg maiden would be worth winning, even if it meant succumbing to the guild's rules. In her soprano youth, the Cleveland-born singer had been featured at the New York City Opera, but she had been "a star" (the designation is Allen's) of the Hamburg Staatsoper since 1964. San Francisco had heard her Louise and Marguerite as early as 1967; for much of her career she continued as a genuine lyric soprano, albeit a healthy-voiced one. Not until the current season did the Metropolitan summon her, and then only for three Evas, including the 8 April premiere. At age forty, her Eva displays the expected idiomatic command of text and phrase that her Hamburg tenure would have inculcated. But authenticity cannot account for the immense charm of her portrayal. Eva is a quicksilver girl and Saunders' voice and interpretive play flicker and shine with delightful piquancy throughout the afternoon. Not a vocal nuance or flight of fancy goes unexplored. Much of Eva's effectiveness lies in projecting tone in the middle voice—Saunders' instrument has the requisite body there. Moreover, it burgeons at the top, touched by silver, but more potent than voices of the Raskin type (though it owns a bit of that singer's tonal sweetness). Her outburst to widower Sachs (this is his moment of temptation) is vocally full and hearty in delivery; she can soar in the upper range, though she does not surge as ardently as a few Evas of the past. After awaiting her quintet launching with keen anticipation, I must confess to some disappointment when it arrives. Eva's heavenly solo phrases are a trial for any artist; they are so exposed and the buildup has been great. Saunders adopts an excessively tiny tone (yes, Wagner wanted a *piano* dynamic), and a rapid vibrato, not hitherto apparent, infects tone and line (even causing a momentary semblance of flat pitch). I think Evas might better forget about containment and paralyzing correctness and rather just sing the phrases, allow the moment to flow forth, fluid, real, and affecting. The whole quintet on this afternoon is a bit too pussy-footedly proper (though one blat of phrase from Cox is a caution in the opposite direction). With that single reservation, Saunders' portrayal ranks high in the broadcast train of Eva interpreters, a list that includes not only Rethberg, but Steber, De los Angeles, and Della Casa. I would have welcomed the opportunity to hear Saunders in what, by career's end, proved to be a considerably varied repertory. The voice eventually matured so that Senta and Sieglinde were within its compass, with as trying a role as Minnie providing a 1980 Covent Garden debut. American artists are ever a game lot.

The comic muse has many faces, as our dip into German, French, and Italian dramas has affirmed. Conceits and foibles form its core, with even a smutch of evil troubling its normally genial surface now and then. Our limited tour suggests that not only Balzac's written page, but opera, too, can expose for our delectation the endearing eccentricity of the human comedy.

Jon Vickers as Énée in *Les Troyens*. Photography by Louis Mélançon. Courtesy Metropolitan Opera Archives.

CHAPTER SEVENTEEN

Metropolitan Premieres

The charge of being merely a museum was—and still is—often leveled at the Metropolitan. Dishonor is not necessarily inherent in the nomenclature. To preserve and present the masterworks of the past is a noble mission. But it is undoubtedly the practical and easy route to take, especially inasmuch as the cultivation of new works has not proved a successful pursuit for general managers since Gatti-Casazza's time. That enigmatic Italian had had the good sense to govern in an age when opera was very much a living art. Of course, it lives even today in performance. Management's record of commission was indeed lax, but, beyond its reliance upon the staple repertory, it did foster the presentation of neglected works by recognized composers. Though the company was not ready to venture into the thicket of "contemporary" opera (or at least those works that employed so-called advanced composition techniques—that had to wait for Levine's supremacy), it added a number of compelling works during the interim years between the end of the Bing reign and the beginning of the Levine regime. An *opera seria* of Rossini (converted from the French *Le Siège de Corinthe* into *L'Assedio di Corinto*), a neglected grand opera of Verdi (originally *Les Vêpres Sicilienne* but translated into *I Vespri Siciliani*), and the immense corpus of Berlioz' *Les Troyens* were introduced. Though here twice disguised, French opera, dominant in the 1800s but sadly neglected in the next century, is given a chance to prove its charms and considerable distinction. In addition, gently dipping its toe into twentieth-century waters, management took on Bartók's *Bluebeard's Castle* and Britten's *Death in Venice*. Janáček's *Jenůfa* had figured in the 1924–25 season, but its neglect over the next half century seems sufficient reason for including it in a chapter that focuses on company enterprise. Each opera provided a welcome opportunity to listeners who were starved for new adventures in opera land.

"Your title is principal conductor here at the Metropolitan Opera, but you look young enough to be my son," remarks Tony Randall, actor and opera devotee, as he begins to interview Maestro Levine during the first intermission of *I Vespri Siciliani* during the broadcast of 9 March 1974.[1] "How old are you?" Caught by surprise, Levine gives a tentative little laugh as he replies: "Thirty." The young conductor wastes no time before he begins to enthuse about his current project, employing that occasionally indiscriminate—but appealing—manner that we will come to know so well over the years. (Sometimes one almost wishes he would not

I Vespri Siciliani
9 March 1974

Elena (Hélène)
Montserrat Caballé
Arrigo (Henri)
Nicolai Gedda
Monforte (Montfort)
Sherrill Milnes
Procida
Justino Díaz
Conductor
James Levine

be so everlastingly upbeat. But, as in his performances, so in interview conversation he refuses to strike a sour note.) Verdi's opera deserves his approbation. His
regard for its quality is apparent in the evident care of his preparation and in his
reading of the neglected work. *Vespri* followed immediately upon the grand trium-
virate of Verdi's early middle age: *Rigoletto, Il Trovatore*, and *La Traviata*. In spite of
that encouraging placement in the Verdi canon, the opera had never been seen on
the Metropolitan stage. (A concert reading had been given in 1967 at Newport,
Rhode Island, under Molinari-Pradelli with Virginia Zeani, Eugenio Fernandi,
Kostas Paskalis, and Bonaldo Giaiotti in the principal roles.) Perhaps it was the
opera's grand design and considerable length—the composer had accommodated
his passion for brevità to the conventions of French grand opera—that underlay
the neglect. The disdain is difficult to understand, for the score is one of the composer's most accomplished middle-period efforts. The gloomy milieu of the subject
matter—the Sicilian massacre of the French at Palermo in 1282—undoubtedly
added further cause for neglect. In producing the opera, the Metropolitan did
better by the ear than the eye: Joseph Svoboda's sets were essentially nothing but
a towering row of steps. At the final curtain, they were strewn with dead bodies—not a pretty picture. But with Caballé as Elena, Milnes and Gedda portraying
father and son (Monforte and Arrigo), and Díaz lurking as the villainous patriot
Procida, the score receives a performance worthy of the master composer.

Both the opera's large-scale and its inner workings are readily accommodated
by Levine's probing mind and efficient baton. Taut and yet vibrant, the performance is notable for its melding of fluidity and precision, a combination difficult
to achieve but immensely rewarding when obtained. David Stivender's chorus is a
model of vitality and exactitude—Levine has it mating perfectly with his orchestra.
That increasingly pliant body does itself proud, whether as soloists or as members
of the varied instrumental combinations that Verdi ladled into his score; the maestro deftly points up their expertise without allowing the opera's generous melodic
profile to be compromised. Levine has often been accused of driving Verdi's operas
with excessive ferocity, so much so that, like the Cole Porter guy whose *Baby Goes
to Town*, you want to "holler Whoa!". Not guilty, I say, at least on this afternoon.
His handling of the well-known overture is a case in point. It is constructed of
melodic and rhythmic motives from the opera proper; Levine deploys them in fair
proportions, placing the disparate elements in mutually advantageous relationships. That is not easily accomplished, in that the overture's formal design is a bit
obvious. Even the opera's big tune—culled from the father–son duet of Verdi's act
three—is discreetly molded. I would prefer a more self-indulgent enjoyment of its
sweep both here and in the duet itself, but I appreciate the maestro's continence
in terms of his overall concept of the opera. When French moderation and Verdian exuberance are joined together, the alignment demands discretion if the brew
is to blend without curdling. (True, a hint of interpretive tidiness can invade the
conductor's music making, but if it be a demerit, it is a slight one.) Of course,
this maestro knows when to kick an overture or finale into overdrive and invariably does so at the right moment in this performance. A pity we cannot hear the
extensive ballet music that the composer fashioned for the French stage. Still, the
opera is long, even when the traditional cuts in the Italian version are employed,
as they are at the Met. Intermissions are confined to two, as the traditional five-act
format of French grand opera is compressed into three acts.

The opera opens well with some Met regulars (Castel, Karlsrud, and especially Dobriansky and Goodloe as Roberto and Bethune) displaying their customary
competence. As ever, Goodloe's well-focused baritone commands attention. Díaz
has been only minimally present on the airwaves for several seasons (Frère Laurent
in 1970, Sparafucile in 1972) and returns to the company after a season's hiatus.
In earlier broadcasts, his voice appeared to have lost some of its timbral luster. His
tone had grown a bit diffuse and gray in color—attributes doubly troubling in
this still young artist. One takes heart from his strong portrayal on this afternoon.
Procida is rather a stick, an all-purpose villain, but Verdi allotted him one of the
best scenes in the opera with his entrance aria. Díaz takes full advantage of the
grandeur of 'O tu, Palermo,' the voice resonant and frequently focused for pointed
thrust. He attempts a *messa di voce* in the introductory recitative—a beat surfaces
(the piece occurs early on in the opera) but that disappears as he moves into the
main body of the aria. True, the tone has a suspicion of haze on it, and size, rather
than compactness, is cultivated. After all, the aria demands strapping tone and if a
bass is to make any effect in this opera, he must do it here. Legato and responsive
phrasing are Díaz assets and the absence of wobble counts as a positive as well.
At the reprise of the opening section, he adds a touch of warmth and tenderness,
and a few well-judged emotive nuances enhance the close. There, the bass' right
to membership in the company's prime ranks is staked, and affirmed, in his big-
voiced cadenza. His strong, assured phrases add to the effectiveness of the act's
concertato, and, though a few ineffectual low notes at the opera's denouement must
be noted, they seem trifling in the face of his splendid vocalism, firm in intent and
now compact of tone, in the conflicting moments of Verdi's fourth act.

In an afternoon of exciting vocalism, Milnes may well claim pride of place.
His sensitive, emotionally telling performance of Monforte's pensive aria ('In
braccie alle dovizie') is perhaps the most satisfying example of his artistry that
I have heard. Over the years quite a few have decried the American baritone's
performance style, characterizing it as grandstand vocalizing too little informed
by interpretive subtlety or vocal niceties; his particular vocal "method" does not
appeal to all connoisseurs of song. The aggrandizement tendency was there from
the first, but interpretations that relied on vocal power and personal swagger
gained greater prominence in Milnes' performances as the years passed. It may
be that was the image he wished to cultivate—it certainly paid big dividends in
recording contracts and public acclaim. And he was happy to oblige, in a sense
to live up to what had become public expectations. Moreover, the swashbuckler
pose seemed natural to his temperament. Above all, a singer's particular "talent
has a right to itself" (to appropriate V. S. Pritchett's defense of a writer's style in
the face of persistent criticism).[2] It was a grand career, especially in his prime years
(that is, before fate dealt him a bad hand). Still, his musicianship, intelligence, and
self-knowledge could have dictated a somewhat different career path, one that
is clearly apparent in his Monforte on this Saturday broadcast. The generalized,
broad brush of a career summary does not always give the whole picture. Some of
those early Milnes performances (and some later ones, as well) tell a story worth
hearing. This is one of them.

On this afternoon, his reading of Monforte's aria and his part in the ensuing duet are worthy to stand with the best vocalism of the era. The composer has
contrived a moment of self-revelation as Monforte longs for the son (Arrigo) who

has been lost to him. Milnes explores the emotional depths that Verdi courted, as he so often did, in father–child scenes. His tone has a sympathetic cast to it, often containing a consistently heady resonance in the upper range that augments the father's pain and serves to magnify his desire for reunion with his child. The voice is entirely at ease, superbly controlled throughout the range and at the several dynamics. When commenting on a few initial broadcast efforts in the sixties, I noted that the singer had not achieved a command of mezza voce, but that deficiency is remedied. It is proudly displayed and expertly deployed (if briefly) when the opportunity presents itself. The father dreams of future happiness and his dreams are suggestively mirrored in the baritone's song. Of course, everywhere in the opera he handles the big moments, both of dramatic recitative and thrusting song, with his customary richness of tone. Even at his aria's close, Milnes lofts a splendid, ringing high F-sharp. Any Verdi baritone knows he must acknowledge his audience.

Each of the father–son duets is grandly vocalized by Milnes and Gedda. The less familiar act-one duet calls forth some vigorous, stentorian top tones from the tenor—and signals that he has a tendency to savor lachrymose effects. The habit can't really tarnish his manly portrayal of the much-troubled son, a young rebel perpetually conflicted by filial and patriotic claims. Because of the son's emotional dilemma, the tenor must rage and declaim with considerable force; a more robust instrument than the artistic Swede owns is called for. But Gedda gives his all whenever stout tone is required and his remarkable technical security sustains his efforts. On the other hand, the melodic contours of Arrigo's music are often enhanced by the elegance and gloss of the Opéra milieu; few *robusto* tenors (Italian or otherwise) could handle the wide-ranging phrases with the suavity that is Gedda's stock in trade. He allows himself a few rambunctious moments, but normally draws the vocal line with sensitivity and precision.

The grander duet for Monforte and Arrigo, its core familiar from employment in the overture, is given its due—which is saying a lot. Gedda's voice takes on a pointed, silvery coloration, augmented by a touch of brass, the alloy necessary to achieve the requisite impact. Milnes makes an affecting moment of the father's appeal to his son, expertly controlling Verdi's expressive phraseology; Levine, ever sensitive to the singer's art, doesn't hurry him along. At the duet's conclusion, Gedda takes up the big tune on his own, showing that he, too, can muscle its soaring phrases with a tenor's pride of possession. He infects Arrigo's solo moment ('Voi per me qui gemete') with self-pity, but I have nothing but admiration for his ease in the aria's high tessitura. This artist is celebrated for his unique command of *voix mixte* and twice he applies it to a high note of the aria; the first try is rather white and soprano-like, but the second is a beautifully colored tone—his technical expertise is always on call. Nothing wrong, either, with the pair of ringing high Bs that he lofts at the aria's end. *Robusto* or no, he brilliantly declaims a critical moment in the long duet with Elena when Arrigo affirms that he has reclaimed the right to die as a patriot. The tenor is able to sound both the high C and D of the final-act duet, producing a rather weird effect as tones go, but nevertheless firm and resolute. Few colleagues would attempt the feat—the audience doesn't quite know what to make of it. I would be remiss not to note the sureness of touch that soprano and tenor exhibit as they execute Verdi's challenging cadenza at the close of their first duet. And a word of approbation must be said for the singers' aplomb in the unaccompanied (barring a few orchestral interjections) quartet. Usually, those a capella episodes are folly laden, but our group of superb musicians brings it off not merely with honor but with admirable result. Milnes is the hero of the quartet, deft and musical, rich toned when the lead is his, but modest in the walking repetitions at its close. The artists respect the composer's (and the conductor's) interpretive framework.

Caballé is in wondrous vocal form. Her several vocal qualities are held in perfect equilibrium on this afternoon. The voice is firm and warmly colored in both the middle and top ranges, and devoid of any trace of acidity at maximum volume; as expected, her tones are dulcet and ethereally breathed when luxuriating in the *piano* dynamic. Chest voice is pungent where needed and free of the ugly graininess that she sometimes has favored. Her command of coloratura is fluent, graceful, and easy. And she is dramatically involved. One cannot always count upon verisimilitude in a Caballé portrayal—she has been known to become overly involved with her own voice, a case of mutual self-love. Today, evidence of her dramatic commitment comes early. Verdi has provided Elena with a lengthy introductory *scena*; its several sections are perfectly calculated to show off our soprano's vocal and interpretive gifts. A Sicilian officer (Dobriansky, his bass sounding comfortably mustachioed—handle-barred, preferably) commands the heroine to entertain his troops with a song. Vocal aficionados perk up when a librettist authorizes a set piece in this manner. Verdi obliged with a varied setting, converting its several moods to dramatic purpose as the patriotic duchess arouses the French populace to near rebellion. The Spanish soprano's recitatives are dignified and given a breadth of utterance worthy of a leader of the folk. Her slow cantilena is expertly fashioned; a long upward portamento to a *pianissimo* high note (as exquisite as a newly budded flower) reminds us of her fondness for similar effects. When blending her registers in mid-voice, she must keep close watch over pitch, but she is on her guard this afternoon; the demerit fails to interrupt our pleasure. The cabaletta-like close with chorus allows her to toss off flashes of fioriture with admirable fluency; a few full-throated high Cs add to the excitement. She caps off the coda with another top C, this time a silvery thread of tone. At several points in the score, Verdi has written half-step descending lines that begin high above the staff. Caballé is just the soprano to execute them with intervallic exactitude, superb control, and disembodied tone. Contrast moments like those with her fervid calls for vengeance and you recognize an artist who is able to paint upon a large canvas—the brush may be broad or fine, at will.

Gedda confides that during the second-act finale Caballé "fainted and fell to the floor," but "came around."[3] He had worried as to how they would negotiate the great duet that began the following act, but notes that she "managed without further mishap." Indeed she does, for in that extended love duet (Verdi's act four; act three, scene one at the Met), the soprano's vocal command again impresses. When she confesses her love for Arrigo in tones of heavenly beauty, the soprano revels in artistic subtleties. But niceties are hardly her only assets. At one point, she executes a scale from high C in a downward cascade over more than two octaves, a spectacularly daring flight. Her Bolero is as fleet and fluent as one might wish. Petit point is her chosen métier for this divertissement. Levine allows her to linger over a few phrases, and she draws them with a fine discretion. The delightful party piece might profit from keener articulation—boleros should sparkle rhythmically—but the soprano substitutes her own brand of charm, delicious in itself. A few stunning top notes heighten the opera denouement's grandeur.

Levine was right to enthuse as he did. The *Vespri* performance is one of the most polished, satisfying broadcast offerings of recent seasons. And a large part of the credit belongs to the young maestro. Verdi did more than his share. The work's melodic bounty, its numerous opportunities for solo display, the variety of ensemble play (including the spacious duets), the intricate orchestral effects, and several compelling theatrical strokes (including offstage chanting monks—shades of *Don Carlo*) are all handled with authority by the still developing composer. The company offered *Vespri* again in the next season, but soon it sank back into Metropolitan oblivion. Perhaps the poverty of Svoboda's visual setting worked against repertory stability.

As Randall remarked, Levine was the Met's principal conductor, but Kubelik went him one better as music director of the company, short-lived though his eminence would be. The Czech conductor stayed long enough to take on the monumental task of bringing Berlioz's *Les Troyens* to the Metropolitan stage for the first time. On the broadcast (16 March 1974) immediately following the *Vespri* airing, we hear the result of his tutelage. In the large cast are Verrett (Cassandre), Ludwig (Didon), Blegen (Ascagne), Dunn (Anna), Kraft (Hécube), Riegel (Iopas), Goeke (Hylas), Lewis (Hélénus), Quilico (Chorèbe), and Macurdy (Narbal). At the center of their concerns is that noblest of tenors, Vickers. Énée is yet another of the independent singer's pivotal career assumptions. At Kubelik's request and with good result, John Nelson is the guest choral master. He will conduct the performances of the following season.

Kubelik's acquaintance with the rare opera, unlike his Metropolitan tenure, was long-lived. He had conducted a famous production at Covent Garden in 1957, a pioneering effort in bringing *Les Troyens* into the repertory. His deep knowledge of its complex makeup as well as his regard for the work are fully apparent in his magisterial treatment of the score. Its varied musical construct and dramatic intensity are well realized in his performance. There are cuts, but what we hear is memorable. The overall impression conveyed is one of tremendous vitality— Berlioz's flamboyant orchestral sonorities are its source, but Kubelik's dynamic management of them sustains the composer's intent. The exultant originality of Berlioz's imagination fills the airwaves. Not all is ferment, of course. (In an intermission discussion of the opera, David Stivender, intending to show how "inclusive" the composer was, asserts that "everything is dumped in." Downes, playing the schoolmaster, is unwilling to let that stand, admitting that dumped in though it be, "everything is wonderfully calculated."[4]). To travel along the composer's unpredictable paths makes for an invigorating afternoon at the opera. Whatever his means, whether "everything" is dumped in or calculated—in actuality, it is more likely a little of both—Berlioz's exploitation of the age-old conflict between the rights and needs of the state and the individual continually leads thought and feeling in unexpected directions.

In multiple ways, time is the conductor's minion. Kubelik acutely propels the composer's brass eruptions; in contrast, he all but stops time's clock in the reposeful moments when Iopas and Hylas offer their songs and, in particular, during the moving pantomime of Andromache, where orchestral tone-painting mirrors her restrained grief. Berlioz often paints on an intimate scale and Kubelik affection-

Shirley Verrett as Cassandre in *Les Troyens*. Photography by Louis Mélançon.
Courtesy Metropolitan Opera Archives.

ately nurses the many solo and novel instrumental combinations. He encourages the pliant shaping of phrases, from both those onstage and in the pit. On the other hand, it is the conductor's sure command of the opera's immense architectural makeup that is his greatest contribution to the performance's success. He brings into focus the conflicting worlds of Troy and Carthage, balancing the former's classical formality with the rhapsodic romanticism of the lover's music.

At the October 1973 premiere, Verrett had assumed the roles of Cassandre and Didon. Ludwig, scheduled for the Carthaginian queen, was unable to sing the dress rehearsal. (Rankin was the disappointed cover who did not gain the prize of the premiere performance.) Management determined, even after Ludwig averred that she could sing opening night after all, that Verrett should undertake the dual assignment. She scored a triumph.[5] For the broadcast, both singers are in their assigned positions (Verrett as Cassandre, Ludwig as Didon) and both perform with responsive control over their luxurious instruments. Both singers' command of their roles, assignments so divergent in character and musical manner, are remarkably assured. Yet the opera might have been better served if the roles had been reversed. I do not suggest that either artist fails to bring her character to life or to embrace her music with wholehearted commitment. Miss Ludwig's voice possesses notable tonal security, its gleaming surface impenetrably solid. Her technical control is a wonder; she is capable of lofting Didon's expansive phrases with savory tone and poised dramatic involvement. Grandeur of utterance is hardly her only weapon. At several moments in Didon's death monologue ('Je vais mourir'), she turns her thoughts inward, adopting a quiet, intimate tone for an affecting farewell to her sister and to her city. As she recalls phrases of the love duet, she spins a lingering mezza voce top tone to magical effect, its silvery cast quite unusual for so timbrally dense a voice as the Berlin-born singer owns. (Hearing her, I find it hard to believe—but believe I must, for so she claims in her memoirs—that she was "indifferent" to much of the composer's music.[6]) Her interpretive range is wide. When, in her opening scene, Didon greets her subjects, Ludwig sends along little runs with fluid ease, but as the monarch urges her people to prepare for war, the mezzo's tones and manner are replete with authority. The queen's royal stance is honored, but more importantly (and more extensively) the woman's heart is exposed. Ludwig's emotional range is large. But nobility most becomes her instrument and her art.

Verrett's instrument is the voice of love (Didon's all-consuming plight) and it invites our affection in return. She serves Cassandre, the prophetess, more than well. Of greater limpidity and with a more engaging float than Ludwig's imperious instrument, the voice is marked by a timbral darkness that is both beautiful and evocative. Its haunting quality breathes an aura of other times; thus Cassandre's prophetic visions gain in credibility and impact, aided also by Verrett's fervid utterance. In her lengthy opening monologue ('Malheureux roi!'), the voice fairly weeps with pain or compassion as she warns of impending disaster. While the mezzo can purl tones of bewitching color and fluidity, she can deploy its proud magnitude as well. The climaxes are thrillingly encompassed with a top voice of considerable amplitude. A few phrases in the mid-low range are less effectively projected, but overall her vocalism, emotion laden and stalwart, is compelling.

Berlioz has filled his canvas with numerous portraits that, in spite of their relative brevity, command our attention; many of them have set pieces filled with

Christa Ludwig as Didon in *Les Troyens*. Photography by Louis Mélançon. Courtesy Metropolitan Opera Archives.

songful phrases. The Met has a talented roster of artists who operate just below divo or diva status and makes fine use of them today. Though all give performances of thorough professionalism and secure vocalism, their portrayals, or at least a number of them, register a notch below what is ideally required. The fit of artist and role is just not quite as tight as it might be. Quilico, for instance, offers advice and sings his love songs to Cassandre with commendable assurance, but years spent in the Verdi baritone Fach have roughened his tone, denying it the ability to conduct the French line with the collected refinement that it deserves. Goeke, too, sings well and his tenor is an attractive, youthful instrument, but it lacks the sheen that can turn Hylas' song of the fields into a sympathetic diversion, creating the atmospheric mood that Berlioz sought before the agitated denouement. Clifford Harvuot, nearing the end of almost three decades of valiant service with the company, owns a baritone of somber character and declaims well, but the descending intonations of Hector's Ghost would be better served by a cavernous bass. Macurdy is one of the company's most valuable artists, hailed for the variety of his portrayals and the solidity of his vocalism, but his timbre is hardly elegant. Indeed, today it is touched by a slight uncouthness—perhaps that is a subtle bit of characterization, since Didon's minister plays an equivocal game as he cautions his queen. Richard T. Gill gives Panthus sufficient stature.

Among the women players, Blegen and Dunn are both effective. The young soprano plays the young son of Énée and thus her light tones are appropriate, though in the midrange they do not project as well as they might. Dunn, on the other hand, gives yet another of her prime quality portrayals. The duet of the sisters (Anna and Didon) is a highlight of the afternoon, the rich timbres of Dunn and Ludwig intertwining to charming effect, their mellifluous exchanges especially poignant within the highly charged dramatic milieu of the opera. Should there be greater contrast between their voices? Perhaps—but then the blend is satisfying as a musical sonority in itself. When Dunn and Macurdy combine in their musings on Didon's emotional state, their vocal colorations complement their points of view. The mezzo's lighthearted play is delightful. I have saved Riegel's Iopas for last. Unlike Goeke, Riegel owns an instrument of distinctive coloration, bright but not harsh—a tenor type suited to the romantic exploits of Hoffmann, for instance. Its character on this afternoon is quite different from that with which he endowed David in the *Meistersinger* broadcast. The French milieu may well be his home: his accurate attack on the high C (heady in resonance) near the end of Iopas' song is as accomplished as his artful voicing of the entire piece.

I have chronicled with admiration the compelling vocalism and forceful characterizations of our two leading ladies. By the opera's end, however, it is Vickers' Énée that registers most strongly. He had played the role in Kubelik's 1957 Covent Garden presentations. Many years have passed since he entered upon the international operatic scene with that celebrated portrayal. One might well wonder if he could re-create it in similarly memorable fashion. Evidently he had been unable to do so at the premiere, or at least that was the word of one of America's most astute critics, who found his voice a "rather ungainly instrument" in a role that "he does not sing very well."[7] Since that review appears in the *Annals* supplement, it is widely circulated. My analysis of Vickers' portrayal at a date almost five months after the premiere is markedly different. The broadcasts have value in that they often provide opportunity for another appraisal of an important portrayal.

On the broadcast, Vickers is in magnificent voice from start to finish. The mannerisms that disturb detractors (and many admirers as well) are in abeyance. (I might mention one, negligible though it is: a kind of "bellows" effect caused by diminishing the tone after taking the note. It afflicts only a few tones in the duet.) He bursts upon the scene, trumpeting the dramatic recitatives that announce Laocoön's death in sizable, but compact, tones, coppery in coloration, and forceful in impact. Berlioz's compositional gambits are exciting in themselves, but Vickers ups the ante with his commanding declamation. Obviously, a hero has arrived. Didon in turn recognizes him as such and accepts his aid in defending Carthage. Why would she not, since the tenor flings out phrases with daunting authority? The high B-flat is as firm and shining as the metal of the real Énée's breastplate. (Vickers' cover Énée William Lewis claims that Vickers always fudged or muffed a few of the role's notorious top notes.[8]) His notes glisten with a golden brilliance before they drop momentarily into baritonal softness as Énée regards Didon. The tenor indeed sounds like a true 'son of the goddess' (Venus), as Didon names him in an aside.

In a later scene, Vickers works a dramatic reverse when he quietly recounts Andromache's fate, the narration causing Didon's violent reaction. Both Ludwig and Vickers, in their separate phrases, launch the grand sequence of quintet, septet with chorus, and love duet with rich, firm complementing tones and expansive phrasing. A bit of *arioso* in the quintet is lovingly laid out by the tenor at a middle dynamic, confirming the stability of Vickers' instrument. The vocal command and dramatic charisma that the tenor has demonstrated thus far are riveting, but he surprises with the magnificence of his vocalism in the love duet. Ludwig, too, sings with comparable control and affective impact. With such large-scale voices, the interpretation is necessarily majestically rendered, rather than intimately murmured; the prescribed moonlight of the setting evidently shone several shades brighter than the heavens normally decree. In the final act, Vickers' dramatic recitatives and aria are even more impressive. There he soars into the upper range with tones of heroic size, resplendent and aureate, entirely focused and assured. The febrile excitement of 'Inutiles regrets' is stunning, the emotional commitment as astonishing as his fearless vocalism. This is Vickers at peak form. According to his biographer, the tenor himself felt that Énée was, from the vocal standpoint, his "finest accomplishment."[9]

Perhaps Kubelik's mission during his few months with the company was fore-ordained: namely, to bring *Les Troyens* to the Metropolitan public. The sheer scope of the opera, scenically and musically, commands so much of a company's resources that it was fated to be a sometime repertory thing. It would reappear sporadically—indeed rarely—over the next two decades, each reappearance enhancing its merit and reaffirming its sui generis importance in the history of opera.

Join me in a traumatic leap from Berlioz' turbulent antiquity to Benjamin Britten's contemplative landscape in his setting of Thomas Mann's *Death in Venice*—different terrestrial worlds, contrasting musical environments. The Metropolitan responded to the British premiere of June 1973 with uncharacteristic alacrity, first offering the work on 18 October 1974. The broadcast followed on 14 December 1974. As in the premiere at Snape, Peter Pears is Aschenbach and John Shirley Quirk assumes the seven varied baritone characterizations. The smaller roles are taken by Velis (Apollo), Garrison (Porter/Tourist), Frederick Burchinal

Death in Venice
14 December 1974

Aschenbach
Peter Pears
Seven Roles
John Shirley-Quirk
Apollo
Andrea Velis
Conductor
Steuart Bedford

(English clerk/Father), and, in the catalytic nonsinging role of Tadzio, ballet dancer Bryan Pitts. Steuart Bedford, who had baptized the opera at Snape, conducts
the broadcast.

For almost a decade, Bedford had been associated with Britten's English Opera Group. Most of his energies were focused there, although a secondary interest in Donizetti's little-known operas also occupied his talents. Not only had the
London-born and based conductor been in at the birthing of the opera, he would
continue to guide it (as well as other Britten operas) into adolescence. Whether
full adulthood, in terms of repertory acceptance, is in the cards for *Death in Venice*
remains a matter of conjecture. But the young conductor's authoritative reading
of the opera on the broadcast can be readily accepted. He understands, and conveys to us, the constantly varied sound world that the composer has devised as a
counterweight to the single-minded dramaturgy of the opera. In his mid-thirties
at the time of the Met premiere, Bedford will return to conduct *Le Nozze di Figaro*
during the next season.

In reality, the opera has only two leading parts (though one of them wears
multiple disguises). With the exception of a few lines sung by the voice of Apollo
(originally for countertenor, but performed in falsetto by Velis), the remainder of
the brief solo roles, which number two dozen or more, are taken by members of
the Metropolitan Studio. The fledgling singers (a few of them considerably more
than novices), trainees in the company's young artists program, add a fresh, appealing sonority to the performance, whether in their solo moments or in the important ensembles. Their healthy young voices provide a vivid contrast to Pears'
sophisticated, world-weary sounding of Aschenbach's turmoil. Of special note are
Emily Golden (the French Mother and the Beggar Woman) and, in a more important role, Frederick Burchinal (Jaschiu's Father and the English clerk). In the
latter vignette, the composer grants the travel office clerk a lengthy accompanied recitative in which he informs Aschenbach of the cholera that is spreading
throughout Venice. Burchinal's baritone is solid but, at this youthful period of
his career, of no particular timbral distinction. Like the other American singers,
he sings the text with clarity. His obvious competence does not quite forecast the
notable career he will have in European theaters and his eventual return to the
Metropolitan as a leading Verdi baritone late in the next decade. The narrative
episode at the travel office is a telling one, although much of its impact depends,
as do so many moments in the opera, on the orchestral underpinning rather than
the vocal line. Here, and in an even more important later episode for Aschenbach
at the opera's close, it is Myfanwy Piper's text, rather than Britten's setting for the
voice, that commands attention.

In the seven baritone roles that may be grouped under the general title of
Aschenbach's nemeses, John Shirley-Quirk contributes greatly to the performance's
success. At first (as the Traveler), his instrument seems rather nondescript, but that
is probably a cagey dodge to allow for varied tonal qualities and musico-dramatic
stances to differentiate his many chores. We hear his basic, attractive timbre most
clearly as the Hotel Manager and, even more, as the Barber. In the latter role, the
singer alternates between a velvety legato and a sprightly staccato that is symbolic
of his snipping profession; the gesture amusingly penetrates the orchestral fabric
as well. (Britten was "not afraid of pictorial effects," Bedford tells us in his intermission commentary.[10]) Legato is his chosen mode whenever the Barber lapses into

Peter Pears and Myfanwy Piper at reception following the Metropolitan
premiere of *Death in Venice* on 18 October 1974.

Italian. Shirley-Quirk's unctuous 'Signore's repeatedly and dexterously lend form to the vocal line and life to the scene. His Leader of the Strolling Players does a job on the Popular and Laughing Songs—he plays in an earthy, grubby fashion, the manner a relative (though Italianate) of music-hall style. Britten wrote the virtuoso assignment of seven roles specifically for Shirley-Quirk. The British baritone, born in Liverpool, had begun his career in 1961 at Glyndebourne and soon came under Britten's aegis (as the Ferryman in *Curlew River*); thereafter, he created roles in each of the composer's new operas. Even in the broadcast performance, one can hear his success at making, as he said, each character "recognizably the same and yet recognizably different," thereby creating a "continuity of character if not of characteristics."[11] Shirley-Quirk would not return to the Met until 1979, when he would be heard as the Music Master (*Ariadne*) and the Speaker (*Zauberflöte*).

Having specified two leading roles, I note that a third character plays a pivotal role in the drama. He is Tadzio, the young Polish boy whom Aschenbach fatefully learns to love. The character, symbolic of so many philosophic concepts (or put more simply, points of view), is mimed by a dancer. He neither speaks nor sings. Britten, however, has given him his own "leitmotiv," a melody in the Lydian mode, and introduced a unique instrumental sound (a vibraphone) when the writer sees Tadzio for the first time. Moreover, when the boy and his friends engage in games on the beach, the orchestral sonority is confined to percussion instruments, of which the xylophone is prominent. Thus, even the radio audience is always aware of Tadzio's presence on the scene. It seems to me that Britten has not been entirely successful in the music he has conceived for the games. The idea of a gamelan simulation to accompany them is a good one, but he has not brought it off—the novelty of the xylophone, marimba, and glockenspiel soon wears off. (Occasionally, the sounds suggest Chinatown as the playground locale. The musical gestures and sonorities are so insistent and repetitive that the hint of an Eastern milieu creeps into Western minds.) Undoubtedly, the stage action aided in holding the interest in these episodes, but they do run on; in particular, the Dionysian dances in Aschenbach's dream sequence wear out their welcome. The composer is far more successful in other episodes of the opera. There, the orchestra, most often in chamber-size combinations, is handled with imagination and taste, the evocative atmosphere well sustained throughout each short scene. In his radio commentary—both the precurtain and intermission features are more agreeable and informative than most of their "educational" ilk—Bedford aptly emphasizes Britten's "economy" in *Death in Venice*, noting that "he doesn't use anything more than is necessary."[12] We are a far cry from that so-called organizational principle of Berlioz where "everything is dumped in."

Now to the heart of the matter, Peter Pears' portrayal of Aschenbach. The tenor, sixty-three years of age at broadcast time and the veteran of a long and distinguished career, is in excellent voice. His control over his unique instrument is near complete. Only in the opening scene does one feel he is marshaling his skill to pull the voice into line; the need to steady tone, to direct it into a legato flow clouds his diction. Thereafter, every word is intelligible. Often, he is aided in that effort by Britten, who has set large portions of Aschenbach's speech in recitative accompanied solely by piano. But Pears offers much that rests on his own merit. Most notable is the quality and durability of the voice itself. His instrument is memorably distinctive, its timbre for many an acquired taste; moreover, it is a taste that, once acquired, may be rejected about two-thirds through a performance as the ear wearies of its often reedy cast. Aural weariness is an ever-present danger in this opera, a work that is essentially a tenor monologue with diversionary episodes. But, wonder of wonders, the voice acquires multiple timbral felicities as the opera proceeds and it gains in thrust and power as well. Built into the instrument, at least at this point in his career, are three distinct sonorities: a grainy baritonal lower voice with an attractive burr or, occasionally, a rasp, the latter employed for expressive purposes; a reedy middle voice; and—most striking—an upper extension that can be heady, almost soprano-like. But, when needed for dramatic pronouncements of short duration, the voice can, even at this late stage, take on quite amazing strength and vibrancy throughout its entire range. Of course, Britten has cannily plotted the role, not only to show off his old friend and partner's best qualities, but to provide him with opportunities to spell himself. The latter is particularly important, since Aschenbach is onstage virtually throughout the entire almost two-and-a-half-hour running time. In their joint interviews, Bedford, recalling how Britten begins act two exactly at the point where act one left off, notes that one could perform the entire opera without "any interval at all." But, he opines, then both he and Pears "would probably be dead by the end—genuinely."[13]

One expects that Pears, in a role created for him, will give a definitive portrayal of Aschenbach, and he does. I was not prepared, however, for the resilience of his instrument, the immense variety of colorations, and the power and eloquence of his projection at key moments. I hope my conversion was not merely an acceptance of actuality, a recognition that, as the only Jane has it, "what prudence had at first enjoined was now rendered pleasant by habit."[14] Some of Pears' phrases are wonderfully vivid, as when (at the end of the first act) the distraught writer cries, 'Don't smile like that! No one should be smiled at like that.' There, pain and terror are realized in sound. A moment to be treasured is the tenor's artful transition from despair to sleep as the dream sequence begins. I liked particularly his sounding of the *arioso* at the end of the third scene, where Aschenbach speaks of the black gondola as 'a vision of death itself.' And here, Britten's orchestral palette is equally fascinating, its employment of glissandi and tinkling harp effects providing a haunting ambience. To hear a portrayal where every inflection, every musical nuance, and each phrase length has been studied with concern for how it will fit into an enveloping interpretative plan always gives particular pleasure. Yet another inspired interpretive moment occurs when the novelist muses upon the intertwining tendrils of Tadzio's beauty and the artist's vocation (scene four); Pears performs the difficult feat of making philosophic thought come alive. Not so, in my opinion, in the critical near-final moments of the opera (scene sixteen). There, I think Britten has let his old friend down. The lengthy recitative meditation (approaching an *arioso* and accompanied by piano and harp) lacks a distinctive musical construct. It need not necessarily be melodic, but it ought to be one that strikes the listener with its uniqueness. As Aschenbach discourses on the Platonic colloquy of Socrates and Phaedrus concerning sensuality's descent into the bleakness of passion, Pears' song revolves, over and over again, around the several notes of his upper voice in a *piano* dynamic. If we are to accept such an esoteric dialogue, lengthy and complex in subject matter, we need something more bracing than Britten has supplied. Even the silvery cast of Pears' top voice, softly intoning in the manner made memorable by his delivery of Grimes' final soliloquy, is not enough to allow the dramatic situation to speak sufficiently to serve as revelation. I am sure the dialogue's content did not faze Pears. The tenor tells Downes, in the second intermission, that he "was educated on the classical side."[15] He mentions his study of certain philosophers and confides that he still reads Latin and can handle Greek, although he admits that modern Greek confounds his youthful study of the language. Tenors don't come like that anymore—as if they ever did. Fortunately, as the final note of the Socrates discourse sounds, the composer's brass and woodwind fugato picks up the dramatic thread to provide the required climax. The quiet magic of the orchestral sonorities as Aschenbach dies and Tadzio walks toward the sea is, in quite a different way, equally telling.

When Aschenbach, early in the opera, senses his interest in the boy may be more than an artist's need for beauty, he half-speaks the line 'There is a dark side to perfection—I like that.' Pears, in a portrayal near to perfection, has been subtly showing us that side, and many more becoming facets of his art, throughout the entire afternoon.

The question remains whether the opera should have been scheduled at the Metropolitan in the first place. Britten utilized so fine an orchestral palette and relied rather heavily on accompanied recitative in this, his last opera; the Met's enormous auditorium militated against success. Bedford himself was well aware of the dangers involved in presenting the opera in so large a venue. He asked the radio audience to "reattune" their ears when listening, cautioning that if they expected to be "overwhelmed by lots of sounds," then they would have "come to the wrong opera."[16] In a way, the radio audience had the advantage over those in the house. They heard the opera in the intimacy of their homes where every nuance, vocal and instrumental, could be savored. Certainly, the opera needed to be made known to the American public and Pears' masterly creation deserved a hearing. Above all, the Met production provided an opportunity to bring one of the century's most distinguished artists to its stage for the first time. To thus honor him, and by so doing, honor itself, was probably reason enough for the Metropolitan venture. Having made the gesture, management brought the tenor back in 1978 to re-create his equally memorable Captain Vere in Britten's *Billy Budd*. Now there's an opera with staying power.

The Metropolitan pursued its admirable goal of adding neglected masterworks to its repertory by next introducing Janáček's *Jenůfa* in December of 1974. The broadcast soon followed. On 21 December radio listeners heard Teresa Kubiak in the title role, Astrid Varnay as the Sexton's Widow, William Lewis as Steva, and, in an unexpected gambit, Vickers as Laca. John Nelson conducted. As earlier noted, the opera had figured in a single previous season (1924–25). Then, Maria Jeritza, Margarete Matzenauer, Rudolf Laubenthal, and Martin Ohman sang the work in German translation under the direction of Bodanzky. The 1974 performance is sung in an English translation by Otakar Kraus and Edward Downes.

Goldovsky, in his intermission feature on the opera, provided a splendid analysis of the second act and probed the character of Kostelnicka (the Sexton's Widow) to good purpose. It is one of his best presentations, doubly valuable as an introduction of an unfamiliar opera to the radio audience. His piano playing of the musical examples is infused with almost orchestral color. In his commentary, he gives a characteristic Goldovsky performance. One shudders a bit at his dramatic

Jenůfa
21 December 1974

Jenůfa
Teresa Kubiak
Widow (Kostelnicka)
Astrid Varnay
Grandmother
Jean Kraft
Laca
Jon Vickers
Steva
William Lewis
Foreman
John Reardon
Conductor
John Nelson

impersonations of the several characters, overly emotive as they are and even unintentionally humorous as he affects different timbres for his charges. It is impossible not to enjoy his exuberance. The virtuoso performance is valuable for his insight into the opera and a fine example of his continuing role as the radio audience's operatic pied piper. Were his strenuous efforts futile? Though well received by the press, the work gained little immediate currency in the Met repertory.

Janáček's operas, especially *Jenůfa*, had already found acceptance on a number of American stages. The Metropolitan was usually a Johnny-come-lately when it came to "twentieth-century" opera. A turn-of-the-century product (composed between 1894 and 1903, and premiered in 1904 in Brno), *Jenůfa* is no folk opera, though the composer's intimate acquaintance with Moravian folksong enabled him to subtly integrate its aura into his compositional style. The work's continuous fabric nevertheless makes room for conventional forms: duets, a trio, a first-act *concertato*, and set pieces for chorus. In the musical sphere, the opera is notable for the innovative use of speech melody in the vocal parts and for considerable orchestral ingenuity; as drama, the composer's humane and heartfelt expression of passionate emotions is front and center. The situations and character confrontations are strong stuff, and yet, quite amazingly, lyricism blooms often, either in short bursts or at some length, unexpected, satisfying, capturing our attention and evoking our sympathy.

You may recall that Nelson, at Kubelik's insistence, had served as guest chorus master for *Les Troyens* during the 1973–74 season. He had in fact conducted the work for his Met podium debut just a week after the premiere under Kubelik. *Jenůfa*, his second assignment with the company, was his own property. One of Jean Morel's products at the Juilliard School, he had begun his pit career at the New York City Opera (1972 with *Carmen*) and conducted a concert version of *Troyens* in that year at Carnegie Hall. The latter occasion had stimulated Kubelik's interest in him. The *Jenůfa* broadcast shows us why. The young conductor (thirty-three at broadcast time) sends the turbulent score along with almost breathless propulsion, each contrast that escaped from the composer's febrile pen made more vivid than the last. But it is not mere youthful spirits that sustain his reading. His command of the score is sure, his integration of orchestral and stage forces astute, not only in their precise mating, but in his pointing up of the focal relationship between the vocal lines and their orchestral counterparts. As a result, a unique synergy between the characters and the orchestra occurs. Nelson understands that the composer's favored technique of infusing the complex orchestral tapestry with motives just sounded in the vocal line is not only an organizational tool, but also the agent of the opera's remarkable dramatic tension. Nelson was a talent that the Met might well have claimed for its own. The symphonic realm beckoned in 1976 when the Indianapolis Symphony took him on for an extended tenure. But opera was in his blood. Santa Fe and Lyon would both know his expertise, and his 1985 appointment as music director of the Opera Theatre of St. Louis ensured that the novice company would profit from his enterprising spirit and his orchestral mastery.

Miss Kubiak is new to our chronicle. Before she undertook Jenůfa, her first venture in the role, the Polish soprano had set foot on the Met stage on a single occasion, as Lisa in *Pique Dame* in January 1973. She would remain a company member for nine seasons over the next dozen years. Five years of appearances in

Lodz had led to her 1970 American debut in Goldmark's *Königen von Saba* at Carnegie Hall. Appearances in Chicago (Tosca, and Ellen Orford with Vickers) and San Francisco (Aida) followed. The roles listed tell us that hers is a healthy instrument, essentially a big lyric soprano. It has most of the virtues and few of the faults of the Slavic-trained soprano. Not for her the acidulous clang of timbre in the upper range or the pervasive tremulousness which can undermine that species' fearsome vocalism. Kubiak's top is her prime weapon. Large and secure, its attractive cutting edge is cushioned by tonal voluptuousness. Moreover, the singer is not loath to spend its capital in generous and spirited outbursts. When the drunken Steva enters, he encounters a blast of soprano tone that should have sobered any alcoholic. We gain another measure of her merit in her quiet, touching vocalism when she and Steva contest over their delayed marriage. But her full-voiced, vibrant exchanges with Laca at the end of the first act show her in home territory. Alone and confused after Kostelnicka has rushed off with her child, Kubiak handles the mood swings of the desperate Jenůfa with complete understanding of her character's plight, her song vacillating between affecting pleading and despair. Her instrument accommodates both modes without losing its natural appeal.

Still, innocence is no part of her timbre. The character would profit from a sound more suggestive of youth, notwithstanding that *Jenůfa*'s has been despoiled by the heartless Steva. And there remains that matter of demerits. In her case, the hint of a gargle imperils the tone in the mid-low range; one has noted it in Slavic women's voices (the excellent Tomowa-Sintow could be guilty of it). Then too, in fast syllabic passages the tone can turn scratchy, a not uncommon trait in voices whose passport to fame is luscious tonal appeal. All is forgiven, however, when in the opera's final moments, Jenůfa agrees to marry Laca. In one of opera's most moving moments, the heroine tells Laca that 'You sinned when you cut my cheek out of love, just as I, too, sinned out of love'; the newfound bond between the lovers exemplifies Janáček's embracing humanity. Kubiak's thrilling top voice and ardent manner enhance this cathartic episode. She is at her best when she can pour out tone with ecstatic generosity, which is exactly what the composer asks of his Jenůfa at the curtain's fall. Though her seasonal tallies with the company would not be overlarge, they held a wide range of roles. Before the decade was out, Met audiences would hear Kubiak as Amelia, Chrysothemis, Giorgetta, Elisabeth (*Tannhaüser*), Butterfly, Tatiana, and Senta. A soprano who can move effectively between the Italian and German milieus is obviously a singer to be prized by a repertory company like the Met.

Throughout the afternoon, clear projection of the English translation is an on-and-off thing. In that regard, Kubiak is the greatest offender—quite naturally, since she is the only non-English-speaking singer in the cast and had only begun to study the language in the last year. She has some moments of clarity in quiet moments, but in the opening act, in particular, one almost despairs of the performance, so incomprehensible are many of her lines. (In her defense, one must acknowledge that unintelligibility is the curse of the singer who operates in the soprano range. Many of them, even in their native language, have not solved the problem of how to combine word and tone, each subtly compromised, into a communicative unity.) Despair departs, however, when a few of the singers of smaller parts appear on the scene. (Of course, Vickers—who, parenthetically, would burst the seams of any small part—is a past master at letting us hear the words.) Kraft and Reardon figure among the reaffirmers, forming their words for maximum comprehensibility. The mezzo's authoritative portrayal of Grandmother Buryja holds some of her most becoming vocalism; she launches the ensemble with good tone and sturdy phrasing. (Oddly, her blessing in the final act is afflicted with a wide tremolo.) Reardon's mill foreman, so cleanly voiced and clearly articulated, is a welcome breath of normalcy when he first enters upon the scene. His lines are few, but their impact is great. Norden, heard as the young boy Jano, whom Jenůfa has taught to read, always drives her points home. Her crystal timbre does most of the job for her. Alma Jean Smith, making her broadcast debut as Steva's prospective bride, Karolka, has a voice of bright timbre and sufficient presence to make her worth watching. As the judge, Richard T. Gill offers a representative example of firm bass tone blended with clean diction, the two neatly poised within a compact legato.

Lewis occupies second-tenor status on this afternoon, and, while he cannot hope to eclipse the mighty Vickers, he seems determined to escape from the Canadian's enveloping shadow. His characterization of the thoughtless Steva is detailed and entirely convincing. The American tenor has the careless stance of the playboy down pat. His song, securely projected, reeks of selfishness and conceit. Emotional extravagance is Steva's mode of expression, whether tormenting Jenůfa with his affairs or reacting with a coward's fear to Kostelnicka's insistence that he marry her foster daughter. Lewis succeeds at both extremes. On some broadcasts, the reliable singer's instrument has lacked individuality or timbral distinction. Today the voice has color, the tone is well focused. Above all, he sings with conviction, turning the outcast of the principal quartet into a potent force in the drama.

Vickers gives one of his characteristic performances. For some, that could be a damning phrase—but not today. The Canadian tenor operates at so high a level of intensity that his stage performances become living projections of his inner self. His portrayal of the bitter Laca is a worthy companion to his larger-than-life representations of Grimes, Samson, and Otello. The voice is in prime shape, the upper register secure and ringing with tone of exceptional density and vibrant color. Even there, his diction is clear. Crooning, that lapse of which he is so often accused, is entirely forsworn. A few might find his treatment of phrase and line a shade overly naturalistic—they flow with a liquid ease that is rather distinct from the more traditional treatment of his colleagues. Portamentos and an occasional slide in or out of a phrase curve can startle. These attributes may well be his attempt to replicate the more fluent idiom of the Czech language. (Though he performed the role in translation, Vickers had indeed sought out a Czech to discover how the original Czech text would be sung.[17]) Or he may be merely affirming his position as the Brando of the operatic stage. His way is as individualistic as that actor's and, in the operatic milieu, he looms as large.

On this afternoon, Vickers' voice blazes forth with complete security, its magnificence quite undimmed by the years. Its heroic size and brilliance continue to amaze, while his control over it remains certain. And he can turn the tables and suddenly caress a sentiment with the utmost tenderness, as he does whenever Laca's love for Jenůfa unexpectedly swells. 'Those cheeks red like roses' is a phrase replete with longing when Vickers repeats Steva's words. 'Won't you take my hand now?' he pathetically asks Jenůfa after Kostelnicka has murdered the child—our hope for her assent becomes as strong as his. But when the mill foreman calls him

'Madman! Madman!' at the end of the first act, so outsized is Vickers' performance that we are tempted to agree. A distinctive feature of his portrayal is the sharp outline he gives to specific short motives; their rhythms and contours are explicitly articulated to resonate in turn in the orchestra, the tenor making clear to us Janáček's compositional method. In their final duet, he soars in the upper ranges of his voice with a thrust and abandon that complements Kubiak's ecstatic song.

Varnay, the heroine of many a Met broadcast during the forties and early fifties, returns to the company after an absence of eighteen years. During that extended hiatus (and even before, coincident in fact with the last years of her Met soprano tenure) she had become a revered favorite of the Bayreuth stage, a creature of Wieland Wagner's innovative productions. Other leading German houses had welcomed her intense, passionate portrayals, especially after Mr. Bing and she came to the parting of the ways in 1956. (Of her relations with the former manager, the soprano remarks that they were "as good as was possible with him."[18] With characteristic honesty, she adds that "we both had our cynicism.") When time dictated a change of Fach, its warnings were heeded, if perhaps not welcomed. Now in her mid-fifties, the onetime soprano had operated in the mezzo range for a decade or more.

Her Kostelnicka had been heard and seen in London, Munich, Düsseldorf, and Vienna. The role is a demanding one, not only dramatically—and one can be sure that Varnay's stage command made her a riveting figure—but, more threateningly for this aging singer, vocally. Numerous large-scale outbursts with critical high notes are the prime obstacles. In the first half of the opera, it is apparent that the Varnay voice, never entirely tractable even in her youth, is hardly a well-oiled instrument. One fears that her later Begbick-type constricted vocalism (as heard in the 1979 *Mahagonny* performances) would make her reappearance merely an event for nostalgia, one made palatable only by the memory of earlier triumphs. Thirty-three years is a daunting time span when measured in terms of an operatic career on the leading stages of the world. Yet other great Wagnerian sopranos have continued to sing the composer's heroines when well into their fifties; but then, most have not made their Met debuts at age twenty-three as Sieglinde and tackled the *Walküre* Brünnhilde a week later. On this afternoon, memory's forgiveness turns out to be, mercifully, not merely a crutch. The second act belongs to Kostelnicka, and when Varnay enters upon the critical scene with Steva ("one of the most pathetic episodes in the entire operatic literature," as Goldovsky put it), her vocalism quite miraculously undergoes a sea change. Great artists have a way of rising to their material. Varnay does on this occasion. The voice (granitic in its solidity, especially on high, still immense in size, and possessed of its uniquely opaque density) begins to sound very like the formidable instrument that made her Elektra sovereign.

Of course, it is not quite the same, not quite as consistently fine—strain still occasionally nudges into the line. But overall, the revenant's second-act scenes with Steva and Laca are an impressive display of vocal power and theatrical art. When Kostelnicka, almost in a hallucinatory state, imagines how the villagers will taunt her about her daughter's disgrace, how they will point their fingers at her, Varnay—in the upper reaches of her voice—pounds out Janáček's descending scale motive with demonic emphases, each note a sledgehammer blow, as though compelling the orchestra to magnify her torment, her fears. They do, repeating the motive over and over. It is a towering moment, the kind of revelation, brief though it be, that perhaps only an artist of Varnay's capabilities could elevate to comparable stature. The episode reminds us that aging artists often have something uniquely their own to offer. In a few quieter moments (when alone with Jenůfa, and later, when the mother confesses that it was fear of her own disgrace, rather than the need to save her daughter from humiliation, that caused her to drown Jenůfa's child) the singer retreats to a humbler utterance, summoning sympathy for the once proud, authoritative moralist. Her portrayal gives legitimacy to Janáček's original title for the opera, commonly translated as *Her Foster Daughter*.

In spite of the triumphant entry of Janáček's opera into the Metropolitan repertory, it would not be heard again by the radio audience for a dozen years. *Jenůfa* would recur thereafter at sporadic intervals. Permanent repertory status should have been its fate, but evidently time was needed before the Janáček mystique could penetrate the conservative breasts of a large portion of the Metropolitan public. The discovery of many other of the composer's imaginative creations remained a happy prospect. But it would be a while.

Remaining for the moment in middle Europe, I turn my attention to Bartók's *Bluebeard's Castle* (*A Kékszakállú herceg vára* in the original Hungarian). The Metropolitan introduced the one-act opera to the radio audience on 22 February 1975. It had first presented the work during a special June Festival season of the preceding year. At that time, and in the broadcast, Shirley Verrett (Judith) and David Ward (Duke Bluebeard) sang in English under Ehrling's direction. The work was coupled with *Gianni Schicchi*.

In contrast to its early championing of Britten's *Death in Venice*, the Met failed to climb on the Bartók bandwagon early on. Janáček redux. After decades of neglect, the Hungarian composer at mid-century had become a pillar of twentieth-century composition, his instrumental works heard everywhere. Even *Bluebeard*, premiered in Budapest in 1918, had gained unexpected réclame with productions in many of the capitals of Europe. In America, the New York City Opera beat the Met to the punch with an early mounting (1952), and San Francisco, Chicago, and Boston had welcomed it. Many professional symphony orchestras throughout the nation had found it an apt concert vehicle, one that lent novelty to their programming. My early acquaintance with the work came from a 1972 concert performance that the Drake University Orchestra and soloists offered during my tenure there. The rich orchestral sonorities made it a natural for symphonic programs; they serve even more effectively to sustain the opera's repute when heard in the opera house.

In regard to the Met, "better late than never" goes down a little hard, especially when the designer's concept for the new production is examined. Instead of the gracious spoken prologue that librettist Béla Balázs provided, an amplified male voice solemnly describes a contemporary world 'of war and destruction, of wealth and poverty,' naming as the 'greatest tragedy . . . the utter isolation of each man.' David Reppa is not content to allow the symbolism of the opera's libretto to speak for itself. The brief words are meant not only to drive home the central theme of the opera, but to prepare the audience for the projections which are utilized to depict the various 'secrets' that lie behind the seven doors. There, upon Judith's command to open the portals, modern images are exhibited in place of the mythic concepts of the original: airplanes and falling bombs fill the armory of

Bluebeard's Castle
22 February 1975
Judith
Shirley Verrett
Bluebeard
David Ward
Conductor
Sixten Ehrling

scene two; skyscrapers rather than jewels occupy the third recess; the weeping faces of war victims despoil the watery fountains of the sixth chamber. Modern production concepts on the Met stage ought to be encouraged, but this hodgepodge seems rather too obvious. Bartók has poured sufficient, if implicit, gloom into his various musical forms and tone-painting effects, while the bursts of light that his orchestration conjure are negated by Reppa's graphic representations. Goldovsky, in a preperformance analysis, lets the radio audience in on the decor and rather patronizingly tries to prepare them for the shock of "modern music," as though this grand score, full to the brim with radiant orchestral pictorialisms, were not readily comprehensible to any opera lover who valued Strauss and Debussy.[19]

Ehrling, like any worthy conductor, shows off the composer's imaginative orchestral palette to good purpose. During the first half—that is, up to the glorious outpouring of the C major tonality as the fifth door opens and exposes Bluebeard's extensive domain—the conductor's exploration of the multifarious symphonic fabric is a bit subdued, the separate units isolated, so that continuity suffers. The opera seems more episodic than need be. His work is never less than effective, however, and the remaining half of the opera is laid out in thrilling fashion. The aching pictorialisms and expressive force of the work are driven home, no more so than in the stunning orchestral crescendo after Bluebeard tells Judith that she is 'queen of all my women.'

In many ways, the orchestra is the most vivid protagonist when it comes to revealing the emotional content and potent symbolism of the opera. Neither Ward nor Verrett can fully contend with its magnificence and come out the victor, though the American mezzo at least gains a draw. The Scottish bass had been a reputable Wagnerian at the Met for several seasons (Hunding, the Dutchman) with appearances as Sarastro and the Grand Inquisitor further defining his métier. His is a sizable voice, but on this afternoon it lacks a commanding presence. The tone seems unnecessarily dull in coloration (gray, or at best, taupe), hollow in resonance, ill suited for a king of legendary stature and (purported) demonic authority. It may be that the timbre has been purposefully dulled down to suggest Bluebeard's loneliness, his 'utter desolation,' as the spoken prologue would have it. If so, the voice fails to take on sufficient thrust even in the king's final apostrophe to Judith, where after the crush of 'tears' at the sixth portal, the character "grows bigger," to use the bass' own words.[20] There, as Bluebeard dwells on his sorrows, Ward does indeed expand his phrasing and add body to his tone—the effect is impressive, in part because of the contrast with what has gone before. But still, one wants more in this revelatory *arioso* than he, even with an artist's clear intent, can offer. He has his moments. 'They have tended to my garden,' Bluebeard says of his former three wives, and Ward (aided by Bartók's sorcery) hits home. He responds well in yet another important moment, grandly intoning, after the spectacular C major orchestral splash, 'All my kingdom lies before you.' And yet, in the ensuing moments of this peroration, the upper voice can sound "stopped" on certain notes, the effect robbing the line of steady sonority. His diction is clean and entirely comprehensible—an annoying abundance of rolled *r*s here and there notwithstanding; that is a point in his favor. But I do not believe he fully comprehends Bartók's text setting, which is based on the typical parlando-rubato of Hungarian song-speech. The composer meant that subtle manipulation to take the curse off his syllabic setting of the text (the latter yet another instance of Debussy at work on his successors). True, in translation we cannot replicate the nuances of the original language, but the bass, for instance, need not give equal weight to the second syllable of 'Open! Open!'—in Hungarian, the first syllable is always stressed.[21]

Verrett fares better in this respect, and in many others. But then, for most of the opera, Judith is the more emotional of the married pair. And, in characteristic Verrett fashion, she plays in an openhearted manner, giving full vent to the bride's changing moods, willingly embracing in turn her anger, her love, her curiosity, her demands, her commands, her self-doubt, and her fears. The singer is not in best voice. Or perhaps, the role challenges her more than is good for her instrument— Bartók's heavy orchestra overwhelms her now and then. Ehrling allows it to do so. A little rasp can interfere with her mid-low recitation (as when Judith first asks about the seven doors) and chest voice must be unduly weighted if certain lines are to be emphatically projected. Many a time her instrument sounds fully extended. Verrett is an artist who feels compelled to "put over" a role, no matter the possible deleterious effect on her instrument. She *will* go after the big moments, and with a fierceness that satisfies her actress soul.

As the fifth door opens, a clean, slightly strained high C affirms her desire to dwell on soprano heights. When allowed to sing at a reasonable dynamic, the upper voice has its familiar burnished cast, the tone owning a liquid spin. She well knows how to exploit contrasting tone colors and qualities of expression for maximum effect. 'It's your castle,' Judith comments after hearing the wall sigh, and the mezzo's soft tones are filled with wonder—but the ensuing 'I heard your castle sighing' (in the mid-voice) is less clearly projected. When she offers her husband her love, we can hear it in her warm tone and delicate phrasing. Several unusual effects reflect her imaginative character plotting: the quiet, haunting, almost childlike tone she wafts as Judith asks about the 'tears'; the weird "harmonic" she sounds at the sixth door, which gives way to a dark, full-throated mezzo embrace of 'Behold me!'; the blunted monotone that she employs (declaiming on a single note as though in a trance) as she tells Bluebeard that she must ask the seventh question; the ghastly chest tone she summons when Judith demands that the king 'Open the seventh and last door!' Even when not ideally cast, Verrett gives a performance where thought dictates before emotion erupts.

After this season's run, Bartók's mythic opera was put into mothballs and not taken out until the 1988–89 season, when Jessye Norman's and Samuel Ramey's large talents and commanding voices thrived under Levine's leadership. For the 1975 broadcast, the opera was paired with *Gianni Schicchi*. Though out of context in this account of premieres, a few words are due that lively masterwork, which premiered in 1918, the same year as *Bluebeard*! Puccini held up his end of the bargain in his dexterous treatment of Dante's rogue and his miserly compatriots. Success is less apparent in the rendering. Ehrling begins in tentative fashion, but soon enough gains control of the intricate score. He does hold its high spirits in a slightly repressive Nordic grip, not quite allowing Italianate bedevilment to bubble up. Flagello's Schicchi won't help much in that regard for, as we know, he loves to sing. I doubt that 'Addio, Firenze' has ever been coddled so mellifluously—no harm in that. But to dictate Buoso Donati's will in a resonance that all but duplicates the natural Schicchi (that is, in this case, Flagello) voice is to turn the logic of the entire plot on its ear. The indulgence spoils the trick, doesn't it?

Gianni Schicchi
22 February 1975

Lauretta
Judith Blegen
Nella
Betsy Norden
Zita
Irene Dalis
Rinuccio
Raymond Gibbs
Schicchi
Ezio Flagello
Simone
Clifford Harvuot
Conductor
Sixten Ehrling

When he offers, in English as was the custom at the Met, his dig at Dante and asks for forgiveness from the audience, the basso does so in a conversational New York manner: Dante be damned and Lauretta's Ponte Vecchio abandoned without a backward look. The young lovers are as American as—well, choose your pie. Blegen sounds weak in much of 'O mio babbino caro,' and the low voice has a disturbing tremolo. The aria, slight but surefire, makes little effect. Raymond Gibbs does better with Rinuccio's enthusiastic paeans to Florence. The voice is narrow in compass, but bright, and youthfully appealing. Best of all, his spirit is willing. His high notes are decent and they retain their color, not lapsing into the white timbre that so many light tenors, of necessity, affect in the upper range. (He does have a bit of trouble on the first syllable of the lofty 'Schicchi,' as he correctly tries to sound the Italian pause between the Cs.) Overall, the performance seems underrehearsed. That seems incongruous. Surely the Donati kin are a close-knit family: each member undoubtedly knows all about every relative's business. These Florentines seem newly met. The enchanting trio where the women dress up Schicchi as Buoso disappoints; Betsy Norden's soprano is all point—and a charming point it is—but the others are nondescript. Elsewhere, Dalis makes most of Zita's interjections count—her long stage experience would hardly allow her to do otherwise—but she doesn't quite have the resonant chest tones that allowed Elmo and Barbieri to elevate the brief part to major status. Though Simone is probably best played by an authoritative bass, Harvuot still has plenty of voice and is effective. Anthony's few lines as Gherardo are a joy; his tenor always pokes through.

Of the two operas, Bartók's was the better served. At least over the air, Reppa's labored symbolism and intrusive projections of the terrors of the modern age could be ignored. Only the composer's imagination is allowed to summon ours in return.

Inserting *Gianni Schicchi* willy-nilly into our consciousness permits me to more easily pull out of the twentieth century and slip back a few generations into Italy's golden age of bel canto opera. Creating an opera for a specific singer, as Britten did for Pears, was nothing new in operatic history. Writing to order was virtually a way of life during the first half of the nineteenth century. Indeed, so many versions of our final Met premiere opera appeared during the first twenty-five years of its existence that any production can choose from a wealth of riches—and might turn it into a confusing polyglot in the process. The opera had a decidedly checkered past. *L'Assedio di Corinto*, broadcast on 19 April 1975, in its original form was an *opera seria* written in 1820 for Naples and titled *Maometto II*. The composer revised it, altered the setting and minimally the plot, and converted it into a French grand opera, first unveiled in Paris in 1826. The French version was quickly translated into Italian as *L'Assedio di Corinto* and the role of Neocle (a tenor in Paris) taken by a mezzo-soprano, as it is in the broadcast. In addition, a Venice production of 1823 had features which contributed to the version that conductor Schippers and scholar J. F. Mastroianni fashioned for the Metropolitan premiere. Schippers, perhaps wishing to serve the needs of his prima donna, also inserted before the third-act finale an aria that Rossini had written for Giuditta Grisi in an 1829 revival at La Fenice, Venice. This may seem quite a mishmash, but all the moves are quite in line with Italian practice during the first half of the nineteenth century. If Rossini would not have been surprised to find his opera tailored to suit the best qualities of a cast or for the needs of a particular theater,

L'Assedio di Corinto
19 April 1975

Pamira
Beverly Sills
Neocle
Shirley Verrett
Cleomene
Harry Theyard
Maometto
Justino Díaz
Conductor
Thomas Schippers

Beverly Sills as Pamira in *L'Assedio di Corinto*. Photography by James Heffernan.
Courtesy Metropolitan Opera Archives.

why should we? The composer himself often participated in the transformations. It seems that, when producing this opera, authenticity is equivalent to freedom of choice. Despite its confusing history, the opera remains remarkable for grandeur of conception; Rossini organized the music into huge formal blocks with considerable continuity between individual components. It is a noble work, its prominent choruses, imaginative orchestration, and moving trios for the principals lending it unusual stature. Some features of *opera seria*, notably the amount of florid singing, continue to be present. Heroic in its music and original in its organizational concepts, the work, impressive even for Rossini, signals the creation of a new grand opera format and style. *Le Siège de Corinth* is more than a way station of operatic history, though in that regard, it anticipates the composer's 1829 pivotal grand opera, *Guillaume Tell*.

If the work seems an unlikely venture for the Metropolitan, its presence is readily comprehensible as a vehicle for the much-delayed house debut of Beverly Sills. For many years a featured member of the New York City Opera and, since her 1966 triumph as Cleopatra in Handel's *Giulio Cesare*, the unchallenged queen of the company, Miss Sills had frequently auditioned for the Met in her salad days. Now she came to the company as a favorite of the American public, trailing a series of recent European triumphs as well. It was in fact her 1969 appearances in *L'Assedio di Corinto* at La Scala (as replacement for the pregnant Scotto) that had certified her prima donna status and eventually led to the Metropolitan production. En route, Bing, after considerable delay, had offered her *Martha*, *Traviata*, *Luisa Miller*, and *Lucia* on various occasions but schedules and desires did not conform.[22] With her in *L'Assedio* are Verrett (Neocle), Theyard (Cleomene), and as the proud Turk, Maometto, Justino Díaz. Schippers (who had been in charge of the La Scala production, where Díaz also scored) is on the podium. He and the four named artists had recorded the opera the previous summer, so understanding and a sense of ensemble had been cultivated in advance.

Schippers' relatively long acquaintance with the opera informs his handling of the grandiose score. The overture begins with a novel double-subject slow introduction, the wind colors chastely sounding the opera's serious mien but soon giving way to dazzling string figurations as the piece trips nimbly along under the maestro's orderly pulse. He paces the opera for maximum grandeur, its large constructs filled with vivid effects, the choral forces emphatic in utterance. Taking to heart the numerous crescendos that animate the score, he propels them to rather feverish heights, creating visceral excitement; I do think that his decided preference for the accelerando when the climax is in sight (as opposed to a subtle quickening of the quality of movement) is an unnecessary enhancement of the composer's built-in ferment. Schippers' reading, though replete with heady excitement, often enough plumbs the noble depths of the composer's conception as well.

In addition to the quartet of principals, the composer wrote a lengthy third-act scene for Jero, the guardian of the graves. A bit anticlimactic, coming as it does late in the long opera, the scene nevertheless is essential. It elevates the theme of patriotism to equal rank with the personal conflicts and prepares us for the tragic denouement. Gill's stern bass is the right vehicle for the task and he performs with admirable seriousness and tonal amplitude. Norden (Ismene) and Best (Omar) have slight assignments but do them well.

Theyard is, in degree of employment and in execution, the least of the quartet of principals. But he is a stalwart performer, his spinto voice carrying enough weight and body to make credible the unlikely match of a leading tenor as father to the leading soprano—the relationship is not something that occurs in everyday opera. The American tenor is at his best in the many dramatic recitatives that Rossini penned for the governor of Corinth. His stern vocal demeanor, its very fierceness, makes one believe that this father could sacrifice a daughter's happiness to patriotic zeal. As in *Hoffmann*, I admire the timbral singularity of his instrument, rather improbably a combination of Corelli (though smaller) and Alagna (though more nasal). That nasality can be troubling, but usually the voice's bright thrusting power nullifies the defect. For the most part, the tenor conscientiously tries to blend in the trios with Verrett and Sills. In the third-act 'Pria svenar,' Theyard's coloratura is acceptable, though Díaz goes him one better, for his roulades are fleet; a stunning high note and two-octave downward leap bring the tenor back into focus. Not all the vocal fireworks are the women's province in this opera.

As Maometto, Díaz gives a remarkably assured performance. Is this Turk practitioner of genocide meant to be this attractive? I have never heard the Díaz voice to be both so securely anchored and so tonally refulgent. For most of the opera, his manner is grand and gracious, an unbeatable combination. Occasionally, when Maometto's wishes are thwarted, Díaz sends forth tone with admirable authority, as any leader should. Pamira renounces her lover at the end of the second act and in response Díaz's delivery is as commanding as one could wish. Everywhere, whether as lover or tyrant, his timbre is vibrant. It calls to mind a young Siepi, the tone resonant and poured forth with prodigality. No haze on its coloration today! And he is amazingly at ease when executing the limited amount of coloratura that Maometto retains in this version. I like particularly the delicious Rossinian swing he gives to his entrance aria; has the fierce leader, purportedly celebrating in the city square of Corinth, momentarily been transported to *Algeri*? A splendid high G at the aria's end confirms his prime vocal condition. Later, he is a sympathetic player in his scenes with Sills, modulating his voice to pair well with her cameo instrument. Blending in thirds a bass voice with a soprano of Sills' type is not an easy task, but Díaz tastefully manages the feat. It is immensely satisfying to hear the bass reaffirm, with interpretive maturity, his youthful vocal promise.

Rossini gave the young officer Neocle two guises. Originally, it was a *travesti* role, a male sung by a contralto. As noted, for the Paris production, the composer rewrote the role for a tenor. Miss Verrett, a mezzo, happily partakes of both versions, obviously playing in pants, but, profiting from Schippers' realignment of the score, she is awarded the grande *scena* that opened the third act of *Maometto II*. And quite a scene it is. As Neocle, the Corinthian warrior, contemplates the coming battle with the Turks, his thoughts range widely—and so did the composer's. Rossini placed the opening dramatic recitative in the upper range, where Verrett's voice, at least at this transitional point in her career, is happiest. There her tones flow meltingly, the fruity timbre allowing a welcome dose of humanity to surface within all the pyrotechnics that dribble from the son of Pesaro's pen. Of course, Verrett will have the opportunity for display as well. Although florid song is not normally her métier, she is equipped for the exercise. A neat *messa di voce* in the recitative sends yet another message of vocal command. The aria proper takes the mezzo voice to the highest of the high before plummeting to the lowest of the low.

The latter range can be a bit gruff, since there Verrett relies heavily upon chest voice, but for the most part the singer handles the scene's vocal challenges with a combination of equanimity and searing conviction. The cabaletta has a surfeit of coloratura fireworks and even there the singer conquers; her trills are adequate and the scales, barring one or two slides in descent, are worthy. Hearing her navigate this scene makes one believe that she could be a plausible Norma. (Would that she had not taken the plunge, however.) At the scene's conclusion, the audience gives her an enormous ovation, their excitement exuberant and unremitting; the response is the most fervent accorded any of the afternoon's artists. Earlier in the opera, Verrett is a brave participant in the series of duets, trios, and *concertato*s, her warm timbre often providing a striking contrast to Sills' silvery point. For the most part, the mezzo keeps her voice in line, corralling her preference for passionate vocalism, so that the two instruments blend affectingly in Rossini's intertwining roulades. For a brief moment in act two, the voice momentarily seems to fail her, the slight rasp infecting her tone—but she soon returns to form. Role immersion is always her primary concern, rather than vocal niceties. Announcer Allen makes a point of telling us that Verrett appears "with mustache" and, at the final bow, she "came striding on stage like a warrior." A conquering hero/ine on this afternoon, she has a right to the warrior's gait.

I have known the Sills voice in live performance throughout a considerable portion of her career. She often has spoken of how conductor Emerson Buckley "conned" her into singing Aida in the 1960 Central City, Colorado, opera festival (my only personal contact with her); the other opera on the bill was *Lucia*, which she thought was her assignment.[23] I remember her Ethiopian princess—the slimmest, fairest of them all—in rehearsals and a half dozen or more performances; many moments profited from the liquidity of her pure-toned song. And of course, the commitment was there. (Adelina Patti—hard to believe—sang the role, so there was some precedent, though a foolhardy one.) In a larger house, it would not have worked at all. At the other end of the career spectrum, I attended a Des Moines concert just a few weeks after the broadcast *Assedio* when the voice sounded tired, tremulous, and occasionally acidulous, hardly the imprint one likes to retain in memory as a final impression of a great artist in live performance. Far more satisfying live events were an inimitable Baby Doe at the New York City Opera (1958) and a fabulous Zerbinetta and a delicious sequence of Mozart arias at Tanglewood in the late sixties. At San Francisco (1971) I thought her fragile, stylistically impeccable Manon was a complete delight. I remember an occasion during her *Aida* season when a few singers were spending an afternoon listening to opera records in my Central City apartment; Sills, after hearing the Cours la Reine aria, remarked that she was tired of seeing a certain interpreter of Manon "clomp around the stage in those sandals." She could never be accused of clomping, either in sandals or with the voice. And after hearing a couple versions of 'Una voce poco fa' (De los Angeles and Simionato), she commented that the Spanish soprano was technically more accurate but "on stage, I bet you couldn't take your eyes off Simionato." In those few words, she succinctly defined the twin poles of her artistry and their convincing admixture; she was mistress of both, the essential technical mastery ultimately trumped by character involvement and stage craft.

And what of the voice on this "long-awaited" broadcast debut, less than two weeks after her house debut in the same opera? (Her July 1966 Donna Anna at

Lewisohn Stadium had been a concert reading.) Now just a month short of her forty-sixth birthday, her career (not counting all those childhood efforts) already spanning twenty-eight years—the latter ones furnished with roles suited more to her stage magnetism than her instrument—she was at the height of her fame. In an otherwise favorable *Times* review of her debut, the critic noted a few questionable areas in the voice and trouble with high notes.[24] Once again, the broadcast serves to provide a corrective by offering another portrayal than the one reviewed in print, this performance one that can be heard again and again over the years. An overview of the artist's career is thus amplified.

But there is more to the story. In a remarkably candid interview taped in June 1975 at the Hollywood Bowl, the soprano discoursed at length about her vocal indisposition on the April 1975 broadcast.[25] She had laryngitis and could hardly speak. She visited Chapin in his office after coming to the house, feeling she could not get through the performance of the lengthy and, to her mind, rather unrewarding role with the amount of voice she had. She at least hoped to cut some arias. But the need to meet the huge radio audience compelled her to go on. She claims her performance was a disaster. (Sills exaggerates, interviewer Martin Bernheimer asserts. He was in the house that afternoon and adds that only those who were deeply acquainted with her work would have guessed she was under par.) She did omit large portions of the score, she avers, never singing with the chorus in order to get through the performance.

The performance may have been a trial for the conscientious Sills, but it was far from a disaster, either for her or the radio audience. (The soprano did acknowledge that the mail response to the broadcast was adulatory—she suspected that the radio muffled her difficulties.) First off, consider those high notes. Sills tackles both the D and E-flat *in alt*, and they are on the button—the tone a bit hard perhaps (you could just call it brilliant), but unflinchingly secure. (Even the soprano was amazed to hear them firmly flashing out—but she never did manage the B-flats, she maintained.) There is some tremulousness in cantilena—the middle voice suffers most from any indisposition. Still even that demerit may be viewed as an expressive device when the pathetic affect is cultivated (but in the first-act 'Ritrovo l'amante,' the affect is overplayed—self-pity can become tedious). And she does tire by the time she reaches the final act. But except for these items, the voice comes through remarkably well, the tone often round (as much as an instrument of her type can be), the timbre—especially in the upper octave—possessing a glinting purity, like a mellow glaze that warms the white chalk body of fine porcelain china. On records, Sills' instrument can sound shallow or acidulous, or even monotonous in its coloration. The wonder of her broadcast Pamira is the voice's timbral variety, sometimes milk-soft, at other moments, especially on high, possessed of a hard, jewel-like brilliance. Often enough the mid-voice (one of those "problem" arias) comes over the air with a fresh, welcoming texture sufficient for her expressive intent. (In the house, it may have been a different matter.) Would the opera be better served by a voice more voluminous, capable of grander dramatic gestures, one carrying within its core a tragic dimension? Of course. But in their place, we hear an artist who builds a portrayal in multiple ways, is musically scrupulous, full of feeling, and in her fioriture absolutely dazzling.

Sills sends off volleys of scales, trills, and arpeggios, roulades sufficient to fill more than one bel canto opera. Her fioriture are often as delicate and fleet as "water-dimples down a tide."[26] The glittering fizz (notably the rapid scale work) of the aria that opens the second act all but makes one dizzy. In contrast, she can convert the fioriture into an expressive tool, capable of limning emotion; in that regard, 'Dal soggiorno' (where Pamira is torn between patriotism and her love for Maometto) benefits from her care. In more dramatic confrontations, as in the duets and trios, her sudden flashes of fioriture thrust into the ensembles with telling effect. Her pointed tone in the act-two finale illustrates her willingness to spend her resources in the service of the drama. In all that glut of coloratura, two brief moments particularly caught my attention: the difficult chromatic descent, at a moderate pace, from a high D, each note sculpted individually, the tone diamantine; and a brilliant high trill that ends in the dying fall of a descending scale in the cadenza of 'Parmi vederlo,' the aria that Rossini wrote for Grisi and that Schippers inserted into the final act. According to Sills, after the performance she went home and, quite needlessly, gave way to tears. In any case, she preferred to play characters rather than pasteboard heroines. She swore that Pamira was a heroine she would be glad to be done with after the 1975–76 run.

We need not unduly lament Miss Sills' late entry to the Metropolitan—she certainly sloughed off any regrets—though she belonged there long before this date. It is her belief that Mr. Bing, whom she later enjoyed as a friend, simply did not want her to sing at the Met. And they, either consciously or unconsciously, irritated one another. It was not because she was a City Opera prima donna, but rather, she quite pertinently notes, that the vehicles of her New York successes were Bing's production misfires, amplifying the comment to contrast her appearances in Manon with the less successful Met production of that opera.[27] Mr. Bing undoubtedly would suggest other reasons for the initial impasse. It would be rewarding to have more Met broadcasts than we do of Sills portrayals, but fortunately, a number of documentations of live performances during the previous decade and a half are preserved. And they represent the voice in its prime.

L'Assedio di Corinto would be repeated during the next season. Then it, too, would vanish, but with more justification than is the case for some of the premieres we have examined. *Assedio* was Sills' creature. By 1980, she would be lost to the Metropolitan and the operatic stage. At least *Jenůfa* and *Les Troyens* would be brought forward at wide intervals for the delectation of future audiences. And there was hope. More venturesome additions to the repertory would be offered when Levine gained full artistic control.

Giovanni Martinelli as Arnold in *Guillaume Tell*. Photography by Mishkin.

CHAPTER EIGHTEEN

Intermission

Upon hearing the first act of *Antony and Cleopatra*, intermission guest Giovanni Martinelli is moved to comment, "I thought the tenor would be the lover."[1] In his book, lovers always are. The grand old lion of the tenorial breed knows what is important in opera. He likes what he has heard. Still, he insists, "I feel the lover should be the tenor," going on to point out that only in *La Juive* does the leading tenor play the father. Martinelli is one among many guests on the parterre floor caught on the fly by interviewer Edward Downes during the first intermission of the opening of the new Met in September 1966. Sir Cecil Beaton is more enthusiastic. His concern is for the stage facilities, which he calls "a designer's dream come true." Marc Chagall, whose murals adorn the lobby of the new Met, prefers to take the high road, remarking (in French) that he is a great lover of humanity and of music. Downes feels that Chagall was "predestined" for the world of opera by his "fantastic imagination and peculiar style of painting." The painter warns him off by noting that he can be a bit contradictory when people ask what he is doing. Most artists prefer to do, rather than to talk.

Fortunately, on the Met's regular-season intermission features, others (assorted singers and administrators, so-called quiz experts) did like to talk. By the mid-sixties, the intermission format was pretty well set in concrete. Analysis of the broadcast opera (or an occasional special feature like William Weaver's Italian travelogues to Verdi and Puccini haunts) dominated the first intermission, and the "Opera Quiz" had a lock on the second, while a bit of variety filtered into the program when a third interlude occurred. Boris Goldovsky, master of all operas, still reigned supreme in the analysis department. The tables were turned on him in 1973 when Downes took him on for "a musical and dramatic analysis of Boris Goldovsky."[2] Downes can hardly get a word in edgewise, the man is so loquacious in telling the story of his life (he barely got through it in two intermissions). Goldovsky, always adept at bringing opera plots to life, treats his own life in like fashion. Irrepressible in his enthusiasm and hardly modest, he drops fascinating bits of information in his familiar rapid-fire manner. Child of the famous violinist Lea Luboschutz, he studied piano with Artur Schnabel in Berlin and Ernst von Dohnányi in Budapest. Before taking up permanent residence in the United States, he determined to learn English while a student at the Liszt Academy in Budapest; he did so by reading P. G. Wodehouse ("for a while I talked just like

Jeeves and Bertie Wooster"). Not content with being a pianist, he determined to be a conductor as well. It was Fritz Reiner at the Curtis Institute who made him study opera: "Anybody can conduct symphonies," Reiner told him. "All my life I hated opera," claims Goldovsky, but, like so many who had tried, he knew that "there was no arguing with Fritz Reiner." He did like theater but was put off opera by the predominant style of operatic acting, not exactly what he had seen in pre-Revolution days at the Moscow Art Theatre. But during twenty summers as head of the opera department at the Berkshire Music Center at Tanglewood, he discovered that "great theater opera was possible because we had such gifted students—they could sing, they could be great musicians, and they could act." Without an ounce of compunction, he pulls out a list of current members of the Met who studied with him at Tanglewood. It is impressive: Curtin, Pracht, Price, Elias, Kraft, Miller, Verrett, Williams, Alexander, Cassily, Franke, Nagy, Shirley, Guarrera, Meredith, Milnes, Díaz, and Macurdy. Even after all these years, he cannot resist proselytizing for his concept of "ensemble opera," the idea that had converted him to a love of opera.

Finally, Downes is able to ask how he came to the Met broadcasts, having noted that the interviews mark Goldovsky's 299th and 301st intermission appearances. "It was an accident" is the reply. When the Met came to Cleveland in 1944, they needed a local fellow for the quiz and Goldovsky was the chosen one. "I was very lucky because I knew all the answers. As a matter of fact, I corrected some of the regular quiz people. And they were wrong and I was right." The following season, the Souvaines decided to inaugurate the musical analysis intermission and Goldovsky was their man. In response to Downes' prompting, he names his favorite intermission, a taped interview with Ponselle for the 1954 *Norma* broadcast.

Notwithstanding his preeminence in the analysis arena, Goldovsky did not reign supreme. Inroads were made on his turf. Downes himself, Met chorus master and conductor David Stivender, and, most authoritatively, musicologist Philip Gossett (Rossini was his specialty) each took a small piece of the analysis pie. A bigger one went to BBC mogul John Culshaw, who pontificated at length about all four operas of Wagner's tetralogy (the 1975 *Ring*) and, his cultivated tones providing a telling counterpoint to Goldovsky's endearingly chewy accent, moved further into the squatter's territory by taking on *Elektra* and *Aida*. But Goldovsky knew how to hold his own; on an earlier *Walküre* intermission, he had put all eight of Brünnhilde's sisters ("horseback-riding Amazons") through their paces.[3] Top that, if you can! Sarah Caldwell, who made her Met broadcast debut conducting *La Traviata* on 14 February 1976, played the neatest trick of all in the analysis game. Always a law unto herself, Miss Caldwell, in complement to her podium commands, provided her own verbal interpretation of the opera during the first *Traviata* intermission.

Even Alberta Masiello had a go at analysis now and then. The longtime Met coach, assistant conductor, and quiz expert turned her hand to the 1973 new production of *L'Italiana in Algeri*. That same year, Cyril Ritchard put her on the spot—a courageous endeavor, for the lady was a formidable, occasionally sassy, interviewee.[4] When pressed, she recounts her early career as a mezzo, most prominently at the City Center, where she sang Carmen, Herodias, Amneris, and Azucena. That ended when she decided "I wasn't pleased with what I was doing. . . . I just never liked my voice tremendously"—a confession few singers would make. But then Masiello's appeal was based on unadulterated opinions. She cites two prominent influences on her as a coach, namely, Fausto Cleva ("I always learned something new") and Maria Callas at the Chicago Opera: "I only played for her—not coached—and learned from her" about phrasing and expression. Masiello knew "some," she says, but Callas "brought it up to the point of ecstasy." Ritchard, charmingly coy throughout the interview, wants to know what advice she gives a singer when the conductor's interpretation differs from Masiello's. "Follow the conductor" is the unequivocal answer.

A few multitalented experts managed to pivot between analysis and quiz spots (much as the erudite Father Owen Lee does today). Among Masiello's many colleagues on the "Opera Quiz," some of the old guard remained: Mary Ellis Peltz, Walter Ducloux, Max de Schauensee, and Sigmund Levarie. The quiz's cast of characters was large. Met second-tier administrators peppered the airwaves: Robert Herman and Paul Jaretzki spread the Bing gospel in the early days of our decade. Chorus master David Stivender and assistant conductor Richard Woitach were frequent contributors. Met stage directors Nathaniel Merrill and Henry Butler, plus across-the-plaza competitor Frank Corsaro—all three at ease when plotting moves—tried their hands at answers. Critics were in demand: Martin Bernheimer (happily, still a witty and perceptive mainstay as of this writing), Eric Salzman, Alfred Frankenstein, Andrew Porter, and John Ardoin. Even Irving Kolodin, chronicler and frequent disparager of the Met, bearded the lions in their den on a couple afternoons. Musicologist H. C. Robbins Landon was allowed in, despite intermission producer Geraldine Souvaine's proclaimed and abiding fear of erudition on her quiz—entertainment was her focus. More to her taste was a special singers' quiz with Bumbry, Crespin, Alexander, and Evans dealing with words without music in March 1969. Later perennials included record company aficionado Terry McEwen (he did a program in 1968 on "Singers: My Favorite Subject"), balanced by John Coveney of Angel Records and RCA Victor's Richard Mohr, who later in the century would become the producer of the intermissions.

McEwen had a stock of stories about singers, including his 1976 comment on *Norma* at Covent Garden in 1952, when Sutherland was confidante Clotilde to Callas' Norma. McEwen had once asked the Australian soprano what her duties were (Clotilde's role consists of only a few words) and she recalled that Callas did not have contact lenses then and couldn't see where the tree was to clip the mistletoe; thus, La Stupenda claimed her main responsibility was to take La Divina by the shoulders and point her in the right direction.[5] (A little firmer hand on Sutherland's part might have profited Callas in traversing her overall career path.) Critic Andrew Porter had his own thoughts on singers in April 1976 but, preferring the historical path, provides illuminating comments on the derivation of the mezzo-soprano ("a fairly modern invention") and defines the (Cornelie) Falcon type of soprano ("like Bumbry").[6] From time to time an audience stray made it on. Bass Alexander Kipnis was invited in during a *Boris Godunov* intermission: he extols the 1975 new production (in Russian) of the opera. Beloved soprano Bidú Sayão (discovered in the audience) was honored on 8 April 1972. Recordings to illustrate her gifts were selected by the experts. Mohr, deeming the soprano "the eternal feminine," chooses Manon's 'Adieu, notre petite table,' and praises her ability to convey "so much emotion through the medium of words."[7] McEwen, fairly bursting with emotion himself, notes that her fragility made you want to "run up on the stage and protect her."

Alexander Kipnis as Boris Godunov.

Bidú Sayão as Manon.

Occasionally an artist (Luigi Lucioni) or actor (Peggy Wood) would be added to the mix. In 1968, a special actors-only quiz featured Cornelia Otis Skinner, John Drew Devereaux (a stage manager as well), and opera-struck Tony Randall. In 1971 Skinner returned to interview Cyril Ritchard—she probably knew all his sins, for I recall seeing the two of them on Broadway in the late fifties in an aptly named trifle called *The Pleasure of His Company*. Randall and Walter Slezak were special cases, for they could be counted on to be on-the-air comedians. Once, when Masiello laments hearing Pinza sing Boris in Italian translation, Slezak follows up with a non sequitur, claiming, "I heard *Lohengrin* in Dutch." He proceeds to sing a few phrases, purportedly in that language, which he translates as "here comes a swan with a boat on it."[8] Osie Hawkins, Met baritone turned executive stage manager, alternated between stern lecturer and provider of comic relief. He liked to tell tales out of school; those of us who knew and liked Osie appreciated them. He combines his two postures when he describes his reluctance to go before the curtain and announce to the public that an artist is indisposed but has consented to sing anyway: "I do not feel that the public should be subjected to paying these prices to hear a sick singer." Bumbry, in one appearance as Amneris, provides an example. He had tried to convince her that there was nothing the matter with her voice, but she insisted on the announcement. He ran into her a few days later and she recounted how, having taped the performance, she had listened and "you know, I sang beautifully." She added that a few friends had called to chide her: "Grace, why did you sing when you were not well?" Point to Osie.[9]

Even opera impresarios were admitted to the experts' circle now and then. In March 1968, Julius Rudel, general director of the New York City Opera, Allen Sven Oxenburg, founder and artistic director of the American Opera Society, and Goldovsky (who had his own opera company), plus conductor George Schick of the Met, were startled when Downes quoted a remark made by Maurice Grau. That gentleman, who ran the Met and Covent Garden when the nineteenth century gave way to the twentieth, claimed that "vocal excellence is worth paying for, but with regard to conductors, no one ever paid a nickel to see a man's back." Rudel takes the comment seriously, averring that a performance without a good conductor was like having a wonderful team of horses and letting them "just take a stage coach by themselves"—they needed someone to give them guidance and to "shape the whole performance." Goldovsky comes to the rescue, affirming that "in an opera performance, nobody should be watching the conductor—all eyes should be on the stage."[10] As for backs, he acknowledged that "we like to see different backs now and then," which is why symphony organizations have guest conductors.

Serious discussion of vocal technique was allowed a hearing now and then. On a 1968 record collector's quiz, the difference between head voice and chest voice is given a going over, with a phrase from *Les Huguenots* heard as recorded by tenors Marcel Wittrisch (head) and John O'Sullivan (chest). Mohr is "not exactly smitten by either one of them," a comment unusually frank for the intermission features; he finds that Wittrisch veers "dangerously close to falsetto" and O'Sullivan is "impressive to listen to in a muscular rather over-the-hill way."[11] Randall opines that "national differences" are at work, while McEwen believes that "physiological differences" enter in as well, adding that "nobody agrees on what are chest notes and what are head notes." No one can accuse them of being pedantic—intermission producer Geri Souvaine must have been pleased. On another quiz focused on

Rosa Ponselle as Mathilde in *Guillaume Tell*. Photography by Mishkin.

Luisa Tetrazzini. Photography by E. F. Foley.

record collecting, George Jellinek, John Ardoin, Andrew Porter, and McEwen, the jolly Englishman, heard Tetrazzini and Ponselle sing, their recordings prompting McEwen to note that bel canto is about the "kind of control" that Ponselle demonstrated in a *Vestale* aria. As to Tetrazzini's fabulous coloratura, he acknowledges that it is difficult to "hit fast notes dead-on," offering in support of that view a remark of Nilsson's: "It is very difficult to sing little notes."[12] After hearing Milanov deftly ascend to a *piano* high C in 'O patria mia' (normally a precarious exercise), McEwen again has a ready quote, citing Russian conductor Emil Cooper's statement that "some operas is easy and some operas is uneasy." Of note is the presence of Magda Olivero in the quiz audience. She hears her ethereal *messa di voce* extolled (an interpolated high note at the end of 'Ah fors è lui') before Ardoin calls her rendition of the aria "one of the most beautiful records ever made."

Another variation on the quiz format involved pianists who played "musical chairs," the question to be answered at the keyboard with an appropriate operatic example. Masiello, Goldovsky, conductor Jan Behr, and critic Paul Hume knew how to play not just the piano, but the game. Another time, pianist Ivan Davis played operatic transcriptions (and very well, too). A pianist of another stripe, Victor Borge, disported with Jascha Silverstein, the Met's principal cellist, in an "Opera News" segment in January 1973—producer Souvaine liked to keep things lively. One 1972 quiz featured the real experts, a crew of experienced Met ushers. One of them recalled a lady who, upon exiting from *Parsifal*, claimed that "Amfortas' pain was all psychosomatic anyway," prompting Downes to note that "she wasn't so far wrong."[13]

Francis Robinson's "Biographies in Music" had first call on the third intermission. Divas as different as Elisabeth Schumann (1968) and Marjorie Lawrence (1971) were given their innings. Naturally, the centenary of Caruso's birth received big play in March 1973—as it should. At the other end of the tenor spectrum, character tenor Alessio De Paolis, killed unexpectedly in a 1964 automobile accident while still a member of the company, was in time given his tribute. Sometimes the anniversary of a current artist's Met debut was celebrated by Robinson: Merrill and Resnik both qualified. The purple-voiced narrator was particularly warm when remembering Risë Stevens' 1938 Met debut thirty years after the event.[14] He traces the schooling lineage of the now-retired (from singing only) mezzo all the way back to the Garcia family, Manuel senior and his genius children, Manuel junior, Maria Malibran, and Pauline Viardot. The latter was the teacher of Risë's own teacher, Madame Schoen-René (who, in Robinson's words, "looked, dressed, and acted like Field Marshal von Hindenburg"). Calling the American mezzo "the finest Orpheus of our time" (the line back to Viardot, the mid-nineteenth-century's prime Orpheus, is suggested), he notes Stevens' antipathy to Amneris after an early Prague tryout in the role. Pertinent to that failed venture is the best advice Schoen-René ever gave the budding diva: "My dear, have the courage to face your faults." The field marshal had the right to be frank, for she "advanced Risë money, cured her Bronx accent, told her how to dress, and took her to Europe." Schick, who had taught her most of her parts, sums up the Stevens career: "Risë was not at her best in the parts where you just stand up and sing; she was too much a creature of the theatre for that."

Others took up the remembrance game, too. John Gutman remembered Mary Garden in 1967. And special artists required special treatment. Weaver

Enrico Caruso as Canio in *Pagliacci*.
Photography by Mishkin.

Lotte Lehmann as the Marschallin in *Der Rosenkavalier*.

talked with Tito Gobbi about *Otello* in 1969, while Downes drew the plum interview—Maria Callas in 1968—and gained another with Karajan in 1969. Jennie Tourel returned to talk with Stivender about *Werther* in 1971. Could there be a better authority? Couples in opera were deemed novel and could be featured: Ludwig and Berry (1967), Lear and Stewart (1969), and the favorites, Sutherland and Bonynge, who came on for several interviews.

Franco Zeffirelli rated an extended conversation on the *Otello* broadcast of 8 April 1972. Downes suggests that the designer/director has broken many traditions with his new *Otello* but Zeffirelli denies breaking "*any* traditions," maintaining he has merely gone back to Shakespeare. His "favorite sport" is to, in effect, "clean the paintings" by removing the layers of "varnish" that have accrued over the ages and thus restore a work to its "original colors."[15] He sounds novel enough when he maintains that *Otello* is not "a drama of jealousy." Jealousy is only the pretext that Iago uses. Any other "trick" would do, because Otello is "an unprotected idealist" and thus immensely vulnerable. Nor is Iago, Zeffirelli maintains, a very subtle villain—he does "a rough job." Well, yes and no. Has he listened carefully to Verdi's setting of 'Era la notte?'

A tribute to Lotte Lehmann on her eighty-fifth birthday was featured in 1973. Coveney, recipient of many letters from the great soprano, read excerpts from a few. One that arrived in the week previous to the intermission related her plans to hear a Salzburg *Tristan*. She inveighed against the gods who had made her instrument neither "dramatic" nor "powerful" enough to undertake Isolde. She knew she might have destroyed her voice if she had sung the role "but it would have been worth the while."[16] A few years earlier, she had written a few words about birthdays, noting that, at her age, congratulations were no longer in order. For her, it is "a day of sadness." The unforgettable Marschallin of an earlier era recalled how "easy" it was when on stage to espouse wisdom and resignation, but at this point in her life she felt only "rebellion. . . . One cannot turn back the clock." Lehmann, as we know from her performances, always felt deeply.

In an unusually generous gesture, Kirsten was invited to speak her farewell to the radio audience on 27 December 1975. Announcer Allen notes that "one of the Metropolitan's greatest artists would like to speak personally with you," citing the double nature of the occasion, for it is Kirsten's thirtieth year with the company, and "with all the fresh bloom still on her voice," she will announce her farewell.[17] The soprano mentions her gratitude to Texaco, noting, perhaps with bittersweet personal knowledge, that before LP records many artists never had the opportunity to record a complete opera and yet could be heard by the radio audience in their complete roles. (Regrettably, in her case the lack was true even after the advent of the LP record.) She describes the "great thrill" it is to be the first prima donna to celebrate thirty years (not seasons) with the Metropolitan. Thanks go to mentor Grace Moore. Not wishing to confuse her farewell to the Met with a cessation of her career, she firmly intones, "No! I am not retiring." But life at her home in California with her "wonderful husband" beckons more insistently and travel will be limited. Of course, she did come back to the Met. As we have seen, management needed her to save a Puccini performance now and then.

The most welcome new intermission feature (begun in 1961) was the "Singers' Roundtable," a kind of informal quiz where the answers were derived from the singers' own experiences. On 15 December 1973, Verrett and Domingo, aided by

Niska and Corena, brought their humor and insights to the table. (However unlikely it seems, at this time Pavarotti was shy of the microphone—Domingo was not.) When Downes wants to know why the tenor relinquished an early desire to be a bullfighter, Domingo, after suggesting that he "gained too much weight," adds that "bull's horns were a lot more dangerous than tomatoes and eggs in the opera house."[18] Verrett, asked to describe her path to divahood, relates how she was a business administration and corporate law major in college and then became a real estate agent in Los Angeles, a vocation seemingly remote from that of opera singer but, to her mind, of value nevertheless. She claims to be "one of the few singers who could read a contract when it was put in front of me." Another roundtable in 1976 featured Milanov, Horne, Guarrera, and Morris. Asked about roles offered in their youth and refused, Horne recalls that as a member of the opera department at USC she was asked to do Carmen at age eighteen. She refused the part. The consequence: "I got an F in Opera."[19] She describes Carmen as "the work-horse of the opera," such a long role and one that calls for "tremendous emotion in the low register." As for Amneris, which she sang in 1964 and then put away until the current season, she cries out that the judgment scene "will just tear your throat apart." On a similar subject, Downes is surprised that Milanov undertook Norma in Zagreb as early as 1939. The inimitable Zinka responds that "it always depends on how you sing and if you know how to do it." She did.

Miss Nilsson received homage as well in a 1974 roundtable. When Downes quotes a line from Strauss' *Capriccio* to the effect that the orchestra can be so loud it kills the singers, he receives a quietly slipped in "How true!" from the Swedish diva—and it's most painful in Wagner and Strauss, she adds. McCracken, another conspirator, suggests "you do very well," while Milnes clinches the tribute with "it's the others who have problems."[20] Nilsson later amusingly describes her auditions with the two previous managers of the Met, Johnson and Bing. Johnson came to Stockholm when she had been with the Swedish opera company for two years and, the manager having suggested she sing for him, she performed the gallows aria from *Ballo in Maschera*. "I had this big beautiful melon hat and I got very dramatic and made a big turn with my head and lost the hat. Mr. Johnson was very kind; he said 'I love your hat.' And then, he ordered me to study more." Nilsson goes on to describe how, six years later, she sang for Bing in Berlin. "Mr. Bing is a great manager but he didn't speak to me at all; he didn't compliment me or anything." Years later she reminded him of the incident saying, "You know you turned me down many years ago." To which Bing replied, "Oh no! That's terrible. What a pity! If I would have taken you at that time, you wouldn't be so difficult to handle now." Birgit loved a bit of kidding on the square.

Most famous of all roundtables was the 18 April 1970 rout where master Downes tried to keep order while Arroyo, Horne, and Sutherland played havoc with decorum. Miss A took the lead in that department, leaving dead bodies not just in the aisles. When Horne notes that she started in big roles in small places, Arroyo chimes in that "the places weren't really small, we made them look small" and off we go. About choice of roles, she dreamt of singing "Madame Butterball." Horne avers that she could never do Octavian, but Arroyo offers a friendly bit of stage business: "You could if you would walk on and back off."[21] There are a few serious moments. Downes wants to know if there is a phrase each one always enjoys singing. Sutherland suggests 'Amami, Alfredo' from the third act of *Traviata*,

Birgit Nilsson.

and Horne loves 'O ihr, der Eide' from Brünnhilde's immolation scene (a role she had not performed onstage but had sung in concert, as she tantalizingly notes). Arroyo grabs hold again, saying she would love to do Salome if "Jackie [Miss Horne] would do the dance." Her most genuinely comic moment comes when Downes wants to know what they would do if a conductor were too slow, too fast, too anything. Arroyo, aware of Sutherland and Horne as Mrs. Bonynge and Mrs. Lewis, pops up: "Divorce him." So many requests came in to the producer that the program was repeated in 1972.

Naturally, opera managers had their own sporting events. They came in at the beginning and the end of most seasons. Mr. Bing's seasonal broadcast appearances and the many tributes awarded him by company members at his retirement are already covered in an earlier chapter. But one remarkable broadcast tribute to him made during the final weeks of his leadership should be noted. Zeffirelli paid it during his April 1972 interview. When Downes states that this was the Italian's first *Otello*, the designer/director responds that two years ago when Bing asked him to do the opera, he readily agreed. Why? Because Bing "understands your

mind, he understands your heart." That is where his "greatness" lies.[22] "He studies the people he works with" and intuitively divines "the right moment for them
to do the right thing." Zeffirelli considers that gift to be "the supreme virtue that
very few people on earth have." Downes interjects, "especially impresarios," but
Zeffirelli won't let that stand. Now he places the verbal laurel wreath on Bing's
expansive brow as he insists that, rather than being merely "an impresario," the
Met's man is "unique."

Chapin, during his brief tenure, would receive no accolades comparable to
that, on or off the air. In addition to the usual seasonal welcomes and farewells,
he came on to plead the Metropolitan's need for financial support. Nancy Hanks,
chairman of the National Endowment for the Arts, joined him in that effort in
March 1974. She brought with her good news. The Endowment would grant the
Metropolitan one million dollars "upon receipt of one million dollars in private
contributions."[23] Chapin had informed her that the broadcasts' "minimum audience is seven million" so she does the math and encouragingly notes, "That's
only fourteen cents per person." In contrast to European subsidies, she finds "the
genius" of the Endowment's procedure is that it encourages "private initiative. . .
. there's no question of control" by the government.

A seemingly more pleasant function fell to Chapin when in April of 1973
he introduced James Levine to the radio audience as the future principal conductor of the company. The articulate Levine describes his plans, noting that, while
management hopes their plans will be a "major improvement," they cannot be
certain of that outcome.[24] He sets forth a key element of the new concept: in order
to provide more rehearsal time, they will cut the number of operas in repertory
from the current twenty-seven to twenty-two for 1973–74. At the end of the intermission, Chapin, who has allowed the members of his team to dominate, rather
unfortunately adds that he thinks it is "marvelous to have somebody else to blame
if something goes wrong." In his case, things did go wrong. On his final seasonal
farewell (19 April 1975), he mentions Anthony Bliss, who is new to the post of executive director that season. Chapin maintains that Bliss' "leadership, [and] business and fund-raising talents" are genuine company assets and avers that "he and
I are working closely together on the affairs of the company."[25] (Chapin's memoirs
reveal those optimistic comments to be prompted by mere courtesy on his part.[26])
With a final salute—"all of us at the Metropolitan look forward to welcoming you
back next season"—he is gone. A few days later, he was informed that his contract
as general manager would not be renewed.

When Bliss takes charge and welcomes the radio audience on the first broadcast of the 1975–76 season, he is able to speak of the "cause for optimism," and
cite the "tremendous momentum within the Met this season."[27] He recognizes
that it is the radio audience that has made the Metropolitan "our national opera
company." This time Levine is hailed as "a man with an intense vision of opera as
a total theatrical experience." The main body of the intermission is given over to
Bliss' remarkable conversation with John Dexter, who makes an initial broadcast
appearance. The Met's director of production, the English-born Dexter states that
his interest in music began "as a rather depraved choir boy," for whom opera,
though he was not then participating, was "almost a mania, certainly an obsession." After spending five years with Lawrence Olivier at the National Theatre,
he was asked to stage Berlioz' *Benvenuto Cellini* for Covent Garden; Gedda (the

Cellini) encouraged him to continue to stage opera. Many years in Hamburg with Rolf Liebermann followed. He was willing to come to the Met because he felt "within this monster" he might be able to create "a working ensemble—inter-working, inter-trusting." In his opinion, since it is not able to compete with subsidized European houses in the money game, the Met needs to develop "a violently creative atmosphere"; he wants to develop a staging format that doesn't require a "tonnage of scenery" or costume "magnificence." Could anything be more diametrically opposed to the Zeffirelli modus operandi?

Dexter's aim is to "stimulate the audience's imagination a little more." In that way he hopes to be able to minimize financial risk by "economically" putting on operas at a modest production level; the slack (if any) will be taken up by astute casting. Over his seven-year tenure the results were indeed positive: *Dialogues of the Carmelites, Lulu, Billy Budd, Mahagonny*, and the *Parade* and Stravinsky triple bills all were notable events in Metropolitan history. (Another manager—Joseph Volpe—remarked in a 2001 intermission that "there was always a conflict with John when it came to standard repertoire."[28] Met management and audiences only accepted Dexter's approach for new additions to the repertory.) The man of the theater left the Met in 1981 (though on call as a consultant until 1984), while Bliss, the man of the ledger books, continued in place. Throughout the 1975 interview, Bliss and Dexter provide a strong contrast in terms of personality, the former correct and formal, Dexter always the original thinker, unafraid to express his ideas in perhaps the most intriguing fashion ever heard on the broadcasts. At the close of the intermission, Dexter suddenly asserts that there was yet another reason for his joining the Metropolitan: "James." He might not have "taken the plunge" otherwise, for he has "never felt so confident about anyone in the theater as I do with James Levine. He is the most extraordinarily sensitive man." Obviously, the young conductor, his name on everybody's lips, is the man of the future.

In January 1975, Chapin had noted that the recently deceased Cross and Tucker would always hold "a big place in our hearts."[29] Tucker had died on Wednesday 8 January 1975. As fate would have it, Robinson had taped a lengthy segment with the tenor on the day before. He had long intended to present the tribute on the following Saturday (11 January) in celebration of Tucker's thirtieth anniversary (thirty years, thirty-one seasons) with the company. At the time only two singers (Scotti, with thirty-four seasons, and Martinelli, with thirty-two) in the Met's ninety-year history had achieved such a record. The tape is unusual in that Robinson had gone on location, catching Tucker working diligently with his accompanist and later in rehearsal for *Cavalleria Rusticana* at the Met, and finally, at home on a Friday evening.[30] The first segment shows the tenor in superior voice, suggesting that he might well have had many more years of high-quality performance ahead of him. At the Met, the tenor reveals himself as both aware of his own worth and demonstrating it as well. He instructs conductor John Nelson about the need for a little pause in a phrase, tells Joann Grillo (covering for Bumbry) not to get angry too soon in the duet because Santuzza is trying to appease Turiddu. Nelson hears more tutelage from Tucker, offered "only because of [my] thirty years of singing *Cavalleria*—not exactly thirty years—I'll take twenty-five, twenty-six." The conductor asserts that Bumbry is used to singing a unison climactic phrase without a break, but Tucker assures him that he will remind Grace of the break he wants to make.

At home, in the third segment, Tucker is the gracious host for the Sabbath dinner. With justifiable pride, he shows Robinson a photograph taken when he received an honorary degree from Notre Dame (pretty good for "a Jewish boy who didn't even finish high school"). In all three segments, the impression of tremendous vitality is indelibly conveyed. Clearly, this is a man dedicated to his profession, one who enjoys life and relishes his prominent position in the operatic world. His many broadcast performances over the thirty years of his Metropolitan career remain the strongest evidence of his quality.

Milton Cross had died on Friday, 3 January 1975 and Robinson paid tribute on the next day's broadcast.[31] The announcer had been the voice of the broadcasts since their inception in 1931; over the next forty-four years he had missed only two broadcasts, when his wife had died two years previous to his death. The bulk of the intermission repeats a 26 December 1970 tribute on the occasion of Cross beginning his fortieth year as announcer. His beginnings in radio are lovingly recounted, including his factotum years on the Westinghouse Slumber Hour. There, Cross ("an unfulfilled singer," according to Robinson) often sang—and we are treated to a rendition of the Slumber Song. Robinson notes that Cross had been in opera so long that "his ordinary speech sometimes becomes operatic." (In an aside, he recalls that people said Mrs. Siddons used to speak in blank verse.) According to Robinson, once when Cross was conversing with a friend while riding on a bus in Rome some years earlier, a lady in front of him, recognizing his voice, turned around and hailed him: "Why, it's Mr. Cross!"

Cross's distinctive voice and diction were giveaway thumbprints. Nobody could say a line like "Scarpia has wreaked his evil vengeance" (15 February 1969) like our announcer. How he enjoyed recounting the macabre details of the final scene of *La Gioconda* (2 March 1968), all but acting them out for us. He could watch and wonder, too, as when, at the conclusion of *Simon Boccanegra* (14 December 1968), he exuberantly exclaimed, "We heard the body fall!—No! It was some kind of fireworks." He was an endearing man—you experienced it all along with him. In act three of a 30 December 1967 *Traviata*, he was astonished at Alfredo's treatment of Violetta: "He actually hit her with the money!" Of Gedda's Tamino (in the 17 January 1970 broadcast of *Die Zauberflöte*), he exclaimed, "What a princely tenor and stalwart prince!" He loved his singers. And he was a company man as well, faithfully reading from the "sensational" reviews when necessary to spin a new opera like *Peter Grimes* (11 February 1967) or *Mourning Becomes Elektra* (1 April 1967).

As Robinson noted, when Milton Cross "referred to the great gold curtain, you were there." The broadcasts went on, but for many they were never quite the same.

Kiri Te Kanawa as Desdemona in *Otello*. Photography by James Heffernan. Courtesy Metropolitan Opera Archives.

CHAPTER NINETEEN

Italian Protein

The operas of Verdi and Puccini are longtime tenants of the Metropolitan airwaves and we anticipate them with the fond regard we reserve for old friends. The two composers preferred to work in contrasting métiers. In *Otello* and *La Forza del Destino*, grand-scale products of the Busetto master, generals and lieutenants contend. Puccini was always more at home in the boudoir than on the battlefield, as his *Manon Lescaut*, *Bohème*, *Butterfly*, and *Tosca* demonstrate. *Turandot* may be a chilling romance but, as antidote, we can warm ourselves in the hothouse theatrics of Leoncavallo's *Pagliacci*.

The 1972 broadcast of *Otello*, an early acquisition for the young Levine, had demonstrated his affinity for Verdi's masterwork. Two years later, the musical and dramatic qualities that were even then potent have been further sharpened to a point where the 9 February 1974 broadcast is almost trenchantly vivid. The bulk of the first act thunders along with controlled fury. There the combination of exactitude and excitement generates a quite wonderful emotional climate, one in which tension, fear, and apprehension are paramount. The storm abates and the choral 'Si calma la bufera' restores our equilibrium, with Levine's shaping of the woodwind chordal interjections so fluent that nature's wind and rain seem to govern their flight. Throughout the afternoon, motives and phrases are continually sculpted for graphic effect. And how well he understands Verdi's musical rhetoric, which is to say, he transforms mere notes into agents of the dramatic action. Not only is the musical syntax of the phrase observed, but punctuation is succinctly applied: octave descents at the end of a phrase become emphatic periods. The excellent chorus is Levine's willing partner in the adventure. Excess is present—sometimes as to volume and, occasionally, in pace (the aftermath of Otello's 'Ora e per sempre addio' flies so swiftly along as to cause aural inebriation). As in 1972, he favors in turn a heady accelerando and a baroque allargando in the final pages of the third-act *concertato*. Command is his in abundance, almost to the point of indulgence. A bit of moderation (the orchestral outbursts after the strangulation—thrilling indeed—are pulverizing explosive volleys) might better balance out Verdi's accounts. And yet any conductor who can get the double basses to play both in unison and in tune (including that hazardous leap of a diminished sixth) as Otello enters the death chamber deserves our eternal gratitude.

Otello
9 February 1974

Desdemona
Kiri Te Kanawa
Otello
Jon Vickers
Cassio
William Lewis
Iago
Thomas Stewart
Lodovico
Paul Plishka
Conductor
James Levine

463

Vickers' Otello, too, is a known quantity and his portrayal adheres closely to the superb performance he offered in the 1972 broadcast. The voice is in fine shape (though a couple of high notes are a bit bruised—but they are there), the timbre golden on high and resonant or, occasionally, ghostly in the lower range. I doubt that those who find his interpretations affected will be offended by his singing on this afternoon. Yes, he betrays a fondness for *morendo* at the end of a phrase, as in the monologue 'Ora e per sempre addio'—but then, the grand portamento at 'ed ora' counts for much. He may employ mezza voce (but a disappointing falsetto at 'acqueto') more than most Otellos do—I class that talent as one of his virtues. The grander moments (a confident, but not a show-off 'Esultate!'; the vengeance duet; his rages at Desdemona) are exultantly declaimed. They contrast markedly with moments of inner emotion: the rapturous mood-setting act-one duet, where husbandly love suffuses the tone and his serene 'Venere splende' is elegantly sustained; the intensely moving monologues of the third act ('Ma, o pianto, o duol!' is shattering in its sadness); and the fourth act ('Oh! Gloria!' opens out in tenorial splendor). These episodes are replete with suffering, but in no instance overplayed so that the Moor's nobility (redolent in Vickers' delivery of 'Niun mi tema's opening lines) is preserved. Otello lives and dies on this afternoon, his tragic obsession as vividly depicted as on any broadcast performance. Milnes, who was often villain to each tenor's Moor, called Vickers "an oak tree, not as vulnerable as Plácido [Domingo]."[1] The difference may have had more to do with relative vocal size than degree of hurt.

Vickers was paired with Lewis in *Jenůfa*, and they line up again with the American offering one of the finest Cassios of broadcast history. Too often the role has been awarded to a tenor who more rightly belongs to the comprimario class when Cassio's dramatic import demands a frontal stance. Lewis supplies it. He and Stewart make the drinking song a rollicking affair and Levine's orchestra adds a raucous good humor that augments their drunken waywardness. Kraft shows why she has become an increasingly valuable member of the company when she confronts Otello in the final act. Plishka, with little to do, has an ambassador's regality of voice and diplomatic musical manners. We need not ask more from a civil servant.

There is nothing civil about Iago, at least in Stewart's conception: knavery is this ensign's occupation. The American baritone, though a survivor of perhaps too many Wagner outings, gives a thoroughly professional reading of the villain. He betrays a complete acquaintance with the role's challenges and traps and, though he cannot conquer all of the former, he foils the latter by negotiating cogently dramatic—if not always musically attentive—ways around them. He tips his villainous hand from the get-go, in the opening scene allowing evil intent to dominate; the menace in his tone tells all. It is seldom entirely absent thereafter. The voice is not overly large, and with Levine intent on volcanic orchestral effects, a singer must make his own way in order to come out on top. Time after time, Stewart does. Able as he is, the artist nevertheless has no genuine mezza voce at his command—he counterfeits it at a few critical moments, and effectively, too; his secretive 'Era la notte' may be a bit of subterfuge, but it works, and the genuine *sotto voce* rendering of Cassio's purported ecstatic memory of his tryst with Desdemona is even better coin. Still, more times than not, he is compelled to ignore Verdi's markings if his Iago is to make his point; the spider's web episode with

Cassio, for instance, conjures only mini-magic—the voice ought to trip along with gossamer lightness. On the other hand, his Credo is upright opera house crowd-pleasing fare, not more, but certainly not less; the baritone's suggestive 'e poi?'s and disdainful 'Nulla' at the close confirm his skill as a singing actor. He puts it over. Boito's addition to Shakespeare will thrive in most throats, especially when Levine's brass intone as grandly as they do here.

An unexpected house and radio debut of a singer who will become a beloved member of the company is always an event to remember. Preservation of the occasion, guaranteed by the broadcast, assuages history's appetite, while opera lovers, always eager to be insiders, are gratified at being present at the baptismal rite. Kiri Te Kanawa's father was of Maori heritage and her mother Irish; Mr. Cross repeatedly pronounces the name as gingerly as though it originated on an alien planet, rather than merely across the Pacific in New Zealand. The twenty-nine-year-old soprano was scheduled for a 7 March debut as Desdemona, but the indisposition of Stratas called her into service a month early. *Grove* tells us that she went on with three hours' notice, since on Saturday morning Stratas was still expected to sing; but Te Kanawa told *Opera News* that she had been alerted on Friday to the possibility of substitution and that she rehearsed the Zeffirelli staging all that day.[2] She had performed the role previously, so an accomplished portrayal seemed in the cards, particularly since her experience included several years at Covent Garden in roles like Micaela, Countess Almaviva, and Amelia Boccanegra. American audiences had made her acquaintance as the Countess in Santa Fe (1971) and San Francisco (1972).

Though there is much to admire in her debut broadcast, her vocalism is not quite as spectacular as memory would have it. Usually, the placement of the microphones will favor a voice if deficiencies of volume make it less than optimal in the house. But much of the time, Te Kanawa's lower octave is all but inaudible over the airwaves. Levine is rather generous with orchestral volume and that may be the culprit, for his pit charges are front and center, often swamping her delicate lower register. She consistently abjures chest voice (barring a few mixed notes in the Ave Maria), and since her line reading is not inherently dramatic, a vacuum occurs. Her interpretive posture is often reticent. She is content to let her tone convey her message. To her credit, she never forces, nor does the voice wobble. Where she does shine, and beautifully, is in the upper octave. There her lovely, fresh tone, poised and luminous, conquers whenever Verdi writes a soaring phrase. The initial moments of the love duet tell her quality, a firm and velvety 'Mio superbo guerrier!' signaling that a superior vocalist has arrived. The observance of the *dolce* marking at 'quanti tormenti' further confirms her artistic intent, while 'Ed io t'amavo per le tue sventure' is nicely sculpted, revealing a sensitive command of line. At some later points in the opera (most often when suffering Otello's rebuke) she affects a childlike tone, perhaps effective as portraiture in that it evokes sympathy, but not serving the music well. Verdi demands more muscle in these moments than Te Kanawa can provide. Time after time one wants a grander line than she commands.

Over the years, we will learn that Te Kanawa's greatest asset is her velvety-smooth laying on of lyric tone—we hear enough of it on this afternoon to be assured of its quality. But oddly, at some moments a vibrato hardens the tone slightly or a bit of skittishness troubles it, as though debut nerves were perhaps at work—though she claims she is cool in a crisis.[3] I believe her. In the quartet, only cool could enable her to so skillfully descend from the high B-flat, forming a perfect union with the orchestral chords. Verdi allows Desdemona to launch the third-act *concertato* and marks her lines *declamato*—the orchestra owns the cantabile. The soprano cannot meet the demand—her voice is too soft, the diction too liquid—and the dramatic moment turns tepid. She manages the upward curve of the grand phrase 'le amare stille del mio dolor' well enough, but the tone evaporates on the descent. In moments like this, Te Kanawa seems an unfinished artist. Her narration at the beginning of the Willow song is again childlike—amazingly so—but most of the aria matches well with her best qualities: the 'Cantiamo's and 'Salce's are neatly turned, the former proudly affirmed, the latter poised and plaintively suggestive. Over the air, the lengthy, low declamation at the beginning of the Ave Maria is barely audible, but the concluding high note is all one could wish. She dies affectingly and the audience takes her to its heart. I had expected to welcome her more graciously, but evidently my memory had embellished the occasion. Te Kanawa will return to the company during the next two seasons in roles well calculated to demonstrate the beauty of her voice and the pliancy of her phrasing: Donna Elvira and the Countess. We know that Mozart and Strauss, rather than Verdi, will be her homeland and look forward to greeting her there.

La Forza del Destino
22 March 1975

Leonora
Lucine Amara
Preziosilla
Joann Grillo
Don Alvaro
Jon Vickers
Don Carlo
Cornell MacNeil
Padre Guardiano
Bonaldo Giaiotti
Melitone
Gabriel Bacquier
Conductor
James Levine

Our Mediterranean sojourn continues as we set sail from Cyprus for Spain. Seville is our destination, not for the barber's tonic, but to encounter the doom-laden characters of Verdi's *La Forza del Destino*. In the broadcast of 22 March 1975, Vickers tries out another Verdi hero (Don Alvaro), pursued by MacNeil's vengeance-driven Carlo. Amara (Leonora), Grillo (Preziosilla), Giaiotti (Padre Guardiano), and Bacquier (Melitone) are the complicit players with Levine once again Verdi's custodian.

The production is "newly staged" by John Dexter but retains the Berman sets (refurbished, however, and filled with new costumes). Of greater moment for the radio audience, the truncated score in use under Stiedry (notorious for its laceration of Verdi's design) has been superseded by a vastly more satisfying version in which almost all of the minor cuts have been opened up. Most important, the entire Hornachuelos inn scene is restored. Preziosilla and her choral colleagues also receive the prominence that Verdi allotted them. The performance thus gains the epical scope that Verdi labored so diligently, albeit not entirely successfully, to impart to the work. Two other items, matters of placement, should be noted. Levine restores the overture to its rightful position before the rise of the curtain; in earlier Met performances, it had been played before the convent scene. In addition, the order of the 'Oh, tradimento! Sleale!' duet for Alvaro and Carlo and the Rataplan (now complete) for Preziosilla and chorus has been reversed. In a right-hand-giveth, left-hand-taketh-away move, Levine, intent on providing a strong second-act curtain, evidently placed more belief in the power of his star tenor and baritone than a mezzo's struggle with the drum corps. (Verdi's four-act opera is converted to three at the Met.)

Levine delivers a taut performance. And it is well that he does, for, as we have noted, the opera is long and at times quite disjunct. Its scope and varied construct require a binding hand. The conductor does not encourage fate to be more numbingly insistent, more voraciously implacable than need be. Where rhythmic energy rather than mass and volume will serve, he is content with the former. The genre episodes, especially those with Preziosilla, are propelled with invigorating vitality, the chorus splendidly alive and precise, leaving no chance for dullness or boredom to set in. Even the Trabucco vignette, often a trial, is painless. Levine keeps it jaunty and Franke abjures any hint of whine. Far from receiving the expected high-powered treatment, the overture—molded from the opera's main themes—profits from Levine's judicious blocking (a stage director's craft) of the varied components, pitting the individual character of each one against its neighbors until he negotiates a quickened dash to the final bar line. With Levine, order is never the enemy of drama, but rather its guide and succor, its accommodating agent and friend.

Giaiotti performs the padre's duties with appropriate seriousness and in a voice that strikes me as more resonant, more agreeable, less hollow-toned than that in some of his other portrayals. Only a touch of coldness remains, but enough so that Guardiano's embrace of the distraught Leonora is too *pro forma*. Still, I count this one of the finer outings for the Italian basso. He and Bacquier square off knowledgeably in their little duet, the latter trying on a headier tone than he normally wears; the change is probably motivated by his desire to provide an effective contrast with Giaiotti's rolling bass. Elsewhere, the French baritone again proves he is a master of theatrical craft, managing to turn Fra Melitone into a character whom one doesn't mind spending time with, a companionable fate not often achieved by other interpreters. He brings into play every technique at his command, both *buffo* and serious, to create a monk of smallness of heart. He curses the poor with a vengeance, but mean as Melitone is, as Bacquier plays him, the monk gains credibility as a man who knows his own mind. And the voice is both sizable and well controlled. Among the shorter roles, Munzer (as Curra) and her mezzo lend spine to Leonora as she plans her escape, while Morris is the finest Marquise in broadcast history. The father's tender regard for his daughter is reflected in his every phrase (including a lovely mezza voce farewell)—that is, until he discovers Alvaro in her bedroom. Rage and anger take over and Morris excels in that department as well. Miss Grillo, stepping in for Nedda Casei, has the difficult assignment of Preziosilla. As noted, she is gifted with more of the vivandière's music than in previous Met outings. That may not be good news, for either the performer or the audience. But in this case, Levine propels these episodes with such crackerjack exhilaration that we and the opera share in the benefits. Grillo's tone is rather scratchy in fast music, but I don't hold it against her in this role, in part because the timbre has a measure of sensuousness as well. A camp follower would need that, if she is to practice her trade. Add in Grillo's willingness to go after things with dash and vitality. She brings off her scenes well enough. One must make do, if you don't have a Stignani in your managerial pocket. There aren't any of that breed around—especially to sing Preziosilla.

MacNeil contributes a performance that satisfies. He is in best vocal form for this stage of his career (occasional rawness of tone, but no beat), never has to force, and expertly judges the amount of voice to spend so that grandeur and musicality are ably joined. As the student at the Hornachuelos inn, he sings forthrightly, executing the dotted rhythms of his simple story with exactitude, the *primo baritono* voice and manner rightly kept in check. No one could anticipate Carlo's murderous intent as he shares in the fellowship. But MacNeil is Herculean in the three duets with Don Alvaro, articulating each phrase with a keen eye to its meaning as well as to vocal solidity. There lies in both his tone and demeanor an intense calm that, far better than fustian rage, conveys the implacability of the brother. Carlo's supreme moment comes as he meditates on Alvaro's supposed death and discovers his true identity. 'Urna fatale' is a fearsome piece, demanding bigness of tone and—in its ornaments and coiling line—more elegance than most baritones can supply. MacNeil is master of both the quantity and the quality. In particular, his negotiation of Verdi's serpentine phrases commands respect; not for him the relief of shortcuts (though, as traditional, the aria is set down a half step from the written score). Nor does he need to bully the music in order to triumph. The cabaletta is similarly well done, and topped by a ringing high G-sharp (a little trouble in getting there). His efforts garner him the most vociferous applause of the afternoon (though Vickers' reward after 'Tu che in seno' is similarly grand).

In a few key regards, the performance is one of unmet expectations. Anticipated interpretive stances, at least those that have been formulated by earlier Met portrayals, need to be revised. The role of Don Alvaro ought to be in an Otello's line, part of his occupation, provided a tenor puts his mind to it. The problem with Vickers' Indian prince is that he does put his considerable mind to it; the result is a little too much intelligent plotting for character and situation—that is ever his way—and not quite enough straightforward vocalism. At a few critical moments, he shortchanges Verdi's transcendent melodies, falling back on that moony introspection that makes his detractors shout "mannerism," when, in fact, an unadorned conduction of line would better satisfy Verdi and expand character portrayal as well. 'Solenne in quest'ora' suffers most from Vickers' introspective inclinations (some might go so far as to call the predilection a vice). In that duet and (though less prominently) in their other confrontations, he and MacNeil inhabit different stylistic worlds. The antinomy is disconcerting. Of course, Alvaro is weak unto death and, inevitably, Vickers' tone is as well; undoubtedly the manner seemed called for by the tenor's realistic interpretive bent, but Verdi and we want nobility rather than self-pity in this sublime moment. For his part, MacNeil pours out voluminous tone and expansive phrasing with traditional Verdian grandeur. Vickers can do that as well, as he shows in many a gratefully received phrase. In the bedroom scene, the weighty ascent at 'il mondo del suo splendore' is executed with masterly control, and his brilliant tone blazes forth at 'Mi segui! Andiam, dividerci il fato.' In the latter phrase, he meticulously observes the *con forza* marking, driving home Verdi's accents on the repeated notes; in contrast, the triple *piano* at 'no, non potrà' also gains his attention. Both nuances confirm his score fidelity. His defense of Leonora's honor after the father's accusation is lusty-voiced vintage Vickers. Throughout the afternoon, the tenor projects the volatility of Alvaro in mesmerizing fashion. An aura of sadness hangs heavy in the air, the mood frequently deepened by remorse, only to give way to brief explosions of rage. Too bad that a few vocal affectations divert attention from his penetrating characterization.

The opening scene with Leonora, quite forthrightly sung by the tenor, promises more than he ultimately delivers. 'Tu che in seno' (the mood defined by a subdued, nonvirtuosic clarinet solo) holds a few splendid moments. The best of them is the grand final note—even this upright tenor knows an audience is out there. At that moment, Vickers flings his tone out into the house with magnificent certitude and receives its approval in return. On the other hand, the climactic curve

Lucine Amara as Aida. Photography by Louis Mélançon. Courtesy Metropolitan Opera Archives.

around the high B-flat (the note a fine one, as many top tones are throughout the performance) suffers from an uneasy traversal of the *passaggio*. 'Or muoio tranquilla' holds a few pitch vagaries. And the tenor *will* abuse his favored attack-and-recede manner, employing the attenuation so frequently within a phrase or even on a single note that preciosity hovers. Then too, here and elsewhere, he assists the attack on some high notes with a preliminary slide, especially if he can utilize an initial vowel as a launching pad for a second vowel (as in 'insiemi'—the two vowels form a single unit and the tone should move quickly to *e* as the resting vowel). Vickers' way makes for some curious Italian. Of course, singers have a right to utilize language to aid their vocalism as necessary, but when overemployed—as it is by Vickers this afternoon—the ploy becomes annoying. But when it comes to big-voiced, grandly drawn pronouncements, events calculated to stimulate crowd-pleasing excitement, never count Vickers out. Both the 'Sleale' and convent duets with Carlo are for the most part sung with forthright phrasing and ringing tone (though 'sulla terra l'ho adorata' is rather too soupy for my taste). And he can rage vigorously and does so in response to Carlo's taunting. The tenor invariably rises to the challenges posed by Alvaro's dramatic perorations; 'al chiostro, all'èremo' at the second-act curtain, for instance, is nobly intoned. In their confrontational duets, the two singers contend as equals, their thrusting voices like two giant, deep tectonic plates rubbing against each other with earth-shaking results.

Vickers' portrayal of Alvaro sends such a mixed message. Verdi's music may suffer in his manipulative interpretation, but the character itself is brought to life through the exploration of multiple facets that others have not defined as well. We know the Canadian singer has the equipment to be a straight-arrow tenor. But he prefers to be a law unto himself, as integrity dictates. For his many admirers, this has not been Vickers' finest hour. Take heart. The future holds more of his inimitable portraits, including new acquisitions like Parsifal (1979) and Handel's Samson (1986).

With Miss Amara, expectations are of quite a different sort. She performs with the consistency and the entirely admirable intention of a professional artist. From first to last, she is in command of her voice and the Verdi idiom. After enjoying a multitude of broadcast appearances in the fifties and early sixties in a wide range of roles (including Aida), Amara had continued to appear on the airwaves during the next decade. But in that period she was confined to her familiar Micaela, Antonia, Liù, and Nedda (plus Ellen Orford, the latter purportedly assigned because of her company loyalty).[4] In house performances, however, during the last decade she had also been appearing in grander roles like Aida, Maddalena, Tosca, Manon Lescaut, and Ariadne. On this afternoon, Leonora comes to her by default; Arroyo was scheduled for the broadcast.

The expectation deficit in regard to Amara comes into play when those with long memories recall other Leonoras, artists whose voices had either more plush or more steel or were more vibrant: singers like Ponselle (the records only), Milanov, Tebaldi, Farrell, and Price, to stay with the Met broadcasts. Arroyo, too, owns a voice of imposing dimensions. Amara's sound is inherently more delicate, at times almost a bit girlish (not inappropriate to the character, but not quite Verdi's soprano). The qualification having been made, I take entirely to heart her portrayal and her performance. Hers is a lovely instrument, the fluency of tone and pearly timbre as fresh today as it was at her *Don Carlo* debut as the Celestial

Voice a quarter century ago. What is different from the early decades of her career is the degree of dramatic involvement, the projection of emotional highlights in the text, the stylistic verity, and, most tellingly, the willingness to spend voice and person at critical moments in commanding fashion. We always knew she could sing. We always recognized her as a thoroughgoing professional, ready to perform an amazing variety of roles at a moment's notice. (No wonder Bing—selfish for his company's health—wouldn't let her wander off to Europe when the offers came.) We always relished the integrity of her musicianship. Now attitude has been added to the mix. A specific revelation, and one that is proof positive of her liberation, is the final high B-flat of her 'Maledizione' at the end of 'Pace, pace, mio Dio!' As expected, her attack is secure, but the tone, initially sounded at a quiet dynamic, expands and grows until an unexpected splendor envelops it, a cutting edge invades it, and excitement inflames the house. I have seldom heard her utter such a tone—and I am a longtime admirer of the Amara voice. One must also salute her *messa di voce* on the initial 'Pace' of the aria as well, and the *piano* attack and crescendo at 'Invan la pace.' The depths of *dolore* cannot be plumbed by such a voice, but the aria rings true, nevertheless. The soprano makes clear that Leonora's cloistered retreat has not brought her the peace she craves. The air of desperation is not only tellingly sounded in this aria, but dominates her characterization throughout the afternoon. I recall seeing Amara during this same period perform the *Trovatore* Leonora with the Houston company and being similarly impressed with her communicative vocalism and dramatic immersion in the character.

Leonora's opening aria, 'Me pellegrina ed orfana,' allows the singer to establish her credentials right off (the *subito piano* at 'Ahi troppo' in the introductory recitative is a lovely effect). Amara sings the aria most affectingly, with many agreeable nuances—the color change at 'Ti lascio, ahimè' is one. Perhaps it is her placement onstage that limits effectiveness in the prayer at the inn—the chorus, as miked, is vibrant and grand. The convent scene is one of the most demanding episodes for a soprano in the Italian repertory and to negotiate it as handily as Amara does is evidence not only of her stamina, but of her worth. Here and there, dulcet tones must do work made for grander instruments, but overall her conviction and projection of text and line carry the day. Linear conduction is her chief weapon and it is resolutely employed throughout the grand *scena*. She seems to pull back momentarily from full-throated vocalism in the later moments of her interchange with Padre Guardiano—probably a wise move in terms of saving voice for the peak moments of the scene. She takes to heart the double *piano* dynamic and *sotto voce* marking of 'La Vergine degli angeli,' her voicing incredibly fine toned for such velvety-voiced monks; again, stage placement may affect the balance.

One of Amara's greatest assets is her fidelity to the score. If occasionally, one senses an air of efficiency in her portrayal, it is a fleeting impression that soon gives way in the face of convincing declamation or heartfelt song. We will hear her in yet another star vehicle, Butterfly, this time substituting for a little-known singer. The opportunity, though at another's expense, is entirely welcome.

Amara is remembered for the preservation of her voice over a long career. Moffo, though her star status continues to be affirmed even today, endured the opposite fate: the disintegration of her voice after about a decade of Metropolitan triumphs and the irrevocable damage to her reputation as she continued to perform. Her final broadcast appearance occurs as Nedda in the *Pagliacci* of 18 Janu-

Pagliacci
18 January 1975

Nedda
Anna Moffo
Canio
James McCracken
Beppe
Robert Schmorr
Tonio
Sherrill Milnes
Silvio
Lenus Carlson
Conductor
John Nelson

ary 1975. With her are McCracken, Milnes, Lenus Carlson (Silvio), and Schmorr (Beppe). John Nelson, remembered for his command of *Jen fa*, is given a chance to try his hand at the standard repertory.

Conductor Nelson is the guiding star of this afternoon's effort; his hand proves to be adept at guiding, and it is his light that gives the performance its major distinction. The introductory prelude tells his quality. Vigor and exactitude are his calling cards, with the individual colors of the orchestral choirs cleanly defined, and delightfully so, the winds sparkling, the horns expressive in their solo. *Stentate, misterioso, con impeto*, Leoncavallo's minute directions are not only followed, but taken to heart, enlivened, made to speak. He sculpts the violin melody for maximum effect, without wallowing in its curves. Here is a musician who belongs in the theater. Drama and music seem indissoluble in his expert fashioning of the score. The intermezzo is the most evocative episode of the afternoon; Nelson knits its several moods into a unified whole. The chorus, too, responds to his leadership in an exuberant, animated fashion so that their lengthy set pieces are not mere fodder in between solo turns. The village of these Calabrians seems to be a livelier, happier place than most performances suggest.

Highlights and lowlights are the order of the day onstage. Schmorr's tenor is too ordinary for Harlequin's song, though he almost makes up the difference with some astute character touches in the little serenade. In his exchanges with Colombina, he again demonstrates his acting skills and the voice is better focused as well. His is the only performance familiar from previous broadcasts. Lenus Carlson, now in his second season with the company, is given a prime opportunity as Silvio. Like many a young American baritone, he owns an attractive voice, the timbre fresh and firm, redolent of healthy youth. His delivery of the grand phrases of the duet is rather too literal for the *verismo* style. It lacks both expanse of line and suavity of expression. He manages all the notes with tonal rectitude, the high ones securely taken, though a bit of temerity may infect the approach to the concluding one. 'Tutto scordiam!' rings true. Time will probably add the necessary interpretive subtlety; the pleasant quality of the voice deserves no less.

Milnes, in the opposite corner, has plenty of know-how and delights in showing it off. The prologue receives a rousing delivery, not devoid, however, of musical or dramatic touches to give it character. His pride is evident as he announces, 'Io sono il Prologo,' and his performance justifies it. One wants a real mezza voce at 'Un nido di memorie'— the text dwells on a 'nest of memories' and Warren's compact, soft tones and gracious conduct of line set the standard for this phrase sequence. Milnes makes a good try, altering the mood, but his soft singing is not in Warren's league. Occasionally, his low voice lacks color and body. We know he has brilliant top notes: the interpolated high A-flat and G are both stunning. (In the duet with Nedda, a high note or two seems oddly swallowed back in the throat— that odd recession is more often than one would like seemingly part of the Milnes "method.") But the top voice opens up grandly in the concluding cantabile of the prologue and, after he gurgitates those brazen concluding top tones, the audience can hardly wait to roar its approval. Thereafter, the role of Tonio calls for a variety of character poses and Milnes, a theatrical creature, knows how to play them for dramatic effectiveness. But he never lets us forget that, beyond the white paint and the red nose, he is a *primo baritono*. One must take him at his word.

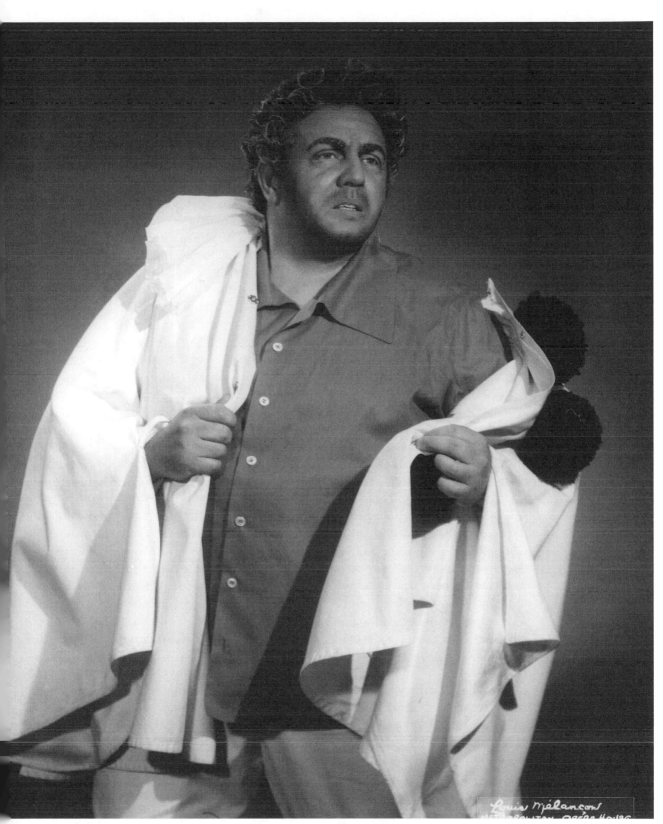

James McCracken as Canio in *Pagliacci*. Photography by Louis Mélançon. Courtesy Metropolitan Opera Archives.

In his initial aria and often thereafter, McCracken's healthy voice could pass for a baritone, so dense and darkly covered are his tones. But when he surges above the staff, the ring and brilliance of his voice assures us of his stature in the tenor ranks. At 'A ventitré ore!' both the high B and A are as strapping and firm as the ridge of a mountain range, and unlike most tenors, who, this early in the opera, like to shortchange the top note and linger on the lower, he sounds a ringing B that takes the honors. The American tenor is in splendid vocal form and the role of Canio seems tailor made for his high-pressure style and dramatic voice. Beef, rather than beauty, is its province. I like his recitative to 'Vesti la giubba' better than the aria itself, although he gives a respectable reading of that strenuous piece. Power, enormity of tone, and heart-on-sleeve theatrics are his tools. He uses them effectively, but a grander curve of phrase and a nobler stance might call forth an even greater response than he receives. Nelson is intent on just such a reading, but the tenor, sensing too slow a pace for his wants (or needs), unabashedly jerks him on at 'E se Arlecchin t'invola Colombina'; singer and conductor thereafter form a perfect union. After all, Nelson has the long postlude to make his point, and does so. More than his conventional reading of the celebrated lament, McCracken's heartfelt singing of 'No! Pagliaccio non son' strikes home. Rather than overt emotions, voice and song are employed to sound his suffering and betray his troubled state. The baritonal resonances that oppress the opening phrases are suggestive in themselves, and when the tenor launches 'Sperai, tanto il delirio accecato m'aveva' his vibrant timbre and burgeoning phrases capture our sympathy. A grand high B-flat takes care of any unfulfilled wishes on the audience's part. When Canio demands that Nedda name her lover, McCracken's fierceness and vocal plenitude are enough to inspire fear in even an innocent wife.

Nedda was hardly an innocent, no matter her affinity for birds. The role is a new one for Miss Moffo. It may seem odd to find a Lucia in the tawdry environment of verismo opera, but recall that Melba performed the role at the Met during the 1890s. Of course, after some short operas (*Bohème*, for instance), management liked to have the Australian diva come before the curtain and sing Lucia's mad scene. In those days, the audience wanted its money's worth. It is well that Moffo does not attempt that feat on this afternoon for her voice is in a shocking state of disrepair. In her favor are a number of top notes that at least resemble their former state, though where velvet once obtained a cutting edge now must do. The upward sweep of the Ballatella's final phrases is a boon to her, but it cannot erase what has gone before nor remedy her largely ineffectual delivery in the scene with Silvio. (One 'Tutto scordiam' helps, however, for her top A is intact.) Much of the role resides in the middle voice, and when Moffo must sing notes within the staff, control flies out the window. A ghastly wobble infects many tones, and sustained notes are clipped short at the ends of phrases—on occasion, when held, the dip down on a final note can be as much of a fourth. Colombina's effectiveness in the play within a play depends on a pinpoint delivery of her doll-like music and even that is beyond the soprano's limited means. Moffo is too experienced a stage person not to rise to the dramatic and musical climaxes of Nedda's final moments. Her top B is a good one and, as if recognizing its quality and, even more, its rarity, she is loath to give it up. At her solo bow, the audience appears to welcome her almost as in days of old. She had been one of the Met's brightest lights of the sixties and one hopes that the memory of her glory days will continue to sustain her.

Moffo was scheduled to sing several performances of Norina later in the season, but they did not materialize. After a few outings as Violetta and a trio of concert Butterflys in the parks series during the 1975–76 season, she and the Met parted company. In her seventeen seasons as a regular company member, she had appeared 199 times at both the old and new Mets and on tour. An operetta duet with Merrill at the 1983 centennial gala was a kind afterthought. In between these events, she attempted to reconstruct her voice and continued to perform occasionally in lesser venues. But the longed-for remontant state eluded her. It is the decade of the sixties that remains her monument.

The Puccini operas live or die in the throats and hearts of their heroines and, in spite of defections (Moffo) and retirements (Kirsten—but in name only), the Metropolitan was well stocked in that category. The composer's popularity continued unabated, so all the favorites plus the recently embraced *Turandot* enlivened the airwaves. In the *Manon Lescaut* broadcast of 29 December 1973, Cruz-Romo—at home in the Verdi operas—tries on that volatile creature for the first time in her career. The performance is in other ways also a venture into the unknown. A new tenor, Carlos Montané, partners her in their adventures in passion and degradation. While Met veterans Anthony (Edmondo), Sereni (Lescaut), and Corena (Geronte) lend a helping or hindering hand, they are subject to Leif Segerstam's presence on the podium, which adds yet another inviting new element to the mix.

The maestro, a Finn, trained at Juilliard but was ultimately faithful to his homeland. He is young (twenty-nine at broadcast time) but clearly a man of parts. Both the Finnish National Opera and the Royal Opera of Stockholm welcomed him in his early twenties, before he became chief conductor at Berlin's Deutsche Oper in 1971. Then Covent Garden (*Tosca*) and Salzburg (*Entführung*) made his acquaintance. But once again the Finnish National Opera claimed him, this time as director—the Savonlinna Festival became his pet project. *Bohème* and *Manon Lescaut* are his debut season assignments. Previous Met conductors of Puccini's first success have included Vigna, Ferraro, Polacco, Papi, Serafin, Antonicelli—all to the manner born. (Yes, Mitropoulos and Adler slipped in there, but the former had a late-career Puccini fetish, while Adler was an in-house takeover man.) Music knows no national boundaries, but from Lucca to Vasa is a far leap. With Segerstam added to Levine and Nelson, is the Met running a boys' camp for conductors? *Wunderkind*s abound. Remember, in the 1974 *Tristan* imbroglio with Vickers and Barlow, Chapin was ready to render unto Segerstam what was Leinsdorf's, though that veteran undoubtedly thought himself securely ensconced in his Wagnerian command post. Wonder boy, indeed. In this broadcast debut, the maestro's youth may be apparent in his search for an individual take on the vibrant Puccini opus. He is half speed demon (first act) and half granite lifter (the final two). Clearly, he knows what he wants. Students and inn guests are propelled along at a breathtaking pace—just keeping up earns a good-conduct medal. Pit and stage are in a disconnect, not in terms of ensemble or of keeping order—except for a slight tussle with the women's chorus, Segerstam has control of that—but rather in each amplifying the other's message. Still, his exuberance is a better tonic than mere routine. And one wants the young people to enjoy themselves. The opera turns tragic at the Le Havre pier and on the Louisiana desert—now the Finn does an about-face. Both episodes are heavily weighted with doom, their pace (especially

Manon Lescaut
29 December 1973

Manon
Gilda Cruz-Romo
Des Grieux
Carlos Montané
Edmondo
Charles Anthony
Lescaut
Mario Sereni
Geronte
Fernando Corena
Conductor
Leif Segerstam

in the roll call) deliberate, at times inexorable. The conductor is intent on making the third act count for more than its brief passage suggests. I found it quite imposing—the roll call of deportees is a gripping episode and Segerstam's reading expands its impact. Throughout the opera, his phrasing is plotted with exceeding care—sometimes the seams show. He wants to pack in so much and the results are occasionally a bit angular. Still, at critical moments he can cultivate a mood, enabling the Puccini flow and surge to have its way with us in the tried-and-true manner. His obvious talent increases anticipation for the *Bohème* broadcast down the line.

Among the comprimario artists, Schmorr adeptly suggests the effeteness of the Dancing Master without resorting to caricature. Castel's Lamplighter sounds like he has been making the rounds for years—he is comfortable in his work and some of the good feeling rubs off on us. Rather than performing menial tasks, in opera lamplighters and night watchmen are there to spread cheer. Anthony, Edmondo in several previous broadcasts, again proves that when he steps out of the character ranks into the romantic spotlight (even in a discretionary manner as Des Grieux's friend) he can form tone and phrase as ingratiatingly as many a leading tenor. Segerstam takes the Madrigal at a somber pace (the text suggests the mood) and Judith Forst profits from the unusual tempo, her tone and phrasing complementing the conductor's intent. As brother and predator, Sereni and Corena, two of the Metropolitan's most valuable veterans, make a meal of the slight fare that Puccini allotted them. They create characterizations of considerable weight, helping to anchor the opera, filling in the corners when the composer is obsessed with his romantic duo. Corena, in spite of his consecrated status in the buffo genre, can convert his timbral burr into menace with hardly the flick of a resonance chamber. His Geronte is in turn a gentleman, a doter on women (he all but licks his lips as Manon dances), and a vile sadist. And each is a believable transformation from the previous pose. Some singers seem made for the stage. On the other hand, Sereni is, and always has been, the singer who comes to sing. And he does so on this afternoon, and very well, too. Heard in his seventh season with the company, he has never sounded better. The voice's manly timbre and bravado finish are proudly displayed during Lescaut's key moment in his sister's boudoir. Indeed, on this afternoon his legato and tonal consistency rival, and in certain ways, exceed, Milnes' allotment. What a hearty and opportunistic brother to Manon the baritone is. He is always out for the big chance and Sereni's voice is sturdy enough to gain it. Lescaut may be willing to help Des Grieux save Manon from deportation, but this baritone makes the sibling seem better fit for helping himself than others. One would not mind sitting opposite him at a gaming table—provided you watched his hand, as well as your own.

Des Grieux is a role made for the greatest tenors. The Met has known many of them in the part, beginning with Caruso at the 1907 premiere, followed by Martinelli and Gigli, with, in broadcasts to this date, Björling, Tucker, and Bergonzi. As if heralding that period where radio casts, once stocked with the proudest of the proud, grow spotty in leading roles, Carlos Montané plays Des Grieux. A Cuban who escaped his homeland in 1962, he became an American citizen. His Metropolitan career would be of short duration and one can only wonder why management placed him in this prominent broadcast assignment. He is experienced in the role, having sung it in Düsseldorf, Berlin, and Seattle, and judg-

Gilda Cruz-Romo as Manon Lescaut. Photography by Louis Mélançon. Courtesy Metropolitan Opera Archives.

ing from his vocal material, he does have a right to tenor rank. The voice is firm and employed with consistency. But the timbre, pleasant in the mid-range at a moderate dynamic, is thrown into another orbit on high. There the voice takes on a decidedly metallic cast, so much so that the ear blanches at his invariably stout—and assured—singing whenever Puccini sends him flying above the staff. While clean, the tone sounds fabricated, offering instead of natural resonance, the cutting sonics of cheap audio. Montané has a good sense of line—his musical qualifications are hardly nil—and he responds to textual stimulus. Still, a bit of *dolcezza* is desirable in a Puccini tenor—'Donna, non vidi mai' demands a caress; Montané cannot supply it. When it comes to Manon, Des Grieux is a firebrand, whether berating her for infidelity or bristling in her defense. He throws voice and person into high gear at the slightest encouragement—and Montané is not loath to follow. In the second-act duet, it is he who best fills the passion quotient, though vocally his work is routine. 'Ah! Manon, mi tradisce' and the fiery aria at Le Havre ('Guardate, pazzo son') are strongly delivered, his best moments of the afternoon. The audience, evidently liking the tenor's brass, shows its approval at his solo bow after the third-act curtain.

In spite of the late-developing popularity of *Manon Lescaut* in the repertory, it had figured in the Met repertory for quite a few seasons. Past performances held a number of memorable creations of the heroine. Puccini had been on hand at the 1907 Met premiere when Lina Cavalieri's beauty obliterated doubts about her voice. Other artists placed decidedly different imprints on the wayward girl. In the teens and twenties, Frances Alda was knowing, while Bori, her successor, gave Manon a demure elegance while being devilishly attractive. The opera faded from the repertory until Johnson revived it in 1949 with Kirsten, charming and suppliant in the title role. (Björling, Hayward, Valdengo, and Baccaloni were her cohorts.) Albanese, passionate and despairing, and Tebaldi, vocally resplendent and placid in temperament, were notable broadcast interpreters.

Not all in that roll call would qualify as singing actresses. But Manon Lescaut is a role that flourishes when interpreted by that rare species. Cruz-Romo's talents in that regard are not of the highest order. But she has been well prepared for this, her first series anywhere in the virtuoso part, by that maven of the opera quiz, Alberta Masiello. Thus the Mexican soprano dutifully employs the distinctive vocabulary of the Puccini idiom, applying it tastefully and with care. Though desperation does not seem quite her most arresting state, it hovers over the last act quite affectingly. Still, more than death's ghostly hand, it is the singer's craft that informs her 'Sola, perduta, abbandonata.' Verdi soprano that she is, Cruz-Romo makes the big moments count and her involvement grows as the aria progresses; the climactic 'Ah' is not only a grand tone, but it speaks of despondency. And the gentle afterthought as Des Grieux returns to her ('Fra le braccia') makes for a heartrending contrast. In her last moments, her cries of 'Io t'amo, t'amo tanto!' are searing. She scores dramatic points in the earlier acts as well; 'Ah! una minaccia funebre io sento!' tellingly exposes Manon's terror when confronting deportation on the docks of Le Havre. I wonder, however, if the verismo terrain (elegant though Puccini's version be) is her natural habitat.

Before Manon crosses the Atlantic, Cruz-Romo exhibits considerable charm in situations where charm matters. Still, her "acting" bits (as when Manon prepares her toilette) come off as a bit studied. Time and more performances may remedy that. Though the role profits from a singing actress's care, the end result will be of little moment if the artist cannot sing. Miss Cruz-Romo is eminently qualified in that regard. The purely vocal challenges are many and varied, with lyric, coloratura, and dramatic soprano components. A light, girlish timbre at the inn establishes both the convent-bound minx' youth and our soprano's credibility. Her 'In quelle trine morbide' is one of the loveliest in broadcast history. The voice, heard now in its full maturity, is as beautiful as one could wish; equalized throughout the range, it blooms on the very secure high notes. She strokes the repeated notes of 'O mia dimora umile' with a gentle *piano*, creating just the intended effect, and executes the difficult low-lying close (elegantly touching the grace notes) with poise and a welcome *délicatesse*. Segarstam doesn't always allow the love duet to overflow with passion à la Mitropoulos, so the soprano must be content to pour out more voice than heart. But she owns such a confident instrument that she comes out the winner, especially in a few unaccompanied moments that have the ring of truth, both as song and as drama. Like most Manons who have preceded and will follow her, she cannot turn 'Lodi aurate' and 'L'ora, o Tirsi' to best account, but her radiant top tones, thrust forth with bright certainty (plus, in the opposite corner, a few delicate trills), rescue them from oblivion. Cruz-Romo, through both her thoughtful characterization of Manon and most particularly, her unmannered, assured vocalism, proves her right to greater acclaim than she received during her fourteen seasons with the company. At this point in her career (1973), the soprano appears to be coming into her own worldwide: debuts at Covent Garden and La Scala were recent conquests and the Vienna Staatsoper is in the offing. Though not a member during the 1974–75 season, thereafter she would belong to the Met for another nine seasons.

Sopranos of various types come and go at the Metropolitan, many stirring hardly a ripple of remembrance in audience members and little interest from opera historians. Enriqueta Tarrés is one of them. A Spanish singer of few appearances in her two seasons with the company, she was scheduled to sing the title role in the *Madama Butterfly* broadcast of 11 January 1975, but Amara took over the glamor part. Joining her are a raft of fine American artists, among them Love (Suzuki), Morell (Pinkerton), and Uppman (Sharpless). Richard Woitach, yet another American, is on the podium.

Woitach is a member of that expert coach-répétiteur-conductor class that the Metropolitan management rightly values highly. *Madama Butterfly* was his broadcast debut as a conductor, but the radio audience was familiar with his extensive knowledge and jocular personality as a frequent quiz participant. His conduct of the opera is eminently successful, both in terms of the professional quality of the performance as a whole and, even more importantly, for the interpretive imprint that he places on the familiar score. His quiz appearances had not prepared us for the sensitive character of his musicianship, and why would they, since it is folly to equate personality traits with artistic worth. Woitach is more of a romantic than most Puccini podium interpreters are wont to be. Strenuous dramatic effects are not cultivated—though they are hardly shunned. Rather, he stresses at every turn the lyrical impulse of the score, reveling in its orchestral colors, piquant or luscious, and shaping phrases with more concern for their musical character than their dramatic potency. The preference is apparent at the very beginning in the unhurried, cleanly articulated soundings of the opening motive; yes, Puccini has

Madama Butterfly
11 January 1975

Cio-Cio-San
Lucine Amara
Suzuki
Shirley Love
Pinkerton
Barry Morell
Sharpless
Theodor Uppman
Conductor
Richard Woitach

marked it *vigoroso*, but Woitach's treatment is not unwelcome—too many string scratches have blemished other performances. The interpretive stance is epitomized in his sensitive, meditative reading of the third-act prelude. Throughout the afternoon, his way lends a more intimate, less harrowing cast to the tale of the abandoned geisha girl. Some might prefer a more traditional thrust at key moments, but Woitach maintains his conception with conspicuous integrity from first to last. And it satisfies. Moreover, he is kind to his singers and they are with him all the way. No wonder the once-designated assistant conductor has this season been elevated to the full conductor ranks.

Castel plugs in as a low-voltage Goro rather than the personality salesman most frequently heard. Vocal unction does not seem to be one of the tricks of his trade. I don't miss it. Christopher sings Yamadori, reminding us that the cherished Cehanovsky, too, gave the enamored prince a songful presence. Thompson (Commissioner) and Harvuot (Bonze), the one a neutral-toned bureaucrat and the other a hard-hearted interfering uncle priest, dutifully fulfill their job descriptions. Love is eminently successful at giving voice to Suzuki's regrets and laments. The voice is warm—essential, if Butterfly is to be comforted—solid in the lower range (which makes for pleasing prayers) and flexible enough for the flower duet. In the latter, Amara's quick leap to the *pianissimo* high B-flat catches her by surprise. Love, like any good Japanese servant, is not overly assertive in the few highly charged moments of the score in which Suzuki participates. To her credit, she doesn't boom out tones for mere display, but remains in character while still administering to her mistress' distress.

Uppman's Sharpless and Morell's Pinkerton are known from earlier broadcasts. The American Consul remains a role agreeable to the baritone's vocal and interpretive talents. In the opening act, a few low tones may have lost their manly burr, but the bulk of the voice has its familiar cast. He salutes America with conviction and continues to deliver sound advice to the wayward lieutenant. The letter-reading scene with Butterfly shows off his best attributes, the sympathetic attitude and warm tones both an encouragement and a caution to the excited Butterfly. Morell has been singing recently in Europe and South America, announcer Allen informs us. Foreign air has done him good. His voice is in prime condition, the phrase shaping and text articulation even more idiomatic than remembered, and the manner, if anything, more assertive. Can this upright tenor be the cad that Giacosa and Illica made of the sailor? (Initially, John Luther Long in his short story formulated Pinkerton's character and then David Belasco in his play cemented it.) Casual in his drinking habits and unthinking in his wedding plans, the Morell Pinkerton is the perfect 'Yankee vagabondo'—the aria is confidently negotiated. The lieutenant is committed to taking his pleasure where he finds it, and our tenor may have a right to gratification—he sings with vibrant tone and thrusts forth ringing high notes whenever Puccini puts them in his way. As Morell begins the love duet, he is appropriately ardent, though his demands hardly seem lascivious, that is, not if we are expected to accept his gentlemanly manner and elegant vocalism as evidence of desire. His interpretive stance complements conductor Woitach's, so all is well. Morell saves a dose of passion for the condemnatory phrases of Pinkerton's third-act farewell to the house of his former happiness, pouring tenorial remorse into its rhapsodic phrases and savoring its treacly sentiments. He comes out a cad, after all.

In many ways, Amara's voice is well suited to Butterfly. The heroine, as Puccini limned her, is a bundle of the pathetic and the brave. She requires a delicacy of touch to complement her diminutive Oriental stature and childlike faith in her love but demands a commanding utterance as the abandoned wife faces loneliness and ultimate despair. The soprano's instrument, while tension-strung, owns an innate sweetness of timbre and she can spin tone most engagingly. Though not broad in circumference, the voice has a taut strength that has enabled her to undertake roles like Aida and Leonora, where dramatic pith is essential. Thus, both of the above-named requisites are fairly met. But to ensure success in this demanding part, those considerable assets need to be placed in the service of character creation; only then can a portrait of heart-piercing appeal be realized. We know the promise is there, especially since we have Amara's Leonora fast in the memory.

At she surmounts the hill overlooking the Nagasaki harbor, Amara certifies her vocal credentials by crowning Butterfly's entrance music with a liquid flight to a stunning high D-flat, as easily attained and scream free as that of any broadcast interpreter. Many of the familiar little character touches are affectingly deployed. For the most part, the soprano keeps them in the middle ground, that is, the *accenti* are not so hard-pressed that they become annoying (though 'uno, due, tre' is harsh counting); a few are not quite deft enough to seem natural to the young heroine. Yet all are in place—Amara is always well schooled and duty-diligent in execution. 'Ieri son salita' is forthrightly presented, a moment of vocal honesty that complements Butterfly's sincerity in adopting her husband's religion. The love duet holds many exquisite phrases, spun with the soprano's customary tonal consistency and an agreeable and compliant sinuosity. The leap to a high *pianissimo* at 'Vogliatemi bene,' an effect that the soprano can easily command, is less than hoped for (the tone thins unexpectedly), but similar moments later in the opera (as in the concluding section of the flower duet) meet the test to lovely purpose. She can be emphatic in surrender as well: 'Si, per la vita' is knifed forth with belief and abandon. Both tenor and soprano latch on to the concluding high note; this time a touch of the scream does infect hers, but the combined effect is audience pleasing.

'Un bel dì' benefits from a bell-like attack that sets the soprano off on an affecting, completely assured, traversal of its overfamiliar phrases. And Amara's exquisitely molded recall of days filled with love, which serves as introduction to that dramatic centerpiece, is equally telling. In that episode, as in the aria, she does achieve that heart-piercing communion that binds us to Butterfly, allowing us to participate in her hopes and disappointments. Throughout the extended scene, Amara demonstrates the fullness of her vocal artistry and a command of character not often credited to her. The letter-reading scene with Sharpless is also well played, the variety of line readings competently explored, the singer's cultivated tones altered to suit the text's demands. I do not believe she is quite as successful in the demanding scene where, in desperation, Butterfly presents Trouble to the consul. The fright, indeed near-terror, that overtakes Cio-Cio-San at the thought of permanent separation from Pinkerton is inadequately realized, either in bounty of voice or intensity of expression. (She does try to rescue it with a dramatic concluding 'Ah morte,' but it seems a bit outsized—stagey—compared to what has gone before.) Nor does she capture the full rapture of the wife's exaltation when she sights the ship (though her crescendo at the close is effective). One feels that the soprano has somehow allowed the dramatic thread of the opera to slacken and the professional singer to take over. But the flower duet is neatly done; a pliant throat and happy spirit—both of which are Amara's in life—take care of its charming furbelows. Oddly, the call for her bridal vestments, a phrase that she ought to make her own, disappoints. The little lullaby that opens the final act—troublesome to some interpreters—is grist for the Amara mill. She floats the high B with the ease of one who could walk on air—a lovely moment. Cio-Cio-San's farewell to her child is yet another episode that seems not to suit the singer's voice and art as well as most of the role. In spite of its tensility, her instrument is ill employed when it must bang away with vehemence in a verismo moment such as the final scene. In the opening phrases (and there the soprano must be commended for the rhythmically exact alternations of 'Tu!' with the orchestral chords), Amara, in an idle search for dramatic verisimilitude, adopts a more open tone to meet the need. In so doing, she denies her most precious asset, namely her comely tone. On the other hand, when the singer again calls upon her best vocal form and applies a silvery float to the concluding high-lying phrases ('O a me, sceso dal trono'), she and her delectable tone seem at odds with the dramatic situation. But Amara greets the final curtain not only with voice intact, but undoubtedly buoyed by the certain knowledge that she has created a believable portrait, one that holds moments, vocal and interpretive, that would do honor to any prima donna.

The following year, Zylis-Gara presents her geisha girl to the radio public, the first of her several radio portrayals. On the broadcast of 3 April 1976, Woitach is again the podium occupant, with a few roles filled by 1975 players (Uppman, Castel, and Christopher). Casei prays as Suzuki, and Dobriansky is her Bonze, while Alexander, the Pinkerton, is the cause of their opposing devotions.

At the curtain's rise, I sense a marginal step-up in conductor Woitach's treatment of the *vigoroso* motivic play, even as the musical gestures of his third-act prelude surge somewhat more vibrantly. Still, his way with the opera remains the very antithesis of, say, the Mehta grandstand play. If occasionally he seems to treasure inordinately the composer's painterly palette and lyrical expressivity, Woitach nevertheless maintains the integrity of his intimate conception of the opera with admirable taste and control. Of the repeat performers, Uppman again exhibits *his* brand of good taste; his tones have their familiar warmth, and may be more resonant than in the previous year. Casei is wrongly cast as Suzuki. Her instrument lacks impact in the lower range and takes on more of a soprano cast as it rises, so the fit between the maid's music and her voice is not ideal. Now and then she displays a welcome mettle that adds to the liveliness of the proceedings, and the love duet allows her to present herself in a more favorable light. Boucher (Commissioner) and Dobriansky are able comprimarios, with the latter convincingly rude and gruff in his denunciations of poor Butterfly.

Alexander is an old hand at Pinkerton's wooing and remorse. The Mississippian had partnered Scotto in her 1966 broadcast debut as Butterfly, and other radio outings (Hoffmann, Anatol, Edgardo, Des Grieux) confirm his stature in the company. He tells *Opera News* that the lieutenant is not really a cad; "ethics change" seems a surprising justification for the character's waywardness, especially coming from so pleasantly uxorious a chap as Alexander.[5] Undoubtedly, the romantic music that Puccini wrote for his jaded male lead allows a tenor to view Pinkerton

Madama Butterfly
3 April 1976

Cio-Cio-San
Teresa Zylis-Gara
Suzuki
Nedda Casei
Pinkerton
John Alexander
Sharpless
Theodor Uppman
Conductor
Richard Woitach

with a less jaundiced eye than does an objective audience member. The American tenor is nearly always in top form, and he is, once again, on this afternoon. In fact, I find the timbre (which seemed to me too nasal on some other broadcasts) to be at its most ingratiating today, its notable plangency blended with the voice's dense core to produce a more mellow tone without any loss of brilliance at the top of the range. Sturdy conduct of line is his forte but, when he chooses, he can inflect a phrase with subtlety and thereby complement the composer's shapely lines; Pinkerton's tribute to American adventurism profits from both modes of expression. While singing with happy assurance there, he is more suited to a lover's tasks than playing at being a Yankee vagabond. He proves it with his sensitive sounding of desire at the close of the first act. In general, the tenor offers a more interesting characterization and more agreeable vocalism than he did in a few of his other broadcast roles. An intelligent artist, he chooses to invest 'Addio, fiorito asil' with a hurt nobility rather than plague it with useless regrets. The high-minded posture may or may not be justified, but the result is preferable to the audible equivalent of a bag of hot tears, which many tenors have favored.

Except for a single season (1973–74), Scotto, whose Butterfly rightfully has earned history's encomium, was a member of the company throughout the seventies and most of the eighties. Yet it is Zylis-Gara whom the management put forth as often as a broadcast Cio-Cio-San. In fact, once a decade was the Italian soprano's allotment from the time of her 1966 radio debut, while Zylis-Gara garnered three hearings from 1976 to 1981. And yet the Polish singer's Butterfly, at least in this first radio outing, is a puzzlement—to quote a Siamese royal source. (The soprano had sung the role on tour in 1974, but this is her first series in the house.) She is surely the most forlorn lepidopteron in broadcast memory. The soprano and Woitach are on the same wavelength. As usual, that makes not only for interpretive bliss but a welcome homogeneity of style. But unbridled joy is not quite my response. The problem is that Woitach's approach, as we have seen, is not inherently dramatic, and when the soprano's languid manner and mournful timbre are added in, the heroine's sorrows tend to wear down the listener. Long-suffering Butterfly is, but the audience need not be. I am a great admirer of the Polish soprano, one of the most satisfying and reliable artists of these decades. Her voice in the house—my memories of her Manon Lescaut and Desdemona are of the fondest—charms and pleases, and when she spends tone at full throttle, tracing arcs of phrase with grandeur, she is a hugely gratifying artist. The timbre, stocked with woodwind colors, is a potent interpretive tool and frequently it serves that purpose on this afternoon. One relishes that magical mix of colors, a palette that can inflect the voice with tonal fullness even when sounded at the softest dynamic—but today a plaintive cast predominates to an alarming degree. That might work well enough as a single component of a characterization, but her geisha girl seldom shows spunk; often the singer fails to take full advantage of those moments when joy or anger animates Butterfly's music. Oh, she recognizes them, gives them a discreet nod, and is content with that. One could regard her way as subtlety squared—and subtlety, if applied as warranted, is a considerable virtue. One more limiting factor must be mentioned. The Polish soprano's articulation of text is cushioned by the texture of her native tongue; the bristling consonants of Italian, that language's overall rhythmic vitality (which could counteract timbral and stylistic languidness), is not called into play. Her legato is delicious and one must savor it, but a price is paid as well. In any case, her Cio-Cio-San is a somber creature. Perhaps it is the soprano's idea of Oriental reserve that she wishes to replicate. But, for theatrical representation, it is better to divine the character of Puccini's geisha in what the composer put on the page.

There you have the case against Zylis-Gara's Butterfly. But its merits are many and exceptional. I count her creation fascinating, more importantly for what it is, rather than what it isn't. Beauties abound. True, the high notes of the entrance music are taken with some caution—she wisely settles for the lower ending. And more power to her. The high note at the end of the love duet, however, is a good one, and throughout the opera her top notes are full and satisfying. At the other end of the spectrum, she counts 'uno, due, tre' charmingly. 'Ieri son salita' shows us her true worth, the legato mesmerizing, the tone luscious. Woitach allows her all the time in the world to work her spell. As I said, they are simpatico. Size of voice is no problem for this soprano, even when Puccini tries his heroine with horns and orchestral *fortes*. Once in a while in the lower voice, she adopts too quiet a dynamic for maximum projection, but normally the middle and low voice sound with frankness and make their mark. In the love duet, passivity and grandeur gingerly mate: 'Io son contento' holds not a hint of coyness (many will welcome her reserve—I prefer delight mirrored in the manner); the *pianissimo* leap in 'Vogliatemi bene' is a delicious morsel; tenor and soprano give the final measures a rousing send-off. Time after time throughout the entire afternoon, Zylis-Gara demonstrates her command of tone, line, and color, weaving them into a fascinating, cascading arc of phrase, or simply letting fall an individual tone with the skill and perceptive placement of a Giverny impressionist fixing a dollop of paint on his canvas.

A beguiling soft attack launches what proves to be a remarkably subdued voicing of 'Un bel dì.' Her *parlante* can hardly be called that, so liquid and intimate are her words; evidently she prefers to revel in an inner vibration of hope rather than to offer a more forthright expression of belief as she imagines Pinkerton's return. The close, however, is vibrant and firm. I doubt that any broadcast soprano has tried so little to "put over" the warhorse aria; undoubtedly that is why audience response is not long or overly fervent. (They make up the deficiency at her solo bow at the opera's end.) At Cio-Cio-San's little tea party with Sharpless and in the ensuing letter scene, she shakes off mournfulness; the charming phrases seem to be a quite natural outflow of Butterfly's character. When she brings forth her child, the soprano allows us to hear the full splendor of her voice, her 'Gioia's replete with pride and belief in future prospects. Her animation as she tries to stab Goro is unexpected and thus doubly pleasing. (Evidently it takes a case of attempted murder to rouse the passions of this singer.) And she celebrates her joy at sighting the *Abraham Lincoln* with grand tones and outward triumph. The flower duet holds exquisite touches (including an unhurried vault to the *pianissimo* high B-flat) before leading on to a deliberate molding of the bridal vestments phrase; I find the manner pregnant with Butterfly's intent as she dons her wedding night garments. The lullaby, appropriately subdued, is capped by a soft, floated high B (maybe a slight hitch there, but more likely merely a change in vibration). Pathos rather than tragedy is cultivated as she agrees to give up her child. The farewell aria (troubled by an odd patch of under-pitch singing near its beginning) convinces by the size of her tones rather than intensity of declamation until a crescendo on the last 'addio' supplies the missing ingredient.

What is one to make of the conflicting descriptions that I have provided? Zylis-Gara is a wonderful singer, one who is imaginative in the application of her considerable vocal resources. She holds to a consistent development of character throughout the afternoon. Subtlety is her confidant, understatement her ally. One may prefer a more open-hearted interpretation, one might even say, a portrayal rooted in Italianate conviction, though that designation need not, by any means, imply lack of subtlety. But the rewards of the Polish soprano's Butterfly are worthy in their own right. Amara's and Zylis-Gara's portrayals are very different conceptions, each to be savored according to one's taste. For my money, an all-embracing palate is the opera lover's best friend.

Passivity is foreign to Tosca's temperament. Zylis-Gara will surely have to set her emotional thermostat higher when playing the Roman diva on the broadcast of 8 February 1975. Bacquier is her attentive police chief, while Anthony (Spoletta) and Christopher (Sciarrone) do his dirty work for him. Corena, the hungry Sacristan, fails to spot Sgarro's Angelotti in the recesses of Sant'Andrea della Valle. But the surprise of the afternoon is the return of Bergonzi as Cavaradossi after an absence of two seasons. Add a zero to that number to reach twenty and you have the extent of conductor Alberto Erede's Metropolitan hiatus. The maestro, remembered for a Met sojourn during the fifties, returns for a single season, thereby augmenting Italian authenticity on the broadcast *Tosca*.

By this time in his lengthy career, Erede is a man who need not spend himself in trying to make an impression. He has a patrician view of this vehement score and deviates not a bit from that stance, even when the composer opens the floodgates of violence during Scarpia's second-act malevolence. For Erede, the famous opening chords are not meant to be world-shaking calling cards—but even so they serve their purpose, musical as much as dramatic. The conductor has lived long with the score and knits its varied strands into a satisfactory whole: Puccini's clever construction, his intricate motivic interplay, and, above all, the work's lyrical bounty are keenly set forth. The format allows the singers to shine and the orchestra to show its proud wares. They play well for the aristocratic Italian maestro. His career had unusual twists and turns. Back in the thirties, he had studied with Fritz Busch and then assisted him in Turin before going on to work with Bing at the Edinburgh Festival. Later, a German administrative post (director of the Deutsche Oper am Rhein) and *Lohengrin* at Bayreuth were among his varied occupations. Ultimately, his numerous recordings of complete operas will become the monuments of his career. His present involvement at the Met is short-lived, but he will be met again as conductor of Puccini's grand Chinese adventure, *Turandot*.

In the broadcast *Tosca*, Corena is the lead-off man, and he comes on strong. The voice, resonant and characterful, seems more sonorous than in recent years. Now in his third decade with the company, the buffo succeeds in suggesting a Sacristan whose good humor can quickly give way to anger and whose piety (the bass devoutly intones the Angelus) will opportunely recede before life's temptations—probably not those of the flesh, but certainly the smaller ones of the stomach and the purse. Sgarro, an ordinary fellow at his entrance, later bestirs himself enough to justify Cavaradossi's patriotic response to his peril. Anthony is a capital Spoletta, a fit companion for the brute who commands his special services. Gabriel Bacquier is the reprobate, having left off Fra Melitone's robes for the more elegant attire of Baron Scarpia. For the most part, his vocalism does not match

Tosca
8 February 1975

Tosca
Teresa Zylis-Gara
Cavaradossi
Carlo Bergonzi
Scarpia
Gabriel Bacquier
Sacristan
Fernando Corena
Conductor
Alberto Erede

his dress—the French baritone is not out to make friends. Menace and the need to cow any who come within his path are immediately apparent in the censorious words he utters as he interrupts the frolicsome choirboys. The fellow leaves no doubt that he has a black heart. Even his courting of Tosca's favor is a bit oppressive. Command is Bacquier's stock in trade and that dominance extends not only to Rome's secret police but to his audience, which values his imaginative, forceful portrayals. And he has the vocal goods for the Te Deum.

A good meal, they say, has the capacity to encourage affability. When this man of business sups at the Palazzo Farnese, he does become a bit more agreeable and the voice grows marginally more supple. But the elegance of a Warren or MacNeil in these private moments (whether alone or with Tosca) is neither Bacquier's intent nor within his means. He is the singing actor par excellence, content with that vocation, insistently plying his trade by relying on dramatic intensity and illuminative word readings more than song to gain his ends. Sadism and vehemence are the stuff of his 'Ha più forte sapore,' but when he speaks to Tosca of his venality and her capitulation, he nurtures the line, allowing insidiousness to penetrate until it gives way to lust in the surging phrases that lead on to his murder. Canny Bacquier is, varying tonal strength with a subtlety here and there before massaging the broad phrases. One is glad when Scarpia receives Tosca's kiss. That means Bacquier has done his afternoon's work well.

Before the second act commences, Peter Allen tells us that the five-minute delay at the beginning of the opera was due to the "sudden indisposition" of Bergonzi, who "sang the first act anyway." The announcer is "happy to tell [us]" that the man from Polisene will sing the remainder of the opera. We share in his pleasure, in spite of not hearing the tenor in prime form. His high notes may be carefully taken, but most often they are astutely managed, that is, attacked well enough to avoid embarrassment, though not with the remembered thrust. Still, the tenor's idiomatic delivery carries the day. At his entrance, the mid-voice is solid and warm. He draws the line of 'Recondita armonia' with a legato so succulent, so proudly expressive of a grand tradition, that the rewards are sufficient even without brilliance at the top. So it goes throughout the afternoon. Actually, his 'Vittoria!'s are stout enough, and the exposed high notes as Cavaradossi and Tosca savor her triumph and the prospect of their freedom are quite creditable. With the final curtain in sight, undoubtedly he felt a modicum of his capital could be safely expended. More treasurable are the soft, velvety tones of 'E lucevan le stelle.' The entire aria is a marvel of vocal control and musical discretion. 'O dolci mani' is further evidence of his subtle artistry; a few phrases remind one of Tagliavini's sweet mezza voce. (Ghosts of broadcasts past always haunt long-lived broadcast devotees.) At the opening of the *Tosca* run, ten days and three performances before the broadcast, the tenor was afflicted with "a sore windpipe."[6] One must admire Bergonzi's dedication in continuing his Metropolitan engagement, and long for the opportunity to hear him again when he can offer the full splendor of his song. But we have doted on his suavity and are all but content.

As Tosca, Zylis-Gara is separated by several degrees from the singer we heard as Cio-Cio-San. Evidently she was merely enjoying what we Vermonters call a blackberry frost, that period in early July when cool temperatures can briefly invade summer warmth. So different is her Tosca voice from her Butterfly voice that both her interpretive intent and her manner of singing the latter role must be regarded (and respected) as a conscious choice on her part. Hardly a touch of her Butterfly's mournful timbre is heard in the church or the Farnese Palace. Few of her customary orchestral wind overtones blow through the ramparts of the Castel Sant'Angelo—and earlier, the Madonna and the police chief have hardly heard their wail, plaintive or grand. They may linger, but they do not dominate. Her Tosca voice, possessed of more centrist qualities, is a precious instrument. Everywhere the tone is forthright and secure, succulently full, the legato flowing as smoothly as the Tiber courses by Sant'Angelo. Zylis-Gara's Roman diva belongs with the broadcast chronicle's finest impersonations of the part—and regular listeners know the number of superior radio Toscas over the years has been legion.

From the moment she enters Sant'Andrea della Valle impatiently—but not imperiously—calling Mario's name, the soprano weaves a potent spell. Her tone holds love's happy burden and she seems reluctant to cultivate a diva's attitude. It rightly takes over when suspicion of the Attavanti surfaces—then her tone becomes acute, her manner accusative. But, for the most part, she charmingly (and deftly—for she glides lightly over the crest of 'Non la sospiri la nostra casetta') jousts with Cavaradossi, tone and manner beguiling, language and phrasing idiomatic. The voice has sufficient size so that anger does not rouse the specter of the shrew, as it does with many a Tosca in these moments. When, in tones soft and seductive, she tells the painter to darken his Magdalene's eyes, she is certain to have her way. No lover could refuse her the accommodation. As the returning diva is taunted by Scarpia, Zylis-Gara embraces Tosca's mood swings with conviction: her 'Traditore!' is not overly damning, but she swears retribution with a zeal that should give even so self-confident a lover as Cavaradossi pause. On this afternoon, her *parlante* is neatly articulated, animated, and persuasive. She has absorbed the idiom of the opera and become mistress of the Puccini mystique.

In the second act, her *lirico spinto* voice is untroubled by either the tumult of the orchestra or the abandon of Tosca's emotions. The round core of her tone is seldom challenged in the turmoil of her struggle with Scarpia. Her top notes are fervently attacked, an occasional hint of strain merely part of the play—their intensity speaks to a welcome dramatic involvement. In response to Cavaradossi's torture, she allows just a touch of that mournful timbre to color her tone as she attends to her lover's hurts. The contrivance is all the more effective for its rarity. 'Assassino' is fiercely belted on high, 'Quanto?' emphatically shouted from the chest, and she infects 'Il prezzo!' with disdain as though the obtuse Scarpia ought to have understood her question. In contrast to her muted delivery of Butterfly's 'Un bel dì,' 'Vissi d'arte' is masterfully projected, one of the loveliest, most affecting readings in broadcast history. Taken at a measured, but not tedious, pace, the twin opening phrases are easily mated with the orchestra's progression; though deceptively simple, the slow descent is not always a comfortable moment for even accomplished sopranos. Thereafter, the soprano's phrases flow with unassuming naturalness, the tone ebbing and flowing to accommodate Puccini's coils and curves. Her 'Perchè's are heartfelt, but she does not intend them to challenge her maker. The prayerful mood is sustained until the confident climax, where the top note is resolute and grand, the next one held long and expertly tapered; the final phrase is uttered more in sorrow than in anger, the soprano maintaining the unity of her conception. When she is in this form, Zylis-Gara offers some of the most delectable vocalism and musicianly interpretations of these Metropolitan decades.

Her song over, now Tosca must take up the knife and do the deed. Zylis-Gara's cries over the prostrate Scarpia are emphatic enough to damn him. Forgiveness is effectively declaimed in a clouded chest tone, but the 'tutta Roma' phrase doesn't quite come off—the measured delivery sounds overly studied. Only that testing moment and, in the final act, her rather contained instructions to Cavaradossi about the mock execution are less satisfying than anticipated. In compensation, she conveys Tosca's inner excitement as she cautions the dead Mario in tiny tones until, as she recognizes Scarpia's deception, fear takes hold of her. Her emphatic 'Avanti a Dio' sounds both Tosca's determination and a diva's triumph.

La Bohème
16 February 1974
Mimì
Montserrat Caballé
Musetta
Marilyn Niska
Rodolfo
Franco Corelli
Marcello
Dominic Cossa
Colline
John Macurdy
Conductor
Leif Segerstam

Prima donnas hold Puccini's heart, but when a divo like Franco Corelli is onstage, pride of place is challenged. In 1974, the tenor is heard as Rodolfo and Calàf, the two roles serving, quite unexpectedly, as his broadcast adieus. Behind-the-scenes manipulations give the *Bohème* broadcast of 16 February 1974 an unusual aura. Pavarotti was scheduled with Amara as his Mimì. The Modena tenor canceled. Corelli agreed to sing a rare radio Rodolfo, whereupon management, perhaps intent on making a high-powered splash, pulled Amara from the cast in favor of Montserrat Caballé. In a singular announcement as he opened the broadcast, Cross read a carefully worded statement, noting that Amara was scheduled, but "has graciously stepped aside" in order to give her sister diva "the opportunity of sharing her first Mimì" with the broadcast public. The American soprano was always a good soldier, but in this instance, grace under fire seems beyond the call of duty. Evidently, Caballé had made it known that she would like to sing the broadcast performance and management acceded.[7] Cross was forced to put the seal of bureaucratic mealy-mouthed unction on the event by adding that "both Madame Caballé and the Metropolitan Opera express their deepest gratitude for [Amara's] generosity." Amen! Miss Caballé's Mimìs were indeed a rare item on the Metropolitan stage. Two seamstresses would be her tally; Corelli's poet loomed considerably larger in numbers, but this is his only broadcast Rodolfo. In attendance on the luminaries are Marilyn Niska (Musetta), Cossa (Marcello), Holloway (Schaunard), and Macurdy (Colline). Segerstam, having conveyed *Manon Lescaut* to the Louisana desert, now savors the nineteenth-century Paris milieu.

As was evident in his *Tosca*, Erede is a patrician master who casts a benign eye upon Puccini's creations. He seems more than ever a man from another century when compared with Segerstam's take on the Lucca master. When it comes to energizing a performance, the young Finn is in the sprinter class. He takes the quartet of bohemians by the nose and leads them a jolly chase. This conductor loves to push the composer's musical gestures to their most extreme interpretive posture, particularly those of a livelier cast. Should he sight a *stringendo*, he clutches it to his bosom with a lover's passion. Even when not indicated, the accelerando is interpretive catnip to him—all that he asks is that the headlong rush heighten the rhetoric of the moment. Often, he expertly captures the shape of a motive (or even an entire musical unit) and polishes its innate character to a gloss; he does so, and agreeably, for instance, with the frisky dotted rhythms that accompany Schaunard's invitation for dinner at Momus. He likes to endow episodes, small or large, with an individual profile, pasting them en route into the mosaic of his overall conception. Hear the dying embers of the poet's manuscript murmur with the gentlest buzz—a delightful orchestral effect. Marvel, if you can catch your breath, at how he propels to orgiastic heights the orchestral interlude that caps the

Franco Corelli as Rodolfo in *La Bohème*. Photography by Louis Mélançon. Courtesy Metropolitan Opera Archives.

quartet's final-act horseplay before the ill Mimì enters their garret. Often enough, Segerstam's gambits effectively vitalize the opera. And when the lovers hold the stage, they and their self-involvement are not shortchanged—the 'Sono andati?' scene is one of the slowest on record. Moderation is not entirely foresworn, of course—one cannot survive in a perpetual whirlwind nor wallow long without rejuvenation. The opening of act one actually receives a tame send-off and the brass chords of the Café Momus are held in check—achieving order seems paramount there. Soon enough, adrenalin takes over and the romp begins anew. It is all grand fun and, Segerstam's control over his forces never being less than secure, his spirited direction drives worry out the door, the jousting bohemians' and ours as well. *Bohème* is, after all, a young man's opera.

The buffo cameos, most often a double assignment, are not only split up, but different in range, with tenor Paul Franke undertaking Alcindoro's complaints and Dobriansky filling Benoit's shoes. The basso plays with uncommon realism. For once, the landlord's pecuniary demands and amorous adventures seem more than a comic turn. His voice and manner are as common as dirt, and their earthiness is Latin Quarter grit. Add in Segerstam's orchestral mockery and the vignette thrives. Schaunard is usually the also-ran of the bohemian quartet, but David Holloway moves him up a notch or two in the garret hierarchy. He is the liveliest baritone to play the musician on the broadcasts. Schaunard's parrot narrative can be dull, but this young singer animates it with individual touches that keep it alive. In the bookend acts, he is personality on the loose—a constant bright light—his modest baritone an able complement to his high spirits. It is well that Holloway's Schaunard lights up the airwaves, for Macurdy is the dourest of philosophers, his stolid vocalism and heavy-hearted stance a letdown in this environment. Perhaps the basso, normally the most conscientious of interpreters, thought the roughhouse antics of the boys needed a counterbalance of sanity. And indeed, when Colline's moment comes, Macurdy sings an affecting farewell to his coat, the voice having gained in focus and color. He makes clear why philosophers abandon tomfoolery when faced with life-and-death situations.

Though their competition is high powered, Niska and Cossa make a brave showing. The soprano's assured voice (its timbre somewhat hard, but basically attractive) and no-nonsense manner give Musetta an unusually candid character. Her capriciousness is downplayed and her practicality brought to the fore. One can well believe the dying Mimì when she tells Marcello that his erstwhile sweetheart is 'assai buona.' A good girl Niska is in her sturdy vocalism as well as in her ministrations to her friend. We hear more of Musetta's lines in the ensembles than most lighter-voiced singers can project. The waltz song may be deficient in charm, but its forthright tone is a tonic as the admirable soprano captures and holds the Momus crowd's attention. When we hear the prompter softly intone 'Brava' as she rests on Musetta's top B, we can echo his approval; he was saluting her in-tempo flash up to the high note. Coaches are like that. Heard in her broadcast debut, Niska was a veteran of the Met's National Company and the New York City Opera, where she performed in a repertory both wide and rare. Several Metropolitan seasons will barely allow this intelligent soprano to demonstrate her worth. Cossa is, along with Caballé, the most satisfying artist of the afternoon. He has an ideal Marcello voice, warm in timbre, the tone expertly focused so that the conversational gambits are pointedly delivered. His instrument may not be overly large (not at all in the Bastianini mold) but it is capable of filling out a phrase and swelling a line with resonant baritone panache. And his song is invariably idiomatic in style and telling in expression. A cultivated singer, Cossa is the most engaging of duet partners. At the Tollgate with Mimì, he settles for being the sympathetic listener. He comforts his poet friend when he needs consolation but pertinaciously questions Rodolfo's reluctance to face the reality of Mimì's illness. Back in the bohemians' garret, the baritone, though he must contend with an outsized partner, holds his own; indeed, when Marcello joins Rodolfo in bewailing their lost loves, Cossa shows his colleague how to mold a line with nary a repugnant huff or grunt. His high F-sharp, hearty and firm, not only affirms his longing for Musetta's provoking lips but confirms his technical dexterity.

And what of our interlopers, the star duo? Corelli sang thirty-four Met Rodolfos. That high tally seems astonishing after hearing his broadcast portrayal. His good looks and exuberant manner are eminent qualifications for this favorite tenor role, making him seem the very picture of a romantic bohemian poet. Perhaps that is enough to explain the frequency of his performances. His tone on this afternoon is touched by an unfamiliar nasality during the opening scene, but soon it acquires its customary luster and remarkable density. He participates in the garret high-jinks with commendable abandon, though occasionally his interjected quick phrases seem almost too frenetic. More problematic is his brusque vocal manner. The Puccini line in this text-driven opera often coruscates along, its twists and turns sometimes so sprightly that Corelli's vocal technique cannot readily accommodate them. At times, his delivery is cumbersome (the grace notes, for instance, are invariably converted into full-time members of the line); often he seems to be shouting. His lunges at high notes, unexpected encroachments on the phrase contour, startle. *Bohème* is essentially an ensemble opera and the tenor's outsized tone, consistent *forte* dynamic, and knobby phraseology are, rather too frequently, rude intrusions into ensemble homogeneity.

Rodolfo just doesn't seem to be the tenor's calling. In a number of roles I have admired those gifts that are uniquely his: the size and density of his tone, especially on high; its robustness, tempered by a vividly romantic coloration; his ardor and intensity; and, above all, the invigorating *slancio* that warms the heart and sets the pulse racing. These are unusual attributes that often convert his musical and technical sins from the mortal to the venial. They do not seem to be quite enough on this afternoon to make his Rodolfo entirely palatable. I would like to have been in the house to hear it, however, for Corelli owns a voice that space not only accommodates but positively relishes. And, taken one by one, many moments have their own appeal. His 'Eureka' is open-hearted; he is quite charming in the key search; he captures the several moods of 'Che gelida manina,' granting a grand arc to the climactic phrase. That demanding traversal holds a stout high B before the aria moves to a quiet close (an odd effect there, as he observes the *fermata*—Puccini's own—on 'piaccia' at some length). In the duet, he and Caballé attack their unison top note ('Ah! tu sol commandi' is Mimì's line) like a pair of refugee Wagnerians. In contrast, the tenor applies a gentle caress to his solo 'Fremon nell'anima' before claiming his sweetheart with the proudest, biggest 'Sei mia!' any lover could possibly summon. The firm high Bs at the duet's close are easily within both singers' compass. The outbursts of the third act are more in Corelli's line and his castigation of Mimì is thrilling—no matter that this Rodolfo is Otello in a frock coat. Soprano and tenor are comfortable in their unison traversal of the quartet's arched final phrase, their coursing musically adept in volume, shape, and pace; both execute a modest *messa di voce* on the penultimate note. At Mimì's death, the tenor goes berserk, offering the most extroverted portrayal of grief in my memory; he fills the airwaves with a spate of interpolated 'No's and man-sized sobs. His final cries of her name are held considerably beyond their appointed length and are less effective for that abuse; they seem more an expression of tenorial vanity than a poet's despair. But then, almost everything Corelli does on this afternoon seems outsized. There is nothing small about him—and for that, we can be grateful.

During this period, Caballé is at the peak of her vocal form and, notwithstanding the circumstances of her assumption of the role, one is grateful to have this lovely memento of her Mimì. The radio is kind to her. (At two points in the opera, the act-one duet and the third-act quartet, Corelli acknowledges the problem of stage verisimilitude—that is, the soprano playing a consumptive—by changing 'mia piccina' to 'mia bambina.') In terms of vocal character and interpretive discretion, the diva is as fragile a heroine as the airwaves have known. Not that she is unwilling to give a climax its due—one could not appear with Corelli and husband tone in the clinches. Her singing at the *forte* dynamic is, in fact, tonally fulgent, without a hint of harshness. But the memory one treasures of her seamstress is the exquisite delicacy, vocal and dramatic, of her portrayal. She paints most often in pastels. The vocalism is so pure, its liquid flow so ecstatically ethereal, that one feels its rarefied air should only be breathed within a cloister's walls.

Of course, this girl of the Paris bohemian milieu ought to be more than a Madonna-like icon. Caballé's Mimì is refinement personified. Never mind, the soprano knows what works for her, and it surely does on this afternoon. Her entrance aria is a model of musicality, the portamentos fluid, the style pristine, untroubled by the liberties the soprano often permits herself. We feel the seamstress' delight in the sun's rays and regret with her the embroidered flower's lack of scent. The 'Addio' is even more remarkable for vocal beauty and stylistic subtlety (including a *messa di voce* on 'rancor'). It is the high point of her performance. Only in a very few phrases does she indulge her preference for omitting text on high and settle for the neutral expression of a vowel. (That habit, if overindulged in this conversational opera, would be deadly.) At the Tollgate, any Mimì, no matter her preference for the inner life, must come out of her shell and deal with her problematic love life. Caballè does. Her account of the lovers' troubling existence is emphatic, full-toned, and convincing. The voice's size is her accomplice in this energetic encounter with Marcello. 'Mi grida ad ogni istante,' her complaint about Rodolfo's incessant jealousy, is strongly delivered, but remains within the conceptual zones she has set for her portrayal. The death scene is all repose and dulcet tone; since this soprano lives in the upper octave, she has no fear of Mimì's exposed phrases. Has there been any tone more downy than that which the soprano applies to 'come è bello e morbido'? Caballé's vocalism is so evanescent that her seamstress seems merely a transient in an earthly world. Puccini loved his Mimì, but I rather doubt it was this one. After viewing a 1900 La Scala performance of *Bohème*, he wrote Toscanini and asked him to tell Emma Carelli (the Mimì) not to play the entire role so "stancamente" (wearily), but rather as Murger had seen and rendered her.[8]

The combination of Corelli and Caballé undoubtedly provided a blockbuster event, but the tenor's excesses and the soprano's refinement, when juxtaposed, are jarring to the listener and ultimately not conducive to performance integrity. Most opera lovers couldn't care less about the anomaly. Maybe they are right. When comets pass in the operatic firmament, the astral concurrence is too unusual, too invigorating, to worry about their not being in the same orbit.

For posterity's sake, the final broadcast of a grand singer, whether intended as a farewell or not, ought to be in a role measured to the size of his talents. Calàf had been just such a portrayal for Corelli ever since the Met relaunched *Turandot* in 1961. On that memorable occasion, Stokowski was at the helm, while Nilsson, Moffo, Guarrera, and Giaiotti joined our tenor in earning a newfound popularity for Puccini's final creation. On the broadcast of 28 December 1974, Ingrid Bjoner tackles Turandot's icy chores and suffers the questions of Corelli's prince. Maliponte is Liù, while Ping and Timur are played by Goodloe and Morris. Erede has another chance to demonstrate his affinity for the Puccini idiom, this time on a grander scale.

Puccini's most spectacular opera may be treated as a walloping good show (with the emphasis on the wallop) or a ceremonial banquet. Our Italian maestro, not unexpectedly, prefers the latter. A stately grandeur is at the heart of his reading. It governs the processions (the composer supplied quite a few), while the crowd's anger and concerns for their welfare are rather chastely encouraged. The conductor knows well how to impose a unity of conception onto a performance. His way is far from undramatic, but he will not be stirred beyond the bounds of (his) good taste. In the hands of more fervent maestros, performances of this opera have not often cultivated that elusive quality. And who can blame them? Yet Erede has a way with him—and it is a classical stance. When he sounds Puccini's emphatic opening strokes, this conductor signals that his China is not the harsh, intemperate environment to which we have been accustomed. That ancient civilization has its own rules and evidently he wants to honor them. Beheadings will be taken in stride. One must admire the conductor's composure, his confidence in Puccini's ability to reflect all the drama that is necessary in the music itself. The Met chorus is his valuable ally, for their splendid tone, emphatic phrasing, and clear diction give the performance the necessary jolt of energy. Their animation in anger and gentility when suppliant are exactly what is needed to counterbalance Erede's aplomb and to complement his unwavering faith in the score's architectural integrity.

Some new interpreters lend interest to the supporting roles. Anthony (Pong) and Velis (Pang) are familiar bureaucrats (and good at their work), but Goodloe has finally been given the opportunity that his attractive baritone warrants. His Ping is exceptionally clean-toned, the voice virile but pointed, so that the trio's ensembles, some of the most vivid we have heard in the opera's considerable broadcast history, are spic-and-span as well. All three spare us any mincing Orientalisms of tone and manner, and when Puccini allots Goodloe a solo passage, the composer is rewarded with some of the afternoon's most attractive vocalism. Morris supplies that as well. Indeed, his bass voice is surprisingly resonant and warm in its lower octave, holding a healthy burr there, while a shining baritonal light penetrates the upper range. His Timur is not all lugubrious lament, for he plays Calàf's father as a middle-aged man rather than the customary ancient. Vigorous and sonorous in

Turandot
28 December 1974

Turandot
Ingrid Bjoner
Liù
Adriana Maliponte
Calàf
Franco Corelli
Ping
Robert Goodloe
Timur
James Morris
Conductor
Alberto Erede

the opening act, he introduces some unusual interpretive touches when kneeling by the dead Liù, employing a dulcet mezza voce to affectingly express Timur's grief.

Miss Maliponte, assuming the role of Liù at the Met for the first time this season, had the temerity to tell *Opera News* readers that the slave girl is "the real protagonist," a belief held by many, but not usually baldly stated by sopranos where the Turandot can read it at performance time.[9] No doubt about it, in her sympathetic music the slave girl can command the affections of the audience. Puccini would not be Puccini if it turned out otherwise. Maliponte gains our affection with the purity of her timbre and the ease with which she floats her *pianissimo* on high. If a Liù has those assets, she is bound to conquer. The floated B-flat at the end of 'Signore, ascolta' is devastating in its shimmering beauty, its gossamer texture comforting after the piercing attack that she applies to launch the note. The third-act episodes are trying to many sopranos because of the high tessitura, but this soprano has no problem in that regard. And she manages to infuse the close of 'Tu che di gel sei cinta' with dramatic meaning, thereby provoking long applause. If the soprano's art is deficient in any area, it may be in pathos—a Puccini requisite. Her manner is perhaps just a bit too efficient, her legato and conduct of line a touch instrumental, to take full advantage of the composer's deliciously bending phrases. More curves and fewer corners, please. But Maliponte is an adorable artist. Her silvery timbre and poised vocalism are always gratefully heard.

The broadcast is the one hundredth company performance of *Turandot*. It is no exaggeration to say that that number is in large part due to Nilsson's galvanizing performance of the title role. The opera had been slow to catch on. Nilsson first assumed the role in only the twenty-eighth Met performance of the opera, and she sang it fifty-one more times. Thus, her imprint on the role is strong, indeed formidable, and unhealthy for any soprano who followed her into the icy heights of the princess' proud isolation. Ingrid Bjoner, a soprano of good repute, though seldom figuring in this chronicle, may be remembered for her Hausfrau Elsa in the 1967 broadcast of *Lohengrin*. During her nine nonconsecutive seasons at the Met she had appeared as Donna Anna, Ariadne, the Empress, and Fidelio. Those assignments would seem to make her a fit candidate to tackle Turandot. She gives a worthy performance. Of course, the initial shock of hearing an ordinary voice intone 'In questa reggia' takes some time to get over after one has been accustomed to the Swedish soprano's blazing tones and confident manner. Confidence the Norwegian soprano also has (she had sung the role about eighty times in Europe), but the tone is best described as blowzy as she launches the great test piece. Before long, however, it gains in body and timbral solidity (or maybe the ears become more accommodating) and soon one realizes she is unafraid of the role's heights or its breadth of phrasing. The top octave is the better half of her instrument, and for the most part she performs honorably in that area; the lower voice can turn shaky at the quieter dynamic. Color changes are not within the scope of her instrument. (It would be hard to recognize her vocal thumbprint in a broadcast quiz.) A few scratchy moments do intrude (when questioning Liù, for instance), or some harshness can surface (a moment or two in the final duet), but her clarity of line and tonal security are valuable assets. The riddles show off her best qualities—one must admire her assured vocalism in these grand moments. Her 'Straniero!' earns high marks for its clean thrust and power. And when she names Calàf 'Amor,' she fixes the top B-flat securely and solidly supports the tone, which is round at its core. The broadcast is the last of the soprano's forty-eight appearances with the company.

How reassuring to come upon Corelli in the environment in which he seems most comfortable and gives greatest pleasure. On this afternoon, his final broadcast, the fifty-three-year-old tenor is in good voice, his instrument only marginally less potent than in his glory days. A top note may be afflicted with a grainier texture now and then, but for the most part the voice throughout the range retains its famously dark, glamorous cast, a curious combination of plushy velvet and resounding steel. The only real indication that he may not be quite what he has been during his fifteen consecutive seasons with the company is the gargled final note of 'Nessun dorma!,' which ends quite abruptly. Elsewhere, he lofts the usual quota of ringing top notes. No tenor on the current roster, and for years to come, thunders forth with the mellifluous brilliance of Corelli. But when he is on his best musical behavior, as he is today, he earns more than a visceral reaction; we are not only beglamored, but experience an affective response. He does manage to find moments in Calàf's energetic music to sound a note of sympathetic regard both for the slave girl, in 'Non piangere, Liù,' for instance, and for himself, as Calàf searches out Turandot's love. Most often, however, he prefers to cause his public's temperature to rise.

At his initial entrance, he seems very much the grand divo of the *Turandot* premiere over thirteen years ago. In the first-act aria, his response to Liù's concern is remarkably contained (for him); the timbral warmth of the middle voice is intact, the musical line conscientiously maintained, and the top voice collected and secure. He answers the riddles with the exuberant enthusiasm of a youth experiencing first love, triumphantly naming 'Turandot' in the third trial. The tenor's ardor is so consuming that one can well believe his prince could sacrifice all for love. The high C is able, only a little less assured than his norm. As if to redress any loss, he offers a patented, lengthy diminuendo on 'morirò'—one of his better ones, at that. When he proposes his own riddle ('Tre enigmi m'hai proposto'), he clothes the generous gesture in an appealing sensitivity. The bulk of the famous third-act aria profits from it as well. There, the tenor's flavorful tone and considerate phrasing are adequate compensation for any diminution in sheer lung power at the climax. He employs that still mighty resource effectively enough in Alfano's duet reconstruction. Even amid the glut of extrovert grandeur, the tenor is able to convert the 'Mio fiore!' address into a romantic reverie, something quite special in the Corelli canon. He can still send out a remarkably potent 'Hai vinto tu!'. Initially addressed to Turandot, those same words (You have won!) may be applied to the tenor. It may have taken some time for those who prefer a more discreet, musicianly style and less muscled vocal manner to fully appreciate Corelli's unique qualities, but in the end, he did conquer us.

The tenor was on the 1975–76 roster, scheduled indeed in *Opera News* for Pollione on the broadcast of 28 February 1976. Alexander sang in his place. His final appearance with the company, after a run of performances in Japan, was as Rodolfo on 28 June 1975 at Wolf Trap Farm Park in Virginia. But the house that had reverberated with his glorious tones for a decade and a half heard him last as Calàf in the very broadcast matinee we have been enjoying. Retirement was patently premature. During his fifteen seasons with the company, he appeared

365 times. Among his nineteen roles, the most performed were Calàf (54 times), Cavaradossi (44), Radamès (40), Rodolfo (34), and Enzo (24). A late-blooming romance with the heroic French repertory allowed him to number Roméo (37 times) and Werther (23) among his trophies.

In *Turandot*, he and Nilsson had often engaged in a not unfriendly, but certainly competitive, contest where decibels and heights were the measure of their worth. The Swedish soprano would have added to the broadcast *Turandot*'s sense of occasion, but it is fair and fitting that, in this, his final house and radio performance, Corelli can claim an uncontested victory.

Régine Crespin as Carmen. Photography by James Heffernan. Courtesy Metropolitan Opera Archives.

CHAPTER TWENTY

Singles and Strauss

The goal is in sight. I take up the final broadcasts of my ten-year survey. In this initial sequence of operas, willful women, strong of purpose, and a quaking czar are at center stage. They each have their troubles, some on the political front, but most prefer to contend in their home environment. Who are they and what causes their pain? Boris, though crowned, is psychologically rent, torn apart by conflicting public and private postures. Our operatic heroines better know what they are about. Carmen's aims are hardly humanitarian, but Beethoven's Leonore is the personification of virtuous intent. Elektra has both her good and bad points, while other Strauss heroines, rather than losing their heads, follow their hearts. The Marschallin does lose a lover—but in Octavian she gains a friend. A questionable trade-off. Ariadne, at first in the same loverless boat, by the final curtain will succumb anew; in the meantime, she pines while Zerbinetta mines the stratosphere on their island paradise. What can a composer do when his work is abused but bow and surrender himself anew to the power of music? That is the only course—and it is open to us.

In the *Fidelio* broadcast of 7 February 1976, Gwyneth Jones, new to our narrative, is heard as Leonore. Blegen repeats her Marzelline, quarreling with new Jaquino Kenneth Riegel, even as Macurdy again plays father Rocco. McIntyre takes over the villain part (Pizarro), while Morris as Fernando has the less prominent but more becoming duty of freeing Jess Thomas' Florestan. Making his broadcast debut is conductor John Mauceri.

Mauceri is yet another of those young conductors whose talents earned them early recognition and a brief berth at the Metropolitan. He led the seasonal premiere of *Fidelio* in January, his company debut. Bernstein—a mentor of the Yale-educated native New Yorker—had been scheduled for most of the run with Mauceri taking over several remaining performances. When the titan canceled, his surrogate was granted the full eleven outings. Only thirty years old at broadcast time, Mauceri had been brought up on Met performances, had assisted Bernstein in the preparation of the Met's 1972 *Carmen*, and gone on to conduct for the Welsh and Scottish National Operas at Spoleto, Santa Fe, and San Francisco. His is a remarkably assured traversal of Beethoven's much-revised score. Notwithstanding the Bernstein connection, his conception decidedly tips toward the classical rather than the romantic mode. Bruno Walter's magic carpet is not Mauceri's

Fidelio
7 February 1976

Leonore
Gwyneth Jones
Marzelline
Judith Blegen
Florestan
Jess Thomas
Jaquino
Kenneth Riegel
Pizarro
Donald McIntyre
Rocco
John Macurdy
Fernando
James Morris
Conductor
John Mauceri

499

transport. (The January premiere was dedicated to the revered maestro.) Oh, he drives the coda of the grander overture and the finale's noisy celebrations with Bernsteinian fervor, but except for the welcome rhetorical flourish that clinches a set piece's momentum, splurges like that are rare. Both overtures (the *Fidelio* played before act one, No. 3 after the dungeon scene) are virtuous, rather than virtuoso, readings. They are lively withal, the curtain-raiser in particular holding some downright jaunty moments; Mauceri seems to be telling us that, in spite of its heroic rescue theme and modern-day anointment as the official monument to humanity, the opera is really quite a homey, intimate drama. Certainly, the opera's first scenes are cast in that mode, so the conductor's warmth of feeling and moderate breadth of phrase are planned with an eye toward the drama ahead. The conductor adapts his manner to suit the majestic scale of *Leonore* No. 3, pacing it more broadly and embracing its roomy architecture and noble sentiments without lapsing into the portentous. Even the march accompanying Pizarro's entrance with his guards rolls along at a lively gait. No horror effects darken the dungeon *Melodram*. His chorus sings with fervor and good tone in the celebratory scene, though I find the prisoners' chorus, one of the most moving episodes in all opera, a bit too healthy to issue from weak, sun-starved men—a bit of ghostly tone on those 'leise's can't hurt. But that is quibbling. Mauceri's prize asset is his ability to keep the pulse of an aria or ensemble alive throughout its length without subverting the composer's purpose. After this season, he would gain prominence at the house across the Lincoln Center plaza before settling into relative permanence on the European opera scene. Evidently, the Met could stand only so many gifted young virtuosos of the baton.

From the assembled cast I expected a higher performance quality than they deliver. As ever, Blegen is the complete professional as to musicianship and vocal acting, but her tone, usually quite appealing but here too often pinched, makes Rocco's child sound not only like a willful daughter, but a disagreeable one. She has her moments. In the duet, the soprano expertly executes the intricate tracery of 'Ich weiss, dass der Arme sich quälet,' and is equally deft in the canon quartet; here and there in her aria Blegen's youthful charm tells—especially as the voice takes on more body. But a Marzelline need not mince, either vocally or interpretively, and shouldn't if she wants to hold on to so excellent a Jaquino as Riegel. It is he who scores most of the points in the opening duet, lifting the performance off to a lively start. The voice has more to it, is more attractive as to tone, than most of the second tenors (first place always goes to Florestan) whom management usually serves up in this role. The difference is that Riegel is a first tenor, one who makes every utterance count, both as to musical shape and character definition. Our third tenor of the afternoon, Douglas Ahlstedt, has the important assignment of singing the First Prisoner's few phrases; his tone is too boyish for this serious episode, so he is compelled to substitute anguish for purposeful song. Thompson's Second Prisoner is in tune with the situation.

Macurdy, McIntyre, and Morris—an alphabet monopoly—are lower-voiced singers of such repute that it is surprising they are uniformly not more satisfying in their respective portrayals of jailer, prison governor, and ambassador—or to put it in terms descriptive of their characters, greedy father, monster, and humanitarian. Macurdy takes some time to warm up. The voice sounds ungainly and doesn't "speak" as well as it can—once again, he may be adopting an uncouth vocal manner in order to highlight Rocco's down-to-earth ways, but the ploy doesn't serve Beethoven's music well. Able musician that he is, he contrives a judicious head tone so as not to unduly overweight the canon quartet with his bass burden. But the gold aria, which articulates the father's creed, could be more emphatic in manner and straightforward in tone. The voice begins to come into its own in the duet with Pizarro—conflict and fear unexpectedly solidify his tone. Both he and Blegen were in better form on the 1972 broadcast. McIntyre, too, performs at a lesser level than his Wotan led me to expect. The voice sounds grubby and his phrasing is slurred in 'Ha! Welch ein Augenblick'; once again, one might excuse it as character responsive—but I wonder. It sounds to me as though the voice could use a bit of shoring up—some vocal rip-rap. He too improves in the duet with Rocco; low-voiced songsters probably respond to a brother's need. Morris doesn't need any encouragement to produce resonant bass tone—though he could use a bit more on one or two low notes. He is always an able singer. One hopes that any Fernando, in addition to liberating the prisoners by fiat, will possess a timbre whose warmth and humanity can refresh their souls. The fine young artist fails to sound that note, at least, not at 'Du schlossest auf des Edlen Grab.' But he does offer a kindly color change as he bids Leonore to remove her husband's chains; and at 'Gerecht, O Gott' his noble stance and sympathetic tone well serve to complement God's righteous judgment.

I wish I could quickly pass over Thomas' Florestan, noting only that he appeared. He makes little effect as the imprisoned husband. So constricted is his tone that Florestan's critical first word, that wounded animal's cry of 'Gott,' is unrecognizable, holding neither a *g* at its beginning nor a *t* at its end, and only a decidedly uncertain and ugly vowel in between. The American tenor labors dutifully, but it is patently a struggle for him to produce tone; the upper range refuses to open up, causing discomfort to performer and audience. His tone remains leathery throughout the act. A few phrases recall the honorable vocalism of earlier years.

Gwyneth Jones had returned to the company as Leonore after a three-year absence that followed her single season series of appearances as Sieglinde in 1972–73. Her European career, a substantial one ever since her Covent Garden debut in 1964 (Lady Macbeth), initially had been grounded in the dramatic soprano roles of the Italian repertory, but two years later she appeared at Bayreuth (Sieglinde) and the German Fach claimed her (though not exclusively). During the last years of her career her vocal vagaries would become legendary, but on the broadcast she is in thorough command of her large, brilliant-timbred voice. In an afternoon of largely undistinguished singing, the Welsh soprano outdistances her colleagues by a good measure. Her Leonore is vocally vibrant and dramatically affecting. In the latter department, those who prefer the Lehmann brand of emotional involvement will find her interpretation of the distraught wife somewhat contained. In Jones' case, it may be that her hold on herself and on her voice must go hand in hand; that in itself would be reason enough to count her carefully plotted portrayal in the plus category. And she does rise to the pivotal dramatic moments with fierce involvement, their emotional impact reinforced by cleanly thrust tones of notable impact. 'Töt' erst sein Weib!' shoots out as surely as a beacon's light, the top tone solid and on the mark—a thrilling moment. Yet her soft singing is steady, pliant, and attractive in tone. So many large-voiced sopranos (and, make no mistake, Jones stands in the forefront of her kind), when refining their tone down to

Gwyneth Jones.

moderate or *piano* dynamics, drain all the color from the voice, neutralizing it as an emotive tool, but on this afternoon Jones retains a healthy core of tone in her quieter moments. Her entry in the canon quartet surprises by its calm assurance and modest tone. Indeed, the soprano seems committed to maintaining a classical vocal stance throughout the opera. Even her speaking voice is for the most part unruffled and gracious. And she blends well with her colleagues in their several ensembles.

The varied and challenging hurdles of 'Abscheulicher! wo eilst du hin?' are conquered without any vocal displacement. Lengthy ascending scales are evenly articulated, the top tones reached with ease and stout on arrival. Much of the lengthy piece lies in the middle voice, and Jones' security (no wobble at any dynamic—there or on high) is reassuring. The aria is Leonore's revelation of self. Without overdramatizing its various parts, the soprano conveys the mood changes of the faithful wife as she moves from initial horror at Pizarro's murderous bent to pathos before experiencing the renewal of hope that enables her to rededicate herself to her husband's rescue. Hers is neither an earth-shaking rendering nor an ear-splitting one, but its stability and confidence speak of an inner strength that makes the wife's disguise and intent plausible. Though dramatically reserved, Jones can make a noise with the best of them: when she learns from Rocco of their imminent dungeon descent, her 'Noch heute!'s blaze with explosive force. Of course, she dominates the dungeon quartet with her strong tone and now fiery purpose. Her sounding of the twisting phrases of 'O namenlose Freude!' is remarkably clear and tonally full; she forms them into units, but each note is cleanly articulated, something more celebrated Leonores seldom manage. Too often the duet comes off as a vocal mare's nest.

One is apt to come to a Jones performance with so many preconceptions (a dangerous state, and one to be avoided at any cost). On this broadcast, her first notes swept them away, banished all fears for the entire afternoon. At her solo bow, Allen tells us that Jones sang Leonore at the 1970 Vienna State Opera Bicentennial celebration of Beethoven's birth. And she will portray Brünnhilde at Bayreuth for the 1976 Centennial *Ring* performances. On this afternoon, the honors seem merited.

Tyrants, who as a class loom large on the operatic scene, most often do meet their deserved fates. Pizarro had no redeeming features but, even though czars can be demonic, Boris Godunov, trapped in conscience-driven torment, does gain our sympathy. In a new production designed by Ming Cho Lee, staged by August Everding, and first unveiled in December 1974, the Metropolitan scored not only in production terms but on the human level with Martti Talvela as an impressive protagonist. Joining him in the broadcast of 25 January 1975 are Dunn (Marina), Theyard (Grigori/Dimitri), Nagy (Shuiski), Dooley (Rangoni), Plishka (Pimen), Gramm (Varlaam), and a host of Met stalwarts in lesser parts. The broadcast performance is one of the company's finest efforts.

Schippers not only guides the performance, but has fashioned a new version for the company. Two changes from previous Metropolitan efforts signal a regard for authenticity in the presentation of the opera—that is, if any production of this much revised score can be considered "authentic." For the first time, the artists and chorus sing the original Russian text; in addition, the orchestration of Mussorgsky will arise from the pit. Gone are the Italian and English translations

Boris Godunov
25 January 1975

Marina
Mignon Dunn
Dimitri
Harry Theyard
Shuiski
Robert Nagy
Rangoni
William Dooley
Boris
Martti Talvela
Pimen
Paul Plishka
Varlaam
Donald Gramm
Conductor
Thomas Schippers

previously employed; banished (at least temporarily) are the much-loved colors of Rimsky-Korsakov's orchestral remake, as well as the touch-ups Rathaus and Shostakovich employed in more recent years. Schippers' effort is based primarily on the composer's 1872 revision but reclaims the psychologically potent St. Basil scene of the 1869 original score. Unwilling to do without any possible riches, the conductor tacks on the Kromy scene to end the opera as Mussorgsky did in 1872. A few smaller internal cuts, especially in the composer's act two (act one, scene five at the Met), are also restored. The Nurse's Song of the Gnat (1872) is cut but the clock sequence added, for that revision is kept. Rangoni, in earlier Met productions suppressed at the end of the Polish act, now reappears, sinister and triumphant.

The composer's spare, bleaker orchestral sound world (the comparison is with Rimsky's flamboyance) mates well with Schippers' no-nonsense interpretive stance. Events in old Russia were swift-moving, according to this conductor's bent. The opening andante motive, in the minor mode and a mood-setting touchstone for the opera, must speak for itself—the conductor does not augment its twists and turns by applying a mournful accent of his own. Every measure of the score is molded into a homogeneous unity in Schippers' well-thought-out conception. The results can be slightly antiseptic, but the conductor's control of his forces, his solicitous shaping of sonorities and phrase details, warrants complete approbation. After all, Mussorgsky's often modal construct, though largely absent in the Polish act, repeatedly casts its own spell, lending a unified tone to both drama and music. The ball-bearing fluency of Schippers' reading, its rather incredible precision (especially in the choral episodes) marginally diminishes the opera's earthy tang— the smell of serfage poverty is not allowed to infect our nostrils. Nevertheless, Schippers' pacing of the score—the conductor seldom lingers to expand emotional response—creates a momentum that enables the individual scenes of the episodic libretto to move with compelling directness. The result is an unusually consistent dramatic tension, sometimes a breath-holding excitement, that upgrades this *Boris*'s credibility and makes its truth not merely historical, but timeless.

Under Stivender's splendid tutelage, the chorus performs with maximum professionalism. While exceptionally well schooled, the chorus' sounding of their newly acquired Russian tongue, especially in the opening scene, fails to take full advantage of the succulent sonorities that reside in the language itself. A first effort is understandably more correct than idiomatic. "Russianness" comes more to the fore in their prominent choral episodes at St. Basil's cathedral and in the Kromy forest. But they never quite command (and cannot be expected to) that black, almost prehistoric-resounding moan—evidently the birthright of Russian basses—that in native performances periodically serves as a vocal and emotional pedal point for the opera.

In the opening scene, a similar deficiency affects some of the afternoon's soloists. Lenus Carlson, as secretary of the Duma Shchelkalov, worries the crowd with the news that Boris will not accept the crown. His splendid high baritone is as firm and attractive as any up-and-coming young singer could hope to provide, the declamation eminently clear. But the moment really demands a weightier sonority, one that will, as in that opening orchestral motive cited above, set the tone for the harrowing voyage that lies before us. Once again, we hear the Russian text but cannot place our feet on Russian soil. Velis quite convincingly plants his

Robert Nagy as Shuiski and Paul Plishka as Pimen in *Boris Godunov*. Photography by James Heffernan. Courtesy Metropolitan Opera Archives.

there. He delivers the Simpleton's laments with unaffected simplicity, sounding the endlessly sighing half-steps in natural tenor tones. Mussorgsky's message is so self-evident that little more is required to send sorrow home to the audience.

As the innkeeper, Batyah Godfrey's vocalism is first rate. Her timbre is invitingly swarthy, her articulation clarity itself; it even holds a suggestion of Russian tang. But she sings her song (delightfully) as an opera singer would, rather than as an on-the-job proprietress should. She probably inherited the inn—her youthful tone seems untouched by business cares. Best's police officer has a nice down-and-dirty feel to him. Among the palace inhabitants, Norden is an exquisitely innocent Xenia. Her uncomprehending sadness is infinitely touching. Boy soprano Paul Offenkrantz, as her young sibling, performs with the professional poise of a veteran. Few unchanged voices are so pungent, so pitch perfect, and so persistently probing as this Fyodor's. When Norden's piping soprano and Offenkrantz's piquant tone combine, their extraterrestrial timbres (hers as sexless as his) create a sonority of enchanting felicity.

Who would expect to encounter Donald Gramm, exquisite singer and principled interpreter, in the dirty rags of a drunken friar? All that art and intelligence can do to make real the impersonation, he does—and does it superbly. His rhythmic emphases (pricking away under the bright spikes of wind tone) help to carry the day in Varlaam's Siege of Kazan set piece. When contending with the border patrol, Gramm trots out a multitude of timbral colors and realistic artifices in a brilliant display of creative ingenuity. It all helps—but he remains the most elegant drunkard in broadcast history. I recall hearing Lorenzo Alvary, one of the genuine character artists on the Metropolitan stage at mid-century, sing Varlaam's Siege aria in a 1953 concert. Without costume or props, he turned it into the most uncouth narrative imaginable, mouthing the language as though it were meat to chew, compelling it to speak volumes of Slavic earthiness. It was a wonderfully theatrical creation where vocal merit was entirely beside the point.

Shuiski and Pimen not only live in different social realms—the one a nobleman, the other a monk—they are opposing symbols of wiliness and goodness. Normally, that means the prince will utter his doublespeak in oily, unctuous tones. Nagy eschews the caricature, and offers in its stead a nobleman confident and strong, his craftiness conveyed by robust, dramatic tones. The straightforward pose provides relief from some distorted portrayals of earlier broadcasts and makes Shuiski a more likely contender for the throne—eventually he did become the czar. A few suggestions of servility on Nagy's part are sufficient to suggest his relationship with Boris. Pimen has to be played straight and Plishka does so. The Ukrainian strain in his heritage (on the mother's side, a genealogically minded *Opera News* charmingly informs us) means he is one up on most of the cast. His sharp consonants and fruity clutch of vowels seem tactile as well as aural. But his performance goes beyond inherited aptitude. Vocal strength, expressive variety, and heartfelt emotion are his more potent weapons. With this portrayal, the American bass, already a near-decade Met veteran, qualifies as a Met star. The czar himself would be in his future. Plishka had intended to play the monk as an ancient, but director Everding wanted a younger characterization. The singer sounds as though he is in the director's pocket as his youthful, rich tones brighten Pimen's tenebrous cell. He pours more than tone, indeed his heart's response, into his description of Fyodor's murder, infusing the narrative—which has been known to come off as a dull exercise—with suspense and dramatic impact. The voice is splendidly resonant, the tale both terrible and touching. In contrast, as though modesty asserts itself before his supposed betters, his account of the miracle when standing in the Duma is simply delivered, but convincingly real. The exchange of the monk's cloth for a monarch's ermine is foreordained.

The Polish scene, so often decried as dramaturgical folly, a sop to operatic convention, has merit as a separate entity—an intriguing diversion. On this afternoon, two assets lend it credibility. Dooley's Rangoni (no Pushkin hangover, but Mussorgsky's own creation) is an effective theatrical portrait. The baritone's voice is firm, the dramatic profile of Marina's confessor strongly limned. (His entrapment of Dimitri is aided by Schippers' scrupulous guidance of the lengthy descending chromatic scale that replicates the priest's reptilian manner.) Dooley's timbre may not be inherently malevolent, but Rangoni's intent to control and manipulate the lovers is explicit in his vocal manner. Obviousness is never central to this artist's credo. Too bad he didn't lay a seductive legato onto the suggestive coils of his little aria—he settles for text articulation. His prey, Marina and Dimitri, are a pair of lovers headed for an unhappy ending. Theyard, whose several performances during these few seasons seem to describe a downward curve, declaims with persistent energy, but is consistently indifferent to musical and textual nuances. A few high notes are touched by strain, and the timbre, initially striking but overall rather insistently brazen, can become tiresome; its nasality is especially trying on the "ee" sounds. He is an energetic performer, both as the awakening Grigori and the troubled suitor. One can never complain about lack of ardor with this tenor and, in truth, he has moments of affecting song when courting Marina. He is at his best as the triumphant pretender riding into the Kromy forest, declaiming with a leader's assurance. In his defense, the role is an ungrateful one, but he does not increase regard for the task.

This season, Dunn, who had figured in two earlier broadcasts of the opera, sings her first Marinas in Russian. As before, she is an admirable Polish princess, for she owns assets—mid-range vocal solidity and overall warmth of timbre—that are singularly suited to the role. They enable her to execute the Polish dance rhythms that pepper Marina's music with both precision and ease. Not for her the squeaks and scratches that many a Marina has served up on previous broadcasts. (In fairness, the fault often has been as much with the composer's setting as with the singer's technique.) The American mezzo had restudied the role when relearning it in the original language (earlier efforts were in English and German—such is the international artist's lot). Her reading of the princess' music is nuance-full. Subtle phrasing turns the Polish intriguer into a more engaging creature than she has a right to be. One would not like to see her banished in the name of either verisimilitude or authenticity. When Marina finally accepts Dimitri's love, seduction vibrates in Dunn's tones, not in blatant assault, but rather in recognition that beauty, both womanly and royal, must receive its reward.

Martti Talvela, the magnificent Finn, had been heard as Hunding in Karajan's 1969 *Walküre* broadcast but had not been on the Metropolitan roster since that debut season. (The Grand Inquisitor was his other occupation that year.) Now he returns in triumph, the focal point of the new production. His physical stature (six foot seven) guaranteed stage dominance; though denied his impressive presence, the radio audience experienced comparable impact. The size and strength of his

Martti Talvela as Boris Godunov. Photography by James Heffernan. Courtesy Metropolitan Opera Archives.

vocalism as well as his detailed characterization of the tortured czar are vivid in the extreme. The voice at some moments seems meticulously cultivated, especially when, vocal finish being appropriate to the mood and situation, he allows song its head. In other episodes, it is rough-hewn, disturbingly sounding on the point of breaking up. The vocal rough edges are employed as graphic revelations of Boris' disintegrating psyche. Still, at times (in the clock scene, especially) one fears for his vocal health, so realistic and hazardously brutal to the voice are his effects. That concern aside, the scene is mesmerizing as Talvela depicts the czar's psychological collapse.

I wonder what Alexander Kipnis, in the house for the performance and an unexpected guest on the intermission quiz, thought of Talvela's all-stops-pulled-out manner. (He described the overall performance as "magnificent."[1]) The legendary Russian bass, well remembered for a couple of Boris performances with the company in the early forties, was never one to abuse his instrument. Of course, it was well stocked with the necessary tools for both song and portraiture, ebony-rich in timbre, almost excessively resonant at one volume extreme and yet possessed of a haunting mezza voce. He conquered while performing within the bounds of healthy vocalism. When speaking of Russian basses, one can't ignore Chaliapin. He had more than his share of innings with Boris—his imprint on the role is greater than anyone's. He usually operated in quite another interpretive sphere from that of countryman Kipnis. Theatrical naturalism was his thing. But, above and beyond the originality of his conceptions—some would call them merely idiosyncratic—he was a master singer.

Talvela may not qualify at that level, but he can sing, as he demonstrates in the long scene with his children that precedes the clock episode. An easy, almost conversational manner is his opening gambit; soon, tonal grandeur invests the 'highest power' monologue. Now the tone pours out of him, as natural as a river's flow—one of Mississippian (or better, Volga-like) proportions. While predominantly densely packed, sonority is often varied by telling gradations. When he speaks of his grief, he allows a slight wail, airy and sorrow-laden (the plaint a common property of men who know the long nights of the far north) to subtly infect his tone. Other scenes are, if anything, underplayed. There is method in that posture. With theatrical craft, he chooses not to stun us with his vocal endowment at his entrance. Indeed, his modulated speeches in the coronation scene actually suggest a man reluctant to ascend Russia's throne. The death scene, while laced with sufficient contrast, is a bit more contained than other interpreters have offered (director Everding favored a lighter touch rather than stagey theatrics). The near-mad czar interrupts the Duma's deliberations with a few weird puffs of tone and an eerie calm descends upon the assembly. In the affecting scene with Fyodor, Talvela relies upon his basic timbre to depict the czar's varied emotions. He can shake the heavens when he implores his son to protect holy church, but turn tender in a trice as daughter Xenia fills his thoughts. In many measured phrases, he allows a singer's vocal artistry to carry the weight of expression—no ill effects from the distortions of the clock scene surface. The result is as powerful as the outsized histrionics of that earlier struggle. One last burst of tone as Boris proclaims he is still czar, the moment enhanced by Schippers' tremendous orchestral crescendo, leads on to his feeble final words, a mumbled cry for God's mercy. Over the airwaves, his collapse and death are physically projected by the series of

Carmen
13 December 1975

Carmen
Régine Crespin
Micaela
Katia Ricciarelli
Don José
William Lewis
Escamillo
José van Dam
Conductor
Henry Lewis

heavy thumps as he rolls down the seven steps leading from the throne. Mighty in his torment and moving in his death, Talvela's Boris ranks with the great ones.

When the broadcast *Carmen* of 13 December 1975 was announced, the cast of Crespin, Ricciarelli, Domingo, and Van Dam promised one of those afternoons where no ciphers would interfere with pleasure. Hopes were dashed in two ways, the one inadvertent, the other planned. Domingo was indisposed and William Lewis was called upon to assume Don José's burden. Scheduled to conduct, and keeping the appointment, was yet another Lewis—Henry, of previous acquaintance. Both gentlemen are honorable practitioners of their trade, but on this afternoon their contributions warrant no more than that, in this case qualifying, designation.

The American conductor has led other broadcasts to considerably better effect, including the 1973 airing of the opera with Marilyn Horne as the gypsy heroine. On this afternoon, he seems preoccupied with speed, deluded in the belief that *Carmen*'s lively ambience can be created through mere motoric drive. No distinctive musical profile emerges from the limitless variety of Bizet's orchestral fabric. One can appreciate the opéra comique mode he adopts in the introductory scenes—better that than an excess of interpretive urgency and dramatic overkill. But ultimately, liveliness mutates into routine, and ensemble between pit and stage becomes merely polite. Occasionally, it is less than that: the chorus at times runs it own show, leading while the conductor follows. It should have tended to its own affairs, for the choral episodes are hardly models of precision, and individual voices often disturb the ensemble blend. Provincial or, if you prefer, ordinary, is the tag one hangs on certain aspects of this performance, and *Carmen* deserves nothing less than a master's care.

At the curtain's rise, Bizet gifted Morales with a plucky opening gambol and, though not long, the part profits from a singer of some elegance. Gene Boucher fills the bill, his French trim, the voice in similarly attractive form. Richard Best is a curiously reserved Zuniga. His lieutenant is a few steps removed from the in-charge bloke preferred by most interpreters. Though vocally he gruffs his way through the role, the bass comes off as a mild-mannered go-along-to-get-along officer whom José could have bested at any time—that is, if he weren't in a permanent funk. The gypsy crew holds its own. The women (Di Franco and Baldwin) perform with greater surety than the men (Velis and Christopher), though Baldwin's tone thickens in the card scene. Di Franco shines there and in the mountain ensemble, her tone compact, her timbre attractive, her manner lively. The quintet roars along at an Indy 500 pace and makes its usual effect, but other readings have sparkled more at a less precipitous pace.

Lewis, though probably the role cover, racked up more than a dozen outings as José with the company so he was no mere junior. He knows his business, and management was wise to keep him around. Still, his is not a "glamor" voice; the notes are all there, but the timbre is less than distinctive. On this afternoon, at least in the initial acts, it sometimes proves aggravating. For much of the opera, he relies on that too-familiar snarl to project tone. From the moment he comes into the picture, his José is an uncommonly aggressive, surly soldier. In the novel, Mérimée's man was certainly no prince of a fellow; indeed, he was a downright blackguard, but Bizet's music tells us that *his* grown-up village boy is rather a different sort of character. The Flower Song is but one proof of the changeover.

Lewis' reading has its moments, but his hurried ascent to a *forte* top tone at the aria's close sounds more like a safety device than a musical prescription; of equal importance, he ruins the composer's novel harmonic sequence under 't'aime' by anticipating the tonic note. The final acts better show his quality. His mountain confrontation with Carmen is dramatically vivid and the decision to hasten to his mother's side convincing, in part because the voice has gained in body and the tone acquired a more agreeable patina. Outside the bullring, he suggests a man who is living on the edge; the tenor's emotional control in the early stages of the encounter enhances the pathos of the final tragedy. Once again, the tone gains in focus, the timbre continues to brighten, and a measure of ring in the upper range aids his desperate pleas. Honorable need not be a trifling epithet.

Miss Ricciarelli had come to the company as Mimì at the end of the previous season and makes her broadcast debut on this occasion. She is destined to become famous. Unfortunately, by the time celebrity claims her, its voracious appetite has to be content with her markedly diminished vocal resources—and the decline from likely star to mere quasar comes much too soon. On this afternoon, however, the Italian soprano was still thought to be something special, and her Micaela gives every evidence that she is. Not quite thirty, she had been before the public a scant half dozen years, beginning in Italian theaters like Parma and Rome, before reaching La Scala in 1973. Covent Garden and Chicago were already on her list before she joined the Met. Her instrument is basically a remarkably fine one, a voice that should have entitled her to become a dominant presence on the operatic scene over the next decades. The timbre is dark, made more interesting by a provocative mix of fruitiness and steel. Indeed, for those who only know the voice in the later years of its disrepair, its fiber is surprisingly firm, the substantial metallic cast entirely reassuring. Hints of that floated, disembodied timbre that she later favored surface now and then (and very beautiful they are), but the thought that they would become the soprano's only reliable resource seems inconceivable.

Interpretively, Ricciarelli is in and out of dramatic focus, sometimes within consecutive minutes. She is subdued when dealing with the playful soldiers—obviously, she doesn't enjoy bantering with their kind. Earnestness, rather than charm, is her principal weapon—not a bad trait for a girl who will go wandering alone in the mountains. But creating a character does not seem on the soprano's mind. Still, a Micaela can survive on voice alone. The soprano purls tone magically in the duet with José. If she begins the aria somewhat tepidly, she makes a strong finish. Indeed, in the thrusting phrases of the middle section, Ricciarelli rouses herself to credible involvement. The voice flows with voluptuous tone in the upper octave. A glorious darkly bronzed timbre takes over in the reprise, where the difficult ascents are well negotiated. Several less than perfect attacks (a bit of sluggishness here, a slide there) indicate some holes in her method—or perhaps a too easygoing nature. Her account of the dying mother's wishes is low-key mush—an emphatic delivery would better motivate the errant son. She makes up the deficiency by injecting some urgency into her final plea. Still, a high degree of dramatic involvement does not seem to be in the cards for this prima donna. Probably few will care about her placidity after they hear the voice's tonal shine and glinting power as it ascends, or, as complement, when she wafts a gossamer *piano* in all parts of her range. Voices like hers are rare in any age. If only they could be nurtured with greater care than was Ricciarelli's fortune.

José van Dam all but walks off with the afternoon's honors—vocal and artistic. The Belgian bass rehabilitates Escamillo, converting the toreador from a macho poster boy into an elegant aristocrat of the arena, one as adept at making a gentlemanly pass at the gypsy temptress as when negotiating a crowd-pleasing *passo* with his cape in the bullring. Though Belgian by birth, French is his "mother tongue," as is evident in his every utterance on this afternoon.[2] The first decade of his career began with small roles at the Paris Opéra, followed by two years with Herbert Graf's Geneva ensemble. Since 1967, the Deutsche Oper in Berlin had been his home company, but Covent Garden, Paris, and Salzburg had welcomed him as well. The voice is big, manly, wonderfully potent in tone, and uniquely timbred—there is none other quite like it. In the Toreador Song, his top tones, grand and solid, bristle with confidence and, though one or two low notes pale (Bizet's setting is notorious for its problematic range), he has total command of the bravura piece. "*Olé*"s in abundance are deserved for his virile reading of the opening stanza and the reward of a bull's tale for his delectable diminuendo entry upon the popular 'Toréador' refrain and subtle tracing of its jaunty tune. A singer who can remove the curse of overexposure from a warhorse is gifted with genius. Van Dam's elegant, decorated 'l'amour' adds an approving period to that status. Most Escamillos are content to rage along with tenor José in their mountain confrontation; our bass-baritone all but shames his rival into submission with his aplomb. His invitation to Carmen is a prospective lover's paean, his dulcet address to her in their little fourth-act duet a poem in sound. A few artists possess such technical security, own so refined a sensibility, that they seem quite set apart from their colleagues, rather like Renaissance sculptured saints secluded in *palazzo* niches. Their rarity, their good deeds, make them almost worthy of idolatry, a state that enhances their untouchability. That is the price they pay for their transcendence. Van Dam is one of those few; De los Angeles, say, another. The prospect of hearing the bass in a variety of roles—he tells *Opera News* he wants to put Escamillo to rest—whets the artistic appetite. Unfortunately, the Metropolitan seemed to have difficulty in weaving his sophisticated art into its plans, and his visits over the years were usually brief and sporadic. Our loss, Europe's gain.

Even as it acquired prospective luminaries in Van Dam and Ricciarelli, the company gained back one of its most accomplished artists when Régine Crespin returned to the fold. In years, she had been absent only two, but the Crespin one had heard in a few seasons that antedated the hiatus was not the great singer whom we remembered as the Marschallin, Tosca, Kundry, and Sieglinde. A period of vocal and personal troubles had all but brought her down and lowered our expectations as well. Carmen is an unusual vehicle for her return. The Metropolitan run represented her first performances of the testing role on any stage, though she had recorded it and sung it in concert. Much jubilation had greeted her initial performance six weeks previous to the broadcast. A return to complete vocal health had been proclaimed by critics who "knew voices," as the saying goes. Much of her broadcast gypsy is vocally enticing, though I would raise a flag concerning a few episodes (in the second act—all the 'Tra la la' business—and a patch or two later on) where the tone in the middle voice sounds less well balanced: it thins and takes on a slight edge. In short, there the voice loses some of its magnetic core timbre. The difference is not enough to impair the overall quality of her performance, which is well sung and fascinating in its detail. At its best, the voice alternates between velvet warmth and copper cool.

With Crespin, language and its messenger, diction, are of paramount importance. The soprano's courting of her native tongue, whether in song or spoken dialogue, gives immense pleasure. Only upon hearing an artist like Crespin (or Van Dam) are we reminded of what we miss in performances of French opera where dutiful or mutilated French either weighs down or trivializes not only the text, but the music itself. The diva's delivery of text (every word intelligible) is crisp, illuminating, vital, or seductive, as the case may be. In spoken dialogue, she runs up and down the scale as though it were an escalator—the range she employs approaches that of Carmen's music itself. The result is pure delight. Actually, "delivery of text" seems inadequate, indeed untruthful, for it implies that articulation is a thing separate from the music, when the two are inseparable, as Crespin repeatedly makes clear. To hear her nonchalantly toss off the Habanera and Seguidilla (insouciantly intimate) is to elevate faith in their simple sophistication a hundredfold; so much heavy breathing has been expended on them, it is a wonder they are still standing. And in them, her voice is at its most beguiling, fluent, full, and secure on top, immensely inviting in its play of colors, vibrant or mellow, as wanted. Throughout the entire first act, she plays with men. They seem like little boys come to gawk when she, bored with their importuning, unconcernedly fondles their libidos as she likens love to an 'oiseau rebelle.' She spares us the usual sexy vocal moves; her way is more sensual than an up-front assault. Even the Gypsy Song, so often a gaggle of desperation, is handled with aplomb by Crespin—and the voice stays true there as well. Her 'l'amour!' at the close of the Toreador Song is velvety deep and *juste*, even as her smiling 'amoureuse' in the quintet seems full of promise. Her disdain when José decides to return to his barracks is quietly intoned—the heat of her disfavor and subsequent disenchantment is saved for later. Crespin's card reading is simplicity itself—undoubtedly she anticipated the fate she finds there. (The soprano believed Carmen was in fact "suicidal."[3]) At the climax, 'La carte impitoyable' receives all necessary emphasis. The 'La mort's are recognized in turn, but for her, though inevitable, death is merely regrettable; no vehement shudders rock her soundings of the word. With the diminuendo that she applies to the final 'mort,' she seems to embrace mortality.

The bullring duet is full of individual touches, beginning with a matter-of-fact greeting ('C'est toi?') to José. When Crespin tells him in world-weary tones that she no longer loves him, the soprano tells *us* that she knows he intends to kill her. The twin 'Libre' phrases do stir her spirit, but she saves her grandest outburst for 'Eh bien! frappe-moi donc,' thrusting forth the opening words before spitting out the remainder in a gnarl of disgust. Perhaps the most idiosyncratic interpretive touch of her portrayal is the mix of disdain and boredom that she lays on the 'ring' phrase—her incredibly quiet, low-voiced 'Tiens' is a world away from other interpreters' snarls as they hurl the ring in José's face. A soft moan is her only concession to death (her stage action at this point evidently included a shocking reaching out to caress her murderer). Miss Crespin has not only returned in triumph, she has done us the favor of allowing Carmen to live again, fascinating us in a way that we had almost forgotten she could.

Carmen's demise was the product of her own intractability. She could afford to be independent, moving in the private sphere as she did. Where political questions are involved, larger questions tend to lead to major disturbance of the psyche. Recall opera's troubled czar. Monarchs like Boris Godunov are not the only operatic creatures to experience dementia. True, Elektra was preoccupied with family, yet her kin played upon the world stage. As the daughter of Agamemnon, she was afflicted by a madness inflamed by vengeance—not a good thing, but in her case understandable. Of course, Strauss garbed it in more flamboyant colors than did Mussorgsky. When it came to orchestration, they lived on different planets.

On the broadcast of 10 January 1976 *Elektra*, absent from the repertory since 1971, is newly cast in the dominant trio of women's parts and guided by a conductor, Heinrich Hollreiser, who makes his house debut. Ursula Schröder-Feinen and Roberta Knie appear as Elektra and Chrysothemis with Varnay, a familiar Elektra in the early 1950s, now undertaking Klytämnestra. Dooley (Orest) and Nagy (Aegisth) are familiars from earlier broadcasts, as are Ordassy (Overseer) and Anthony (Young Servant).

Hollreiser, Munich-born, was a well-tutored product of the German opera circuit, where he progressed from coach to conductor (Wiesbaden, Mannheim) before Böhm in 1942 invited him to return to his home city with the Bavarian State Opera. In turn *Generalmusikdirektor* at Düsseldorf, principal conductor at the Vienna Staatsoper and at the Berlin Deutsche Oper, he found a home at Bayreuth and enjoyed guest performances throughout Europe. A pedigree studded with the most hallowed European stages excites anticipations beyond the norm and Hollreiser doesn't disappoint. That record also carries with it an indoctrination in the traditions of Strauss performance, and the conductor affirms that tutelage in his middle-of-the-road interpretation. All the nuances of the score are acknowledged. The orchestral flow of the composer's intricate web of motives is consummately woven into a continuous flow, while the layering of orchestral sonorities remains scrupulously clean even when the Strauss bellows is pumping its maximum wind storms. He is not afraid to let the orchestra belch tone to mimic turmoil onstage but his is not the turbulent ride nor the ecstatic immersion in Grand Guignol that some broadcast conductors have provided. Hollreiser's musical and dramatic ploys are explicit, graphically sculpted as Strauss intended, and convincing.

In the opening scene, the five maids (Godfrey, Love, Munzer, Di Franco, and Weidinger) are an able group, a little more well behaved than suits their dramatic function, with the first- and last-named respectively offering some distinction of timbre and tone. Anthony's young servant has grown more emphatic since his 1966 outing—both his tenor and the servant have aged during the decade. Nagy's Aegisth is stout voiced and sounds appropriately befuddled by Elektra's on-again-off-again treatment. Dooley, after a tepid start—Orest's low range limits his high baritone's effectiveness—rises to the climactic moments of the recognition scene with an actor's touch and a musician's affective delivery.

Varnay, already introduced in her mezzo-soprano guise as Kostelnicka during the previous season, seems as self-confident when depicting the queen's malevolence as she was when exposing Elektra's fixation in her towering 1952 portrayal of the deranged daughter. Genes, once again at work. The great artist is in excellent vocal form. Of course, the role's grotesquerie allows the interpreter considerable divergence from normal vocal standards; it even invites it, that is, if Klytämnestra's fears and hungers are to register as worthy of her daughter's fulminations. On that score, Varnay is ahead of the game. Her voice, large, metallic, hard toned, is built for confrontation (though in her youth she effectively put it to more benign uses). On this afternoon, the low- and mid-voice are rock solid and the relatively few ascents into the upper range are ably negotiated with none of the problems at the break that can affect her late-career portrayals. Indeed, she

---

Elektra
10 January 1976

Elektra
Ursula Schröder-
Feinen
Chrysothemis
Roberta Knie
Klytämnestra
Astrid Varnay
Aegisth
Robert Nagy
Orest
William Dooley
Conductor
Heinrich Hollreiser

launches some splendid top tones (including the critical G-sharp as the queen seeks sacrificial bloodshed in return for a good night's sleep). The entire scene between mother and daughter, one of the several highpoints of the drama, is crafted with masterly insight by Varnay. The voice's solidity in the lower range allows her to pungently project Klytämnestra's account of her weird dreams. She even manages to evoke momentary sympathy for the troubled mother as she recalls earlier familial associations. But as she leaves the stage, the singer emits a series of wild, maniacal laughs and shrieks calculated to send shivers up the spine. They do.

Roberta Knie, though a native Oklahoman, like so many Americans in these opportune years, earned her operatic spurs in the German provincial houses. A dozen years before her Met house debut on this broadcast afternoon, she had first appeared at Hagen in repertory as varied as Sieglinde, Minnie, the Countess, and Agathe. Freiburg and then Austria's Graz heard her as well. Her repertory expanded to include Fidelio, Senta, and Salome with additional outings in the Italian terrain: Desdemona, both Verdi Leonoras, Manon Lescaut, and Tosca. Her United States stage debut as Isolde in Dallas had occurred only a few months before she came to the Met. The voice is certainly a healthy instrument, resilient in the upper octave, where its metallic cast and firm tones with minimal vibrato have a laser-beam objectivity. In the middle low range, the instrument is of more ordinary character. She performs with unabated strength, but her casting in this role goes against the grain. Elektra is the stronger sister, Chrysothemis the weaker, less tormented creature who longs for their old family life. Contrast between the two voices (recall the ideal Nilsson/Rysanek lineup) ought to amplify the dramatic construct of the opera, but that desirable effect is nullified by Knie's inherently commanding timbre. Hers is a voice that creates angles and inhibits arcs when shaping phrases. Beyond that observation, her performance is thoroughly professional with a few blazing moments that demonstrate her right to tread the Met stage. Management did not overprize her abilities—after a few Chrysothemis appearances she would be absent until 1981, when she returned for a single Isolde as replacement for Gwyneth Jones. A decade or two later, I think they would have placed a greater value upon her services.

Schröder-Feinen, too, would have a Met career of short duration. But hers is a different story. She had come to the house as early as 1970, first appearing as Chrysothemis. Indeed, the character of her voice would seem to qualify her best for that sisterly assignment. Still, she is an artist of immense sensibility, owning an instrument that is a veritable aural coat of many colors, any one of which she can don with the flick of a vocal cord. Elektra was not a new role for her—productions had been mounted for her in Berlin and Hamburg—but throughout her career, she had resisted being typecast. In her native Gelsenkirchen, her repertory included Aida (1961), Handel's Cleopatra, Oscar, Salome, Turandot, and Bess (in Gershwin's opera). (Now, there is either a vastly gifted singer or a foolhardy one.) Düsseldorf later in the decade knew her as Kundry and Brünnhilde, and from 1971 on Bayreuth valued her warrior maid, her Senta, and Ortrud. The Salzburg and Edinburgh festivals claimed her as well. Her Met performances would be few in number (only sixteen), which perhaps accounts for her delayed broadcast debut as Elektra, six years after her initial house appearance.

The wait was worth it. Schröder-Feinen gives a ravishing reading of the treacherous role, replete with sensitive interpretive touches and furnished with vocal nuances, both subtle and grand. Her performance, rapturously received by the audience at the opera's end, is captivating on several fronts. The voice is a singular one. As noted, it assumes different guises at will and always in response to the text or action. Nevertheless, its makeup is consistent overall, the timbre in the lower octave complex and a little shrouded, the coloration intriguing; the upper voice's silver is occasionally cast of shining steel, but more often sugar-coated. It is decidedly not the Elektra voice to which we have become accustomed, though Rysanek's instrument, too, was outside the norm for the daughter of Agamemnon. But Schröder-Feinen's lower range is solid, devoid of wobble, its color here darkened to suit the low axis and mournful, vengeance-prone mood of the opening monologue. At first, this Elektra seems rather contained, a creature who lives more by her wits than her passions. That soon changes. Her reading is as far removed—a polar distance—from Nilsson's powerhouse interpretation (heard in the previous two broadcasts) as two artists of merit can be and still remain conscientious purveyors of the composer's message. In its imaginative character, the German diva's Elektra has a fascination similar to that evoked when Welitch first brought her incandescent Salome to the airwaves in the late forties.

Elektra's entrapment of her mother in their grand *scena* together is subtly plotted, the craft of the daughter evident in the soprano's seductive manner and appealing tones. Schröder-Feinen owns a firm high C but she is also mistress of the high *pianissimo*, an uncommon attribute (except for Rysanek) among interpreters of the role. She delights in introducing it, *subito* and finely controlled, at unexpected moments; sometimes they move, via a magisterial crescendo, to a stout *forte*. They startle in the opening monologue and inhabit, most searingly, the recognition aria: 'Traumbild, mir geschenktes Traumbild' is literally plucked out of the ether. The sweet-and-sour timbre of her voice in the ambiguous colloquy with her long-lost brother is effectively exploited, and the heart of the scene ('O lass deine Augen mich seh'n!') receives quite the most fascinating reading of broadcast history. Her phrasing is languorous in the extreme, as though drug induced, touched even by "blue" notes, and so suggestive of a trancelike state as to produce a hypnotic response from her auditors. The *pianissimo* high B-flat of 'erhobenes Gesicht,' a stunning effect, tugs at the heartstrings. All the subtle vocal nuances combine to suggest a woman passing out of normalcy into an otherworldly state, love and madness intermingling in transfixing fashion. Does she court the accusation of quixotism, stray outside the interpretive zones, in the effort? I think not. In any case, the results are mesmerizing. Hollreiser's fluent accompaniment augments the mood, as does the hold-your-breath tension that he cultivates after the sibling's duet. Varnay's grotesque cries inflate the horror tally as Klytämnestra feels Orest's death blows. Though, as noted, their voices hardly suggest the sisters' contrasting temperaments, in their final joy-infused duet Schröder-Feinen and Knie satisfy with their confident, potent vocalism. The German diva revels in Elektra's high tessitura, as timbral steel, silver, and sugar meld into a cathartic ecstasy. The audience, at her solo bow immediately after the curtain's fall, erupts with passionate approval. The soprano will be heard again as the Dyer's Wife in the 1978 revival of *Die Frau ohne Schatten*, but, oddly and regrettably, retirement from the operatic stage would claim her a year later. At the time still in her early forties, the singer had been perhaps too eager to revel in the grandest roles of the repertory and, having once obtained them, been overly generous in dispensing her vocal wealth. Evidently the expected quota of a career's length could not be endured. Two decades of portrayals comparable to this Elektra would probably be sufficient reward for most singers.

Artists new and familiar inhabit the opera that Strauss penned after *Elektra*. As the curtain opens on an eighteenth-century Viennese boudoir, we discover that Zylis-Gara has welcomed a new Octavian, Tatiana Troyanos, to her bed. Old friends Blegen (Sophie), Edelmann (Ochs), and Dooley (Faninal) cavort in Levine's first radio reading of *Rosenkavalier*. For garnishment, Pavarotti sings the Italian aria. High-priced fare indeed on the broadcast of 27 March 1976.

Rosenkavalier is a siren call to conductors, bidding them to podium virtuosity beyond the norm and in the process adding to the opera's radiance by creating their own celestial light. Levine does not go down that tempting path. His is a centrist reading, its even tenor sounded in the measured character of the boudoir pair's lovemaking in Strauss' graphic introduction. Brazen it is not, but expeditious enough to serve the composer's purpose. Even the opening horn call is not overblown, Levine's insouciant shaping a nose-flip that signals comedy ahead. His waltzes gleam, though the Viennese lilt is not savored as succulently as I, who, like the Marschallin, have ridden on Prater lanes strewn with chestnut leaves, might prefer. And yet, *Gemütlichleit* hovers discreetly in his phrases, though it did not always among Hofmannsthal's characters. When Strauss' orchestral bumps and grinds surface, they are savored by the conductor—sometimes, in fact, he gives them an emphatic salute. He doesn't hurry the trio. Rather, it emerges grander than usual (Zylis-Gara and Troyanos see to that); the conductor's expansive embrace of Strauss' triumphant ensemble is both summary and soothing. Acquaintance with Levine's modus operandi over his initial half decade with the company has led us to expect his consummate command over—and a willing response from—his orchestral charges. The mutual respect between conductor and players is no mere accommodation, but rather a pact made in recognition of Levine's gifts.

Laboring in the comprimario vineyards are several of the Metropolitan's superior character players. Velis adeptly scatters Valzacchi's poisonous words like clattering pebbles; Love is his able accomplice, reading the letter with comic flair, but too labored in her third-act upward flight when posing as the Baroness. Baldwin's duenna is healthier of tone than most of her predecessors, and welcome for that. The solid-voiced Anthony (Innkeeper) and Booth (Police Commissioner) anchor the horseplay at the inn.

Strauss could not have ordered up a better Italian Tenor than Signor Pavarotti; the man already occupied that italicized slot in the mind of a large public. On this afternoon, he earns that right by his secure negotiation of the trying phrases of 'Di rigori armato.' The little upward run is clean and fluent and his top notes satisfy. He molds a finer legato in the rerun ('Ma si caro'), so much so that Ochs' rude interruption, theatrically a clever invention of the creative duo, is all the more to be regretted. He doesn't take a curtain call, having hurried home to rest before the evening's *Bohème*. Caballé will be his Mimì. Those were the days.

The Faninals may be a nouveau riche family, but Dooley would be at home in the best operatic society. In unusually blooming voice, his father of the bride is nervous, irate, beaten—as called for—but the voice and art are upper class all the way. Blegen's Sophie won the soprano her Metropolitan spurs a few seasons ago and she plays with comparable assurance today. As before, her bartered bride is half naif, half willful foot stomper. Her father can't handle her, and one wonders if

Der Rosenkavalier
27 March 1976
Marschallin
Teresa Zylis-Gara
Sophie
Judith Blegen
Octavian
Tatiana Troyanos
Italian Singer
Luciano Pavarotti
Faninal
William Dooley
Baron Ochs
Otto Edelmann
Conductor
James Levine

Octavian is taking on more than he can manage. The soprano's tone on this after-noon is not the most blandishing—to make up for its modest size she must apply sufficient point for it to carry in a house of Metropolitan proportions. Occasionally, mostly in agitated moments (and her sassy Sophie does seem to be in a perpetual stew), it grates on the ear. But she is a delightful interpreter, a sterling musician, and, for the most part, her vocalism delights with its purity of line and keenly etched tone. Her 'himmlische' leaps are accurate and certainly not insipid; critics considered them inappropriate to a teenager at the 1913 Met premiere when the beautiful Anna Case sang them. With Blegen, who sounds like a teenager, they come off as the natural effusion of a girl who reads 'Dem Ehrenspiegel Oester-reichs' for pleasure—and to get one up on her Rosenkavalier. I wonder if she had an ulterior motive in learning all those names of the young count.

Of course, Ochs is a boor, and Sophie's escape, preplanned or on-the-spot in-spiration, was in the cards. Because his resources are diminished, Edelmann's suitor is somewhat less of an impediment to happiness than most Barons. After all, the man is pushing sixty (born in 1917) and had been a broadcast Ochs as far back as 1956. The bass-baritone, born near Vienna, has the baron's patter ingrained in his subconscious; as he pets Sophie, the bass savors her in an idiomatic 'Schultern wie ein Henderl!' (Tender as a pullet), a delectable slip into the vernacular. So settled in his voice are Hofmannsthal's word marathons that they fall from his lips as easily as rain falls from heaven. He cannot storm and thunder as of old, but then his Baron was always a gentlemanly boor; Ochs may be so regarded, his gentility being a family inheritance, the bad habits evidently acquired. But there is nothing heavenly about his vocalism today. The tone is virtually devoid of bass resonance, so we can't indulge our liking for the rascal—in opera, thin tone implies an inher-ent meanness of spirit. Indeed, beery tone is always an asset in this role, especially in the act-two waltz finale. On this afternoon, Edelmann plays more as a charac-ter singer than a star in the spotlight. A generous sprinkling of vocal tricks—the well-earned stock in trade of a lengthy career—gets him over the more treacher-ous hurdles (although those puny falsettos on a couple high notes are hardly coin-age of the Straussian realm). This is his last season with the company. A return to the old glory haunts is a temptation few artists can resist, and, on this afternoon, no permanent damage is done to Edelmann's professional standing.

Not every Tosca will a Marschallin make. Zylis-Gara's vocal splendor and discerning musicality qualify her for the task. The role is beloved of sopranos who relish the opportunity to play a heroine whose complexity can only be revealed by a subtle probing of her character. The Polish soprano is first and foremost a singer—at least, the beauty of her voice, its savory legato, and her careful mold-ing of dynamics are so fine that one's attention settles on them. To some extent, these prize attributes work against her Marschallin. Her liquid legato, which in itself invites immersion, inhibits text articulation. When discerningly inflected, Hofmannsthal's words open up the princess' heart and, in the monologues, allow us to see into her soul. Sometimes the soprano achieves that end, as in her emo-tional reading of 'bis in mein Herz hinein . . . alles zergeht wie Dunst und Traum.' Words are the princess' friends, but Zylis-Gara does not always seem willing to admit them to her inner circle. Still, she is often so adept at applying a vocal inflec-tion or a musical subtlety that a comparable revelatory result is gained. A pity the text is not always equally responsive to her inquiring touch.

Vocally, her performance is a complete delight. By this time, we know that her soprano is one of the more luscious voices in the present company. Moreover, it is entirely obedient to her wishes. No hit-or-miss foibles mar her vocalism. Her technical security, wedded as it is to a keen musicality, can turn a phrase or an aria into a feast of vocal treats. While she is bound to shine when lofting tones on high, her middle and low voice are full toned and solid as well; since much of the Marschallin's part lies in that range, her phrases readily penetrate Strauss' sometimes overly assertive orchestral fabric.

Interpretively, Zylis-Gara's Marschallin is a charming creature. She can toss off a lightly nuanced phrase ('Quinquin, es ist ein Besuch,' for instance) with playful ease. Again Hempel, an idiomatic Marschallin, instructs us, as she recalls how Strauss told her he had written the role with "graceful, easy, parlando singing" in mind.[4] Yet Zylis-Gara's aristocratic, gracious poise is, at least in public, never in doubt; at the inn, for instance, she handles Ochs with care, not quite imperious in manner, but pointedly commanding. In the first-act monologues, she calls into play the mournful wind colors of her flexible instrument. At times, those memorable episodes become overlaid with a not unsuitable morose tinge: the clock's tick-tocks call it forth, and even the prospect of Onkel Greifenklau is touched by timbral sorrow. (Would not the princess have looked forward to the visit with pleasure?) Yet the role often allows her a delicious play of phrase and there the soprano is invariably at her best. The 'silberne Ros'n' phrase is exquisitely sounded; the top tone, though neither *piano* nor silvery, is nevertheless deliciously tapered and jewel-like in coloration. A few celebrated phrases may be rather too carefully sculpted, but her considerate placement of their every note and word commands regard. 'Und in dem "Wie" da liegt der ganze Untershied' is one of those studied gambits; the soprano's choice of colors and conscious blend with the wind instruments in the pit, however, make her reading magical in its own right. She opens the trio with a sure-throated molding of 'Hab mir's gelobt'—the tone may harden slightly as she rounds its curve, but the exposed passage is finely executed. Her phrases in the remainder of the trio are deployed like bands of honed steel that contribute to an uncommonly vibrant reading of the opera's ensemble highlight. I prefer to think that the portamento that binds her 'Ja, Ja' suggests a gracious, perhaps easy, acceptance of the unexpectedly quick realization of her 'heut oder morgen' prophecy. Zylis-Gara's princess deserves a full and happy future life.

Troyanos, in voice and temperament, is a mezzo-soprano of unusual distinction. A native New Yorker, the mezzo had behind her a decade's success on European stages to recommend her. Hamburg was her home company. Charlotte, Dido, Poppea, Orfeo, Adalgisa, Cherubino, and the Strauss roles, acquired in that secure German cocoon, proclaim an all-embracing repertory. She had scored in Aix-en-Provence and Vienna, and at Covent Garden too. Her instrument's brilliant coloration, its tonal edge, above all its tensility, conspire to make vivid her every utterance. She could not hide her light either under a bushel or in any demure posture if she tried. And who would want her to? Her theatrical temperament, ardent, even fiery, dictates the all-out nature of her interpretations. (Quite surprisingly, one author maintains that her temperament was either "unusually placid or unusually well-controlled."[5] But then, artists in private are seldom what they appear to be on stage.) An athletic singer, she is an end-zone combatant who wants to win.

At the curtain's rise, Troyanos voices Octavian's satisfaction in radiant tones and with exalted feeling. Her 'Bub' is an unusually commanding lover for a seventeen-year-old. The voice's quick vibrato is well under control today, sometimes even smoothed away into a liquid flow, molten and always attention-getting. The voice holds a carefully doled-out batch of sweet secrets as well: she lofts a velvety *piano* in the duet with Sophie, and the presentation of the rose contains suggestive hints of it as well. And back in the princess' boudoir, her dulcet 'Das weiss niemand' is a meltingly lovely calling card. Still, her primary currency is a rich, fruity tone. Her voice and art vibrate with emotional vitality. As my friendly neighborhood sommelier might say—and does—of a favorite wine, her voice "has a long finish"; like a healthy cabernet that grows and spreads on the palate, her tones invade and reverberate in the ear. What a telling contrast the two lovers make, Troyanos all youthful passion, Zylis-Gara rightfully mature in manner and controlled in vocalism—their very professional selves are emblematic of their stage characters. When jousting with lecher Ochs, Troyanos brooks no contest: "Mezzo Overmatches Bass" would be the headline if Octavian's assault had reached the pages of the *Wiener Abendpost*. At the inn, his/her Mariandel is more a personage than the usual mere comic turn, for the mezzo employs a variety of vocal techniques (chest, nose, harmonic overtones, her natural tone, and, most frequently, sounds so immature as to suggest the puerile voice of a stunted Olympic gymnast). At every turn, she is an inventive singer. Troyanos' control over the final phrase of the concluding duet is exemplary (as is Blegen's), one of the most accomplished ascents in broadcast history. Allen tells us that she will sing Carmen on tour in Boston and Amneris next season. A grand career lies before her.

A week before the *Rosenkavalier* broadcast the airwaves welcomed yet another Strauss comedy. Though her Composer is a backstage participant, Troyanos again sparks a performance on the 20 March 1976 airing of *Ariadne auf Naxos*. Caballé (Ariadne), Welting (Zerbinetta), Alberto Remedios (Bacchus), and Alan Titus (Harlekin) are the uncongenial island dwellers. Even Dooley's Music Master must bow to Levine's controlling vision.

Once again the maestro's control governs, but his vision is not so clear sighted as one might have expected. He does not seem to have quite found the pulse of Strauss' mélange of the buffa and *seria* genres. The pace is off. It isn't necessarily a question of tempos, although he does give the comedians a run for their money. (Expert as that group of male players is at their trade, they do survive and cross the finish line in tandem with the conductor.) He opens the prologue in modest fashion, the restraint shortchanging Strauss' motivic play. In this curious operatic adventure, the accommodations dictated by genre mixing require a touch so adept that it doesn't come obligingly to even this maestro's perceptive mind. Nor do they inform his shaping hand. Initially, I suspected his tepid manner merely implied that he was saving his big guns for the opera itself, where the thematic matter augments stage action, but irregularities surface there as well. As noted above, the charm of a few commedia dell'arte episodes is sacrificed, or at least neutralized, by his rigorous gait. In contrast, the final scene, in which Bacchus and Ariadne team up, is beset with languors. It seems interminable. (But then, I often have felt that Strauss is, even for him, too long-winded in this extravagantly expansive conclusion. Of course, he had to provide a counterbalance to Zerbinetta's display piece in order to safely anchor the opera in port.) Still, no Levine performance is devoid of

Ariadne auf Naxos
20 March 1976

Ariadne
Montserrat Caballé
Zerbinetta
Ruth Welting
Composer
Tatiana Troyanos
Bacchus
Alberto Remedios
Music Master
William Dooley
Harlekin
Alan Titus
Conductor
James Levine

Tatiana Troyanos as the Composer in *Ariadne auf Naxos*. Photography by James Heffernan. Courtesy Metropolitan Opera Archives.

skillfully negotiated turns, of surging orchestral sonorities, of phrases seductively molded. Satisfaction lurks around every corner. Though not up to his own standard, his *Ariadne* has its patches of lyrical beauty and (in the prologue) managed mayhem. Very few broadcasts coincide with the seasonal premiere of a work, as does this afternoon's offering. Usually there is time for a shakedown before sending it out over the ether. Levine owns to a great affection for the opera, finding it "so clever, fluent, so irresistibly subtle at times."[6] A few in-house readings before the broadcast probably would have benefited both conductor and work.

As directed by Strauss in his 1916 prologue, the Major-domo sets the bizarre adventures of the opera proper in motion. Castel displays his disdain for the artists assembled to entertain his master with complete confidence in his superiority over these theatrical artisans. The terms of their engagement are articulated with a mixture of boredom and nose-elevated scorn. Thus Castel sets the tone with admirable composure, and Velis' Dancing Master, agreeable to any artistic humiliation as long as his fee is paid, is an equally accomplished foil, eager and nimble in articulation—and he has the greater task of singing his words. In the prologue, Hofmannsthal and Strauss fashioned numerous character portraits. Their send-up of a prima donna is a treat, and Caballé takes full advantage of it: her humorous, uncomprehending 'Was ist das?' is stuffed with diva self-importance, its grossness as authentic as Bratwurst on a bun. No player on this afternoon deserves greater commendation than Dooley. He can wear his Music Master stripes with pride. The voice retains its invigorating bloom, and his rhythmic vitality, prompted by carefully considered musical and text relationships, enlivens every move he makes. He is quite simply the real thing.

The opera itself is overloaded with nymphs—but no shepherds, *Gott sei Dank*!. (The commedia dell'arte quartet must suffice in their place.) Najade (Christine Weidinger), Dryade (Munzer), and Echo (Norden) never escape their union, which, however, is not as blissful in terms of tonal match as the ear would wish. (Sometimes one wonders if casting directors have ears. In Norden's case, I think her presence may have been based solely on her ability to lightly replicate Ariadne's mournful cry—she has the perfect echo voice.) Able all three are, but Norden's bright timbre—sometimes enchanting, at other moments unnerving—makes for a difficult blend. Her rapid coils (and the part is loaded with them) come out as awkward spikes rather than graceful curves. Weidinger and Munzer are tonally pleasing and at home in water or forest, or so their accomplished song would indicate. The comedians are an agreeable group and bound to satisfy the richest man in Vienna. Even there a bit of mismatching occurs, for the usually reliable Anthony (Scaramuccio) occasionally blunders in a bit too raucously, disturbing the even tenor of the comedians' ensemble blend; he is perhaps unaware that Truffaldino, according to century-old tradition, is the preferred clumsy member of the group. Richard T. Gill would rather be a team player and is, in both tone and manner. Ahlstedt is excellent as the naive Brighella, his attractive voice suggesting boyish belief and his musicianly shaping of phrases a delight. Whenever the young tenor is the lead-off man, he brightens the scene.

Alan Titus, destined for a career of considerable importance, makes his Metropolitan debut on this occasion. His lyric baritone, firm and of inviting timbre, is just the thing for Harlekin's romantic persona. The New Yorker's elegant singing of 'Lieben, Hassen, Hoffen, Zagen' leaves no doubt that Zerbinetta will be his before the final curtain. Though still a very young man, his experience was large, for he had sung the Celebrant in the world premiere of Bernstein's *Mass* as a mere stripling. Many contemporary roles had come his way, but Pelléas in the Netherlands and Papageno in San Francisco were already in his pocket, with Monteverdi's Nero in Houston and Rossini's Figaro with the New York City Opera on his schedule. He would become a fixture with the latter company before emigrating to Europe and earning a prominent place for himself on the German stages. He is a markedly engaging artist. Evidently the Met found him superfluous—they were well stocked with baritones of his type. Who could have predicted that, a quarter century down the road, he would end up as a Bayreuth Wotan?

Though peopled with a fascinating group of well-defined characters, the prologue belongs to the Composer, and Troyanos' quicksilver vocalism makes it doubly her own. She grabs hold of central stage and never lets go. In artistry, the mezzo is in the same league as compatriot Dooley, only she plays for bigger stakes. It comes as no surprise that the most authentic portrayals come from the two American artists who have spent a decade or more imbibing the idiom and polishing the style on German stages. They know their way around. The young Composer is even more impetuous (and within a far more compact time zone) than his operatic cousin, Octavian. Troyanos sends off sparks at her entrance, the voice at once warm, vibrant, and penetratingly brilliant. Only when he (she) dreams up a new melody does the young man let his guard down. There the soprano takes advantage of the lapse to lower her vocal temperature; she lofts 'Du allmächtiger Gott!' with deliciously mellow tone, a timbral warmth that she spends rather too sparingly in her normally exuberant, forthright portrayals. A few top tones, taken *subito piano*, are more dulcet than one has a right to expect from so intensely collected a voice. Few mezzos can have raged as explosively at artistic philistines as this American songstress. Her open-hearted nature is proper fodder for Zerbinetta's seductive tactics and, cause leading to effect, the Composer's disappointment when he learns that her cajoling pretence was deceptive is expressed in a towering combination of anger and hurt. Before her music master reappears, the singer offers some exquisite, almost vibrato-free soft notes as the young man muses on Zerbinetta's invitation to love; soon his newfound maturity is apparent in Troyanos' joyful, resolute, almost swaggering vocal stance. The dynamic ascents of the Composer's ode to music at the prologue's close push even Troyanos' instrument to its limits. But her vocal bands are stout, her heart is big, her courage game, and her song exhilarating as the curtain nears. The 'heilige Kunst' of music has been well served.

Her temporary prologue playmate, Zerbinetta, is a coloratura mouthful. Ruth Welting, too, makes her first appearance on the Metropolitan stage in the broadcast. The Memphis-born soprano's artistry had been polished by Luigi Ricci in Rome before the New York City Opera gained her expertise in roles ranging from Lucia to Zerbinetta. Thus the Met management knew what it was buying when it contracted for her commedia minx (a portrayal that later in the year Covent Garden also acquired). Let us acknowledge one thing from the start: Welting is a pint-sized coloratura in a quart-sized part. Her voice, whetted to a fine point, is, though abetted by skillful deployment, small for the house. She manages to put over the monster aria more as a vocal actress than an expert in fioritura, fearlessly tackling what may be the supreme challenge of her repertory. She skips through its coloratura traps without the slightest trepidation, tossing off the trills, the ascending scales, the top tones (her E-flats *in alt* are assured, even tenacious—

though hard in timbre) with admirable nonchalance. She shows her hand right off: character portrayal will be her passport to audience acceptance. When she first addresses the 'Grossmächtige Prinzessin,' she does so with an audible vocal bow, respectful but personality-driven. Similar gambits in tighter spots carry her on to victory. The audience loves her and of course applauds on cue to allow Strauss his jocular put-down of their ingrained need to respond to a high note. What they heard in the house may well have been considerably less than the mikes picked up, but it was enough to earn their regard. Never mind that she failed to flip up to the arpeggio's top note in Zerbinetta's crowning cadenza. Actually, some of Welting's most affecting moments occur in the prologue, where she draws a taut 'Ein Augenblick ist wenig'; she nurses its grateful melodic expanse with surety of line and compact tone. And Levine enhances the moment, summoning from the orchestra a mood of welcome calm. The American soprano skitters delightfully with her fellow comedians in the opera itself. She knows how to make the most of her carefully marshaled assets. Over the next decade, Welting would be a some-time visitor to the Met, appearing as Olympia (just her ticket), Sophie and Fire in *L'Enfant et les Sortilèges*.

The *seria* lovers are novel entities. One seldom finds Miss Caballé in the Strauss milieu during her mature career, and tenor Alberto Remedios makes his Metropolitan debut as Bacchus. It is not a part for a debut—too treacherous. Luckily, the Liverpudlian tenor had two decades' experience to sustain him, the bulk of it gained as a mainstay of the English National Opera. Sutherland had taken him up for lyric roles (Faust, Edgardo, Alfredo) in her Australian touring company, and Covent Garden claimed him in 1966 (Dimitri, Florestan, Aeneas). He soon mutated into a reputable Wagnerian for the Sadler's Wells' English-language *Ring* productions. Remedios owns an attractive tenor, its timbre unusu-ally warm for one who labors most often in the Wagnerian arena. The tone is mainstream, so manly that initially it seems as though for once a godlike Bacchus will emerge from Circe's illicit embrace. Alas! the voice is a bit short on top. A few high notes unexpectedly fall away, the support briefly withering at the exact mo-ment when an exuberant thrust is required. Nor does his instrument seem quite large enough for the burden that Strauss has laid upon it. If the opera is to end with triumphant grandeur, Bacchus' final peroration really needs more expansive phrasing and resplendent tone than the tenor can summon. Still, if his means are less than is required for the task, Remedios' attributes are not negligible. That ap-pealing timbre is balm for ears that too long have suffered the dried-out voices and tonal flapping of the usual Bacchus genus. Often he sounds virile enough to make his occasional lapses on high dwindle in importance. Indeed, he does manage to handle more than one critical climax with secure and vibrant tone. But Bacchus is a role that uses up tenors the way a boa constrictor devours a rabbit. Remedios suffers that fate, for he fades out of the Metropolitan picture after this worthy ef-fort. England would continue to savor his Wagnerian heroes in the years ahead. More moderate-sized houses made them plausible there.

Caballé's Ariadne may be accounted an anomaly. By this time in her career, she had become the acknowledged queen (her supremacy not entirely accepted by the Sills and Sutherland camps, to be sure) of a large spectrum of the Italian reper-tory. Songbirds that escape their habitat can expect trouble in foreign lands, and the Spanish soprano's forays into the Strauss realm have not been accepted as rea-sonable ventures by everyone. Still, the singer was no novice on that terrain. She had recorded Salome, and in the first decade of her career had appeared at Basle not only as the Judean princess but as Arabella and Chrysothemis. In 1965, Glyndebourne knew her Marschallin, and one year Vienna awarded her its gold medal as the season's best Straussian. The credentials are there. It is clear that the singer early on had set her sights on the heavenly heights where the composer's heroines live. Evidently, she remained intent on gaining entry into those Elysian fields.

Then why this resistance? Certainly, her stage deportment came into the picture. But Ariadne was much more plausible in terms of dramatic action than most of her roles; the girl lives on a shell, immersed in one of the most static environments in all opera, a security blanket of inactivity for Caballé. Some detractors object to her Mediterranean aural gloss, deeming it not sufficiently idiomatic for the Strauss roles, as though bel canto lyricism is a blight not to be visited upon Teutonic holies. Strauss was in love with the soprano voice and I rather think he would have found the Spanish diva's vocalism too enchanting to be forsworn. After all, he had tried to get singers as diverse as lissome-voiced Elisabeth Schumann and Puccinian Geraldine Farrar to sing Salome. (Yes, physical considerations were involved as well.) Of course, idiomatic language is another concern. Glottals Caballé owns (though happily they are not abundant today), but gutturals are not part of her vocal makeup. Her soprano thrives in a vowel-drenched ambience. Without doubt, these demerits hardly make her a scofflaw. Interpretively, her predilection is for pathos, rather than *Schmerz*, the favored attitude of her German sisters. The forsaken heroine, as Strauss conceived her in musical terms, utters not only an introductory wail, but exists in a perpetual *cri de coeur*. One can play her either way, that is, for pain or for pity. On the broadcast, Caballé bathes Ariadne in tonal fluidity.

The role lies low for her, as it does for many sopranos whose ease in the stratosphere meets the Strauss standard. The opening phrases of 'Es gibt ein Reich' are a trial for her instrument. But she is handy with reinforcements. The diva relies on a chest voice in the nether area. It is not a particularly attractive part of her equipment. And yet, even in the middle-low range of the voice, her tone is often full and colored with a slightly musky timbre of attractive cast. When the cagey composer comports Ariadne on high, he can exact an exorbitant price. If a soprano be ill endowed in that range, let her beware. Caballé, however, can pay tribute in full. She offers ravishing phrases of a silken *morbidezza* (Italianate, yes—or should I coin them Spaniardate?—but then, the shimmering gleam of a German soprano is but a sister under the skin). Her crescendos are monuments of control—thrilling, not only in their ultimate power, but in the finesse with which she manages the aggrandizement. In the concluding duet, her vocalism is tangibly sensuous, producing an aureate rapture that, idiomatic or not, is as revelatory of Ariadne's temerity, her fears, and ultimately her passionate need, as one could wish. (Only in one important phrase series—'Sind meine Schmerzen mir auf immer genommen?'—does a harsher tone momentarily startle.) More than one critic on the scene did not take favorably to Caballé's Ariadne (nor to the performance as a whole, for that matter). Listening in the house (rather than in a home-and-radio environment) can alter aural perception, and the stage action—or lack of it— plays a part in that discrepancy. The radio audience, however, can invoke fantasy to complement the audible ecstasy of Caballé's song.

We are lucky that way.

Frederica von Stade as Rosina in *Il Barbiere di Siviglia*. Photography by James Heffernan. Courtesy Metropolitan Opera Archives.

CHAPTER TWENTY-ONE

Finale for a Decade

A feast of Italian operas, old favorites and a few rarities, brings the new Met's initial decade to a close. Comedies that feature the Almavivas (a touch of Teutonic influence there) and irrepressible Figaro lead off. A pair of Bellini works not often heard of late at the Met highlights sopranos of legendary renown. Puccini's three one-acts return to their legitimate home, brought together again after more than a half-century separation. Add in two warhorses, one a little shopworn (in the minds of some, Ponchielli's *La Gioconda* is not to be suffered—but I do, and gladly), the other a late-career masterwork by the grandest Italian of them all. Verdi's *Aida* allows us to go out in style.

The 20 February 1976 broadcast of *Le Nozze di Figaro* enlists players new to the company and artists previously not heard in their roles. Te Kanawa (Countess), Valente (Susanna), Elias (Cherubino), Norden (Barbarina), and Stewart (Almaviva) all appear in new broadcast assignments. Making broadcast debuts are Stafford Dean (Figaro) and Andrew Foldi (Bartolo). Steuart Bedford, remembered for conducting the Met premiere of Britten's *Death in Venice*, returns for his second season, this time placed in charge—surprisingly—of one of the gems of the repertory.

Normally, the prize assignment of the Mozart opera buffa has been reserved for conductors well seasoned by years of experience and, one hopes, expertise. But, as we have seen, youth on the podium has become a Metropolitan fetish of late. There's nothing wrong with that when they deliver. I am of one and a half minds about Bedford's Mozart. His overture is as brisk as we have heard on the broadcasts—fleetness can be a virtue. But there, and rather frequently throughout the afternoon (the grand second-act finale being one instance), the British maestro seems unwilling to allow those gracious moments of relaxation—not of tempo, but of manner—that would permit a Mozart melodic motive or phrase to shine, to flower just enough to vary the motoric pulse of the musical progress. He is fond of the *fortepiano*, sometimes exaggerating the effect, and chordal interjections can be as abrupt as gunshots; in 'Non più andrai,' one would think Cherubino was receiving canon salutes in anticipation of his military career. He does keep things lively. Occasionally his stage colleagues have to hop to keep up with him. A good deal of the humor is lost when the players' comic timing is ruffled by too hurried a pace: all those questioning 'Sua madre's and 'Suo padre's need loving care. At other times—including the fourth-act finale—his tempos are measured and con-

Le Nozze di Figaro
20 February 1976

Countess
Kiri Te Kanawa
Susanna
Benita Valente
Cherubino
Rosalind Elias
Marcellina
Jean Kraft
Almaviva
Thomas Stewart
Figaro
Stafford Dean
Bartolo
Andrew Foldi
Conductor
Steuart Bedford

siderate of the singers. Often he shapes an introductory motive as an individual architectural unit that will be savored in the ensuing piece, thus enhancing the graphic character of both the small and larger units. The double image continues throughout the afternoon. Obviously a man of talent, Bedford evidently pleased management with his reading for they invited him back to conduct the opera again in the 1976–77 season (though the premiere went to Leopold Hager—there may be something in that).

Of the smaller parts, Betsy Norden delivers Barbarina's little aria with unaffected charm, her distinctive tone and naive manner not only suiting its subdued pathos but serving to foreclose recrimination as she twits her master on his romantic dalliance with her. Could she have become the Met's own Graziella Sciutti? Best plays Antonio as straight man, not mining his rustic ways for comic effect as old-timers once did. It works. Schmorr is not afraid to allow Curzio his moment in the comic sun; it works for him as well. Velis is granted the right to perform Basilio's fourth-act aria and, singing with agreeable tone, deserves the reward. Elsewhere, his touch, unction's oil blended with the discreetly malicious, is deftly applied. Velis' ensemble playing manages to make Mozart's singing master almost as substantial a personage as Rossini's more imposing Basilio. 'La Vendetta' is normally a feature of most performances of the opera and Foldi also gains it. The voice is rather too mellifluous for a buffo turn, so the Budapest-born bass does not attempt one. When this Bartolo seeks revenge, he means business. His pleasure in taking vengeance is obvious and, though the timbre is a little dull and doesn't project with utmost clarity, it suffices to guarantee the singer future seasons with the company. Foldi, already in his mid-fifties, had made his initial appearance in the previous season as Alberich, the casting an indication of the American-trained singer's value to the company as a versatile repertory artist. Bartolo's companion in meanness is played by Jean Kraft. Her scratchy vocalism (that is what she sees fit to offer) serves as a clever tool to help characterize the petulant Marcellina. The mezzo has plenty of voice and more than holds her own in the duet with Susanna. Foldi does not have a monopoly on company worth, for everywhere a sure comic touch affirms Kraft's own merit. Her expansive 'Rafaello' introduces the sextet with a pride appropriate to a mother denied. She proves Marcellina's right to motherhood by adopting a more attractive tone and manner to comfort her newly acquired son when he suspects Susanna of straying.

Both master and servant contribute novel portrayals. Stewart has not thus far appeared as a Mozartean on the broadcasts. He has done heavier lifting in the Wagner camp and lately taken on some of the more demanding challenges in the French and Italian repertory. I imagine his demonic Don Giovanni has its points, but his Almaviva ultimately proves dispiriting. On this afternoon, his vocalism is too bluff; the tone—especially in the lower range, where his favored gnarl is operative—is frequently gruff. Moreover, he has an unexpected fondness for lagging just a fraction outside the beat so that his ensemble playing can be obstructive.

Of course, his professional experience tells at every turn. He is nothing if not assured in his portrayal. The conception, however, seems off key. From the moment of his entry into his servant's room, he plays a mean-spirited, bullying master; few aristocratic traits, other than an obvious aura of command and palpable disdain for the rights of others, are in this Count's makeup. When he learns of Cherubino's presence in Susanna's room, he rages like a veteran of the

Velletri battlefield. Perhaps this intelligent baritone is intent on demonstrating why the French revolution was inevitable. Whether to his credit or not, that goal is achieved. But his obstreperous manner ought at least to recede when love is his pursuit. Even in 'Crudel! perchè finora,' conquest comes more by right than vocal charm—Mozart surely intended something more than mere aggression when he wrote the aching curves of 'Mi sento dal contento.' Still, it must be admitted that Stewart's voice has gained in attractiveness by the time he engages in this serious courting; its manly timbre might well be enough to win most maidens—but not our Susanna. Lust is so clearly his preoccupation that the Count comes off as a predator. Of course, he was—though probably not in his *seigneur* mind. The aria is grandly thrust forth, the tone strong and well focused. The delivery would be more at home in a Verdi opera, but Stewart's reading is undeniably well sustained by professional know-how. He even articulates—a pseudo-staccato does the trick—the concluding triplets with greater clarity than most Almavivas manage. Unfortunately, the troublesome high F-sharp is precarious. I do wonder why Rosina would want to hold on to this Count. There may be something to her flirtation with Cherubino after all.

It seems that Stafford Dean had made his reputation almost exclusively as Figaro and Leporello. The thirty-eight-year-old British bass had appeared at Glyndebourne and Sadler's Wells in the mid-sixties and was later welcomed at Covent Garden and the Scottish Opera. Stuttgart followed before he became a regular guest artist with the Munich Opera. His Met debut as Figaro occurred a few weeks before his broadcast debut. His instrument is attractive, albeit quite different from the bass voice normally heard on the international circuit. It is essentially a *basso cantante*—or to put it more accurately, a *basse chantante*, for the timbre and legato remind me of nothing so much as early-twentieth-century French basses like Marcel Journet or Pol Plançon. A hint of the *voix sombre* lingers in Dean's dark tones and luxuriant legato. His Figaro is a paradox. In the recitatives, he is uncommonly deft, introducing many novel touches that fill out the character nicely. (He actually sounds as though he is measuring that room.) Thus, I had expected the arias to be miracles of liveliness, replete with similarly vibrant interpretive strokes. Both 'Se vuol ballare' and, to a lesser extent, 'Non più andrai' are wrapped in a dark velvety legato—quite an intriguing vocal color—and executed with a musicianly drawing of phrase that is, to my mind, ill suited to the situation and to Figaro's mercurial character. Still, Dean's somber timbre and menacing glower in the 'ballare' aria serve notice that the servant will challenge his master. Further to his credit, the high Fs are taken full voice with no loss of that basic timbre, something few basses manage with comparable surety. In the military aria, the suave viola-like tincture continues to please but one wishes he would enliven its phrases with rhythmic vitality.

Often in the ensuing acts, a phrase here, a line there shows the cultivated artist to great advantage. He does possess the weight of voice to sustain Figaro's purpose. Dean's fourth-act solo holds some fascinating touches. In the introductory recitative, he favors a beguiling mezza voce to sound his hurt and regret; in the aria, he intones 'il resto nol dico' with sinister quietude, the repetitions effectively contrasting with the head voice employed in the higher alternating phrase. The vocal line climbs relentlessly upward at 'non sento pietà' and Dean's crowning 'no, no, no, no' are the cries of a wounded animal. The singer best shows his worth as

Figaro invokes Venus and Vulcan in the garden farce: 'Tutto è tranquillo e placido' is as suavely conducted as those early French practitioners (cited above) could have provided. Ultimately, the American public probably was too accustomed to Figaros who offered high-powered vocalism and magnetic stage presences (Pinza and Siepi are the models) to be willing to accept Dean's novel and even aristocratic domestic.

Elias gives what may be her finest broadcast performance. The voice, almost abnormally trim on most occasions, is in exceptional condition on this afternoon, equalized throughout the range, the conduct of tone completely assured, the timbre as finely honed as possible without tipping into harshness. Her line is firmly drawn. These attributes turn 'Voi, che sapete' into one of the more delightful broadcast readings of its measured perfection. Bedford prefers a no-nonsense tempo, so the mezzo is not permitted to savor the aria's subtle curves, but her straightforward delivery complements the boy's youthful assurance. 'Non so più cosa son' is a horse of a different color and the mezzo rides it to victory as well. Its churning phrases are so securely in the Elias voice that she is able to suggest the youth's bewilderment at his rampant sexuality without losing an iota of vocal poise. Elias is now in her twenty-third season with the company and her vocal health is such that it comes as no surprise to find her still active (though in character parts) after crossing over the millennium.

Valente is a lovely Susanna. Her voice, not overlarge, is so distinguished by its lemony sweet timbre on the staff and exquisite shine on high that she gives the servant status beyond her station. As the manipulator of all about her, Susanna deserves that elevation. The soprano is even-handed, both in her musicality and her plotting, never overemphasizing her moves, but every note, every word is in its proper place and given its tonal reward. As is evident in the opening duets with Figaro, she controls him by pretty ways—aural and interpretive—rather than by command. She can dress Cherubino without losing either her vocal or maidenly poise, and she saves her mistress from embarrassment over the locked key and its aftermath with the lightest mockery. Untouched by excessive coyness, the supple phrases that she wafts in 'Crudel! perche finora' are bound to entrap the Count in their modest coils (though no encouragement would be needed with this rake). Her seductive conduct of line, ingenuous in its simplicity and abetted by her piquant timbre, turns the garden aria into a promise that Figaro could never refuse. In her unhurried caress of the concluding measures, she makes clear her invitation to her beloved, the 'incoronar' run and concluding garland both exquisitely traced. Employment of appoggiaturas has increased a notch or two—though it is far from uniform—as several artists, Dean and Valente among them, favor them. They favor us in turn by their recognition of eighteenth-century practice.

Te Kanawa captures the honors of the afternoon. If her broadcast Desdemona indicated her quality, her Contessa not only confirms it, but grants her immediate status in that most circumscribed of theatrical categories: star. Though the term is much abused, it sits comfortably on the New Zealander's shoulders. From first note to last, her vocalism is celestial on this afternoon. Few singers at their entry can perform 'Porgi amor' with comparable tonal firmness or the complete technical control that our diva displays. The tone is full, creamy, luscious—what you will—and her control of breath a marvel. The ascent to the high A-flat is as smooth and unruffled as though she were stroking a baby's cheek. Her composure is remarkable. (In the later stages of her career, that too often turned into a demerit, but it becomes her Countess.) The core of warm sound, unhindered by the slightest hint of harshness, is not confined to the set pieces—it turns even her recitatives into tonal bouquets. And she is lively in her play with her sister sopranos in their second-act folderol.

When heard against Valente's slighter instrument, one realizes the healthy size of Te Kanawa's lyric soprano. Thus, triumph in the challenging phrases of 'Dove sono' is assured. They flow from her obliging throat in full bloom. The introductory accompanied recitative is salted with a welcome bit of fire. One expects a more reflective tone in the opening phrases of the aria—the volume level is rather too high—but she saves that mood for the reprise, which she sings in a cool *pianissimo*. It is the totality of her remarkably mature delivery that most impresses. She is not much given to individual interpretive gestures. Like that of Meredith's lark, her song is "seraphically free of taint of personality," the phrase employed by me both as salute and rebuke. But Mozart thrives on a gracious, fluent conduct of line and Te Kanawa is complete mistress of it. Other sopranos have allowed a suggestive aura of tristesse to permeate their reading, subtly intensifying the wife's unhappiness; our soprano is content to let her *pianissimo* turn the reprise into a reverie over past happiness. A major ovation is her reward. The Letter Duet is as satisfying as the arias. The contrast between the voices of mistress and maid is apt, Te Kanawa's so refulgent, Valente's so sweetly accommodating. And there the New Zealand soprano demonstrates her musicality in the light pressure she applies to the dissonant notes, appoggiaturas that Mozart wrote into the vocal line. Te Kanawa's acknowledgement of them enhances expression. Those with long memories recognize that in Te Kanawa we have a Contessa who, though different in many respects, may be ranked with luminaries like Steber and Della Casa.

The operatic time machine allows us to turn back to happier days for the Almavivas, when the Count courted Rosina and that young lady had as yet no claim upon his name. In the 31 January 1976 broadcast of *Il Barbiere di Siviglia*, Von Stade plays with such aristocratic charm that their marriage seems inevitable. Ryland Davies is the happy recipient of her love, while Richard Stilwell plays the factotum who foils the devious practices of Corena (Bartolo) and Morris (Basilio). John Nelson—yet another of the youth contingent—is the man in the pit.

To move from the grandeur of *Les Troyens* and the earthy drama of *Jenůfa* (Nelson's previous Met charges) to the effervescent comedy of *Barbiere* requires more than a quick-change artist on the podium. The comic touch is not available to every aspirant. It does not come readily upon call, even for conductors as gifted as our American maestro. He lays such a serious hand upon Rossini's score that the opera's bubble of frivolity is in danger of being pricked before we reach the second-act finale. Actually, to better appreciate his quality, the several acts of the opera (three at the Met) might be better heard in reverse order. At the opera's end, the conductor's method—certainly not his madness, there is too little of that—becomes clear and his honor is reclaimed. Unfortunately, live performances are not subject to reverse replays. Nelson knows what the buffa genre, especially when Rossini is involved, requires: "This kind of music can't be conducted . . . it must be released," he astutely observed.[1] But conduct is precisely what he does. Overconducts, I would say. He has obviously studied the score assiduously and is intent on savoring every succulent morsel of its rich orchestral detail, desirous of lay-

Il Barbiere di Siviglia
31 January 1976

Rosina
Frederica von Stade
Almaviva
Ryland Davies
Figaro
Richard Stilwell
Basilio
James Morris
Bartolo
Fernando Corena
Conductor
John Nelson

ing out its magisterial construct with the devotion of a newly converted disciple. But evidently it takes time for acolytes to acquire the light touch of their elders. Nelson is never heavy handed in his pursuit, but the elusive sparkle that is the lifeblood of the buffa genre is certainly not pervasive. On the other hand, though Nelson may hold the reins tightly, he doesn't settle for mere lockstep movement. The "release" that he desires may not be his to provide on this afternoon, but he does give us something valuable in its place. At first, I thought it was uncertainty, a bit of tentativeness on the conductor's part, that inhibited the opera's progress; but (and here is where reverse playback enters in) it then became apparent that Nelson intends to treat each and every one of Rossini's graphic musical gestures with respect. His eye and ear are ever concerned with making clear the grand scope of the opera's design. That is a novel approach to apply to a comedy. His treatment of the second-act finale in particular demonstrates his preoccupation with the opera's overall construct. There each section is well considered as to its place and function in the totality of the composer's architectural plan. The individual numbers of the third act reinforce his emphasis upon structural integrity. The result is pleasing (and revealing) in its own right. Seldom has so much of the music of *Barbiere* been made to sound in such proud beauty as Nelson offers in this, his first venture with operatic comedy. I should love to hear his reading of the opera a few years down the road when time may have relaxed his hold but not obscured his obvious reverence for the score.

The stage is peopled with intelligent performers, but fortunately they don't let their smarts get in the way of giving a performance. Corena, of course, can't ever do anything else—but give a performance, that is. His Bartolo, much heard on the airways, is presented here as in unspoiled infancy; after all these years, the conception and the song are free of distortion, as they have not always been in the past. But comedy lives within the very sound of his sonority, and he is such an old hand at the grasping doctor's machinations that he needs do little to put a smile on our faces. At his entrance—and he hardly sings a note there—the audience is thrown into lengthy stitches of laughter. He is in good voice and skillfully wends his way through the notorious intricacies of his aria, doing so with an assurance and big-time tonal burl that reaffirms his status as the leading buffo bass of his era. He and Goodloe (a capital Fiorello) are the only hangovers from earlier broadcasts. Munzer contributes to the high standard of vocalism with her first-class rendering of Berta's aria. But isn't the servant supposed to add to the comedy quotient? The able mezzo neglects that part of her job. Morris, though new to Basilio's antics, well serves both the vocal and comic demands of his role. The malicious humor of 'La calunnia' (sung in C) is well projected, though the voice is a little weak at the bottom; the top rolls out in splendor (as it will later on, when the music master says goodnight in the 'Buona sera' ensemble of the last act). A little assist from the podium in sending rumor more fleetly along its devious path might have encouraged the singer to shuck off his slightly studied air.

Welsh tenor Ryland Davies is heard in his broadcast debut. A decade on the British stages, with forays at Berlin, Munich, and Salzburg, had allowed his cultivated art to mature. San Francisco and Chicago were also favored haunts. During these decades, the role of Almaviva was difficult to cast for maximum quality. Two choices, then and now, are open to management. The first would be a tenor whose appeal resides almost entirely in his timbre, the vocal velvet compensating (but only partially) for ineptitude in Rossini's ever-present roulades. The second is a singer adept in fioriture and, most often, musical to his fingertips, but with tone so white (or so blatantly open) that it curdles even as it sounds, surely a dear price to pay for a few clean notes of coloratura. But then, to hear the composer's traceries mauled beyond recognition is equally hard to take. Davies' voice is not made of velvet, but neither does its timbre cause hackles to rise. Indeed, as the opera progresses, a slight baritonal heft when playing the drunken soldier and attractive head tones when Almaviva poses as the loving music master place him among the better masquerading suitors. He is adept at fioriture, seldom needing an aspirant to spur them on. And not only are the very tips of his fingers musical but—more to our purpose—so is his every utterance. He has all the ingratiating nuances and technical devices of the *tenore di grazia* down pat and displays them to good advantage in his serenade and on every warranted occasion thereafter. Clearly, he is possessed of that intelligence I mentioned above. And he, too, gives a performance, as detailed and sure-footed as one could wish. Does one miss the velvet? Most assuredly.

At this period of her lengthy career, Von Stade was beginning to come into her own. Her period of apprenticeship in minor roles on the Met stage was several years behind her and a fast expanding international career was in process. Paris, Glyndebourne, Covent Garden, and Salzburg had already become acquainted with her refined artistry. On the broadcast, her bewitching vocalism and endearing person demonstrate why public and press were beginning to bandy about the seldom bestowed accolade "beloved"—perhaps a more treasured sobriquet than the more frequent "great" or too readily applied "legendary." Her Rosina is not the usual minx of everyday operadom. The plaint in the mezzo's timbre makes the maiden less a footloose partner in the amorous escapades and more of a believable progenitor of the Contessa that Mozart (with Beaumarchais' help) made of her. The singer's phrasing suggests that Rosina is at heart a more sensitive creature than the years have taught us to expect. We hear a breath of Von Stade's sensibility in her very first utterance as she repeats Almaviva's phrase—it wafts into the ether with a wistful charm. 'Una voce poco fa' does not overly disturb that posture—there is nothing deceptive in her claim to be 'docile,' nor spiteful when she claims to turn into a 'vipera' when crossed. Clearly, her bravura attitude is mostly façade. But she is intent on her goal and thus not false to Rossini's intent. This Rosina knows how to get her way, but will earn it by a quiet persistence and a belief in love's felicity.

Von Stade's coloratura, though not the most astonishing in brilliance or clarity, is nevertheless assured (a sparkling trill is among her assets) and attractive in tone. In some ways, its very equitability is a relief from the aggressive brilliance of some mezzo interpreters of the role. The fioriture flow smoothly and trippingly in the duet with Figaro. Occasionally, they assume an appropriately grander cast, as when she performs 'Contro un cor' in the lesson scene. Her rendition of Rossini's original aria represents the high point of her vocal performance. Its far-ranging phrases are etched with aristocratic elegance, touched here and there with an adorable delicacy—both the mezzo's musicality and her technical prowess are affirmed. A brief episode denied most Met Rosinas occurs when Bartolo blackens Lindoro's character toward the end of the final act; Von Stade's sorrowful response, an exquisite moment of pathos, is the more affecting as heard within

Nelson's conception of the opera. The mezzo leaves off sorrow when she learns that Lindoro and Almaviva are one and the same; in its place, her joyous, loving song is infectious in its forthright vocalism and expression. Those attributes apply as well to Stilwell and, in some degree to Davies (his voice most attractive in this episode and his musical discretion again apparent). The three artists run up and down and around and over the coloratura traps of Rossini's excessive exuberance with the nonchalance of technical wizards.

Stilwell came to the Metropolitan earlier in the season as Guglielmo and here makes his broadcast debut. Before the public a scant six years, he had already been acclaimed (most prominently as Pelléas) in Europe as well as America. A 1970 debut at the New York City Opera had led to engagements in Santa Fe, Glyndebourne, Washington, DC (Ulisse in the American premiere of Monteverdi's opera), Hamburg (Billy Budd), and Chicago (Orfeo). When not involved in this specialized repertory, he had found time to create roles in several American operas. Figaro is a role more in the mainstream than those listed. His fitness for the assignment is never in doubt. Unless one prefers the booming voice of a Ruffo-type baritone in the role (which I confess I do not), Stilwell's perfectly placed instrument, virile in timbre and agile in execution, is just the thing for the barber's glittering music and mercurial personality. The factotum is an in-charge kind of guy and the American baritone's every word and tone affirm that status. The entrance aria, so often bruised in execution and overinterpreted, receives as lively a reading as yet heard on the broadcasts. Every note, every bit of patter, every tone is distinctly in place, top tones are strong and attacked spank on—in short, his is the most elegant of renderings, but with exuberance rampant. The singer's musicianship and intelligence are patently apparent, but not for a moment do they inhibit character portrayal or dim the performer's bright light. In the duet with Almaviva, Stilwell's deft interpretive touches lend it the vitality that the conductor has partially subdued; the rhythmic dash of his repeated 'Eccolo's under Almaviva's florid line is just one of his inventive nuances here and elsewhere throughout the afternoon. An admirable example of his technical expertise occurs in that duet at 'Il tutor si fiderà'; there he executes a leap from a low tone to a top note, taking it full voice and then executing a well-controlled diminuendo before descending with subtle gradations of tone in the ensuing phrase. Taken *in toto*, the musicality of the exercise pleases exceedingly. 'Dunque io son' shows off the clarity and tonal fire of his fioriture—he sings all the roulades in full voice. And once again he offers a delightful rhythmic subtlety with his merrily bouncing 'Donne, donne's, the reiterations a flickering salute to woman's eternal mystery. His vibrant 'Guarda Don Bartolo' lends a firm foundation to the fleet embroidery of Von Stade and Davies in the composer's monumental *concertato*, 'Fredda ed immobile.' A similar professional shine animates the three singers' final trio. Whenever Stilwell is on stage, he works a wonder: the slightly pedantic tinge that Nelson, quite unconsciously no doubt, has allowed to infect the performance is dissipated by the sheer vitality of the baritone's tone and the exuberance of his playing. America has produced a number of excellent baritones of Stilwell's type over the last half century, but none merited greater Metropolitan service than this young artist. Repertory was ever a problem for singers of his (and Von Stade's) kind in large houses like the Met. While he would return with considerable frequency to the company, Stilwell would make the bulk of his career in other venues.

After our sojourn with singers for whom the accolade of artist was more appropriate than star, we return to operas where the presence of a Caballé, a Sutherland, or a Pavarotti was essential if they were to reach the Metropolitan boards. Throw in Verrett and Milnes and the airwaves are bound to crackle with front-and-center vocalism. They do in broadcasts of a pair of Bellini operas. On 28 February 1976 *Norma*, the most exclusive—in terms of presence in the everyday repertory—of anointed Italian masterworks, returns for the delectation of the radio public. Actually, the decade of the seventies was a good one for the difficult-to-cast opera. The title role was the stumbling block, but as long as Sutherland (two broadcasts in 1970) and Caballé (heard in 1973 as well as in the current offering) were on hand and willing, *Norma* could flourish. Verrett (Adalgisa) joins the soprano in the melodious duets, with Alexander and Michalski (Oreveso) completing the quartet. A new podium occupant, Gianfranco Masini, is the chosen guide.

The Italian maestro, his beginnings including the usual Italian provinces, Prague and Budapest, had been closely associated with Caballé during several seasons at the Teatro del Liceo in Barcelona. Not only had they collaborated on *Adriana Lecouvreur* in London and *Elisabetta, Regina d'Inghilterra* in Aix-en-Provence, they had also recorded the two operas. The statistics suggest that the Met might again be indulging in prima donna whims where the diva drags along a favorite conductor who will accommodate her interpretive ways without fuss. The suspicion proves to be an unworthy one, for Masini gives one of the finest readings of the opera to be heard at the Met in decades. His sense of Bellinian style is near-infallible. His musicianly molding of phrases, pacing of set pieces, and superb plotting of the architectural layout of this grandly conceived masterwork are immensely gratifying. Every phrase is shaped with sensitivity. True to his Italian heritage, he is not ashamed to allow a tune to roll comfortably along; he savors its rhythmic swing and, moreover, avoids any hint of vulgarity in the process. To pummel a supporting chord or orchestral motive with a brutal *fortissimo* where a considerate *forte* will serve the purpose seems anathema to him. Even the composer's martial music is more amiable when marshaled by Masini's accommodating hand. As with Levine, one of his most agreeable talents is the ability to propel an accompanying motive or an "oom-pah-pah" with a well-judged pulse, whether vibrant or relaxed, and sustain it over long passages, thereby providing a singer with the fluid support that in turn allows her (I refer to Caballé or Verrett) to phrase with expressive flexibility. The chorus, in general singing with becoming tone or (as in the 'Guerra! Guerra!' ensemble) appropriate vitality, is not quite as well attuned to his musical subtleties as the orchestra—the difference probably a matter of inadequate rehearsal time. Or perhaps it is a misconnect between the Met's exemplary chorus master Stivender and Masini. (A false entry by a wind instrument a few measures into the overture suggests time limitations as the more likely culprit.) One questionable episode—and it is an important one—is his treatment of the composer's grand buildup to the cymbal crashes in the fourth-act finale; his way (a rather too aggressive accelerando, followed by a broad ritard, before giving way to a magisterial rounding of the climax), while sounding the essence of these sublime moments, seems a bit too calculated, so that the searing emotion of the magnificent phrases is slightly dampened. Everywhere else, his sensitive conception and masterly execution command only admiration. Masini returned to conduct *Butterfly* and *Rigoletto* (mostly on tour) during the 1977–78 season. Prob-

Norma
28 February 1976

Norma
Montserrat Caballé
Adalgisa
Shirley Verrett
Pollione
John Alexander
Oreveso
Raymond Michalski
Conductor
Gianfranco Masini

ably a bit more diva patronage would have been required to enable us to have the further benefit of his skills.

The opera belongs to the ladies. Still, Michalski makes a valuable contribution to the afternoon's pleasure. Oroveso is dignified in act one and angry in the final act, with nothing in between. Reams of rolling bass tone will do the trick in both cases. The New Jersey bass can't quite supply that, but his tone is so perfectly collected, his timbre so warmly attractive, and his interpretive gestures so knowing that his limited opportunities rank among the performance pluses. Not so much can be said for our Pollione. Of course, when one expects Corelli and gets Alexander in his place, a broadcast devotee may experience the kind of paroxysm that shortens listening life. The tenor's effort is honest, his technique solid, his tone stout—if slightly overfed—and his musicianship sound. But his Pollione is a dull fellow. For the drama to obtain believability in its triangular relationships, it requires a Pollione who sounds like a Roman general, one preferably gifted with an Italianate timbre of steely tinge. That will take him safely through the opening acts. If he can summon a bit of pathos for the final scene, so much the better, but if he lacks both attributes and hews safely to a middle ground—as Alexander does—not much will come of it. The Mississippian sounds a fine high C—razor-sharp in attack and tone—and never drops his guard in his contests with his twin loves. Pollione, though the pivot of the plot, is, in some musical respects, a cipher, and Alexander hasn't the means to elevate him beyond that status. The fault is not entirely his, for the role lies low; the original Pollione, Domenico Donzelli, owned a dark voice, heavily weighted in the lower octave, whereas Alexander thrives as he ascends. After his first-act *scena*, the audience gives him a good hand in appreciation of his secure vocalism and brave attempt at impersonating an army man.

Caballé's Norma has the virtues familiar from her 1973 broadcast of the role. A few distinctions between then and now may be made, namely that her very top tones are a little harsher in timbre on this occasion and that her characterization is marginally more dramatic today than in the earlier reading. These are distinctions without the proverbial difference, however. (Her Norma and Callas' priestess are, as to vocal qualities and dramatic projection, so antithetical as to make comparisons unprofitable.) Caballé remains a first-class interpreter of this challenging soprano assignment. Her dramatic recitatives are most frequently declaimed with fullness of tone and authoritative manner. Rarely does she abuse her delectable *pianissimo* by imposing it where a grander tone would better suit the fervor of passion or the nobility of thought. Her 'Casta diva' is perhaps slighter in weight of tone than is desirable if we are to fully savor the aria's rhapsodic melodic line, but her largely soughed reading is arresting in its own way—and this time the syncopations that launch Norma's burgeoning coloratura descents are all in place. When she confronts Pollione with his treachery in the second-act trio, she lashes out with commendable fury, her acidulous attack on the high Cs veritable cries of pain. I do like the rhythmic vitality that Caballé applies to the opening phrases of 'Oh, di qual sei tu vittima.' The contrast between the breadth of her recitatives as Norma contemplates killing her children and the tonal balm that she applies to 'Teneri, teneri figli' when she relents is highly effective; Caballé's conduct of the bending line of the *arioso* is scrupulous. Some might find these block ministrations too much on the surface, but pure song and vocal mastery are compelling advocates for Caballé's practice. She dominates the final act as a Norma should, strong and authoritative in her fury; even more notably, she puts her technical command to good purpose, proffering an exquisite *messa di voce* or floating an extended cadenza (and doing so with seemingly endless breath). Though begun too quietly, 'Qual cor tradisti' profits from her command of varied timbral colors, contrasting dynamics, and subtly applied expressive devices. Pathos (her reliance on the quieter dynamics is probably excessive) rather than grandeur is the interpretive mood that she cultivates in the final pages of the opera.

Verrett is new to the role of Adalgisa, having sung it for the first time (in a staged performance) only a week before the broadcast. By this point in her career, the transition to soprano that she was intent on making has been fully achieved. She will prove it by singing her first Normas later in the season when on tour with the company. To tackle both soprano roles in Bellini's opera within the space of two months would seem foolhardy for most singers, but the American soprano welcomes a challenge. (Recall her desire to sing both Cassandre and Didon at the Met premiere of *Les Troyens*.) Today we are accustomed to mezzo-soprano interpreters of Adalgisa, but Bellini wrote it for Giulia Grisi, a high soprano who created Elvira in *I Puritani* (the role that Sutherland sings in this season's revival of the opera). Grisi was also a famous Norma, so Verrett's double duty, from the historical standpoint, is not out of line, though the latter's early career was founded along very different lines from that of her illustrious predecessor. And there is the rub. Ultimately, the results of the vocal makeover were not entirely salutary either for her career or her audience. Had he been in her camp, old fight trainer Gus D'Amato might have cautioned her (and other ambitious mezzos) with the plain words with which he had advised many a young fighter who wanted to move up to a heavier weight category: "People born round don't die square."[2] The quality of Verrett's Norma will have to wait for another day's consideration, but her Adalgisa is through and through a lovely creation, expertly vocalized and beautifully characterized.

In her extended entry scene, Verrett's tone floats with gratifying serenity. No trace of mezzo weight burdens it, while happily the voice continues to wear its familiar soft timbral glow. The singer's modest manner and dulcet tones are entirely in keeping with the priestess' youth. As remarked before in these pages, Verrett's artistry has the ability to immediately provoke not just one's interest, but a sympathetic response. She does so again in her very first phrases; thralldom continues throughout the afternoon. The middle-upper voice purls deliciously in the duet with Pollione. As Adalgisa attempts to repulse the proconsul's lovemaking, Verrett takes advantage of the opportunity to play at a higher dramatic pitch. Her command of this emphatic singing mode is vivid and complete, an effective foil for her poised vocalism during the rest of the opera. The top notes are either easily encompassed or strongly attacked with assurance (they include a stunning leap to a D-flat *in alt*); at the other end of the vocal spectrum, no residue of the register break with which most mezzos must contend troubles her song. Nor is there any sign of the slight rasp that has occasionally infected her low voice on previous broadcasts. As of this performance, the transformation has worked no harm.

The duets of the second and third acts are test pieces for both sopranos. Caballé and Verrett prove their worth time and again as, at ease with Bellini bel canto, they spin phrases of his extended melody or fly fleetly through his intricate roulades. In their joint efforts, Verrett relies for the most part on a gracious interpretive stance, guiding her dulcet tone as complement to Caballé's more brightly timbred voice. Their coloratura passages, whether solo or in tandem, are handily negotiated, indeed, well mastered (though both sopranos can slither down a scale where cleaner articulation would be welcome). Still, it is their cantilena that most satisfies. Both singers and their conductor relish the rhythmic swing of the second-act duet when the music surges like the slow lapping of waves—the effect is hypnotic, causing one to become immersed in the quality of movement and the eloquence of their song. Verrett swathes the opening of 'Mira, o Norma' in plaintive pastel tones before her sister soprano takes up the melody with the utmost delicacy. Of course, they should exuberantly flaunt the jaunty coloratura that Bellini doled out in the duet's cabaletta, and for the most part they do. Verrett does sound oddly reserved at this moment—a bit more gusty tone on her part would make a more exciting curtain. (The composer's second act is split into two at the Met.) Throughout the afternoon, conductor Masini picks up any lapsed threads, binding up Bellini's masterwork with a rare and loving understanding.

I Puritani
13 March 1976

Elvira
Joan Sutherland
Enrichetta
Cynthia Munzer
Arturo
Luciano Pavarotti
Riccardo
Sherrill Milnes
Giorgio
James Morris
Conductor
Richard Bonynge

The composer's final opera, *I Puritani*, had not been heard at the Metropolitan for more than half a century. A new production for Sutherland and Pavarotti was unveiled only a few days before the *Norma* broadcast and brought to the airwaves two weeks later on 13 March 1976. Joining them are Munzer (Enrichetta), Milnes (Riccardo), Morris (Giorgio Walton), and, in lesser roles, Jon Garrison as Bruno Robertson and Philip Booth as Gualtiero Walton. Bonynge is again on hand to husband his wife's first Metropolitan venture as the unfortunate Elvira.

The opera's Metropolitan history was surprisingly brief. It had figured in only two seasons and then for a total of seven performances, only four of them at the major house. Sembrich had briefly laid claim to Elvira during the Met's first season, abetted by Roberto Stagno and Giuseppe Kaschmann. In the seasons 1918–1920, conductor Roberto Moranzoni had guided Maria Barrientos, Hipolito Lazaro, Giuseppe de Luca, and José Mardones through their paces without gaining for Bellini's work the favor that it deserved. Nor would the present revival fifty-six years after its last performance entirely remedy that situation, though the merits of the present production were beyond cavil. Periodic revivals (1983, 1986, 1991) at least would keep the work alive in public memory.

In the 1976 broadcast, Bonynge, a recognized authority on early-nineteenth-century bel canto style, demonstrates that he has earned the right to that accolade. More pertinent to our purpose, the Australian has become a conductor who can not only hold a performance together but also sustain dramatic impetus while preserving the opera's musical continuity and formal design. He gets things off to a good start by artfully juxtaposing the disparate blocks of the opening scene: the drum rolls, the soldier choruses, the Puritan's quiet hymn topped by Elvira's flowing line—all fall neatly into place. When he has only an accompaniment figure to work with, he knows how to keep it—and thus the singer's song—buoyant. Ready with the whip hand as needed, he never allows the ensembles to fall into routine. Most important, he savors the Bellinian pathos without allowing it to turn maudlin. His way with Elvira's mad scene is notable for the lyrical continuity of the orchestral fabric; the composer's elegiac melodic beauties are honored to the full. Bonynge has a superb cast to complement his efforts, but still a large portion of the performance's quality originates in the pit.

Joan Sutherland as Elvira and Luciano Pavarotti as Arturo in *I Puritani*. Photography by James Heffernan. Courtesy Metropolitan Opera Archives.

At the curtain's rise, Garrison's firm tenor ably fulfills his task of leading the Puritans in prayer. Familial relationships seem a bit out of line since Elvira's father (Gualtiero) allows his brother Giorgio to claim his daughter's attention throughout most of the opera. As the father, Philip Booth makes the transfer of affections seem logical, his gruff bass solid but remote from the bel canto aura that Morris' Giorgio creates. Indeed, both Morris and Milnes perform with considerable sensitivity in their major foray into bel canto land. In Riccardo's lengthy first-act scene, the baritone sings 'Ah, per sempre io ti perdei' with stylistic restraint and tonal moderation. The richness of his timbre is apparent—he cannot hide that—but neatly concentrated so as to better conduct Bellini's fluid melodic line in this sympathetic expression of his love for Elvira. He is adept at handling the small moments of fioriture and the cadenza is well executed. (In his *Opera News* interview, Bonynge noted that most male singers of today had not "taken the trouble" to learn how to do ornamentation, making an exception, however, in the baritone's case: "With a singer like Sherrill Milnes, of course, I think perhaps one can do more.")[3] On this afternoon, Milnes does more. His only indulgence—and who can blame him, for it is probably period-wise—is a superbly negotiated high note at the aria's close. Thereafter, Riccardo's duties are second-line, but Milnes discharges them more than ably. The dispute with Arturo over Queen Enrichetta and, in the second act, Riccardo's condemnation of the cavalier allow him to call into play his more familiar stalwart tone and manly interpretive stance. Even there, he remains reasonably within the framework of the opera's style, and during Elvira's mad scene he conducts his long-breathed supportive phrases with admirable restraint and flexible line. The same may be said of Morris in those moments.

The young American bass performs Giorgio in what must be deemed, in career terms, a breakthrough portrayal. Vocal suavity is the keynote of his success. His portion of the duet with Elvira is notable for its subtlety (most apparent in finely tuned gradations of tone and volume) and his manner is as tenderhearted as Sutherland's. Giorgio's aria ('Cinta di fiori') is a difficult piece to bring off, the repetitious leaps of a sixth often cumbersome as negotiated by many bassos. Morris etches them with delicate portamentos and touches them with liquid tone to good effect; he fills the entire aria with mellow vocalism, frequently calling to his aid an assured mezza voce. The voice is at its best in the upper range—one low note is extremely modest, but no matter. Interpretively, his sympathetic posture is disturbed only by a moment or two of excess emotion. While admirable in most respects, the two men's performance of the grand duet that concludes the second act does not quite measure up to the demands of the situation. Here Morris' vocal youth shows, at least in the initial moments—one wants a more commanding manner and grander tone—and even Milnes doesn't supply as much vocal protein as expected. Before launching 'Suoni la tromba,' however, Morris gets off a splendidly majestic phrase, and he finds the right rhythmic impulse for the tune itself. Bonynge's broader pace and square rhythms in their unison reprise come to the rescue, providing the spine that satisfies the celebrated duet's call-to-arms virility. Milnes' high A-flat helps too, rousing the audience to vociferous response.

I must confess that I do not find this to be one of Miss Sutherland's finest afternoons, at least as her singing comes over the airwaves. Of course, she is magnificent in her coloratura endeavors and gives an affecting performance of the on-again-off-again heroine. Curiously, the voice sounds slightly muffled, rather too delicate, in portions of the first act. It may be due in part to her stage place-ment. (I am not, of course, referring to Elvira's initial offstage positioning, which is dictated by the libretto.) Her duet with uncle Giorgio is quite fine, but 'Son vergin vezzosa,' one of opera's most dazzling set pieces, does not quite make the expected effect. Her fioriture trip out of her throat as expeditiously as usual—no fault-finding there—and some subtle nuances and elegant touches of phrase com-mand regard, but somehow the buoyancy of Bellini's *polacca* is muted. Applause is brief and surprisingly muted as well. It would be heretical to suggest that Elvira just may not suit the diva as well as some of her other heroines, particularly since hers is a celebrated creation and opening night reviews were glowing. To consider it from a different angle, the role may suit her style and temperament overly well, at least in the mad scene. When her mournful tone in the mid-voice and slightly droopy phrasing are combined with the exquisite pathos of 'Qui la voce,' dolor receives more than its due. And she does pick at the melody rather than allowing it to flower in all its serene remembrance of Arturo. One wants to turn plebeian and shout out—however irreverently—just sing it! She appears to have had a relapse in terms of clarity of diction. It isn't merely a case of wanting to hear the words—clean articulation of text adds its own musical and rhythmic contribution to the phrase line.

Taken in its totality, her performance is loaded with vocal felicities, chief among them the fabulous Sutherland trill—a few of them sound even more full toned than usual. Top notes are to order throughout the afternoon. And in the cabaletta of the mad scene, her tone acquires its full bloom, the several down-ward scales are brushed exquisitely with liquid tone, the ornamented repeat is astounding in its flashing tracery. She caps it all with a crystalline E-flat *in alt*. Now the audience response is worthy of her splendid effort. In the final act, her delicate vocalism and pinpoint coloratura charm. Before the final curtain, prima donna prerogatives are honored as the diva propels a burst of coloratura fireworks over the assembled company's sustained support. Healthy tone and a blithe spirit make the episode one of the most enjoyable moments of the afternoon. In the house, heads must have been nodding to one another, as if to say, "This is what we came for." One of the few certitudes in the uncertain world of operadom is the knowledge that Sutherland always delivers. We come to her performances with such high expectations. Was I a bit disappointed on this afternoon? Yes. Does she remain the most spectacular vocalist in her repertory, one of the wonders of the operatic world? Without a doubt. (During her era, the wonder number may have been more than seven.) Her incomparable mastery of bel canto technical resources and her elegance in their execution have a hallowed place in operatic history.

It need not lessen the diva's accomplishment to note that Pavarotti's perfor-mance on this occasion is even more striking. Though the contest is close, it is he who carries off the honors of what has been an afternoon of remarkable vocalism. How reassuring it is to hear him perform with complete command of his instru-ment and wholehearted commitment. Coming upon him in his prime makes re-grets about late-career behavior recede into nothingness. Any tenor who tackles Arturo has to contend with the notorious stratospheric notes (D and F) that the composer confidently wrote into the part for Rubini. Of course, they were not sung from the chest in his time, but there they are, and to offer them in a sickly falsetto when all around them is refulgent tone simply won't do today. Our tenor wisely declines to attempt the high F and performs 'A te, o cara' down a half-tone, so that the high D is correspondingly lowered. He succeeds in conquering the D-flat in confident fashion and lofts another excellent pair of them later in the opera. Remember that his spurt of fame had come when he acquired the title "tenor of the high Cs," after striking nine of them in *La Fille du Régiment*. In my mathematical book, three or four high D-flats more than equal nine high Cs. With that chore out of the way, we can move on to more important matters.

The Pavarotti voice is a marvel on this afternoon. His tone is so luxuriant, so fruity in its overtones, so brilliant in plangency. At the first sounding of 'A te, o cara,' the sheer splendor of the voice startles, even after all these years of almost too great familiarity with his instrument. Complementing the voice's vibrancy is the tenor's dramatic involvement. His recitatives are alive and, on occasion, downright emphatic; an early example occurs when Arturo hears about the prisoner queen, and the fiery manner continues in his exchanges with Enrichetta. (As the unhappy queen, mezzo Munzer discharges her brief duties with commendable fervor.) The several little flights of fioriture that fall to Arturo are handled with clarity and stylistic aplomb (Bonynge has done well in tutoring all his soloists). Offstage for the entire second act, the tenor claims center stage during the final act. There his full-throated singing and ardent manner justify the primacy Bellini granted Arturo. His presentation is necessarily quite removed in its vocal character and dramatic puissance from the elegant vocalism and manner with which Rubini and Mario—according to report—swathed Arturo's music and person in the nineteenth century. The informative Chorley, writing of an 1844 *Puritani* performance that starred the husband and wife team of Giulia Grisi and Giovanni Mario, thought that there was "too much of the *enfant gâté* in his singing."[4] Though Mario's voice was deemed "delicious" (that adjective tells us a lot), the tenor "dispatched" the third act's demanding tasks with "indifference." Certainly, there is nothing of the "spoiled child" in Pavarotti's playing of the act. He introduces more vocal colors than we suspected the voice owned in the opening dramatic recitatives; their varied emotional content is fully explored. Soon he takes up the melody of "their" song (Arturo had taught it to Elvira) and the voice is at its most beautiful; it fairly bursts with rich tone until a neat touch of mezza voce (not merely whispered breath, for once) rounds off the final phrase. In the duet 'Nel mirarti un sol istante,' Pavarotti is refreshingly at ease in the high tessitura and maintains his ardor without sense of strain. 'Vieni, fra queste braccia' is taken down a half-tone; at its close, both artists' efforts to bring the house down achieve their desired end. The tenor launches the final ensemble ('Credeasi misera') with appropriate seriousness, investing its line with a credible nobility.

All the high-powered talent in *Puritani* guaranteed the "great success" with which Peter Allen credited the new production in his final remarks. The announcer himself calls up the specter of that bygone age which I have cited, going so far as to make a favorable comparison between our four principals and the famous Puritani quartet who created the roles of Elvira, Arturo, Riccardo, and Giorgio: Giulia Grisi, Giovanni Battista Rubini, Antonio Tamburini, and Luigi Lablache. The Met management had indeed put its best foot forward in *Puritani*. When it came to bringing *La Gioconda* back to the boards, evidently the cupboard was not so full. On the broadcast of 10 April 1976, a cast of Arroyo (Gioconda), Rankin (Laura), Chookasian (Cieca), Matteo Manuguerra (Barnaba), and Morris (Alvise)—admi-

La Gioconda
10 April 1976

Gioconda
Martina Arroyo
Laura
Nell Rankin
La Cieca
Lili Chookasian
Enzo
Misha Raitzin
Barnaba
Matteo Manuguerra
Alvise
James Morris
Conductor
Giuseppe Patanè

rable artists all, but a bit short of star power—are the headliners. Tenor Misha Raitzin (Enzo) makes his broadcast debut, as does conductor Giuseppe Patanè.

The Italian conductor came to the company to take charge of the revival of *Gioconda*, which had been out of the repertory for seven seasons. When last heard, it had been converted into a vehicle for the much-loved Tebaldi, one that she and her rabid fans deemed appropriate to her reworked voice. The lengthy hiatus provided the opportunity for a considerable restudy of the opera. Within the Montresor sets, new in 1966, John Dexter restaged the opera for an almost entirely new crew of principals. That Patanè had done much to reshape the musical contours of the opera as well is evident in his broadcast reading. He is an old hand at *Gioconda*, having recently conducted it for Rysanek (!) at the Deutsche Oper in Berlin, where he had for a number of seasons been in charge of Italian repertory. The genes were inherited—he was the son of conductor Franco Patanè. More important, they are authentic. His operatic indoctrination came about in a time-honored way; that is, while in his twenties, he progressed from répétiteur and assistant conductor (Teatro San Carlo) to possession of the podium in his own right. Over the last decade both San Francisco (1967) and Chicago (1969) had learned his worth.

His overview of the opera and his detailed shepherding of its rich cargo of melody are the best things to happen to the much-maligned score in Met decades. He believes in the opera and that belief, coupled with his thorough knowledge of the nineteenth-century Italian operatic idiom, results in a strikingly spacious, and curiously sensitive, performance. The maestro, now in his mid-forties, proves that "sensitive" is no misnomer, although few would think to apply it to *Gioconda*. Grandeur is what the score needs, and Patanè is no slouch in that area either; solemnity, too, is enhanced by his sensibility. Give him the chance to shape a proud Ponchielli melody and he will lovingly embrace it, mold its arching contours, and bring it home with both crowd-pleasing fervor and musicianly manners. His touch is equally effective when handling large ensembles, whether applying a light hand and an easy gait to the opening chorus of Venetians at the regatta or managing the considerable feat of converting the sailor's chorus with Barnaba into an ingratiating barcarole; an elegant swing transforms 'Pescator, affonda l'esca' into a delightful gambol far from the bumpy ride it often receives. Best of all is the architectural scope he achieves in the large-scale *pezzo concertato* at the Cà d'Oro. His sure-footed pacing allows Ponchielli's phrases to roll out in granitic blocks of sound, bringing the opera to a stunning climax.

The lead-off player in that concerted ensemble is new tenor Misha Raitzin. Giorgio Lamberti had sung the premiere and Morell was scheduled for the broadcast, so the tenor is third man on. The broadcast would be his only Met Enzo and one can see why. Not that his performance doesn't have its pluses as well as its minuses. On the credit side of the ledger is a hint—only a hint—of Gigli-like sweetness in the middle voice; Slavic tenors, when not of the Otello breed, sometimes do have that milky quality, pleasant enough when they don't overly squeeze its fruity core. High notes are a little unreliable, for he is a jump-ball tenor—one never quite knows where the voice will land. 'Cielo e mar,' however, holds several worthy top tones. He cannot match Manuguerra's potent vocalism in their first-act duet—Raitzin's curse is puny indeed. But the big aria shows why he is on hand to cover other Met tenors (and gain credit in his own right for some fine

Dimitris—he is on home turf there). He sets the mood with a quiet sounding of the opening phrase and, when operating within the staff, the voice is attractive. A bit of a sob now and then helps him along—for at least a century, tenors have been wont to disguise their technical deficiencies in that abused fashion—and handles the concluding 'Ah, vien's reasonably well. The final note is quite secure, though by the time it reaches its end only a terminal squeeze allows release—otherwise strangulation would surely have set in. In the duet with Laura, his gently sweet tone in the middle voice is again pleasant, but he and Rankin are a mismatch; her more potent, though shaky, vocalism dominates. For the *Gioconda* moon to descend tranquilly into the sea, two vocalists more gifted than this pair are required. (My plot summary says that, after setting fire to his ship, Enzo "dives into the sea"—yet another tenorial self-sacrifice that I always eagerly anticipate.) Being more of a lyric tenor than the robust type required for the third-act *concertato*, Raitzin can't fill the need at this important juncture. Patanè's majestic postlude does. In the last act, whether preparing to kill or commend Gioconda, the tenor sounds committed to his task. The Met would keep him around for five seasons over the next decade.

His inamorata, Nell Rankin, all but has a patent on the role of Laura Badoero. During her twenty-four seasons with the company, she has performed the role on six of the nine broadcasts of the opera since her initial radio outing in 1952. Initially, her voice sounds shopworn, especially in the middle and low range. That poses problems for her in the second-act duets, but the top voice can still project quite splendidly. After her middling effort with Enzo, the Alabama mezzo, trouper that she is, pulls one out of the hat and gives a rousing performance of 'Stella del marinar'; she tops it off with a proud high A, lovely in timbre and texture, a note that would do credit to any budding mezzo. The conductor molds the concluding section ('Scenda per questa fervida orazione') with some subtlety and Rankin performs in kind; his way allows her to shape the climaxes to good effect. She more than holds her own in the wild exchange with Gioconda; Rankin has been over this terrain so often that a bit of chest voice here and a soaring top note there will turn the trick for her every time. This performance will write *finis* to her string of broadcast Lauras, and indeed she will be heard no more at the Met after this season.

Even as Rankin lives for the vocal highs, her sister singer, Lili Chookasian, loves the depths. Her rock-solid tones are reassuring in the opening terzetto. Density below and brass above give her vocalism considerable presence. When bestowed with such plenitude, those attributes are perhaps a bit more than the gentle 'Voce di donna' can bear; by the end of the piece, even her huge voice seems a bit overweighted by its burden. Still, a mother equipped with such authority and emotional solidity is bound to be a support to a girl in love. Morris arrives in time to save her from Barnaba's machinations, but his good deeds end with that act. From there on out, evil and the macabre are his preoccupations. The young bass is not equipped for such grand plotting. Alvise's aria operates on two levels, often descending into a range where Morris cannot manufacture sufficient tone. In those moments, the aria swallows him up. Fortunately, some rolling phrases in the upper range are well within his abilities, though his final top F all but gets away from him; fortunately, his young cords produce a strained tone that at least saves him from embarrassment. He greets his ball guests with greater assurance and firmer tone as Alvise prepares to expose his wife's catafalque. (Before viewing that grisly scene, the guests are in for a treat. Patanè takes the tawdry out of the Dance of the Hours, sculpting its phrases—especially the slow melodic portions—for maximum graphic effect.) After Morris' superb bel canto outing in *Puritani*, the bass ought to have been spared a journeyman effort for which he was patently miscast.

As Gioconda, Arroyo is both magnificent and aggravating, sometimes managing to provoke both responses in successive phrases. The street singer ranks as one of the heaviest soprano roles of the Italian repertory, requiring not only the ability to loft tones of size and color but to project in the middle and low voice with gusty certainty and dramatic fervor. In fulfilling the first half of that tall order, the American soprano is on a par with any who might attempt the role. We know only too well that inadequacy in the low voice will limit a number of celebrated Gioconda moments from receiving not only full value, but even a down payment. The concluding 'tenebrous' phrases of 'Suicidio' are the most prominent of these lacunae, but there are many others. Her ill-sounding chest tone (oddly infantile in quality), when coupled with a perfunctory declamatory style, is hard to take. She sings Gioconda's opening phrases at the curtain's rise in her best maidenly manner, tone and manner blander than remembered. But we need not give way to despair. When Arroyo can linger in her upper octave, she produces some of the most vibrant, luxuriant sounds to be heard from any soprano on the current roster. It may be treason even to think it, but her 'Enzo adorato, ah, come io t'amo'—phrases to be judged forever by dear Zinka's rendition—rivals that celebrated Gioconda's handling of the moment. The Croat's ravishing *pianissimo* attack is not hers to command, but the full-throated splendor of her B-flat is ravishing, the lead-in phrase is equally satisfying, and both brief phrases are delicately laced with engaging portamentos. Things are looking up. She makes something touching and lovely of the Angelus episode with chorus; the voice may disappear at the end of a phrase, but the grand arcs of melody are affectingly sung. She is not quite a match for Rankin in the bestial duet, but remember, this is the soprano's first *Gioconda* series and she is up against an old hand. Patanè insists on not trashing the piece, but rather fills it with delightful hesitations and subtle propulsions, so the two combatants can't charge through it as though riding horses home to the barn. Once again, Arroyo's top-voice splendor comes to her rescue, as it does in the following duet with Enzo. From the vocal standpoint, her 'Suicidio' has many glorious moments, but it lacks a convincing dramatic posture and the aforementioned weak close robs her of complete triumph. In the grand recitative that follows, Gioconda must change moods with chameleon rapidity—sometimes it occurs on alternate words—and this is territory incognito for this well-behaved soprano. Too bad that Arroyo so often seems to be just trying on a role, as though it were an outfit that she is not yet ready to wear for company. But her scene with Enzo has a few high-flying phrases that alone are, as they say, worth the price of admission. Neither she nor her partners make their terzetto the transfiguring moment we want it to be—I lay part of the blame on Ponchielli. Her coloratura invitation to Barnaba is exceedingly agreeable in tone but so straightlaced—as flirtation goes—that I doubt that it would have deceived the spy as to any amorous receptivity on her part.

That gentleman, one of the most despicable villains in all opera, is meat for Manuguerra's well-practiced art. The baritone, born in Tunis of Italian parents but French-acclimated, was a late entrant in the operatic sweepstakes. He began in Lyon, moved on to the Paris Opéra in 1966, arrived in America two years later (Seattle), and made his Met debut as Ashton in 1971. Perhaps it is his long French apprenticeship that has added an extra fillip of elegance to his sturdy vocalism. The timbre, however, is blessedly Italianate, a becoming mix of Amato's forthright delivery blended with a suggestive De Luca lyricism, with neither quite the grandeur of the former's instrument nor the sweetness of the latter's. His mastery of the Italian late-nineteenth-century operatic idiom is complete and he has the technique to realize his intentions with vocal surety. No Barnaba can hope to succeed without a vocal snarl, and Manuguerra concocts a good one. But it is the firmly centered tone and manly timbral glint that he brings to 'O monumento!' which furnish the aria with more declamatory strength and melodic curves than most baritones have discovered in its severe phrases. As for 'Pescator, affonda l'esca,' that is where the fillip of elegance comes in handy. Mr. Manuguerra is an artist. One deft touch before he gives the de rigueur sardonic laugh at the final curtain clinches his right to the title. After he shouts that he has murdered Gioconda's mother, Barnaba utters "she cannot hear me"; there Manuguerra sounds a hint of regret, quietly intoning the words—perhaps his pursuit of her was more than lust. The baritone is an ideal partner for the new maestro's way with Italian opera. Patanè would return with some frequency over the next decade. His Italianate suavity and savory tastefulness provided an instructive alternative to Levine's more streamlined conduct of the Italian repertory.

Il Trittico:
Gianni Schicchi
3 January 1976

Lauretta
Evelyn Mandac
Nella
Betsy Norden
Zita
Lili Chookasian
Rinuccio
Raymond Gibbs
Schicchi
Ezio Flagello
Simone
Raymond Michalski
Conductor
Sixten Ehrling

Life in Italy over the centuries was not all torture and pain, at least if we are to accept Puccini's Florence as an informative surrogate for Ponchielli's Venice. Of course, during Gianni Schicchi's time—several centuries before Alvise and Barnaba did their dirty deeds—the Inquisition was hardly the topic of the day. And Schicchi's skulduggery was small potatoes compared to the ploys of the doge's secret service. But later on in seventeenth-century Tuscany, even life in a religious community had its lighter moments: the sisters of *Suor Angelica* dealt with the everyday concerns of a bee sting, lost lambs, and a craving for sweets. Angelica herself had other things on her mind, but then, downgraded princesses are bound to be a bit neurotic. At any rate, the nun's tasks were probably more pleasant than those of twentieth-century toilers on a Parisian barge. Illicit love, however, was common to both environments. And in all centuries.

The Metropolitan determined that Puccini's disparate characters, products of the company womb in the 1918 world premiere of *Il Trittico*, deserved to be reunited. In December 1975, they did just that with in-house mountings of *Il Tabarro*, *Suor Angelica*, and *Gianni Schicchi*; staff members Fabrizio Melano and David Reppa respectively directed and designed. The Met had kept the operas apart for fifty-five years. In fact, it had not offered *Suor Angelica* since 1920 and *Il Tabarro* was definitely a sometime visitor. Only *Gianni Schicchi* had proven to be a useful filler for bills that featured operas as varied as *Elektra*, *Bohème*, *Salome*, and *Pagliacci*. On the broadcast of 3 January 1976, Sixten Ehrling is in charge of the family reunion, retying the tenuous bonds of Puccini's neglected orphans.

Though it may appear perverse, reverse is the order of the day. I begin with the most familiar of the trio. In the 1975 broadcast of *Schicchi*, it was apparent that humor was not Ehrling's strong suit. The surprise of the 1976 airing is the conductor's newfound exhilaration. One can hear his delight in the bursting energy of the score, a treasure he had kept hidden in the earlier reading. Graphic nuances abound, often enhanced by shapely musical formulations. One is the encompassing curve he applies to 'O Gianni Schicchi, nostro salvatore!' as Buoso Donati's relatives gratefully hail the parvenu as their savior because he appears to agree to each request for part of the spoils. Not only is the overall pace of the opera quickened, but the composer's orchestral tone-painting is highlighted so that the airwaves crackle with his comic touches. A similar enhancement strengthens the characterizations of the assembled relatives. How much more alive they are as they express their gluttonous joy at their prospects, how much more depressed in their fear of deprivation. Standouts among them are Baldwin (Ciesca), Anthony (Gherardo), Boucher (Marco), and especially Michalski (taking over from last year's Harvuot, the newcomer's resonant bass not only authoritative in judgments, but displaying the cultivation appropriate to Simone as a former mayor of Florence). Richard Best lisps along as an operatic general practitioner should. Chookasian does triple duty on this afternoon, appearing in all three operas. Her Zita howls effectively here and there, but perhaps the *Angelica* princess' hard heart has dampened her spirits and cooled her voice. Norden is another triple threat. Her spirits (and that inimitable resonance) remain high. She delights in etching the trio's curving phrases with her piccolo-like tone.

Gibbs' tenor is a bit more mature than in the 1975 broadcast, the gain reminding us that he began his Met career as a baritone (Morales) before moving quickly on to roles like Roméo and Narraboth. Rinuccio suits his optimistic outlook and timbral brightness. *His* spirits seem untouched by care, so confident is he that Schicchi can rescue his amorous hopes. One can hear him, evidently intent on proving that he is no tenorino, adding weight and darker color to his tone throughout the performance—a dangerous procedure. As Gibbs moves through the assertive phrases of 'Firenze è come un albero fiorito,' sure enough, he courts disaster, cracking twice on the B-flat of 'Schicchi.' (Of course, the *i* vowel is murderous on high.) He keeps his confidence, however, and thereafter sings with ringing tone—baritonal weight now nicely balanced with tenorial headiness—and shapes the opera's concluding phrases with a friendly, triumphant expansiveness. Evelyn Mandac, in her broadcast debut, makes 'O mio babbino caro' the endearing moment it ought to be. (One wearies of hearing the slight piece turned into 'Vissi d'arte' when taken out of context.) The tone of the Manila-born, Juilliard-trained soprano is slightly metallic, but attractively so—copper is the tincture; the voice has more point and carrying power than the usual soubrette type can muster. As the aria proceeds, the fluency of her phrasing and the charm of her piquantly colored voice become apparent. In spite of her merits, she would not long figure in the Met's plans. Blegen had a corner on her market.

Flagello seems more interested in creating a character in this broadcast than in 1975, where he rather rambled through the role. The voice retains its customary velvety bass resonance, but he introduces more variety of color and phrase so that Schicchi's craft and quality register more strongly. Occasionally, he allows the voice its full bloom—his is an impressive instrument. He puts vanity aside long enough to counterfeit Buoso's voice for the doctor (a bit of nasality and a velvet downgrade do the deed), but in the end, he cannot forgo his vocal wealth when dictating the will. Once again, I can hardly believe that Florentines could be so easily duped. A touch of slyness infects his self satisfied tone as he pretends to accept the relative's requests. His suggestive 'Addio, Firenze's are liquid molasses,

Ezio Flagello as Gianni Schicchi. Photography by James Heffernan. Courtesy Metropolitan Opera Archives.

both in color and smoothness. Overall, Flagello manages to give the deceiver a slight pomposity that serves as a permissible substitute for Schicchi's customary rascality. De Luca, his baritone ringed with sweetness, was probably a lighthearted schemer in the 1918 premiere. Our bass' rogue is rather a tame character, hardly warranting Dante's punishment. When Flagello asks the audience to 'give me the benefit of your forgiveness'—if they have enjoyed themselves—this time the request seems reasonable enough.

Suor Angelica's music, at least for the first half hour, is quite innocuous, and Ehrling doesn't (or can't) do much to lend it significance. His interpretive stance for this slight confection is a shade pedantic, rather too literal. In the opening episode, he does allow us to hear an echo of the pace of *Tabarro*'s Seine, but the progress is transformed into a simpler format appropriate to the convent. (The connection is subtle, but enough to indicate that Puccini was serious about maintaining his *Trittico* as a single entity.) The contrast, musical and dramatic, between the two operas is stark. One moves from the clotted gray hues of *Tabarro* to the transparency and occasional sprightliness of the sisters' alternately playful or prickly environment. *Angelica*'s lightness and simple tonality do make more sense with *Tabarro* as foil.

All of the afternoon's sisters are worthy of their calling. Baldwin's Monitor is firm voiced and authoritative, but benign, in dispensing punishments; Munzer's Nurse can be flustered—bees on the loose would make one nervy; and Batyah Godfrey's voice as Teacher provides valuable timbral contrast. When her slightly sepulchral instrument is juxtaposed with Norden's angelic tones, earth and heaven are in aural alignment. The latter's Sister Genovieffa is a delight. Could the young soprano be wearing ballerina toe shoes under her nun's habit? Her pinpoint accuracy of pitch and attack sheds rays of sunlight into the everyday world of her colleagues. Though Kraft's bleak and hoary timbre is worlds away from Norden's, the mezzo casts a spell of her own. When the Abbess informs Angelica of the Princess' visit, Kraft, by her stark, stern delivery commands our attention as readily as Norden's innocent prattle had.

With the coming of the Princess, the opera springs to life. Chookasian's magisterial contralto tones are the rightful province of a princess, especially one so forbidding and unbending as Angelica's aunt. The Chicago native can be imposing without having to toughen her tone, nor does one feel that she has sharpened it on a whetstone before quitting her *palazzo*. Interpretively, Chookasian finds little variety in the aunt's pronouncements; but then, her dramatic function is one giant put-down and vocally she plucks the single string of disapprobation.

We know from grander assignments that Cruz-Romo's instrument is a healthy one: her tone is devoid of wobble or undue vibrato; her timbre is equalized throughout its range; the round core at its center minimizes acidulousness and lends assurance to her conduct of line. These are the attributes of a well-schooled singer and intelligent practitioner. Yet the tone is not quite mellow enough in itself to suggest Angelica's suppliant character or to evoke full sympathy for her sorry plight. At times, indeed, her tone seems, if not hard, a little unforgiving. Of course, the former princess has moments of command, irritation, and self-indulgence so that Cruz-Romo may be on to something distinctive in her characterization. (I wonder how Farrar portrayed her at the premiere.) The Mexican soprano's Angelica is no sugary, forlorn waif. She plays her straight in her dealings

Suor Angelica
3 January 1976

Angelica
Gilda Cruz-Romo
Genovieffa
Betsy Norden
Princess
Lili Chookasian
Conductor
Sixten Ehrling

with the sisters, allowing a bit of the nun's prickly personality to surface now and then, but forthrightly acknowledging Angelica's innate kindliness. She holds her own with the Princess. When the hard-hearted aunt refuses to respond to her questions, the niece becomes agitated and turns confrontational, her tone not inappropriately touched by harshness, but still preserving its timbral solidity. We hear the first indication that the soprano can soften her tone, lend it a modicum of delicacy, as she pleads for 'clemenza' and 'pietà'; it surfaces again as Angelica takes comfort in her younger sister's approaching marriage. Now we can glimpse the dramatic arc that the artist's portrayal will traverse.

Ehrling is at his best in the expansive interludes, whether the dynamic is quiet or grand. The orchestral peroration that precedes the aria is particularly heartfelt—not overdramatized, but lovingly phrased. Cruz-Romo is a match for the vocal challenges of 'Senza mamma, o bimbo, tu sei morto!' She begins affectingly, offering contrast at the little outburst 'E tu sei morto,' notches the volume up or grades it down as appropriate, and summons a welcome sweetness at 'Oh! dolce fine d'ogni mio dolore.' The mini-climax ('Quando potrò morire?') is tonally expansive and free of harshness. Sobs and theatrics are mercifully minimal. (But surely, when Angelica names her child 'un angelo del cielo,' her voice, as well as the word, should reflect the anointing.) Cruz-Romo's clean attack on the final high note is enhanced by a well-judged diminuendo. If her rendition of the aria is not quite the heart-crushing trauma it can be, as vocalism it is both assured and compelling. Her best moments come in the ensuing, more dramatic episode where she can let out her spinto voice to her heart's content. The several top Cs are on pitch and confident, but a cooler glaze, a slight hardness rather than the wished-for bloom, settles on them. Her manner is singularly devoid of wonder or suggestive of mystery as she prepares the suicide herbs—here she is too much the vocalist rather than a singer acting with the voice. Her farewell to her sister nuns, for instance, is merely obligatory—ordinary fare. The little downward octave glides are affectingly done, quite touching, but her sobs continue throughout the final choral scene, an odd effect since restraint has been the watchword of her portrayal. Angelica's ecstatic state is not quite realized at the opera's close. Our belief in the miracle, difficult to accept at any rate in Puccini's bland creation, is doubly challenged. A little more imagination, a deeper involvement, is required if Angelica is to be fully accepted into the composer's gallery of sympathetic heroines. Scotto will achieve that distinction when she takes on Angelica (along with Giorgetta and Lauretta) later in the month. Her triumph in the three roles (comparable to a soccer game hat trick) foreshadows her controversial ascendancy to the grander Italian repertory during the Levine regime.

For maximum effect, *Suor Angelica* requires the help of a great singing actress, but Puccini's deft touch and astute characterizations are usually sufficient to carry *Gianni Schicchi* to triumph. Still, it is the masterful construction, musical and dramatic, of *Il Tabarro* that gives the *Trittico* its much-needed backbone. The only previous radio outing in 1946 (with Albanese, Harshaw, Jagel, Tibbett, and Lazzari, under Cesare Sodero's direction) provided early acquaintance with the opera's strong profile. But I marvel anew at the composer's skill. His orchestral tone-painting ladles river atmospherics and a Parisian aura over the entire score. Concurrently, he molds character vignettes with brief but telling strokes: Tinca (Anthony, sounding like a tenor of rank), Talca (Booth, dusky of tone and earthy

Il Tabarro
3 January 1976

Giorgetta
Teresa Kubiak
Frugola
Lili Chookasian
Luigi
Harry Theyard
Michele
Cornell MacNeil
Conductor
Sixten Ehrling

in manner), and best of all, his wife, Frugola, brought to life in the hearty, sonorous tones of Chookasian. Rock solid of voice, the American singer conveys the ragpicker's satisfaction with her lot, her joie de vivre. She blithely tosses her songs out upon the riverbanks, an admirer of her own eccentricity. Most mezzos get the register bends in these skittish ditties, but Chookasion carries her contralto weight up and down the range with no sign of strain or timbral change. Like Giorgetta, she can dream. Her wish is for a house in the country ('Ho sognato una casetta'); the dream may not be realized, but we imagine she can handle disappointment (her name, Frugola, means 'the lively one'). Jon Garrison has his songs, too. His are for sale and his clean-cut tenor ought to seal many a deal.

The three principals provide strong characterizations as well. Theyard has had his ups and downs during his relatively brief Met career, but he scores as Luigi. His tenor has the fiber of a stevedore built in, strong-muscled as it is, but it carries as well an innate sensual component within the timbre that makes Giorgetta's dalliance believable. Beyond those qualities, Theyard permits flicks of romantic yearning to infect a line here and there. Passion may not be the only motivation for Giorgetta's obsession. But it is the hard life he leads as a laborer on the Seine that is the core of Luigi's being—there a man must drown regret in drink in order to escape his desolate existence. Theyard's passionate, defiant singing of 'Hai ben ragione,' in which the stevedore enunciates his credo, is hair-raising. His tenor bangs away at the declamatory phrases at the top of his range, each note as cutting as the lash of a whip on his weary back. The destructive force of those repeated tones, their hopeless belligerence, mirrors the hard-nosed inevitability of his life.

Miss Kubiak may not be in best voice. A slight rasp can be heard rather frequently when she declaims in the middle-low part of her voice. Perhaps the rasp is a normal component of her instrument's makeup. Giorgetta doesn't offer her the flights of song that Jenůfa did, but Puccini provides enough opportunities to show off the bright bloom of her upper voice. The Polish soprano takes advantage of them, often to thrilling effect. More unusual, however, is her ability to suggest the desultory character of the wife's humdrum life on the barge. In spite of her Puccinian dreams of a better existence, Kubiak exposes the common streak in Giorgetta's nature. One would need it to survive in that environment. She makes the wife's involvement with Luigi and her harshness to her husband seem essential to the woman's nature. The loss of her child has further hardened her. When this Giorgetta muses on the difficulty of finding happiness, one can believe her. She has been there. Happiness will not be Giorgetta's reward in life. (Claudia Muzio, the creator of the role, would have understood her condition only too well.) The soprano adopts a tender tone in her quiet, mournful attempt at reconciliation with Michele before Luigi's body, hidden in the cloak, rolls out in the Grand Guignol finale. It can hardly have been the first time that Giorgetta has attempted to close the unbridgeable gap between reality and dreams. Kubiak and Theyard, strong of voice and passionate in utterance, are lovers outside the operatic norm.

Michele is only a brooding presence for the major part of the score, but when his turn comes, he claims the opera as his own. Possession is certain when a powerhouse baritone like MacNeil's is wielded with a veteran's sure-voiced capability. The singer grabs the closing episodes by the throat and wrings his triumph from them as assuredly as the cuckolded husband takes Luigi's life into his hands when

Cornell MacNeil as Michele in *Il Tabarro*. Photography by James Heffernan. Courtesy Metropolitan Opera Archives.

the stevedore returns for his assignation with Giorgetta. Even in the early stages of the opera, the sheer bulk of MacNeil's tones in his few lines establishes Michele as a man to be reckoned with. A Gobbi might well uncover complex depths in the barge owner; MacNeil rightly places his faith in tone and line. His instrument is of superior quality on this afternoon, solid, its initial touch of rawness, even coldness, mating well with the husband's hard manner. When he pleads with Giorgetta, hoping to revive the happier relationship they knew before the death of their child, MacNeil allows a muted sadness to steal into his tone; warmth infects it, but nothing can drive out the cold that possesses his inner being. The moving climax to his plea fails to soften Giorgetta's revulsion. Left alone, the baritone names his wife 'whore,' with a growl that would do credit to the hound of the Baskervilles. With magnificent tones and breadth of phrase he plots his retribution. A stunning high G caps the monologue. He lofts another one, confidently poised, as the curtain falls.

Ehrling, not quite convincing when husbanding *Suor Angelica*'s slight wares but ably embracing *Schicchi*'s fount of humor, has a masterly feel for the pacing of *Tabarro*. The mesmerizing flow of orchestral tone suggests the river's ceaseless coursing; sometimes Ehrling cultivates its graceful flow; at other moments he sends it surging on. River control establishes conductorial hegemony from the first measures. Drama and music are wedded intrinsically without resorting to cheap theatrics or overplaying the composer's vivid orchestral portraiture. Yet he is attentive to Puccini's novel harmonic touches and cherishes the weird organ-grinder dance episode. The conductor never allows the drama to slacken or the musical momentum to bog down. When the three operas are retained in the next season's repertory, they will be under the care of Levine, who ranked the *Trittico* with *Bohème* as "a masterpiece."[5] Puccini's orphans have found at least a temporary home.

One-acts were not on Verdi's schedule. He preferred a larger canvas. The master gained a grand one when he settled on a ceremonial opera set in Egypt during the time of the pharaohs. With Levine as tour guide, *Aida* is bound to be an exciting trip, even if the Sphinx is not on the itinerary. On the broadcast of 6 March 1976, Price is Aida, Horne tackles Amneris, the young Domingo undertakes to save 'la patria,' MacNeil rages as a father manqué, and Giaiotti pulls behind-the-scenes strings. Obviously life on the Nile is a high-content experience. The broadcast will ring down the curtain on my chronicle as the Met proudly displays its quality wares.

As it came from Verdi's pen, *Aida* turned out to be not as heroic as it might have been. Except for a touch of bellicosity in the opening scene ('Guerra! Guerra!' resounds insistently) and the grandiose triumphal scene, the work is astonishingly intimate, essentially a conventional love triangle with a father–daughter relationship superimposed. Maestro Levine is just the man to knit the public and private manners into a convincing whole. The preludes to acts one and three share his penchant for efficient musicianship and hint at the path the stage action will take. A slim thread of violin tone opens the opera, but the vibrant low strings soon take over and before long Levine sights an *incalzando* (how he loves an *incalzando*); his happy heart leaps with anticipation and the music takes flight. But rarely does bullet-train propulsion (most aptly applied at moments like the 'inni leviamo ad Iside' section of the triumphal scene) drive him and us over the edge. The third-

Aida
6 March 1976

Aida
Leontyne Price
Amneris
Marilyn Horne
Radamès
Plácido Domingo
Amonasro
Cornell MacNeil
Ramfis
Bonaldo Giaiotti
Conductor
James Levine

act prelude plinkings are held to a perfect time-trot—that is one way to hold the piece together, even if the aura of the Nile is shortchanged. The act-one Ballabile and act-two dances are devilishly fleet, the latter in particular cracklingly alive as the orchestra enjoys displaying its virtuosity. The conductor, as ever, is sensitive to his singers' needs, though he resists pampering them. (I rather think that Verdi would not have minded a bit more indulgence in that regard.) Lovely ethereal choral effects in the temple scene create their own aura. In the triumphal scene, the choral sonority is surprisingly modest and the impact is somewhat muted. Indeed, there hangs over the performance just a hint of business as usual. But when it is the Levine brand of usual, a high standard is the operative factor. This seasonal run is the conductor's first Met husbanding of *Aida*, but the performance moves on ball bearings, Levine's expert tutelage by now having permeated all facets of Met music making. Homage must be paid and will be for decades to come.

Baldwin's priestess is an energetic incantor, and Anthony delivers a message with assurance, even when the news is bad. The low-voiced male trio, too, know their business. Though he is the newest member of the group, Morris' King sings as though his subjects were ever on his mind. The role (a debut assignment for the twenty-three-year-old bass in 1971) lies in the best part of his firm, bright voice and he sings with confident authority. By this time, Giaiotti is practically an honorary member of the operatic priesthood; his Ramfis sounds as though he may have officiated at a few too many rites. The voice is a good one but his bored manner is neither confessional nor retributive. In the judgment scene, no Radamès with an ounce of tenorial pride is going to give in to him. MacNeil is the regular of the group. His Amonasro has been round the Nile bases often enough to know that he has only two at-bats. (The Ethiope, as far as acts go, is shortchanged—he comes late and leaves early.) MacNeil can both bewail the fate of his Ethiopian comrades in the face of Egyptian injustice—his baritone has the size and timbral appeal to plead effectively—and thunder away at his daughter's perfidy, though he does it a shade less violently today than in his prime. But when it comes to the serious business of enlisting her in his cause, his grand line and swelling tone are bound to win back a daughter's loyalty. MacNeil's voicing of the supreme Verdian appeal 'Pensa che un popolo vinto, straziato,' touched this time by a knowing sadness, is simply glorious.

Daughters who are conflicted by a father's command and a lover's desire have a hard time of it, whether they exist only on the operatic stage or figure in newspaper headlines. Miss Price makes Aida's torment vividly clear on this seasonal return to what had been a signature role after several years of neglect. She had consciously avoided the assignment, blithely telling an interviewer that she preferred not to perform any more "on-my-knees" roles.[6] The great soprano had not been heard on the broadcasts since her 1974 Donna Anna; by this career date, she was intent on avoiding "overexposure"—a stance that rightly had driven Mr. Bing into near-apoplexy. At any rate, we welcome her with the immutable regard that her vocalism on many a broadcast of the sixties deserves. Warning flags, however, must be sent up the celebratory flagpole. One must not expect the pristine vocalism, the crystalline tone and supple line of those years. The artist has now become the prima donna. That of course has its own satisfactions, especially for an operatic public that loves to worship and to be wowed. To achieve that end, grand gestures are essential and Price delivers them. Aida's modest music at her entry allows the soprano to gather her resources, and when she reaches 'Ritorna vinci-tor!' she is ready to display her diva wares. The piece is assuredly frenetic. Aida's plight, torn as she is between country and lover, is desperate and the soprano plays that mode for all it is worth. Effects are her concern, and some of them border on vulgarity, including a slight howl in her portamentos, and an emotional delivery of the concluding prayer. It is all highly effective, even thrilling, but one longs for the adorable simplicity with which she once implored the gods. Now it is the gallery gods who must be appeased.

Nor does the voice always quite sound like the Price of old. On occasion dur-ing the afternoon, it seems thinner. In the final duet, for instance, 'Vedi? di morte l'angelo' is oddly articulated and tonally edgy—one might not actually recognize the voice in this incarnation. There are plenty of moments, however, when it is very much the voice we remember, where its incomparable shine is proudly pre-sented. The first-act trio holds some exquisite vocalism. She comes into her own in the second-act colloquy with Amneris; I relaxed upon hearing 'Ah! pietà ti prenda del mio dolor'—there the idol dropped the public mask. Now both the familiar silken glint and luxuriantly glossy tone are at her disposal. They inform a good deal of the duets with Amonasro and Radamès. With her father, 'Ah! ben ram-mento quegl' infausti giorni!' has the remembered nobility of phrase and fullness of tone. With her lover, the repeat of 'Là tra foreste vergini' has a near-gossamer spin. Unfortunately, she hurtles rather crudely through 'Nella terra avventurata.' Put the best face on it and call it dramatic involvement. Indeed, it is passionately sung and she and Domingo create the kind of excitement that gladdens even hard-hearted opera lovers. I do like the conspiratorial intimacy she adopts when Aida first suggests their flight ('Fuggiam gli ardori inospiti'). 'O patria mia' is the core of an Aida portrayal and I wish I could admire Price's current interpretation. Where once a silvery float created an ethereal tonal world that was uniquely hers, now it is replaced by emphatic effects, slurred legato, excessive portamentos, and that insidious howl. The final A is taken full voice (luxuriance incarnate, it is true) rather than the exquisite *piano* of yore. Both ascents are well managed, the second to a high C that is far more cutting than the easy tone of memory and tenaciously made to stay in place. Give her full credit—few singers could manage that chal-lenge with comparable brilliance. Elsewhere, the Price top notes are still intact, and for many their magnificence will be sufficient reward.

Admirers of Price's artistry are apt to find this report unnerving, as I do. I offer two palliatives. First, one can be content to revel in the diva's current ex-travagant expenditure of her still potent vocal resources; much remains to enjoy. Conflict rears its head when she is set up against her former self. That contest is a losing battle. A more pertinent assuagement, for me at least, is that over the next decade I often heard the soprano sing far better than on this broadcast. Perhaps we can regard this afternoon's performance as an aberration. At least, until the next time.

In addition to Miss Price's increasingly rare presence, the afternoon holds our first opportunity to hear one of America's favorite singers in the guise of a Verdi mezzo-soprano. It was to be a posture that Marilyn Horne hereafter would not often assume. She has the assets to make her venture an entirely plausible one, even for the paramount Rossini coloratura mezzo of her era. One of those assets is the voice's tonal consistency throughout its entire range—no problem about the dreaded mezzo break with this diva. Then, too, an Amneris must be secure on high and confident down low, and Horne more than qualifies on both counts. Her top voice on this afternoon is indeed resplendent—not even the violent ascents at the close of the judgment scene try her full-throated ease in riding their treacherous paths. And we know how she can boom a baritonal low note at will. As Amneris, she avoids that frequently criticized device that she loved to exploit in her comic Rossini roles, rightly preferring to employ chest voice as part of the wide-ranging Verdian line. Miss Horne always comes to sing. She takes advantage of every opportunity to demonstrate, as have some predecessors, like Castagna and Cossotto, and even today's Zajick, that a Verdi mezzo can win approval with considerate vocalism as much as from boffo effects. If a phrase be marked *grazioso*, she will honor it—not always with maximum tonal warmth, since the timbre is a shade metallic, especially when she must marshal tone against late-nineteenth-century orchestral forces; but invariably her phrasing and interpretive stance convey the message. Amneris' three-pronged declaration of love ('Ah! vieni, amor mio ravvivami') is a case in point. Her tone is neither *piano* at its inception nor particularly caressing, but her refulgent *espansione* (Verdi's directive) in the upper range is replete with desire and the conduct of line and tonal control are remarkable. Many other instances of similar skill could be cited. We hear one of the era's finest musical minds at work. Words, however, are not really her thing and we know how Verdi begged Maria Waldmann, the Amneris of the La Scala premiere, to "study the words" assiduously and to do so "with no singing."[7] He valued their vivid presentation.

Like any astute Amneris, Horne saves her full battery for the judgment scene and there she spends some vocal capital, but fortunately, not so liberally as to imperil future encounters with her specialty. Still, her efforts bespeak the generosity that is hers in life as well as in song. Astutely, at every turn she allows acute rhythmic emphases to carry part of the load—and it does. When she encounters a string of quarter notes—as at 'Voi la terra ed i Numi oltraggia' (and there Levine's orchestra swamps her as well)—the going gets harder. But she is a born survivor. If her Amneris is not quite the genuine article—that is, cast in the Stignani or Simionato mold—Horne certainly provides an excellent facsimile of one. When, with immense confidence and resonant tone, she rides over the crest of 'de' miei pianti la vendetta or dal ciel,' she does sound like the real thing, and I, for one, am willing to grant her the right to the Verdi idiom. But I will be even more responsive to restraint in the face of temptation. Let her not swim in the Nile nor haunt the mountains of Biscay.

The object of both Horne's and Price's affections was to have been McCracken, but it is Domingo who is entombed with Aida on this afternoon. Radamès is not a role that the young tenor often performed at the Met. The martial cast of the music does not always show him to best advantage. Yet, on this afternoon, our future Otello proves to be an excellent general and adept lover. At his entrance, the voice's customary warmth is augmented by a dramatic vigor that enlivens the recitative to 'Celeste Aida' and later keeps the troublesome phrases of that aria in line. His is not a rhapsodic reading; no portamentos, for instance, grace Verdi's upward phrase thrusts. But he gets the job done and, in the process, offers some fine B-flats. A slight frog or rasp momentarily threatens the final one before, after a quick release, he sounds the Toscanini-authorized four-note low conclusion. (I once heard Domingo quite surprisingly assert that tenors would be hooted off the stage if they included Caruso-type portamentos in the aria. I thought they were Verdi's. Just how an artist can preserve the composer's intent while necessarily adhering to the performance practice of one's own era can be, to put it mildly, a dilemma.) Thereafter, Domingo has no problem with top notes: 'immenso Fthà!' and 'Io resto a te' are full-toned, noble, and assured. What more could one ask of a tenor? Well, precisely what Domingo delivers elsewhere in the opera. Over the years, Domingo has generally been credited with—accused of, if you prefer—what I would call a panoramic view of a role, where the broad outlines are fully charted at the expense of subtle interpretive gestures. Of course, Radamès is a role made up of interpretive building blocks, so the panoramic serves both him and Verdi very well. Not that Domingo doesn't call his musicality into play when he spots a likely candidate for an interpretive salute. As he stands before the god Ptah (the Met's version of Fthà), he clothes 'Nume, che Duce ed arbitro' in a vocal caress, its line lovingly guided. And a tenor who can sing those galloping phrases at his entry in the Nile scene with vitality and accuracy (a perfect union with the orchestra, for a change) is both a divo and a musician. A similar brio enhances the couple's transport as they contemplate escape. When dishonor overtakes Radamès, Domingo is dramatically vibrant; he, Price, and MacNeil heat up the airwaves with their overt playing of this theatrical moment. He is equally effective in the confrontation with Amneris where his determination not to renounce Aida is manifest in his emphatic vocalism. In the final scene, the tenor takes Verdi's injunction (*voce cupa*) to heart, the velvety soft tone and an intimate manner complementing the silence of the tomb. His portion of the duet, whether ardent or resigned, is musically phrased and sung with admirable control. Of course, he cannot sing the final phrases *piano* any more than most tenors can, and Price, who undoubtedly could if she would, chooses not to. Thus, the otherworldly aura that Verdi so successfully limned in his music is not fully realized. Miss Horne's pleas for 'pace' will have to be enough to satisfy, if not the composer, the gods on high and those in the house. The quality of the Met's *Aida* on this broadcast is more than sufficient to uphold Verdi's view that "this opera is certainly not one of my worst."[8]

Our tour of Italian opera suggests, admittedly with some foreknowledge, that the era of the two tenors is just around the corner. Domingo and Pavarotti will come to dominate Metropolitan planning to a degree unheard of since the Caruso era. Of course, it took two of them to contest the Neapolitan immortal's singularity.

James Levine. Courtesy Metropolitan Opera Archives.

CHAPTER TWENTY-TWO

Levine Takes Hold

"Well, Jimmy, every time we talk together," Anthony Bliss exclaimed, "I become increasingly excited by the accomplishments that I can see ahead for the Metropolitan Opera under your leadership."[1] The executive director's enthusiasm for his young colleague, James Levine, spills over the airwaves on the final broadcast of the 1975–76 season.

Bliss had in effect taken control of the opera administration in the summer of 1975 after the board failed to renew Schuyler Chapin's contract as general manager. That office would remain vacant for a half dozen years (in 1981 the title was granted to Bliss), but a gifted trio effectively filled the void. In addition to Bliss, John Dexter was named director of production—since 1974 he had been in charge of stage operations. Levine had served as principal conductor since 1973, and on the 1976 seasonal farewell broadcast Bliss announced his rise to the position of music director, his responsibilities to begin with "the beginning of the coming season" (1976–77). The young conductor's influence on the musical aspects of the company was already strong. Now he officially assumed responsibility for the most important component of the opera company's activities, the very reason for its existence, both in regard to daily performances and planning for the future. The Levine era, which would stretch into the twenty-first century, now begins.

Bliss' enthusiasm was no PR pose. The seemingly unbounded energy and contagious zeal of Levine would prove to be invaluable assets, second only to his musical qualifications in their importance to the Metropolitan's future. During the Chapin regime, the financial condition of the company had become rocky beyond belief. The troubled decade that had begun in 1966 with the move to Lincoln Center was plagued thereafter by financial and labor union problems; upon Bing's retirement, a period of greater uncertainty had set in under the tentative leadership of Chapin, a well-intentioned second-in-command type who, as earlier noted, had been thrust into the prime post upon Goeran Gentele's death. Dire warnings were issued frequently to the radio audience throughout the 1974–75 and 1975–76 seasons concerning company survival; in a January 1975 radio interview, Chapin had noted that the deficit for that season would be nine million dollars: "time is running out," he averred.[2] Appeals for contributions filled the airwaves, with artists and administrators the chief solicitors. Happily, by the time Bliss announced Levine's newly acquired authority, he was able to report that for the first time since 1969, performance attendance had reached just under 95 percent of capacity and that the base of support had been substantially broadened (in the year just ended, about 150,000 people had contributed to the Metropolitan). Still, the path ahead was not secure and Bliss ended the final 1976 intermission with not one, but two pleas for continuing contributions, stressing "the enormous financial difficulties that beset us" due to present and past deficits.[3] But his overall stance was upbeat. And, in that regard, he could have had no greater ally than Levine, who, though more enigmatic than his outwardly candid behavior suggested, possessed an optimist's courage.

Of greatest importance for the radio audience were Levine's plans for the coming seasons. In response to Bliss' invitation, the new music director enunciated his credo: to produce "every time the curtain goes up" a performance at the "Metropolitan standard," that is, one that is "cast . . . conceived . . . and rehearsed as well as possible." Any new leader might articulate the same goals upon assuming the managerial reins. With Levine, however, the capabilities he had already demonstrated enhanced belief, encouraging the radio audience in their hope that his words went beyond mere good intentions. The frequency of the word "possible" in his statement underlines the pragmatic element in Levine's makeup that was symptomatic of his building-block approach toward his work. Give him time enough to teach and guide and he might well be able to mold the company in his own image. Still, he feared that economic and practical problems would make the realization of his goals harder than at any time in company history. Bliss, too, acknowledged that "we are going to make mistakes" and may be unable to "fulfill our objectives because of the intense competition for certain performers or for financial reasons."

Levine then became more specific about the direction in which he intended to take the company, noting especially the need to introduce the "real twentieth-century masterpieces," for which, he claimed, there is "an ever increasing audience." (Time would prove him right on that score. In yet another intermission interview a quarter century later, general manager Volpe noted that, in the 2000–01 season, *Lulu*—under Levine, of course—played to 96 percent capacity.[4]) In addition, he intended to add lesser-known operas by recognized masters of earlier centuries. And, as the third prong in his program, he planned to continue to refurbish acknowledged popular masterworks. New productions in the coming season conformed to those principles: *Lohengrin* and *La Bohème* fit the masterpiece category; Massenet's *Esclarmonde* (for Sutherland) and Meyerbeer's *Le Prophète* (for Horne) had certainly been "less heard"; and Poulenc's *Dialogues of the Carmelites* and Berg's *Lulu* qualified as twentieth-century gems. Most notable are the Metropolitan premieres of the twentieth-century operas, the emphasis upon this aspect of the repertory being particularly dear to Levine's heart. In addition to his leadership of *Lulu*, the new music director planned to conduct *Lohengrin* and *La Bohème*. Each of these operas, too, may be viewed as an indicator of future important paths for the conductor and the company. *Lohengrin* would be Levine's first venture onto Wagnerian terrain at the Metropolitan; that grand corpus would become increasingly prominent in his future career endeavors. On 15 March 1977, the new *Bohème* inaugurated the enormously successful televised opera series on the Public Broadcasting System under the rubric *Live from the Met*. (In that same 2001 interview, Volpe was not so sanguine about the television venture, claiming that the size of the viewing audience was not large enough to justify the money the Met put into it. For him, the telecasts were not as important as the radio broadcasts.)[5]

It could not be known at the time, but the most important long-range benefit of Levine's appointment would be his ongoing involvement with the company during three-plus decades. The gain in continuity outweighed any desire for greater variety of conductorial supervision of new productions and important occasions, the majority of which henceforth would belong to Levine. And, under Bliss' management financial security eventually did return to the company, its solvency enduring into the first year or two of the twenty-first century under Volpe's stern, canny leadership. Bliss, Dexter, and Levine had set things off on the right path, with the maestro the long-term standard bearer of his proclaimed Metropolitan ideal.

While orchestral and choral forces would prosper immeasurably under Levine's leadership during the next decades, the quality of vocalism offered would depend, as Bliss had made clear, on the ability to attract to the Met stage artists of the first rank. As we have seen, even during the troubled decade of our chronicle, great artists and grand performances often were offered to the radio audience. Fortunately, in the late seventies, there were still giants in the singing world and increasingly Levine's presence at the helm would encourage their presence on the Metropolitan stage. He inherited a company of high quality. We know these artists well, for they have been the pillars of our broadcast enjoyment. A few had departed: Della Casa, Tucci, Moffo, Tebaldi, Tucker, Corelli, Merrill, Siepi, and Tozzi. But remaining, for greater or lesser service, were an array of sopranos that would honor any age: Sutherland, Price, Caballé, Rysanek, Nilsson, Lorengar, Stratas, Amara, Freni, Zylis-Gara, Crespin, Maliponte, Cruz-Romo, Sills, Te Kanawa, Lear, Jones, Arroyo, and Scotto. Nor was the company shy of quality mezzos, for numbered among their members were Ludwig, Cossotto, Resnik, Horne, Von Stade, and Troyanos. (Bumbry and Verrett, erstwhile mezzos, current sopranos, may be placed in either category.) Exceptional tenors were still on call: Gedda, Bergonzi, Vickers, McCracken, Burrows, Domingo, and Pavarotti. The baritone and bass ranks were less full, but on hand were MacNeil, Milnes, McIntyre, Stewart, and Corena and Talvela, plus the budding Morris and Plishka.

But before long, the crop of magnificent artists who had dominated the company after the watershed years of the late fifties and early sixties would gradually leave the scene of their Metropolitan triumphs. Miss Nilsson's participation, for example, would be quite limited in the future, so the heroic Wagner operas inevitably suffered neglect (or, if performed, a measure of abuse). Most Wagnerians, when she left the scene, must have felt that, like Walter Scott's *Redgauntlet* heroine, she "put the sun . . . into her pocket." Her Brünnhilde had hailed it ('Heil dir, Sonne!') often enough to claim possession. New artists of merit would indeed enter the company, not as replacements for departed favorites (one should never expect or look for replication) but worthy in their own right. Nevertheless, the supply appeared to dwindle over the next half dozen years or so. Distinguished singers like Ileana Cotrubas, Edita Gruberova, Eva Marton, Anna Tomowa-Sintow, Julia Varady, Mariella Devia, and Margaret Price came but did not linger overlong. The men whom we wished had been more permanent visitors included José Carreras (a 1974 debutant), René Kollo, Siegfried Jerusalem, Gösta Winbergh, Bernd Weikl, Yuri Mazurok, Sesto Bruscantini, Thomas Allen, Jorma Hynninen, and

Kurt Moll. All these fine artists were welcome, but the times prescribed a new order. Few in that long list remained long enough to set a company tone the way artists like Milanov, Steber, Tucker, and Warren, for instance, had at mid-century, or the way many of the singers named above (Tebaldi, Corelli, and Rysanek, for example) had over the next two decades. Several new artists did become more or less permanent Metropolitan tenants, singers like Kathleen Battle (her sojourn famously ruptured), Håkan Hagegård, Catherine Malfitano, Carol Vaness, Jessye Norman, Dawn Upshaw, Leo Nucci, Juan Pons, and Samuel Ramey. Of the previous generation of artists, Scotto would play an increasingly prominent role in the daily life of the Met. Two singers, Domingo and Pavarotti, did put their mark upon the company to a remarkable degree. We have been the fortunate recipients of their enduring commitment to the Metropolitan. And in the years surrounding the millennium, not only did Levine gain an ally in Valery Gergiev, but a number of artists of high merit (Fleming, Voigt, Mattila, Heppner, Alagna, Vargas, Florez, Hampson, Hvorostovsky, Terfel, and Pape, to name only a few) joined the company. They came mostly for single (or at best two) productions, so their quality regrettably was seldom enough to guarantee an elevated standard for everyday repertory performances. But their presence gives hope for the morrow. In 1976, at the end of his remarks on his debut interview as music director, Levine prophesied that "over the next few years we will be able to bring the Metropolitan into a new and very great era."[6] I am glad that he has been on hand to make the attempt.

Decades of broadcasts lay in Levine's, and our, future. Then the unthinkable happened. In the early years of the new century, opera lovers were struck by a thunderbolt. Chevron Texaco decided to terminate its sponsorship of the broadcasts after the 2003–04 season. For more than six decades they had sustained us in our Saturday afternoon habit. Manager Volpe (who unexpectedly scheduled his own departure in 2006) soon vowed that cold turkey would not be our lot. The broadcasts would continue—new sponsors would be sought. And he hinted that, as had happened so often in the Metropolitan's troubled financial history, solicitation of the radio audience might provide a way out. The Save the Met Broadcasts Campaign was launched. Despite a healthy response from faithful listeners, this time adequate sustenance has not yet come from that quarter. The Campaign continues. Fortunately, corporate benevolence (Toll Brothers) and foundation magnanimity for the time being sustain our hopes.

Whatever the fate of the broadcasts over the coming decades, those broadcasts already secured—over seventy years of operatic treasure—are certain to retain their documentary importance, their capacity to inform, and, of greatest moment, their power to please. They are history come alive.

CHECK No. 1473   NEW YORK, December 12, 19 30

Manufacturers Trust Company
513 FIFTH AVENUE, Cor. 43RD STREET

PAY TO THE ORDER OF Giuseppe de Luca #11

SIX HUNDRED NINETY SEVEN DOLLARS FIFTY CENTS   DOLLARS.

METROPOLITAN OPERA COMPANY

Frank Garlichs.
TREASURER

$ 697.50

CHECK No. 1520   NEW YORK,   Jan. 29 1938

THE FIFTH AVENUE BANK OF NEW YORK 1-76
530 FIFTH AVENUE, N. W. Cor. 44TH STREET

PAY TO THE ORDER OF Gina Cigna ##C# $ 400.00#

FOUR HUNDRED DOLLARS   DOLLARS,

METROPOLITAN OPERA ASSOCIATION, Inc.

Frank Garlichs
TREASURER

Edward Johnson

THE CHASE NATIONAL BANK 1-74 / 210   32
OF THE CITY OF NEW YORK
TIMES SQUARE BRANCH, SEVENTH AVE. AT 41st ST.

EMPLOY. NO. 1548

PAY TO THE ORDER OF ETTORE BASTIANINI

MO. 02 | DAY 03 | YR. 56

PAY EXACTLY 374 DOLLARS AND 00 CENTS $ 374 00

PAY THIS AMOUNT

METROPOLITAN OPERA ASSOCIATION, Inc.
PAY ROLL ACCOUNT

S   PAYROLL DEPT.   AUTHORIZED SIGNATURE

Metropolitan Opera checks signed by Giulio Gatti-Casazza (for Giuseppe de Luca), Edward Johnson (for Gina Cigna), and by Rudolf Bing and Max Rudolf (for Ettore Bastianini).

Notes

Metropolitan Opera Annals 1966–76 refers to *Metropolitan Opera Annals: Third Supplement, 1966–1976*, compiled by Mary Ellis Peltz and Gerald Fitzgerald, published by the Metropolitan Opera Guild and James T. White & Company, New York, 1978.

CHAPTER ONE

1   Rudolf Bing, *5000 Nights at the Opera* (Garden City, NY: Doubleday, 1972), pp. 307–308.
2   Martin Mayer, "The Elaborately Practical Theater," *Opera News*, 17 September 1966, p. 16.
3   Bing, *5000 Nights*, p. 308.

CHAPTER TWO

1   Frank Merkling, "This Week," *Opera News*, 17 December 1966, p. 2.
2   Richard Strauss and Romain Rolland, *Correspondence*, ed. Rollo Myers (Berkeley: University of California Press, 1968), p. 166.
3   Erich Leinsdorf, *Erich Leinsdorf on Music* (Portland, OR: Amadeus Press, 1997), p. 190.
4   Hugo von Hofmannsthal to Richard Strauss, 15 April 1922, in Hanns Hammelmann and Ewald Osers, ed. and trans., *A Working Friendship: The Correspondence between Richard Strauss and Hugo von Hofmannsthal* (New York: Random House, 1962), p. 351.
5   Strauss & Rolland, *Correspondence*, p. 166.
6   Irene Dalis, "Between Two Worlds," *Opera News*, 17 December 1966, p. 16.
7   Hofmannsthal to Strauss, 25 July 1914, in Hammelmann and Osers, *A Working Friendship*, p. 209.
8   Ibid.
9   Christa Ludwig, *In My Own Voice: Memoirs* (New York: Limelight Editions, 1999), p. 137.

10   Ibid., p. 124.

11   Harold C. Schonberg, review, performance of 2 October 1966, *New York Times*, quoted in *Metropolitan Opera Annals 1966–76*, p. 17.

12   Strauss to Hofmannsthal, 8 March 1920, in Hammelmann and Osers, *A Working Friendship*, p. 335.

13   Hofmannsthal to Strauss, 10 March 1920, in Hammelmann, p. 336.

14   John W. Freeman, "Plus One," *Opera News*, 10 December 1966, p. 13.

15   Eric Salzman, "The World of Wieland Wagner," *Opera News*, 21 January 1967, p. 8.

16   *The Music Criticism of Hugo Wolf*, trans. and ed. Henry Pleasants (New York: Holmes & Meier Publishers, 1978), p. 147.

17   Ann M. Lingg, "Made to Measure," *Opera News*, 21 January 1967, p. 16.

18   Ludwig, *In My Own Voice*, p. 85.

19   Ibid., p. 86.

20   Irving Kolodin, review, performance of 19 February 1967, *Saturday Review*, quoted in *Metropolitan Opera Annals 1966–76*, pp. 21–22.

21   Pleasants, *Criticism of Hugo Wolf*, p. 115.

22   Giuseppe Verdi to Clara Maffei, 29 January 1853, quoted in Mary Jane Phillips-Matz, *Verdi: A Biography* (Oxford: Oxford University Press, 1993), p. 309.

23   Rudolf Bing to Max Rudolf, 27 June 1951, Met Archives.

24   Elizabeth Bowen, *Friends and Relations* (Harmondsworth, England: Penguin Books, 1943), p. 81.

25   Paul Fresnay, "Verdi à Paris," *Voltaire*, 29 March 1886, quoted in Marcello Conati, ed., *Encounters with Verdi* (Ithaca, NY: Cornell University Press, 1984), p. 168.

26   *Verdi: The Man in His Letters*, ed. Franz Werfel and Paul Stefan, trans. Edward Downes (New York: Vienna House, 1973), p. 359.

27   Jeannie Williams, *Jon Vickers: A Hero's Life* (Boston: Northeastern University Press, 1999), p. 153.

28   Bruce Burroughs, "Serene Lucine: The Celestial Voice," *Opera Quarterly* 9, no. 1 (1992): p. 96.

CHAPTER THREE

1   Martin Mayer, *High Fidelity, Musical America*, quoted in *Metropolitan Opera Annals 1966–1976*, p. 21.

2   Williams, *A Hero's Life*, p. 149.

3   Bing, *5000 Nights*, p. 201.

4   Max Loppert, "Jon Vickers on *Peter Grimes*," *Opera*, August 1984, p. 840.

5   Bing, *5000 Nights*, p. 211.

6   Elizabeth Forbes, "Communicator," *Opera News*, 11 February 1967, p. 16.

7   Martin Mayer, *The Met: One Hundred Years of Grand Opera* (New York: Simon & Schuster and the Metropolitan Opera Guild, 1983), p. 308.

8 Douglas Watt, review, performance of 17 March 1967, *New York Daily News*, quoted in *Metropolitan Opera Annals 1966–76*, p. 22.

9 Marvin David Levy, "Music of the Spheres: Sputnik?" *Opera News*, 27 January 1958, p. 28.

CHAPTER FOUR

1 Gerald Fitzgerald, "Charmer," *Opera News*, 3 December 1966, p. 16.

2 Fritzi Scheff, "Tales of an Enfant Terrible: Chapters from the Unpublished Memoirs of Fritzi Scheff," *Opera News*, 24 January 1944, pp. 10–11.

3 Eugene Rizzo, "D Is for Deutekom," *Opera News*, 31 October 1970, p. 25.

4 Ann M. Lingg, "A Hard Life," *Opera News*, 8 April 1967, p. 13.

CHAPTER FIVE

1 Harold Rosenthal, "Anna Moffo" [biographical notice], *The New Grove Dictionary of Opera* (New York: Grove's Dictionaries of Music, 1992), vol. 3, p. 421.

2 Peter G. Davis, *The American Singer* (New York: Doubleday, 1997), p. 467.

3 Beverly Johnson, quoted in the *New York Times*, 5 May 1977.

4 Francis Rizzo, "The Pinnacle," *Opera News*, 4 April 1970, p. 16.

5 Paul Jaretzki to Bing, 17 June 1963, Met Archives.

6 Robert D. Daniels, "A Sense of Timing," *Opera News*, 27 December 1966, p. 20.

7 Rizzo, "Pinnacle."

8 Paul Jackson, *Sign-off for the Old Met: The Metropolitan Opera Broadcasts: 1950–1966* (Portland, OR: Amadeus Press, 1997), p. 492.

9 Ann M. Lingg, "Speaking of *Cav/Pag*," *Opera News*, 13 February, 1971, p. 24

10 James A. Drake, *Richard Tucker: A Biography* (New York: E. P. Dutton, 1984), pp. 236, 237.

11 Bing to Richard Tucker, 6 November 1957, Met Archives.

12 Quoted in Rick Lyman, "Watching Movies with Barry Levinson: Telling Stories Simply," *New York Times*, 26 April 2002.

13 Drake, *Richard Tucker*, pp. 186–190.

14 Robert D. Daniels, "Fleet and Flexible," *Opera News*, 13 April 1968, p. 27.

15 Donal Henahan, review, performance of 10 October 1967, *New York Times*, quoted in *Metropolitan Opera Annals 1966–76*, p. 41.

16 Robert D. Daniels, "Out of Egypt," *Opera News*, 13 January 1968, p. 26.

17 Harold Schonberg, review, performance of 19 September 1968, *New York Times*, quoted in *Metropolitan Opera Annals 1966–76*, p. 40.

18 Regina Resnik, telephone interview with author, 26 March 1995.

19 Bing, *A Knight at the Opera* (New York: G. P. Putnam's Sons, 1981), p. 169.

20 Frank Merkling, "This Week," *Opera News*, 20 April 1968, p. 2.

21 Piotr Ilyich Tchaikovsky to Modest Tchaikovsky, 18 July 1880, in Piotr Ilyich Tchaikovsky, *Letters to His Family: An Autobiography*, trans. Galina von Meck (New York: Stein and Day Publishers, 1981), p. 246.

22 Jackson, *Sign-off for the Old Met*, p. 350.

23 Winton Dean, *Bizet* (London: J. M. Dent & Sons, 1975), p. 226.

CHAPTER SIX

1 Conrad L. Osborne, review, performance of 8 February 1968, *Financial Times* (London), quoted in *Metropolitan Opera Annals 1966–1976*, p. 43.

2 Julian Budden, *The Operas of Verdi* (New York: Oxford University Press, 1973), vol. 1, p. 446.

3 Virgil Thomson, "Strauss and Wagner," in *Music Reviewed: 1940–1954* (New York: Vintage books, 1967), p. 82.

4 Julian Budden, *The Operas of Verdi* (New York: Oxford University Press, 1978), vol. 2, p. 102.

5 Harvey E. Phillips, "Backstage with Boccanegra," *Opera News*, 14 December 1968, p. 26.

6 Leinsdorf, *Erich Leinsdorf on Music*, p. 236.

7 Verdi to Giulio Ricordi, 18 March 1899, quoted in William Weaver, *Verdi: A Documentary Study* (New York: Thames and Hudson, n. d.), p. 251.

CHAPTER SEVEN

1 Plácido Domingo, *My First Forty Years* (New York: Penguin Books, 1984), p. 71.

2 Ibid., pp. 73–74.

3 Ibid.

4 Ippolito Valletta, in the *Nuova Antologia*, quoted in Budden, *Puccini: His Life and Works* (Oxford: Oxford University Press, 2002), p. 199.

5 William Ashbrook and Harold Powers, *Puccini's Turandot: The End of the Great Tradition* (Princeton, NJ: Princeton University Press, 1991), p. 143.

6 Speight Jenkins, "The Unknown Princess," *Opera News*, 22 March 1969, p. 30.

7 Donal Henahan, review, performance of 25 March 1968, *New York Times*, quoted in *Metropolitan Opera Annals 1966–76*, p. 44.

8 Giacomo Puccini to Rosina Storchio, 22 February 1904, in Eugenio Gara, ed., *Carteggi Pucciniani* (Milan: G. Ricordi, 1958), p. 261.

9 Mary Jane Phillips-Matz, *Puccini: A Biography* (Boston: Northeastern University Press, 2002), p. 146.

10 Puccini to Carlo Clausetti, 9 August 1895, in Gara, *Carteggi Pucciniani*, p. 117.

11 Robert C. Marsh, *Dialogues and Discoveries: James Levine—His Life and His Music* (New York: Scribner, 1998), p. 113.

12 Harold Schonberg, *New York Times*, quoted in *Metropolitan Opera Annals 1966–1976*, p. 75.

13 Steven Blier, on "Singers' Hall of Fame," Met broadcast, 15 January 2000.

CHAPTER EIGHT

1 Anthony Trollope, *Can You Forgive Her?* (London: Oxford University Press, 1968), p. 204.

2 Erich Leinsdorf, *Cadenza* (Boston: Houghton Mifflin, 1976), p. 98.

3 Speight Jenkins, "Enchantress," *Opera News*, 10 February 1968, p. 14.

4 Ludwig, *In My Own Voice*, p. 88.

5 Régine Crespin, *On Stage, Off Stage: A Memoir*, trans. G. S. Bourdain (Boston: Northeastern University Press, 1997), p. 170.

6 Bing, *5000 Nights*, p. 346.

7 Carolyn Abbate, *Unsung Voices: Opera and Musical Narrative in the Nineteenth Century* (Princeton, NJ: Princeton University Press, 1991), p. 215.

8 Mary Garden and Louis Biancolli, *Mary Garden's Story* (New York: Simon & Schuster, 1951), p. 95.

9 Crespin, *On Stage, Off Stage*, p. 172.

10 Ibid., p. 165.

11 Bing, *5000 Nights*, p. 348.

12 Ibid., p. 346.

13 Ibid.

14 C. J. Luten, "Self-made Maestro," *Opera News*, 3 April 1971, p. 27.

15 *Cosima Wagner's Diaries*, ed. Martin Gregor-Dellin and Dietrich Mack, trans. Geoffrey Skelton (New York: Harcourt Brace Jovanovich, 1977), p. 714.

CHAPTER NINE

1 Arnold Schoenberg to Alban Berg, 11 January 1926, in *The Berg–Schoenberg Correspondence: Selected Letters*, ed. Juliane Brand, Christopher Hailey, and Donald Harris (New York: W. W. Norton, 1987), p. 342.

2 Berg to Schoenberg, 13 March 1926, Brand, Hailey, and Harris, *Berg–Schoenberg Correspondence*, p. 344.

3 Henry Krehbiel, review, performance of 23 December 1909, *New York Herald Tribune*, quoted in William H. Seltsam, *Metropolitan Opera Annals* (New York: H. W. Wilson Co. and the Metropolitan Opera Guild, 1947), p. 212.

CHAPTER TEN

1 Bing, *5000 Nights*, p. 356.

2   Ibid., p. 350.

3   Ibid., p. 359.

4   Raymond Ericson, review, performance of 25 October 1971, *New York Times*, quoted in *Metropolitan Opera Annals 1966–1976*, p. 111.

5   Theodore Fenner, *Leigh Hunt and Opera Criticism: The "Examiner" Years, 1808–1821* (Lawrence: University Press of Kansas, 1972), p. 207.

6   Glenn Loney, "Nature Translated," *Opera News*, 15 April 1972, p. 21.

7   John Warrick, *Carl Maria von Weber* (New York: Macmillan, 1968), p. 212.

8   David Bamberger, "An Opera for Grown-ups," *Opera News*, 25 December 1971/1 January 1972, p.18.

9   Harold Schonberg, review, performance of 6 November 1967, *New York Times*, quoted in *Metropolitan Opera Annals 1966–1976*, p. 41.

10   Ernest Newman, *Stories of the Great Operas and Their Composers* (Garden City, NY: Garden City Publishing, 1928–30), vol. 3, p. 267.

11   Bing to Herman and Jaretzki, 24 August 1964, Met Archives.

12   "Biographies in Music: Francis Robinson," Met broadcast, 8 January 1972.

13   Reynaldo Hahn, *On Singers and Singing: Lectures and an Essay*, trans. Léopold Simoneau (Portland OR: Amadeus Press, 1990), p. 217.

14   Henry Krehbiel, review, performance of 20 April 1894, *New York Tribune*, in *The Metropolitan Opera: The First Twenty-five Years 1883–1908*, Paul E. Eisler (Croton-on-Hudson, NY: North River Press, 1984), p. 193.

15   W. J. Henderson, review, performance of 20 April 1894, *New York Times*, ibid.

16   Ibid., p. 192.

17   Quoted in Gale F. Wiley, "The New Barry . . .," *Opera News*, 29 January 1972, p. 26.

18   Ibid.

19   Debussy to Ernest Chausson, in François Lesure, ed., and Roger Nichols, ed. and trans., *Debussy Letters* (London: Faber and Faber, 1987), p. 62.

20   Debussy to Hector Dufranne, 26 October 1906, in Lesure and Nichols, p. 173.

21   Debussy to André Messager, 9 May 1902, in Lesure and Nichols, p. 126.

CHAPTER ELEVEN

1   Eugène Delacroix, quoted in Tom Prideaux et al, *The World of Delacroix 1798–1863* (New York: Time Inc., 1966), p. 92.

2   Bing, *5000 Nights*, p. 203.

3   John W. Freeman, "Böhm in Italian," *Opera News*, 8 April 1972, p. 26.

4   Sherrill Milnes, *American Aria: From Farm Boy to Opera Star*, with contributions by Dennis McGovern (New York: Schirmer Books, 1998), p. 91.

5   Martin Mayer, review, performance of 25 February 1972, *High Fidelity/ Musical America*, quoted in *Metropolitan Opera Annals 1966–1976*, p. 114.

6   Julian Budden, *The Operas of Verdi* (New York: Oxford University Press, 1981), vol. 3, p. 21.

7   "Sir Rudolf Bing: Twenty-two Metropolitan Years," Met broadcast, 22 April 1972. Cyril Ritchard interviews Bing.

CHAPTER TWELVE

1   "Sir Rudolf Bing: Twenty-two Metropolitan years," Met broadcast, 22 April 1972. Cyril Ritchard interviews Bing; Metropolitan Opera artists sing tributes.

2   *Nicolai Gedda: My Life and Art*, as told to Aino Sellermark Gedda (Portland OR: Amadeus Press, 1999), p. 174.

3   Ibid., p. 175.

4   Frank Merkling, "Four-Year Term," *Opera News*, 14 January 1967, p. 16.

5   Joseph Volpe, interview by Robert Marx, Met broadcast, 2 December 2000 ("Met Marathon").

CHAPTER THIRTEEN

1   George S. Moore, "In Memoriam: Goeran Gentele," *Opera News*, pp. 8–9.

2   Dean, *Bizet*, pp. 294–95.

3   Ibid., p. 221.

4   Lorna Levant, "The Cast," *Opera News*, 12 January 1974, p. 19.

5   Ibid.

6   Ibid.

7   Saint-Simon, quoted in Pierre Schneider et al, *The World of Watteau: 1684–1721* (New York: Time Inc., 1967), p. 32.

8   Harvey E. Phillips, "A Tenor of Line," *Opera News*, 6 January 1973, p. 23.

9   Ibid., p. 24.

10   Marsh, *Dialogues and Discoveries*, p. 34.

11   Rosa Ponselle, interview by Boris Goldovsky, "Opera News on the Air," initially broadcast 27 March 1954, repeated on Met broadcast of 17 March 1973.

12   Gerald Fitzgerald, "Good Colleagues," *Opera News*, 17 March 1973, p. 21.

13   Renata Scotto and Octavio Roca, *Scotto: More than a Diva* (Garden City, NY: Doubleday, 1984), p. 77.

14   Irving Kolodin, *The Metropolitan Opera, 1883–1966* (New York: Alfred A. Knopf, 1966), p. 608.

15   Verdi to Antonio Lanari, 21 January 1847, quoted in Werfel and Stefan, *Verdi*, p. 121.

16   Verdi to Francesco Maria Piave, quoted in Phillips-Matz, *Verdi*, pp. 331–32.

17   Harvey E. Phillips, "Mr. and Mrs. Macbeth," *Opera News*, 3 February 1973, p. 15.

CHAPTER FOURTEEN

1   Verdi to Ricordi, 10 July 1871, in Hans Busch, coll. and trans., *Verdi's Aida: The History of an Opera in Letters and Documents* (Minneapolis: University of Minnesota Press, 1978), pp. 182–83.
2   Drake, *Richard Tucker*, pp. 255–257.
3   Francis Robinson, "Tribute to Richard Tucker," *Opera News*, 8 February 1975, p. 8.
4   Robert Jacobson, "Viewpoint," *Opera News*, 8 February 1975, p. 5.
5   John Gruen, "Lucky Star," *Opera News*, 6 December 1975, p. 18.

CHAPTER FIFTEEN

1   Fenner, *Leigh Hunt*, p. 210.
2   Robert Jacobson, "And a New Marschallin," *Opera News*, 23 February 1974, p. 14.
3   Frieda Hempel, *My Golden Age of Singing*, annotated by William R. Moran (Portland OR: Amadeus Press, 1998), p. 122.
4   Schuyler Chapin, *Musical Chairs: A Life in the Arts* (New York: G. P. Putnam's Sons, 1977) pp. 359–367; Leinsdorf, *Cadenza*, pp. 296–303; Williams, *A Hero's Life*, pp. 185–189.
5   Williams, *A Hero's Life*, p. 188.
6   Chapin, *Musical Chairs,* pp. 363–64.
7   Leinsdorf, *Cadenza*, p. 300.
8   Ibid.
9   Williams, *A Hero's Life*, p. 185.
10 Leinsdorf, *Cadenza*, p. 302.
11 Williams, *A Hero's Life*, p. 188.
12 Hofmannsthal to Strauss, 6 June 1910, in Hammelmann and Osers, *A Working Friendship*, p. 58.
13 Leinsdorf, *Cadenza*, p. 302.
14 Chicago Lyric Opera broadcast, intermission, 16 May 2001.
15 Leinsdorf, *Cadenza*, p. 296.
16 Donal Henahan, review, performance of 5 March 1975, *New York Times*, quoted in *Metropolitan Opera Annals 1966–1976*, p. 174.
17 Raymond Erickson, review, performance of 15 March 1975, *New York Times*, 16 March 1975.
18 Richard Wagner to Anton Pusinelli, 12 January 1870, *The Letters of Richard Wagner to Anton Pusinelli*, ed. and trans. Elbert Lenrow (New York: Vienna House, 1972), p. 225.
19 Gustave Flaubert to Ivan Turgenev, quoted in Herbert Lottman, *Flaubert: A Biography* (New York: Fromm International Publishing, 1990), p. 272.

CHAPTER SIXTEEN

1 Chapin, *Musical Chairs*, p. 352.
2 Pleasants, *Criticism of Hugo Wolf*, p. 79.
3 Joan Sutherland and Richard Bonynge, interviews by Terry McEwen, "Opera News on the Air," Met broadcast, 2 February 1974.
4 Quaintance Eaton, *Sutherland and Bonynge: An Intimate Biography* (New York: Dodd, Mead, 1987), p. 154.
5 Ibid., p. 155.

CHAPTER SEVENTEEN

1 "Opera News on the Air," Met broadcast, 9 March 1974.
2 V. S. Pritchett, *The Gentle Barbarian: The Life and Work of Turgenev* (New York: Random House, 1977), p. 63.
3 Gedda, *My Life and Art*, p. 107.
4 "Opera News on the Air," Met broadcast, 18 March 1974.
5 Chapin, *Musical Chairs*, pp. 345–46.
6 Ludwig, *In My Own Voice*, p. 92.
7 Peter G. Davis, review, performance of 22 October 1973, *London Times*, quoted in *Metropolitan Opera Annals 1966–1976*, p. 153.
8 Quoted in Williams, *A Hero's Life*, pp. 184–85.
9 Ibid., p. 141.
10 "Peter Pears and Steuart Bedford Analyze *Death in Venice* with Edward Downes," intermission feature, Met broadcast, 14 December 1974.
11 Barbara Fischer-Williams, "Singing-Actor Shirley-Quirk," *Opera News*, 14 December 1974, p. 26.
12 "Pears and Bedford Analyze *Death in Venice*," pre-curtain feature.
13 Ibid., intermission feature.
14 Jane Austen and Another Lady, *Sanditon* (New York: New American Library, 1976), p. 11.
15 "Pears and Bedford Analyze *Death in Venice*," intermission feature.
16 Ibid., pre-curtain feature.
17 Williams, *A Hero's Life*, p. 196.
18 Robert Jacobson, "Varnay Revisited," *Opera News*, 21 December 1974, p. 24.
19 "Musical and dramatic analysis of Bluebeard's Castle by Boris Goldovsky," Met broadcast, 22 February 1975.
20 Deborah Seabury, "Sharing the Bill," *Opera News*, 22 February 1975, p. 15.
21 George Jellinek, "First and Only," *Opera News*, 22 February 1975, p. 12.
22 Robert Jacobson, "At Long Last!," *Opera News*, 19 April 1975, p. 22–23.
23 *Central City Opera: Looking Back over Sixty Years 1932–1992* (Central City Opera House Association, 1992), p. 12.

24 Harold Schonberg, review, performance of 7 April 1975, *New York Times*, quoted in *Metropolitan Opera Annals 1966–1976*, p. 175.

25 Beverly Sills, interview by Martin Bernheimer (taped in June 1975 after a rehearsal for opening night of the Hollywood Bowl; broadcast on KDIB-PBS, 30 September 1975).

26 George Meredith, "The Lark Ascending" in *Minor Victorian Poets*, ed. John D. Cooke (New York: Charles Scribner's Sons, 1928), p. 303.

27 Sills, interview by Bernheimer.

CHAPTER EIGHTEEN

1   Met broadcast, intermission, 16 September 1966.

2   Boris Goldovsky, interview by Edward Downes, Met broadcasts, 20 January 1973 and 10 February 1973.

3   Boris Goldovsky, "Boris Goldovsky with 8 Valkyries" (commentary), Met broadcast, 16 December 1972.

4   Alberta Masiello, interview by Cyril Ritchard, "Opera News on the Air," Met broadcast, 7 April 1973.

5   "Opera Quiz," Met broadcast, 6 March 1976.

6   Andrew Porter, "Singers: High, Low and In Between" (commentary), "Opera News on the Air," Met broadcast, 10 April 1976.

7   "Opera Quiz," Met broadcast, 8 April 1972.

8   "Opera Quiz," Met broadcast, 3 January 1976.

9   "Opera Quiz," Met broadcast, 24 January 1970.

10 "Opera Quiz," Met broadcast, 23 March 1968.

11 "Opera Quiz," Met broadcast, 16 March 1968.

12 "Opera Quiz," Met broadcast, 5 April 1975.

13 "Opera Quiz," Met broadcast, 15 April 1972.

14 "Biographies in Music," Met broadcast, 7 December 1968.

15 Franco Zeffirelli, interview by Edward Downes, "Opera News on the Air," Met broadcast, 8 April 1972.

16 John Coveney, "Honoring Lotte Lehmann's Eighty-fifth Birthday," Met broadcast, 24 February 1973.

17 Dorothy Kirsten, farewell speech, Met broadcast, 27 December 1975.

18 "Singers' Roundtable," Met broadcast, 15 December 1973.

19 "Singers' Roundtable," Met broadcast, 20 March 1976.

20 "Singers' Roundtable," Met broadcast, 2 March 1974.

21 "Singers' Roundtable," Met broadcast, 18 April 1970.

22 Franco Zeffirelli, commentary, "Opera News on the Air," Met broadcast, 8 April 1972.

23 Schuyler Chapin, conversation with Nancy Hanks, Met broadcast, 2 March 1974.

24 Schuyler Chapin, seasonal farewell, Met broadcast, 21 April 1973.

25 Schuyler Chapin, seasonal farewell, Met broadcast, 19 April 1975.

26 Chapin, *Musical Chairs*, pp. 397–400.

27 Anthony A. Bliss, welcoming remarks, "Opera News on the Air," Met broadcast, 6 December 1975.

28 Joseph Volpe, end-of-season interview, Met broadcast, 21 April 2001.

29 Schuyler Chapin, remarks, Met broadcast, 25 January 1975.

30 Francis Robinson, tribute to Richard Tucker, Met broadcast, 11 January 1975.

31 Francis Robinson, tributes to Milton Cross, Met broadcasts, 26 December 1970 and 4 January 1975.

CHAPTER NINETEEN

1 Milnes, *American Aria*, p. 91.

2 Robert Jacobson, "Kiri," *Opera News*, May 1974, p. 26.

3 Ibid.

4 Bing, *5000 Nights*, p. 201.

5 Gerald Fitzgerald, "Cherry Blossom Time," *Opera News*, 3 April 1976, p. 35.

6 Donal Henahan, review, *New York Times*, 31 January 1975.

7 Burroughs, "Serene Lucine," p. 41.

8 Puccini to Arturo Toscanini, 27 December 1900, in Gara, *Carteggi Pucciniani*, p. 204.

9 Lorna Levant, "People of Peking," *Opera News*, 28 December 1974, p. 25.

CHAPTER TWENTY

1 "Opera Quiz," Met broadcast, 25 January 1975.

2 Karl F. Reuling, "Vivat Van Dam," *Opera News*, 13 December 1975, p. 34–35.

3 Crespin, *On Stage, Off Stage*, p. 113.

4 Hempel, *My Golden Age*, p. 100.

5 Martin Mayer, "Tatiana! American Mezzo Comes to the Met," *Opera News*, 20 March 1976, p. 22.

6 Marsh, *Dialogues and Discoveries*, p. 107.

CHAPTER TWENTY-ONE

1 Barbara Fischer-Williams, "Joining the Fun," *Opera News*, 24 January 1976, p. 35.

2 Quoted by sports columnist Ron Borges, *Boston Globe*, 18 December 2002.

3 Stephen Wadsworth, "Bonynge on Bel Canto: Interpreting the Early 19th Century," *Opera News*, 28 February 1976, p. 20.

4   Quoted in Elizabeth Forbes, *Mario and Grisi: A Biography* (London: Victor Gollancz, 1985), p. 65.

5   Marsh, *Dialogues and Discoveries*, p. 113.

6   Stephen E. Rubin, "Price on Price," *Opera News*, 6 March 1976, p. 17.

7   Verdi to Ricordi, 6 December 1871, in Busch, *Verdi's Aida*, p. 260.

8   Verdi to Opprandino Arrivabene, 9 February 1872, in Busch, *Verdi's Aida*, p. 281.

CHAPTER TWENTY-TWO

1   Anthony A. Bliss, seasonal farewell, Met broadcast, 17 April 1976.

2   Schuyler Chapin, remarks, Met broadcast, 25 January, 1975.

3   Anthony A. Bliss, with James Levine, seasonal farewell, Met broadcast, 17 April 1976.

4   Joseph Volpe, end-of-season interview, Met broadcast, 21 April 2001.

5   Ibid.

6   James Levine, seasonal farewell, Met broadcast, 17 April 1976.

METROPOLITAN OPERA

SEASON 1970 – 1971   LINCOLN CENTER PLAZA

Saturday Afternoon, December 19, 1970, at 2:00

SUBSCRIPTION PERFORMANCE

LAST TIME THIS SEASON

VINCENZO BELLINI

Norma

Opera in four acts   Libretto by Felice Romani

Conductor: Richard Bonynge

Production by Paul-Emile Deiber

Sets and costumes designed by Desmond Heeley

Stage Director: Patrick Tavernia

Norma	Joan Sutherland
Adalgisa	Marilyn Horne
Pollione	Franco Tagliavini
Oroveso	Ezio Flagello
Clotilda	Carlotta Ordassy
Flavio	Rod MacWherter

Chorus Master: Kurt Adler

Musical Preparation: Alberta Masiello

This production of NORMA *was made possible by a generous and deeply appreciated gift from Mrs. John D. Rockefeller, Jr.*

KNABE PIANO USED EXCLUSIVELY

The audience is respectfully, but urgently, requested not to interrupt the music with applause

THIS PERFORMANCE WILL END AT APPROXMATELY 5:40

Program for broadcast of *Norma* on 19 December 1970.

Operas and Casts of the Broadcasts 1966–1976

Major roles in all broadcast performances from 1966–67 through 1975–76 are listed in this table. Italicized dates indicate performances discussed in detail in the text. Symbols preceding the performance date indicate a translation from the original language into English (E), French (F), or Italian (I).

Adriana Lecouvreur (Cilea)

Date	Conductor	Adriana	Princess	Maurizio	Michonnet	Abbé	Bouillon	Quinault
19 Apr '69	Cleva	Tebaldi	Dalis	Corelli	Colzani	Franke	Meredith	Plishka

Aida (Verdi)

Date	Conductor	Aida	Amneris	Radamès	Amonasro	Ramfis	King	Messenger
25 Feb '67	Schippers	Price	Bumbry	Bergonzi	Merrill	Hines	Sgarro	Nagy
20 Jan '68	Schippers	Tucci	Dalis	McCracken	Milnes	Giaiotti	Sgarro	Nagy
3 Jan '70	Molinari-Pradelli	Price	Dalis	Thomas	Merrill	Macurdy	Michalski	MacWherter
26 Dec '70	Cleva	Arroyo	Bumbry	McCracken	Colzani	Flagello	Plishka	MacWherter
24 Feb '73	Molinari-Pradelli	Arroyo	Bumbry	Tucker	MacNeil	Tozzi	Morris/Karlsrud	MacWherter
6 Mar '76	Levine	Price	Horne	Domingo	MacNeil	Giaiotti	Morris	Anthony

Antony and Cleopatra (Barber)

Date	Conductor	Cleopatra	Charmian	Iras	Octavia	Caesar	Antony	Enobarbus	Alexas	Agrippa
16 Sep '66	Schippers	Price	Elias	Amparán	Pracht	Thomas	Díaz	Flagello	Michalski	Macurdy

Ariadne auf Naxos (Strauss)

Date	Conductor	Ariadne	Zerbinetta	Composer	Bacchus	Music	Mtr. Harlekin	Echo	Najade
28 Mar '70	Böhm	Rysanek	Grist	Lear	King	Dooley	Uppman	Clements	Pracht
20 Mar '76	Levine	Caballé	R. Welting	Troyanos	Remedios	Dooley	Titus	Norden	Weidinger

L'Assedio di Corinto (Rossini)

Date	Conductor	Pamira	Ismene	Neocle	Cleomene	Maometto
19 Apr '75	Schippers	Sills	Norden	Verrett	Theyard	Díaz
17 Jan '76	Woitach	Sills	A. J. Smith	Verrett	Di Giuseppe	Díaz

Un Ballo in Maschera (Verdi)

Date	Conductor	Amelia	Oscar	Ulrica	Riccardo	Renato	Sam	Tom
6 Apr '68	Schippers	Price	Peters	Rankin	Prevedi	Merrill	Alvary	Sgarro
30 Jan '71	Molinari-Pradelli	Arroyo	Peters	Dunn	Domingo	Merrill	Plishka	Dobriansky
27 Jan '73	P. H. Adler	Cruz-Romo	Robinson	Dalis	Tucker	Milnes	Morris	Best
6 Dec '75	H. Lewis	Ross	Peters	Forrester	Morell	Merrill	Michalski	Booth

Il Barbiere di Siviglia (Rossini)

Date	Conductor	Rosina	Berta	Almaviva	Figaro	Basilio	Bartolo	Fiorello
* 7 Nov '68 (TV)	Bonynge	Berganza	Love	Alva	Sereni	Tozzi	Corena	Boucher

*Taped for broadcast in Japan, televised on 4 January 1969

Date	Conductor	Rosina	Berta	Almaviva	Figaro	Basilio	Bartolo	Fiorello
11 Jan '69	Bonynge	Peters	Love	Alva	Sereni	Tozzi	Corena	Boucher
20 Feb '71	Schippers	Horne	Kraft	Di Giuseppe	Milnes	Tozzi	Corena	Gibbs
7 Apr '73	Levine	Horne	Kraft	Di Giuseppe	Prey	Tozzi	Corena	Goodloe
2 Mar '74	Pritchard	Elias	Love	Goeke	Walker	Tozzi	Flagello	Holloway
31 Jan '76	Nelson	Von Stade	Munzer	Davies	Stilwell	Morris	Corena	Goodloe

Bluebeard's Castle (Bartók)

Date	Conductor	Judith	Bluebeard
E 22 Feb '75	Ehrling	Verrett	Ward

La Bohème (Puccini)

Date	Conductor	Mimì	Musetta	Rodolfo	Marcello	Schaunard	Colline	Benoit
4 Feb '67	Cleva	Stratas	Bower	G. Raimondi	Sereni	Harvuot	Tozzi	Alvary
25 Jan '69	K. Adler	Tucci	Fenn	Labò	Walker	Goodloe	Díaz	Corena
24 Jan '70	Cleva	Tebaldi	C. Carson	Tucker	Walker	Boucher	Siepi	Plishka
6 Mar '71	Cleva	Kirsten	Boky	Kónya	Sereni	Goodloe	Hines	Best
20 Jan '73	H. Lewis	Lorengar	Boky	Tucker	Walker	Goodloe	Plishka	Dobriansky
16 Feb '74	Segerstam	Caballé	Niska	Corelli	Cossa	Holloway	Macurdy	Dobriansky

Boris Godunov (Mussorgsky)

Date	Conductor	Marina	Dimitri	Rangoni	Boris	Pimen	Varlaam	Shuiski
25 Jan '75	Schippers	Dunn	Theyard	Dooley	Talvela	Plishka	Gramm	Nagy
24 Jan '76	Kord	Dunn	W. Lewis	Meredith	Talvela	Gill	Michalski	Nagy

Carmen (Bizet)

Date	Conductor	Carmen	Micaela	Frasquita	Mercedes	Don José	Escamillo	Zuniga
20 Apr '68	Lombard	Bumbry	Freni	Sukis	Baldwin	Tucker	Díaz	Meredith
15 Mar '69	Mehta	Resnik	Raskin	De Paul	Forst	Tucker	Díaz	Meredith
6 Feb '71	Morel	Baldani	Amara	De Paul	Forst	Domingo	Merrill	Meredith
1 Jan '72	Örvös	Baldani	Amara	De Paul	Love	Tucker	Merrill	Morris
10 Mar '73	H. Lewis	Horne	Amara	Amara	Love	McCracken	Krause	Gramm
12 Jan '74	H. Lewis	Horne	Amara	Weidinger	Baldwin	McCracken	Reardon	Dobriansky
13 Dec '75	H. Lewis	Crespin	Ricciarelli	Di Franco	Baldwin	W. Lewis	Van Dam	Best

Cavalleria Rusticana (Mascagni)

Date	Conductor	Santuzza	Lola	Lucia	Turiddu	Alfio
7 Feb '70	Bernstein	Bumbry	Casei	Ordassy	Corelli	Cassel
13 Feb '71	Cleva	Cossotto	Casei	Kraft	Di Giuseppe	Meredith
18 Jan '75	Nelson	Bumbry	Grillo	Ordassy	Theyard	Colzani

Les Contes d'Hoffmann (Offenbach)

Date	Conductor	Olympia	Giulietta	Antonia	Nicklausse	Hoffmann	4 Villains	4 Servants
10 Apr '71	Baudo	Boky	Crespin	Amara	Von Stade	Gedda	Bacquier	Velis
2 Feb '74	Bonynge	Sutherland	Sutherland	Sutherland	Tourangeau	Theyard	Stewart	Velis

Così Fan Tutte (Mozart)

Date	Conductor	Fiordiligi	Dorabella	Despina	Ferrando	Guglielmo	Alfonso
22 Jan '72	Pritchard	Zylis-Gara	Elias	Stratas	Bottazzo	Uppman	Berry
20 Dec '75	Kord	C. Carson	Tourangeau	Boky	Di Giuseppe	L. Carlson	Corena

Death in Venice (Britten)

Date	Conductor	Aschenbach	7 Roles	Apollo	Tadzio	Porter	Clerk/Father	Mother/Beggar
14 Dec '74	Bedford	Pears	Shirley-Quirk	Velis	Pitts	Garrison	Burchinal	Golden

Don Carlo (Verdi)

Date	Conductor	Elisabetta	Eboli	Carlo	Rodrigo	Philip	Inquisitor	Friar	Voice
I 14 Feb '70	K. Adler	Kabaivanska	Bumbry	Corelli	Merrill	Tozzi	Michalski	Karlsrud	Kalil
I 22 Apr '72	Molinari-Pradelli	Caballé	Bumbry	Corelli	Milnes	Siepi	Macurdy	Plishka	Amara

Don Giovanni (Mozart)

Date	Conductor	Anna	Elvira	Zerlina	Ottavio	Giovanni	Leporello	Masetto	Commandant
28 Jan '67	Böhm	Sutherland	Lorengar	Hurley	Gedda	Siepi	Corena	Uppman	Giaiotti
4 Jan '69	Varviso	Arroyo	Zylis-Gara	Elias	Schreier	Siepi	Flagello	Uppman	Macurdy
20 Mar '71	Krips	Moser	Zylis-Gara	Pilou	Gedda	Siepi	Corena	Uppman	Plishka
3 Mar '73	Maag	Moser	Lorengar	Elias	Shirley	Siepi	Flagello	Uppman	Macurdy
13 Apr '74	Levine	Price	Zylis-Gara	Stratas	Burrows	Milnes	Berry	Michalski	Morris
1 Feb '75	Rudolf	Moser	Te Kanawa	Peters	Burrows	Morris	Flagello	Michalski	Gill

Don Pasquale (Donizetti)

Date	Conductor	Norina	Ernesto	Malatesta	Pasquale	Notary
5 Dec '70	Franci	Grist	Kraus	Krause	Corena	Carelli

Elektra (Strauss)

Date	Conductor	Elektra	Chrysothemis	Klytämnestra	Aegisth	Orest	Overseer
10 Dec '66	Schippers	Nilsson	Rysanek	Resnik	King	Dooley	Ordassy
27 Feb '71	Böhm	Nilsson	Rysanek	Madeira	Nagy	Stewart	Ordassy
10 Jan '76	Hollreiser	Schröder-Feinen	Knie	Varnay	Nagy	Dooley	Ordassy

L'Elisir d'Amore (Donizetti)

Date	Conductor	Adina	Giannetta	Nemorino	Belcore	Dulcamara
16 Mar '68	Cleva	Peters	Clements	Kraus	Sereni	Corena
19 Feb '72	Franci	Scotto	Di Franco	Bergonzi	Sereni	Corena
6 Apr '74	Rudolf	Blegen	Di Franco	Pavarotti	Reardon	Flagello

Falstaff (Verdi)

Date	Conductor	Alice	Nannetta	Meg Page	Quickly	Fenton	Falstaff	Ford
16 Dec '67	Amaducci	Curtin	Raskin	Miller	Barbieri	Alva	Flagello	Guarrera
1 Apr '72	Dohnányi	Tebaldi	Peters	Grillo	Resnik	Alva	Gobbi	Paskalis
5 Apr '75	Levine	Lear	Valente	Grillo	Barbieri	Ahlstedt	MacNeil	Stewart

La Fanciulla del West (Puccini)

Date	Conductor	Minnie	Wowkle	Johnson	Rance	Sonora	Larkens	Jake
14 Mar '70	Behr	Tebaldi	Von Stade	Kónya	Colzani	Harvuot	Gibbs	Macurdy

Faust (Gounod)

Date	Conductor	Marguerite	Siebel	Marthe	Faust	Valentin	Méphistophélès	Wagner
24 Dec '66	Lombard	Tucci	Baldwin	Love	Alexander	Walker	Díaz	Christopher
18 Jan '69	Varviso	Lorengar	Baldwin	Love	Gedda	Merrill	Siepi	Christopher
26 Feb '72	Rich	Zylis-Gara	Von Stade	Godfrey Ben-David	Domingo	Sereni	Tozzi	Christopher
30 Dec '72	Benzi	Boky	Forst	Love	Gedda	Manuguerra	Macurdy	Sgarro

Fidelio (Beethoven)

Date	Conductor	Leonore	Marzelline	Florestan	Jaquino	Pizarro	Rocco	Fernando
2 Jan '71	Böhm	Rysanek	Blegen	Vickers	Dickie	Berry	Tozzi	Macurdy
11 Mar '72	Wallat	Silja	Blegen	Brilioth	Goeke	Dooley	Macurdy	Plishka
7 Feb '76	Mauceri	G. Jones	Blegen	Thomas	Riegel	McIntyre	Macurdy	Morris

La Fille du Régiment (Donizetti)

Date	Conductor	Marie	Marquise	Duchesse	Tonio	Sulpice	Hortensius
25 Mar '72	Bonynge	Sutherland	Sinclair	Welitch	Di Giuseppe	Corena	Velis
6 Jan '73	Bonynge	Sutherland	Resnik	Kraft	Pavarotti	Corena	Velis

Die Fledermaus (Johann Strauss)

Date	Conductor	Rosalinda	Adele	Orlofsky	Eisenstein	Alfred	Falke	Frank
E 7 Jan '67	Allers	Costa	Peters	Carlisle	Reardon	Sergi	Gramm	Bottcher

Der Fliegende Holländer (Wagner)

Date	Conductor	Senta	Mary	Erik	Steersman	Dutchman	Daland
27 Jan '68	Klobucar	Rysanek	Williams	Parly	Olvis	MacNeil	Tozzi
31 Jan '70	Böhm	Rysanek	Chookasian	Kónya	Shirley	Dooley	Macurdy

La Forza del Destino (Verdi)

Date	Conductor	Leonora	Preziosilla	Alvaro	Carlo	Guardiano	Melitone	Marquis
9 Mar '68	Molinari-Pradelli	Price	Pearl	Corelli	Merrill	Hines	Corena	Sgarro
12 Feb '72	Veltri	Price	Casei	Bergonzi	Paskalis	Siepi	Corena	Karlsrud
22 Mar '75	Levine	Amara	Grillo	Vickers	MacNeil	Giaiotti	Bacquier	Morris

Die Frau ohne Schatten (Strauss)

Date	Conductor	Empress	Dyer's Wife	Falcon	Nurse	Voice	Emperor	Barak	Messenger
17 Dec '66	Böhm	Rysanek	C. Ludwig	Ordassy	Dalis	Amparán	King	Berry	Dooley
8 Mar '69	Böhm	Rysanek	C. Ludwig	Ordassy	Dalis	Godfrey Ben-David	King	Berry	Dooley
16 Jan '71	Böhm	Rysanek	C. Ludwig	Ordassy	Dalis	Godfrey Ben-David	Nagy	Berry	Dooley

Der Freischütz (Weber)

Date	Conductor	Agathe	Ännchen	Max	Ottokar	Kilian	Caspar	Hermit	Cuno	Samiel
15 Apr '72	L. Ludwig	Lorengar	Mathis	Kónya	MacWherter	Dobriansky	Feldhoff	Macurdy	Karlsrud	Ebert

Gianni Schicchi (Puccini)

Date	Conductor	Lauretta	Nella	Zita	Rinuccio	Schicchi	Simone	Spinelloccio
22 Feb '75	Ehrling	Blegen	Norden	Dalis	Gibbs	Flagello	Harvuot	Best
3 Jan '76	Ehrling	Mandac	Norden	Chookasian	Gibbs	Flagello	Michalski	Best

La Gioconda (Ponchielli)

Date	Conductor	Gioconda	Laura	Cieca	Enzo	Barnaba	Alvise
15 Apr '67	Cleva	Tebaldi	Elias	Baldani	Morell	MacNeil	Siepi
2 Mar '68	Cleva	Tebaldi	Cossotto	Dunn	Bergonzi	MacNeil	Giaiotti
10 Apr '76	Patanè	Arroyo	Rankin	Chookasian	Raitzin	Manugerra	Morris

Götterdämmerung (Wagner)

Date	Conductor	Brünnhilde	Gutrune	Waltraute	Siegfried	Gunther	Alberich	Hagen
23 Mar '74	Kubelik	Hunter	Rankin	Dunn	Brilioth	Dooley	Rintzler	Rundgren
29 Mar '75	Ehrling	Nilsson	Rankin	Reynolds	Thomas	Dooley	Rintzler	Rundgren

Hansel and Gretel (Humperdinck)

Date	Conductor	Hansel	Gretel	Gertrud	Witch	Sandman	Dewfairy	Peter
E 23 Dec '67	Allers	Elias	Stratas	Chookasian	Dönch	Sukis	Armstrong	Walker
E 25 Dec '71	Allers	Elias	Stratas	Chookasian	Velis	Potter	Di Franco	Walker
E 27 Dec '75	Allers	Elias	Weidinger	Kraft	Velis	A. J. Smith	Norden	Walker

L'Italiana in Algeri (Rossini)

Date	Conductor	Isabella	Elvira	Zulma	Lindoro	Taddeo	Haly	Mustafà
8 Dec '73	Örvos	Horne	Weidinger	Love	Alva	Uppman	Boucher	Corena
4 Jan '75	H. Lewis	Horne	Weidinger	Love	Di Giuseppe	Uppman	Boucher	Corena

Jenůfa (Janáček)

Date	Conductor	Jenůfa	Jano	Barena	Widow	Grandmother	Laca	Steva	Foreman
21 Dec '74	Nelson	Kubiak	Norden	Di Franco	Varnay	Kraft	Vickers	W. Lewis	Reardon

Lohengrin (Wagner)

Date	Conductor	Elsa	Ortrud	Lohengrin	Telramund	Herald	King Henry
21 Jan '67	Böhm	Bjoner	C. Ludwig	Kónya	Berry	Milnes	Macurdy
10 Feb '68	Klobucar	Arroyo	Dvoráková	Kónya	Cassel	Milnes	Macurdy

Lucia di Lammermoor (Donizetti)

Date	Conductor	Lucia	Alisa	Edgardo	Arturo	Ashton	Raimondo	Normanno
31 Dec '66	Bonynge	Sutherland	Sukis	Tucker	Marek	Colzani	Ghiuselev	Nagy
1 Feb '69	Franci	Moffo	Ordassy	Gedda	Anthony	Bruson	Giaiotti	MacWherter
21 Apr '73	Molinari-Pradelli	Scotto	Ordassy	Alexander	Goeke	Sereni	Plishka	MacWherter

Luisa Miller (Verdi)

Date	Conductor	Luisa	Federica	Laura	Rodolfo	Miller	Walter	Wurm
17 Feb '68	Schippers	Caballé	Pearl	Williams	Tucker	Milnes	Tozzi	Flagello
11 Dec '71	Levine	Maliponte	Dunn	Myhal	Alexander	MacNeil	Giaiotti	Plishka

Macbeth (Verdi)

Date	Conductor	Lady Macbeth	Macduff	Malcolm	Macbeth	Banquo	Physician
3 Feb '73	Molinari-Pradelli	Arroyo	Fr. Tagliavini	MacWherter	Milnes	R. Raimondi	Karlsrud

Madama Butterfly (Puccini)

Date	Conductor	Cio-Cio-San	Suzuki	Kate	Pinkerton	Sharpless	Goro	Bonze	Yamadori
18 Mar '67	Molinari-Pradelli	Scotto	Casei	Love	Shirley	Bottcher	Velis	Alvary	Christopher
30 Mar '68	Gardelli	Stratas	Casei	Pearl	Morell	Uppman	Velis	Scott	Christopher
7 Mar '70	Molinari-Pradelli	Arroyo	Baldwin	Forst	Alexander	Uppman	Franke	Best	Boucher
17 Apr '71	Franci	Lorengar	Miller	Myhal	Shirley	Guarrera	Schmorr	Karlsrud	Boucher
30 Mar '74	Baudo	Kirsten	Casei	G. Ben-David	Kónya	Christopher	Schmorr	Harvuot	Holloway
11 Jan '75	Woitach	Amara	Love	A. J. Smith	Morell	Uppman	Castel	Harvuot	Christopher
3 Apr '76	Woitach	Zylis-Gara	Casei	Ordassy	Alexander	Uppman	Castel	Dobriansky	Christopher

The Magic Flute (Mozart) (see *Die Zauberflöte*)

Manon Lescaut (Puccini)

Date	Conductor	Manon	Madrigal	Des Grieux	Lescaut	Geronte	Edmondo	Dance Mtr.
23 Mar '68	Molinari-Pradelli	Tebaldi	Baldwin	Alexander	Guarrera	Michalski	Anthony	Velis
29 Dec '73	Segerstam	Cruz-Romo	Forst	Montané	Sereni	Corena	Anthony	Schmorr
8 Mar '75	P. H. Adler	Kirsten	Kraft	Alexander	Walker	Michalski	Garrison	Schmorr

Martha (Flotow)

Date	Conductor	Lady Harriet	Nancy	Lionel	Plunkett	Tristram	Sheriff	Innkeeper
E 3 Feb '68	Allers	Fenn	Elias	Alexander	Gramm	Alvary	Plishka	Christopher

Die Meistersinger von Nürnberg (Wagner)

Date	Conductor	Eva	Magdalene	David	Walther	Sachs	Kothner	Beckmesser	Pogner
14 Jan '67	Rosenstock	Fenn	Miller	Dickie	Kónya	Tozzi	Walker	Dönch	Flagello
28 Dec '68	Rosenstock	Fenn	Miller	Driscoll	Kónya	Tozzi	Knoll	Dönch	Flagello
15 Jan '72	Schippers	Lorengar	Love	Driscoll	King	Adam	Gramm	Kusche	Flagello
17 Apr '76	Ehrling	Saunders	Baldwin	Riegel	Cox	Stewart	Uppman	Leib	Macurdy

Mourning Becomes Electra (Levy)

Date	Conductor	Lavinia	Christine	Helen	Adam	Orin	Peter	Ezra	Jed
1 Apr '67	Mehta	Lear	Collier	Sukis	Milnes	Reardon	Bottcher	Macurdy	Michalski

Norma (Bellini)

Date	Conductor	Norma	Adalgisa	Clotilde	Pollione	Flavio	Oroveso
4 Apr '70	Bonynge	Sutherland	Horne	Ordassy	Bergonzi	MacWherter	Siepi
19 Dec '70	Bonynge	Sutherland	Horne	Ordassy	Fr. Tagliavini	MacWherter	Plishka
17 Feb '73	Cillario	Caballé	Cossotto	Ordassy	Cossutta	Anthony	Tozzi
28 Feb '76	Masini	Caballé	Verrett	Ordassy	Alexander	Anthony	Michalski

Le Nozze di Figaro (Mozart)

Date	Conductor	Countess	Susanna	Cherubino	Marcellina	Almaviva	Figaro	Basilio	Bartolo
9 Dec '67	Rosenstock	Della Casa	Freni	Stratas	Williams	Krause	Siepi	Franke	Corena
11 Apr '70	Krips	Zylis-Gara	Stratas	Elias	Casei	Krause	Siepi	Franke	Plishka
21 Feb '76	Bedford	Te Kanawa	Valente	Elias	Kraft	Stewart	Dean	Velis	Foldi

Orfeo ed Euridice (Gluck)

Date	Conductor	Orfeo	Euridice	Amor	Spirit
9 Jan '71	Bonynge	Bumbry	Tucci	Peters	Pracht

Otello (Verdi)

Date	Conductor	Desdemona	Emilia	Otello	Cassio	Iago	Lodovico	Montàno
11 Mar '67	Mehta	Caballé	Love	McCracken	Lorenzi	Gobbi	Michalski	Harvuot
8 Apr '72	Böhm	Zylis-Gara	Love	McCracken	Di Giuseppe	Milnes	Plishka	Goodloe
9 Dec '72	Levine	Zylis-Gara	Kraft	Vickers	Goeke	Quilico	Michalski	Goodloe
9 Feb '74	Levine	Te Kanawa	Kraft	Vickers	W. Lewis	Stewart	Plishka	Goodloe

Pagliacci (Leoncavallo)

Date	Conductor	Nedda	Canio	Beppe	Tonio	Silvio
7 Feb '70	Cleva	Stratas	Tucker	Velis	Guarrera	Cossa
13 Feb '71	Cleva	Stratas	Tucker	Schmorr	MacNeil	Cossa
18 Jan '75	Nelson	Moffo	McCracken	Schmorr	Milnes	L. Carlson

Parsifal (Wagner)

Date	Conductor	Kundry	Flowermaid	Parsifal	Amfortas	Klingsor	Gurnemanz	Titurel
3 Apr '71	L. Ludwig	Dalis	Robinson	Kónya	Stewart	Meredith	Siepi	Macurdy
20 Apr '74	Steinberg	J. Martin	Pracht	Thomas	Stewart	Meredith	Macurdy	Morris

Pelléas et Mélisande (Debussy)

Date	Conductor	Mélisande	Geneviève	Yniold	Pelléas	Golaud	Arkel	Physician
29 Jan '72	C. Davis	Blegen	Chookasian	Klein	McDaniel	Stewart	Tozzi	Harvuot

La Périchole (Offenbach)

Date	Conductor	Périchole	Paquillo	Andres	Pedro	Panatellas	Tarapote	Prisoner
E 23 Jan '71	Allers	Stratas	Uppman	Ritchard	Gramm	Franke	Alvary	Velis

Peter Grimes (Britten)

Date	Conductor	Ellen	Mrs. Sedley	Auntie	Peter	Balstrode	Boles	Swallow	Rev. Adams
11 Feb '67	C. Davis	Amara	Madeira	Chookasian	Vickers	Evans	Franke	Michalski	Schmorr
5 Apr '69	C. Davis	Amara	Madeira	Chookasian	Vickers	Evans	Franke	Michalski	Schmorr
24 Mar '73	Ehrling	Amara	Kraft	Chookasian	Vickers	Gramm	Franke	Morris	Schmorr

I Puritani (Bellini)

Date	Conductor	Elvira	Enrichetta	Arturo	Bruno	Riccardo	Giorgio	Gualtiero
13 Mar '76	Bonynge	Sutherland	Munzer	Pavarotti	Garrison	Milnes	Morris	P. Booth

Das Rheingold (Wagner)

Date	Conductor	Freia	Fricka	Erda	Loge	Wotan	Alberich	Mime
22 Feb '69	Karajan	Mangelsdorff	Reynolds	Chookasian	Stolze	Adam	Kelemen	Velis
15 Feb '75	Ehrling	Pracht	Dunn	Chookasian	Peterson	McIntyre	Rintzler	Ulfung

Rigoletto (Verdi)

Date	Conductor	Gilda	Maddalena	Duke	Rigoletto	Monterone	Sparafucile	Marullo
8 Apr '67	Gardelli	Peters	Amparán	Gedda	MacNeil	Michalski	Giaiotti	Goodloe
7 Dec '68	Cleva	Moffo	Love	Bergonzi	Merrill	Díaz	Michalski	Boucher
5 Feb '72	Veltri	Robinson	Grillo	Tucker	Merrill	Morris	Díaz	Gibbs
10 Feb '73	Levine	Grist	Grillo	Pavarotti	Wixell	Morris	Macurdy	Harvuot
22 Dec '73	Baudo	Boky	Grillo	Di Giuseppe	Manuguerra	Morris	Flagello	Harvuot

Roméo et Juliette (Gounod)

Date	Conductor	Juliette	Stéphano	Gertrude	Roméo	Tybalt	Mercutio	Capulet	Laurent
13 Apr '68	Molinari-Pradelli	Freni	Baldwin	Love	Gedda	Anthony	Reardon	Michalski	Macurdy
18 Apr '70	Lombard	Pilou	Baldwin	Kraft	Corelli	Anthony	Reardon	Harvuot	Díaz
31 Mar '73	Rich	Boky	Forst	Love	Corelli	Anthony	Cossa	Harvuot	Macurdy
7 Dec '74	H. Lewis	Blegen	Munzer	Love	Corelli	Anthony	L. Carlson	Mazzieri	Gill

Der Rosenkavalier (Strauss)

Date	Conductor	Marschallin	Sophie	Octavian	Marianne	Singer	Faninal	Ochs	Valzacchi	Annina
8 Feb '69	Böhm	Rysanek	Grist	C. Ludwig	De Paul	Gedda	Knoll	Berry	Velis	Elias
28 Feb '70	Böhm	Rysanek	Raskin	C. Ludwig	De Paul	Gedda	Knoll	Berry	Velis	Love
14 Apr '73	Strasfogel	Rysanek	Blegen	Minton	Ordassy	Alexander	Meredith	Berry	Velis	Baldwin
23 Feb '74	Böhm	Lear	Mathis	Fassbaender	Ordassy	Goeke	Dooley	Jungwirth	Velis	Miller
27 Mar '76	Levine	Zylis-Gara	Blegen	Troyanos	Baldwin	Pavarotti	Dooley	Edelmann	Velis	Love

Salome (Strauss)

Date	Conductor	Salome	Herodias	Page	Herod	Narraboth	Jokanaan	Nazarene	1st Jew
18 Mar '72	Böhm	Rysanek	Dalis	G. Ben-David	Stolze	MacWherter	Stewart	Macurdy	Anthony
5 Jan '74	Levine	Bumbry	Resnik	G. Ben-David	Ulfung	W. Lewis	Shadur	Michalski	Anthony

Samson et Dalila (Saint-Saëns)

Date	Conductor	Dalila	Samson	Priest	Old Hebrew	Abimélech	Philistines	Messenger
8 Jan '72	Baudo	Bumbry	McCracken	Bacquier	Macurdy	Plishka	Schmorr, Goodloe	Anthony

The Siege of Corinth (see *L'Assedio di Corinto*)

Siegfried (Wagner)

Date	Conductor	Brünnhilde	Forest Bird	Erda	Siegfried	Mime	Wanderer	Alberich	Fafner
15 Mar '75	Ehrling	Nilsson	Norden	Chookasian	Thomas	Ulfung	McIntyre	Rintzler	Macurdy

Simon Boccanegra (Verdi)

Date	Conductor	Maria/Amelia	Maid	Gabriele	Simon	Paolo	Fiesco	Pietro
14 Dec '68	Molinari-Pradelli	Tucci	Brewer	Shirley	MacNeil	Milnes	Hines	Sgarro
19 Jan '74	Ehrling	Maliponte	Webber	Tucker	Wixell	Shadur	Tozzi	Sgarro

La Sonnambula (Bellini)

Date	Conductor	Amina	Lisa	Teresa	Elvino	Notary	Rodolfo	Alessio
21 Dec '68	Bonynge	Sutherland	Boky	Pearl	Alexander	Franke	Giaiotti	Plishka

Suor Angelica (Puccini)

Date	Conductor	Angelica	Princess	Genovieffa	Monitor	Head Mistress	Abbess	Nurse
3 Jan '76	Ehrling	Cruz-Romo	Chookasian	Norden	Baldwin	Godfrey Ben-David	Kraft	Munzer

Il Tabarro (Puccini)

Date	Conductor	Giorgetta	Frugola	Luigi	Tinca	Song Seller	Michele	Talpa
3 Jan '76	Ehrling	Kubiak	Chookasian	Theyard	Anthony	Garrison	MacNeil	Booth

Tosca (Puccini)

Date	Conductor	Tosca	Cavaradossi	Spoletta	Scarpia	Angelotti	Sacristan	Sciarrone
13 Jan '68	Mehta	Crespin	G. Raimondi	Velis	Bacquier	Harvuot	Plishka	Christopher
15 Feb '69	Schick	Nilsson	Domingo	Velis	Dooley	Sgarro	Plishka	Christopher
10 Jan '70	Molinari-Pradelli	Tebaldi	Kónya	Schmorr	MacNeil	Harvuot	Corena	Boucher
12 Dec '70	Molinari-Pradelli	Ross	Bergonzi	Franke	Colzani	Sgarro	Plishka	Christopher
8 Feb '75	Erede	Zylis-Gara	Bergonzi	Anthony	Bacquier	Sgarro	Corena	Christopher

La Traviata (Verdi)

Date	Conductor	Violetta	Flora	Alfredo	Gastone	Germont	Douphol	Dr. Grenvil
25 Mar '67	Prêtre	Moffo	Baldwin	Morell	Anthony	Merrill	Bottcher	Sgarro
30 Dec '67	Cleva	Moffo	Williams	Alexander	Anthony	Sereni	Goodloe	Sgarro
21 Mar '70	Rich	Pilou	Kraft	Bergonzi	Goeke	Milnes	Goodloe	Sgarro
13 Jan '73	Molinari-Pradelli	Cruz-Romo	Kraft	Di Giuseppe	Anthony	Merrill	Goodloe	Sgarro
14 Feb '76	Caldwell	Shane	Munzer	Burrows	Ahlstedt	Wixell	Goodloe	Karlsrud

Tristan und Isolde (Wagner)

Date	Conductor	Isolde	Brangäne	Tristan	Sailor	Melot	Kurwenal	Marke
18 Dec '71	Leinsdorf	Nilsson	Dalis	Thomas	Goeke	MacWherter	Dooley	Tozzi
26 Jan '74	Leinsdorf	Barlow	Dunn	Vickers	Ahlstedt	W. Lewis	Dooley	Macurdy

Il Trovatore (Verdi)

Date	Conductor	Leonora	Azucena	Inez	Manrico	Ruiz	Di Luna	Ferrando
18 Feb '67	Molinari-Pradelli	Arroyo	Cvejic	Love	Tucker	Marek	Merrill	Michalski
29 Mar '69	Mehta	Price	Bumbry	Ordassy	McCracken	Anthony	Milnes	Macurdy
13 Mar '71	Mehta	Arroyo	Verrett	Myhal	Tucker	Anthony	Sereni	Michalski
17 Mar '73	Cillario	Caballé	Cossotto	Kraft	Domingo	Castel	Merrill	Vinco

Les Troyens (Berlioz)

Date	Conductor	Cassandre	Didon	Ascagne	Anna	Hécube	Énée	Iopas	Hylas	Hélénus	Narbal
16 Mar '74	Kubelik	Verrett	C. Ludwig	Blegen	Dunn	Kraft	Vickers	Riegel	Goeke	W. Lewis	Macurdy

Turandot (Puccini)

Date	Conductor	Turandot	Liù	Calàf	Emperor	Pang	Pong	Ping	Timur
3 Dec '66	Mehta	Nilsson	Freni	Corelli	Caruso	Nagy	Anthony	Uppman	Giaiotti
22 Mar '69	Mehta	Lippert	Arroyo	McCracken	Caruso	Velis	Anthony	Guarrera	Giaiotti
21 Feb '70	K. Adler	Nilsson	Amara	Domingo	Schmorr	Velis	Anthony	Uppman	Giaiotti
27 Apr '74	Örvös	Ross	Moser	Corelli	Schmorr	Velis	Anthony	Goodloe	Macurdy
28 Dec '74	Erede	Bjoner	Maliponte	Corelli	Schmorr	Velis	Anthony	Goodloe	Morris

I Vespri Siciliani (Verdi)

Date	Conductor	Elena	Ninetta	Arrigo	Monforte	Vandemont	Procida
I 9 Mar '74	Levine	Caballé	Munzer	Gedda	Milnes	Karlsrud	Díaz
I 12 Apr '75	Levine	Niska	Munzer	W. Lewis	Milnes	Karlsrud	Plishka

Die Walküre (Wagner)

Date	Conductor	Sieglinde	Brünnhilde	Fricka	Siegmund	Wotan	Hunding
24 Feb '68	Klobucar	Rysanek	Nilsson	C. Ludwig	Vickers	Stewart	Ridderbusch
1 Mar '69	Karajan	Crespin	Nilsson	Veasey	Vickers	Adam	Talvela
16 Dec '72	Leinsdorf	G. Jones	Nilsson	Baldani	Vickers	Stewart	Macurdy
1 Mar '75	Ehrling	J. Martin	Nilsson	Dunn	Vickers	McIntyre	Rundgren

Werther (Massenet)

Date	Conductor	Charlotte	Sophie	Werther	Schmidt	Albert	Johann	Bailiff
27 Mar '71	Lombard	Elias	Robinson	Corelli	Castel	Reardon	Dobriansky	Gramm
4 Mar '72	Behr	Elias	Boky	Corelli	Anthony	Cossa	Best	Gramm

Wozzeck (Berg)

Date	Conductor	Marie	Margret	Major	Captain	Andres	Fool	Wozzeck	Doctor
E 12 Apr '69	C. Davis	Lear	Pearl	Nagy	Franke	Anthony	Velis	Evans	Gramm

Die Zauberflöte (Mozart)

Date	Conductor	Pamina	Queen	1st Lady	Papagena	Tamino	Papageno	Speaker	Sarastro
4 Mar '67	Krips	Raskin	Peters	Pracht	Di Franco	Shirley	Uppman	Cassel	Macurdy
6 Jan '68	Rosenstock	Lorengar	Deutekom	Pracht	P. Welting	Schreier	Uppman	Meredith	Hines
17 Jan '70	Skrowaczewski	Zylis-Gara	Popp	Fenn	Di Franco	Gedda	Prey	Cassel	Hines
23 Dec '72	Maag	Maliponte	Moser	Pracht	Di Franco	Burrows	Reardon	Gramm	Sotin
15 Dec '73	Maag	Moffo	Shane	Pracht	Di Franco	Alva	Gramm	Meredith	Hines

Gala Performance

22 Apr '72 (TV)   (Honoring Sir Rudolf Bing on his retirement after twenty-two years as general manager)
Levine, Bonynge, Molinari-Pradelli, K. Adler, Rudolf (conductors); Gniewek (violin)
Peters, Milnes, Stratas, Stewart, Plishka, R. Raimondi, Moffo, Arroyo, Sutherland, Pavarotti, Robinson, MacNeil, Kirsten, Corena, Flagello, Caballé, Domingo, Bumbry, Crespin, Sereni, Amara, Di Giuseppe, Siepi, Tucker, Merrill, Price, Resnik, Tucci, Dalis, Macurdy, McCracken, Kónya, Elias, Hines, Lorengar, Rysanek, Vickers, Zylis-Gara, Corelli, Nilsson.

Miscellaneous

10 Apr '75 (TV)   (Televised on 27 April 1975)
"Look-in" Student Performance, Danny Kaye, master of ceremonies
Levine (conductor): Blegen, Sills, Elias, Di Giuseppe, Merrill, Morris
La Traviata (Act I) Levine: Maliponte, Munzer, Carreras, Anthony, Goodloe, Karlsrud

26 Sep '75   Met Marathon (concert)
Katz, Masiello, Woitach (pianists): Quilico, Horne, Hines, Lear, Díaz, Kubiak, Corena, Arroyo, Dunn, Gedda, Macurdy, Capecchi, Maliponte, Lamberti

Lauritz Melchior as Tannhäuser. Photography by Mishkin.

Metropolitan Opera Historic Broadcast Recordings

For each performance listed below, the name of the conductor appears first, followed by the names of the lead singers.

The professionally mastered Historic Broadcast recordings are available from the Metropolitan Opera in return for a contribution to the Metropolitan Opera Fund. Some of the recordings may be out of print. Inquiry may be made to

Metropolitan Opera Association
Lincoln Center
New York, NY 10023

Carmen
17 April 1937

Papi; Ponselle, Burke, Maison, Huehn

Der Rosenkavalier
7 January 1939

Bodanzky; Lehmann, Stevens, Farell, Schorr, List

Simon Boccanegra
21 January 1939

Panizza; Rethberg, Martinelli, Tibbett, Warren, Pinza

Otello
24 February 1940

Panizza; Rethberg, Martinelli, Tibbett, Moscona

Le Nozze di Figaro
7 December 1940

Panizza; Rethberg, Albanese, Novotná, Brownlee, Pinza, Baccaloni

Un Ballo in Maschera
14 December 1940

Panizza; Milanov, Andreva, Castagna, Björling, Sved, Cordon

Tannhäuser
4 January 1941

Leinsdorf; Flagstad, Thorborg, Melchior, Janssen, List

Tristan und Isolde
8 February 1941

Leinsdorf; Flagstad, Thorborg, Melchior, Huehn, Kipnis

597

Fidelio
22 February 1941

Walter; Flagstad, Farell, Maison, Huehn, Janssen, Kipnis

Die Walküre
2 December 1944

Szell; Bampton, Traubel, Thorborg, Melchior, Janssen, Kipnis

Madama Butterfly
19 January 1946

Cimara; Albanese, Browning, Melton, Brownlee

La Gioconda
16 March 1946

Cooper; Milanov, Stevens, Harshaw, Tucker, Warren, Vaghi

Roméo et Juliette
1 February 1947

Cooper; Sayão, Benzell, Björling, Brownlee, Moscona

Salome
19 January 1952

Reiner; Welitch, Höngen, Svanholm, Sullivan, Hotter

Elektra
23 February 1952

Reiner: Varnay, Wegner, Höngen, Svanholm, Schöffler

Andrea Chénier
4 December 1954

Cleva; Milanov, Warfield, Del Monaco, Warren, Baccaloni

Les Contes d'Hoffmann
3 December 1955

Monteux; Peters, Stevens, Amara, Miller, Tucker, Singher

Tosca
7 January 1956

Mitropoulos; Tebaldi, Tucker, Warren, Corena

Otello
8 March 1958

Cleva; De Los Angeles, Del Monaco, Warren, Moscona

Turandot
4 March 1961

Stokowski; Nilsson, Moffo, Corelli, Guarrera, Giaiotti

La Sonnambula
30 March 1963

Varviso; Sutherland, Scovotti, Gedda, Flagello

In addition to the complete operas listed above, several collections of excerpts are also available. The Metropolitan Opera Historic Broadcast Centennial Collection 1935–1959 features highlights from twenty-five seasons of broadcasts. The James Levine Anniversary Collection 1971–1996 includes broadcast excerpts from the maestro's twenty-five-year career at the new Met.

1908 1935

FAREWELL LUNCH
BY
GIULIO GATTI-CASAZZA

❖

Cocktails

❖

Olives and Celery
Hors d'Oeuvres

❖

Cold Turkey, Chicken, Roast Beef, Tongue, Virginia Ham

❖

Vegetable and Lettuce and Tomato Salads

❖

Ice Cream and Petit Fours

❖

Demi Tasse

Metropolitan Opera House
New York
April 22, 1935

Emil Katz
Caterer

Farewell luncheon by Giulio Gatti-Casazza on 22 April 1935. Menu autographed by Artur Bodanzky, Geraldine Farrar, Kirsten Flagstad, Rosina Galli, Giulio Gatti-Casazza, Edward Johnson, Rosa Ponselle, Arturo Toscanini, and Herbert Witherspoon.

Select Bibliography

Alda, Frances. 1937. *Men, Women and Tenors*. Boston: Houghton Mifflin Company.

Ardoin, John. 1977. *The Callas Legacy*. New York: Charles Scribner's Sons.

_____. 1994. *The Furtwängler Record*. Portland, OR: Amadeus Press.

Beecham, Sir Thomas. 1943. *A Mingled Chime: An Autobiography*. New York: G. P. Putnam's Sons.

Belmont, Eleanor Robson. 1957. *The Fabric of Memory*. New York: Farrar, Straus and Cudahy.

Bing, Sir Rudolf. 1972. *5000 Nights at the Opera*. Garden City, NY: Doubleday.

_____. 1981. *A Knight at the Opera*. New York: G. P. Putnam's Sons.

Björling, Anna-Lisa, and Andrew Farkas. *Jussi*. Portland, OR: Amadeus Press.

Bloomfield, Arthur. 1978. *The San Francisco Opera: 1922–1978*. Sausalito, CA: Comstock Editions.

Caruso, Enrico, Jr., and Andrew Farkas. 1990. *Enrico Caruso: My Father and My Family*. Portland, OR: Amadeus Press.

Casanova, Carlamaria. 1995. *Renata Tebaldi: The Voice of an Angel*. Dallas, TX: Baskerville Publishers.

Chapin, Schuyler. 1977. *Musical Chairs: A Life in the Arts*. New York: G. P. Putnam's Sons.

Christiansen, Rupert. 1984. *Prima Donna*. New York: Viking Penguin.

Cone, John Frederick. 1983. *First Rival of the Metropolitan Opera*. New York: Columbia University Press.

_____. 1993. *Adelina Patti: Queen of Hearts*. Portland, OR: Amadeus Press.

Crespin, Régine. 1997. *On Stage, Off Stage*. Boston: Northeastern University Press.

Davenport, Marcia. 1967. *Too Strong for Fantasy*. New York: Charles Scribner's Sons.

Davis, Peter G. 1997. *The American Opera Singer: The Lives and Adventures of America's Great Singers in Opera and Concert, from 1825 to the Present*. New York: Doubleday.

Davis, Ronald L. 1966. *Opera in Chicago*. New York: Appleton-Century.

De Schauensee, Max. 1962. *The Collector's Verdi and Puccini*. Philadelphia: J. B. Lippincott.

Dizikes, John. 1993. *Opera in America: A Cultural History*. New Haven: Yale University Press.

Downes, Olin. 1957. *Olin Downes on Music*. New York: Simon & Schuster.

Drake, James A. 1984. *Richard Tucker: A Biography*. New York: E. P. Dutton.

———— and Kristin Beall Ludecke. 1999. *Lily Pons: A Centennial Portrait*. Portland, OR: Amadeus Press.

Eames, Emma. 1927. *Some Memories and Reflections*. New York: D. Appleton and Co.

Eaton, Quaintance. 1957. *Opera Caravan: Adventures of the Metropolitan Opera on Tour: 1883–1956*. New York: Farrar, Straus and Cudahy.

————. 1968. *The Miracle of the Met: An Informal History of the Metropolitan Opera 1883–1967*. New York: Meredith Press.

————. 1987. *Sutherland and Bonynge: An Intimate Biography*. New York: Dodd, Mead & Co.

Eisler, Paul E. 1984. *The Metropolitan Opera: The First Twenty-Five Years 1883–1908*. Croton-on Hudson, NY: North River Press.

Erskine, John. 1950. *My Life in Music*. New York: William Morrow.

Farkas, Andrew, ed. 1989. *Lawrence Tibbett: Singing Actor*. Portland, OR: Amadeus Press.

Farrar, Geraldine. 1938. *Such Sweet Compulsion*. New York: Greystone Press.

Farrell, Eileen, and Brian Kellow. 1999. *Can't Help Singing: The Life of Eileen Farrell*. Boston: Northeastern University Press.

Fiedler, Johanna. 2001. *Molto Agitato: The Mayhem Behind the Music at the Metropolitan Opera*. New York: Nan A. Talese/Doubleday.

Fitzgerald, Gerald, and Jean Seward Uppman, eds. 1989. *Annals of the Metropolitan Opera: The Complete Chronicle of Performances and Artists*. 2 vols. Boston/New York: G. K. Hall and the Metropolitan Opera Guild.

Flagstad, Kirsten, and Louis Biancolli. 1952. *The Flagstad Manuscript*. New York: G. P. Putnam's Sons.

Garden, Mary, and Louis Biancolli. 1951. *Mary Garden's Story*. New York: Simon & Schuster.

Glackens, Ira. 1963. Yankee Diva: *Lillian Nordica and the Golden Age of Opera*. New York: Coleridge Press.

Goldovsky, Boris. 1984. *Good Afternoon, Ladies and Gentlemen!: Intermission Scripts from the Met*. Bloomington: Indiana University Press.

Gruber, Paul, ed. 1993. *The Metropolitan Opera Guide to Recorded Opera*. New York: W. W. Norton and the Metropolitan Opera Guild.

————. 1997. *The Metropolitan Opera Guide to Opera on Video*. New York: W. W. Norton and the Metropolitan Opera Guild.

Hamilton, David, ed. 1987. *The Metropolitan Opera Encyclopedia: A Comprehensive Guide to the World of Opera*. New York: Simon & Schuster and the Metropolitan Opera Guild.

Hart, Philip. 1994. *Fritz Reiner: A Biography*. Evanston, IL: Northwestern University Press.

Hines, Jerome. 1982. *Great Singers on Great Singing*. Garden City, NY: Doubleday.

Horowitz, Joseph. 1994. *Wagner Nights: An American History*. Berkeley: University of California Press.

Jackson, Paul. 1992. *Saturday Afternoons at the Old Met: The Metropolitan Opera Broadcasts 1931–1950*. Portland, OR: Amadeus Press.

———. 1997. *Sign-off for the Old Met: The Metropolitan Opera Broadcasts 1950–1966*. Portland, OR: Amadeus Press.

Jacobson. Robert. 1974. *Reverberations: Interviews with the World's Leading Musicians*. New York: William Morrow.

Jeritza, Maria. 1924. *Sunlight and Song: A Singer's Life*. Trans. Frederick H. Martens. New York: D. Appleton and Co.

Kirsten, Dorothy, with Lanfranco Rasponi. 1982. *A Time to Sing*. Garden City, NY: Alfred A. Knopf.

Kolodin, Irving. 1936. *The Metropolitan Opera 1883–1935*. New York: Oxford University Press.

———. 1966. *The Metropolitan Opera 1883–1966: A Candid History*. New York: Alfred A. Knopf.

Lawrence, Marjorie. 1949. *Interrupted Melody*. New York: Appleton-Century-Crofts.

Lee, M. Owen. 1995. *First Impressions: Twenty-one Great Operas Explored, Explained and Brought to Life from the Met*. New York: Oxford University Press.

Lehmann, Lotte. 1938. *Midway in My Song*. New York: Bobbs-Merrill.

———. 1948. *My Many Lives*. New York: Boosey & Hawkes.

Leider, Frida. 1966. *Playing My Part*. Translated by Charles Osborne. New York: Meredith Press.

Leinsdorf, Erich. 1976. *Cadenza*. Boston: Houghton Mifflin.

———. 1997. *Erich Leinsdorf on Music*. Portland, OR: Amadeus Press.

Ludwig, Christa. 1999. *In My Own Voice*. New York: Limelight Editions.

Marsh, Robert C. 1998. *Dialogues and Discoveries: James Levine: His Life and His Music*. New York: Scribner.

Matz, Mary Jane. 1955. *Opera Stars in the Sun: Intimate Glimpses of Metropolitan Personalities*. New York: Farrar, Straus & Cudahy.

Mayer, Martin. 1983. *The Met: One Hundred Years of Grand Opera*. New York: Simon & Schuster, and the Metropolitan Opera Guild.

McGovern, Dennis, and Deborah Grace Winer. *I Remember Too Much: 89 Opera Stars Speak Candidly of Their Work, Their Lives, and Their Colleagues*. New York: William Morrow.

Mercer, Ruby. 1976. *The Tenor of His Times: Edward Johnson of the Met*. Toronto: Clarke, Irwin & Co.

Merkling, Frank, John W. Freeman, and Gerald Fitzgerald. 1965. *The Golden Horseshoe: The Life and Times of the Metropolitan Opera House*. New York: Viking.

Merrill, Robert, with Robert Saffron. 1976. *Between the Acts: An Irreverent Look at Opera and Other Madness*. New York: McGraw-Hill.

The Metropolitan Opera: The Radio and Television Legacy. 1986. New York: Museum of Broadcasting. Exhibition.

Mili, Gjon and Mary Ellis Peltz. 1960. *The Magic of Opera: A Picture Memoir of the Metropolitan*. New York: Frederick A. Praeger.

Milnes, Sherrill. 1998. *American Aria: From Farm Boy to Opera Star*. New York: Schirmer Books.

Moore, Grace. 1944. *You're Only Human Once*. Garden City, NY: Garden City Publishing.

Moran, William R., ed. 1990. *Herman Klein and the Gramophone*. Portland, OR: Amadeus Press.

Nash, Elizabeth. 1981. *Always First Class: The Career of Geraldine Farrar*. Washington, D.C.: University Press of America.

O'Connell, Charles. 1949. *The Other Side of the Record*. New York: Alfred A. Knopf.

Opera Cavalcade: The Story of the Metropolitan. 1938. New York: Metropolitan Opera Guild.

Peltz, Mary Ellis. 1950. *Behind the Gold Curtain: The Story of the Metropolitan Opera: 1883 to 1950*. New York: Farrar, Straus and Co.

Peltz, Mary Ellis, and Gerald Fitzgerald, eds. 1978. *Metropolitan Opera Annals: Third Supplement 1966-1976*. Clifton, NJ: James T. White & Co.; New York: Metropolitan Opera Guild.

Phillips-Matz, Mary Jane. 2000. *Leonard Warren: American Baritone*. Portland, OR: Amadeus Press.

Pinza, Ezio, with Robert Magidoff. 1958. *Ezio Pinza: An Autobiography*. New York: Rinehart & Company.

Pleasants, Henry. 1966. *The Great Singers: From the Dawn of Opera to Our Own Time*. New York: Simon & Schuster.

Ponselle, Rosa, and James A. Drake. 1982. *Ponselle: A Singer's Life*. Garden City, NY: Doubleday.

Porter, Andrew. 1978. *Music of Three Seasons: 1974–1977*. New York: Farrar Straus Giroux.

————. 1981. *Music of Three More Seasons: 1977–1980*. New York: Alfred A. Knopf.

————. 1989. *Musical Events: A Chronicle: 1983–1986*. New York: Summit Books.

Prawy, Marcel. 1970. *The Vienna Opera*. New York: Frederick A. Praeger.

Rasponi, Lanfranco. 1982. *The Last Prima Donnas*. New York: Alfred A. Knopf.

Robinson, Francis. 1979. *Celebration: The Metropolitan Opera*. Garden City, NY: Doubleday.

Rosenthal, Harold. 1958. *Two Centuries of Opera at Covent Garden*. London: Putnam.

Roussel, Jean-Jacques Hanine. 1997. *Giulietta Simionato: How Cinderella Became a Queen*. Dallas, TX: Baskerville Publishers.

Rubin, Stephen E. 1974. *The New Met in Profile*. New York: Macmillan.

Sachs, Harvey. 1978. *Toscanini*. Philadelphia, PA: J. B. Lippincott.

Sargeant, Winthrop. 1973. *Divas*. New York: Coward, McCann & Geoghegan.

Schwarzkopf, Elisabeth. 1982. *On and Off the Record: A Memoire of Walter Legge*. London: Faber & Faber.

Scott, Michael. 1977. *The Record of Singing: To 1914*. New York: Charles Scribner's Sons.

_____. 1979. *The Record of Singing {To 1925}*. New York: Holmes & Meier Publishers.

_____. 1988. *The Great Caruso*. New York: Alfred A. Knopf.

_____. 1992. *Maria Meneghini Callas*. Northeastern University Press.

Scotto, Renata, and Octavio Roca. 1984. *Scotto: More than a Diva*. New York: Doubleday.

Seltsam, William H., ed. 1947. *Metropolitan Opera Annals: A Chronicle of Artists and Performances*. New York: H. W. Wilson and the Metropolitan Opera Guild.

_____. 1957. *Metropolitan Opera Annals First Supplement: 1947–1957*. New York: H. W. Wilson and the Metropolitan Opera Guild.

_____. 1968. *Metropolitan Opera Annals Second Supplement: 1957–1966*. New York: H. W. Wilson and the Metropolitan Opera Guild.

Seroff, Victor I. 1980. *Renata Tebaldi: The Woman and the Diva*. North Stratford, NH: Ayer Company Publishers.

Sheean, Vincent. 1956. *First and Last Love*. New York: Random House.

Smith, Patrick J. 1983. *A Year at the Met*. New York: Alfred A. Knopf.

Spotts, Frederic. 1994. *Bayreuth: A History of the Wagner Festival*. New Haven: Yale University Press.

Steane, J. B. 1992. *Voices, Singers and Critics*. Portland, OR: Amadeus Press.

_____. 1993. *The Grand Tradition: Seventy Years of Singing on Record*. Portland, OR: Amadeus Press.

_____. 1996. *Singers of the Century*, vol. 1. Portland, OR: Amadeus Press.

_____. 1998. *Singers of the Century*, vol. 2. Portland, OR: Amadeus Press.

_____. 2000. *Singers of the Century*, vol. 3. Portland, OR: Amadeus Press.

Steber, Eleanor, with Marcia Sloat. 1992. *Eleanor Steber—An Autobiography*. Ridgewood, NJ: Wordsworth.

Stevens, Risë. 1959. *Subway to the Met: Risë Stevens' Story*. Garden City, NY: Doubleday.

Taubman, Howard. 1994. *The Pleasure of Their Company: A Reminiscence*. Portland, OR: Amadeus Press.

Thompson, Oscar. 1937. *The American Singer*. New York: Dial Press.

Thomson, Virgil. 1947. *The Musical Scene*. New York: Alfred A. Knopf.

_____. 1967. *Music Reviewed: 1940–1954*. New York: Vintage Books.

Traubel, Helen, with Richard G. Hubler. 1959. *St. Louis Woman*. New York: Duell, Sloan and Pearce.

Truxall, Aida Craig, ed. 1991. *All Good Greetings: Letters of Geraldine Farrar to Ilka Marie Stotler 1946–1958*. Pittsburgh: University of Pittsburgh Press.

Tuggle, Robert. 1983. *The Golden Age of Opera with the Photographs of Herman Mishkin*. New York: Holt, Rinehart and Winston.

Walter, Bruno. 1944. *Theme and Variations*. New York: Alfred A. Knopf.

Wayner, Robert J., ed. 1976. *What Did They Sing at the Met?* New York: Wayner Publications.

Weaver, William, and Simonetta Puccini, eds. *The Puccini Companion*. 1994. New York: W. W. Norton.

Williams, Jeannie. 1999. *Jon Vickers: A Hero's Life*. Boston: Northeastern University Press.

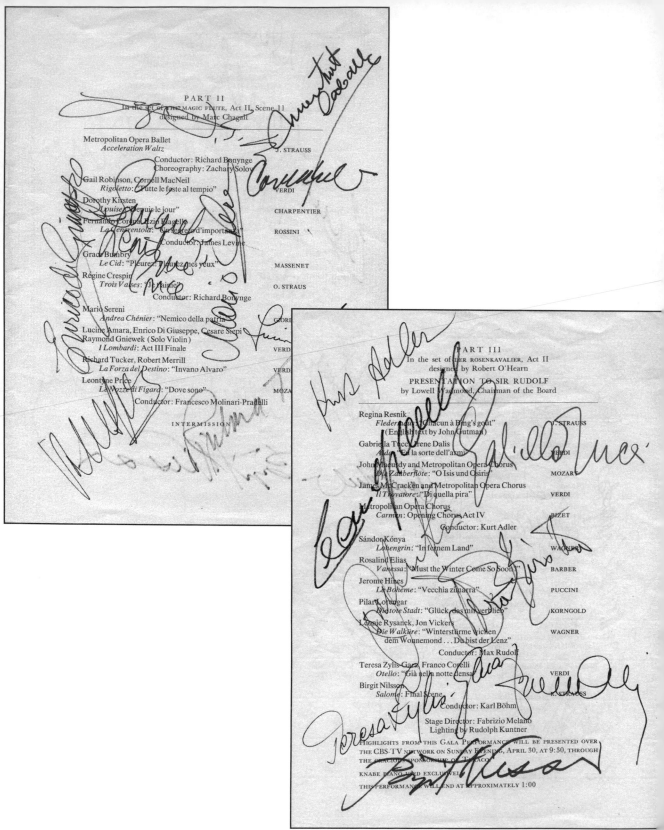

Program for gala performance honoring Sir Rudolf Bing, 22 April 1972. Part II (left, autographed by Lucine Amara, Carlo Bergonzi, Montserrat Caballé, Régine Crespin, Enrico Di Giuseppe, Cornell MacNeil, Leontyne Price, Mario Sereni, Richard Tucker) and Part III (right, autographed by Kurt Adler, Franco Corelli, Dorothy Kirsten, Birgit Nilsson, Leonie Rysanek, Gabriella Tucci, Jon Vickers, Teresa Zylis-Gara).

Index

Beneath each artist's name, specific roles in the broadcasts critiqued are listed in alphabetical order (a key to shortened opera titles appears below). To find the page reference for each role, turn to the Index to Operas Critiqued, where the cited opera includes the names of the featured artists in each performance.

Joan Sutherland as Norma sings 'Casta diva.' Photography by Louis Mélançon.
Courtesy Metropolitan Opera Archives.

Index to Operas Critiqued

Page references to broadcast performances of operas critiqued in the text appear in boldface preceding the date of the broadcast.

Aida (Verdi)

	Date	Conductor	Aida	Amneris	Radamès	Amonasro	Ramfis	King	Messenger
328	24 Feb '73	Molinari-Pradelli	Arroyo	Bumbry	Tucker	MacNeil	Tozzi	Morris/Karlsrud	MacWherter
553	6 Mar '76	Levine	Price	Horne	Domingo	MacNeil	Giaiotti	Morris	Anthony

Antony and Cleopatra (Barber)

	Date	Conductor	Cleopatra	Charmian	Iras	Octavia	Caesar	Antony	Enobarbus	Alexas	Agrippa
3	16 Sep '66	Schippers	Price	Elias	Amparán	Pracht	Thomas	Díaz	Flagello	Michalski	Macurdy

Ariadne auf Naxos (Strauss)

	Date	Conductor	Ariadne	Zerbinetta	Composer	Bacchus	Music Mtr.	Harlekin	Echo	Najade
207	28 Mar '70	Böhm	Rysanek	Grist	Lear	King	Dooley	Uppman	Clements	Pracht
520	20 Mar '76	Levine	Caballé	R. Welting	Troyanos	Remedios	Dooley	Titus	Norden	Weidinger

L'Assedio di Corinto (Rossini)

	Date	Conductor	Pamira	Ismene	Neocle	Cleomene	Maometto
438	19 Apr '75	Schippers	Sills	Norden	Verrett	Theyard	Díaz

Un Ballo in Maschera (Verdi)

	Date	Conductor	Amelia	Oscar	Ulrica	Riccardo	Renato	Sam	Tom
145	30 Jan '71	Molinari-Pradelli	Arroyo	Peters	Dunn	Domingo	Merrill	Plishka	Dobriansky
323	27 Jan '73	P. H. Adler	Cruz-Romo	Robinson	Dalis	Tucker	Milnes	Morris	Best
335	6 Dec '75	H. Lewis	Ross	Peters	Forrester	Morell	Merrill	Michalski	Booth

Il Barbiere di Siviglia (Rossini)

	Date	Conductor	Rosina	Berta	Almaviva	Figaro	Basilio	Bartolo	Fiorello
293	7 Apr '73	Levine	Horne	Kraft	Di Giuseppe	Prey	Tozzi	Corena	Goodloe
531	31 Jan '76	Nelson	Von Stade	Munzer	Davies	Stilwell	Morris	Corena	Goodloe

Bluebeard's Castle (Bartók)

	Date	Conductor	Judith	Bluebeard
435	22 Feb '75	Ehrling	Verrett	Ward

La Fanciulla del West (Puccini)

	Date	Conductor	Minnie	Wowkle	Johnson	Sonora	Rance	Larkens	Jake
174	14 Mar '70	Behr	Tebaldi	Von Stade	Kónya	Harvuot	Colzani	Gibbs	Macurdy

Faust (Gounod)

	Date	Conductor	Marguerite	Siebel	Marthe	Faust	Valentin	Méphistophélès	Wagner
246	26 Feb '72	Rich	Zylis-Gara	Von Stade	Godfrey	Ben-David / Domingo	Sereni	Tozzi	Christopher

Fidelio (Beethoven)

	Date	Conductor	Leonore	Marzelline	Florestan	Jaquino	Pizarro	Rocco	Fernando
210	2 Jan '71	Böhm	Rysanek	Blegen	Vickers	Dickie	Berry	Tozzi	Macurdy
227	11 Mar '72	Wallat	Silja	Blegen	Brilioth	Goeke	Dooley	Macurdy	Plishka
499	7 Feb '76	Mauceri	G. Jones	Blegen	Thomas	Riegel	McIntyre	Macurdy	Morris

La Fille du Régiment (Donizetti)

	Date	Conductor	Marie	Marquise	Duchesse	Tonio	Sulpice	Hortensius
296	6 Jan '73	Bonynge	Sutherland	Resnik	Kraft	Pavarotti	Corena	Velis

Der Fliegende Holländer (Wagner)

	Date	Conductor	Senta	Mary	Erik	Steersman	Dutchman	Daland
179	27 Jan '68	Klobucar	Rysanek	Williams	Parly	Olvis	MacNeil	Tozzi
182	31 Jan '70	Böhm	Rysanek	Chookasian	Kónya	Shirley	Dooley	Macurdy

La Forza del Destino (Verdi)

	Date	Conductor	Leonora	Preziosilla	Alvaro	Carlo	Guardiano	Melitone	Marquis
265	12 Feb '72	Veltri	Price	Casei	Bergonzi	Paskalis	Siepi	Corena	Karlsrud
466	22 Mar '75	Levine	Amara	Grillo	Vickers	MacNeil	Giaiotti	Bacquier	Morris

Die Frau ohne Schatten (Strauss)

	Date	Conductor	Empress	Dyer's Wife	Falcon	Nurse	Voice	Emperor	Barak	Messenger
9	17 Dec '66	Böhm	Rysanek	C. Ludwig	Ordassy	Dalis	Amparán	King	Berry	Dooley

Der Freischütz (Weber)

	Date	Conductor	Agathe	Ännchen	Max	Ottokar	Kilian	Caspar	Hermit	Cuno	Samiel
224	15 Apr '72	L. Ludwig	Lorengar	Mathis	Kónya	MacWherter	Dobriansky	Feldhoff	Macurdy	Karlsrud	Ebert

Gianni Schicchi (Puccini)

	Date	Conductor	Lauretta	Nella	Zita	Rinuccio	Schicchi	Simone	Spinelloccio
437	22 Feb '75	Ehrling	Blegen	Norden	Dalis	Gibbs	Flagello	Harvuot	Best
546	3 Jan '76	Ehrling	Mandac	Norden	Chookasian	Gibbs	Flagello	Michalski	Best

La Gioconda (Ponchielli)

	Date	Conductor	Gioconda	Laura	Cieca	Enzo	Barnaba	Alvise
89	2 Mar '68	Cleva	Tebaldi	Cossotto	Dunn	Bergonzi	MacNeil	Giaiotti
542	10 Apr '76	Patanè	Arroyo	Rankin	Chookasian	Raitzin	Manugerra	Morris

Götterdämmerung (Wagner)

	Date	Conductor	Brünnhilde	Gutrune	Waltraute	Siegfried	Gunther	Alberich	Hagen
383	23 Mar '74	Kubelik	Hunter	Rankin	Dunn	Brilioth	Dooley	Rintzler	Rundgren
386	29 Mar '75	Ehrling	Nilsson	Rankin	Reynolds	Thomas	Dooley	Rintzler	Rundgren

Hansel and Gretel (Humperdinck)

	Date	Conductor	Hansel	Gretel	Gertrud	Witch	Sandman	Dewfairy	Peter
230	25 Dec '71	Allers	Elias	Stratas	Chookasian	Velis	Potter	Di Franco	Walker

L'Italiana in Algeri (Rossini)

	Date	Conductor	Isabella	Elvira	Zulma	Lindoro	Taddeo	Haly	Mustafa
394	8 Dec '73	Ötvos	Horne	Weidinger	Love	Alva	Uppman	Boucher	Corena

Jenůfa (Janáček)

	Date	Conductor	Jenůfa	Jano	Barena	Widow	Grandmother	Laca	Steva	Foreman
430	21 Dec '74	Nelson	Kubiak	Norden	Di Franco	Varnay	Kraft	Vickers	W. Lewis	Reardon

Lohengrin (Wagner)

	Date	Conductor	Elsa	Ortrud	Lohengrin	Telramund	Herald	King Henry
19	21 Jan '67	Böhm	Bjoner	C. Ludwig	Kónya	Berry	Milnes	Macurdy
185	10 Feb '68	Klobucar	Arroyo	Dvořáková	Kónya	Cassel	Milnes	Macurdy

Die Meistersinger von Nürnberg (Wagner)

	Date	Conductor	Eva	Magdalene	Walther	David	Sachs	Kothner	Beckmesser	Pogner
16	14 Jan '67	Rosenstock	Fenn	Miller	Kónya	Dickie	Tozzi	Walker	Dönch	Flagello
231	15 Jan '72	Schippers	Lorengar	Love	King	Driscoll	Adam	Gramm	Kusche	Flagello
410	17 Apr '76	Ehrling	Saunders	Baldwin	Cox	Riegel	Stewart	Uppman	Leib	Macurdy

Mourning Becomes Electra (Levy)

	Date	Conductor	Christine	Lavinia	Helen	Adam	Orin	Peter	Ezra	Jed
48	1 Apr '67	Mehta	Collier	Lear	Sukis	Milnes	Reardon	Bottcher	Macurdy	Michalski

Norma (Bellini)

	Date	Conductor	Norma	Adalgisa	Clotilde	Pollione	Flavio	Oroveso
85	4 Apr '70	Bonynge	Sutherland	Horne	Ordassy	Bergonzi	MacWherter	Siepi
306	17 Feb '73	Cillario	Caballé	Cossotto	Ordassy	Cossutta	Anthony	Tozzi
535	28 Feb '76	Masini	Caballé	Verrett	Ordassy	Alexander	Anthony	Michalski

Le Nozze di Figaro (Mozart)

	Date	Conductor	Countess	Susanna	Cherubino	Marcellina	Almaviva	Figaro	Basilio	Bartolo
55	9 Dec '67	Rosenstock	Della Casa	Freni	Stratas	Williams	Krause	Siepi	Franke	Corena
60	11 Apr '70	Krips	Zylis-Gara	Stratas	Elias	Casei	Krause	Siepi	Franke	Plishka
527	21 Feb '76	Bedford	Te Kanawa	Valente	Elias	Kraft	Stewart	Dean	Velis	Foldi

Orfeo ed Euridice (Gluck)

	Date	Conductor	Orfeo	Euridice	Amor	Spirit
212	9 Jan '71	Bonynge	Bumbry	Tucci	Peters	Pracht

Otello (Verdi)

	Date	Conductor	Desdemona	Emilia	Otello	Cassio	Iago	Lodovico	Montàno
36	11 Mar '67	Mehta	Caballé	Love	McCracken	Lorenzi	Gobbi	Michalski	Harvuot
269	8 Apr '72	Böhm	Zylis-Gara	Love	McCracken	Di Giuseppe	Milnes	Plishka	Goodloe
316	9 Dec '72	Levine	Zylis-Gara	Kraft	Vickers	Goeke	Quilico	Michalski	Goodloe
463	9 Feb '74	Levine	Te Kanawa	Kraft	Vickers	W. Lewis	Stewart	Plishka	Goodloe

Roméo et Juliette (Gounod)

	Date	Conductor	Juliette	Stéphano	Gertrude	Roméo	Tybalt	Mercutio	Capulet	Laurent
102	13 Apr '68	Molinari-Pradelli	Freni	Baldwin	Love	Gedda	Anthony	Reardon	Michalski	Macurdy
105	18 Apr '70	Lombard	Pilou	Baldwin	Kraft	Corelli	Anthony	Reardon	Harvuot	Díaz

Der Rosenkavalier (Strauss)

	Date	Conductor	Marschallin	Sophie	Octavian	Marianne	Singer	Faninal	Ochs	Valzacchi	Amina
350	14 Apr '73	Strasfogel	Rysanek	Blegen	Minton	Ordassy	Alexander	Meredith	Berry	Velis	Baldwin
354	23 Feb '74	Böhm	Lear	Mathis	Fassbaender	Ordassy	Goeke	Dooley	Jungwirth	Velis	Miller
514	27 Mar '76	Levine	Zylis-Gara	Blegen	Troyanos	Baldwin	Pavarotti	Dooley	Edelmann	Velis	Love

Salome (Strauss)

	Date	Conductor	Salome	Herodias	Page	Herod	Narraboth	Jokanaan	Nazarene	1st Jew
240	18 Mar '72	Böhm	Rysanek	Dalis	G. Ben-David	Stolze	MacWherter	Stewart	Macurdy	Anthony
360	5 Jan '74	Levine	Bumbry	Resnik	G. Ben-David	Ulfung	W. Lewis	Shadur	Michalski	Anthony

Samson et Dalila (Saint-Saëns)

	Date	Conductor	Dalila	Samson	Priest	Old Hebrew	Abimélech	Philistines	Messenger
243	8 Jan '72	Baudo	Bumbry	McCracken	Bacquier	Macurdy	Plishka	Schmorr, Goodloe	Anthony

Siegfried (Wagner)

	Date	Conductor	Brünnhilde	Forest Bird	Erda	Siegfried	Mime	Wanderer	Alberich	Fafner
379	15 Mar '75	Ehrling	Nilsson	Norden	Chookasian	Thomas	Ulfung	McIntyre	Rintzler	Macurdy

Simon Boccanegra (Verdi)

	Date	Conductor	Maria/Amelia	Maid	Gabriele	Simon	Paolo	Fiesco	Pietro
331	14 Dec '68	Molinari-Pradelli	Tucci	Brewer	Shirley	MacNeil	Milnes	Hines	Sgarro
	19 Jan '74	Ehrling	Maliponte	Webber	Tucker	Wixell	Shadur	Tozzi	Sgarro

Suor Angelica (Puccini)

	Date	Conductor	Angelica	Princess	Genovieffa	Monitor	Head Mistress	Abbess	Nurse
549	3 Jan '76	Ehrling	Cruz-Romo	Chookasian	Norden	Baldwin	Godfrey Ben-David	Kraft	Munzer